INTRODUCTION TO KNOWLEDGE BASE SYSTEMS

INTRODUCTION TO KNOWLEDGE BASE SYSTEMS

Richard Frost

MACMILLAN PUBLISHING COMPANY
NEW YORK

First published in Great Britain by Collins Professional and Technical Books 1986.
First American publication by Macmillan Publishing Company 1986.

Macmillan Publishing Company
866 Third Avenue, New York, NY 10022

Collier Macmillan Canada, Inc.

Printed in the United States of America

Printing: 1 2 3 4 5 6 7 8 9 10   Year: 6 7 8 9 0 1 2 3

Library of Congress Cataloging-in-Publication Data

Frost, R. A. (Richard A.)
   Introduction to knowledge base systems.

   Bibliography: p.
   Includes index.
   1. Expert systems (Computer science) 2. Data base
management. I. Title.
QA76.76.E95F76 1986   006.3'3   86-12796
ISBN 0-02-948490-1

This book is dedicated to
my mother Lillian and my father Leslie
who have always encouraged my academic interests

Contents

Contents

Preface

This book evolved from a desire which I had to make available to a
wider group of computer scientists the notions and techniques which
have been used and developed by researchers working in the domain of
automated knowledge processing. When I first took an interest in this
subject some five years ago, I was actively involved in research in
database technology and had given related courses to undergraduate
students at The University of Strathclyde. The first impression I had,
when reading the literature on automated knowledge processing, was that
the subject is extremely difficult. Many of the papers I read assumed
an understanding of topics such as formal logic and linguistics which
are not in the mainstream of computer science as generally taught in
universities and polytechnics. When I looked to the literature to gain
a better understanding, I found that most descriptions of logics, for
example, were written by logicians for logicians. Very few publications included descriptions of how the techniques could be used in
automated knowledge processing, and in those that did so the descriptions were at a level beyond the comprehension of most undergraduate
students. I decided, therefore, to attempt to describe these techniques, and their application to knowledge processing, in a way that
could be understood by advanced students of computer science.

In order to achieve my objectives, I began by writing sets of notes on
various topics related to knowledge base systems. These notes were
given to final year undergraduate and postgraduate students who were
working on related projects. During the course of two years, these
notes underwent much revision. The final versions, which make up this
book, are at a level which I believe is appropriate for advanced undergraduate students. The notes are currently being used as reading
material for a course in Knowledge Base Systems which I give at The
University of Glasgow.

Acknowledgements

This book was conceived whilst I was a lecturer in the Department of
Computer Science at the University of Strathclyde, and drafts of the
first five chapters were written there. Subsequently, I obtained a
position in the Department of Computing Science at the University of
Glasgow where the book was completed. Colleagues and students at both
institutions have helped me a great deal during the two years in which
I have been working on this project. In particular, Professors Malcolm
Atkinson, Andrew Colin, Denis Gilles, Andrew McGettrick and Douglas
McGregor have given me encouragement in my studies, and amendments to
the text have been suggested by Saeed Al-Amoudi, Peter Buneman (who was
on sabbatical from the University of Pennsylvania), Jack Campin, Mike
Coombs, Bill Findlay, Simon Garrod, Robin Harper, Mungo Henning, John
Hughes, Ioannis Kidonakis, Chong Lim, Stephen McInnes, Hugh Noble (of
Robert Gordon's Institute of Technology, Aberdeen), Christian Okoye,
Dimitris Phoukas, Mohammad Riaz, Odd Snahre and Mohamed Zouardi.

Much of the material in the text originated as notes for courses which
I have given at the Universities of Strathclyde and Glasgow. These
notes were typed by Christine Soutar and Helen McNee, and I would like
to thank both for their secretarial help. I am also indebted to David
Watt for allowing me to adapt extracts from his notes on Grammars and
Translators and use them in Chapter 11.

As each chapter was written, the publishers arranged for it to be
refereed both in the UK and in the US. Many of the anonymous referees
made useful comments which enabled me to improve the text and I am
grateful to them. My thanks go also to Bernard Watson and Janet Murphy
of Collins, and Wendy Gibbons and Maxine Frieze, who had the unenviable
task of editing and preparing the camera-ready copy.

Last, but by no means least, I would like to thank my family: my wife
May, our son Stephen, and our parents Mr and Mrs Frost and Mr and Mrs
Henderson. May has constantly encouraged me during the two years that
I have been involved in this project, and when I have been writing at
home Stephen has provided many amusing distractions which have helped
me to keep my work in perspective.

Notes for Lecturers

Lecturers considering the adoption of this book for courses which they give may be interested to know how the notes on which the book is based have already been used in university courses and in industry:

USE AT THE UNIVERSITY OF GLASGOW

At the time of writing, the author is responsible for three undergraduate degree courses given by the Department of Computing Science at the University of Glasgow. Two of these courses are Junior Honours (third year) courses and the other is a Senior Honours (fourth year) optional course. At present, all Senior Honours courses given by the Department of Computing Science are optional and students choose a combination of courses to suit their interests and abilities.

Various sections of the book are used in the courses for which the author is responsible:

JUNIOR HONOURS 'DATABASE' COURSE

- Students are required to read the material in chapter 3 ahead of the lectures.

- Twenty one-hour lectures are given, two per week for ten weeks. These lectures introduce the material in chapter 3, put it in context and explain some of the more difficult concepts.

- Students are required to submit answers to between one and three exercises per week, taken from the exercises on chapter 3 given in appendix 1.

- Students are required to undertake a mini-project. An example of such a project is the implementation of a simple database system based on inverted lists with a menu-driven user interface.

- Students have access to the INGRES and dBASE II database management systems and are given informal tuition in their use.

JUNIOR HONOURS 'GRAMMARS AND TRANSLATORS' COURSE

- Students are required to read the material in chapters 2 and 11 ahead of the lectures.

- Twenty one-hour lectures are given, two per week for ten weeks. These lectures introduce the material in chapters 2 and 11, put it in context and explain some of the more difficult concepts.

- Students are required to submit between one and three exercises per week, taken from the exercises on chapter 11 given in appendix 1.

- Students are required to undertake a mini-project. An example of such a project is the implementation of a relational calculus query language processor which can be used as an end-user interface to the database system which was constructed as part of the Database Course.

SENIOR HONOURS 'KNOWLEDGE BASE SYSTEMS' COURSE

- Students admitted to this course are required to have completed the above two courses.

- Students are required to read the material in chapters 4, 5, 7, 8 and 9 ahead of the lectures.

- Twenty one-hour lectures are given, two per week for ten weeks. These lectures introduce the material in chapters 4, 5, 7, 8 and 9, put it in context and explain some of the more difficult concepts.

- Students are required to submit answers to selected exercises from appendix 1.

- Students have access to a set of tutoring programs which include:

    (a) A propositional logic tutor which consists of a clause form translator and various automatic theorem provers.

    (b) An 'intelligent' database system which is based on the theory and incomplete relational structure approach (see chapter 5).

    (c) A knowledge base system based on first order predicate logic and the theory only approach (see chapter 5).

    (d) A flexible expert system which demonstrates most combinations of search strategies.

    (e) An inference system capable of reasoning under uncertainty.

- Students also have access to Prolog and LISP and various expert system shells. Informal tuition on the use of these systems is given.

The above notes describe the courses as given in the academic year 1985-6. It has been planned to expand the Knowledge Base Systems Course to forty hours of lectures in the academic year 1986-7. The first half of the new course is concerned with formal logic including non-classical logics (i.e. chapters 4 and 6). The second half of the course is concerned with advanced database systems and expert systems (chapters 5, 7, 8, 9 and 10).

USE IN OTHER COURSES
Various sections of the book have been and are being used as essential or recommended reading for Computer Science courses given at the University of Strathclyde - for example, chapter 3 in a twenty-lecture database course given to postgraduate students on a 'conversion' diploma, and chapter 4 in a twenty-lecture logic programming course given to final year undergraduate degree students.

Sections of the book are also recommended reading for postgraduate
students involved in research in A.I.-related areas at the Universities
of Glasgow, Strathclyde and Manchester, at Birkbeck College, London
University, and at technical colleges in Glasgow and Aberdeen.

USE IN INDUSTRY
Sections of the book have been and are to be used as reading material
in various courses given to industry. These 'courses' range from half-
day seminars on specific subjects such as 'the semantic integrity of
databases', to one-week courses which are closely related to the
Knowledge Base Systems Course described above.

1 Introduction

1.1 AN INTRODUCTION TO THE BOOK

The knowledge which a human being 'carries in his head' is encoded somewhere in his neural system. Possibly, it is stored in networks of nerves involving synaptic connections of variable electro-chemical conductivities; a kind of soft-wired circuit whose structure and function can be modified through experience. The exact physiology involved is not known. However, studies have shown that over the last 30,000 years or so there has been little change in the memory and mental processing power of individual humans, yet during this time there has been a marked increase in mankind's ability to store and process knowledge. This is largely due to improvements in techniques for the communication of knowledge, together with the development of methods for the mechanistic processing of knowledge.

In the early stages of mankind's social evolution, gestures and speech were used to communicate knowledge. Subsequently, the transitory medium of speech was augmented with more durable kinds of knowledge representation including paintings, pictorial hieroglyphics and the written word. Concurrently with this growth of techniques for communication, mankind was developing methods for the routine manipulation of knowledge to augment his ability to think. For example, mathematical notations and systems were developed to facilitate numerical calculation, formal logics were developed to facilitate reasoning, and libraries and filing systems were developed to facilitate the management of large collections of knowledge. In more recent times, we have seen great advances through the invention and use of mechanical, electronic and optical systems for the communication, storage and processing of knowledge. For example, database management systems are able to accommodate multi-user access to large volumes of uniformly formatted facts, expert systems are able to reason with complex rules as well as simple facts and several systems are available which can understand subsets of natural language.

Currently, there is a growing interest in the design and implementation of knowledge base systems. This book is about such systems. We begin, in this chapter, with a discussion of what constitutes a knowledge base and a knowledge base system. This is followed by a discussion of how notions and techniques from database technology, formal logic, expert

1

systems work and natural language understanding research may be integrated to provide a theoretical and practical foundation for the
development of computerised knowledge base systems. In chapter 2, some
notations for the representation of knowledge are briefly described.
This chapter may be regarded as an introduction to various approaches
which are described in more detail in subsequent chapters. Chapter 3
describes the current state of database technology. This is an important chapter since many of the techniques which have been developed for
database management are applicable to knowledge base management. In
addition, those systems which some people refer to as fifth generation
database management systems may be regarded as a particular type of
first generation knowledge base system.

Chapter 4 contains an introduction to formal logic. This subject is
regarded by many people as being somewhat difficult to understand.
Consequently, we have tried to make the discussion of it as readable
as possible and for this reason we have presented most results without
giving formal proofs. However, references are included to what we
think are relatively clear expositions of what has been omitted.
Readers who are interested in research in knowledge base systems are
advised to follow up these references. However, this is not necessary
for those who have more practical objectives. In chapter 5 we show
how logic may be used to formalise various aspects of database technology. We include discussions of conventional database systems and
of deductive database systems. The advantage of such formalisation is
that it provides a clear understanding of what is meant by, for
example, 'semantic integrity checking', and also of the limitations of,
for example, using PROLOG to implement deductive database systems.
Chapter 6 begins with a discussion of the limitations of the use of
classical logic as a basis for automated knowledge processing and continues by describing various non-classical logics which have been
developed to overcome these limitations.

In chapter 7, we briefly outline various calculi which have been
developed for reasoning with uncertain and/or inconsistent knowledge.
This is followed in chapter 8 by a description of the production rule
based approach to knowledge processing and its use in expert systems.
The latter part of chapter 8 includes a discussion of how the calculi
described in chapter 7 may be used in expert reasoning. We do not
regard the production rule based approach as being in competition with
the use of logic. We believe that they have much in common, particularly in the search strategies which have been developed for theorem
proving and problem solving.

In chapter 9, we introduce various methods for the representation of
knowledge which we call 'slot and filler' methods. Most of these
methods have been developed by people working on natural language processing systems. They differ from logic and the production rule based
approach in that they make use of structural relationships between
statements as well as statement 'content'. For example, in propositional
logic the order in which propositions are written has no meaning,
whereas in the frame-based approach (a particular kind of slot and
filler approach) 'related' assertions are grouped together into frames,
and frames are related in frame-structures whose purpose is, amongst
other things, to guide search. Again, we do not regard the slot and

filler approach as being in competition with logic or the production-rule based approach. They have much in common, and in chapter 9 one or two of their similarities are explicitly described.

Chapter 10 describes the functional approach to knowledge representation. This approach is currently of interest to researchers who are trying to integrate knowledge processing routines with programming language capabilities.

In chapter 11, we describe various programming languages which may be used as knowledge base systems and/or to implement knowledge base systems. This section is highly relevant since many of the languages are described by reference to notions which have been introduced earlier in the book.

In chapter 12, a very brief overview is given of various types of hardware which have been developed, or are under development, and which could be used as components of knowledge base systems. The brevity of this chapter does not reflect the importance that we attach to the subject. Many of the techniques for automated knowledge processing have been developed to overcome the limitations of conventional computer architectures. The development of special hardware for knowledge base systems is likely to have a great impact on their capabilities. Unfortunately, the limitation of space prevents us from discussing hardware in detail. References are, however, given to the literature in which more informative discussions may be found.

In chapter 13, we list some of the knowledge base systems which are currently available.

Chapter 14 summarises the various approaches that have been described in earlier chapters. A case is made for work leading to the identification of a semantic framework with which to categorise these approaches. We conclude with a list of topics which we regard as deserving further study and hope that this list will encourage some students to embark on research activities related to knowledge base systems work.

1.2 KNOWLEDGE BASES

In section 1.1, we used the term 'knowledge base' without defining what was meant by it. Unfortunately, at present, there is no widely accepted definition and the term is used by different people to mean different things. In this book the term knowledge base is used to mean 'a collection of simple facts and general rules representing some universe of discourse'. The meanings of the terms 'simple fact', 'general rule' and 'universe of discourse' will become apparent as we progress through the book. (In some respects the term 'complex fact' might have been more appropriate than 'general rule'. However, for consistency, we shall use the term 'general rule' throughout this discussion.)

A knowledge base may consist of more simple facts than general rules as, for example, in a knowledge base representing a train timetable. On the other hand, it may consist of more general rules than simple facts - as, for example, in a knowledge base representing good chess moves.

Most knowledge bases are distinct from conventional databases in that they typically consist of *explicitly* stated general rules as well as explicitly stated simple facts. Databases, on the other hand, typically consist of a large number of explicitly stated simple facts together with a relatively small number of *implicitly* stored general rules.

For example, consider an application involving the management of hospital in-patients. A requirement that a date of birth must be recorded for all patients would be enforced in a different way in a conventional database system than it would in a knowledge base system. In a conventional database system, every patient record would contain a field for the date of birth. In addition, there would be data entry and validation rules that would require the operator to input some value for the date of birth when a patient record is created. In contrast, in a knowledge base system the requirement that patients must have a date of birth would be expressed explicitly, possibly as a formula of a language of first order predicate logic. Such a formula looks like, and can be handled by the computer as, a mathematical expression:

$$\forall x \ (x. \in . \ patients) \rightarrow \exists y \ (x. \ hasdateofbirth. \ y)$$

which may be read as 'for all x, if x is a member of the set of patients, this implies that there exists a y such that x has date of birth y'. The symbols in the formula have the following meanings:

$\forall$ means   'for all'

$\in$ means   'member of set'

$\rightarrow$ means   'implies'

$\exists$ means   'there exists'

The difference between the approaches used in conventional database systems and knowledge base systems is that in the former the requirement for a date of birth is 'hardwired' into both the record structure and the programs, whereas in the latter the requirement is stated explicitly in one place and in a form that enables the system to use it as a piece of knowledge for whatever task is required. In addition, it is in a form that could be easily modified should that become necessary.

In this example, the explicit rule is expressed in a formal language called a 'first order predicate' language. By 'formal' we mean that the language is well-defined in the sense that (a) rules exist for the construction of legal expressions and (b) rules exist such that the meaning of legally formed expressions can be derived from the meaning of the components of those expressions.

Formal languages and notations for the representation of knowledge are important since they enable the resulting representations to be interpreted correctly by people other than those who encoded them. They are also important because they enable knowledge to be reasoned with automatically. However, there are problems with the formal languages which are currently available: they are limited in their expressive power, and the associated methods which are used for automatic reasoning are not very efficient. Consequently, people have developed alternative, less formal notations for the representation of knowledge. Some of these notations are described later in the book.

You may ask why a natural language such as English is not used for the representation of knowledge in knowledge base systems. One of the reasons is that natural languages are not formal languages and therefore do not exhibit the advantages described above. No one has yet been able to identify all of the rules which determine the structure and meaning of 'legal' sentences in any natural language. If someone could do this, then it might be possible to write computer programs to understand natural languages. However, there is doubt that a rule based approach to natural language understanding is appropriate since the meanings of many sentences expressed in a natural language can only be determined given the context in which they appear.

For example, consider the following sentence:

'Do not let the side down.'

This sentence has two quite distinct meanings, depending on whether it is said by a football coach to a player or by a construction worker to a crane operator. This dependence on context and on the knowledge of the interpreter suggests that it may be impossible to write general purpose algorithms for the processing of sentences of natural language.

Another reason why natural languages are not used for knowledge representation in knowledge base systems is the lack of uniformity in the structure of natural language sentences. This creates problems when we attempt to store and process such sentences efficiently using computers. Many methods which have been developed in database technology and automatic reasoning are only applicable to uniformly formatted and structured data.

1.3 KNOWLEDGE BASE SYSTEMS

We have defined a knowledge base as a collection of simple facts such as (John works for IBM) together with general rules such as (all humans are either male or female). A 'knowledge base system' (KBS) is a set of resources - hardware, software and possibly human - whose collective responsibilities include storing the knowledge base, maintaining security and integrity, and providing users with the required input/output routines, including deductive retrieval facilities, so that the knowledge base can be accessed as required. Knowledge base systems, as currently discussed in the literature, are distinct from conventional database systems in four ways:

(a)   Knowledge bases typically contain *explicitly represented rules* as well as simple facts (as discussed above).

(b)   Knowledge base storage structures typically have *low structural semantic content* compared with database structures (as discussed above).

5

(c)   Knowledge base systems include components for the *automatic maintenance of semantic integrity* in addition to components for syntactic checking as found in conventional database systems (see later).

(d)   Knowledge base systems include components which can make inferences over the knowledge base, thereby providing a *deductive retrieval facility* (see later).

KBSs are also distinct from 'expert systems' which are most often designed for specific tasks such as mineral prospecting, medical diagnosis, fault-finding and proving mathematical theorems. KBSs might be used as components in expert systems. However, their use is not limited to this. They can be used as general purpose sophisticated database systems or as components of 'special function' systems such as pattern recognition systems.

The distinction between KBSs and 'fifth generation database systems', as defined by Nijssen (1984) is not so clear. A reasonable approach is to regard fifth generation database systems as belonging to a particular type of KBS in which the rules are relatively few and relatively static. The notion of conceptual 'schemas' in fifth generation database systems reflects the stability of the general rules and the use to which the rules are put.

A simple architecture for an unsophisticated knowledge base system is given in fig. 1.1.

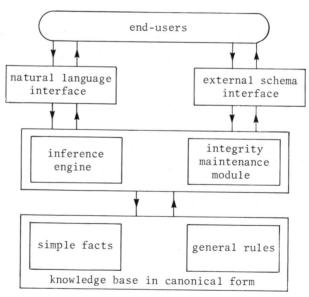

Figure 1.1 A simple architecture for an unsophisticated knowledge base system

1.4 CURRENT DEVELOPMENTS IN KBS COMPONENTS

Research groups are currently working on various aspects of KBSs. For example:

(a) Hardware is being developed for the mass storage of simple facts represented in data structures with low structural semantic content.

(b) Hardware is being developed to speed up reasoning with rules expressed in languages such as PROLOG and LISP.

(c) Methods are being developed for the automatic maintenance of the semantic integrity of knowledge bases using rules expressed in languages based on formal logic.

(d) Methods have been developed to speed up deductive retrieval by mixing theorem proving techniques from sorted first order predicate logic with relational algebraic operations such as division and projection as used in relational database systems. Extensions to PROLOG are also being investigated. For example, a new sorted logic has been developed recently and is being implemented as an extension to PROLOG.

(e) The use of logic to express and reason with knowledge involving uncertainty, beliefs, time, and so on, is being investigated.

(f) Methods have been developed which allow multiple user-views (external schemas) of knowledge which is stored in some standard canonical form. Also some progress has been made in the automatic translation of statements expressed in natural language to statements expressed in a canonical form.

These, and other research developments, are described in more detail later in the book.

1.5 INTEGRATION OF CONCEPTS AND TECHNIQUES FROM DATABASE TECHNOLOGY, FORMAL LOGIC, EXPERT SYSTEMS WORK AND NATURAL LANGUAGE PROCESSING RESEARCH

Progress in the design of knowledge base systems is benefiting greatly from an integration of concepts and techniques which have evolved in the disciplines of database technology, formal logic, expert systems work and natural language processing. Database techniques have been developed to accommodate multi-user access to large volumes of uniformly formatted simple facts, formal logics allow more general statements as well as simple facts to be expressed and reasoned with, research in natural language processing has provided some approaches to the representation of complex objects, sequences of events, and vague knowledge, and work on expert systems has provided techniques for dealing with uncertain knowledge.

The storage and manipulation of knowledge is highly dependent on the way in which it is represented. This, in turn, depends on the way in which the universe of discourse is perceived or viewed. In database work, four views are commonly used: the hierarchical, network, relational and binary relational views. In formal logic, parts of the universe are viewed as 'mathematical' structures such as first order relational structures. In natural language processing the universe is viewed as a more complex structure, parts of which can be modelled using more complex representations such as frames for objects and scripts for event sequences.

In order to provide a basis for the integration of concepts from database technology, formal logic, expert systems work and natural language processing, we introduce the notion of a view of the universe defined as 'a set of concepts and rules which can be used to formulate and rationalise one's perception of parts of the universe'. Such views help one to identify, name, classify and represent those components and processes which constitute that part of the universe in which one is interested. Well defined views are necessary in order that parts of the universe may be represented in a consistent way and the resulting representation interpreted correctly by processes using the same view.

Different views are used to build different representations for different purposes, as illustrated in fig. 1.2. For example, if some part of the universe is to be analysed using Newtonian mechanics, then an appropriate view is one which regards that part as consisting of objects whose positions in space can be accurately defined. If, however, the same part is to be analysed using quantum mechanics, then an appropriate view is one which regards the universe as consisting of objects whose positions in space are given by probability distributions.

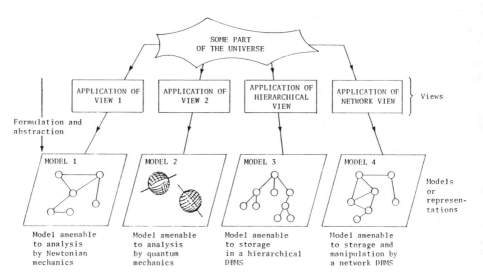

Figure 1.2 Different views of the universe

In database work, views of the universe help designers to choose appropriate data structures for the storage of knowledge. For example, some views require the designer to distinguish between 'entities', 'attributes' and 'relationships'. Entities might then be represented by records, attributes by fields in records and relationships by access

8

paths between records. The notion of a view is closely related to the notion of a database *data model*. However, data models are primarily concerned with data storage and provision of access paths, whereas views are concerned with our perception of reality.

In formal logic, parts of the universe are regarded as constituting 'mathematical' structures. For example, in first order predicate logic, parts of the universe are regarded as first order relational structures each consisting of a set of entities with first order relations and functions defined on this set. The 'first order relational' view in mathematics is similar to the relational view used in database work.

Views provide various means for the rationalisation of 'imaginary' as well as concrete objects. For example, in some views sets are regarded as instances of a special type of entity, whereas in other views sets are treated like all other entities and the set-membership relation like any other relation. As an example, consider a set of people consisting of John, Jim and Mary where John is married to Mary. Representation of this universe of discourse will differ according to whether sets are treated like other entities or not, as illustrated in fig. 1.3.

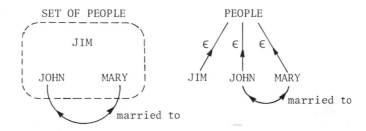

Figure 1.3 Two different views of the same slice of reality

The view chosen will also determine the way in which one accommodates intellectual processes such as generalisation and abstraction. This is discussed in more detail in chapter 2.

The identification and evaluation of appropriate views of the universe is of fundamental importance to advancement in the design of knowledge base systems. You may ask what characterises a 'good' view. Our belief is that views should not be based on a particular type of storage structure. We do not want to make the same mistake as was made when database systems and database management systems were being developed. Many database views, especially the hierarchical and the CODASYL network views, are highly dependent on storage structure implementation considerations. Now that more powerful hardware and new data structures have been developed, much of the theory and many of the algorithms which were designed for hierarchical and CODASYL network database systems are becoming obsolete. We should try to avoid a similar situation occurring in work on knowledge base systems.

Note, however, that we are not saying that choice of appropriate views should ignore implementation considerations. We are saying that such considerations should not be the main criteria when views are evaluated.

We also believe that views should not be chosen which are based on one type of formal logic. It would appear that no single logic has been developed, or is likely to be developed, which has all of the express-ive power and all of the knowledge processing functions which might reasonably be expected in a general purpose knowledge base system.

Another important factor in the evaluation of views is the ease with which the knowledge representation can be mapped into other represen-tations based on different views. Different users of a knowledge base are likely to perceive the universe of discourse in different ways, i.e. they are likely to use different views. It is important that the knowledge in the knowledge base be presented to them in an appropriate form.

We begin our study of knowledge base systems, therefore, with a dis-cussion of knowledge, knowledge representation and the views of the universe which underly different knowledge representation formalisms.

2 Knowledge, Knowledge Representation and Views of the Universe

2.1 KNOWLEDGE

2.1.1 DEFINITION OF KNOWLEDGE

In this book, the definition of the word 'knowledge' which is adopted derives from the meaning ascribed to it in the current literature on knowledge base systems:

> 'Knowledge is the symbolic representation of aspects of some named universe of discourse.'

As such, we regard a piece of knowledge as being a 'model' of some aspect of some named universe of discourse. The universe of discourse may be the actual universe or some non-actual universe such as a universe in the future, a make-believe universe depicted in fiction, a universe existing in an individual's beliefs, etc.

The following are examples of pieces of knowledge represented in natural language:

(a) John is married to Sally.
(b) John is an employee of the AIA company.
(c) All employees of AIA have salaries greater than $50,000.
(d) All employees of AIA know that they should have a good lifestyle.
(e) John does not think that he has a good lifestyle.
(f) Anyone who knows that he should have a good lifestyle and does not think that he has a good lifestyle is disappointed.
(g) In order to determine if someone is disappointed, do the following: (i) find out if he works for AIA, (ii) find out if he does not think that he has a good lifestyle, and (iii) use the knowledge in (f) above to determine if he is disappointed.

The pieces of knowledge above model aspects of some universe of discourse which have varying degrees of complexity. Knowledge (a) is perhaps the simplest. It models the binary relationship of *marriage* between the two entities John and Sally. Knowledge (b) is a little more complex in that it models the binary relationship of *employment* between the entities John and AIA, and it also models the *set membership* relationship between AIA and the set *companies*.

11

The pieces of knowledge (c), (d) and (f) model general properties of aspects of the universe of discourse which are related in some way. Knowledge (g) models a procedure which can be used in the universe of discourse for obtaining knowledge.

The definition of 'knowledge' given above agrees quite well with the meaning ascribed to it in everyday usage. For example:

> (a) When we say that an encyclopaedia contains a large amount of 'knowledge', we are referring to the large number of symbolic representations (words, pictures, graphs, etc.) which are present in it.

> (b) When someone participates in a general 'knowledge' quiz, he demonstrates his knowledge by translating the internal representations which exist in his brain into external representations which are given as written or spoken answers.

> (c) If someone asks you if you 'know' what happened to Saruman in Tolkien's book *The Lord of the Rings*, he is asking you if you have in your brain a representation of a particular aspect of the fictional universe which was constructed and described by Tolkien in his book.

These last two examples illustrate the need to identify the universe of discourse to which the knowledge relates. General knowledge quizzes usually involve representations of the actual universe, whereas the knowledge requested in question (c) above involves the representation of some aspect of a fictional universe. If the universe to which a symbolic representation relates is not known, then that symbolic representation does not constitute knowledge.

We now discuss the relationship of 'knowledge' to the notions of 'data' and 'information'.

2.1.2 DATA

We define 'data' as 'the symbolic representation of simple aspects of some named universe of discourse'.

This definition is in agreement with the use of the word data in data processing and database terminology. The following are examples of pieces of data:

> (a) John is married to Sally.
> (b) John works for the AIA company.
> (c) The average salary of AIA employees is $59,500.

As such, we regard the word data as referring to a particular type of knowledge: the representation of *simple* aspects of some given universe of discourse.

2.1.3 INFORMATION

The 'information content' of a piece of knowledge is a measure of the extent to which that piece of knowledge tells you something which you did not previously know. Consequently, a piece of knowledge can have different information contents for different people.

For example, suppose that we have two people: P1 who knows that it is raining in Glasgow and P2 who knows that there is an even chance of it raining or not raining in Glasgow. Suppose that they both receive a piece of paper which contains the message:

'IT IS RAINING IN GLASGOW'

Both P1 and P2 have been given the same piece of knowledge. Since P1 already knows that it is raining in Glasgow the message has no information content for him. However, the message does have an information content for P2. Furthermore, the quantity of information can be measured and is one bit (see below for a definition of a 'bit'). This notion of information derives from information theory developed by Shannon (1948). Shannon defined 'information' in such a way that the amount of information obtained by the receiver of a message is related to the amount by which that message reduces the receiver's uncertainty about some aspect of the universe of discourse.

It is unfortunate that the word information is used in current computer jargon with meanings other than the precise meaning ascribed to it by Shannon. It is unfortunate because it is useful in real applications to talk about the information content of a body of knowledge. For example, it is not worthwhile providing a decision maker with a knowledge base if the knowledge base has no information content for that decision maker. In this book, we adhere to Shannon's definition of 'information'.

The following is an informal introduction to information theory which we include to emphasise the distinction between the notions of knowledge and information.

A brief introduction to information theory

Consider some part of the universe (U) which must have one and only one of the possible states (a, b, c, d, e, f) at some time (t). Knowledge about U (based on past observation) indicates that the probabilities of U having a particular state at time t are:

$$pa \simeq 0.5$$
$$pb \simeq 0.49$$
$$pc \simeq 0.005$$
$$pd \simeq 0.004$$
$$pe \simeq 0.0009999$$
$$pf \simeq 0.0000001$$

Note: To obtain absolutely accurate probabilities, U would have to be observed for an infinite length of time, hence $\simeq$ is used which means 'approximately equal to'.

These probabilities indicate that, based on past experience, there is a one in two chance that U will have state a at time t (pa $\simeq$ 0.5) but only a one in 10,000,000 (pf $\simeq$ 0.0000001) chance that U will have state f at time t.

Now consider the following cases:

13

(1) At time t1, you receive knowledge d1 representing the fact that U has state a.

(2) At time t2, you receive knowledge d2 representing the fact that U has state f.

Intuitively, it would seem reasonable that d1 conveys less information than d2 to *a receiver who knows the probability distribution*, since such a receiver would half expect (would be half certain) that U has state a, and would be nearly certain that U would have a state other than f. In other words, the message that is least expected conveys more information.

To formalise the measure of information conveyed to some receiver R, by some message d representing part of the universe U, having state i, Shannon proposed the following formula:

information conveyed = $-\log_2 p_i$ bits

where p_i is the probability with which R expects U to have state i. Applying this formula to cases (1) and (2) above gives:

case	knowledge	p_i	information content
1	d1	0.5	$-\log_2 0.5 = 1$ bit
2	d2	0.0000001	$-\log_2 0.0000001 = 23.25$ bits

In the extreme case, where only one state j is possible (i.e. $p_j = 1$), the information conveyed by any knowledge representing the situation 'U has state j' is zero, since $\log_2 1 = 0$. This means that if you already know the state of some part of the universe, then knowledge representing that state conveys no information to you. (However, such knowledge would convey information to someone who doesn't know the state.)

2.1.4 SOME PHILOSOPHICAL CONSIDERATIONS

The definition of knowledge given in 2.1.1 ignores some interesting philosophical considerations. For example, what do we mean when we say that someone 'knows' something? Philosophers have debated this for many years and one definition which prevailed for a time was that:

'A justified belief in a true proposition constitutes knowledge.'

However, imagine a secretary who works in an office with an electric clock on the wall. In all the time that the secretary has worked in that office, the clock has always been correct. One morning, a manager walks through the door and asks the secretary what time it is. The secretary looks at the clock and tells the manager that it is ten o'clock exactly.

Now it happens that the clock, unknown to the secretary, stopped exactly twenty-four hours earlier hence, fortunately, it does happen to be ten o'clock. Would it be correct to say that the secretary knew it was ten o'clock?

14

The secretary was justified in believing that it was ten o'clock because the clock had always been reliable in the past. In addition, the proposition that it was ten o'clock was true because, luckily, it happened to be ten o'clock when the manager walked into the office. Yet it somehow does not seem to be correct to say that the secretary 'knew' that it was ten o'clock.

This and other philosophical considerations are beyond the scope of this book, and the definition of knowledge which we have chosen is a working definition which is in reasonable agreement with the meaning ascribed to it in everyday usage and in the current literature on knowledge base systems. For a readable account of the related philosophical considerations, the interested reader is referred to Bradley and Swartz (1979).

2.2 KNOWLEDGE REPRESENTATION FORMALISMS

In this section, various knowledge representation formalisms including natural language, conventional file/record structures, languages of formal logic, production rules, frames and certain others are introduced. In each case we give examples, discuss the expressive power of the formalism and make some comments on the suitability of the formalism for use in computerised knowledge base systems. In no case do we discuss in detail the storage, management and manipulation of the knowledge representations in computers. Such topics are discussed in later chapters. This section may be regarded as an overview of the knowledge representation formalisms which are considered in the book.

2.2.1 THE REPRESENTATION OF KNOWLEDGE IN NATURAL LANGUAGE

The ability to articulate thoughts in the spoken and written word is one of the most obvious skills which sets man apart from the other creatures which inhabit this planet. Not only can natural language be used to represent what obtains in the actual world; it can also be used to represent what will obtain, what might obtain, what should obtain, what we would like to obtain, etc. Thus man can reflect and discuss with fellow man that which will happen in the future, that which might happen if such and such an action were taken, that which should happen if everyone obeyed the law, that which we would like to happen, and so on.

There is much that we cannot express in natural language. For example, feelings of emotion are often difficult to express, and contents of art cannot adequately be put into words. However, much can be expressed and natural language is perhaps the most powerful knowledge representation formalism that we have.

Computerised knowledge base systems would, ideally, contain knowledge bases comprising sentences of natural language. Unfortunately, this is not yet possible for three reasons:

(a) Natural language is ambiguous, e.g. 'the girl guides fish'. Such ambiguity is generally resolved by reference to the context in which the sentence appears but the way in which humans do this is not yet fully understood.

(b) At present the syntax and semantics is not fully known for any natural language. The syntax of a language comprises the rules

15

which determine the structure of all allowed sentences of
that language. (The word 'syntax' has a similar meaning to
the word 'grammar'.) The semantics of a language comprise a
set of rules which determine how meaning can be ascribed to
sentences of that language.

(c)   There is little uniformity in the structure of sentences in a
      natural language. Most techniques which have been developed
      for managing large collections of knowledge require the know-
      ledge to be represented in a reasonably uniform format.

These three factors hinder the automatic processing of natural
language. Notwithstanding, much progress has been made in removing
these obstacles. In particular, the work of Montague (1974) has led
to a number of fruitful developments. Montague's work is referred to
further in chapter 6.

2.2.2 THE REPRESENTATION OF KNOWLEDGE IN DATA PROCESSING AND CONVENTIONAL DATABASE SYSTEMS

In the early days of automated data processing, knowledge was encoded
on punched cards which were stored in boxes. Subsequently, knowledge
was encoded on magnetic tapes and magnetic disks as records grouped
into files. Such representation of knowledge is perhaps the most commonly used representation in current data processing and database
applications, although other representations involving relations and
tuples (see below) are becoming more frequently used. In this sub-
section, we give examples of knowledge represented as files of records
and also as relations. We include descriptions of various file organisations. However, in this chapter we do not describe the systems
which manage such collections of knowledge. A sub-set of such systems,
called 'database management systems' is discussed in detail in
chapter 3.

Records

A 'record' is a collection of one or more named fields each of which
contains the symbolic representation of some aspect of the universe of
discourse. Typically, records are of a particular type and the fields
within a record are also of a particular type. For example, the
following defines a 'person record' type by naming the fields and
specifying the type of symbolic representation each field can accommodate:

```
person record = {     name : max 20 characters
                       age  : 3 digits in range 000-120
                       sex  : male or female
             marital status : married, bachelor, spinster,
                                  divorced, widowed, or engaged
   first names of children : up to 10 names each max 15 characters}
```

An example of an instance of this record type is:

J J ADAMS
025
male
married
Sally
Richard
Bob

This example illustrates the hierarchical physical structure of records. The field named 'first names of children' has three entries: Sally, Richard and Bob. Such fields are sometimes called 'repeating groups'.

A record instance typically represents a single entity in the universe of discourse. The record above represents the person called J J ADAMS. The field values represent other entities to which the entity called J J ADAMS is related. To emphasise this point, we can depict the above record as a directed graph where P stands for the person represented by the record:

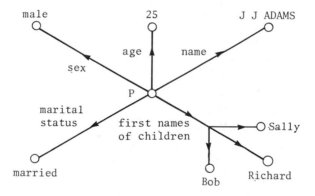

As such, a record may be used to represent the relationships which a single entity has with other entities.

The advantage of using records in automatic knowledge processing derives from their uniform format. Generally, the fields in records are specified as having fixed lengths in terms of the number of characters or digits which they can hold. In addition, the number of 'repeats' in a repeating group is generally restricted to be less than some fixed upper bound. Space which is not used in a record is filled with blanks thus ensuring that all records of the same type are of equal length. This fixed format facilitates the storage of records and the subsequent location of records with given field values. In chapter 3, sub-section 3.3.6, various ways in which records may be organised for retrieval are described.

The processing of records in order to obtain new knowledge, e.g. to obtain the average age of employees of the XYZ company, is also facilitated by the uniform format of records.

The main disadvantage of using records to represent knowledge, however, also derives from their fixed format. The addition of an extra field, or the extension of an existing field to accommodate a longer sequence of symbols (e.g. to extend a name field from 20 to 30 characters), can be extremely costly in a conventional data processing or database environment. (Again see chapter 3.) Another disadvantage derives from the fact that the contents of records are generally chosen for one particular use of the knowledge base. Other uses which would benefit from alternative record structures are therefore generally much less efficient.

Records can be related to other records in various ways, as described in the paragraphs which follow.

Conventional files/contiguous storage

A conventional file consists of a contiguous collection of records which are all of the same type and which are all related in some way. By 'contiguous' we mean that the records are stored in physical proximity. They might be stored one after another on a magnetic tape. For example, all person records representing employees of the XYZ company might be held as follows:

XYZ employee file

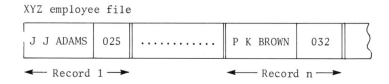

← Record 1 →   ← Record n →

As such, a set of conventional files can be used to represent the binary relation linking companies to employees. A 'binary relation' is a set of pairs such as:

employment relation = {<XYZ, P1>, <XYZ, P3>, <ABC, P2>....}

where, for example, XYZ and ABC are identifiers of companies and P1, P2, P3, etc., are identifiers of employees.

Binary relations can be categorised as 'one-to-one', 'one-to-many', 'many-to-one', and 'many-to-many'. The meaning of these categories may be illustrated by reference to different types of employment relation:

Type of employment relation	Meaning
One-to-one	A company can employ at most one employee and an employee can be employed by at most one company.
One-to-many	A company can employ many employees but an employee can only be employed by one company.
Many-to-one	A company can only employ one employee but an employee may be employed by many companies.
Many-to-many	A company can employ many employees and an employee can be employed by many companies.

Of course, the employment relation is generally regarded as being a one-to-many relation, and in this case a set of file/record structures as described above can be used to represent the relation: one file has many records, and a record only appears in one file.

Suppose, however, that we have the not uncommon situation in which people have more than one job. The employment relation is now many-to-many. Such a situation can only be represented using the file/record structure if records are replicated. For example, suppose that the person called P K BROWN is employed by the ABC company as well as by the XYZ company. We can only represent this using files and records if P K BROWN's record is duplicated and put into ABC's employee file. Such replication of records is best avoided for two reasons:

(a) Multiple copies require extra space for storage.

(b) Multiple copies can lead to inconsistencies if some copies of the record are updated while other copies are inadvertently left unchanged.

Consequently, conventional file structures are best used to represent one-to-many relations rather than many-to-many relations. One-to-many relations are often called 'hierarchical' relations and are typically depicted as tree structures:

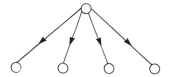

at most one parent

many sons

Notice that the hierarchical physical structure of records which derives from the presence of repeating groups does not mean that *records* are restricted to representing one-to-many relations only. The field values within a record may occur in many other records.

Consequently, in systems which use conventional files, one-to-many and many-to-many relations can be represented by record/field links, one-to-many relations can be represented by file/record links without record replication, and many-to-many relations can also be represented by file/record links if records are replicated (or if some kind of pointer structure is used, as described below).

Records linked by pointers

Instead of relating records through physical proximity, records may be related by the use of 'pointers'. For example, the fact that XYZ employs J J ADAMS and P K BROWN can be represented as follows:

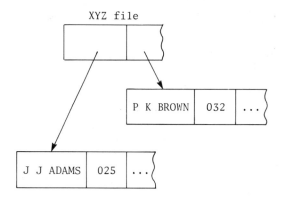

The pointers are typically implemented by the use of physical addresses. For example:

XYZ file

215	867

where 215 is the address (possibly on magnetic disk) at which J J ADAMS' record is located and 867 is the address at which P K BROWN's record is located.

One advantage of pointers is that they can be used to represent many-to-many relations without replication of records. For example, if P K BROWN also works for ABC, we simply put the address of his record in ABC's file:

ABC file

867		

Pointers can also be used to relate records in 'network' structures. For example:

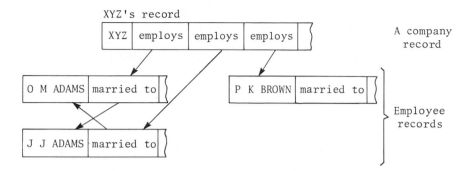

This represents the situation in which XYZ employs Mr ADAMS, Mrs ADAMS and P K BROWN (who is unmarried). Network structures are discussed in more detail in chapter 3.

There are three disadvantages to using pointers:

(a) The pointers (addresses) take up space.

(b) Son records which are related in the same way to a single father file or record may be scattered about in physical storage, unlike the conventional file/record approach in which they would all be held in physical proximity. Certain types of knowledge processing are consequently less efficient: for example, calculation of the average age of all employees of the XYZ company.

(c) When a record is moved from one physical address to another, all fields pointing to it must be updated.

Relating records by use of key fields

Instead of using physical addresses as pointers, we can use 'unique record identifiers'. For example, if we are certain that all employees have different names then we can use the name field as the employee record identifier. In our example this would result in a 'company' record structure such as:

$$\boxed{\text{XYZ} \mid \text{O M ADAMS} \mid \text{J J ADAMS} \mid \text{P K BROWN}}$$

This overcomes problem (c) above which is associated with the use of physical addresses. Fields which are used to identify records in this way are called 'key fields'.

The use of n-ary relations to represent knowledge

The relational approach to the representation of knowledge in computer systems was developed by Codd (1970). 'Relations' are superficially similar to files of records but differ in several respects:

(a) Relations consist of a collection of 'tuples' where a tuple is like a record but is not allowed to contain repeating groups, i.e. tuples are flat. For example, the knowledge in J J ADAMS' record on page 17 could be represented by three 5-place tuples:

J J ADAMS	025	male	married	Sally
J J ADAMS	025	male	married	Richard
J J ADAMS	025	male	married	Bob

This set of tuples constitutes a quinary relation (n-ary relation with n=5) since there are 5 components for each tuple. In mathematical terms, we would say that the relation is defined over 5 domains.

(b) Unlike files which may only be used to represent one-to-many mappings (unless records are replicated or pointers are used), 'Codd relations' can be used to represent many-to-many mappings. For example:

Employment relation

XYZ	J J ADAMS	025	. . . . .
XYZ	P K BROWN	032	. . . . .
ABC	P K BROWN	032	. . . . .
XYZ	O M ADAMS	021	. . . . .

(c) All fields in a tuple must contain values; no fields are allowed to be blank.

(d) All tuples in a relation must be distinct. No such constraint applies to conventional files.

The examples above may give the impression that relations constitute a highly redundant form of knowledge representation. However, such redundancy is not a necessary feature of this approach. Redundant relations can be decomposed or 'normalised' to produce equivalent sets of non-redundant relations. For example, see the set of non-redundant normalised relations on the following page.

Notice that tuples in one relation are related to tuples in other relations by the use of key fields. For example, the first tuple in the 'person' relation is related to all three tuples in the 'parent/child' relation through the key field value 'J J ADAMS'.

R1: Employment

XYZ	J J ADAMS
XYZ	P K BROWN
ABC	P K BROWN

R2: Person

J J ADAMS	025	male	married
P K BROWN	032	male	single

R3: Marriage

J J ADAMS	O M ADAMS

R4: Parent/child

J J ADAMS	Sally
J J ADAMS	Richard
J J ADAMS	Bob

Various advantages are claimed for the relational approach compared with the use of conventional files. For example:

(a) Due to the similarity between 'Codd relations' and mathematical relations, well-defined operations from relational theory can be used to manipulate relational knowledge bases. Such operations include selection, projection and join. The select operator constructs a new relation by taking a *horizontal* subset of an existing relation, i.e. all rows of an existing relation that satisfy some condition. For example, consider the relation R1 above. The effect of the operation:

SELECT R1 WHERE COMPANY = XYZ GIVING R5

would be to produce the following relation:

R5

XYZ	J J ADAMS
XYZ	P K BROWN

Due to the well-defined nature of the relation manipulation operations, it is easier to construct general purpose query languages for querying relational knowledge bases than it is to construct such languages for conventional file systems.

(b) A relational knowledge base can be expanded to include new types of knowledge more easily than can a conventional file system. The addition of a column to a relation is generally less troublesome than the addition of a field to a record type.

The relational approach to knowledge representation is discussed in more detail in chapters 3 and 5.

The use of binary relations to represent knowledge
If the relational approach is restricted to binary relations, we obtain
a method called the 'binary relational' approach. The following is an
example of a binary relational knowledge base:

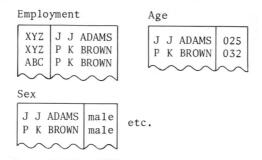

Employment

XYZ	J J ADAMS
XYZ	P K BROWN
ABC	P K BROWN

Age

| J J ADAMS | 025 |
| P K BROWN | 032 |

Sex

| J J ADAMS | male |
| P K BROWN | male |

etc.

Alternatively, the 'type' of each relationship can be encoded explicitly and all binary relationships stored in one place. For example:

XYZ	employs	J J ADAMS
XYZ	employs	P K BROWN
ABC	employs	P K BROWN
J J ADAMS	aged	025
P K BROWN	aged	032
J J ADAMS	sex	male
P K BROWN	sex	male

Various advantages derive from this approach:

(a)   The uniformity of the knowledge representation results in
      simplified storage and manipulation of knowledge.

(b)   Many-to-many relations can be represented with no replication
      of knowledge.

(c)   It is even easier than in the relational approach to add new
      knowledge to the knowledge base.

(d)   If tuples are labelled, it is possible to represent higher-
      order relationships. For example, to represent the situation
      in which 'Bob thinks Bill likes Sue', we could use two tuples
      as follows:

Relationship id	Subject	Relation	Object
R1	Bill	likes	Sue
R2	Bob	thinks	R1

Disadvantages of the binary relational approach include the following:

(a)   A large amount of space is generally required. Although

24

knowledge is not replicated, since all representations are explicit, the knowledge base will be considerably larger than if conventional files were used.

(b) Since related tuples (i.e. tuples which have a field in common) cannot always be stored in physical proximity, the retrieval of collections of related knowledge can take more effort than if conventional files were used. In the example above, it would be possible to store all tuples which contain the value XYZ in proximity, but this could prevent us storing all tuples with value J J ADAMS in proximity. In a conventional file system, the contents of a record are generally chosen to comprise a collection of knowledge which is generally required to be retrieved at the same time.

The binary relational approach to knowledge representation is discussed in more detail in chapter 3.

The representation of knowledge in programs
In conventional data processing and database applications, knowledge is stored in programs as well as in data structures as described above. Such a representation of knowledge is discussed in sub-section 2.2.8 later in this chapter.

Summarising the representation of knowledge in data processing and database systems
Apart from the knowledge which is stored in programs, the knowledge which is held in conventional data processing and database systems typically represents only 'simple' aspects of some universe of discourse. We can represent entities and relationships between entities, but not much else. This does not mean to say that such systems are not important. Much of the knowledge which is required in the everyday management of organisations is of this simple nature. Consequently, we have devoted a whole chapter, chapter 3, to a discussion of database technology. Many knowledge bases will contain a large amount of simple knowledge (i.e. data) and the theory and techniques which have been developed in database technology to manage large collections of data will have their use in knowledge base systems.

2.2.3 THE REPRESENTATION OF KNOWLEDGE USING LANGUAGES OF FORMAL LOGIC
From the early days of civilisation man has been engaged with fellow man in philosophical discussion. In order to facilitate the expression and justification of arguments, various 'formal logics' have been developed. Typically, a formal logic consists of (a) a language for expressing knowledge about certain aspects of some universe of discourse, and (b) rules for manipulating formulas expressed in that language. Thereby, formal logics provide a means to perform and explicate reasoning. (We give a more precise definition in chapter 4.)

In this sub-section, we are concerned only with the languages of formal logic. A more general discussion of logic and its relevance to knowledge base systems is given in chapters 4, 5 and 6.

The Backus-Naur method for defining the syntax of languages
Before giving examples of languages of formal logic, it is appropriate

to introduce a method which is now in common use for clearly expressing the syntax rules of such languages (and of other languages including programming languages). The syntax rules of a language determine how legal sentences or well-formed formulas (wffs) of that language may be constructed. As such, the word 'syntax' has a meaning somewhat similar to the word 'grammar'.

The method that we are about to describe is a slightly modified form of a notation popularised by Backus and Naur when they used it to define the syntax of the programming language Algol in 1958. Since then, this notation has been called the 'Backus-Naur Form' often abbreviated to BNF.

The symbols of BNF which are commonly used include :: = which means 'consists of', | which is used to separate alternatives and < and > which are used to enclose non-terminal symbols. A 'terminal' symbol is simply one of the symbols that we use when writing a sentence of the language. A 'non-terminal' symbol is the name of one of the sub-structures of a legal sentence.

To exemplify the use of BNF, consider a language in which the only legal sentences or well-formed formulas are:

        2 + 2 =
        2 + 1 =
        1 + 2 =
        1 + 1 =

That is, in this language there are only four wffs. To define this language, we begin by giving a BNF expression which specifies the legal structure of a wff in terms of its components, some of which may be non-terminals:

        <wff> :: = <oneortwo> + <oneortwo> =

The terminal symbols that we have used so far are '+' and '='. The non-terminal symbols are 'wff' and 'oneortwo'. This means that all wffs of our example language consist of a sub-formula called a oneortwo followed by the terminal symbol + followed by another oneortwo followed by the terminal symbol =.

We have not yet stated what a oneortwo is, therefore we need to write down another syntax rule giving the following complete BNF specification for our example language:

        <wff> ::= <oneortwo> + <oneortwo> =

    <oneortwo> ::= 1 | 2

This additional rule states that a oneortwo consists of the terminal symbol '1' or the terminal symbol '2'.

For clarity, in this book, we shall omit the angled brackets, and list the set of terminal symbols of the language at the beginning of the grammar specification. Thus the syntax, or grammar, of our example language may be specified as follows:

        terminals = {1, 2, +, =}
        wff   ::= oneortwo + oneortwo =
        oneortwo ::= 1 | 2

Alternatives may also be specified using a slightly different notation. Instead of using the symbol '|', we can put alternatives on separate lines. For example:

```
oneortwo ::= 1
             2

operator ::= +
             -
             /
             *
```

When we specify a grammar in this book, we use one or the other of
these methods depending on which is most easily read.

An advantage of using a BNF-type notation for specifying the syntax of
a language is its conciseness. For example, consider a language with
the following grammar G1:

```
terminals = {1, 2, 3, 4, 5, 6, 7, 8, 9, +, -, /, *, =}
wff      ::= digit operator digit =
digit    ::= 1 | 2 | 3 | 4 | 5 | 6 | 7 | 8 | 9
operator ::= + | - | / | *
```

This grammar defines a language with 324 wffs, an example of which is:

```
4 * 3 =
```

In addition, grammars can be used to produce wffs automatically. For
example, if some random element were introduced into the process, the
grammar above could be used to generate simple arithmetic tests automatically. Furthermore, grammars can be used in the construction of
programs called 'parsers' which can check a sentence (formula) to see
if it is a sentence of the language, i.e. to see if it is well formed.
To illustrate how this might be done, consider the following sentence:

```
4 * 3 =
```

To see if this is a wff of the grammar G1 above, we begin by looking
to see if the sentence has the structure given by the first syntax
rule in G1:

```
wff ::= digit operator digit =
```

In order for the sentence to conform with this rule, (a) 4 must be an
allowed digit, therefore we look at the second rule and find that 4
is an allowed digit; (b) * must be an allowed operator, therefore we
look at the third rule and find that * is an allowed operator; (c) 3
must be an allowed digit, therefore we look at the second rule and
find that 3 is an allowed digit; (d) the last symbol must be =, which
it is. Therefore we can conclude that the sentence 4 * 3 = is a wff
of G1.

We are now in a position to describe some of the languages of various
branches of formal logic. We begin with the simplest: propositional
logic.

Languages of propositional logic
Consider the following sentences:

27

(a) Pat is a man.
(b) Pat is a man and Jan is a woman.
(c) Pat is married to Jan or Pat is married to Sue.
(d) Not Sue is a man.
(e) If Pat is married to Jan then not Pat is married to Sue.
(f) Pat is married to Jan.

The simple or atomic propositions which are contained in these sentences are:

Pat is a man.
Jan is a woman.
Pat is married to Jan.
Pat is married to Sue.
Sue is a man.

The logical connectives which are contained in the sentences are:

and
or
not
if....then

If we use the symbols ∧, ∨, ¬ and → in place of the connectives 'and', 'or', 'not' and 'if....then' respectively, and if we use single letters to stand for atomic propositions, we can express the sentences above as follows:

(a') P
(b') [P ∧ Q]
(c') [R ∨ S]
(d') ¬T
(e') [R → ¬S]
(f') R

where P stands for 'Pat is a man', etc. These sentences are all wffs of a propositional language which may be specified by the following grammar G2:

terminals = $\{∧, ∨, ¬, →, P, Q, R, S, T..Z, [,]\}$

wff   ::= ¬wff|wff ∧ wff|wff ∨ wff|wff → wff|atomic formula|[wff]

atomic
formula ::= P|Q|R|S|T.....

One advantage of expressing knowledge in this way, compared with using files and records, is that we can express alternatives using ∨, negation using ¬ and implication using →. There is no facility, in file/record structures, for expressing such notions (unless the knowledge is partly encoded in the programs which access the file/record structures). The ability to express implication means that propositional logic allows us to express simple 'rules', such as:

[P ∧ Q] → [S ∨ T]

roughly meaning 'if P and Q are true, then S or T is true'.

Another advantage of expressing knowledge as sentences of a language of propositional logic is that the rules of propositional logic can be used to infer new knowledge from the knowledge that we have. For example, one rule of propositional logic is called 'modus ponens' and states that:

from the formulas α and [α → β] we can infer the formula β

where α and β are any wffs of propositional logic. Using modus ponens and the formulas (e') and (f') above, we can infer the formula ¬S. That is, using propositional logic, we can infer that 'not Pat is married to Sue' from the knowledge expressed in sentences (e) and (f). This trivial example illustrates how propositional logic can be used to facilitate reasoning. The subject is discussed in more detail in chapter 4.

A disadvantage of propositional logic is the non-uniform structure of the wffs. For example, both of the formulas below are wffs of the grammar G2 given above:

(a) P
(b) [[[P ∨ Q] ∧ [R ∨ ¬S]] → [P ∨ [Q ∧ [S ∨ T]]]]

Such non-uniformity can give rise to problems when we want to process knowledge automatically. In chapter 4, we show how arbitrary formulas of propositional logic can be converted to a form called 'clausal form' which is more uniform than the standard form exemplified above.

First order predicate logic

The atomic propositions (or atomic formulas) of propositional logic are semantically indivisible as far as the logic is concerned. That is why we can use single letters in their place without loss of meaning with respect to the logic. As such, propositional logic provides no facilities for expressing specific knowledge about individuals or general knowledge about classes of individuals. First order predicate logic, on the other hand, allows us to do this. The following are all wffs of predicate logic:

(a) man(Pat)
(b) [man(Jan) ∨ woman(Jan)]
(c) married(Pat, Jan)
(d) ∀x∀y[[married(x, y) ∧ man(x)] → ¬man(y)]
(e) ∀x∃y[person(x) → has mother(x, y)]

Sentence (a) states that Pat is a man, (b) states that Jan is a man *or* a woman, (c) states that Pat is married to Jan, (d) states that *for all* x and *for all* y *if* x is married to y *and* x is a man *then* y is not a man. Sentence (e) states that *for all* x, *there exists* a y such that if x is a person *then* y is the mother of x, i.e. if an entity is a person, then that entity must have a mother.

The 'predicate symbols' used in the examples above are:

man	has mother
woman	person
married	

The 'constant symbols' used in the example above are:

    Pat
    Jan

The 'variable symbols' used in the examples above are:

    x
    y

The logical connectives of predicate logic are those described for propositional logic, plus:

    ∀ meaning 'for all'
    ∃ meaning 'there exists'.

One advantage of expressing knowledge as sentences of first order predicate logic is that we can express generalisations such as those given in sentences (d) and (e) above. Another advantage of first order predicate logic is that, as with propositional logic, rules exist which can be used to infer new knowledge from existing knowledge. For example, from (a), (c) and (d) above, we can infer the formula:

    ¬man(Jan)

And from this formula and the formula (b) above, we can infer the formula:

    woman(Jan)

The way in which these, and inferences in general, are performed in first order predicate logic, is described in chapter 4.

Sorted predicate logic
Sorted logics are similar to predicate logics but differ in that the variables are 'typed'. Variables are anotated with a type specifying the kind of entity which the variable can stand for - that is, the 'denotation' of the variable. The following is an example of a wff of a language of sorted predicate logic:

    ∀x/person, ∀y/person[married(x, y) → married(y, x)]

There are many other types of non-classical logic: for example, non-monotonic logic, modal logic, temporal logic and intensional logic. Such logics are discussed in chapter 6.

2.2.4 CONSTRUCTING A PARSER FOR A LANGUAGE OF PROPOSITIONAL LOGIC
Before going on to describe other types of knowledge representation, our discussion of formal logic concludes with an explanation of how to construct a parser for a propositional language called PROPLANG.

A 'parser' is a program which can be used to check character strings to see if they are well-formed formulas of a given language. As we shall see later, parsers can be extended to create (i) interpreters which carry out tasks specified by the parsed strings, and (ii) translators which translate strings from one form to another. For example, we show how to convert the PROPLANG parser into an interpreter for a database query language, i.e. into an interpreter which retrieves and manipulates data from a database in order to answer queries expressed in the query language. We also show how to convert the PROPLANG parser into a translator which translates formulas written in PROPLANG to a particularly uniform format called 'clausal form' (which is described in detail later on).

It is extremely useful for computer scientists in general, and knowledge base system designers in particular, to be able to construct interpreters and translators for various languages. Fortunately, most computer science courses cover this subject during the third or fourth year. For readers who have not taken such a course, the following discussion should serve as a useful introduction. For a more complete introduction to the subject, readers are referred to chapter 11.

The PROPLANG language
The following strings are well-formed formulas of the PROPLANG language:

[(johnwalks) ∨ (johnruns)] ;

[(johnwalks) $\Rightarrow$ ¬(johnruns)] ;

PROPLANG differs from the language defined by the grammar G2 given earlier in that atomic formulas of PROPLANG are strings of characters enclosed in round brackets rather than single capital letters as in G2. We have chosen to define PROPLANG in this way for two reasons: (i) more meaningful examples of propositional formulas can be expressed and (ii) later on we show how the PROPLANG parser, as defined, can be extended to derive a parser for a language of predicate logic.

The grammar of PROPLANG
The grammar that we use to define PROPLANG, as shown on page 32, is somewhat different from the grammar G2 given earlier.

In this specification, 'a' stands for 'atomic formula', and 'ε' stands for 'empty' or 'nothing'. The 'director set' column is explained later. The grammar can be explained as follows: a well-formed formula (wff) of PROPLANG consists of an expression (exp) followed by a semicolon (;) (rule (a)); an expression consists of an atomic formula 'a', or a not symbol '¬' followed by an expression, or an opening square bracket '[' followed by an expression followed by a list followed by a closing square bracket ']' (rule (b)). And so on.

The reason that we have defined the grammar of PROPLANG in this way is that it allows us to construct a particularly simple type of parser called a 'recursive descent parser' (see below).

The lexical scanner
Before describing how to construct the recursive descent parser for PROPLANG, we explain how to construct a module called a 'lexical scanner' which is used to pre-process formulas so that they are in a form which is more suitable for parsing.

PROPLANG GRAMMAR

	Productions		Director set
(a)	wff	::= exp;	'a', '¬', '['
(b)	exp	::= a	'a'
		¬exp	'¬'
		[exp list]	'['
(c)	list	::= > exp	'>'
		∧ conjlist	'∧'
		∨ disjlist	'∨'
(d)	conjlist	::= exp conj	'a', '¬', '['
(e)	conj	::= ∧ conjlist	'∧'
		ε	']'
(f)	disjlist	::= exp disj	'a', '¬', '['
(g)	disj	::= ∨ disjlist	'∨'
		ε	']'

The objective of the lexical scanner is to simplify the 'syntactic surface structure' of formulas without affecting their meaning. For example, the symbol '⇒' can be replaced by '>' without loss of meaning. In addition, if the parser is only being used to determine if formulas are well-formed, then atomic formulas may be replaced by the symbol 'a'. For example, consider the formula:

[(johnwalks) ⇒ ¬(johnruns)];

If we are only wanting the parser to test this formula to see if it is well-formed, we can convert it to:

[a > ¬a];

The lexical scanner performs this conversion, and the symbols which are output by the lexical scanner are called 'tokens'. In effect, the lexical scanner removes details which are irrelevant as far as parsing is concerned. A generally useful method of constructing a lexical scanner is to draw a state diagram and then to design a function containing a corresponding case statement. Although we could construct a simpler lexical scanner for PROPLANG (since it is a relatively simple language) we shall use this general method as an example.

The state diagram
The state diagram for the lexical scanner for PROPLANG is given in fig. 2.1. This diagram can be explained as follows: whenever the scanner looks for the next token, it may be thought of as being in the state represented by the node containing '*'. It then looks at the next character on the input string: if it is a space it is ignored, if it is '[' then the scanner delivers the token '[', likewise for ']', '∧',

'v', ';', and '¬'. If the next character is '(' then the scanner looks at the following character: if this character is a space or one of 'a' to 'z', it is ignored and the scanner looks at the next character. If the next character is ')', then an atomic formula has been recognised and the scanner can deliver the token 'a', and so on.

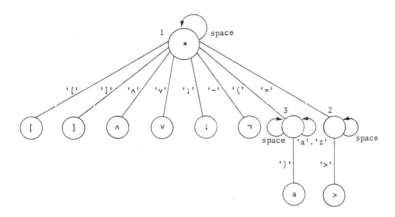

Figure 2.1   State diagram for a lexical scanner for the language
PROPLANG

If, at any point, the scanner finds a character in the input string which is not compatible with the state diagram, it indicates that it has identified a lexical error. For example, consider the following string:

    [(john aged 2) & (jill aged three)];
         ↑ ↑

There are two lexical errors in this string, at the positions indicated. Numerical digits are not allowed in atomic formulas of PROPLANG as we have defined it. (However, it would be a simple matter to extend the scanner to accommodate numbers.)

Use of a case statement
The first half of the PROPLANG parser program, which is given below, contains a procedure called 'read formula' which reads the formula to be parsed into an array called 'formula'. It also contains a function called 'getok' which scans the characters in the formula in order to identify the next token which it delivers as a result.

The lexical scanner in the function 'getok' is implemented as a case statement within a while loop. The correspondence between this case statement and the state diagram is clarified by reference to the numbers 1, 2 and 3 which are used on the state diagram to identify non-terminal nodes, and in the case statement to identify cases.

Although the code in the function 'getok' could be made more concise, the advantage of not doing so is twofold: (i) it is easy to debug lexical scanners which are constructed in this way and (ii) it is easy to

33

modify lexical scanners which are constructed in this way should the
need arise.

Constructing the parser for PROPLANG

The grammar which we have specified above is said to be an 'LL1 grammar'.
The first L stands for 'Left to right scanning', the second L stands
for 'constructing a Leftmost derivation', and 1 stands for 'at most 1
token lookahead is required to uniquely determine which of the productions should next be applied'. (These terms are defined in chapter 11.)

The 'director set' column of the grammar shows us that PROPLANG is a
1-token lookahead language, since the possible next tokens associated
with each production are *distinct*. For example, when starting to
parse a formula, the first production is used, and the only legal next
tokens are 'a', '¬' and '['. (Any other token would signify that the
formula is not well formed, i.e. that a syntax error has been made.)
A description of how to design LL1 grammars, and how to convert non-LL1
grammars to equivalent LL1 grammars, is beyond the scope of this discussion. The interested reader is referred to chapter 11.

Designing LL1 grammars is perhaps the hardest part of language processing. Constructing a parser for an LL1 language is relatively
straightforward. All one needs to do is to write a procedure for each
production, as illustrated in the second half of the PROPLANG parser
program which follows.

Note: Strictly speaking, the program below is not a parser but a
'recogniser'. However, in chapter 4 we show how to extend this program
to be a parser. Language and parser design are discussed in much
greater detail in chapter 11.

```
program proplangparser( input , output ) ;
 var formula : array [1..80] of char ;
     charpos : integer ;
     k : char ;
procedure readformula ;
 var i : integer ;
 begin
  for i := 1 to 80 do formula[i] := '' ;
  writeln( 'enter a formula' ) ;
  i := 1 ;
  read( formula[i] ) ;
  while ( i < 79 ) and ( formula[i] < >';' ) and not eoln
   do begin
        i := i + 1 ;
        read( formula[i] ) ;
      end ;
  formula[i+1] := ';';
  readln ;
 end ;
function getok : char ;
 var i : integer ;
     c : char ;
     tok : char ;
```

```
    procedure error ;
      begin
        writeln( 'lex error at pos', charpos ) ;
        tok := 'e'
      end ;
  begin
  tok := '*' ;
  i := 1 ;
  while tok = '*'
   do begin
     charpos := charpos + 1 ;
     c := formula[charpos] ;
     case i of
       1 : begin
            if c = ' '
              then i := 1 ;
            if c in ['^', 'v', '-', ';', '[', ']']
              then tok := c ;
            if c = '='
              then i := 2 ;
            if c = '('
              then i := 3 ;
            if not (c in [' ', '^', 'v', '-', ';', '[', ']', '=', '('] )
              then error ;
           end ;
       2 : begin
            if c = ' '
              then i := 2 ;
            if c = '>'
              then tok := '>' ;
            if not (c in [' ', '>'] )
              then error
           end ;
       3 : begin
            if c = ' '
              then i := 3 ;
            if c in ['a'..'z']
              then begin
                    i := 3
                  end ;
            if c = ')'
              then tok := 'a' ;
            if not (c in [' ', ')', 'a'..'z'] )
              then error
           end ;
       end ;
   end ;
  writeln( 'token is', tok ) ;
  getok := tok
  end ;

  procedure parse ;
   var tok : char ;
   procedure wff ;     forward ;
```

35

```
procedure exp ;      forward ;
procedure list ;      forward ;
procedure conjlist ; forward ;
procedure conj;      forward ;
procedure disjlist ; forward ;
procedure disj;      forward ;
procedure wff ;
  begin
     exp ;
     tok := getok ;

     if tok  < > ';'
        then writeln( ' ; expected' )
  end ;
procedure exp ;
 begin
  if not( tok in ['a', '-', '['] )
    then writeln( 'a, -, or [ expected' )
    else case tok of
          'a': begin
               end ;
          '-': begin
                  tok := getok ;
                  exp
               end ;
          '[': begin
                  tok := getok ;
                  exp ;
                  tok := getok ;
                  list ;
                  tok := getok ;
                  if tok  < > ']'
                     then writeln( '] expected' )
               end
          end ;
  end ;
procedure list ;
  begin
    if not ( tok in ['>', '^', 'v'] )
        then writeln ( ' >, ^, or v expected' )
        else case tok of
              '>': begin
                     tok := getok ;
                     exp
                   end ;
              '^': begin
                     tok := getok ;
                     conjlist
                   end ;
              'v': begin
                     tok := getok ;
                     disjlist
                   end ;
              end ;
      end ;
```

```
procedure conjlist ;
  begin
    exp ;
    tok := getok ;
    conj
  end ;
procedure conj ;
  begin
    if not ( tok in ['^', ']'] )
      then writeln( '^ or ] expected' )
      else case tok of
             '^': begin
                    tok := getok ;
                    conjlist
                  end ;
             ']': begin
                    charpos := charpos - 1
                  end
           end ;
  end ;
procedure disjlist ;
  begin
    exp ;
    tok := getok ;
    disj
  end ;
procedure disj ;
  begin
    if not ( tok in ['v', ']'] )
      then writeln( 'v or ] expected' )
      else case tok of
             'v': begin
                    tok := getok ;
                    disjlist
                  end ;
             ']': begin
                    charpos := charpos - 1
                  end
           end ;
  end ;
begin
 charpos := 0 ;
 tok := getok ;
 wff
end ;
procedure printformula ;
 var i : integer ;
 begin
   writeln( 'the formula you typed in is' ) ;
   for i := 1 to 80
     do write( formula[i] ) ;
   writeln ;
 end ;
```

```
begin
writeln('THIS IS A PROPLANG PARSER');
writeln;writeln;
writeln('enter formula such as [(peter walked)v(peter ran)];');
writeln;writeln;
repeat
  readformula ;
  printformula ;
  parse ;
  writeln( 'type e to terminate any key to continue' );
  readln( k )
until k = 'e'
end.
```

An example trace of the execution of the PROPLANG parser
Consider the following string:

    [(johnwalks) v (johnruns)] ;

The lexical scanner would produce the following sequence of six tokens
one at a time on each call of the function 'getok':

    [a v a] ;

The recursive procedures which constitute the parser would be called
as follows for this sequence of tokens:

```
call wff
   call exp
      recognise '['
      call exp
         recognise 'a'
      call list
         recognise 'v'
         call disjlist
            call exp
               recognise 'a'
            call disj
               recognise ']' (hence recognise ε)
               backspace (so that ']' can be recognised again)
      recognise ']'
   recognise ';'
```

2.2.5 THE REPRESENTATION OF KNOWLEDGE IN PRODUCTION RULE BASED SYSTEMS

What is a production rule based system?
A production rule based system consists of:

    (a) a set of rules called production rules
    (b) a database management system
    (c) a rule interpreter

Note that these production rules are distinct from productions in grammars. A 'production rule' is a condition/action pair of the form:

    if C then A

where C is some condition which has to be satisfied by the data in the database before the rule can be applied and action A taken. An example of a production rule is:

    if red spots and fever and school age *then* patient has chicken pox

The 'database management system' of a production system manages a database which consists of a number of facts relevant to a particular problem for which the production system is being used.

The 'rule interpreter' is a program which identifies applicable rules, i.e. rules whose condition part is satisfied, and determines the order in which applicable rules should be applied.

Expert systems
'Expert systems' are systems which tackle problems regarded as being difficult and requiring expertise. Such systems are often implemented as production systems where:

    (a)   The production rules represent a body of expert knowledge relevant to some problem domain, e.g. medical diagnosis.

    (b)   The database contains facts about the particular problem being solved, e.g. symptoms and results of tests for a particular patient.

    (c)   The rule interpreter acts in a way which is comprehensible to the expert system user. For example, it may be appropriate in some cases for the rule interpreter to solve the problem by applying rules in the same order as would a human expert.

We discuss the mechanics of production systems in more detail in chapter 8. At present we are only interested in the representation of knowledge in such systems.

The representation of knowledge in a production system
As mentioned above, two types of knowledge are represented in a production system:

    (a)   general knowledge relevant to the problem domain

    (b)   specific knowledge relevant to a specific application of the production system

The specific knowledge may be represented using any of the conventional data processing or database techniques which have been briefly described in sub-section 2.2.2 and which are described in detail in chapter 3.

The general knowledge, however, is typically stored as a set of rules of the form:

> *if* C *then* A

where C may be a compound expression, as illustrated in the rule:

> *if* [C1 AND C2] OR [C3 AND NOT C4] *then* A

Uncertain knowledge may also be expressed by inclusion of 'certainty factors'. For example:

> *if* C *then* A *with* certainty 0.7

The certainty factor may represent a truly probabilistic measure of the likelihood of C implying A or it may simply be a measure of some expert's belief that C implies A. The meaning and use of certainty factors are discussed in more detail in chapters 7 and 8.

Advantages and disadvantages of representing knowledge as production rules

One advantage of using production rules is the modularity of such an approach compared with a procedural representation. For example, consider the following set of production rules:

> *if* C1 AND C2 AND NOT C3 *then* A1
>
> *if* C1 AND C3 *then* A2
>
> *if* C3 AND NOT C1 *then* A3

An equivalent procedural representation is:

> *if* C1
> > *then if* C3
> > > *then* A2
> > > *else* if C2
> > > > *then* A1
> > > > *else* do nothing
> > *else if* C3
> > > *then* A3

Suppose we want to add the knowledge that:

> *if* [NOT C2 OR NOT C1] AND NOT C3 *then* A4

It would be easier to add this as a fourth production rule than to modify the procedural representation.

A further advantage of production rules is that they can capture useful probabilistic or judgemental knowledge which humans often use in their reasoning.

A disadvantage of production systems is the current lack of formality
in the descriptions of them and of the reasoning processes which they
use. However, due to the similarity between production rules and the
formulas of formal logic, many of the well-defined methods and theorems
of formal logic can be applied to production systems. This point is
discussed further in later chapters.

2.2.6 THE REPRESENTATION OF KNOWLEDGE IN SLOT AND FILLER SYSTEMS

The languages of formal logic and rules in production systems allow us
to represent various aspects of the universe. However, they do not,
in general, allow us to structure this knowledge to reflect the 'structure' of that part of the universe which is being represented.

'Slot and filler' representations, on the other hand, include facilities for representing structure. Slot and filler formalisms include
'frames', 'nets', 'conceptual dependency structures' and 'scripts'.

In frames, all assertions about a particular entity are held together.
Frames are then linked together in frame structures, which represent
entity-set membership relations and relations such as the sub-set relation between entity sets. In conceptual dependency structures, all
assertions about an action or an event are held together. In scripts,
all assertions about a particular sequence of events, such as 'going
to a restaurant' are held together.

In the frame, conceptual dependency and script based approaches, the
notion of 'stereotype' is accommodated. For example, one can represent
a stereotypical person as a frame and a stereotypical outing, such as
going to a restaurant, as a script.

Slot and filler approaches facilitate pattern recognition, inference
of generic properties (such as the property of 'being warm-blooded'
which entities of type person have), handling of default values (such
as the property of 'having two legs' which we can assume that an entity
of type person has, unless we are told otherwise), and the detection of
errors and omissions in a body of knowledge.

The slot and filler approach is described in more detail in chapter 9.

2.2.7 THE REPRESENTATION OF KNOWLEDGE IN THE FUNCTIONAL APPROACH

In the functional approach, the universe of discourse is regarded as
consisting of 'entities' and 'functions'. For example, students and
courses may be regarded as entities, and the function 'course of' may
be defined to map students to sets of courses.

'Properties' of an entity are often derived from properties of entities
to which it is related. For example, the 'instructor of a student' may
be defined as the 'instructor of any course which the student takes'.
The advantage of the functional approach is that it allows one to treat
such 'derived' properties as primitive. This is accommodated in DAPLEX
(which is a particular implementation of the functional approach), by
the notion of 'derived functions'. DAPLEX is discussed in more detail
in chapter 10.

One of the problems with knowledge representation (in general) is that
no single 'view' of reality is likely to be appropriate for all users

41

and all applications. Even the definition as to what constitutes an 'entity' is not straightforward. For example, some users of a knowledge base system might want to regard 'enrolment' as a relation mapping students to courses, whereas other users might want to regard 'enrolments of students on courses' as entities which have relationships with other entities such as dates. To accommodate this, DAPLEX allows the construction of separate 'user views' of a knowledge base. These user views may be specified in terms of derived functions. Consequently, complex relationships between views may be accommodated. For example, consider the following derived functions:

(a) DEFINE Instructor(Student) $\Rightarrow\!\!\gg$ Instructor(Course(Student))

(b) DEFINE Enrolment( ) $\Rightarrow\!\!\gg$ COMPOUND OF Student, Course(Student)

Definition (a) allows the user to regard students as being directly related to instructors, and (b) allows the enrolment of a student on a course to be regarded as an entity. (The notation used here is explained in chapter 10.)

Other functional approaches are more closely based on the functional theory of types. In this theory, the universe of discourse is regarded as consisting of 'entities', 'truth values' and 'functions'. The notion that a set may be regarded as a function (the characteristic function of the set) is of central importance in this approach. For example, given a set of entities E and a subset SE of E, we can define the characteristic function, fSE, of SE as follows:

$$fSE(x) = T \text{ if } x \in SE$$
$$= \perp \text{ if } x \notin SE$$

for all $x \in E$

where $T \equiv$ true, and $\perp \equiv$ false

A function space may now be constructed on the primitive objects of type 'entity' and 'truth-value'. The set of types is defined as follows:

(a) e is the type 'entity'

(b) t is the type 'truth value'

(c) if a and b are types, then $\langle a, b \rangle$ is a type (objects of this type are functions from objects of type a to objects of type b)

Examples of types are:

$\langle e, t \rangle$ which is the set of all functions from entities to truth values. Objects of this type may also be regarded as entity sets or unary relations.

$\langle e, \langle e, t \rangle\!\!\gg$ is the set of all functions from entities to functions from entities to truth values. Objects of this type may also be regarded as two place relations.

For example, suppose that Fido is a dog, and that John, Mary and Bill are entities of type person. In the functional approach this situation would be regarded as follows:

The function 'person' is of type <e, t>, and is defined such that:

{ person(Fido) = ⊥
  person(John) = T
  person(Mary) = T
  person(Bill) = T }

This function may also be depicted as:

```
| 'person' is of type <e, t>      |
|---------------------------------|
| Fido  →  ⊥                      |
| John  →  T                      |
| Mary  →  T                      |
| Bill  →  T                      |
```

Suppose, also, that John is married to Mary. This may be depicted as:

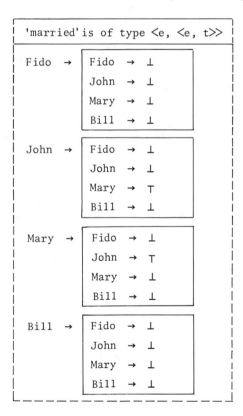

Languages which are based on this approach are called 'type theoretic' languages. Such languages are discussed in more detail in chapter 6, where we show that they have greater expressive power than languages of first order predicate logic.

2.2.8 THE REPRESENTATION OF KNOWLEDGE IN PROGRAMMING LANGUAGES

If we require a computer to carry out a task then we must specify instructions to it in a precise manner. Formal languages have been developed especially for this purpose and are called 'programming languages'. Examples of relatively well known programming languages are COBOL, FORTRAN, BASIC, Algol 60, Algol 68, PL/I, Pascal, and Ada. These languages are all 'procedural', or sequential, and are also relatively general purpose.

During the last few years, there has been a growing interest in other types of programming language. For example, in non-procedural languages such as PROLOG, in symbol processing languages such as LISP, in data definition and manipulation languages such as DAPLEX and PS-Algol, in database query languages such as SQL and QBE, and in frame system building languages such as KRL. These and other languages are described later in the book.

In most of the widely used languages there is a clear distinction between 'data' and 'procedures' whereas, in languages such as LISP, 'data' and 'procedures' have an equivalent form which allows data structures to be executed as procedures, and procedures to be modified as data. This and other differences between the various types of programming language will become apparent when the languages are discussed in following chapters.

Irrespective of its type, a programming language may be regarded as a knowledge representation language. In fact, one of the most important tasks to be accomplished before writing a program is translation of the data of the problem being solved into a manipulable form. In doing this, the programmer must take into account data types and structures of the languages available to him: the choice of a language implies the choice of a set of data structures. Since the appropriate choice of data structures is fundamental to good program design, the data structures which are available in a programming language have great influence on the quality of programs.

Many high-level languages provide the following types of data structure:

    integer

    real

    boolean

    character

    array

    record

    pointer

    file

Other languages, such as LISP, make use of generalised, dynamic data structures (in LISP these are of type 'list'). Emphasis in LISP is on the application of functions to arguments rather than on the assignment of values to variables. Hence, LISP programs may be regarded as expressions which are to be evaluated with respect to previously defined (or 'primitive') functions.

In non-procedural languages such as PROLOG, the programmer does not have to concern himself with the flow of control through the program (i.e. the order in which statements are to be executed) to the extent which is required in a procedural language. Recursion is used instead of iteration ('looping'), and the order in which statements are obeyed is mostly determined by the language interpreter.

Each programming language has its own vocabulary, its own grammar (set of syntax rules) and its own semantics (set of rules depicting the meaning of well-formed statements). A good introduction to the formal definition of programming languages can be found in McGettrick (1980).

The representation of knowledge in programming languages is discussed in more detail in chapter 11.

2.3 VIEWS OF THE UNIVERSE

In the previous section various formalisms which may be used for the representation of knowledge were briefly described. In the following chapters these formalisms are discussed in much greater detail. We define them more precisely, and discuss various methods which have been developed for processing the knowledge which is represented using them. When reading the following chapters, and the literature which is referenced in them, you may notice that many of the methods which have been developed for processing the knowledge which has been represented according to one formalism have similarities to methods which have been developed for processing the knowledge which has been represented according to other formalisms. For example, many of the methods which have been developed in formal logic have much in common with the methods developed for use in production rule based systems.

On recognising such similarities, you may feel that it would be worthwhile to integrate those methods which have much in common. You would find, however, that such integration is hindered by the different terminologies which are used in the literature to described methods which have been developed in different areas of knowledge processing. In this sub-section, a notion which may alleviate this difficulty is introduced: the notion of a 'view of the universe'.

Irrespective of the notation which is used to represent knowledge, it is always necessary for the 'representer' to perceive the universe and 'conceptualise' that part which he or she is wanting to represent. The notation which is used to convey the represented knowledge to another person is always defined in terms of some 'intuitively appealing' semantic concepts such as 'entity', 'relationship', 'set', 'negation', and so on.

Ideally, it would be possible to define a set of semantic primitives which could be used to define all knowledge representation formalisms.

However, this is not feasible. Attempts have been made, but they usually result in lengthy philosophical discussion. A more pragmatic approach is to identify a set of commonly used semantic concepts and to employ these concepts in the definition of knowledge representation formalisms. Hopefully, the result would be such that 'similar' formalisms (i.e. those which differ only in superficial syntactic structure) could be identified. The ultimate aim would be to categorise various formalisms, such as file/record structures, languages of logic, production rules, frames, scipts, etc., and to identify some generally useful concepts and algorithms for knowledge representation and manipulation. An attempt to do this is being made in Britain by a working party chaired by the author of this book (Frost, 1985). At present, we have done no more than identify a set of commonly used semantic concepts which are listed below. We have not yet determined how useful these concepts are, but we are currently attempting to do this by using the concepts to define a wide range of knowledge representation formalisms.

A set of commonly used semantic concepts

entity	
entity set	(the notion of 'type' is related to this)
attribute	(in the author's opinion these are no different from entities and entity sets)
attribute set	
relationship	
relation	
function	(characteristic functions can be used to define entity sets as discussed in chapter 6)
the truth-value 'true'	
the truth-value 'false'	
the truth-value 'unknown'	
time	
proposition	(a statement which is true or false)
name	(in the author's opinion, a name is an entity)
variable	
logical negation	(NOT, a special function)
conjunction	(AND, a special function)
disjunction	(OR, a special function)

→	(material implication, see chapter 4)
possible world	(as defined in modal logic, which is described in chapter 6)
possible truth	(as defined in modal logic)
necessary truth	(as defined in modal logic)
strict implication	(as defined in modal logic)
agent	(the 'knower' or believer in epistemic logic, as discussed in chapter 6)
proof	(as defined in logic)
rule	(entity set membership rules, etc.)

We have not attempted to give precise definitions of these concepts, since they were chosen intuitively and we recognise that they will require a good deal of reworking before a really useful set can be identified. However, we have included this list because we feel that it will be useful, when you read the following chapters, to consider the basic semantic concepts on which the various knowledge representation formalisms are founded. For example, when reading about database systems it will be useful to regard the file/record approach as being founded on the notions of entity, entity set, attribute, attribute set and relation. When reading about logic, it will be useful to regard classical predicate logic as being founded on the notions of entity, relation, function, truth, falsity, negation, conjunction, disjunction, variables, and so on.

In this book, the term 'view of the universe' is used to denote a set of semantic concepts and rules which can be used to formulate and rationalise one's perception of parts of the universe. As hinted at in chapter 1, it is felt that an understanding of the various views of the universe which underlie different knowledge representation formalisms is essential to the development of a theory of knowledge processing. Categorisation of knowledge processing techniques, according to the views of the universe on which they are based, will help us to understand these techniques and to integrate them when building complex knowledge base systems.

We now begin our study of knowledge representation formalisms by considering those concepts which have been developed in the domain of database technology.

3 Database Concepts

3.1 INTRODUCTION

So far various methods and notations for the representation of knowledge have been described. In our discussion we have made a distinction between simple facts such as (John is married to Sally) and complex facts such as (all humans are male or female). The representations of simple facts are traditionally referred to as 'data' and, due to the uniform format of data, the processing of this type of knowledge is particularly amenable to automation.

Large collections of data are called 'databases'. In this chapter, various concepts and methods which have been developed to facilitate database management are described. We begin with a discussion of databases, database systems, and database management systems (DBMSs). This is followed by a brief outline of commercially available DBMSs. We conclude with some comments on fifth generation DBMSs, i.e. those DBMSs which are likely to be used on fifth generation computers.

The concepts described in this chapter are very relevant to knowledge processing. That part of a knowledge base which can be represented in a uniform format can be stored in a database system. In many ways, fifth generation DMBSs may be thought of as a particular type of first generation KBS in which the complex facts are relatively few and relatively static.

3.2 WHAT IS A DATABASE?

A database is a collection of regularly formatted data which is accessed by more than one person and/or which is used for more than one purpose.

The database might be a large collection of similar data such as that relating to airline seat reservations, or it might consist of various related data such as that used in an integrated accounting system.

There are several advantages in using a single shared database in which the data is generally stored only once rather than maintaining several separate, possibly non-disjoint files:

    (a)   Resources may be saved if the data is collected and stored without duplication. In addition, economies of scale might

48

apply if all of the data is stored in one place under one management.

(b)   The data may be put to more use than if it were stored separately.   If a new user or new application requires use of data which is already in the database, then in many cases such a requirement can be readily met.   If, on the other hand, the required data is stored at several locations under various managements, then a great deal of time and effort might be required to gain access to it.

(c)   The data is likely to contain fewer errors.   In particular, inconsistencies in the data are likely to occur less frequently.   One of the problems of keeping several separate non-disjoint sets of data is that some copies might be updated while other copies are overlooked.   A similar problem might occur if you keep two diaries.   When two supposedly identical files contain contradicting data they are said to be inconsistent.   This problem occurs to a lesser extent if a database is used since, in general, there is less redundancy (duplication) of the data.

Of course, it could be argued that there are several disadvantages of using databases.   For example:

(a)   The data must be transmitted from the sources to the central database and from the central database to the end-users.

(b)   Security and privacy constraints must be enforced on access to the database to prevent unauthorised reading or changing of data.   This is likely to be more complicated than if the data were held in several separate files.

(c)   Standard data formats need to be created and adopted by all users of the database.

However, it could also be argued that these last two considerations are not really disadvantages but are practices which should be adopted whether or not a database is used.   If this view is taken, then an additional advantage of using a database is that it compels organisations to adopt worthwhile practices.

Irrespective of whether or not the above tasks are regarded as disadvantages, they still need to be carried out if a database is to be used.   In addition, several other tasks arise as a consequence of using a database.   They are collectively known as database management tasks and are carried out by a system called a 'database system'.

3.3   DATABASE SYSTEMS

3.3.1   WHAT IS A DATABASE SYSTEM?

A database system is a set of resources whose collective responsibilities include the following:

(a)   Storing the database.

(b) Maintaining database security by enforcing privacy and
integrity constraints and by providing the necessary back-up
for recovery from hardware/software breakdown.

(c) Providing users/uses with the necessary input/output routines
so that the database can be accessed as required.

In this book, it is assumed that a major component of the database
system is a computer and that the database resides in some form of computer storage.

3.3.2 THE FUNCTIONAL ARCHITECTURE OF DATABASE SYSTEMS

The functional architecture of many existing database systems is given
in fig. 3.1. By 'functional' we mean that this architecture indicates
the different functions or facilities which are available in many database systems. The architecture does not necessarily depict the
physical construction of such systems.

As can be seen from fig. 3.1, database systems can comprise up to nine
modules. These modules are described in the next nine sub-sections.

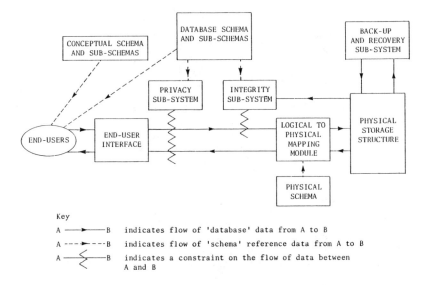

Figure 3.1 An ideal architecture for a database system

3.3.3 THE CONCEPTUAL SCHEMA

What is a conceptual schema?
The starting point for the design of a database system is some abstract
and general description of that part of the universe which is to be
represented by data in the database. (This part of the universe is
often called the 'universe of discourse'.) The abstract description is
called a 'conceptual schema'.

For example, the conceptual schema might contain (i) a list of the
types of *entities* involved: employees, departments, machines, parts,

etc.; (ii) a list of the interesting *relations* between these entity types: employees work in departments, machines are built from parts, etc.; and (iii) a list of the *integrity constraints* which apply: e.g. 'if employee A manages employee B and employee A works in department D, then employee B must also work in department D'.

The conceptual schema is a description of reality and not of data. Consequently, it does not refer to access paths, privacy constraints and the like. Information about this part of the system is contained in the 'database schema' which is described in the next sub-section.

Uses of conceptual schemas

The conceptual schema has several uses in the context of database system design:

(a) It can be used at the start of the design process to integrate the interests of the various end-users.

(b) It is a useful description for communication with non-technical end-users. The application area is described without reference to access requirements or physical storage considerations and is therefore free of technical jargon.

(c) It helps the designer to build a more durable database system. By looking at the conceptual schema, the designer can identify those access paths which, although not required now, may be required at some time in the future. The database system can then be designed so that these access paths could be easily accommodated if required.

(d) Once the database system has been designed, the conceptual schema may be used to introduce potential users to it. This is particularly important if the system is being considered for transfer to, and use at, another site. The conceptual schema may help identify any fundamental differences between the organisation at the new and original sites. Such differences might require extensive alterations to be made to the system before it can be used at the new site and are best identified early.

Formal specification of conceptual schemas

Conceptual schemas are generally written in English, if at all. Often, the database system designer keeps such information in his head. However, there are good reasons why a more formal approach should be used:

(a) The meaning of the resultant conceptual schemas would be less ambiguous.

(b) The logical consistency of the schemas could be determined if the conceptual schema definition language were 'decidable' in the strict mathematical sense. This would allow some types of mistakes in the designer's perception of the application area to be identified.

(c) It might be possible to use formally defined constraints to maintain the semantic integrity of the database automatically.

An example of a conceptual schema
Consider the conceptual schema shown in fig. 3.2. This schema is specified using a modified binary relational approach and describes an
application area comprising employees, companies, departments, machines
and parts. Relations between these entity types are depicted by named
arcs in the schema. The 'cardinality' of the relations is given by the
label underneath (or to the right of) the arc. For example, an employee
is allowed to manage up to 20 employees but an employee may not have
more than one manager.

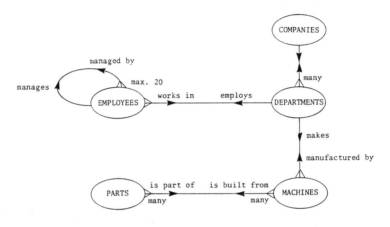

Figure 3.2 A conceptual schema

Problems in creating conceptual schemas
One of the most difficult problems in creating the conceptual schema is
in obtaining the agreement of all potential users of the system that
the schema represents the application area correctly. This is largely
due to the many exceptions which are often allowed to override the
general rules which govern organisational structures. For example, it
might be true that in most cases an employee is only allowed to have
one manager, but this might be overruled in the case of secretaries.
Although such exceptions complicate the specification of the conceptual
schema, it is better that they are identified early on in the design
process. Failure to do so could result in the need to introduce ad hoc
extensions to the system at a later date.

Conceptual sub-schemas
That part of the conceptual schema which is of interest to a particular
end-user or group of end-users is called a 'conceptual sub-schema'.
Ideally, sub-schemas should be presented to end-users in the form most
appropriate for them. For example, some end-users might prefer a
diagrammatical description, whereas others might be more at home with a
record-like notation. Sub-schemas have similar functions to schemas;
however, their use is oriented to end-users rather than to database
system designers.

3.3.4 THE DATABASE (OR LOGICAL) SCHEMA

What is a database schema?
This is a description of the data which is stored in the database and
specifies what data elements are stored and what access paths are
provided between these elements. The database schema also contains
specifications of privacy, as well as integrity, constraints. It is
somewhat similar to the conceptual schema, but is a description of data
rather than of reality. Some aspects of reality which are described in
the conceptual schema will not be represented by data in the database
schema. Note, however, that the database schema does not specify how
the data is actually stored or how access paths are provided. (Ideally
it should *not* refer to files, records, sets or the like.) It is,
therefore, an implementation-independent description, and for this
reason is sometimes referred to as the 'logical schema'.

That part of the database schema which is of interest to a particular
end-user or group of end-users is called a 'database sub-schema'.
Ideally, a sub-schema should be specified using the notation which is
most appropriate for the use to which it is being put. Database sub-
schemas have several uses: (i) they can be referred to by application
programmers to see what access paths are available in that part of the
database in which they are interested, (ii) similarly, they can be
referred to by end-users when they are using a report program generator
or formulating queries, etc., using a query language provided, and (iii)
they can be used to divide the database into units for the specification
of privacy constraints. For example, a sub-schema could be defined for
which all users have read access but only one specified user has write
(update) access.

Before the database schema can be specified, the database system designer must carry out several tasks. These include:

    (a) constructing the conceptual schema
    (b) identifying the required data
    (c) analysing the data
    (d) specifying the input/output packages

We have discussed (a) already. A brief description of steps (b) to (d)
now follows.

Identification of required data
Having constructed the conceptual schema, the system designer is in a
position to identify which parts of the application area should be represented by data, and when and how this data should be presented to the
users. The art of doing this falls within the scope of systems analysis. It involves a thorough understanding of the application area and
an ability to determine the real value of the data to the organisation
for which the database system is being built. Many books have been
written on this subject. However, it should be noted that systems
analysis is not yet a science but is a skill that may only be acquired
through practical experience in conjunction with extensive reading. A
good reference to start with is Gane and Sarson (1977).

Data analysis
Once the required data has been identified, the next step involves the

definition and classification of this data. This task may be facilitated by the use of methods which are gaining acceptance as comprising
a well defined discipline called 'data analysis' of which much has been
written, e.g. BCS (1978), King (1977), Gradwell (1975) and Perkinson
(1984). The result of the first stage of data analysis is a 'data
dictionary' which is a description of all data items which are to be
processed by the system.

The data dictionary might consist of a manually supported set of forms,
or it might be maintained by a computer-based system. A typical data
dictionary allows the designer to record the following properties of
each data item:

- name
- synonyms
- definition, i.e. description of the real world entity which it
  represents
- type, e.g. string, integer, real, etc.
- format
- access constraints
- relationship to other data items

Discussion of the use of data dictionaries can be found in BCS (1976),
Canning (1981), Lomax (1978) and Van Duyn (1982).

Specification of input/output packages
After the data dictionary has been constructed, the next step in the
specification of the end-user interface is to determine how groups of
data items should be packaged for input to and output from the system.
Most techniques used for data analysis also provide facilities for such
specification. However, many of the techniques describe the packages
in terms of the data structures which are to be used for the physical
storage of the database. For example, packages are often described as
records or files. Such an approach confuses what the system is required to do (i.e. what packages of data are to be made available to the
users) with how the system is to do this (i.e. how the data is to be
stored - as files of records of relations, etc.). Ideally, at this
stage, the designer should be able to specify the required packages
with as little reference to implementation details as possible. For
example, instead of stating that 'package A consists of an employee
record, printed on paper, which is generated by the user entering an
employee number at a terminal', a better specification would be that
'package A consists of an employee number, name and salary, on human
readable hard copy media, which is generated by the user entering an
employee number at one of several specified locations'.

This method of specification gives the designer more freedom when designing other aspects of the system. A few techniques have been developed which support this approach and an example of the use of one is
given in fig. 3.3 (Warnier, 1974). However, none of these techniques
has yet gained wide acceptance though some are recommended in recent
books on systems analysis, e.g. Cougar, Colter, Knapp (1982) and
Perkinson (1984).

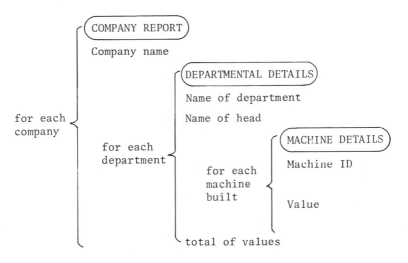

Figure 3.3 An implementation independent specification of output required

We have said little about how the contents of the input/output packages are identified. In general, it is not a simple matter of asking the users what packages they want. This might provide a starting point but should not be regarded as a means of achieving a final input/output specification. The designer needs to rationalise the user's require-ments in order to construct a minimal set of requirements. This pro-cess involves three stages:

(a) Determine what input/output packages each user requires.
(b) Construct the data dictionary.
(c) Determine what minimal set of input/output packages would meet the total set of requirements for each user.

Such minimisation would, in general, require a degree of compromise. For example, some users might be provided with packages containing more data than was strictly necessary whereas others might have to use two packages with cross-referencing to obtain the data they require. In many cases, however, users may be quite tolerant of such a compromise and the designer should always consider minimisation of input/output packages since this would normally result in a simpler database system.

Another factor which must be taken into account when deciding on the input/output package structure concerns data privacy. This will be discussed later.

Specification of the database schema
At this stage, the designer will have created three 'documents': (i) a description of the application area (the conceptual schema), (ii) a def-inition and classification of the data items which are to be manipulated by the system (the data dictionary) and (iii) a specification of the characteristics of the various packages of data which are required by the users. The designer will also have gathered information concerning

55

the privacy and integrity of the data and this will have had some influence on the choice of the input/output package contents.

The next step is to specify the total data content of the database and the characteristics of the access paths required through this data. It is this specification which is called the 'database schema'.

Like conceptual schemas, database schemas are often written in English. However, some data dictionary systems are sophisticated enough to be used for database schema definition. Care must be taken to distinguish between data analysis and database schema definition. Data analysis is concerned with the definition and classification of the data which is to be manipulated by the database system. Database schema definition is concerned with the use of this data: what access paths are required, what privacy constraints should be imposed and so on.

Irrespective of what notation is employed for specification, it is useful to think of the database schema as a network such as that shown in fig. 3.4. The nodes represent types of data, and the directed arcs represent access paths between data types. In a complete schema the nodes would contain information which might include:

- the data type name
- a definition of the data type or a reference to the data dictionary where the definition may be found
- a list of the various formats in which the data is required by the various input/output packages
- a list of the users and/or packages which are allowed access to the data type
- a list of the integrity constraints which apply to the data type, e.g. 'age of employee cannot exceed 70'

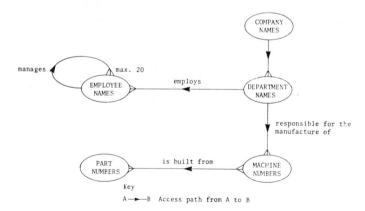

Figure 3.4 A simple database schema (incomplete)

The arcs of the network are labelled with information which might include:

- the name of the access path or relation which the arc represents, e.g. 'built from'

- a definition of the relation or a reference to the data dictionary where the definition can be found
- a list of the uses of the access path, e.g. package 15 uses each
  access path of this type twice per week in employee order, package
  57 uses one random path of this type once per week
- a summary of the access path use
- a list of the users/packages which are allowed to follow the
  access path
- a list of the integrity constraints which apply, e.g. 'an employee
  may not be related to more than one department'

When creating the database schema, the designer should refer to the conceptual schema as well as the input/output package specification. This
will aid prediction of what access paths might be required by future
applications. For example, although the current input/output package
specification might not indicate a need for an access path from machine
to department, the system designer should establish whether or not such
a requirement might arise in the predicted lifetime of the system. If
such a requirement is likely then this should be mentioned in the database schema.

In many ways, the database schema may be thought of as a specification
of what the database system is required to do. It describes what data
is to be stored and what access paths are to be provided. Notice, however, that no mention is made of how the access paths are to be implemented. It is for this reason that the database schema is sometimes
referred to as the 'logical schema' to distinguish it from the physical
or internal schema which is described below.

3.3.5 THE PHYSICAL (OR INTERNAL) SCHEMA

The physical schema is a description of the physical structure of the
database. If, for example, conventional indexed sequential files (fig.
3.5) are used to store the database then this will be stated in the
physical schema. It will also contain details of record formats,
blocking factors, etc. The physical schema is constructed as an essential part of the design process. However, it may also be used as an
integral part of the operational database system as discussed later.

The distinction between the conceptual, database and physical schemas
may be clarified by an example in which all three schemas are specified
in English:

Conceptual schema: the universe of discourse consists of 20 com-
                    panies, each of which employs between 50 and
                    200 employees; employees work for a single
                    company and have a unique age.

Logical schema: the logical data structure is based on the
                    relational data model and consists of a single
                    relation with domains 'employee name', 'age'
                    and 'company'.

Internal schema: the relation is held as an indexed sequential
                    file (described below) with employee name as
                    key, together with a set of inverted lists
                    (described below), one for each company.

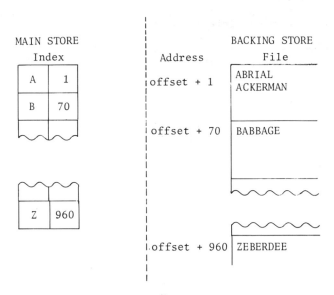

Figure 3.5 An indexed sequential file

3.3.6 THE PHYSICAL STORAGE STRUCTURE AND DATA STRUCTURES

The structure in which the database actually resides is called the 'physical storage structure'. It typically consists of hardware such as disk drives, tapes or large RAM stores, together with programs which manipulate various data structures which are mapped on to this hardware. Such data structures might include arrays, sequential files, indexed sequential files, hash tables, trees, relations, inverted files, networks and the like. Some of these data structures are described below.

Definition of a data structure

A data structure is a collection of elements, related in some way, each of which can have a value together with a set of data manipulation operations allowed on the collection. For example, consider a fixed-size array:

	e1	e2	e3	e4
A =	6	5	5	8

(a)   This array consists of four elements: e1, e2, e3 and e4, each of which has an integer value.

(b)   A 'physical order' relation R is defined over the set of elements such that R = {<e1, e2>, <e2, e3>, <e3, e4>} meaning e1 comes before e2, etc.

(c)   The operations allowed on A are: direct access to the ith element, where $(1 \leqslant i \leqslant 4)$, and change of value of an accessed element.

Data structure type

Data structures may be classified according to properties such as:

(a) the number of elements in the structure
(b) the type of elements in the structure
(c) the type of relations defined over the elements
(d) the type of operations allowed on the structure

Operations allowed on structures include:

(a) direct access to an element by position in the structure (as in arrays)
(b) direct access to an element by name (as in a record)
(c) change of value of an element
(d) removal of an element (cannot be done in a fixed-size array)
(e) change of relationships between elements (cannot be done in an array)

For example, the data structure A above is of type 'array of four integers'. This would be expressed as follows in the Pascal programming language.

    A : array [1..4] of integer;

Examples of data structure types

The following list identifies some commonly used data structures:

Simple types: integer
               character
               boolean
               real

Complex types: array
                bit map
                string
                queue
                stack
                record
                list
                direct-access file
                sequential file
                indexed sequential file
                SID file
                tree
                hash table
                graph
                multi-list
                inverted list
                bit list
                inverted file
                transposed files
                B-tree
                dynamic hash table

```
Database data
structures:       hierarchical structure
                  network structure
                  relational structure
                  binary relational structure

Knowledge
structures:       formal languages
                  production rules
                  slot and filler structures
```

Some of these data structures have already been described in chapter 2. We now describe a few more. The database data structures and the knowledge structures are not included here as they are dealt with later. Neither do we include the common data structures such as arrays, lists, trees, sequential files, etc., since we assume that the reader is already familiar with them. If not, we refer the reader to Tremblay and Sorenson (1985). The data structures that we do describe are those which are relatively new and are useful for storing large collections of data. The notion of associative stores is discussed later in this chapter, and the notion of 'abstract data types' and 'persistent' data stores in chapter 11.

Hash tables

A hash table consists of a number of addressable locations, each of which is capable of holding one or more records. To place a record in the table, its key is transformed into an address within the range of table addresses by the use of a hash function, (see fig. 3.6). Hash tables can provide very fast access to records. There is no need to search through the whole set of records as the key of the record required can simply be transformed to an address, using the same hash function that was used to place the record in the table. We then look at that address to see if the required record is there.

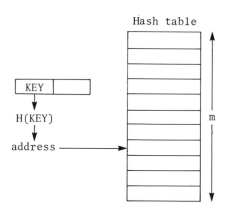

H is a hash function

Figure 3.6   A hash table

Hash functions

A hash function H is defined on a domain of values which includes the keys of all of the records to be stored. The range of the function is some given segment of integers, say 1 to m where m is the number of addressable locations in the hash table.

As an example of a hash function, consider the following: suppose m = 20 and we want to store records whose keys are character strings. A possible hash function is:

(a) Add the alphabetical positions of all letters in the key

e.g. SMITH = 19 + 13 + 9 + 20 + 8 = 69

(b) Divide the sum by 20 and take the remainder

e.g. 69/20 = 3 with remainder 9

(c) Add one to the remainder

e.g. 9 + 1 = 10

The result is guaranteed to lie in the range 1 to 20, and is the location in which to store the record. For example, the record with key 'SMITH' goes into location 10.

Collisions

Various hash functions have been developed to spread records evenly throughout the table. Nevertheless, there will be times when two or more keys are transformed to the same address. This is called 'collision'. There are two commonly used methods for resolving collisions: 'probing' and 'chaining'.

Probing or open addressing

In probing, unoccupied locations are found for records whose 'home address' is already full. Linear probing is the simplest method and uses a cyclic linear probe sequence (see fig. 3.7):

H(key), then H(key) + 1, then H(key) + 2, ..., M, 1, 2...

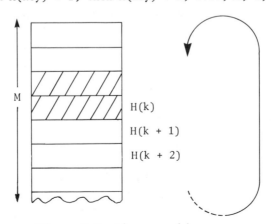

Figure 3.7 Linear probing

Various other types of probing have been developed to overcome some of the disadvantages of linear probing. See Tremblay and Sorenson (1985).

Collision resolution with chaining

An alternative approach to that of open addressing for collision resolution is to use indirect addressing which allows elements to be linked to their home addresses in the table. Methods using this approach are commonly called 'chaining' methods. An example of a chaining method which uses linked lists is illustrated in fig. 3.8.

Hash table   Lists of colliding records

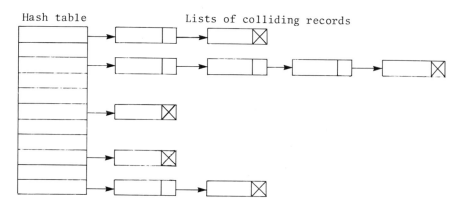

Figure 3.8   Collision resolution using chaining

Deletions from hash tables

Whenever there are deletions from a hash table which uses probing, the addresses at which these occur cannot merely be reset to a value meaning 'no record at this position'. This is because when a search for another record encounters such a value the search will terminate and the search routine will assume, perhaps erroneously, that the searched-for record is not in the table. Instead, therefore, a special code signifying a deleted item should be used.

Where chaining has been used to overcome collisions deletions are somewhat easier to handle since links in the chain can be adjusted to effect the required deletion.

Overflow

One of the major disadvantages of the hashing method is the static storage allocation. The number of records must be estimated in advance and physical storage space allocated accordingly. If it is necessary to increase the size of the hash table then all records currently in the table must have their hash codes recalculated and stored at new locations in a larger table. An interesting method of recalculating hash codes when the hash table size is increased is given by Bays (1973).

If storage requirements for a hash table are underestimated, the number of overflow records will be large and this will slow down searching and updating. If the storage requirements are overestimated, storage utilisation will be low and storage space wasted.

Dynamic hash tables

A relatively new record organisation called 'dynamic hashing' was designed by Per-ake Larson (1978). The organisation is based on normal
hashing but the allocated storage space can easily be increased and
decreased without rehashing. The expected storage utilisation is
approximately 69%. The proposed scheme requires the maintenance of a
relatively small index structured as a forest of binary trees.

Let the set of records to be stored at a certain time be denoted by
$R = \{r1, r2, \ldots, rN\}$. N is not fixed and may vary with time. A
record ri is assumed to contain a unique key ki. To simplify this
description, the records are assumed to be of fixed length. The data
structure consists of:

(a) A set of M addressable locations each of which has a capacity
of C records. (From now on it will be assumed that the method
is used in a two-level storage environment, and that the
'locations' mentioned above are 'blocks' - a block being a
convenient unit of transmission to and from a disk.)

(b) An index to these blocks.

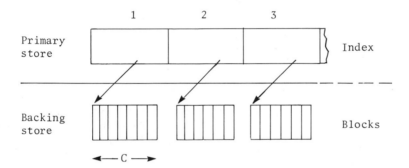

(c) A hashing function H1 which is used to distribute the records
among the blocks. The function is a normal hashing function,
the only difference being that the value H1(ki) is used to
define an entry point in the index and does not directly refer
to a block. The block is found by means of the pointer in the
corresponding index entry.

(d) A forest of binary trees to accommodate overflow. When the
file is initialised, no binary trees exist. However, sooner
or later a block will overflow, i.e. when we try to insert a
record into a block that is already full. When this happens,
we split the block in two and update the index by extending
the tree downwards, as illustrated in fig. 3.9.

When the number of records decreases, the allocated storage space can
also be decreased. When the number of records in two brother blocks
becomes substantially less than the capacity of one block, the two are
merged and the corresponding tree adjusted.

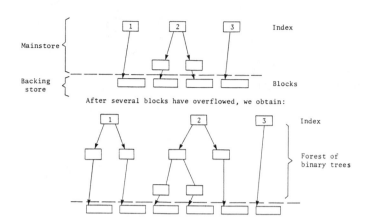

Figure 3.9 Blocks are split when they become full

Notes
The splitting of blocks is achieved as follows.

A second hashing function H2 is applied to the keys of the records in the block to be split. The value H2(ki) gives a given sequence of bits, such as 010011000111000... Since this binary sequence can be used to determine a unique path in a binary tree, record insertion can proceed.

When inserting a record ri with key ki, the root of the search tree in the index is first located by computing H1(ki). We can then compute H2(ki) which gives us a binary sequence. The path uniquely determined by this sequence can be scanned until a terminal node is reached. This node contains a pointer to the block in which the record is to be stored (see fig. 3.10). If the block is already full, the node is split into two nodes, a new block is allocated and the records divided into the left and right block depending upon their binary sequences.

It is suggested that the binary sequence should be generated by a pseudo-random number generator. Such a generator is designed to return 0 or 1 with probability 0.5 when called. This ensures that records are equally distributed between the two blocks provided that H2 is a reasonable hashing function. The random number generator must be of the type where the generated sequence is uniquely determined by the seed, i.e. it may not be repetitive. Note, however, that calls to such a generator by equal seeds will always result in the same binary sequence being generated. For example:

call RANDOM(9), would always return the sequence 0111000...

To make the generated binary sequence uniquely determined by the key of the record, the seed for the generator is computed from the key. Therefore the hashing function H2 is defined on the set of keys and has a range which is a subset of the allowable seed points for the generator in use. H1 and H2 *must* be different functions.

64

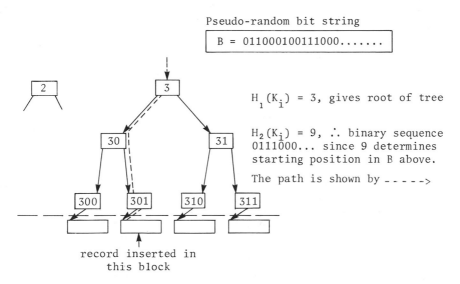

Pseudo-random bit string

$B = 011000100111000.......$

$H_1(K_i) = 3$, gives root of tree

$H_2(K_i) = 9$, $\therefore$ binary sequence 0111000... since 9 determines starting position in B above.

The path is shown by $\text{-----}>$

record inserted in this block

Figure 3.10   Inserting a record into a dynamic hash table

The advantages of dynamic hashing are:

(a)   It can accommodate collections of data which vary in size.
(b)   The backing store file is always about 69% full.
(c)   Any record can be retrieved with only one or two accesses to backing store.

Refinements and variations
In the preceding discussion, we have assumed that records are of fixed length. This assumption is not crucial; the algorithms can be easily modified - we just keep account of the occupied space in each block instead of the number of records.

The use of explicit pointers to represent the tree structure makes for heavy main store requirements. It is possible to store search trees in consecutive storage without using pointers, as in the 'heapsort' method of sorting.

B-trees
The expected number of memory accesses per retrieval (i.e. the path length) in a completely balanced binary search tree of N elements is log to the base 2 (N + 1) - 1. However, if instead of a binary search tree one were to use an m-ary search tree (i.e. a tree in which the number of successors of any given element was m) one would expect much shorter path lengths. In a completely balanced m-ary tree the expected number of accesses per retrieval is log to the base m (N + 1) - 1 which means m-ary trees (m > 2) are better than binary trees for searching.

However, one problem associated with the use of m-ary trees is that an excessive amount of storage can be wasted if many of the link fields are allowed to be empty. Therefore, an m-ary tree can be used, but with certain constraints - the resulting structure being called a 'B-tree'. B-trees were developed by Bayer and Mcreight (1972).

Basically, a B-tree is a balanced m-ary ordered tree T which satisfies the following conditions:

(a) Every node except the root and terminal nodes has x successors where $m/2 \leqslant x \leqslant m$.

(b) The root has at least 2 successors (unless it is the only node).

(c) A non-leaf node with k successors is an ordered list of k - 1 keys.

(d) Leaf nodes are lists of records.

(e) The ith successor of a node with (k - 1) keys is a B-tree containing nodes whose keys lexicographically precede the ith key of that node. The kth successor of a node with (k - 1) keys is a B-tree containing nodes whose keys lexicographically succeed the (k - 1)th key of that node.

For example, a B-tree with m = 5 is shown in fig. 3.11.

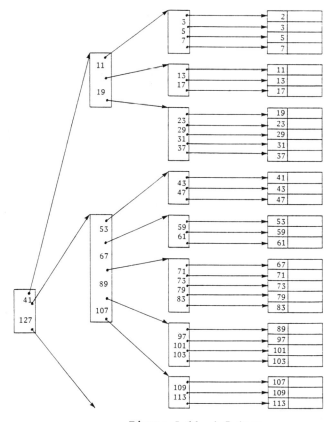

Figure 3.11   A B-tree

The parameter m is determined by the page size and data characteristics. For example:

if the page size is = 600 bytes
and the key size is = 10 bytes (including pointers)
then the maximum number of keys in a node = 59
therefore, the maximum number of successors of a node = 60
therefore, m = 60

B-trees are very suitable for database design, because:

(a) A two level storage is used.

(b) The dependence upon physical device level is confined to only
     one parameter, i.e. page size.

(c) A high performance is obtained in all four basic operations
     of retrieval, modification, insertion, and deletion.

(d) A high performance is obtained in batch processing since
     records at the leaves are in lexicographical order.

(e) A fairly good storage occupancy is achieved.

The B-tree is one example of a class of data structures called 'dynamic
structures' because it is dynamically reorganised during update to provide a balanced search tree at all times. If we want to insert a new
record with key 60 into the tree shown in fig. 3.11, simply change the
appropriate node as follows:

On the other hand, if we want to insert a new record with key 27 there
is no room since the corresponding node on level 3 is already 'full'.
In this situation the node is split into two parts, with three keys in
each part and passing the middle key up to the next level. The resulting tree shown on page 68 preserves all of the B-tree properties.

Multilists

A multilist is a data structure in which records are linked in different ways by several interwoven lists. Each list typically links
records having some field value in common. The 'next' record in a
particular list is identified by a 'pointer' which is stored in the
record which precedes it in the list. A pointer to the first record
in a list, together with the number of records in that list, is usually
maintained in a directory of some kind. An example of a multilist
structure is given in fig. 3.12. If the directory is large then some
kind of hashing scheme may be used to find the list head for a given
<field name, value> pair.

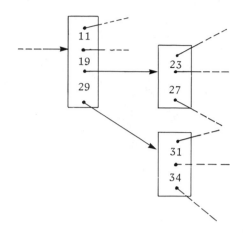

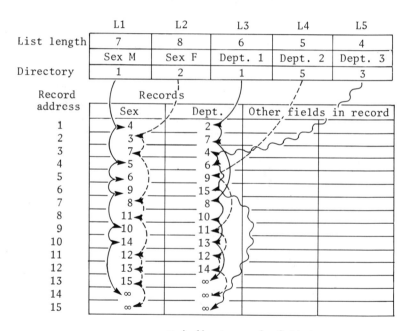

∞ indicates end of list

Figure 3.12 A multilist structure

Multilist and conjunctive queries

As mentioned, the directory also contains the length of each list, and this is extremely important when handling conjunctive queries such as:

Which male people work in dept. 3?

To service such a query we look up the directory to see which of the lists L1 or L5 is the shortest, and then proceed to process it.

The greatest disadvantage of the multilist organisation is that in order to respond to a conjunctive query, all records corresponding to the term having the shortest list *must* be individually brought into main memory for examination.

The principal advantages are the simplicity of programming and the flexibility in performing updates (since records can easily be inserted into linked lists).

Inverted lists

One way of overcoming the major disadvantage of the multilist approach (i.e. the need to access all records on the shortest list in a con-junctive query) is to remove all linkages from the records and to place the pointers corresponding to some list L in a separate index. Such indexes are called 'inverted' lists or files. Inverted lists corres-ponding to the multilist structure given in the previous sub-section are shown in fig. 3.13. Note that records are ordered on the NAME key. This would be the case if the majority of queries were on NAME, or if the file was processed sequentially against batched updates ordered on NAME.

Advantages of inverted lists:

- The inverted lists allow quick response to queries such as 'print names of all males who work in dept. 1'. We simply determine which record addresses appear in lists L1 *and* L3, namely record addresses 1 and 10, and retrieve the two corresponding records. (Compare this to the multilist approach in which all 6 records of the shortest list L3 would have to be retrieved.)

- Good for keeping track of file statistics for secondary access. An extra numeric field in the inverted list can be incremented each time a particular secondary key is used.

Disadvantages of inverted lists:

- The first disadvantage of inverted lists is duplication of data. The same data is held both in the record file (e.g. the depart-ment of an employee) and in the inverted list (i.e. the record address for that department). Therefore, valuable storage space is occupied.

- The second disadvantage arises from the first. Because data is duplicated, a double updating process is required.

- Inverted lists cannot be used for fields which can have many values, with few records having the same value.

Bit lists

An inverted list may be represented as a bit list, or bit string, as follows: For each inverted list L1 a bit string b1, N bits long is created, where N = number of records in the file.

Directory of inverted lists

	Sex=M	Sex=F	Dept. 1	Dept.2	Dept. 3
	L1	L2	L3	L4	L5

Inverted lists

L1	1,4,5,6,9,10,14
L2	2,3,7,8,11,12,13,15
L3	1,2,7,8,10,13
L4	5,9,11,12,14
L5	3,4,6,15

Record address   Main file

Record address	Name	Sex	Dept.	
1	Abbott	M	Dept. 1	
2	Aristotle	F	Dept. 1	
3	Bristol	F	Dept. 3	
4	Chutney	M	Dept. 3	Backing store
5				
6				
7				
8				
9				
10				
11				
12				
13				
14				
15				

Figure 3.13 An inverted list structure

If a particular record r1 whose address relative to the other records in the main file is j, has a field value corresponding to a particular list L1 then the jth bit in the bit list b1 is set to 1. For example, consider the inverted lists described in the previous sub-section. The corresponding bit lists are shown in fig. 3.14.

An advantage of using bit lists is that boolean combinations of simple queries can be easily performed, because computers can manipulate bit lists at relatively high speed.   (For example, see below for an application of bit lists.)

Record address	Main file on backing store			Bit lists in main store				
	Name	Sex	Dept.	Sex M	Sex F	Dept. 1	Dept. 2	Dept. 3
				b1	b2	b3	b4	b5
1	Abbott	M	Dept. 1	1	0	1	0	0
2	Aristotle	F	Dept. 1	0	1	1	0	0
3	Bristol	F	Dept. 3	0	1	0	0	1
4	Chutney	M	Dept. 3	1	0	0	0	1
5				1	0	0	1	0
6				1	0	0	0	1
7				0	1	1	0	0
8				0	1	1	0	0
9				1	0	0	1	0
10				1	0	1	0	0
11				0	1	0	1	0
12				0	1	0	1	0
13				0	1	1	0	0
14				1	0	0	1	0
15				0	1	0	0	1

Figure 3.14   A bit list structure

The disadvantages of using bit lists are the same as for inverted lists.

As an example of an application of bit lists, consider the following employee file:

Employee no.	Name	Sex	Dept.	Hourly rate	Location
1	Graham	F	1	4.00	J
2	Lewis	M	1	4.00	B
3	Hunter	F	2	2.00	B
4	Coley	M	3	6.00	J
5	Spitzen	M	4	4.00	B
6	Corbles	F	4	6.00	J
.	.	.	.	.	.
.	.	.	.	.	.
.	.	.	.	.	.
1000					

We may want to list all employees earning £6.00 per hour, all employees at location J, etc. This problem can be solved by making use of 11 bit lists. The length of each list is 1000 bits and for the six records given the bit lists would be:

Field value	Bit list
Male	010110 ....
Female	101001 ....
Dept. 1	110000 ....
Dept. 2	001000 ....
Dept. 3	000100 ....
Dept. 4	000011 ....
Rate 2.00	001000 ....
Rate 4.00	110010 ....
Rate 6.00	000101 ....
Location B	011010 ....
Location J	100101 ....

71

To provide an easy mode of system interaction, it is desirable to create a non-procedural command language, such that commands have the format:

LIST employees [specifications]

e.g.   LIST employees [DEPT4 ∧ LOCATIONJ]

In response to such a command, the following action would take place in the retrieval system:

(a)   The bit lists corresponding to DEPT 4 and LOCATION J are retrieved (000011 and 100101 respectively).

(b)   The logical conjunction, as indicated by the operator ∧ is calculated (000011 & 100101 = 000001).

(c)   The corresponding record(s) is retrieved and listed under appropriate headings:

Employee no.	Name	Sex	Dept.	Hourly rate	Location
6	Corbles	F	4	6.00	J

The logical operators which may be used within the specifications of the query might be:

∨ - OR
∧ - AND
¬ - NOT

Inverted files

With inverted lists, a problem arises in inverting on a field which has a large number of possible values. In such a case it is impractical to hold a list for each possible value of the field. Instead each list holds a range of values and the actual value of the field is held next to each record address.

Value range	No. of records in range	Record address/Value (examples)				
AA-FZ	156	......	117/AP	11/DC	3334/EA	......
GA-KZ	297	......	86/JS	....		
LA-PZ	42	......	2475/NX	....		
QA-UZ	51	....				
VA-ZZ	27	......	4628/VP	19/WT	5320/YH	......

For example, the record with address 86 has a value of JS.

An advantage of inverted files is that it is possible to invert on every field in the record, no matter how many values it may have. Consequently, retrieval on single keys is in most circumstances quite efficient.

Transposed files

Instead of storing a series of records, a file may be 'transposed' by storing a 1-dimensional array for each field. The values for any logical record appear in the same relative position within each array as shown in fig. 3.15.

	1 Stock no.	2 Stock desc.	3 Pack size	4 Unit	5 Stock level
Record 1	0010902	BAKED BEANS	24	A2	510
Record 2	0011257	SPAGHETTI HOOPS	12	A5	4791
Record 3	0011271	SPAGHETTI HOOPS	6	A10	295
Record 4	0100020	SOAP POWDER BRAND A	24	XL	15000
Record 5	0100228	SOAP POWDER BRAND B	30	SM	999
Record 6	0100235	SOAP POWDER BRAND B	24	XL	4927
Record 7	0103007	SOAP POWDER BRAND X	18	L	1507
Record 8	0110016	W/U LIQUID	36	SM	427

Figure 3.15 Transposed files

Choosing an appropriate data structure

Each of the data structures described above has advantages and disadvantages compared to the other data structures. This must be taken into account by the designer when choosing an appropriate structure. For example, sequential files are readily available in most programming languages and are ideal for sequential processing but do not support random access. Hash tables, on the other hand, provide very fast random access but do not provide sequential access. In order to make the choice, the designer must have a thorough knowledge of such performance characteristics. Fortunately, several studies have been carried out which contribute to our understanding of these factors. For example:

- sequential files (Shneiderman and Goodman, 1976)
- indexed sequential files (Wiederhold, 1983)
- transposed files (Batory, 1979)
- inverted files (Claybrook and Yang, 1978)
- hash tables (Severence and Duhne, 1976)
- B-trees (Nakamura and Mizoguchi, 1978)
- relations (Chamberlin, 1976)

Relations are described in detail later in this chapter.

An example of a physical storage structure

For a simple database schema, a simple data structure might suffice. For example, given the database schema in fig. 3.15, an appropriate

73

physical storage structure might consist of a single sequential file of employee records sorted into employee name order.

For more complicated database schemas, more complicated physical storage structures are likely to be required. It may be necessary to integrate several of the data structures above and it is frequently necessary to duplicate data in order that sufficiently efficient access paths are provided. Even database schemas which are only slightly more complicated than the above example require careful design.

Consider the database schema shown in fig. 3.16. This schema might have been constructed for a system in which a telephone directory is to be stored and used to find numbers for given names *and* names for given numbers. (Notice that these example schemas are incomplete. Details which are irrelevant to the present discussion have been omitted.) An indexed sequential file of records containing name and number might suffice for access from name to number. However, access from number to name would be hopeless. For a successful search 50,000 records on average would have to be scanned; for an unsuccessful search, all 100,000 records would require to be examined! A reasonable solution to this particular problem requires the data to be duplicated, thereby providing fast access in both directions. For example, two hash tables - one using the name as hash key and the other using the number as hash key - might constitute an appropriate physical storage structure.

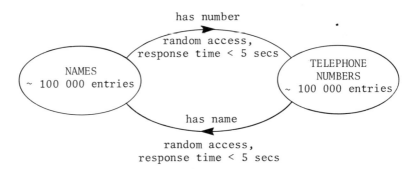

Figure 3.16 Telephone directory database schema

3.3.7 THE END-USER INTERFACE

The 'end-user interface' is that part of the database system which is available to end-users. It typically consists of VDU screens, keyboards, printers and user-friendly software. This software includes application programs, report program generators and query languages.

The 'application programs' when executed allow end-users to enter, retrieve and update data in the database. Application programs can be written to present data to the users in the form most appropriate for them. Little knowledge of the database is needed to use an application program. The end-users need only be aware of the integrity constraints which apply to the data and the meaning of the 'prompt' messages which are issued by the application program.

Use of the report program generators and query languages, however, does require a knowledge of database contents and access path provision. A 'report program generator' (RPG) is a utility program which helps end-users create 'reports'. The end-user specifies the data content and format of the report required and the RPG creates a report program which, when executed, obtains the necessary data from the database and displays it according to the format specified. Whenever an up-to-date report is required, the end-user simply re-runs the report program.

The RPG is often used to generate programs for outputting reports which are required on a regular basis. Query languages, on the other hand, are often used to meet one-off requests for data or to provide a 'browsing' facility with which the end-user can navigate his way round the database.

Before a query language can be used, the user needs to know what access paths are available in the database. This information can be obtained by reference to the relevant database sub-schema. Similarly, application programmers need to refer to relevant database sub-schemas when they construct application programs.

3.3.8 DATA INDEPENDENCE AND THE LOGICAL TO PHYSICAL MAPPING MODULE

Data independence
'Data independence' is a term used by the database community to describe the extent to which the physical storage structure of a database system is independent of the application programs (and other components of the end-user interface) which access it. The main advantage of data independence is that the databases in a data independent database system may be extended or moved on to a new physical storage structure with minimal effect on the rest of the system.

In the early days of database work, it became apparent that data independence could be improved if the end-user interface accessed the data base indirectly using commands which referred to the database schema. The translation of these logical commands to physical commands which manipulate the physical data structure directly is called 'binding'. In early-bound systems, binding takes place when application programs are compiled. In late-bound systems, binding takes place when the commands are executed and in some cases this translation is carried out by a centralised logical to physical mapping module. Late-bound systems are more data independent than early-bound systems since no recompilation of application programs is necessary when the physical storage structure is changed.

3.3.9 THE PRIVACY SUB-SYSTEM

What is privacy?
Database 'privacy' is defined as a property of the database which reflects the extent to which the data is protected against unauthorised access. The 'privacy sub-system' protects the database from unauthorised access. Ideally, privacy constraints are expressed in the same logical language that is used by the application programs and are then incorporated into the database schema. When end-users attempt to input or output packages of data (via the application programs) the privacy sub-system refers to the database schema to see if such access is allowed, and then acts accordingly.

Design of the privacy sub-system

Privacy requirements are first identified during the construction of
the conceptual schema. If English is the language used then the schema
might contain a statement such as: 'A and B are the only employees who
are allowed to know the salaries of other employees.' During the subsequent design of the database schema, such statements are converted
into 'access constraints' which are couched in terms of data elements
and access paths, i.e. in the ideal case, in terms of the nodes and
arcs of the database schema. For example, the requirement above might
be converted to the constraint: 'Users A and B are the only users who
are allowed to follow the access paths linking employees to salaries.'
The access constraints are then taken into account when the physical
storage structure is designed. However, the actual mechanisms for
enforcing the constraints are best contained in a separate module or
sub-system called an 'arbiter'.

Two advantages derive from this approach:

(a) The design process is facilitated. All access control mechan-
     isms reside in one module and a single standard approach may
     be used for their implementation.

(b) The resulting system is more data independent than it would be
     if the access control mechanisms were built into the physical
     storage structure.

Ideally, complete 'data independence' of privacy constraints may be
achieved since the access constraints need never be couched in terms
of physical data structures (i.e. files, records, relations and so on).
If access requests are issued by input/output application programs in
some logical language as discussed previously then the arbiter can enforce the constraints, as expressed in the database schema, without
any reference to the physical storage structure (see fig. 3.1). The
arbiter would be a relatively simple program which would perform the
following functions:

(a) Identify the user.

(b) List the nodes and/or arcs of the database schema which cor-
     respond to that part of the database which the user is trying
     to access.

(c) Consult the access constraints to see if such access is allow-
     ed. If so, then permit access; else take some action as
     defined in the database schema.

Design of the privacy sub-system involves decisions concerning how
users/uses are to be identified - for example, by user names and passwords or by machine readable identity cards - how access rights for an
identified user are to be stored and retrieved and what actions should
be taken when an attempt is made at unauthorised access to data. The
actual mechanics of access control might involve the use of a security
matrix (Conway, Maxwell and Morgan, 1972) or of an access matrix
(Fernandez, Summers and Coleman, 1974). In both of these techniques
the columns of the matrix represent data elements and the rows

represent users. The elements M(i,j) of the matrix specify access
rights of user i to data j.

In practice, most privacy sub-systems are not designed to exhibit data
independence as discussed above. Application programs tend to issue
access requests in terms of physical rather than logical data structures and the columns of the access matrix, if one is used, tend to
represent physical storage structures such as files, records, relations and so on. In many cases, not even this level of modularisation
is used and access constraints are implemented in an ad hoc manner as
follows:

(a) Privacy constraints are specified in terms of an individual
user's rights to access specific parts of the physical storage
structure, e.g. employee file, manager record, salary field.

(b) Some of the constraints are implemented by restricting access
to relevant input/output programs and/or data files.

(c) Other constraints might require ad hoc procedures to be
written to reside within the input/output application programs. Such procedures are used to constrain access to those
parts of the database which are not regarded as 'units of
data' by the operating system. For example, if a particular
user is allowed to read some but not all of the fields in a
certain type of record, then such control cannot be enforced
by use of passwords in a file oriented operating system and
an ad hoc procedure would have to be written.

Although much has been written on the subject of database privacy,
most of this material is concerned with the social implications of
insecure data. However, some publications do consider the mechanics
of privacy control and the system designer can refer to these when
building the privacy sub-system, e.g. Denning and Denning (1979).

3.3.10 THE INTEGRITY SUB-SYSTEM

We define database 'integrity' as a property which reflects the extent
to which the database is an accurate model of that part of the universe
which it represents. The 'integrity sub-system' is responsible for
maintaining integrity by protecting the database against invalid (as
opposed to unauthorised) alteration.

Errors in the data occur for a number of reasons and protection must be
provided for each, for example:

(a) Parts of the universe are observed incorrectly before they are
represented by data, e.g. a thermometer might not be calibra-
ted correctly. Incorrect input data results.

(b) Observations are not made frequently enough, e.g. an employee
might be represented as working in department M when in reality the person has been transferred to department N.

(c) Data is corrupted in coding, transcription, and/or transmission.

(d) Errors are introduced through concurrent update, e.g. user 1 reads balance B at time T1, adds X to B and overwrites the original balance at time T2. User 2 repeats the process, reading at time T3, adding Y to the balance, and writing at time T4. If T1<T3<T2<T4 and X≠0 then the balance will be in error.

(e) Data is corrupted in storage through hardware faults.

Various techniques have been developed to reduce the occurrence of such errors or to detect them when they occur. Many of these techniques are well understood and their use is common practice. For example, parity checks are used to detect errors in data transmission and locks are used to reduce errors due to concurrent update. A concise description of these methods is given by Wiederhold (1983). But some aspects of the problem are very poorly understood. For example, the problem of 'out-of-date' data has not received much attention in the literature. However, Klopprogge (1981) has addressed this question in a recent publication and makes some interesting suggestions as to how the time dimension might be taken into account.

Semantic integrity

Other aspects of the problem are poorly understood although some progress has been made. One of these aspects is concerned with semantic integrity. By 'semantic integrity' we mean the compliance of the database with constraints which are derived from our knowledge about what is and what is not 'allowed' (or sensible) in that part of the universe which is represented by data in the database. The maintenance of semantic integrity involves preventing data which represents a disallowed state of the universe from being inserted into the database. The procedures which maintain semantic integrity detect semantic errors, inform the user that an error has taken place and prevent data from being inserted into the database. The design of these procedures is similar to the design of the security sub-system:

(a) Integrity constraints are identified during construction of the conceptual schema and are encoded as statements such as 'no employee may have two salaries' and 'it is unlikely that anyone has an age greater than 110'.

(b) These contraints are then couched in terms of data elements and access paths and constitute part of the database schema, e.g. 'only one access path between an employee and a salary is allowed' and 'no element of type age may be greater than 110'.

(c) The constraints are then taken into account when designing the physical storage structure.

(d) Mechanisms are designed for the enforcement of the integrity constraints.

Integrity constraint enforcement

Ideally, the enforcement mechanisms should be grouped together into a single program similar to the privacy arbiter. In practice, however, this is rarely done. The reason is that semantic integrity constraints can be of varying degrees of complexity and the subject is not yet well enough understood for a general purpose integrity checking algorithm to have been developed. Consequently, ad hoc procedures tend to be written and embedded in the application programs which handle the data input packages. For example, the application program which allows users to enter new employee records might have a procedure for checking that the entered age is not greater than 110.

The disadvantage of this ad hoc approach is that the code for checking a single integrity constraint might appear in many different application programs. This is particularly undesirable if the integrity check requires the database to be interrogated. However, if this is not the case there is an advantage in the approach: some integrity checking can be done 'off-line'. Input packages may be generated and checked at remote locations before being batched for input.

The maintenance of integrity is a difficult and poorly understood subject. However, it is of crucial importance that the database system is designed so that confidence in the accuracy of the data can be maintained at the required level. Notice that we have not said that the database should be completely correct. That would be unrealistic. What is important is that the database is sufficiently accurate for the use for which it is intended. The designer must remember that integrity checking can be expensive. One of the criteria is to find the right compromise between correctness and cost.

The 'automatic' maintenance of integrity is described later in this chapter.

3.3.11 THE BACK-UP AND RECOVERY SUB-SYSTEM
The back-up and recovery sub-system is the module which re-builds the database after corruption due to hardware or software failure. Recovery from such corruption is achieved by the use of locking strategies, transactions, back-up files and recovery routines.

Locking strategies
The 'locking strategy' determines how the database should be partitioned into units for update. The units might be fields, records, files or some larger sections of the database. While a copy of the unit is being updated, the original is locked to prevent any access to it. When the update is complete, the new version of the unit replaces the old version and the update is thereby committed. Should the system fail during update then the original remains intact. In some cases, the unit might not be copied but locked for exclusive use by the transaction which updates it directly (rather than updating a copy of it). If the system fails during update in this situation then the old version is reinstated by the use of back-up files and recovery routines, as explained later.

The locking process also serves to prevent errors arising from concurrent update.

Transactions
The use of transactions is closely related to the locking strategy.

A 'transaction' is a collection of database accesses which are regarded as comprising a unit of processing as far as the locking routines are concerned. The choice of transaction size is determined by other factors in addition to recovery. For example, the 'logical' units of work as seen by the user will have some influence on the choice of transaction content.

Back-up files
The 'back-up files' typically consist of a journal file and dump files. The journal is normally a sequential file held on tape which contains copies (or images) of database units before and/or after they are updated, together with copies of the transactions which update them. The dump files consist of copies of the whole or parts of the database which are taken periodically. For example, a copy of one-seventh of the database may be taken every day, or a copy of the whole database may be taken once a week.

Recovery routines
The 'recovery routines' determine how a correct version of the database may be reinstated after system failure. Ideally, the database should be returned to the state it was in just before the failure. Various techniques have been developed, two of which may be simply described as follows:

(a)   Roll-back or backward recovery. The journal file is scanned to identify the before-images of the units which were being updated when the system failed. These before-images are reinstated.

(b)   Roll-forward or forward recovery. A copy of the database (or that part of the database which has been corrupted) is obtained from the most recent dump file and loaded. The journal file is then used to bring the database up to the state it was in just before failure. After-images can be used directly or transactions which occurred since the dump can be automatically re-run.

Roll-back can be used to deal with deadlock (where two transactions lock units of the database required by each other and thereby prevent each other from completion), run-unit failure (where a transaction terminates prematurely) and communication/write errors which corrupt a single locked unit of the database.

Roll-forward is generally used when the failure has affected a large section of the database and the extent of corruption is not restricted to the units which were active at the time of the failure. This occurs, for example, with disk-head crash.

Design of the recovery sub-system
Design of the recovery sub-system involves decisions concerning how often dumps should be taken, how big the locked units and transactions should be, and what information should be recorded on the journal file. To a large extent the recovery sub-system is dependent on the physical storage structure, and the design of these two parts of the system should be carried out concurrently.

3.3.12 ADVANTAGES OF THE FUNCTIONAL ARCHITECTURE AS OUTLINED

The advantages of the functional architecture of database systems described so far are felt in all stages of the system life cycle. For
example, the design stage is facilitated by the modular structure and
by the fact that the application programs and the integrity and privacy
sub-systems all refer to the database in logical terms. Each of these
modules can be designed independently and the designers need not be
concerned with the implementation details of the physical storage
structure used. Use of the system is facilitated by the presence of
the conceptual and database schemas. End-users can refer to these
schemas to clarify their understanding of the application area and to
find out what data is stored in the database. Maintenance of the system is facilitated to a large extent by the logical to physical mapping
module. As mentioned, the introduction of new hardware and/or operating system has minimal impact on the system if this module is present.

In practice, few existing systems conform to the ideal architecture.
This is largely because of difficulty in designing the logical to
physical mapping module. In general, application programs communicate
with the data storage structure directly and privacy and integrity controls are embedded in these application programs.

3.4 DATABASE MANAGEMENT SYSTEMS

The design of a database system from scratch would involve the following tasks:

- specification of the conceptual schema
- specification of the input/output requirements
- specification of the database schema
- specification of the physical storage structure
- design of the privacy sub-system
- design of the integrity sub-system
- design of the back-up and recovery sub-system
- design of the input/output application programs and RPG and
  query languages

As can be seen from reading section 3.3, such design would be a difficult and tedious process. Fortunately, database systems need not be
designed in this way. Since the designer can use a database management
system to assist in the task. A 'database management system' (DBMS) is
a collection of procedures, documentation aids, languages and programs
to facilitate the design and implementation of database systems.

(Readers with no conception of what a DBMS is like may find it worthwhile to have a quick look at sub-section 3.5.5 before continuing. In
that sub-section we describe the use of a very simple and user-friendly
DBMS which is available on micro-computers. The system, called dBASE
II, is very limited in the facilities it provides but is extremely useful as an introduction to database work. With a little guidance, the
average person can learn to use dBASE II within a few hours.)

Typically, a DBMS is based on a general purpose storage structure which
can be tailored to meet the requirements of various database systems.
The system generally comes equipped with privacy, integrity and recovery sub-systems which can also be tailored for particular requirements.

More sophisticated DBMSs provide facilities for the generation of application programs from specifications written in very high-level languages. Much of the designer's work is already done.

Ideally, it should be possible to use a single DBMS to implement many various database systems: for example, it should be possible for one person to use a DBMS to implement a shop floor reporting system and for another person to use the same DBMS to implement an integrated accounting system. However, this ideal has not yet been achieved. Some DBMSs are better suited to certain types of application than others.

The following list identifies some of the better known commercially available DBMSs:

> IMS
> IDMS
> TOTAL
> ADABAS
> dBASE II
> DB2
> INGRES
> IDS
> S2000
> IMAGE

3.4.1 COMPONENTS OF AN IDEAL DBMS

Ideally, a DBMS should contain:

- a *conceptual schema definition language* which is powerful (allowing any organisational structure to be described), natural to use and decidable (that is, the consistency of schemas written in it can be determined)

- a *data dictionary system* together with guidelines for data analysis

- an implementation independent *input/output package specification language* which can be used to describe useful packages of data

- an implementation independent *database schema definition language* which can be used to specify privacy constraints, security requirements and access path requirements

- a general purpose *symmetrical data storage structure* (by symmetrical it is meant that all access paths which are provided in the structure have equal efficiency)

- a *logical to physical mapping module*

- a general purpose *privacy sub-system*

- a general purpose *integrity sub-system*

- a general purpose *back-up and recovery sub-system*

82

Database Concepts

- an *application program generator*

- a *report program generator*

- a general purpose *query language*

Given such an ideal DBMS, the creation of a database system would simply involve the following steps:

(a) Construct the conceptual schema using the language provided. This would include a definition of integrity constraints and inference rules.

(b) Perform a data analysis study and create a data dictionary. This would involve definition of the meaning and format of data items and the specification of useful packages of data items. For example, a package P1 might be specified as:

    P1
    _____

    customer name
    address
    balance

(c) Describe the privacy and back-up and recovery requirements in the logical language provided.

(d) Specify some of the application programs using the high-level language provided in the application program generator module. For example, an application program specification may include statements such as:

    display 'please enter customer name';
    read cname;
    retrieve P1 with customer-name = cname;
    display 'please enter amount to be credited or debited';
    read amount;
    add amount to balance of P1;
    replace P1;

The data storage structure and general purpose integrity and recovery mechanisms would then be configured automatically, as would the application programs. The designer would not need to know how the data was stored since all communication with the physical storage structure would be carried out by the logical to physical mapping module.

Notice also that the designer need not specify all of the database schema since, in the ideal DBMS, all relations in the conceptual schema would be implemented as access paths with equal efficiency in the physical storage structure. Therefore the conceptual schema and the database schema would be identical in this respect.

The ideal architecture as described above also displays a high degree of data independence. Since all relations in the conceptual schema are represented by access paths with equal efficiency in the data storage structure, any new end-user requirements can be accommodated by simply specifying the new input/output packages and the application programs which use them. If the required data is there, it can readily be accessed.

3.4.2 LIMITATIONS OF EXISTING DBMSs

Unfortunately, currently available DBMSs are not ideal. Although researchers are developing fully automatic components, no single DBMS has yet been produced which can automatically generate a complete database system from its specification. In general, the DBMS user must become involved with implementation details as well as system specification. In particular, the DBMS user must be fully conversant with the data storage structure underlying the particular DBMS being used (largely because of the common absence of a logical to physical mapping module). Integrity constraints, privacy controls, input/output requirements and so on are typically specified in terms of the underlying storage structure. Two important consequences of this are:

(a) The database system designer's task is complicated by the need to be conversant with the terminology of the data storage structure used by the DBMS.

(b) The expressive power of the various specification languages provided by the DBMS (e.g. schema specification language, query language, etc.) tends to be limited to correspond to the limitations of the underlying data storage structure.

The second point is very important and deserves further explanation. Suppose that we have a DBMS which is based on a hierarchical storage structure (such a system is described in more detail later). It is probable that the specification languages which are provided by that DBMS are limited in their expressive power in such a way that they can only be used to describe hierarchically structured organisations and hierarchically structured access paths. In order to use such a DBMS, the designer and the end-users must perceive the application area as consisting of a set of hierarchical structures. That is, they must use a hierarchical view of the universe. This may not be the most natural view to use and, of more importance, it may not be powerful enough to accommodate all of the organisational structures which the user wants to model in the database.

Before discussing database views in more detail, three other shortcomings of currently available DBMSs should be mentioned:

(a) They do not provide data independence to the extent outlined for the ideal system. In general, when a database system has been designed and implemented using a commercial DBMS, it is relatively inflexible. Any new input/output requirements which crop up may often only be accommodated by major reorganisation of the database and physical schemas, followed by extensive modification or re-compilation of existing application programs. This is a consequence of two factors. Firstly, the views of the universe which underly most commercial DBMSs are asymmetrical, resulting in asymmetrical conceptual schemas, asymmetrical database schemas, and asymmetrical physical storage structures. The effect is that some access paths are implemented more efficiently than others and some access paths are not implemented at all. New input/ output requirements may require the application area to be viewed in a different way and new access paths to be provided by modification to the data storage structure. Secondly, the absence in most currently available DBMSs of a central logical to physical mapping module means that modification to some part of the data storage structure may have an impact on many existing application programs which use that part.

(b) Yet another way in which currently available DBMSs do not match up to the ideal as described concerns the extent to which they automate the implementation of database systems. In general, the data storage structure is automatically con- figured from the database schema, and the necessary back-up and recovery sub-systems are provided. However, in most cases, the construction of application programs is left to the DBMS user. High-level database commands such as INSERT, FIND and DELETE may be provided but the programs in which these commands appear must be constructed by the user. Integ- rity constraints,and sometimes privacy controls,are typically implemented as ad hoc procedures embedded in application pro- grams.

(c) One final criticism of currently available DBMSs concerns their architecture. In many systems, the distinction between conceptual, database and physical schemas is not clear. Often, only two schemas are used: the database (or logical) schema, and the physical schema. Furthermore, these tend to overlap. One consequence of this is that a designer using a DBMS to facilitate the implementation of a database system, must immediately start thinking in terms of the data structure used by that DBMS. Often, the designer commences by performing a data analysis study and then goes on to specify the database schema using a notation which refers to components of the DBMS data storage structure. Integrity and privacy constraints are also specified using this notation. The result is that no implementation independent specification of the application area, or of the user requirements, is ever constructed. If a new DBMS is introduced at some later date then the whole sys- tem may have to be re-specified as well as re-designed. This is most likely if the new DBMS uses a different view to the one being replaced.

Notwithstanding the shortcomings discussed above, the use of a DBMS can simplify design and implementation of database systems - perhaps not to the extent which one would ideally like, but at least their use is a vast improvement on designing database systems from scratch.

3.4.3 DATA MODELS, VIEWS OF THE UNIVERSE AND CATEGORIES OF DBMS

As mentioned earlier, DBMSs contain general purpose data structures which can be tailored to meet the requirements of particular applic- ations. These structures are abstract structures in the sense that they can be implemented in various ways using arrays, files, trees, hash tables, inverted lists, and so on. Traditionally, these abstract structures are called 'data models'. The seven most commonly used data models are:

(a) the hierarchical data model
(b) the network data model
(c) the CODASYL network (or DBTG) data model
(d) the relational data model
(e) the entity relationship attribute model
(f) the binary relational data model
(g) the functional data model

It is important when choosing a DBMS that the user is aware of the data model underlying it. This is because the user of a DBMS must perceive the universe of discourse according to the view of the universe which is the basis of the data model of that DBMS. For example, most DBMSs which are based on the hierarchical model are based on a hierarchical view which distinguishes between 'entities' and 'attributes' and in which one-to-many relations between entities are allowed but many-to-many relations are not.

In the following sub-sections, a brief description is given of the seven views of the universe which are closely related to the seven models mentioned above. Much has been written on the relative merits of these approaches and those arguments are not repeated here. A good account of them can be found in Tsichritzis and Lochovsky (1982). DBMSs can be categorised according to which view they use. Knowing the limitation of the view used by the DBMS under consideration, it is possible to perform at least an initial appraisal of the usefulness of that DBMS without going into the technical details of its construction.

The description of database views which are given in this and the following sub-sections are not definitive. We have tried to present simple descriptions of each view which conform to the widest (most general) interpretation of their meaning rather than the particular meanings which they are given when used in the context of a particular DBMS. For example, the following description of the hierarchical view refers to the generally accepted features of this view rather than the specific features in IMS terminology. (IMS is an acronym for Information Management System, which is a widely used 'hierarchical' DBMS.) The reason for this approach is that the discussions which follow are of general applicability and should enable the reader to appreciate *some* of the limitations and strengths of the seven different types of DBMS. Specific limitations and strengths of a particular DBMS may only be identified by reference to literature which contains a detailed (and usually lengthy) description of that DBMS.

3.4.4 THE HIERARCHICAL VIEW

The hierarchical view regards the universe as consisting of entities, attributes and relationships. Entities are related to other entities in tree structures such as those shown in fig. 3.17. The nodes of the trees are entities and the arcs (or branches) are relationships between entities. Entities at the top of trees are called 'roots'. Roots may be related to any number of lower-level dependent entities and each of these may be related to any number of lower-level dependents, and so on.

86

If entity X is a dependent of entity Y, then Y is called the 'father'
of X and X the 'son' of Y.

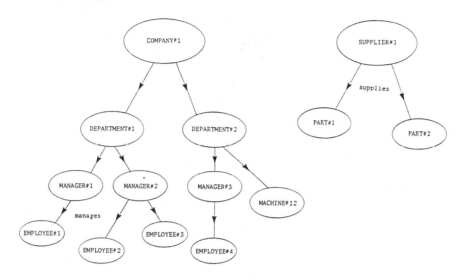

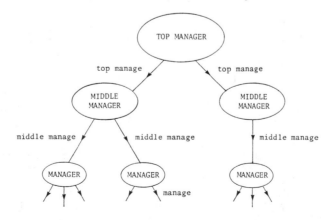

Figure 3.17 A hierarchical organisation

An entity set is a set of entities and a relation is a set of relationships. All relationships from a given relation must link father
entities from at most one entity set to son entities from at most one
different entity set. For example, all relationships of type 'manages'
must link a father entity from the 'manager' entity set to a son entity
from the 'employee' entity set. This means that this view cannot be
used to model the situation in which managers manage other managers.
The user would have to perceive such a situation as shown in fig. 3.18.

The major constraint of the hierarchical view is that *entities
may be related to at most one father entity.*

Figure 3.18 A hierarchical view of management

We now consider attributes. An attribute is regarded, in the hierarchical view, as a property of an entity (e.g. height, age, address) which has no meaning (or more correctly, no interest) on its own. Unfortunately, no clear definition has ever been given of the terms 'entity' and 'attribute', and the user of the hierarchical view must refer to examples for guidance. An entity may be related to many attributes and an attribute may be related to many entities. Therefore, the single father restriction governing the relationship between entities does not apply to relationships between entities and attributes. Situations such as that shown in fig. 3.19 can be modelled by the hierarchical view.

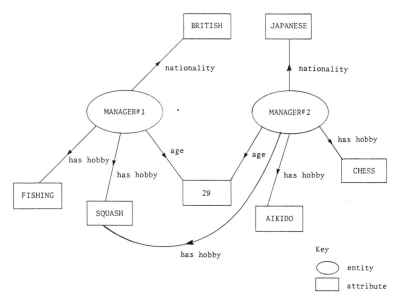

Figure 3.19 Relationships between entities and attributes

Notice that we do not attempt to give a formal definition of the terms 'entity' and 'attribute'. A rough guideline is that if you ever want to find out something about an object then it should be regarded as an entity; otherwise, it is an attribute. For example, if you want to use the data model to produce a list of all managers who are aged 29, then 'age 29' should be regarded as an entity and not an attribute.

Shortcomings of the hierarchical view
The hierarchical view leads to an asymmetrical perception of the universe in two respects:

(a) The tree structure implies that relationships between entities have *direction*. The concept of father and son enforces this.

(b) 'Things' of the real world are classified as entities or attributes. There would appear to be no rationale for this distinction. Consider the colour of a plant. The colour is of as much interest to an artist as the plant is to a gardener.

88

The asymmetry of the view leads to asymmetric models and, in the context of database work, to asymmetric implementation of access paths through data models. In general, hierarchical trees are represented by hierarchical data structures. Random access to elements in such structures is efficient only if it involves traversal down through the tree and traversal from entities to their attributes.

Applicability of the hierarchical view

The main advantage of the hierarchical view is that those parts of the universe which can be modelled using this view can be easily represented by hierarchical data structures. For example, entities can be mapped to files, records or fields in records, and attributes can be mapped to fields within records (the word 'record' is used here with its traditional meaning). An example of a hierarchical data structure is shown in fig. 3.20.

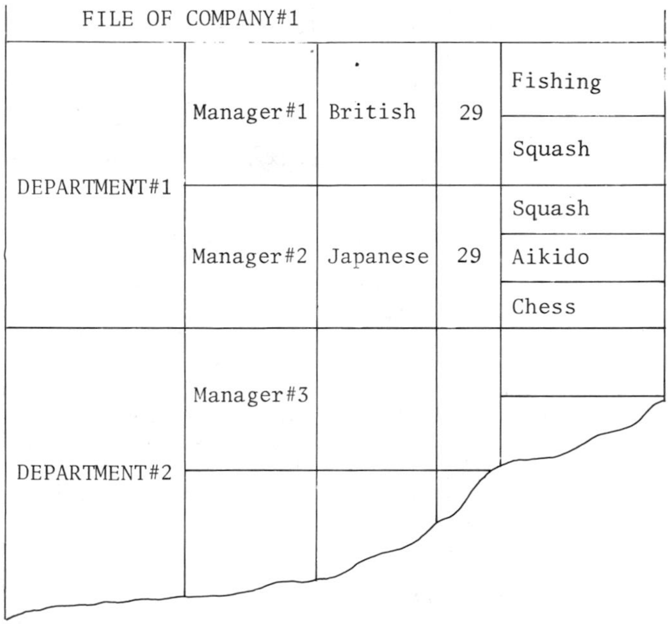

FILE OF COMPANY#1				
DEPARTMENT#1	Manager#1	British	29	Fishing
				Squash
	Manager#2	Japanese	29	Squash
				Aikido
				Chess
DEPARTMENT#2	Manager#3			

Figure 3.20 A hierarchical data structure

Note, however, that problems may still occur with such a data structure even though it models a truly hierarchical situation:

(a) If a record is deleted then it is possible that some information might be inadvertently lost from the system. For example, if two departments were to be amalgamated then care would need to be taken to ensure that all employees in these two departments were assigned to the new department before the old department records were erased.

(b) As mentioned, some access paths are implemented more efficiently than others. For example, in fig. 3.20 the retrieval of data about a given manager is quite straightforward if the department and company in which he works are known (i.e. if we have sufficient information to select a 'tree' and traverse it from root to the branch required). On the other hand, if we want a list of the - probably few - managers who practice the martial art of Aikido then we would have to search through all of the files, examining all of the records.

We conclude, therefore, that the hierarchical view should only be used (i) when the situation to be modelled is truly hierarchical and (ii) when the required access to, and manipulation of, the resulting database is also hierarchical in the sense that access to data is only required to be to and down trees and from entities to attributes, and insertion and deletion of data is only required to be 'branch at a time'. If this is the case, the hierarchical view will lead to simple data structures and simple data manipulation algorithms.

In practice, many 'hierarchical' DBMSs do not require the user to perceive the universe according to the hierarchical view as described above. The views are not, in general, so constraining. However, this requires some entities to be regarded as existing in more than one place. The database must then contain redundant representations of entities (in addition to the redundant representation of attributes which is the case in most data structures) or make use of pointers. Most hierarchical DBMSs can easily accommodate models of truly hierarchical situations but the accommodation of non-hierarchical situations is possible only at the expense and danger of duplication of data and/or the creation of secondary indexes or the use of pointers.

3.4.5 THE NETWORK VIEW
In the network view the same distinction is made between entities and attributes as is made in the hierarchical view. However, the 'allowed' structures linking entities are much less constrained. Entities may be related to any number of other entities. An example of a model which has been constructed using the network view is given in fig. 3.21.

The network view can be used to readily create models of most organisational structures that we are likely to want to represent by data. However, the actual storage of such data models is more complicated and/or less space efficient than is the storage of hierarchical models. One method of implementation is to map entities to records, attributes to record fields and to represent relationships between entities by pointers as illustrated in fig. 3.22.

3.4.6 THE DBTG (OR CODASYL NETWORK) VIEW
In 1971, the Data Base Task Group (DBTG) of the CODASYL programming language committee published a report (DBTG, 1971) which contained definitions and guidelines for the construction of databases and database management systems. Systems which are based on these recommendations are called CODASYL or DBTG systems.

The DBTG report includes a description of a language called a data description language (DDL) which can be used for the specification of data models. The view of the universe which underlies this language may be regarded as a 'constrained' network view. The constraints are not as severe as those of the hierarchical view but are sufficient to ensure that all data models which can be built by use of the DBTG view can be readily accommodated by the 'set' data structure which is also defined by DBTG.

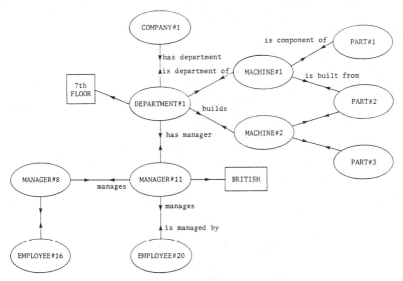

Note: Some arc labels have been omitted for clarity

Figure 3.21   An example of an unconstrained network situation

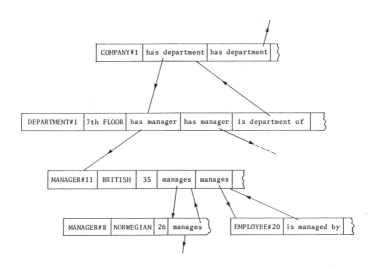

Figure 3.22   An example of an unconstrained network data structure

The DBTG 'set' data structure

Because the DBTG view is closely related to the DBTG 'set' data structure, it is useful to consider this structure before we consider the
view. The reason for some of the characteristics of the view will then
be more apparent.

The data structure which is used in a DBTG system is called a DBTG set.
A 'set occurrence' is a collection of records one of which is the
'owner' and the others 'members'. In hierarchical terms, the owner is
the 'father' and the members are the 'sons'. (Notice that a DBTG set
has little in common with a mathematical set.) Figure 3.23 illustrates
three set occurrences of the same 'set type'. Relationships which are
represented in occurrences of a set type must be of the same type.

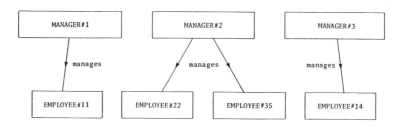

Figure 3.23   Three set occurrences of the same type

A DBTG set occurrence is like a hierarchical data structure consisting
of two levels only. The constraints which govern the presence of
records in DBTG sets are:

(a)   All owner records of occurrences of the same set type must be
      of the same record type. Notice that member records may be
      of different types, as shown in fig. 3.24.

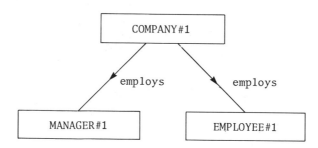

Figure 3.24   Members of a DBTG set may be of different record type

(b)   The owner record type of a set type must be different from
      the types of the member records. For example, the structure
      illustrated in fig. 3.25 is not allowed.

(c)   A member record is only allowed to appear at most once in set
      occurrences of the same type. This means that a record may
      only have one 'father' with respect to a particular relation-
      ship type. For example, the structure illustrated in fig.

3.26 is not allowed. Notice, however, that this does not preclude a record from having more than one father provided that the record is related to those fathers in different ways, i.e. a record may be a member of more than one set occurrence provided that these are occurrences of different set types.

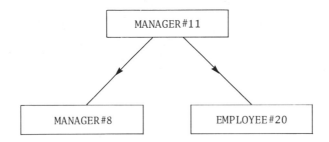

Figure 3.25 An illegal set with owner type the same as one of the member types

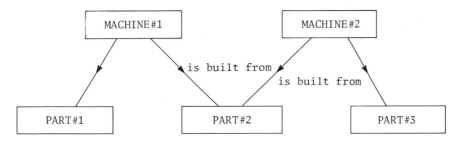

Figure 3.26 An illegal DBTG set

Use of connection records in DBTG sets

The usefulness of DBTG sets can be extended by use of 'connection records', as follows:

(a) Records of the same type may be indirectly related by the introduction of connection records as shown in fig. 3.27. Two set types are used both of which have the same connection records as members. Because these two types are different, a single connection record may occur once as a member in a set occurrence of both.

(b) 'Many-to-many' relations between two record types may be accommodated by the introduction of connection records as shown in fig. 3.28. Two set types are used in this example: MC and PC. Owner records of MC are of type machine and owner records of PC are of type part. MC and PC have the same connection records as members.

(c) Relationships which involve more than two records may also be handled by the introduction of a connection record as shown in fig. 3.29. This record structure represents the fact that 'person 1 bought object 5 from person 6 at place 4'. This is how n-ary relationships between entities are represented in the DBTG view.

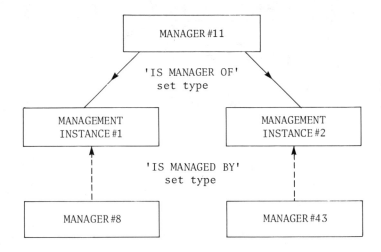

Figure 3.27 Relationship between two records of the same type

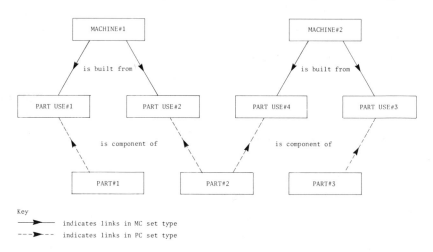

Figure 3.28 Many-to-many relation using connection records

Connection records may contain knowledge as shown in fig. 3.30. This may be necessary to improve the efficiency of some of the access paths which may be required by the user. For example, to find all of the parts used in the construction of machine 3 requires the system to:

(a) Locate the set occurrence with machine 3 record as owner.

(b) Access all connection records which are members of this set occurrence.

(c) Look at the part field of each of these connection records to find the part number.

If the connection records did not contain the part field or a pointer to part records then the system would have to look through all occurrences of the PC set type to find the part used.

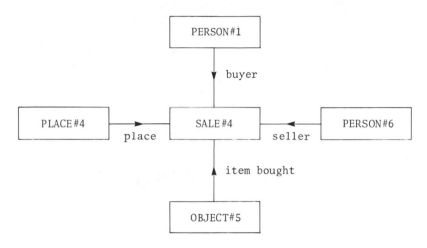

Figure 3.29 A relationship between four records

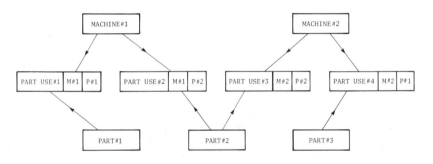

Figure 3.30 Connection records may contain information

The DBTG view

We now look at the view of the universe which underlies the DBTG recommendations. This view has never been formally defined and the discussion which follows does not attempt to do this. We simply present an outline of the view in order that the reader may gain an understanding of what is involved in using a DBTG system.

Like the hierarchical view, the DBTG view regards the universe as consisting of entities and attributes. Entities are related to other entities and these relationships are classified as belonging to relations. Relationships are perceived as having a direction from what we shall call the 'father' entity to the 'son' entity.

An entity may be the father of any number of sons. However, two
entities of the same type may not be directly related (other than by
the fact that they are of the same type). Also, an entity may only
occur once as a son in a relationship of a given type (i.e. an entity
may not have more than one father with respect to a given relation).

As an example of the use of the view, consider the situation shown in
fig. 3.21 (this model was built with the use of the unconstrained network view). This situation when perceived using the DBTG view may be
modelled as shown in fig. 3.31. Notice that the arrows do not necessarily indicate the user's access requirements. They indicate the DBTG
set structure which must be used. Access in the direction of the arrow
will therefore be provided. However, if access in the other direction
is required then either (a) additional sets must be provided or (b)
member records will have to contain pointers to owners, as discussed
earlier.

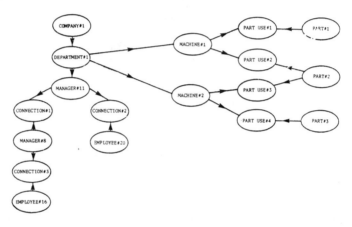

Figure 3.31 An example of a DBTG model

Applicability of the DBTG view
The DBTG view can be used to model most situations which can be modelled by the network view. However, this use is complicated by the need
to introduce connection records. In addition, the DBTG set structure
is asymmetric (access from owner to member is implemented in a different way to access in the other direction). This asymmetry is reflected
in the DBTG view which complicates the construction of data models.

3.4.7 THE RELATIONAL VIEW
The relational view (Codd, 1970) regards the universe as consisting of
entities, entity sets and relations. A relation is a set of n-tuples
$<e1, e2, e3, \ldots\ldots\ldots, en>$ where entity e1 belongs to entity set E1,
e2 belongs to entity set E2, and so on. A relation may be represented
by a table as illustrated in fig. 3.32. This relation models a situation in which departments make machines, machines consist of parts and
the quantity of each part in each machine is known.

One difference between relational storage structures and files of
records is that each entry in a relation is 'flat'. Compare the relation in fig. 3.32 with the file of records shown in fig. 3.33.

Relations are therefore more symmetrical, and this symmetry is enhanced by the fact that the order of the columns in a relation is not significant.

Dept	Machine	Part	Quantity
D1	M1	P1	20
D1	M1	P2	40
D1	M2	P2	10
D1	M2	P3	20
D1	M2	P4	4

Figure 3.32 An example of a relation

DEPARTMENTAL FILE

Machine	Part	Quantity
M1	P1	20
	P2	40
M2	P2	10
	P3	20
	P4	4

Figure 3.33 A file of records

Now consider a situation in which departments also employ people and are situated at known locations. In all, six entity sets are involved:

- departments
- locations
- employees
- machines
- parts
- quantities (of parts)

Location	Department	Employee	Machine	Part	Quantity
London	D1	E1	M1	P1	20
London	D1	E1	M1	P2	40
London	D1	E2	M1	P1	20
London	D1	E2	M1	P2	40
London	D1	E1	M2	P2	10
London	D1	E1	M2	P3	20
London	D1	E1	M2	P4	4
London	D1	E2	M2	P2	10
London	D1	E2	M2	P3	20
London	D1	E2	M2	P4	4
...etc.					

Figure 3.34 A 'poor' relational model

The 'unthinking' use of the relational view as described so far could result in one large relation, as shown in fig. 3.34. This is, obviously, a 'poor' model of the situation for two reasons:

(a) There is a great deal of redundancy. For example, the fact that machine M1 is made in department D1 is modelled in four places.

(b) Different types of relationships between entities are modelled in the same way. For example, consider the first tuple in the relation. The relationship between E1 and 20 (quantity) is indirect, whereas the relationship between E1 and D1 is direct; yet they are both modelled in the same way.

These undesirable features can be eliminated as follows:

(a) The 'artificial' linking of machines with employees can be removed by replacing the large relation by two smaller ones. Essentially, we recognise that a machine is only related to an employee by virtue of the fact that it is one of many machines which are made by a department which employs many people. We say that there is a 'multi-valued dependency' between machines and employees. This dependency can be 'factored out' as shown in fig. 3.35.

(a) Department/employee relation

Location	Department	Employee
London	D1	E1
London	D1	E2

(b) Department/machine relation

Department	Machine	Part	Quantity
D1	M1	P1	20
D1	M1	P2	40
D1	M2	P2	10
D1	M2	P3	20
D1	M2	P4	4

Figure 3.35 Relational model after the multivalued dependency between machines and employees has been factored out

(b) We now recognise that there still exists some redundancy in the model. Notice that each tuple in the department/machine relations contains information about the use of a particular part in a particular machine. The quantity value in a tuple refers to the part *and* the machine on which it is used. It would be meaningless to say that 'the quantity of P2 used was 40' without saying which machine was involved. We say that the quantity is 'fully dependent' on the machine/part pair. This is not true for the department. Department is only

dependent on the machine involved; therefore we can 'factor'
this column out as shown in fig. 3.36.

Location	Department	Employee
London	D1	E1
London	D1	E2

Machine	Part	Quantity
M1	P1	20
M1	P2	40
M2	P2	10
M2	P3	20
M2	P4	4

Department	Machine
D1	M1
D1	M2

*Figure 3.36 Relational model after the department/machine links
have been factored out*

(c) We have not removed all redundancy from the model: there still
exists an asymmetry in the department/employee relation.
Employees are directly related to departments but are only
indirectly related to department location, yet these direct
and indirect links are represented in the same way. This may
be resolved by replacing the troublesome relation by two relations as shown in fig. 3.37.

Department	Employee
D1	E1
D1	E2

Department	Location
D1	London

Machine	Part	Quantity
M1	P1	20
M1	P2	40
M2	P2	10
M2	P3	20
M2	P4	4

Department	Machine
D1	M1
D1	M2

Figure 3.37 The final model

We now have a better model consisting of relations which are said to
be 'fully normalised'. We achieve this by a rather unsystematic factoring process. In general, a fully normalised relational model can be
built by the systematic application of well defined normalisation
rules. These rules are described in more detail in (Kent, 1983), for
example.

Notice in fig. 3.37 that each tuple now refers to a single entity *or a
single relationship* and that each tuple contains a model of some of the

direct links which this entity *or relationship* has with other entities
or relationships. For example:

   (a)   Tuple <D1, E1> in the department/employee relation refers to
        entity E1 and represents the link which this entity has with
        the department D1.

   (b)   Tuple <M1, P1, 20> in the machine/part relation refers to the
        relationship between machine M1 and part P1 and represents the
        link which this relationship has with quantity 20:

(quantity)

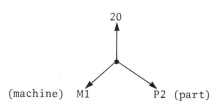

(machine) M1   P2 (part)

We see therefore, that the relational view is more symmetrical than the
DBTG view since relationships which involve more than two entities can
be modelled in the same way as relationships between two entities. For
example, consider the situation in which 'A bought item B'. This can
be modelled as:

Buyer	Item bought
A	B

Now suppose we want to qualify this relationship by stating that 'A
bought B from C'. This three-entity relationship can be modelled as:

Buyer	Item bought	Seller
A	B	C

The extension to the model is relatively straightforward.

Now consider what would be involved if a DBTG view were used. The
initial model would be as shown in fig. 3.38. The appearance of C on
the scene requires a 'new' entity to be introduced, as shown in fig.
3.39. A consequence of this is that the data structure in which the
DBTG model is stored could require extensive modification. In a DBTG
system new sets would have to be created with a new type of connection
record as member. In a relational system the model could be stored as
a set of tables, one for each relation. The addition of columns to

100

tables is likely to be less of a problem.

Figure 3.38 A relationship involving two entities

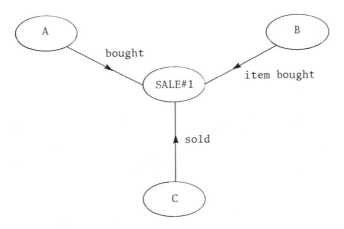

Figure 3.39 A relationship involving three entities

Applicability of the 'normalised' relational view

The normalisation process is quite complicated and consequently, the
relational view requires a certain amount of expertise to be used correctly. However, a number of advantages derive from its use:

(a) It is powerful and can accommodate most situations which we
     might want to model.

(b) The resulting structure is reasonably symmetrical and does
     not reflect the (possibly short-lived) access requirements of
     users to any great extent.

(c) The structure can be mapped into storage with relative ease.
     For example, one approach is to use direct access files with
     inverted indexes, one for each column which the user wants to
     use as a key.

3.4.8 RELATION MANIPULATION AND QUERY LANGUAGES

Various languages have been developed for querying relational databases.
These languages may be divided into two types: those based on relational algebra and those based on relational calculus. The languages which
are based on relational algebra are procedural languages which allow
database programmers and end-users to manipulate relations using relational algebraic operators in order to obtain the results they require.
The languages based on relational calculus, on the other hand, are
declarative languages which allow end-users to specify exactly what
data they require without having to specify how that data is to be
obtained from the relations available in the database.

Before giving examples of such languages, we describe relational algebra and relational calculus in more detail.

3.4.9 RELATIONAL ALGEBRA

Relational algebra consists of the traditional set operations of union, intersection, difference and Cartesian product, together with some special relational operations. The four most commonly used relational operations are:

- selection
- projection
- join
- division

In addition, there is another operation which we shall call 'projection*' and which we include because it is used later in this book.

The simplest way to explain these operations is by example. Consider, therefore, the relations given in fig. 3.40. These (not fully normalised) relations constitute a simple 'company database' and each of the relational algebraic operations will now be described with reference to this database.

Selection

The SELECT operator creates a new relation from an existing relation by selecting only those rows (tuples) which have some specified values in given columns. For example, consider the command:

R4 = SELECT R1 WHERE SEX = 'FEMALE'

Execution of this command would cause the following relation to be created:

Relation R4

EMP-NAME	SEX
LEWIS	FEMALE
JONES	FEMALE
GREEN	FEMALE

The condition for selection may be more complex. For example:

R5 = SELECT R3 WHERE (DISCOUNT RATE = 10) AND (BALANCE > 500)

The complex condition may be any expression containing the connectives AND, OR, NOT, =, >, $\geqslant$, <, and $\leqslant$.

Projection

The PROJECT operator creates a new relation from an existing relation by selecting only those columns which have been specified and by removing any redundant rows (tuples) which might arise in the new relation. For example, consider the following command:

R6 = PROJECT R2 OVER DEPT, DEPT-TEL-EXT

Execution of this command would cause the following relation to be created:

Relation R6

DEPT	DEPT-TEL-EXT
ACCOUNTS	3133
PERSONNEL	2786
MANUFACTURING	2482

Notice that there are two stages in the execution of a projection:

(a) Create a relation with the columns specified.

(b) Remove any redundant tuples (i.e. if two tuples are identical then one must be removed).

Relation R1

EMP-NAME	SEX
Smith	male
Rodgers	malc
Lewis	female
Jones	female
Jenkins	male
MacIntosh	male
Green	female

Relation R2

DEPT	EMP-NAME	DEPT-TEL-EXT
Accounts	Lewis	3133
Personnel	Smith	2786
Manufacturing	Jones	2482
Accounts	Green	3133
Manufacturing	Rodgers	2482
Manufacturing	MacIntosh	2482
Manufacturing	Jenkins	2482

Relation R3

CUSTOMER	DISCOUNT RATE	BALANCE
AI Company	10	+1000
Greaves & Son	5	+ 200
Allied Bakeries	10	+ 600

Figure 3.40 A relational database

Projection*

The PROJECT* operator is similar to the PROJECT operator but differs in that the columns which are *not* wanted are specified. For example, consider the following command:

R7 = PROJECT* R3 WITH RESPECT TO BALANCE

Execution of this command would cause the following relation to be created:

Relation R7

CUSTOMER	DISCOUNT RATE
AI COMPANY	10
GREAVES & SON	5
ALLIED BAKERIES	10

Later on in this book we use the PROJECT* operator where we introduce the notation πx to stand for 'project with respect to column x'. Using this notation, the command above may be re-expressed as follows:

R7 = πBALANCE R3

Joining

The operator JOIN takes two relations which have one or more columns in common and creates a new relation by concatenating tuples which have the same value in a specified common column. For example, consider the following command:

R8 = JOIN R1 and R2 OVER EMP-NAME

Execution of this command would cause the following relation to be created:

Relation R8

DEPT	EMP-NAME	SEX	DEPT-TEL-EXT
PERSONNEL	SMITH	MALE	2786
MANUFACTURING	RODGERS	MALE	2482
ACCOUNTS	LEWIS	FEMALE	3133
MANUFACTURING	JONES	FEMALE	2482
MANUFACTURING	JENKINS	MALE	2482
MANUFACTURING	MACINTOSH	MALE	2482
ACCOUNTS	GREEN	FEMALE	3133

Division

The operator DIVIDE takes an n-ary relation (the dividend) and a unary relation (the divisor) and produces an (n - 1)ary relation (the quotient). The unary relation must be defined on the same domain as one

104

of the domains in the n-ary relation. An (n - 1)ary tuple will appear in the quotient if and only if it appears in the dividend with *all values* which appear in the unary relation. For example, suppose that we have the following relations:

Relation R9   Relation R10

SEX
FEMALE
MALE

DEPT	SEX	DEPT-TEL-EXT
PERSONNEL	MALE	2786
MANUFACTURING	MALE	2482
ACCOUNTS	FEMALE	3133
MANUFACTURING	FEMALE	2482
ACCOUNTS	FEMALE	3133

Consider the following command:

    R11 = DIVIDE R10 BY R9

Execution of this command would cause the following relation to be created:

Relation R11

DEPT	DEPT-TEL-EXT
MANUFACTURING	2482

<MANUFACTURING, 2482> is the only entry in R11 since this is the only tuple which appears in R10 with both values of 'FEMALE' and 'MALE' which are present in R9.

An alternative form of the DIVIDE operator is illustrated by the following example:

    R12 = DIVIDE R10 WITH RESPECT TO SEX

Execution of this command would cause a relation R12 to be created which contains all tuples which appear in R10 *with all values* in the domain SEX. That is:

Relation R12

DEPT	DEPT-TEL-EXT
MANUFACTURING	2482

<MANUFACTURING, 2482> is the only tuple in R12 since it is the only tuple which appears in R10 with the two values: 'MALE' and 'FEMALE' which constitute the domain SEX.

We use this form of the divide operator later on in the book where we introduce the notation δx to stand for 'divide with respect to the domain of column x'. For example, using this notation, the command above may be expressed as follows:

    R12 = δSEX R10

Examples of the use of the relational algebraic operators
Suppose that we have access to the relational database given in fig. 3.40. Some examples are now given of how queries might be formulated using relational algebra.

   (a) List all employees who work in the manufacturing department:

         TEMP = SELECT R2 WHERE DEPT = 'MANUFACTURING'
         ANSWER = PROJECT TEMP OVER EMP-NAME

   (b) List all departments which employ both male and female employees:

         TEMP1 = JOIN R1 AND R2 OVER EMP-NAME
         TEMP2 = PROJECT TEMP1 OVER DEPT, SEX
         ANSWER = DIVIDE TEMP2 WITH RESPECT TO SEX.

3.4.10 RELATIONAL CALCULUS

Relational calculus is a notation for expressing the definition of some new relation in terms of some given collection of relations. The required relation is described using a first order language involving predicate symbols, the logical connectives ∧, ∨, ¬ and →, the quantifiers ∀ and ∃, and variables which range over tuples of given relations. ∀ is called the universal quantifier and ∃ is called the existential quantifier.

As an example, consider the relational database given in fig. 3.40 and the following queries expressed in relation calculus:

   (a) Obtain the employees of the manufacturing dept:

         {<R2.EMP-NAME> | R2.DEPT = 'MANUFACTURING'}

       The curly brackets indicate that the expression denotes a set of tuples (a relation), the vertical line stands for 'such that', the term preceding the vertical line represents a typical member (tuple) of the required relation and the term following the vertical line is a condition representing the defining property of the set. The value of this set is the relation:

EMP-NAME
JONES
RODGERS
MACINTOSH
JENKINS

(b) For each of the employees, give the sex, and the telephone number of the department in which that employee works:

  {<R1.SEX, R2.DEP-TEL-EXT> | R1.EMP-NAME = R2.EMP-NAME}

The value of this set is the relation:

SEX	DEPT-TEL-EXT
MALE	2786
MALE	2482
FEMALE	3133
FEMALE	2482

Notice that the redundant tuples have been removed from the answer. That is, a male(s) works in the department with telephone number 2786, a female(s) works in the department with telephone number 3133, and both a male(s) and female(s) work in the department with telephone number 2482.

(c) Obtain a list of the customers with a discount rate of 10% and a balance greater than £500:

  {<R3.CUSTOMER> | R3.DISCOUNT-RATE = 10 ∧ R3.BALANCE > £500}

The value of this set is the relation containing the tuples <AI COMPANY> and <ALLIED BAKERIES>.

(d) Obtain a list of the departments and their telephone numbers which employ at least one female employee:

  {<R2.DEPT, R2.DEPT-TEL-EXT> |
                  ∃X (X ∈ R1 ∧ X.EMP-NAME = R2.EMP-NAME
                              ∧ X.SEX = 'FEMALE')}

The value of this set is the relation:

DEPT	DEPT-TEL-EXT
ACCOUNTS	3133
MANUFACTURING	2482

In this example, X is a variable whose value ranges over the relation R1. This restriction on the range of X is specified by the statement X ∈ R1.

An alternative method of specifying this query is as follows:

  RANGE OF X IS R1

{<R2.DEPT, R2.DEPT-TEL-EXT> |
$\exists$X (X.EMP-NAME = R2.EMP-NAME $\land$ X.SEX = 'FEMALE')}

In English, this expression defines the set of all those
tuples consisting of DEPT and DEPT-TEL-EXT values obtained by
taking the DEPT and DEPT-TEL-EXT values from tuples of R2
whose EMP-NAME value is equal to the EMP-NAME values in tuples
of R1 whose SEX value = 'FEMALE'.

(e) Obtain a list of those departments which do not employ a
female:

RANGE OF X is R1
RANGE OF Y is R2

{<R2.DEPT> | $\forall$Y (Y.DEPT = R2.DEPT $\rightarrow$
$\forall$X (X.EMP-NAME = Y.EMP-NAME $\rightarrow$ X.SEX $\neq$ FEMALE))}

In English, this defines the set of tuples consisting of a
DEPT value obtained from a tuple T of R2 such that for all
tuples Y in R2, if Y.DEPT = T.DEPT then for all tuples X in
R1, if X.EMP-NAME = Y.EMP-NAME then X.SEX $\neq$ FEMALE.

(f) Obtain a list of those departments which employ all of the
female employees:

RANGE OF X IS R1
RANGE OF Y IS R2

{<R2.DEPT> | $\forall$X (X.SEX = 'FEMALE' $\rightarrow$ $\exists$Y (X.EMP-NAME =
Y.EMP-NAME $\land$ Y.DEPT = R2.DEPT))}

In English, this expression defines the set of all tuples
consisting of a DEPT value obtained by taking the DEPT value
from tuples T in R2 such that for all tuples X in R1, if
X.SEX = 'FEMALE' then there exists at least one tuple Y in R2
such that X.EMP-NAME = Y.EMP-NAME and Y.DEPT = T.DEPT. In our
example this set is empty.

Advantages of relational calculus
(a) Once familiar with relational calculus, the user will find
that even complex queries can be expressed simply and concisely.

(b) Relational calculus is non-procedural and statements expressed
in it simply define what the user requires. This simplifies
its use and enables the computer to determine the most efficient method of obtaining the answer.

(c) Relational calculus, as defined by Codd (1972), is 'relation-
ally complete'. This means that any relation which can be
derived from any set of relations can be defined, using relational calculus, in terms of those relations.

Various relational database query languages have been developed which
are based either on relational algebra or on relational calculus. Some
of these languages are described in the next sub-section.

Visitas del Domingo 7 de Febrero de 1588
para mi Papá, en su periodo
de recuperación:

Ruben y Mildred
Esquía y Mauricio
Ronde. Rios
Oswaldo y Nieves
Omaira y Laurencio

Otros que han estado pendientes
Enrique Zamora
Jorge y Belkis
Perucho e Icilia
Odremán - Nuñez

3.4.11 EXAMPLES OF RELATION MANIPULATION AND QUERY LANGUAGES

Relational algebra
Various database systems and languages have been developed which are
based on relational algebra. These include:

MacAIMS (Strnad, 1971)
IS/1, later renamed PRTV (Todd, 1976)
LINUS (Honeywell, 1980)
ASTRID (Gray and Bell, 1978; Gray, 1984)

One of these, the ASTRID language, may be considered as an example.

ASTRID
The ASTRID language is based on full relational algebra together with
the standard algebraic operations on numbers. It also contains extra
operators, including the following:

(a) 'extend by' which allows new relations to be created contain-
     ing extra columns whose values are derived arithmetically from
     other columns in the relation.

(b) 'group by' which allows values to be computed arithmetically
     from values in a group of tuples.

(c) 'rename' which allows columns to be re-named.

As an illustration of the use of these extra ASTRID operators, consider
the relational database in fig. 3.40 together with the ASTRID expression:

NEWREL1:= R3 extend by [baltimesdisc:= discount rate*balance]
                                    - discount rate - balance

Execution of this statement creates the following relation:

CUSTOMER	BALTIMESDISC
AI COMPANY	10000
GREAVES & SON	1000
ALLIED BAKERIES	6000

Note that '- discount rate' removes the discount rate column.

Now consider the following statement; count gives the number of occurrences of a given department:

NEWREL2 := R2 group-by [dept creating Number := count()]

Execution of this statement creates the following relation:

DEPT	NUMBER
ACCOUNTS	2
PERSONNEL	1
MANUFACTURING	4

All of the standard relational algebraic operations such as selection, projection, etc., are available in ASTRID.

Relational calculus

Various languages have been developed which are based on relational calculus. These include:

ALPHA	(Codd, 1971)
DEDUCE	(Chang, 1976)
DEDUCE 2	(Chang, 1978)
FQL	(Pirotte & Wodon, 1974)
ILL	(Lacroix & Pirotte, 1974)
QUEL	(Stonebraker, Held & Wong, 1975)
QUERY-BY-EXAMPLE	(Zloof, 1977)
SEQUEL 2	(Chamberlin et al, 1976)
SQUARE	(Boyce et al, 1975)
TAMALAN	(Vandijk, 1977)
SQL	(Astrahan & Chamberlin, 1975)

Comparisons of these languages are given in Pirotte (Jan, 1978), and in Lacroix and Pirotte (1976) where a list of 66 queries expressed in 10 different languages can be found. One of these, the QUEL language, is described below as an example.

QUEL

QUEL is based on relational calculus. Relations can be created as follows:

    create R1 (EMP-NAME = C20, SEX = C6)

Execution of this command would create a relation called R1 with two domains: EMP-NAME and SEX. The format C20 means that EMP-NAME can take values of up to twenty characters. Other formats are I for integer and F for floating point.

The basic QUEL command for extracting data from relations is the retrieve command. For example:

    range of X is R1
    retrieve (X.EMP-NAME)
         where X.SEX = 'FEMALE'

Execution of this command would retrieve the names of all female employees from the database in fig. 3.40.

Complex conditions can be constructed using 'and' and 'or', but QUEL

does not allow universal quantification and all variables are implicitly assumed to be existentially quantified. (Universal and existential
quantifiers are described in detail in chapter 4, section 4.3.)

Relations can be updated using QUEL as, for example:

 range of X is R3
 replace X (DISCOUNT = 12) where X.CUSTOMER = 'GREAVES & SON'

Execution of this command changes GREAVES & SON's discount to 12.

Integrity constraints may be expressed in QUEL as, for example:

 range of X is R3
 integrity X.DISCOUNT $\geqslant$ 0 and X.DISCOUNT $\leqslant$ 30

Such integrity constraints are implemented by modifying users' requests
before execution so that they cannot violate any relevant constraints.
For example, the update command given above would be modified by adding
the constraint with appropriate instantiation:

 range of X is R3
 replace X(DISCOUNT = 12)
   where X.CUSTOMER = 'GREAVES & SON'
   and
   (X.12 $\geqslant$ 0 and X.12 $\leqslant$ 30)

QUEL also provides some 'aggregate' operators which are not available
in pure relational calculus. These are:

 count : number of occurrences
 countu : number of unique occurrences
 sum : sum of values
 sumu : sum of unique values
 avg : average (sum/count)
 avgu : sumu/countu
 max : maximum value
 min : minimum value
 any : (1 if any tuple satisfies condition, 0 otherwise)

These operators can, amongst other things, be used to obtain the same
effect as could be obtained if universal quantification were possible.
For example, given the relations in fig. 3.40, we can obtain a list of
all those companies which do not employ a female:

 range of X is R1
 range of Y is R2
 retrieve (Y.DEPT-NAME)
   where count(X.where Y.EMP-NAME = X.EMP-NAME and
          X.SEX = 'FEMALE') = 0

3.4.12 THE BINARY RELATIONAL VIEW

Many of the problems of existing DBMSs derive from the views of the
universe on which they are based. Hierarchical and network systems
require the designer to distinguish between entities and attributes at
an early stage in the design process. This distinction is really an

implementation consideration: entities map to records and attributes
to fields within records. Conceptually, there is no difference. Something which is regarded as an attribute by one person may be thought
of as an entity by another. As far as the database system designer is
concerned, we recommend that he look at access requirements to make the
decision. If we never want to know anything about an 'object' X, then
X may be regarded as an attribute and may be mapped into a field of a
record. In most hierarchical and network DBMSs it is very inefficient
to access records by giving values of fields unless these fields constitute the record key, i.e. unless the fields identify the entity
which the record represents. Examples of things which are frequently
regarded as attributes include height, address, age, year-of-manufact-
ure and so on. Such things are often represented by fields in records.
It is then quite difficult to access, for example, all employees of
'age 30'. In general, all employee records would have to be scanned.
If this and other similar access paths were required to be used on a
regular basis, then it would be better to treat 'age 30' as an entity
and link employees to it using whatever entity-entity linking mechanism
is available in the DBMS being used: e.g. father-son links in IMS or
owner-member links in IDMS (both discussed later).

The problem is that once a thing has been regarded as an attribute and
mapped to a field in a record, it generally requires extensive reorganisation of the database system to subsequently regard this thing as an
entity. Notice that the relational view does not suffer from this
problem to the extent that hierarchical and network views do.

Another difficulty which derives from existing views concerns the complications which are caused by their asymmetry. In all of the views
considered so far, relationships between 'things' are asymmetric. In
the hierarchical view the relationship is 'directed' from father to
son and in the DBTG view the direction is from owner to member. In
both of these views, direction is also from entity to attribute. In
the relational view, relationships are regarded as being of two types:
relationships between elements of a tuple and relationships between
tuples. For example:

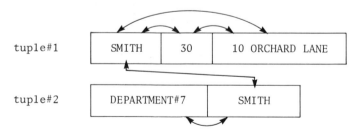

In effect, 'things' are represented by fields within tuples (e.g. 'age
30' and '10 ORCHARD LANE') or by the tuple itself (e.g. the 30 year old
person called SMITH who lives at 10 ORCHARD LANE is represented by
tuple#1). The problem is that this asymmetry (which really reflects
the storage structure) complicates data manipulation. End-users and
application programmers must learn how to use different types of access
path, e.g. from owner to member and member to owner, from tuple to

field within a tuple, and from tuple to tuple. In addition, these asymmetrically specified relationships are typically implemented in asymmetrical storage structures.

The specification and enforcement of integrity and privacy constraints also suffer from the asymmetry of the conceptual and database schemas which derive from the asymmetric views. Many proponents of the binary relational view would claim that, ideally, no distinction should be made between entities and attributes and all relationships between 'things' of the real world should be perceived and represented in a consistent way. All relationships which are of interest should be represented by access paths with equal efficiency.

A view of the universe which demonstrates these features is called the simplified binary relational (SBR) view (Frost, March 1983). The SBR may be informally defined as follows:

(a) The universe is regarded as consisting of entities with binary relationships between them.

(b) A binary relationship can link an entity to at most one other entity or to itself.

(c) Entity sets such as 'EMPLOYEES' are treated as abstract entities.

(d) ∈, the set-membership relation, is treated like any other binary relation.

As example of the use of the view, consider the following SBR model:

MANAGER#1.	∈.	MANAGERS
MANAGER#1.	NATIONALITY.	BRITISH
MANAGER#1.	HOBBY.	FISHING
MANAGER#1.	WORKS IN.	DEPARTMENT#1
DEPARTMENT#1.	MAKES.	MACHINE#1

The only asymmetry in this model concerns the names of the relationship type, e.g. the last triple is equivalent to :

MACHINE#1. MADEIN. DEPARTMENT#1

In all other respects, the view is symmetrical.

SBR data structures
An SBR physical storage structure is a data structure into which data representations of binary relationships may be inserted, and from which data representations of binary relationships may be deleted and/or retrieved. Data representations of binary relationships are often called

'triples'. Triples are inserted singly, and are deleted and/or retrieved in sets. Such sets have one or more fields in common. The
common field(s) correspond to the search key(s) which were used in the
deletion or retrieval request. Thus we may think of a binary relational storage structure as a box which stores triples. For example:

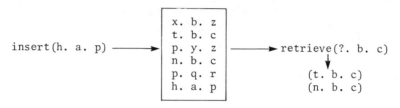

That is, the command retrieve(?. b. c) would cause the following set
of triples to be retrieved:

{(t. b. c), (n. b. c)}

Feldman (1965) introduced the term 'simple associative forms' (SAFs)
for the eight basic ways in which triples may be retrieved. These
eight forms may be denoted as:

    retrieve(a. b. ?)
    retrieve(?. b. c)
    retrieve(a. ?. ?)
    retrieve(?. b. ?)
    retrieve(?. ?. c)
    retrieve(a. ?. c)
    retrieve(?. ?. ?)
    retrieve(a. b. c)

The eighth SAF yields true or false depending on whether the triple is
in the database. The seventh SAF causes a database dump. Other SAFs
yield sets of triples which match on the given fields. For example,
(?. b. ?) retrieves all triples with b as relationship type. Not all
SBR-like structures provide all eight SAFs.

The distinction between an SBR structure and a binary relational
structure is not great: in an SBR structure, set-membership relationships are stored like all other relationships. For example, the fact
that 'David is an employee' is stored as (David. ∈. employees). Much
of the following discussion applies equally well to binary relational
structures as to SBR structures.

Some of the advantages and disadvantages of binary relational systems
will now be described.

Schema specification is straightforward
Schema specification using the binary relational view is straight-
forward if a conceptual schema definition language such as SCHEMAL
(Frost, 1983) is used. Examples of SCHEMAL expressions are:

    ∀x (x. ∈ . husbands) → ¬(x. ∈ . bachelors)
    ∀x ∃y (x. ∈ . people) → (x. hasmother. y)

The first expression states that 'for all x, if x is a member of the
set of husbands, then x may not be a member of the set of bachelors'.
The second expression states that 'for all x, if x is a person, then
there exists some y such that y is the mother of x'. In section 3.8.2
we show how constraints expressed in SCHEMAL may be enforced automatically in a DBMS based on the binary relational view.

A consistent conceptual framework may be used throughout the system design

If an SBR-like view is used during analysis and specification of database systems, as is increasingly the case - see for example Shave
(1981) - then its use as the basis for the storage mechanism means that
a consistent conceptual framework may be applied throughout much of the
design work. The consequent simplification in system design was first
noted by Levien and Maron (1967), Feldman and Rovner (1969), Ash and
Sibley (1968), and Titman (1974) who also noted that a simple uniform
design should lead to a more reliable system.

Simple interface with other modules of the database system

The interface between an SBR structure and other modules consists of
three procedures:

    insert(triple)
    delete(partial specification of triple)
    retrieve(partial specification of triple)

Retrieval requests such as 'list all employees of IBM' may be met by
issuing a simple retrieval call (IBM.employs.?) which delivers only
that data which has been requested. As Ravin and Schatzoff (1973) point
out, the application programmer need not be concerned with details of
file/record structure, and no more workspace than that required to
store the requested data is needed. In addition, the task of retrieving collections of data and formatting them according to some user
specifications is straightforward. This is discussed later, in the
section which deals with SBR query languages.

In particular, mapping end-user views to the storage structure is simplified. One of the tasks of a DBMS is to help database implementors
provide different end-users with different 'views' of the data held in
the data storage structure. Pelagatti et al (1978) claim that this can
best be achieved if the data is regarded as consisting of basic unstructured facts (triples) which can be combined to construct the different
user-views. The mapping of 'external' end-user views is further simplified if the data is actually stored as a set of triples as it is in
an SBR data storage structure.

File design is no longer necessary

File design is one of the most difficult tasks in database system design. This is illustrated in the following example:

    A system is to store data about parts, suppliers of parts, and
    machines which are constructed from these parts. Suppose the sys-
    tem is required to output (i) the description and stock-on-hand
    for a given part and (ii) the stock-on-hand and supplier of all
    parts used in the construction of a given machine.

Even for this simple example, the choice of an appropriate storage structure is complicated. Consider the structure in fig. 3.41 consisting of two hash tables. At first sight it might appear to be a reasonable solution. However, closer examination identifies several shortcomings, which include:

(a) Part/stock-on-hand relationships are replicated many times. Since these are volatile relationships, database consistency will be difficult to maintain.

(b) Updating stock-on-hand for a given part will be difficult.

(c) Part/supplier relationships are replicated many times, thereby wasting space.

Hash on part   Hash on machine

Part	Stock on hand	Description

Machine	Part	Stock on hand	Supplier

Figure 3.41 A storage structure consisting of two hash tables

The problem is two-fold. In the first place, system specifications need to be more comprehensive than that given above. In the second place, even if a complete set of requirements is available, there are many combinations of data structure which might fit, and the choice of the most appropriate is difficult. If, however, an SBR structure is available then specification and analysis of requirements is not so critical. This is because all conceptual access paths may be implemented with equal efficiency in an SBR structure. As far as the storage of data is concerned, the designer has little else to do other than decide what SAFs are required. In the example above, only retrievals of the form: retrieve (a.b.?) and retrieve (?.b.c) are necessary.

Multi-attribute retrieval is readily accommodated

Suppose that the system described above was also required to output lists of parts supplied by a given supplier and used as components on a given machine. This type of query is known as a 'multi-attribute' query. To accommodate such requirements into the overall design policy one should first analyse them in order to produce an integrated set of access path requirements.

Unfortunately, multi-attribute queries cannot be analysed without assuming something about the implementation strategy. For example, the query above might be analysed and reduced to two parts: (i) access the set of suppliers, go to the given supplier and then to the parts supplied, and (ii) access the set of machines, go to the given machine, and then to its component parts. However, this analysis assumes that

116

the query will be met by retrieving the set of parts supplied by a given supplier and the set of parts used on a given machine, followed by computing the intersection of these two sets. This may not be the most appropriate strategy if, for example, there are only a few parts per machine and only a few suppliers who supply many thousands of parts each. A more appropriate strategy might be to retrieve all the parts for a given machine and then, for each one of these, find out if it is supplied by the given supplier.

The situation is simplified if an SBR structure is used. Access paths for multi-attribute queries need not be analysed in the way described above because all conceptual links between entities which the user might want to use, are represented by equally efficient access paths. The choice of method for servicing a multi-attribute query may be left to the application programmer since all possible methods will be available to him.

Data independence is improved

Johnson (1968) and Titman (1974) recognised some time ago that use of an SBR-like storage structure should improve data independence. Data independence refers to the independence of a database and the application programs which use it. In a data independent system, application programs are insulated from the effects of changes made to the database, its organisation and the physical devices on which it is stored. New types of data and application programs may be added with minimal effect on existing programs.

SBR structures provide maximum flexibility with respect to the addition of new types of entity and relationship: relevant triples are simply inserted. If all eight SAFs are available, any new application program whose data requirements can be met by the contents of the database may be added without making changes to the database structure or to existing programs.

The disadvantages of binary relational systems include the following:

N-ary relationships have to be reduced to binary relationships

Relationships of the form 'a bought b from c' must be converted to three binary relationships before they can be stored in an SBR structure. This conversion requires the explicit naming of the implied entity which is of type 'sale', giving, for example:

```
(sale 1. buyer. a)
(sale 1. itembought. b)
(sale 1. seller. c)
```

The introduction of such explicit names is regarded by some, for example Date (1977), as a major drawback of the binary relational approach. However, as discussed later in the sub-section on the NDB system, this disadvantage may not be as great as at first appears.

Multi-attribute retrieval may be inefficient

Use of an SBR structure for multi-attribute retrieval might not be very efficient, irrespective of the way in which the structure is implemented. To illustrate this, consider an example given by Martin (1975):

Retrieve (the names of) all 18-year-old unemployed actresses with experience in movie-acting, and talents for singing and sky-diving.

The bracketed clause has been added - Martin may have been a little optimistic in his original retrieval request!

Using an SBR structure, one could issue the commands:

```
retrieve(?. aged. 18)
retrieve(?. job-status. unemployed)
retrieve(?. profession. actress)
retrieve(?. talent. singing)
retrieve(?. talent. sky-diving)
```

and then form the intersection of the delivered sets to obtain the required data. This is probably faster than having to do a sequential search through the whole database, which would be necessary if the data were stored as a file of records: (name, age, job-status, profession, experience, talents) ordered on name. However, the search would be even faster if the data were stored as a file of records together with appropriate inverted list/file indexes. The shortest list, possibly talent = sky-diving, could then be used and the records of sky-divers examined to see if they were 18-year-old unemployed singing movie-actresses.

The retrieval strategy using an SBR structure could be improved by re-trieving the smallest set: possibly (?.talent.sky-diving), and then for each member of this set issuing retrievals to see if the member met the other requirements. However, it is unlikely that the SBR structure could compete with tailor-made structures for given types of multi-attribute retrieval, whatever strategy were used.

Groups of related entities must be retrieved separately
A major disadvantage of SBR structures is that 'related' entities such as a person's name, age and salary must be retrieved separately. The application programmer must issue three separate retrieval requests. In a conventional system such related entities could be grouped together, given a group name, and retrieved as a group (for example, in a record).

Batch processing techniques may not guarantee improved performance
The method of collecting transactions, sorting them and running them against a sorted master file is called 'batch processing'. Techniques of this kind are often used to speed up processing since disk-head movement is minimised. Such improvement is unlikely to be achieved with an SBR structure since the 'fields' of each 'master record' have to be retrieved independently and are unlikely to reside together on disk.

3.4.13 IMPLEMENTATION OF BINARY RELATIONAL SYSTEMS
SBR-like structures have a long history, dating at least from the work of Levien and Maron (1967) on a system called the Relational Data File (RDF). The next system to appear was the LEAP programming language (Feldman and Rovner, 1969). Development and extension of some of the LEAP ideas is found in a system called TRAMP (Ash and Sibley, 1968).

The LEAP structure has also been used to develop an extension of the programming language PL/1 (Symonds, 1968). This work led to the construction of the SAM system (Crick and Symonds, 1970) and from that to the Relational Memory (RM) (Lorie and Symonds, 1971). RM was further extended to support n-ary relations and evolved into the Extended Relational Memory (XRM) (Lorie, 1974) which has been used as a storage sub-system for the query languages SEQUEL, GMIS, FXRAM and QUERY-BY EXAMPLE.

Later work on SBR-like structures is largely unrelated to earlier systems. Titman (1974), for example, makes no reference to any earlier work when describing his experimental system. Titman's work has been cited in a paper describing the PeterLee Test Vehicle (Todd, 1976), and directly influenced the design of the NDB system (Sharman and Winterbottom, 1979). Another system which uses a structure similar to that proposed by Titman is the WELL system developed by Munz (1978). However, Munz does not refer to Titman's work nor to the NDB system. NDB is described in more detail in section 3.5.9.

A different approach has been made by Futo et al (1977) who investigated the efficiency of the PROLOG programming language in making deductions over a binary relational database (see later).

All of the structures described above require, on average, more than one access to backing store to retrieve a triple. This situation can be overcome if the data is duplicated and held in several dynamic hash tables.

Special purpose hardware is also being developed for binary relational systems. This includes the FACT machine (McGregor and Malone, 1984) and the Intelligent File Store (IFS) (Lavington et al, 1984).

A survey of binary relational data structures can be found in Frost (1982).

3.4.14 IMPLEMENTATION OF A BINARY RELATIONAL QUERY LANGUAGE

Our discussion of the binary relational approach concludes with a brief description of how one might go about implementing a simple binary relational query language. It is hoped that this will give the reader a feel for what would be involved in implementing query languages in general.

Suppose that we wanted to ask queries such as:

(a) Retrieve all employees of IBM aged 24, together with all employees of ICL aged 32.

(b) Retrieve all employees of IBM who are married and who live in Glasgow.

We could design a binary relational language in which these queries may be expressed as follows:

(a)' $[[(x. \text{ worksfor. IBM}) \wedge (x. \text{ aged. } 24)] \vee$
$[(x. \text{ worksfor. ICL}) \wedge (x. \text{ aged. } 32)]];$

(b)'   [(x. worksfor. IBM) ∧ (x. marriedto. ANY) ∧
                                       (x. livesin. Glasgow)];

where ∧ stands for 'and', and ∨ stands for 'or'.

A Backus-Naur specification of an LL1 grammar for this language would
include the following productions:

```
wff       ::=  exp ;

exp       ::=  triple     <retrieve and stack the list of values
                            substituted for x>
          |  [ exp list ]

list      ::=  conjlist
          |  disjlist

conjlist  ::=  exp conj    <form intersection>

conj      ::=  conjlist
          |  ε

disjlist  ::=  exp disj    <form union>

disj      ::=  disjlist
          |  ε
```

where ε stands for 'empty', conj stands for 'conjunction', disj stands
for 'disjunction', and the strings inside the angled brackets describe
actions to be carried out when the parser reaches that point in a parse
of a query. Specifically:

- After the parser finds a triple, it should retrieve a set of
  triples from the database which match that triple and create a
  list of entities from these triples for the unknown value of the
  variable. For example, if the triple were (x. worksfor. IBM),
  the action would be to retrieve all triples from the database
  with 'works for' in the middle field and 'IBM' in the last field,
  and then form a list of all of the entities in the first field of
  these triples. The parser should then put this list on a stack.

- After the parser finds a conj it should take the top two lists
  off the stack, form a new list which is the intersection of these
  two lists, and put this new list on to the stack.

- After the parser finds a disj it should take the top two lists
  off the stack, form a new list which is the union of these two
  lists, and put this new list on to the stack.

When the parse is complete there will be one list on the stack containing the answers to the query.

Therefore, to implement this query language we simply create a parser
as described in chapter 2, create procedures for retrieving entities
matching a triple, for intersecting lists of entities, for uniting
lists of entities, and for pushing and pulling lists from a stack.
Calls to these procedures are then placed in the parser at appropriate
points. For example, the 'retrieve' procedure call should be placed
in the exp procedure so that it is executed if a triple is found, and

the 'intersect' procedure call should be placed in the conjlist procedure such that it is executed after conj is called.

As illustration of the method, consider the query (a)' above. The
parser would act as follows when parsing this query:

```
call query
   call exp
      recognise [
      call exp
         recognise [                        ·
         call exp
            recognise triple
            retrieve and stack a list of values of x where
            (x. worksfor. IBM) is in the database
         call list
            recognise ∧
            call conjlist
               call exp
                  recognise triple
                  retrieve and stack a list of values of x where
                  (x. aged. 24) is in the database
               call conj
                  recognise ε (i.e. not recognise ∧)
               pull 2 lists off stack and form the intersection
                  list and put this list on the stack
         recognise ]
      call list
etc.
```

This simple query language can be extended quite easily to a complete
application programming language in which code such as the following
can be written:

```
[(?x. worksfor. IBM) ∧ (?x. aged. 25)];
for all x [(x. marriedto. ?y);
          display(x, y)];
(x. hassalary. ?s);
display ('total salary of all 25 year old employees of IBM is',
                                                        sum(s)).
```

This code retrieves all 25-year-old employees of IBM and then lists
each of these employees together with the person he or she is married
to. It then retrieves the 'bag' s of all salaries of all these
employees and displays the sum of the values in s. The word 'bag' is
used deliberately to distinguish the collection from a set (s, for
example, could contain duplicate entries).

3.4.15 THE ENTITY RELATIONSHIP ATTRIBUTE MODEL/VIEW

In this approach, the universe of discourse is regarded as consisting
of entities such as 'people', and values such as 'ages'. There are
'relationships' between entities. In addition, entities have values
as 'attributes'. For example:

aged — John $\xrightarrow{\text{married to}}$ Sally

24 $\xleftarrow{}$ (an attribute) (a relationship)

Entities are grouped into 'entity sets'. 'Relationship sets' are relations where the domains are entity sets. An attribute is a mapping
between an entity set such as 'people' and a value set such as 'age'.
The approach is based on the notion that there is a distinction between
relationships between entities, and relationships between entities and
attributes.

This notion seems reasonable when considering examples such as the one
given above. However, it becomes less easy to justify with examples
such as the following:

entity 1 ———— has name ———————— Mary

(the name) Mary ——————— originated in ———— Hebrew

Should 'Mary' be regarded as an entity or an attribute?

One of the best known entity relationship attribute approaches is that
of Chen (1976).

3.4.16 THE FUNCTIONAL MODEL/VIEW
In this approach, the universe of discourse is regarded as consisting
of objects and functions. It is not discussed here, since a chapter
is devoted to it later in the book.

3.4.17 COMMENTS ON DATA MODELS/VIEWS
Seven data models/views which are commonly used in database work have
been mentioned.

The hierarchical, network and CODASYL network views may be regarded as
record-based approaches. The long history of use of these approaches
has had a strong effect on the acceptance of the more recent views.
Many database practitioners still regard the relational view and other
views which followed it with much scepticism.

The relational view is becoming the dominant view used in new database
products. The development of non-procedural data manipulation languages based on relational calculus has made some relational systems
simple enough for the novice to use. In addition, the fact that the
relational approach is founded on well-defined mathematical notions
has facilitated the development of 'intelligent' relational database
systems which have deductive capabilities and can maintain semantic
integrity automatically. Such systems are discussed in more detail in
chapter 5.

The binary relational approach has also been used as the basis for the
development of intelligent database systems. It has much in common
with the relational approach. However, some researchers, including

122

this book's author, regard its simplicity as being of great help in the design of the complex algorithms which are used for deduction and integrity maintenance. The main advantages and disadvantages of this approach when used in non-deductive database systems were discussed in sub-section 3.4.12.

Interest in the functional approach is growing, and this approach is described in chapter 10. One of its greatest advantages over the other approaches is that it can be used to represent 'higher-order' knowledge (see chapter 6).

A brief description now follows of some of the database management systems which are commercially available.

3.5 EXAMPLES OF COMMERCIALLY AVAILABLE DBMSs

Commercially available DBMSs can be loosely classified according to the view on which they are based since the view underlying a particular DBMS has an influence on all its aspects. For example, relational DBMSs have tabular data structures, relational schema definition languages and data manipulation languages which are based on relational algebra or relational calculus. However, it should be recognised that such a classification is only a rough guide. Many 'hierarchical' systems, for example, also allow network structures to be modelled if the user is willing to fiddle with the system. The classification, therefore, only indicates which organisational structures can be *readily* modelled by the DBMS concerned.

It should also be mentioned that the facilities which are provided by various DBMSs differ greatly and, consequently, the view on which a DBMS is based may not be a critical factor in its assessment for use. For example, a DBMS which is based on the unconstrained network view will have a powerful (and simple) modelling capability but is of limited applicability if it does not provide adequate security mechanisms.

The brief descriptions which follow are intended to provide the reader with a 'feel' for various DBMSs which are available. More detailed descriptions may be found in texts such as Cardenas (1979), Date (1977), Kroenke (1977), Robinson (1981), Tsichritzis and Lochovsky (1977), Online (1983) and Perkinson (1984).

3.5.1 IMS

IMS (Information Management System) is a hierarchical system produced by IBM and is one of the most widely used DBMSs. The storage structure consists of a collection of trees. Nodes in a tree may only have one parent, therefore networks may only be readily represented by the duplication of nodes. However, IMS does provide a way to avoid such duplication by 'virtual pairing' in which nodes are stored only once and their virtual presence in other trees is provided by means of pointers.

In IMS, what we have called the database schema consists of a specification of all of the types of 'trees' which are stored in the database, including those which have virtual nodes. Database sub-schemas consist of specifications of sets of 'logical' tree-types each of which is a sub-set of one of the tree-types defined in the database schema. A logical tree-type is defined on a tree-type and may omit one or more of the nodes (apart from the root node) together with all dependents of that node. Note, however, that IMS terminology is quite different from that employed here. For example, records are called 'segments' and database sub-schemas are called 'program specification blocks'.

IMS uses a host language approach in which database commands are issued as procedure calls from within programs written in languages such as PL1, COBOL or assembler. The set of procedure calls available constitutes a language called DL/1. Commands in this language include:

GET UNIQUE	GU
GET NEXT WITHIN PARENT	GN
GET NEXT	GN
REPLACE	REPL
INSERT	ISRT
DELETE	DLET

The unit of retrieval is a node and the meaning of 'next' is the next node to the right on the current level of the tree. DL/1 is a relatively easy language to master, but requires the user to navigate paths through the database.

IMS provides a data dictionary facility which is itself a hierarchially structured database system.

Database privacy may be maintained in several ways, including:

(a) The definition of sub-schemas to exclude those trees and branches of trees which are not allowed to be accessed by a given user or group of users.

(b) Encryption of data before storage.

(c) Use of passwords to restrict access to certain sub-schemas and application programs.

IMS provides back-up and recovery by means of dump/restore and checkpoint/restart utility programs. All database modifications are records on a system log.

IMS software allows concurrent access to a database. When a run unit updates a record, that record is locked to prevent access by other run units until the updating run unit terminates. If the run unit terminates abnormally then the IMS software 'rolls back' all updates made by that run unit. If 'deadlock' occurs (i.e. two run units lock data required by each other so neither can terminate) IMS terminates one, rolls its updates back and lets the other carry on to successful termination. The run unit which was rolled back is then allowed to start again.

IMS is a complex system and a more detailed account may be found in Walsh (1979).

3.5.2 IDMS

The IDMS database management system is based on the CODASYL DBTG recommendations. These recommendations refer to other aspects of DBMSs, not
just to the 'set' data structure as already discussed. Specifications
of the architecture, schema definition language and data manipulation
language are also given. IDMS adheres quite closely to these recommendations, and the following may be regarded as an introduction to many
other CODASYL DBTG systems as well as IDMS.

The IDMS data model consists of 'records' which are related in 'sets'.
The constraints on set membership are the same as those outlined for
the DBTG model discussed earlier.

The database schema is defined by the use of a data description language (DDL) which is somewhat like COBOL. An example of an IDMS schema
is given in fig. 3.42(a). This schema is depicted graphically in fig.
3.42(b). Notice that a schema is simply a generalisation of a data
model. The arrows in the example graphical schema indicate that there
are two set types: one has machine type records as owner, the other has
part type records as owner and both have part-use type records as member.

IDMS also provides a 'device media control language' (DMCL) which is
used by the designer to specify some of the details of the mapping of
the logical model on to the storage media. An example of a device
media control specification is given in fig. 3.43.

The designer is also required to specify a set of sub-schemas. As it
was defined earlier, a sub-schema is a sub-set of the database schema
which is of interest to a particular user or group of users. In IDMS,
a sub-schema consists of a name, the name of the device media specification used, the name of the schema used and a description of the areas,
records and sets which comprise that part of the database concerned.
Privacy locks may be defined, names can be changed from those used in
the database schema and 'logical' records may be declared which are
sub-sets of records declared in the database schema (fields may be
omitted, for example).

IDMS application programs typically consist of:

(a) Commands to invoke a particular sub-schema, e.g. INVOKE SUB-
SCHEMA SUB-1 OF MACHINE.

(b) Commands to open an area for the mode of operation required,
e.g. OPEN AREA MACHINE-AREA USAGE-MODE IS RETRIEVAL.

(c) Commands to manipulate records, e.g. FIND.

Records may be found in various ways. If the record has been declared
with location mode CALC then it can be found by supplying the hash
field value. For example:

MOVE 124 TO MACHINE-NUM

FIND MACHINE RECORD

```
SCHEMA DESCRIPTION.
SCHEMA NAME IS SMACHINE.

FILE DESCRIPTION.
FILE NAME IS MACHINE-FILE ASSIGN TO MDB.
FILE NAME IS JOURNAL          ASSIGN TO JMDB.

AREA DESCRIPTION
AREA NAME   IS MC-AREA
     RANGE  IS 1001 THRU 1050
     WITHIN FILE MACHINE-FILE FROM 1 THRU 50.

RECORD DESCRIPTION.
RECORD NAME IS MACHINE.
RECORD ID   IS 100.
LOCATION MODE IS CALC USING MACHINE-NUM.
WITHIN MC-AREA AREA.
   03 MACHINE-NUM PIC9(4).

RECORD NAME IS PART-USE.
RECORD ID   IS 200.
LOCATION MODE IS VIA USES-PART SET.
WITHIN MC-AREA AREA.
   03 USE-NUM    PIC9(8).
   03 QUANTITY   PIC9(6).
```

```
RECORD NAME IS PART.
RECORD ID   IS 300.
LOCATION MODE IS CALC USING PART-NAME
     DUPLICATES ARE NOT ALLOWED.
WITHIN MC-AREA AREA.
   03 PART-NUM 9(6).
   03 PART-NAME X(12).
SET DESCRIPTION
SET NAME   IS USES-PART.
   ORDER IS FIRST.
   MODE  IS CHAIN.
   OWNER IS MACHINE NEXT DBKEY POSITION IS 1.
   MEMBER IS PART-USE NEXT DBKEY POSITION IS 1.
     LINKED TO OWNER OWNER DBKEY POSITION IS 2.
     MANDATORY AUTOMATIC.
SET NAME   IS-USED-BY.
   ORDER IS FIRST.
   MODE  IS CHAIN LINKED TO PRIOR.
   OWNER IS PART NEXT DBKEY POSITION IS 1.
                 PRIOR DBKEY POSITION IS 2.
   MEMBER IS PART-USE NEXT DBKEY POSITION IS 3.
                      PRIOR DBKEY POSITION IS 4.
     LINKED TO OWNER OWNER DBKEY POSITION IS 5.
     MANDATORY AUTOMATIC.
```

Figure 3.42(a) An IDMS database schema

Figure 3.42(b) A DBTG database schema

```
DEVICE MEDIA DESCRIPTION.
DEVICE MEDIA NAME IS DMACHINE OF SCHEMA NAME SMACHINE.

BUFFER SECTION.
   BUFFER NAME IS DM-BUFFER.
   PAGE CONTAINS 512 CHARACTERS.
   BUFFER CONTAINS 8 PAGES.

AREA SECTION.
   COPY MACHINE-AREA AREA.
```

Figure 3.43 A device media specification

The machine record with machine member equal to 1234 would be found and then regarded as the current record of the record type MACHINE. Any subsequent references to this record type or to sets of which this type is an owner will refer, respectively, to record 1234 and to the particular set occurrence of which this record is owner.

For example, to find the first part-use record which is related to machine 1234 one could write:

FIND FIRST RECORD OF USES-PART SET.

This locates the first member record of the USES-PART set occurrence of which machine 1234 is owner. This part-use record is now the current member record of this set occurrence.

To find and retrieve the part record related to the current part-use record we need to go from member to owner in the IS-USED-BY set. This is achieved by writing:

OBTAIN OWNER RECORD OF IS-USED-BY SET.

To find the next part-use record (for machine 1234) one could write:

FIND NEXT RECORD OF USES-PART SET.

INVOKE, OPEN AREA, FIND and OBTAIN are some of the IDMS procedures which may be called from within the host language being used. Resultant application programs are put through a pre-processor before being compiled. Pre-processors for use with COBOL and PL/1 are available and these enable database manipulation operations to be included as direct· procedural extensions to these two languages.

Creation of an IDMS system is, therefore, a four stage process:

(a) Design, declaration and compilation of the database schema.

(b) Design and compilation of the device media control specification.

(c) Design, declaration and compilation of the sub-schemas.

(d) Design, coding and compilation of the application programs which include embedded data manipulation language (DML) commands such as INVOKE and FIND, etc.

Only the device media control, sub-schema and application program object modules are required for processing the database. The database schema is not required. Its function is to assist in building the other components.

3.5.3 TOTAL

TOTAL is a relatively simple DBTG-like system which is widely used.

The data storage structure is similar to the set structure of DBTG. Two types of file are used: master files which contain master records (or owner records in DBTG terminology) and variable files which contain member records. Owners are related to members by means of linked lists as shown in fig. 3.44.

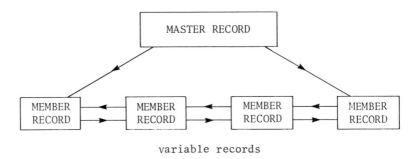

variable records

Figure 3.44 The TOTAL data structure

The whole structure may therefore be thought of as a multi-list structure. Direct access from member to owner may be provided by hashing. The structure is similar to the DBTG structure except that the variable files may not also be master files. Therefore, hierarchies of depth greater than two may only be accommodated by means of 'connection' records as shown in fig. 3.45.

The records of master and variable files are records in the conventional sense, consisting of data items and groups of items called elements. Application programs can access elements of records and can construct 'logical' records made up of elements from several physical records, thereby demonstrating a degree of data independence.

TOTAL provides no mechanism for checking the format of data input. However, it does provide a privacy sub-system and constraints may be expressed at data item level if required.

Two supporting software packages are available: SOCRATES which is a
report program generator, and ENVIRON/1 which is a real-time general
tele-processing monitor which supports the concept of logical terminals
and re-entrant application programs.

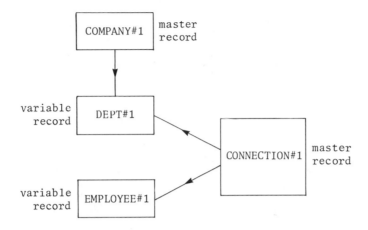

Figure 3.45 Hierarchy representation in TOTAL

3.5.4 ADABAS

ADABAS is a network oriented DBMS, although it does have some relational features. The logical data model of ADABAS is network structured in
that entities may be represented by records and these records may be
linked to any number of other records (up to a maximum which is dictat-
ed by implementation considerations). The physical storage structure
consists of files of records together with inverted indexes held in the
'ASSOCIATOR'. Records are linked by means of common field values. To
facilitate access, the system can be told to create inverted indexes
which correspond to the linking of records by common field value. To
do this, the user tells the system to 'couple' the two files involved
'on' the relevant fields. An inverted list index is then generated
automatically. Two files may only be coupled if the records in one
contain field values matching field values of records in the other.

Each record has a unique internal sequence number (ISN) assigned to it,
and it is these ISNs which are used in the inverted indexes.

Data compression techniques are used to reduce the size of files.
Phonetic searching facilities are available, and an encoding/decoding
mechanism is provided to improve privacy. Fields may be added to
records dynamically, thereby demonstrating a degree of data independence.

For batch processing, ADABAS may be interfaced with COBOL, FORTRAN,
PL/1 or assembler. For on-line processing it can be interfaced with
TSO, CICS, INTERCOMM, TASKMASTER and ENVIRON/1. Database commands are
implemented as procedure calls to a procedure called ADABAS which takes
several parameters, one of which specifies the database command to be
invoked. A query language called ADASCRIPT is available.

3.5.5 dBASE II

dBASE II is a relatively simple relational DBMS which is available on several microcomputers. The system is usually supplied on a floppy disk and may be thought of as an extension to the computer's operating system.

dBASE II does not provide any facilities for the construction or storage of the conceptual schema, nor does it contain a data dictionary. Therefore the initial analysis and specification of the database system has to be done manually. However, this is not too much of a burden for the type of database system which is likely to be implemented using dBASE II.

Once the structure of the relations (files) which you are going to store has been decided on (i.e. once you have created the database schema), dBASE II can be used to help build a database system to manage these relations. The commands which are available in dBASE II can be used to create relations (called files or databases in dBASE II terminology), to add tuples (called records) to relations, to locate tuples with given field values, to sort relations, to create reports from relations, to join two relations, and so on. In addition, there are facilities for creating application programs (called command files) consisting of several dBASE II commands packaged under one name. In the following, examples of the use of some of these commands are presented to give the reader an idea of what it is like to use dBASE II. The full stop (dot) in front of each command is the prompt which is displayed by the computer when it is waiting for you to enter the command.

. *set default to b*

This command (or something like this command) is necessary in many implementations of dBASE II to tell the computer that the data in the database is (or is to be) stored on the disk in disk drive 'b'. That is, the user puts the system disk into drive 'a' and his own disk into drive 'b' of the computer before issuing the command. If this is not done, the system will automatically assume that the database resides on the system disk (i.e. the disk in disk drive 'a').

. *create studentfile*

This tells the computer that you want to create a new file (relation) called 'studentfile'. After issuing this command, the computer would ask for the record structure of this file. You could respond by typing:

```
name, c, 20
age, n, 3
dept, c, 10
```

This tells the computer that the records (tuples) in the relation 'studentfile' each contain a name field which consists of 20 characters, an age field which is a 3-digit number, and a department field which consists of 10 characters. This specification constitutes part of the database schema as defined in earlier sections of this chapter.

The computer now asks if you want to put any records into the relation. You would normally answer yes. The computer responds by providing a

screen format so that you can enter records easily. You might, for
example, enter the following records:

    john   25 physics
    david   18 chemistry
    susan   20 chemistry

To terminate the entry of records, simply press the return key by
itself.

. *create deptfile*
This tells the computer that you want to create a file (relation)
called 'deptfile'. This file might have the following format which
you enter:

    deptname, c, 10
    head, c, 20
    extension, n, 4

You might enter the following records:

    physics   prof atom   3422
    chemistry prof molecule   1644
    geology   prof rock   4457

. *use studentfile*
This tells the computer that you want to use the relation 'studentfile'. All commands that you now issue will operate on the relation
'studentfile' until you issue another 'use' command with a different
relation name.

. *insert*
This tells the computer that you want to insert one or more new records
into the file which is currently in use. The computer responds by displaying a screen format which will allow you to enter new records. For
example, you might enter:

    peter   17 geography

This record would be inserted into the relation 'studentfile' in this
case since 'studentfile' is the file currently in use.

. *sort on name to sfile*
This tells the computer to make a sorted copy of the relation which is
currently in use. The copy is sorted on the 'name' field and is called
'sfile' - or whatever name you want to use.

. *use sfile*
This tells the computer to make 'sfile' the current file in use.

. *list*
This tells the computer to display the records of the relation currently in use. In this example, the computer would respond by displaying:

131

```
david          18 chemistry
john           25 physics                [note that these are sorted]
peter          17 geology
susan          20 chemistry
```

. *locate all for dept = 'chemistry'*
This tells the computer to locate all records in the current relation
in which the 'dept' field contains the value 'chemistry'. The computer
responds with the position in the relation of the first record which
fulfils this condition. To display this record, type:

. display

The computer then displays the record. For example:

david   18 chemistry

If you want the computer to locate the next record which meets the condition above, enter the command:

. continue

This must be followed by the display command to display the located
record (if any). The 'continue' and 'display' commands can then be
used to display all records in the relation which meet the condition.

. *report*
This command can be used to create a report form file for displaying
specified information from a relation in a user-defined format. The
output can then be directed to the VDU screen or the printer. The
following is an example of the type of dialogue with the computer which
follows the issue of this command.

Computer response	User response
ENTER REPORT FORM NAME:	report1
ENTER OPTIONS, M=LEFT MARGIN ETC	press return for default setting
PAGE HEADING? Y/N	y
ENTER PAGE HEADING	report 1/student
DOUBLE SPACE REPORT? Y/N	n
ARE TOTALS REQUIRED? Y/N	n
COL WIDTH. CONTENTS 001	20,name
ENTER HEADING:	studentname
002	6, age
ENTER HEADING:	age
003	press return key to terminate specification

The computer now displays the report according to the report format as
specified. In our example, the computer displays the following:

PAGE NO. 00001

      report1/student

studentname	age
david	18
john	25
peter	17
susan	20

If the user wants to use the same report format at some later date, he
need not specify it fully. For example, to use the report format
'report 1' to produce a report from relation 'studentfile', we would
issue the commands:

  . use studentfile
  . report

The computer responds, as above, with ENTER REPORT FORM NAME:. If we
respond with 'report1', the computer will immediately use the specification of 'report1' as given above and will display the following:

PAGE NO. 00001

      report1/student

studentname	age
peter	17
john	25
david	18
susan	20

This facility means that report format files, once created, can be used
as required at later dates.

. *use sfile (followed by)* . *select secondary*
These commands cause the relation 'sfile' to be stored in the secondary
storage area. They are necessary for the 'join' command described
below.

. *use deptfile (followed by)* . *select primary*
These commands cause the relation 'deptfile' to be stored in the primary storage area. They are necessary for the 'join' command described
below.

. *join to newrel for dept = deptname*
This command tells the computer to create a new relation called 'newrel'
by 'joining' the two relations in primary and secondary storage 'over'
the fields 'dept' and 'deptname'. In our example, the tuples in
'newrel' will consist of tuples from the 'sfile' relation concatenated
with tuples from the 'deptfile' relation where the 'dept' field in the
'sfile' tuple = the 'deptname' field in the 'deptfile' tuple.

. *use newrel (followed by)* . *list*
These commands tell the computer to display the contents of the 'newrel'
relation illustrating the effect of the join command. The computer responds with the following output:

david	18	chemistry	chemistry	prof	molecule	1644
john	25	physics	physics	prof	atom	3422
peter	17	geology	geology	prof	rock	4457
susan	20	chemistry	chemistry	prof	molecule	1644

. *modify command*

This command tells the computer that you want to create an application
program (or command file) consisting of a package of commands. The
computer responds by asking for the name of the command file. You respond by entering a name such as prog1. The computer then goes into a
screen edit mode allowing you to create a program. For example, you
might type the following:

```
use deptfile
do while .not. eof
display
skip
enddo
return
```
[now terminate input - on some computers you do this by pressing
the control key and W simultaneously]

The program which you have created tells the computer to display all
of the tuples in the relation 'deptfile'. The 'do while .not. eof'
command causes the computer to repeat the instructions down to the
'enddo' command while it has not reached the end of file. The 'display'
command tells the computer to display the current record. The 'skip'
command tells the computer to move to the next tuple in the relation.

. *do prog1*

This command tells the computer to execute the commands which are contained in the command file called 'prog1'. The computer responds by
displaying all of the tuples in the relation 'deptfile' as expected.

The examples above illustrate some of the facilities provided by dBASE
II. More information can be obtained in for example Byres (1984).

Note that dBASE II is a very simple system. It does not provide privacy or back-up facilities, and does not have a query language. However,
it is ideal for introducing users to database concepts.

3.5.6 INGRES

INGRES (Stonebraker et al, 1975) is a relational DBMS which was developed at the University of California, Berkeley. It is available on
DEC PDP-11 and VAX computers and runs under the UNIX operating system.
Relations may be manipulated in INGRES by use of the QUEL language
which has already been described. Integrity and privacy constraints
may also be expressed in QUEL.

Versions of INGRES are available which provide host language interfaces
to Pascal, FORTRAN and C.

INGRES is a late-bound system whose database schema is very dynamic
and flexible. New relations can be created by users while they are
processing data. (See section 3.6 for a discussion of binding.)

134

Relations can be held in one of four different structures:

isam   : indexed sequential access method
hash   : hash table
heap   : unkeyed and unstructured (tuples held in arrival order)
heapsort: heap with tuples sorted and duplicates removed

In addition, each of these structures has a compressed version: cisam, chash, cheap and cheapsort. In the isam, cisam, heap, cheap, heapsort and cheapsort structures, one or a collection of domains (columns) must be specified as primary key.

3.5.7 DB2

DB2 is IBM's latest relational database product. It supports the relational query language SQL and QUERY-BY-EXAMPLE. DB2 is a complex system and its description is outside the scope of this discussion. A specification of DB2 can be obtained from IBM.

3.5.8 NDB

NDB (Sharman and Winterbottom, 1979), which was later re-named 'Data Mapping Program', is a binary relational DBMS which was developed at the IBM Hursley laboratories in the mid-seventies. The major object- ives of the design were flexibility and ease of use. In order to achieve these objectives, NDB has the following features:

* Database creation and restructuring is program controlled.

* Binary relationships may be retrieved using 'subject/relation' or 'object/relation' pairs as key.

* The data structure is automatically reorganised at regular intervals to improve response time.

A generalised linked-list structure is used to store the triples. Entities are represented by three fields. The first field contains a pointer to the entity set to which the entity belongs, the second field contains a pointer to the binary relationships in which the entity is involved, and the third field contains a 'value' representing the entity. The value may be a variable length name such as 'Part# 1234', or it may be null in which case the three-field structure itself acts as an internal identifier. Relationships are represented by linked structures such as the one shown in fig. 3.46(a). A similar structure is also used to provide access from an entity set to its members, as shown in fig. 3.46(b). The complete interlinked structure is very much like a graph. Access to data in NDB is always via entity sets. For example, a query corresponding to (John. employedby. ?) must be qualif- ied by a statement to the effect that (John. ∈ . people).

NDB has been used for a number of applications at different locations and has met with a good user-response. The binary relational approach has often been criticised as being 'unnatural' in that it requires users to create unnatural names (identifiers) for n-ary relationships, where n > 2. Experience with NDB has demonstrated that this is not the case. The names which have to be created are quite natural, and in many cases refer to 'concrete' entities. For example, consider the tertiary relation shown on page 136.

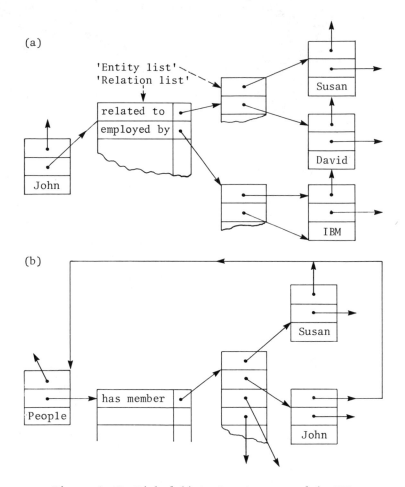

Figure 3.46 Linked list structures used in NDB

STUDENT	EXAM	MARK
SMITH	MATHS	80
JONES	MATHS	74
SMITH	CHEMISTRY	76

If this were to be represented using the binary relational approach, a name would have to be created for each tuple. However, each tuple corresponds to a 'script', i.e. to the booklet containing the student's answers to the questions. Therefore, the following, quite natural, names could be used:

```
(SMITH. wrote. SCRIPT#1)
(SCRIPT#1. forexam. MATHS)
(SCRIPT#1. givenmark. 80)
(JONES. wrote. SCRIPT#2)        (etc.)
```

136

Another criticism of the binary relational approach concerns the 'extensibility' of the schemas. For example, suppose that we had the schema:

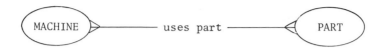

and entries such as the following in the database:

(M#1. usespart. P#1)

There is a problem if we want to add 'number of parts used' data to the database. The schema would have to be restructured as follows:

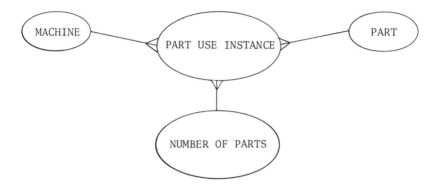

and the database entries would have to be converted to entries such as:

(M#1. has part use. PARTUSEINSTANCE#1)
(P#1. is used in. PARTUSEINSTANCE#1)
(PARTUSEINSTANCE#1. has number. 20)

Early experience with NDB showed that many-to-many relations such as the MACHINE/PART relation are often required to be extended in this way. Therefore, it was found to be good design policy to *always* expand many-to-many relations when they first arose in the systems analysis study. That is, if a many-to-many relation is identified during analysis it should be replaced by two one-to-many relations before the database system is designed. This approach has proven useful, and many NDB applications which were designed in this way have been running for several years without schema modification.

3.6 USING A COMMERCIAL DBMS

What you get
A commercial DBMS package typically consists of one or more of the following:

(a) Software to extend the user's operating system - for example, to accommodate concurrent access to the database.

(b) Software routines which can be CALLed from a host language such as COBOL, FORTRAN, PL/1, C, Pascal, etc. These routines may be regarded as additions to the standard functions or library routines which are already available in the host language. Examples of database routines are procedures to FIND, DELETE or INSERT units of data.

(c) Utility programs which may be executed as normal jobs in the existing or extended operating system. Such programs might be used, for example, to create, save or restore the database. Some DBMS packages include report program generators, query languages and data dictionary systems as sets of utility programs.

How you use it

The creation of a database system using a commercial DBMS typically involves the following tasks:

(a) *Analyse the end-user requirements.* The DBMS package may contain advice on how to do this, but it is unlikely. Cougar, Colter and Knapp's book on advanced system development/feasibility techniques is useful reading material (Cougar, 1982).

(b) *Create the conceptual schema.* The conceptual schema is constructed according to the view of the universe which underlies the DBMS being used. Note that an unconstrained network schema should be constructed before the DBMS is chosen. This schema should then be used as one of the factors affecting the choice of DBMS. However, once the DBMS has been purchased the conceptual schema should be rewritten according to the view underlying that DBMS.

(c) *Construct conceptual sub-schemas.* Conceptual sub-schemas are constructed for each set of end-users.

(d) *Perform a data analysis study and create the data dictionary.* The DBMS package may contain programs to help you do this. If not, it might be worthwhile investing in a data dictionary system to complement the DBMS.

(e) *Construct the database schema.* Many commercial DBMSs provide a mechanism for the formal specification of the database schema. In some cases a data description language (DDL) is provided. Essentially, the construction of the database schema requires the designer to map the conceptual schema into the abstract data structures provided by the DBMS being used. For example, with relational systems, the designer maps the conceptual schema into relations in the system and decides on, say, the order and format of columns.

(f) *Compilation of the database schema.* In most systems, the database schema is 'compiled' and the DBMS configures the physical storage structure automatically. The system may ask the user to input blocking factors, type of data compression scheme and type of index method required. However, other implementation aspects are taken care of automatically.

138

(g) *Specify the database sub-schemas.* Some DBMSs allow the user to specify database sub-schemas using the DD/L. Sub-schemas are often used to provide a level of privacy control by specifically excluding parts of the database from users who are only allowed to use that sub-schema. Sub-schemas may also be used to add an additional degree of data independence. For example, records may be defined in the sub-schema which are made up from parts taken from several different records in the database schema. Such composite records are often called 'logical records'.

(h) *Compile the database sub-schemas.* In many cases, the sub-schemas are compiled by the DBMS and the resultant object modules contain all of the necessary knowledge to map the logical structures of the sub-schema into the physical storage structures. That is, the compiled sub-schemas are stand-alone object modules which can be linked to various application programs. This is the case in IDMS, for example. In other cases, the sub-schema modules do not contain the mapping information which is necessary to locate data in the physical storage structure. This information is held in the database schema object module. The sub-schema modules only contain that information which is necessary to map logical sub-schema structures into the structures of the database schema. In this case, only when an application program is executed does the linked sub-schema object code refer to some repository of mapping information in order to obtain the information necessary to locate data in physical storage.

From this, we can see that the physical storage mapping information is introduced in two ways (i) with some DBMSs the sub-schema object modules contain the mapping information and these modules may be incorporated into application object modules by link editing - in this case, the application programmer refers to a logical data structure and the sub-schema module converts this logical description to physical locations; (ii) in other DBMSs, the mapping information is not made available until the application program is executed - in this case, the programmer refers to logical records and these are mapped into database structures by the information in the sub-schema module. Only when the application program is executed are the database schema structures mapped into physical locations. The mapping information necessary to do this is held in a 'logical to physical mapping module' (which might be part of the database schema itself). The mapping module is therefore part of the operational database system and is not just referred to in the compilation sub-schemas. (In practice, the logical to physical mapping information is often scattered about in various programs.)

In case (i) above the system is said to be 'early-bound', and in case (ii) the system is 'late-bound'. The idea of binding is very important. Late-bound systems are more data independent than early-bound systems. In a late-bound system, a change in the organisation of the physical storage structure

only requires the mapping module to be changed. Application
programs and sub-schemas are left unchanged and do not need
to be re-compiled.

(i) *Creation of the back-up and recovery programs.* Commercially
available DBMSs vary greatly in the way in which they handle
back-up and recovery. Some provide utility programs which
can be used directly to SAVE and RESTORE, ROLL-BACK or ROLL-
FORWARD a database. Others require designers to build programs for these tasks.

(j) *Loading of the database.* Special purpose utility programs
are typically provided for the initial loading of the large
quantities of data which constitute the database. This task
could be carried out by writing and running application programs which insert data piecemeal, but this is likely to be
too time-consuming.

(k) *Creation of application programs.* Once the database has been
loaded, it may be manipulated by application programs which
are often written in some host language. Such programs typically start by declaring the sub-schema which is to be used.
That part of the database may then be manipulated by means of
CALLS to DBMS routines such as FIND, DELETE, etc., as required

A good account of the database system design process can be found in
Perkinson (1984).

3.7 LIMITATIONS OF EXISTING DATABASE MANAGEMENT SYSTEMS

Data independence is not supported
Currently available DBMSs do not support data independence to any grea
extent. Even in relational systems the addition of a column to a rela
tion can be problematical.

The co-existence of external schemas is not supported
In many database applications, end-users will be interested in different sub-sets of the universe of discourse. This is often accommodated
by the use of conceptual and logical sub-schemas. Such sub-schemas
allow sub-sets of the database to be defined but do not satisfy the
requirements which some end-users might have to view parts of the data
base structured according to a data model other than the one on which
the system is based. For example, consider a database system which is
based on a hierarchical data model. Hierarchical sub-schemas could be
defined for users who are content to see the database as a set of file
of records with repeating groups. However, other users may prefer to
see the database as a set of relations in third normal form. An
appropriate relational sub-schema would then have to be created. Such
sub-schemas are called 'external schemas'.

The co-existence of external schemas may be achieved by using algorith
which map data and commands, structured and expressed in terms of one
data model, to equivalent data and commands expressed in terms of some
other data model. The difficulty of constructing such algorithms wou
appear to be related to the difference in the structural semantics of
the data models involved in the mappings. For example, consider a

hierarchical database comprising a file of person records, each of which consists of a 'person name' field and a repeating group of two 'parent name' fields. The explicit data content of this file could easily be mapped into a relation with domains 'person name' and 'parent name'. Each person record would be mapped into at most two tuples. However, the implied integrity constraint that 'a person may have at most two parents' would be lost unless it were mapped into an explicit representation in some code which restricts the type of updates allowed on the person/parent relation. This constraint is embedded in the structural semantics of the hierarchical database.

Currently available DBMSs do not support the co-existence of external schemas to any great extent. In relational systems, end-user views may only be defined in terms of projections, selections and joins on relations and not in terms of, say, records with repeating groups. The difficulty of supporting co-existence would appear to be partly due to the structural semantics of the hierarchical, network and relational data models on which conventional DBMSs are based.

Semantic integrity checking is not automatic
Another shortcoming of currently available systems is that they do not use conceptual schemas as integral components which are accessed by automatic integrity checking and inference sub-systems. Conceptual schemas are being used more frequently during requirements analysis and for reference by potential users. However, the information which they contain is re-coded explicitly in application programs or implicitly in choice of data structure and provision of access paths.

Deductive retrieval is not supported
Only a few of the DBMSs which are currently available provide a 'deductive retrieval' facility. Deductive retrieval involves the inference of data which is not stored explicitly from data which is stored explicitly. For example, if we know that Pat is male, and that someone may not be both male and female, then we can deduce that Pat is not a female even though this fact has not been given explicitly.

The end-user interfaces are not very friendly
Most commercially available DBMSs are relatively difficult to use. In particular, many of the systems based on the hierarchical and DBTG network views require trained staff to set up a database system and to produce application programs for end-users. The relational systems are a little better. For example, an inexperienced user can learn how to use dBASE II in two or three hours, and INGRES in a day or two.

Most database manipulation, query and report generation languages are either difficult to use or limited in their capability. Exceptions are those languages based on relational calculus. These languages allow users to express what data they want without having to specify the procedural operations necessary to obtain it. However, most of these languages have the disadvantage of being 'unnatural' in the sense that queries expressed in them do not resemble the equivalent query in natural language.

In short, most existing DBMSs are not 'friendly' enough for an untrained person to use.

Most DBMSs are based on inappropriate hardware
Another criticism of conventional database management systems is related to their implementation. Because they are based on conventional computer hardware, they suffer in performance. Conventional hardware locates data by position whereas the main requirement in database applications is to locate data by content. That is, the 'logical' specification of required data is given in terms of 'semantic values', e.g. 'RETRIEVE RECORD WITH NAME = SMITH', and the DBMS must convert this 'logical' specification to a physical address on backing store in order to retrieve the required data. In the last ten years techniques have been developed to speed up this conversion or to eliminate it altogether by the use of content addressing schemes. Special-purpose processors and computers have been developed which use these techniques.

At present, very few DBMSs are based on special-purpose hardware. IBM's System 38 is perhaps the only widely used commercial system which is. This sytem speeds up database management tasks and improves security by means of micro-coded high-level database instructions.

In the next section some features are described that may be found in DBMSs which are currently being developed and which will be available in the future. We shall call these 'fifth generation' DBMSs since they are designed to run on fifth generation computer hardware.

3.8 FIFTH GENERATION DATABASE MANAGEMENT SYSTEMS

3.8.1 AN ARCHITECTURE FOR FIFTH GENERATION DBMSs
Recognition of the limitations of conventional approaches to database work has resulted in a reconsideration of DBMS architecture. It has been proposed (see, for example, van Griethuysen, 1982 and Nijssen, 1984) that fifth generation DBMSs will need to place more emphasis on conceptual schemas and that their underlying data models will need to have low structural semantic content. The resulting architecture is in some ways simpler than that of conventional DBMSs - the database schema is no longer necessary since the conceptual schema takes over its function as the co-ordinating module in the operational database system.

Nijssen (1984) has proposed an architecture for fifth generation DBMSs which is an extension of the architecture published in the report of the International Standards Organisation (van Griethuysen, 1982), which is itself an extension of the three schema architecture endorsed in the earlier report of the American National Standards Institute (ANSI, 1977). A slightly modified version of Nijssen's architecture is illustrated in fig. 3.47. A more complete architecture developed from this is given in fig. 3.48 (see page 144).

Nijssen refers to the database as an 'information base' and defines its contents as a set of 'deep structure elementary sentence instances' each of which is a predicate with an ordered set or tuple consisting of the kind of thing, the kind of naming convention and the name of the specific thing itself. Sentences are allowed to function as things in other sentences.

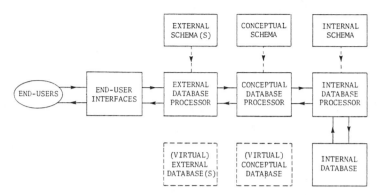

Figure 3.47 A starting point for an architecture for fifth generation database systems

Nijssen gives the following examples of instances of deep structure elementary sentences:

```
The president...................................(kind of thing)
                with name......................(kind of naming
                                                 convention)
               J F Kennedy..................(name for specific
                                                 thing)
was married to..............................(predicate)
the spouse...................................(kind of thing)
               with first name................(kind of naming
                                                 convention)
                   Jacqueline...................(name for specific
                                                 thing
This........................................(name for specific
                                                 sentence instance)
marriage....................................(kind of sentence)
was established on...........................(predicate)
the date.....................................(kind of thing)
               with American date code.........(kind of naming
                                                 convention)
                9/12/1953....................(name for
                                                 specific thing)
```

Nijssen's approach is similar in some respects to the use of an irreducible n-ary relational data model as proposed by Hall et al (1976). The external, conceptual and internal schemas which have been described earlier correspond to the descriptions given by Nijssen for these components.

If the binary relational view were used as the basis for a fifth generation DBMS then the 'deep structure' elementary sentence instances would all be of the form:

relationship id   entity id   relationship type   entity id

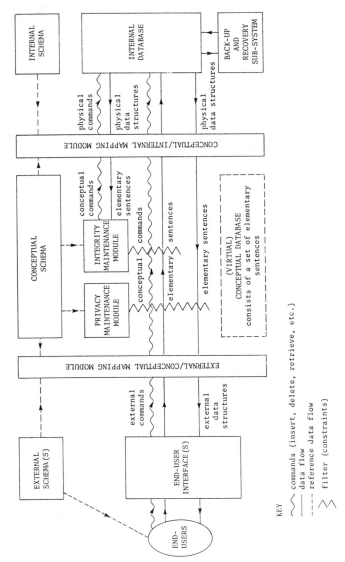

KEY

$\sim\sim$ commands (insert, delete, retrieve, etc.)

$\sim$ data flow

- - - reference data flow

$\gtrsim$ filter (constraints)

Figure 3.48 A more complete architecture for fifth generation database systems

and Nijssen's example above would be represented as follows:

b#1	E#1	has name	J F Kennedy
b#2	E#1	∈	President
b#3	E#2	has first name	Jacqueline
b#4	E#2	∈	Spouse
b#5	E#1	partner in	E#3
b#6	E#2	partner in	E#3
b#7	E#3	∈	Marriages
b#8	E#3	established on	9/12/1953
b#9	9/12/1953	∈	American date codes

There is a growing interest in the binary relational view and it is thought by many (see, for example, Alvey, 1984) that this view might be appropriate as a basis for the development of fifth generation DBMSs. In many parts of this book, examples based on the binary relational view are used to illustrate methods for the manipulation of knowledge. This is partly because we feel that the view is likely to be used in many future systems and partly because it simplifies explanation of the methods described.

3.8.2 AUTOMATIC SEMANTIC INTEGRITY CHECKING
Not only will fifth generation DBMSs be expected to be more flexible and data independent than current systems; they will also be expected to have more powerful integrity checking mechanisms. These will include more powerful syntactic (type checking and spelling) routines and also more powerful semantic integrity checking routines.

What is semantic integrity?
By 'semantic integrity' we mean the compliance of the database with constraints derived from our knowledge of what is and is not 'allowed' in that part of the universe which is represented by the data in the database. The maintenance of semantic integrity involves preventing data which represents a disallowed state of the universe from being inserted into the database.

Some approaches to the automatic maintenance of semantic integrity
A straightforward approach for the maintenance of semantic integrity follows from suggestions by Abrial (1974) and Florentin (1974). It involves two steps:

(a) Provide the database implementor with a language for specifying semantic constraints.

(b) Use the constraints to vet data which is presented for insertion into the database.

Ideally, the database implementor should be able to specify constraints which are then used by the system to maintain semantic integrity automatically. However, this approach must be viewed with caution. Firstly, for languages in general it is undecidable whether the constraints expressed in it are themselves consistent (see chapter 4). Secondly, vetting data against a complex integrity constraint might require access to a large portion of the database; the system must be capable of optimisation.

145

The first problem can be solved only if the language in which the constraints are expressed is decidable. The second problem can be explained as follows: given a constraint, the system must be capable of determining how costly it is to apply that constraint - ideally, this cost should be estimated when the constraints are being formulated thereby allowing the user to replace 'expensive' constraints with 'cheaper' ones.

This may be illustrated with an example. Given a 'parent' relation, a semantic constraint might state that the sub-graph containing only edges labelled with 'parent' must be cycle free (i.e. no one may be his own ancestor). Checking this constraint is likely to be expensive. If the database also contains birthdates, then the constraint above could be replaced by a constraint which states that the birthdate of the parent must precede the birthdate of the child.

These considerations, however, have not deterred the development of the two step approach, and progress has been achieved through the work of Abrial (1974), Florentin (1974), Eswaran and Chamberlin (1975), Stonebraker (1975), Hammer and McLeod (1975), Biller and Neuhold (1978) Pelagatti, Paolini and Bracchi (1978), Roussopoulos (1979), Mylopoulos, Bernstein and Wong (1980), Brodie (1980), Borgida and Wong (1981), Shipman (1981), and Frost and Whittaker (1983).

Florentin (1974) was one of the first to propose that predicate calculus could be used for the precise specification of semantic integrity constraints. However, he goes on to state that the manipulation of a logical formula is likely to be too tedious to be useful as a practical method for the maintenance of semantic integrity. This conclusion is accompanied by a reference to work carried out by Robinson (1967).

The papers by Eswaran and Chamberlin (1975) and Stonebraker (1975) are concerned with the maintenance of semantic integrity of relational databases. Constraints are specified in two relational query languages SEQUEL and QUEL respectively. (We have already given a brief description of how constraints expressed in QUEL are enforced.)

A more general approach is claimed to have been made by Hammer and McLeod (1975). Although they describe their work in the context of a relational database system, they go some way towards the design of a special-purpose constraint specification language. Several useful examples of constraints are presented in Hammer and McLeod's paper.

Biller and Neuhold (1978) also recognise the need for generality and point out that it would be difficult to translate an integrity constraint formulated in terms of one specific view (e.g. the relational view) into constraints expressed in terms of some other view (e.g. the hierarchical view). Consequently, they developed an abstract conceptual view which uses the concepts of entity, entity type and relation. Constraints are expressed in terms of this view in a language called LDDL. Although LDDL has a simple semantic basis, it has a complex syntax. For example, there are seven different kinds of 'type' definition.

Pelagatti, Paolini, and Bracchi (1978) discuss semantic integrity in

146

relation to their main topic of 'mapping external views to a common data model'. For this reason they restrict their attention to two types of constraint, 'cardinality' and 'equivalence' constraints. They suggest a technique similar to that proposed by Abrial (1974) for expressing cardinality constraints.

The next significant contribution was made by Roussopoulos (1979) with his language CSDL. CSDL facilitates the specification, modification and examination of constraints through high-level support facilities.

Another major step forward was made by Mylopoulos, Bernstein and Wong (1980) in their design of a language called TAXIS. Semantic integrity constraints are regarded as pre-requisite or result conditions of transactions which must be met if the effect of the transaction is to be accepted. Mylopoulos et al give several examples of semantic integrity constraints. Their main contribution is in recognising that constraints defined over one class of entities or transactions should be automatically inherited by sub-sets of that class.

Borgida and Wong (1981) have given two formal specifications of the semantics of the TAXIS language, one of which is based on axioms and partial correctness assertions and is intended for verifiers who wish to show that the system maintains database integrity.

A somewhat different approach has been proposed by Brodie (1980) who suggests that data type tools can be used for the definition of semantic constraints and for the maintenance of semantic integrity. Strong typing is provided in a Pascal-like type system embedded in a language called BETA. For example, specification of the type 'person object' might be:

```
type
   person = object name      :  nametype;
                   number    :  social-insurance;
                   sex       :  (male,female) unordered
                   address   :  address type;
                   title     :  (professor,tutor,student);
                   keys      :  name, number
                   dependencies names → address|sex|title
           end object;
```

Enforcement of the semantic constraints implied by this specification may then be carried out automatically by normal type-checking routines. For example, the constraint 'person objects may only be of sex male or female', which is implied in the above, is easily enforced. However, it is not easy to see how more complex constraints such as 'a person may not be the son of someone born at a later date than himself' could be expressed in a type declaration. Brodie's work is interesting because it questions the notions which are used to distinguish between syntax and semantics.

More recently Shipman (1981) has designed a data definition and manip-ulation language called DAPLEX. This language is based on a conceptual view called the 'functional' view. Constraints may be expressed in DAPLEX as, for example:

DEFINE CONSTRAINT NativeHead(Department) = >
Dept(Head(Department)) = Department

which states that a department's head must come from within the department. DAPLEX is described in more detail in chapter 10.

A *method which can be used with binary relational DBMSs*

The following method was specifically designed to facilitate automatic
constraint enforcement. It was developed by Frost and Whittaker (1983)
for use with a binary relational (BR) DBMS. In this method, constraints
are expressed in a language called SCHEMAL. This language is a sub-set
of first order predicate logic which is restricted to binary predicates
and does not include function symbols. (First order predicate logic is
described in detail in chapter 4.)

Note that a BR database consists of a set of binary relationships or
triples such as:

(e1. ∈ . student)
(e1. named. peter)
(e1. livesin. london)

These triples state that the entity e1 is a student called Peter who
lives in London.

The following constraints will be used as examples in this discussion:

C1 : members of the set of husbands may not also be members of the
set of bachelors

C2 : only students may enrol for something

C3 : an employee's manager must also be an employee

C4 : professors may not earn more than £30,000

C5 : male persons are only allowed to marry if they are older than
18 years

C6 : no two entities may have the same name and address

C7 : a department can only have one manager

C8 : no one can set an exam unless he teaches someone who is a
student

C9 : all employees who work in the same department must have the
same manager

C10: the only relations which lecturers are allowed to participate
in are of type 'teaches' and 'sets exam'

C11: a married person may not become a single person

C12: an employee's salary may not be reduced

C13: the professors' average salary may not exceed £26,000

C14: an employee's salary must exceed deductions

Constraint C2 is interpreted as meaning that an entity may not be enrolled for a course unless that entity is known to be a member of the

set of students. For example, the data 'entity#3 is enrolled for English' may not be inserted into the database unless that database already contains the data 'entity#3 is a member of the set of students'. Similar interpretations apply to constraints C3, and C5. C11 and C12 constrain the way in which the database may be updated rather than extended.

Rules C1, C2 and C6 above may be expressed in SCHEMAL as follows:

C1': (X. ∈ . husbands) → ¬(X. ∈ . bachelors)
C2': (X. enrolledfor. Y) → (X. ∈ . students)
C6': (X. named. n) ∧ (X. livesin. a) ∧ (Y. named. n) ∧
                    (Y. livesin. a) → (X. identicalto. Y)

These rules may be read as follows *according to the semantics of SCHEMAL:*

C1':   'if an entity is a member of the set of husbands then it must not be a member of the set of bachelors'

C2':   'if an entity is enrolled for anything, then it must be a member of the set of students'

C6':   'if two entities have the same name and address, then they must be identical'

SCHEMAL is limited in its expressive power and cannot be used to express constraints such as C8, C10, C13 or C14. Also, it is not clear how it would be used in relation to C11 and C12.

We now describe how constraints which are expressed in SCHEMAL may be enforced automatically.

Informal overview of the method
A BR database exhibits semantic integrity with respect to a set of SCHEMAL constraints if all (possibly partial) instantiations of these constraints which are generated by the triples in the database are true. If any instantiation is false then the database does not exhibit semantic integrity. An instantiation of a constraint is derived by the substitution of variables in that constraint by entities. For example, the triple (e1. ∈ . bachelors) gives the following instantiation of constraint C1:

  (e1. ∈ . husbands) → ¬(e1. ∈ . bachelors)

The integrity of a database can be maintained by checking that all new instantiations of constraints which can be generated by a new triple would be true if that triple were in the database. If so, the triple may be inserted into the database; otherwise it is rejected.

Using this approach, the maintenance of database integrity involves a five-stage process:

(a)   The constraints are specified in SCHEMAL by the database implementor. For example:

     C2'   (X. enrolled for. Y) → (X. ∈ . students)

(b) The constraints are then converted to a particularly simple form called 'clausal form' (described in more detail later). An example of a constraint in clausal form is:

C2"   {(X. ∈ . students), ¬(X. enrolled for. Y)}

which may be read as 'either X is a student or X is not en-rolled for anything'. C2" has the same meaning as C2'.

(c) When the system receives a triple TI to be inserted into the database, the system attempts to match it against the con-straints in clausal form. For example, the triple (el. enrolled for. physics) matches constraint C2" above.

(d) For every constraint C which is matched by TI, the set of new (possible partial) instantiations of C which can be obtained from TI and the database are generated. For example, the set of new instantiations of C2" above, which can be obtained from the triple (el. enrolled for. physics), consists of one instan-tiation only, irrespective of the database contents:

{(el. ∈ . students), ¬(el. enrolled for. physics)}

(e) The new instantiations are then evaluated, assuming that the new triple were in the database. If the instantiations are all true then the triple may be put into the database; other-wise it is rejected. For example, the triple (el. enrolled for. physics) may only be inserted if the triple (el. ∈ . students) is already in the database. If this triple is not in the database then the instantiation of C2" above is false.

The process is now described more precisely, defining the terms intro-duced, and showing how stages (b) to (e) may be carried out automatic-ally.

Conversion of constraints to clausal form

A SCHEMAL constraint in clausal form consists of a 'disjunction of literals', where a literal is a triple or the negation of a triple. An example of a constraint in clausal form is:

C1"   {¬(X. ∈ . bachelors), ¬(X. ∈ . husbands)}

which may be read as 'either X is not a bachelor or X is not a husband'. Other examples are:

C2"   {(X. ∈ . students), ¬(X. enrolled for. Y)}

C6"   {(X. ident. Y), ¬(X. named. N), ¬(X. lives in. A),
                        ¬(Y. named. N), ¬(Y. lives in. A)}

which correspond to C2' and C6' above.

Some SCHEMAL constraints transform into more than one constraint in clausal form. For example:

(X. ∈ . vegetables) → [¬(X. ∈ . animals) ∧ ¬(X. ∈ . minerals)] transforms into the two constraints:

{¬(X. ∈ . animals), ¬(X. ∈ . vegetables)}
{¬(X. ∈ . minerals), ¬(X. ∈ . vegetables)}

The automatic translation of formulas to clausal form is described in more detail in chapter 4 where predicate logic is considered in more detail.

Matching a triple against a constraint

The method which we are describing assumes that all triples in the database are variable free. This assumption is reasonable for many database applications.

A variable free triple TI matches a constraint C if there is at least one triple TC in C which corresponds to TI. Two triples, TC and TI, correspond if:

      (i)   TI = TC

OR (ii) TI and TC have identical second fields AND

         (a)   TI and TC have identical first fields AND the third field of TC is a variable

    OR (b)   TI and TC have identical third fields AND the first field of TC is a variable

    OR (c)   the first and third fields of TC are variables

For example:

(e2. ∈ . bachelors) matches C1'' above
(e3. named. peter) matches C6'' above

Instantiations of constraints

An instantiation of a constraint is obtained by the consistent substitution of *all* of its variables by entities.

A partial instantiation of a constraint is obtained by the consistent substitution of *some* of its variables by entities. For example, the following is a partial instantiation of constraint C2'':

{(e4. ∈ . students), ¬(e4. enrolled for. Y)}

The set of new (possibly partial) instantiations of a constraint C, which is obtained from a matching triple TI, is generated by calling the recursive procedure p-instant below for each triple TC in C which corresponds to TI. Notice that the set generated will depend upon the database into which TI is being proposed for insertion. (The procedure is written in pseudo-Pascal.)

```
proc p-instant (triple TI, TC, constraint C);
var sub : boolean; TDX : array [ ] of triples;
begin
substitute variables in TC by equivalent entities in TI;
make the same substitution(s) throughout C;
sub := false;

for each triple TX in C still containing one or two variables
do begin
    TDX := retrieve(TX);
    if TDX isn't empty
        then sub := true;
            for each TD in TDX
                do begin
                    p-instant(TD, TX, C)
                end


    end;
if sub = false
    then print(C)


end;
```

Notes

(a)   Constraint C is an array of literals representing a constraint. For example:

(el. $\in$. students)	$\neg$(el. enrolled for. Y)

(b)   TDX is an array of literals, none of which contain a negation sign.

(c)   The statement commencing 'substitute variables in TC by equivalent...' is not a comment on the code following it but is shorthand for a number of statements, details of which are not given.

(d)   The procedure generates all new instantiations of C which can be obtained from TI due to its correspondence to TC in C.

(e)   The boolean variable 'sub' is used to flag when no more variable substitution can be made. At this point a new (possibly partial) instantiation has been generated and is printed. The call print is replaced later by a procedure call to evaluate the instantiation.

(f)   TDX := retrieve(TX); causes the set of triples which correspond to TX to be retrieved from the database and put into TDX.

The algorithm p-instant is actually a variant of the recursive formulation of the solution to the eight queens problem (Wirth, 1976). The array of constraints corresponds to the chess board and instantiation of variables to the placing of queens in positions.

The initial call of p-instant substitutes the entities from the triple to be inserted into corresponding variables in C. Subsequent recursive calls substitute the remaining variables in all possible ways according to the triples in the database. Sometimes, it may not be possible to substitute all of the variables. In these cases, partial instantiations are generated. To illustrate the process, consider the following examples:

Suppose that the database contains the triples:

```
(e1. ∈       . students)
(e1. named  . peter  )
(e1. livesin. london  )
(e2. named  . peter  )
(e3. livesin. london  )
(e4. named  . peter  )
```

and suppose that the following constraints hold:

```
C2"   {(X. ∈ . students), ¬(X. enrolled for. Y)}
C6"   {(X. ident. Y), ¬(X. named. N), ¬(X. livesin. A),
                      ¬(Y. named. N), ¬(Y. livesin. A)}
```

Example 1
   If TI = (e4. ∈ . students) then this matches C2" because TI corresponds to (X. ∈ . students). With TC = (X. ∈ . students), the call p-instant (TI, TC, C2") generates the single partial instantiation:

   I1:   {(e4. ∈ . students), ¬(e4. enrolled for. Y)}

no other triples in C2" correspond to TI, therefore no further substitutions can be made, consequently I1 is the only new instantiation of C2" which is generated.

Example 2
   If TI = (e2. enrolled for. physics) then this matches C2" because TI corresponds to TC = (X. enrolled for. Y). The call p-instant (TI, TC, C2") generates the instantiation:

   I2:   {(e2. ∈ . students), ¬(e2. enrolled for. physics)}

no other triples in C2" correspond to TI, therefore this is the only instantiation generated.

Example 3
   If TI = (e5. livesin. london) then this triple matches C6" because TI corresponds to TC = (X. livesin. A). The call p-instant (TI, TC, C6") generates the instantiations:

   I3:   {(e5. ident. e5), ¬(e5. named. peter),
                ¬(e5. livesin. london), ¬(e5. named. peter),
                                 ¬(e5. livesin. london)}

   I4:   {(e5. ident. e2), ¬(e5. named. peter),
                ¬(e5. livesin. london), ¬(e2. named. peter),
                                 ¬(e2. livesin. london)}

I5: {(e5. ident. e4), ¬(e5. named. peter),
¬(e5. livesin. london), ¬(e4. named. peter),
¬(e4. livesin. london)}

I6: {(e5. ident. e3), ¬(e5. named. peter),
¬(e5. livesin. london), ¬(e3. named. peter),
¬(e3. livesin. london)}

The triple (e5. livesin. london) also corresponds to the triple (Y. livesin. A) in C6". The set of instantiations obtained from this correspondence is similar to the set above.

Notice that the set of new instantiations of C is obtained from a triple in conjunction with the database for which the triple is being tested.

For reasons which will be apparent later, the evaluation of two types of instantiation will be considered.

Evaluation of instantiations in which no further variable substitution can be made
These instantiations may be completely variable free or may contain triples with variables for which there is no corresponding triple in the database, e.g. I1 above with variable Y. Such (possibly partial) instantiations are true if they contain at least one literal which is true.

A literal which contains a negation sign is true if the triple it contains is false; otherwise it is false. A literal which does not contain a negation sign is true if the literal it contains is true; otherwise it is false. For example, if the triple (e1. ∈ . students) is true then the literal (e1. ∈ . students) is true and the literal ¬(e1. ∈ . students) is false.

A triple is assumed to be true (i) if it is the triple being tested for input, OR (ii) if a corresponding triple is stored in the database, OR (iii) if its evaluation is true. Triples such as (john. ident. john) and (10. < . 100) can be evaluated to produce true or false. The assumption here is that if a triple is missing from the database or is not being proposed for input then the corresponding fact is false. This is the 'closed world assumption' as discussed by Minker (1982), and described in more detail in chapter 5.

From this it can be seen that instantiation I1 is true, and I2 is false with respect to the example database above.

Evaluation of instantiations where further variable substitution is possible
Such instantiations are generated as intermediate results by p-instant and are not printed out. For example, in the derivation of I5, the following instantiation is generated as an intermediate result:

{(e5. ident. Y), ¬(e5. named. N), ¬(e5. livesin. london),
¬(Y. named. N), ¬(Y. livesin. london)}

An intermediate partial instantion is true irrespective of further variable substitution if either:

it contains at least one literal with no negation sign and a variable free triple which is true; or

it contains at least one literal with a negation sign and a triple (which may or may not be variable free) which is false

Similarly, an intermediate partial instantiation is false irrespective of further variable substitution if it contains no literals which could become true by such substitution - that is, if each one of its literals is either:

a literal with no negation sign and with a triple (which may or may not be variable free) which is false; or

a literal with a negation sign and with a variable free triple which is true

Accepting or rejecting triples

As mentioned earlier, the integrity of a database D with respect to a set of constraints C can be maintained by checking each triple TI proposed for input, to make sure that all new instantiations of C which are generated by TI and D would be true if TI were in the database. So far, methods which could be used to carry out this checking automatically have been described. However, such an approach assumes that the database already exhibits semantic integrity which is then maintained. A simple solution is to start with an empty database and then check every triple proposed for input. This solution assumes that an empty database exhibits semantic integrity with respect to any set of constraints. This is *not* true. Therefore, a restriction must be imposed on the type of constraints allowed so that we can assume that an empty database exhibits semantic integrity. The restriction is not severe and may be thought of as a point of clarification as far as the user is concerned:

The set of integrity constraints must not contain any constraints consisting of one literal with no negation sign and with a variable free triple. For example, constraints such as:

(e11. ∈ . companies)

are not allowed. This constraint states that e11 must be known to be a member of the set of companies at all times; therefore an empty database does not satisfy this. A database implementor wishing to make this constraint could do so by putting the triple (e11. ∈ . companies) into the database before it is handed over to the user community.

Efficiency considerations

It can be seen that the procedure p-instant could generate a large number of instantiations in some cases. Fortunately, it is not always necessary to generate all of these explicitly:

(a) If an instantiation, in which no further variable substitution can be made, is found to be false then the whole process can terminate and the triple may be rejected.

155

(b) If an intermediate instantiation is found to be false irrespective of further substitution (as described earlier), then the whole process can terminate and the triple may be rejected.

(c) If an intermediate instantiation is found to be true irrespective of further substitution (as described earlier), then further substitution of that instantiation is not necessary and the current call of p-instant can terminate. An extreme example of this is where a triple TI matches a constraint C because it corresponds to a literal which does not contain a negation sign. In this case, all possible instantiations of C which are generated by TI must be true.

The revised version of p-instant is as follows:

```
proc p-instant (triple TI, TC, constraint C);
var sub : boolean; TDX : array [ ] of triples;
begin

substitute variables in TC by equivalent entities in TI, make the
same substitution(s) throughout C:

if C is false irrespective of further substitutions
    then goto reject
    else if C is true irrespective of further substitutions
        then do nothing

        else begin sub := false;

            for each triple TX in C still containing
                                      one or two variables
                do begin
                    TDX := retrieve(TX);
                    if TDX isnt empty
                        then sub := true;
                        for each TD in TDX
                            do begin
                                p-instant(TD, TX, C)

                        end

            end;

            if sub = false
                then if C is false
                    then goto reject

        end

end;
```

The statement 'goto reject' causes the process to terminate and the triple to be rejected. A goto has been used for clarity and for efficiency. Whenever an instantiation is found to be false the whole process can terminate and there is no need for recursive 'ascent'. If the triple is not rejected, it may be inserted into the database.

To illustrate the process, consider the following examples:

Take the example database given earlier and suppose that the constraints C2" and C6" hold:

C2"   {(X. ∈ . students), ¬(X. enrolled for. Y)}
C6"   {(X. ident. Y), ¬(X. named. N), ¬(X. livesin. A),
                    ¬(Y. named. N), ¬(Y. livesin. A)}

Example 1
   Try to insert TI = (e8. ∈ . students):

   (a)   Match C2".

   (b)   Take the substitution {X := e8} giving:

            {(e8. ∈ . students), ¬(e8. enrolled for. Y)}

   (c)   The literal (e8. ∈ . students) is true irrespective of
         further substitution (since it contains the triple being
         proposed for insertion), therefore no further substitution
         is necessary. Therefore, we can assume that all instan-
         tiations of C2" generated by TI are true, and TI may be
         inserted.

Example 2
   Try to insert TI = (e3. named. peter):

   (a)   Match C6".

   (b)   Make the substitutions {X := e3, N := peter} giving:

            {(e3. ident. Y), ¬(e3. named. peter),
                      ¬(e3. livesin. A), ¬(Y. named. peter),
                                     ¬(Y. livesin. A)}

   (c)   Find the corresponding triple (e3. livesin. london) in the
         database, and make the substitution {A := london} giving:

            {(e3. ident. Y), ¬(e3. named. peter),
                   ¬(e3. livesin. london), ¬(Y. named. peter),
                                     ¬(Y. livesin. london)}

   (d)   Find the corresponding triple (e1. named. peter) and make
         the substitution {Y := e1} giving:

            {(e3. ident. e1), ¬(e3. named. peter),
                   ¬(e3. livesin. london), ¬(e1. named. peter),
                                     ¬(e1. livesin. london)}

   (e)   No more substitutions can be made, therefore this instan-
         tiation is evaluated and found to be false.

   (f)   No more instantiations of C6" need be generated and no
         more constraints need be matched. TI is rejected.

Example 3
   Try to insert the triple TI = (e5. named. james)

   (a)   Match C6".

   (b)   Make the substitutions {X := e5, N := james} giving:

$$\{(e5. \; ident. \; Y), \; \neg(e5. \; named. \; james),$$
$$\neg(e5. \; livesin. \; A), \; \neg(Y. \; named. \; james),$$
$$\neg(Y. \; livesin. \; A)\}$$

(c) Try to find a triple corresponding to (e5. livesin. A) in the database, since there is no such triple, the literal (e5. livesin. A) must be true, therefore further substitution of this instantiation is not necessary and p-instant can terminate its current call.

(d) We have not finished yet - we must also test the instantiations resulting from the substitution {Y := e5, N := james}. We will find that all such instantiations are also true.

(e) Since no more literals in C6'' correspond to TI, we can accept TI for insertion because it has not been rejected.

Limitations of the method

There are many limitations to the method described above, including the following:

(a) Since SCHEMAL contains no constructs for dealing with sets, constraints such as C13 and C14 cannot be accommodated.

(b) Since SCHEMAL does not allow variables to be existentially quantified, constraints such as C8 cannot be accommodated. (See chapter 4 for a discussion of existential quantification.)

(c) The method requires the whole database to be locked while integrity checks are being carried out for a single triple. Only when a triple has been rejected or accepted can another triple be considered. This situation can be alleviated somewhat since two triples can be tested simultaneously if the constraints which they match are totally unrelated.

A more serious criticism of the method is that it is not based on a well-defined semantics. For example, consider the meanings of the following constraints:

C1':   (X. $\in$. husbands) $\rightarrow \neg$(X. $\in$. bachelors)
C2':   (X. enrolledfor. Y) $\rightarrow$ (X. $\in$. students)

The method described above interprets these constraints as follows:

(a) C1' in clausal form is {$\neg$(X. $\in$. husbands), $\neg$(X. $\in$. bachelors)}. Therefore, either $\neg$(X. $\in$. husbands) or $\neg$(X. $\in$. bachelors) must be true. By the closed world assumption, $\neg$T is true if T is absent from the database. Therefore, either (X. $\in$. husbands) or (X. $\in$. bachelors) must be absent from the database. If one is present, the other may not be inserted.

(b) C2' in clausal form is {$\neg$(X. enrolledfor. Y), (X. $\in$. students)}. This means that (X. enrolledfor. Y) must be absent or (X. $\in$. students) must be present. Therefore, if

158

(X. ∈ . students) is absent then (X. enrolledfor. Y) may not
be inserted.

As such, these constraints define 'pre-requisite' conditions which must
be satisfied before certain triples can be inserted into the database.
However, they may also be used for inference - for example, C1' might
be read as for all x, if (X. ∈ . husbands) is in the database then we
can infer that ¬(X. ∈ . bachelors) is true.

A problem arises when we use rules for inference as well as for integrity checking. In order to determine if a triple T is true it is
necessary (a) to see if it is in the database and (b) if it is not in
the database, to see if it can be inferred from the database by use of
the inference rules.

At this point, the reader may begin to appreciate the usefulness of
more formal approaches to integrity checking. Such approaches are
described later on (in chapter 5) and are based on the well-defined
semantics of formal logic described in chapter 4.

3.8.3 DEDUCTIVE RETRIEVAL

Not only will fifth generation DBMSs be expected to be flexible and to
provide automatic semantic integrity checking; they will also be
expected to provide deductive retrieval facilities. That is, they will
be expected to be able to deduce 'implied' data from the data which is
held explicitly in the database. For example, consider the following
inference rule expressed in a language of predicate logic:

$$\forall x \forall y \forall z [(x. \text{ tallerthan. } y) \wedge (y. \text{ tallerthan. } z)] \rightarrow (x. \text{ tallerthan. } z)$$

This rule states that 'for all x, for all y and for all z, if x is
taller than y and y is taller than z, then x is taller than z'. Suppose
that we have the following facts in a database:

(John. tallerthan. Sally)
(Sally. tallerthan. Jean)

A deductive retrieval facility would be able to deduce that John is
taller than Jean even though this fact is not held explicitly in the
database.

Various attempts have been made to augment conventional DBMSs with deductive retrieval facilities. For example DEDUCE (Chang, 1976 and 1978)
is a deductive query language designed for use with relational DBMSs.
DEDUCE allows one to state inference rules, integrity constraints and
queries which are answered deductively.

Many of the deductive systems which have been built are based on formal
logic, described in detail in chapter 4. In chapter 5, we show how
methods of formal logic can be used to formalise both semantic integrity checking and deductive retrieval facilities in various types of
database system.

3.8.4 IMPROVED END-USER INTERFACES

Fifth generation DBMSs should have sufficiently friendly end-user interfaces that naive users can learn how to use them with only one or two hours of instruction. In addition, the database manipulation and query languages should be 'natural' to use in the sense that they should resemble sub-sets of natural language.

Some progress has been made in the development of 'natural language interfaces' to DBMSs. Such work includes the development of the following systems:

REL (Thompson and Thompson, 1975)
CONVERSE (Kellog et al, 1971)
LSNLIS (Woods, Kaplan and Nash-Webber, 1972)
RENDEZVOUS (Codd, 1974)
TORUS (Mylopoulos et al, 1976)
PHLIQUAI (Scha, 1977)
PLANES (Waltz, 1978)
ROBOT (Harris, 1977)
IQS (Cullinane, 1980)
INTELLECT (EDP, 1982)
EUFID (Templeton and Burger, 1983)

3.8.5 SPECIAL HARDWARE

As mentioned in section 3.7, most existing DBMSs are based on inappropriate hardware. However, special database hardware using content addressing schemes has been, and is being, developed. Such systems include:

CASSM (Su and Lipovski, 1975)
RAPS (Ozkarahan et al, 1975)
STARAN (Batcher, 1977)
CAFS (ICL, 1977)
DBC (Banerjee et al, 1979)
FACT (McGregor and Malone, 1984)
IFS (Lavington et al, 1984)

These systems are mentioned in chapter 12 where the use of special-purpose hardware in general purpose knowledge base systems as well as in fifth generation DBMSs is discussed.

3.9 CONCLUDING COMMENTS

This chapter has discussed databases, database systems, and database management systems (DBMSs). This was followed by a brief description of examples of commercially available DBMSs. The limitations of such systems were then identified and the properties and functions which are to be expected in fifth generation DBMSs were outlined. These properties and functions include: greater flexibility (data independence), automatic semantic integrity checking, deductive retrieval, more friendly end-user interfaces and architectures based on special-purpose hardware.

In the following chapters, methods which might be used to provide such properties and functions are discussed. However, we do not describe these methods solely in the context of database work. As mentioned earlier, database systems may be thought of as a particular type of knowledge base system in which the set of general rules (i.e. the schema) is relatively small and static. This particular characteristic means that some of the methods described in the following chapters will be more appropriate than others for use in database systems.

4 An Introduction to Formal Logic

In chapter 2, various notations for the representation of knowledge were described, and in chapter 3, we reviewed various techniques for the management of large collections of regularly formatted representations of simple facts. We now turn our attention to methods for automatic 'reasoning' with knowledge. In this and subsequent chapters, we show how computers can be programmed to 'think'. In particular, we describe methods by which computers (a) can recognise contradictions in a body of knowledge and (b) can deduce new knowledge which follows from knowledge which it has been given.

The following very informal discussion of what is meant by 'reasoning' serves two purposes: firstly, it provides a simple introduction to what is generally regarded as a difficult subject and, secondly, it demonstrates the need for rigorous definitions and precise specifications of methods. Such definitions and specifications are the subject matter of formal logic. Unfortunately, many texts on formal logic are principally concerned with formal definitions and exclude discussion of their application. We have tried to avoid this shortcoming but should warn the reader that this chapter contains many definitions which must be fully understood if later chapters are to be appreciated. Effort spent on this chapter will be well rewarded since it provides the necessary foundation for an understanding of many of the techniques used in advanced knowledge base systems work.

In trying to make definitions in this chapter as simple as possible, we may have been less rigorous than some readers might feel we should have been. More precise definitions can be found in *The Dictionary of Logic* (Marciszewski (ed.) 1981) and in the references given at appropriate places in the text.

4.1 A GENERAL OVERVIEW OF LOGIC

4.1.1 A VERY INFORMAL DISCUSSION ABOUT REASONING
The simplest type of reasoning which humans carry out involves the manipulation of propositions. We begin, therefore, by giving some examples of simple propositions which are called atomic formulas:

    P1: Frederick is a man
    P2: Sally is a woman

```
P3 : Frederick is married to Sally
P4 : Fido is a dog
P5 : Sally owns Fido
P6 : Scamp is a dog
```

More complex propositions can be constructed from combinations of
simple propositions by use of the words OR, NOT, IF...THEN and AND.
For example:

```
P7 : Pat is a man OR Pat is a woman
P8 : Jan is NOT a woman
P9 : IF Frederick is married to Sally THEN Sally is married to
     Frederick
P10: Frederick is a man AND Sally is a woman
```

Arbitrarily complex propositions can be constructed in this way.

So far, we have not stated which of the propositions above are true
and which are false. The assignment of truth values to propositions
can be stated explicitly as follows:

```
A = {Frederick is married to Sally := true,
     Scamp is a dog                 := false}
```

where the curly brackets denote a set, and the symbol := means 'has
the value'. That is, a truth assignment is a set of statements each
of which assigns a value of true or false to a proposition.

An alternative method of specifying a truth assignment, is to list an
equivalent set of propositions all of which are assumed to be true
(such statements are called 'assertions'). Any proposition P which
is assigned a value of false by the truth assignment is written as the
assertion 'not P'. For example, the following set of assertions is
equivalent to the truth assignment A above:

```
S1 = {Frederick is married to Sally,
           not Scamp is a dog}
```

Consistency checking
There are various ways in which we can reason about a truth assignment.
For example, we might want to see if it contains a contradition - that
is, if it contains a proposition that has been assigned both a value of
true and a value of false. If it does, it is said to be 'inconsistent';
otherwise it is said to be 'consistent'. For example, S1 above is consistent. However, consider the following set of assertions:

```
S2 = {Jan is NOT a woman,
      Jan is a woman AND Jan is tall}
```

Intuitively, we can see that S2 is inconsistent since it assigns both
a value of true and a value of false to the proposition 'Jan is a
woman'. Neither of these assignments is explicit in S2 but can be
made so by our understanding of the words NOT and AND. That is:

(a)   Jan is NOT a woman is equivalent to

      Jan is a woman := false

(b)   Jan is a woman AND Jan is tall is equivalent to

      {Jan is a woman := true,
       Jan is tall   := true}

Deduction

Given that we have a consistent truth assignment, we can undertake
another kind of reasoning called 'deduction' or 'inference'. For
example, consider the following consistent set of assertions:

      {Pat is a man OR Pat is a woman,
             Pat is NOT a woman}

Although this set does not contain the assertion 'Pat is a man' explicitly, this assertion can be inferred as follows:

(a)   Pat is a man OR Pat is a woman means that one of the following
      must hold:

      Pat is a man   := true
      Pat is a woman := true

(b)   Pat is NOT a woman means that the following does NOT hold:

      Pat is a woman := true

(c)   From (a) and (b) we can infer that the following assignment
      must hold:

      Pat is a man   := true

The need for formality

Consider the following set of assertions:

      S3 = {Pat is not a woman,
             IF Pat is married to Jan THEN Jan is married to Pat,
             IF Jan is married to Pat AND Pat is a parent of Bill
                 THEN Pat is not a man OR Jan is the mother of Bill,
             Pat has blue eyes AND Pat is a man   }

Is S3 consistent, Can we deduce from S3 that Jan is the mother of
Bill? It may take us several minutes to answer these questions and
our answers will depend on our interpretation of what is meant by NOT,
IF...THEN, AND and OR.

Now suppose that we want either to justify our answers or to write a
computer program to accept the set of assertions S3 and give us answers
automatically. We shall have to be much more precise (formal) in our
definitions of NOT, IF...THEN, AND and OR. We shall also have to be
much more precise in what we mean by 'reasoning'. In particular, we
shall have to define exactly how to check for consistency and how to
perform inference. This is where formal logics can help us. Within
any one of the many branches of logic there are systems each of which
consists of (a) a well defined language for the representation of knowledge, and (b) well defined methods for reasoning.

For example, systems of the branch of logic known as 'classical propositional logic' can accommodate reasoning of the kind discussed above. However, such systems are limited in the type of knowledge that can be expressed and in the type of reasoning that can be performed. Consequently, logicians have developed other types of logic such as predicate logic, sorted predicate logic, non-monotonic logic, modal logic, temporal logic, belief logic, fuzzy logic, intensional logic and many others.

Before these logics are discussed individually, we present an introduction to logic in general. Much of this introduction is strictly only applicable to classical propositional and first order predicate logic, both of which are described in detail in later sections of the chapter. However, this introduction also paves the way for the understanding of other logics, many of which are described in chapter 6. We begin by considering the languages of logic.

4.1.2 LANGUAGES OF LOGIC
Assertions about parts of the universe may be formulated in a precise and unambiguous way by use of formal languages. For example, consider the following formulas expressed in a language of propositional logic:

(a) (Pat is a boy) $\vee$ (Pat is a girl)
read as '(Pat is a boy) or (Pat is a girl)'

(b) (Pat is a boy) $\rightarrow \neg$ (Pat is a girl)
read as 'if (Pat is a boy) is true then (Pat is a girl) is false', or more correctly '(Pat is a boy) implies not (Pat is a girl)'

(c) (John is a boy) $\wedge$ (Jill is a girl)
read as '(John is a boy) and (Jill is a girl)'

Syntax
The syntax of a formal language determines how legal statements called 'well formed formulas' (wffs) of that language may be constructed by combining simple components called 'atomic formulas' using logical connectives such as:

$\wedge$ - and
$\vee$ - or
$\neg$ - not
$\rightarrow$ - implies

The syntax of a language consists of a set of rules which determine which formulas are well formed and which are not. (See chapter 2, section 2.2.3 for a discussion of syntax rules.)

Semantics
The semantics of a formal language determine how meaning may be ascribed to atomic formulas, and how this meaning can be extended to give meaning to wffs in which the atomic formulas occur. In many logics, formulas may only be assigned values of true or false. The semantic effect of the logical connectives is then often defined by use of truth tables. For example, the following truth table, in which T stands for

165

true and ⊥ for false, defines the effect of the logical connectives of propositional logic:

A	B	A ∧ B	A → B	A ∨ B	¬A
T	T	T	T	T	⊥
T	⊥	⊥	⊥	T	⊥
⊥	T	⊥	T	T	T
⊥	⊥	⊥	T	⊥	T

A and B stand for any formulas such as (Pat is a boy), [(Scamp is a dog) ∧ (Frederick is married to Sally)], etc.

The definitions of ∧, ∨ and ¬ are in agreement with the everyday usages of the words 'and', 'or' and 'not'. The definition of →, however, may not be in agreement with everyone's idea of what 'if...then' or 'implication' means. Notwithstanding, the definition of → given by this truth table is the definition which holds in propositional logic. In chapter 6, section 6.4, we describe formulations of implication which are used in other logics. Some of these formulations agree more closely with the commonly understood meaning of 'if...then'.

Truth assignments

A 'truth assignment' is a function which assigns a value of true or false to each member of a set of atomic formulas. A truth assignment is appropriate to a formula F if it assigns a truth value to every atomic formula in F. For example, consider the formula (Pat is a boy) → ¬(Pat is a girl). An appropriate truth assignment is:

$$\alpha = \{(\text{Pat is a boy}) \; := \text{true},$$
$$(\text{Pat is a girl}) := \text{false}\}$$

Any truth assignment, @, can be extended to a function, @', that assigns a truth value to every formula to which @ is appropriate. This extension follows from the semantic definition of the logical connectives. For example, the truth assignment α above can be extended to a function α' which includes the following assignments as well as the ones above:

(a) (Pat is a boy) ∧ ¬(Pat is a girl) := true,
(b) (Pat is a boy) → ¬(Pat is a girl) := true,
(c) ¬(Pat is a boy)   := false, etc.

Satisfiability

Let @ be some truth assignment and let @' be the function obtained by extending @. For any formula F for which @ is appropriate, if @'(F) is true, then we say variously, that @ 'satisfies' or 'verifies' F or that F is 'valid' in @. For example, α above satisfies the formula (b) above.

A formula or set of formulas is 'satisfiable' if there is at least one truth assignment which satisfies it. The examples (a), (b) and (c) given above are all satisfiable formulas. The following is an example of an unsatisfiable formula:

(Pat is a boy) ∧ ¬(Pat is a boy)

166

This formula, which may be read as '(Pat is a boy) and not (Pat is a boy)', is unsatisfiable since neither of the following truth assignments are satisfying truth assignments and they are the only appropriate truth assignments that exist:

    @1 = {(Pat is a boy) := true}
    @2 = {(Pat is a boy) := false}

Universal validity

A formula or set of formulas is 'universally valid' if every truth assignment which is appropriate to it satisfies it. The following is an example of such a formula:

    (Pat is a boy) ∨ ¬(Pat is a boy)

This formula is universally valid since both @1 and @2 satisfy it and these are the only appropriate truth assignments. Universally valid formulas of propositional logic are called 'tautologies'.

Equivalence

Two formulas are 'equivalent' if they are assigned the same truth value by every (extended) truth assignment which is appropriate to both. Equivalence is denoted by the logical connective ↔. The following is an example of an equivalence:

    [A → B] ↔ [¬A ∨ B]

where A and B stand for any wff.

Logical consequence

A formula F is said to be a logical consequence of a formula, or set of formulas, S, if F is satisfied by all truth assignments which satisfy S. Logical consequence is denoted by:

    S ⊨ F

The following is an example of logical consequence:

    {A ∨ B, ¬A} ⊨ B

Another way of expressing this is to say that B follows from (A or B) and not A. We can demonstrate that this logical consequence is correct by drawing a truth table in which each row corresponds to an appropriate truth assignment:

A	B	A ∨ B	¬A	B	
T	T	T	⊥	T	
T	⊥	T	⊥	⊥	
⊥	T	T	T	T	✓
⊥	⊥	⊥	T	⊥	

The ✓ symbol identifies those truth assignments which satisfy both A ∨ B and ¬A. Since there is only one such truth assignment and B is also satisfied by this truth assignment, we know that B is a logical consequence of the set {A ∨ B, ¬A}.

Satisfiability, universal validity, equivalence and logical consequence are all semantic properties of formulas and the use of truth tables (or equivalent methods) to determine these properties is called 'semantic reasoning'.

4.1.3 FORMAL DEDUCTION SYSTEMS

Given a set of wffs, S, it is possible to derive or deduce logical consequences of S by methods other than those described above. In particular, it is possible to deduce logical consequences of S by syntactic operations alone. That is, by structurally manipulating S, without reference to truth values, it is possible to derive new formulas which are guaranteed to be logical consequences of S. The systems by which this is done are called 'formal deduction systems'. There are various types of formal deduction system and the type which will be described here are called 'axiom systems'.

An axiom system consists of a formal language such as those described already, a set of inference rules, and a set of logical axiom schemas (or 'logical axioms' for short).

Inference rules

The 'inference rules' define the syntactic operations by which new formulas can be generated from given formulas - that is, they allow deductions to be made. Examples of inference rules are the following, in which P and Q stand for any wff:

R1:   From P → Q and P, infer Q. This rule is called 'modus ponens'.

R2:   If F is a universally valid formula, then so is F' where F' is obtained from F by the consistent substitution of any sub-formula in F by any other sub-formula. For example, if B ∨ ¬B is a universally valid formula, then so is A ∨ ¬A. This rule is called the substitution rule or 'substitution' for short.

Logical axioms

The 'logical axioms' comprise a set of templates for some of the universally valid wffs of the formal language. The set of logical axioms of an axiom system is generally *chosen such that all universally valid formulas of the language can be generated from it* using the inference rules of the axiom system.

Formal proofs

The derivation of a formula F from a set of formulas S using an axiom system A, is called a formal deduction or 'formal proof' of F from S in A. A formal proof of F from S in A is a finite sequence F1, F2, ..., Fn, of formulas such that F = Fn and for each i, $(1 \leqslant i \leqslant n)$:

either   (a)   Fi is a logical axiom of A

or   (b)   Fi ∈ S

or   (c)   Fi is generated from previous formulas of the sequence according to one or more of the inference rules of A

where ∈ stands for 'member of the set'.

The existence of a formal proof of F from S in A, is denoted by:

$$S \vdash_A F$$

Example

As example of a trivial formal proof, consider the following:

(a)   axiom system =
$$\begin{cases} \text{logical axioms : } \{P \lor \neg P, \\ \quad\quad \neg\neg P \to P, \\ \quad\quad [P \land Q] \to P, \\ \quad\quad [P \land Q] \to Q\} \\ \text{inference rules: R1 and R2 from above} \end{cases}$$

(b)   S = {(Pat is a student) ∧ (Pat is a girl),
        (Pat is a girl) → (Pat is human)}

(c)   The formula to be proved is (Pat is human).

The proof proceeds in three stages:

(i) Using the 4th logical axiom and the inference rule R2 we can infer the following formula:

[(Pat is a student) ∧ (Pat is a girl)] → (Pat is a girl)

(ii) From the formula derived in (i), the first formula in S, and the inference rule R1, we can infer the following formula:

(Pat is a girl)

(iii) From the formula derived in (ii), the second formula in S, and the inference rule R1, we can infer the following formula:

(Pat is human).

Hence the proof is complete.

The purpose of the logical axioms may now be apparent. They serve as fodder for the derivation mechanism. Their universal validity means that they can be used in any proof whatsoever in the logic defined by the axiomatisation. Note that the set of logical axioms in this example is not complete, in that not all universally valid formulas can be generated from it.

Commonly used inference rules

Modus ponens and substitution are only two of several rules of inference which are used in everyday reasoning. Other rules include the following, where P and Q stand for any wff:

R3:   conjunction

from P and Q, infer P ∧ Q.

R4:   simplification

  from P ∧ Q, infer P.

R5:   addition

  from P infer, P ∨ Q.

R6:   transposition

  from P → Q, infer ¬Q → ¬P.

R7:   hypothetical syllogism

  from P → Q and Q → R, infer P → R.

R8:   disjunctive syllogism

  from P ∨ Q and ¬P, infer Q.

Axiom systems vary in the choice of inference rules and logical axioms. Some inference rules are closely related to particular logical axioms. For example, the rule R4 and the logical axiom [P ∧ Q] → P are 'equivalent' in the sense that the logical axiom can be used to infer P from P ∧ Q when used in conjunction with the rule modus ponens.

Axiom systems are not the only type of formal deduction system. Other systems have been built which contain only inference rules and no logical axioms. These are described in more detail in section 4.2.

4.1.4 SOUNDNESS AND COMPLETENESS

Soundness
A formal deduction system A is said to be 'sound' if all of the formulas which can be derived from any set of formulas S using A, are also logical consequences of S. Soundness is denoted by:

$$S \vdash_A F \quad \text{implies} \quad S \vDash F$$

That is, in a sound system, if a formula F can be derived from a set of formulas S, then we can be quite certain that F is a logical consequence of S. Soundness is an essential property of any useful formal deduction system.

Completeness
If, for some formal deduction system A, every logical consequence of any set of formulas S can be derived from S using A, then A is said to be 'complete'. Completeness is denoted by:

$$S \vDash F \quad \text{implies} \quad S \vdash_A F$$

Completeness is a desirable though not essential property of a useful formal deduction system.

It can be seen that the inference rules of a sound system must be closely related to the semantic definitions of the logical connectives of the

language of that system. However, it should be noted that although
inference rules are themselves obtained (or justified) using some argument involving semantics, their use in formal proofs involves purely
syntactic operations.

4.1.5 THEORIES AND THEOREM-PROVING

Theories

A theory consists of a formal system together with a set of wffs which
are known to be true in some set of intended interpretations. These
wffs are called the 'proper axioms' of the theory. The following is
an example of a set of proper axioms:

S = {P1: (Ali is a man) ∨ (Ali is a woman)
　　　P2: ¬[(Ali is a man) ∧ (Ali is a woman)]
　　　P3: (Pat is a man) ∨ (Pat is a woman)
　　　P4: ¬[(Pat is a man) ∧ (Pat is a woman)]
　　　P5: [(Ali is married to Pat) ∧ (Ali is a man)] →
　　　　　　　　　　　　　　　　　　　　　　(Pat is a woman)
　　　P6: [(Ali is married to Pat) ∧ (Ali is a woman)] →
　　　　　　　　　　　　　　　　　　　　　　(Pat is a man)}

The intended interpretations of a theory are those truth assignments
which satisfy all proper axioms of the theory according to the rules
of the formal system. For example, the following are some of the intended interpretations of the theory T' which consists of a sound and
complete axiomatisation of propositional logic together with the set S
of proper axioms given above.

@1 = {(Ali is a man)　　:= true,
　　　(Ali is a woman) := false,
　　　(Pat is a man)　　:= true,
　　　(Pat is a woman) := false,
　　　(Ali is married to Pat := false}

@2 = {(Ali is a man)　　:= false,
　　　(Ali is a woman) := true,
　　　(Pat is a man)　　:= false,
　　　(Pat is a woman) := true,
　　　(Ali is married to Pat) := false}

@3 = {(Ali is a man)　　:= true,
　　　(Ali is a woman) := false,
　　　(Pat is a man)　　:= false,
　　　(Pat is a woman) := true,
　　　(Ali is married to Pat) := true}　　　(etc.)

The theory T holds for situations in which 'Ali is a man or a woman
but not both', 'Pat is a man or a woman but not both', and in which
'if Ali is married to Pat and Ali is a man then Pat must be a woman',
and 'if Ali is married to Pat and Ali is a woman then Pat must be a
man'.

The theory above is a 'social' theory. There are other types of theory.
For example, a scientific theory is a theory whose proper axioms are
verified through being used to predict the outcome of experiments.

Powerful theories are able to correctly predict the outcome of experiments well before the experiments are technically feasible. For example, Einstein's theory of relativity states, among other things, that inertial mass and gravitational mass are equivalent. This theory was used to correctly predict the results of an experiment involving the earth and the moon many years before the invention of lasers and man's landing on the moon made the experiment feasible.

Database theories, which are called 'schemas' in database technology, are theories whose proper axioms represent the laws which govern the structure and properties of organisations such as hospitals, manufacturing plants, banks, etc.

Theorem-proving

A 'theorem' of a theory is a formula which has a formal proof in that theory. The fact that F is a theorem of a theory T is denoted by:

T ⊢ F

For example, suppose that we have a theory T'' which consists of the proper axioms S above together with the following axiom system:

    logical axioms = {L1: [P → Q] → [¬P ∨ Q],
                        L2: ¬[P ∧ Q] → [Q → ¬P],
                        L3: [P ∧ Q] → [Q ∧ P],
                        L4: [P ∨ Q] ∨ R → [P ∨ Q ∨ R],
                        L5: ¬[P ∧ Q] → [¬P ∨ ¬Q]}

    inference rules = R1, modus ponens
                       R2, substitution
                       R7, hypothetical syllogism

The following is a theorem of the theory T'':

[¬(Ali is married to Pat) ∨ ¬(Ali is a man) ∨ ¬(Pat is a man)]

The proof proceeds as follows:

(a) From P4, L2, R1, R2 infer the following:

F1: [(Pat is a woman) → ¬(Pat is a man)]

(b) From P5, F1, R1, R7 infer the following:

F2: [[(Ali is married to Pat) ∧ (Ali is a man)] →
                                        ¬(Pat is a man)]

(c) From F2, L1, R1, R2 infer the following:

F3: [¬[(Ali is married to Pat) ∧ (Ali is a man)] ∨
                                        ¬(Pat is a man)]

(d) From F3, L5, R1, R2 infer the following:

F4: [[¬(Ali is married to Pat) ∨ ¬(Ali is a man)] ∨
                                        ¬(Pat is a man)]

(e) From F4, L4, R1, R2 infer the following:

F5: [¬(Ali is married to Pat) ∨ ¬(Ali is a man) ∨
                                        ¬(Pat is a man)]

Theorems of formal deduction systems

The formulas which can be derived within a formal deduction system alone with no proper axioms are theorems of that deduction system itself. The theorems of a complete and sound deduction system are all of the universally valid formulas of the language of that deduction system.

Consistency

A theory T is 'inconsistent' if and only if (iff):

$$T \vdash F \quad \text{and} \quad T \vdash \neg F \quad \text{for some formula F}$$

T is 'consistent' iff it is not inconsistent.

4.1.6 PURELY SYNTACTIC THEOREM-PROVING

Given some theory T, we can prove whether or not a formula F is a theorem of T by repeatedly using the inference rules of the formal deduction system and thereby deriving new valid formulas. Examples of this approach have been given. This approach is regarded as using purely syntactic reasoning since it involves only the structural man-ipulation of formulas. The consistency of a theory T may also be determined in this way in some cases by generating *all* theorems of T and checking to see if any formula F and its negation ¬F are derived, in which case T is inconsistent.

4.1.7 PURELY SEMANTIC THEOREM-PROVING

One can sometimes determine whether or not a formula F is a theorem of a theory T in a sound and complete deduction system by constructing a truth table to see if F is valid in all satisfying truth assignments of T. For example, consider a trivial theory T''' which has the follow-ing proper axioms:

¬P   where P might stand for (Pat is a woman)
P ∨ Q   where Q might stand for (Pat is a man)

We can prove that Q is a theorem of T''', in a sound and complete axio-matisation of propositional logic, by constructing the following truth table:

| | | PROPER AXIOMS | | THEOREM TO BE PROVED | |
P	Q	¬P	P ∨ Q	Q	
T	T	⊥	T	T	
T	⊥	⊥	T	⊥	
⊥	T	T	T	T	✓
⊥	⊥	T	⊥	⊥	

Q is a theorem because it is true in all cases in which ¬P and P ∨ Q are true. In theories of sound and complete deduction systems, the syntactic and semantic approaches to reasoning are equivalent. Note, however, that this method is not always feasible, as will be seen when we consider first order predicate logic.

Semantic reasoning can also be used, in some cases, to determine whether a theory T is consistent or not. A truth table is constructed for all truth assignments which are appropriate to T. If no truth assignment satisfies T then T is inconsistent; otherwise it is consistent. For example, consider a trivial theory T'''' of propositional logic which has the following proper axioms:

    ¬P
    P ∧ Q

We can show that T'''' is inconsistent by constructing the following truth table:

P	Q	PROPER AXIOMS		CHECK FOR A MODEL
		¬P	P ∧ Q	
T	T	⊥	T	x
T	⊥	⊥	⊥	x
⊥	T	T	⊥	x
⊥	⊥	T	⊥	x

Since there is no truth assignment (i.e. no line) in which ¬P and P ∧ Q are both true, the theory is inconsistent.

4.1.8 REFUTATION PROCEDURES

Instead of applying purely syntactic or purely semantic reasoning, one can apply syntactic procedures followed by semantic checks in order to determine whether a formula F is a theorem of a theory T. One such approach involves the following steps:

(a) Add the negation of F to the set of proper axioms S of the theory T to obtain a new set of formulas S' = S U ¬F, where U is the set union operator.

(b) Repeatedly apply inference rules to S' to derive new formulas which are then added to S'.

(c) Test S' for satisfiability.

(d) If S' and therefore S U ¬F is unsatisfiable, then F must be a theorem of T.

Such procedures in which the formula being tested is negated are called 'refutation' procedures.

As example, consider the following formulas expressed in the language of propositional logic:

    S = {P ∨ Q,
         P → ¬Q,
         Q   }

To prove that ¬P is a theorem of S, we proceed as follows:

(a)   Add the negation of ¬P to S giving:

        S' = {P ∨ Q,
               P → ¬Q,
               Q,
               P   }

(b)   Apply the inference rule, modus ponens, to formalise in S':

        From P → ¬Q and P infer ¬Q

(c)   Add ¬Q to S' giving S" = {P ∨ Q,
                                P → Q,
                                Q,
                                P,
                                ¬Q}

(d)   S" is unsatisfiable since it contains Q and ¬Q, therefore ¬P
      must be a theorem of any theory of propositional logic whose
      proper axioms include S.

4.1.9   DECIDABILITY

So far, examples have been given of theorem-proving and consistency
checking which are 'decidable'. That is, we have assumed that it is
at least theoretically possible to determine whether or not a formula
is a theorem of some theory or that a theory is consistent. Although
this may be possible in some cases, it is not possible in all. Purely
syntactic methods are only guaranteed to terminate in a finite amount
of time if there are only a finite number of deductions that are possible, or in the event that the formula searched for is indeed a theorem.
Purely semantic approaches are only guaranteed to terminate in a finite
amount of time if there are only a finite number of truth assignments,
or in the event that the given formula is not a logical consequence of
the theory.

Two particular logics will now be considered in detail: propositional
logic and first order predicate logic. Propositional logic is too
limited in its expressive power to be of much use in knowledge base
systems. However, its simplicity makes it useful as an introduction
to the more complicated first order predicate logic.

4.2   CLASSICAL PROPOSITIONAL LOGIC

Well-formed formulas (wffs) of classical propositional logic are constructed from atomic formulas and the logical connectives ∧, ∨, ¬, →
and ↔. For example, the following are wffs of classical propositional
logic:

(a)   it is hot ∨ it is cold
      read as 'it is hot or it is cold'

(b)   it is hot → ¬it is cold
      read as 'if it is hot this implies that it is not cold'

(c)   [it is hot ∧ ¬it is raining] → it is a fine day
      read as 'if it is hot and it is not raining this implies that
      it is a fine day'

Notice that atomic formulas of classical propositional logic, e.g. 'it is hot', 'it is cold', 'it is raining' and 'it is a fine day' are propositions which are semantically indivisible as far as the logic is concerned. Atomic formulas can be consistently replaced by letters such as P, Q, R and S without loss of meaning as far as the logic is concerned. For example, the wffs above could be expressed as follows:

    P ∨ Q
    P → ¬Q
    [P ∧ ¬R] → S

where:

    P stands for 'it is hot'
    Q stands for 'it is cold'
    R stands for 'it is raining'
    S stands for 'it is a fine day'

The system of classical propositional logic has been well known since the publication in 1910 by B. Russell and A.N. Whitehead of the first volume of their *Principia Mathematica*. Since then, various axiom systems (or axiomatisations) have been defined for classical propositional logic. They differ as follows:

(a) In the symbols used to represent atomic formulas. This is a trivial difference.

(b) In the choice of logical connectives used as primitive. All other connectives are then defined in terms of the primitives.

(c) In the rules of inference used.

(d) In the choice of logical axiom schemas. Any choice of axiom schemas is adequate if it can be used in conjunction with the inference rules to derive all tautologies of propositional logic. In such cases the axiomatisation is said to be complete.

4.2.1 AN AXIOM SYSTEM FOR PROPOSITIONAL LOGIC

As example of an axiom system for classical propositional logic, consider the following system which uses ¬ and → as primitive connectives. This system is similar to that defined by Lukasiewicz (1929). The system may be defined in four parts: syntax of the language, semantics of the language, the logical axiom schemas and the inference rules:

Syntax of the language
We shall refer to the language of this axiom system by the name LO. The syntax of LO is defined by the following context-free grammar:

    terminals = {P, Q, R, S, T, ¬, →, [,]}
    nonterminals = {wff, atomicformula}
    production rules:
        wff ::= atomicformula
            | wff → wff
            | [wff]
            | ¬ wff
        atomicformula ::= P|Q|R|S|T

(See chapter 2, section 2.3, for an explanation of this notation.)

Examples of well-formed formulas of LO are:

    P
    Q
    P → Q
    [P → Q]
    ¬P
    [P → Q] → [¬P → Q]

Instead of the letters P, Q, R, S, T, character strings are sometimes used to stand for atomic formulas. For example:

    it is raining → ¬it is dry

Such character strings are used when it is appropriate to give meaningful examples.

If α and β are wffs of LO, then the following abbreviations are also defined for the language:

    DF1:   α ∧ β for ¬[α → ¬β]
    DF2:   α ∨ β for ¬α → β
    DF3:   α ↔ β for [α → β] ∧ [β → α]

The semantics of LO
The semantics of LO, and of all languages of propositional logic, define formulas to have values of 'true' or 'false', and the logical connectives to have the effect indicated by the following truth table. Note that we have redundantly specified the effect of the abbreviations DF1, DF2 and DF3 above.

P	Q	¬P	P → Q	P ∧ Q	P ∨ Q	P ↔ Q
T	T	⊥	T	T	T	T
T	⊥	⊥	⊥	⊥	T	⊥
⊥	T	T	T	⊥	T	⊥
⊥	⊥	T	T	⊥	⊥	T

The formulas P ∧ Q and P ∨ Q are called, respectively, the 'conjunction' and 'disjunction' of P and Q.

All of the connectives of classical proposition logic, i.e. ∧, ∨, ¬, → and ↔, are strictly 'truth-functional'. That is, given the truth values of the components of a well-formed formula containing a connective, the truth value of the formula is always uniquely determined. For example, it is of the very essence of the meaning of '∧', that a conjunction of the form P ∧ Q will be true just exactly when both components P and Q are true, and false otherwise.

Given the truth table definitions of the logical connectives, the wffs of propositional logic can be thought of in input-output terms. When certain truth values are fed into a formula, the formula guides us in using the truth tables to calculate an output truth value. This truth value is the value of the formula. For example, consider the formula:

P → [Q ∧ [[P ∨ Q] → [R ↔ P]]]

If we have a truth assignment @ = {P := T, Q := ⊥, R := T} then the formula above can be replaced by:

T → [⊥ ∧ [[T ∨ ⊥] → [T ↔ T]]]

Since the truth tables for ∨ and ↔ inform us that T ∨ ⊥ = T and T ↔ T = T, this amounts to:

T → [⊥ ∧ [T → T]]

and since T → T = T, this amounts to:

T → [⊥ ∧ T]

but since ⊥ ∧ T = ⊥, this amounts to:

T → ⊥

which, by the truth table for →, amounts to ⊥. This demonstrates how the truth values of formulas can be computed from the truth values of their components.

The logical axiom schemas and inference rules
Lukasiewicz's axiomatisation of classical propositional logic contains three axiom schemas:

AS1: [¬P → P] → P
AS2: P → [¬P → Q]
AS3: [P → Q] → [[Q → R] → [P → R]]

together with two rules of inference:

(a) Modus ponens: from P and P → Q infer Q

(b) Substitution: once F has been established as a theorem, one may assert as a theorem any other formula G obtained from F by uniformly replacing all the occurrences in F of some propositional variable by any formula whatsoever - for example, from [¬P → P] → P one can assert [¬A → A] → A as a theorem using the substitution rule.

Lukasiewicz's axiomatisation of classical propositional logic, as described above, is a particularly concise although somewhat obscure 'complete axiomatisation'. The objective of a complete axiomatisation is to provide an economical list of logical axioms from which *all* tautologies can be derived as theorems by the rules of inference of the axiom system (in this case, modus ponens and substitution).

An example of the use of the axiom system above
Consider a theory T which consists of the axiom system above plus the following proper axioms:

PA1: it is raining ∨ it is snowing ∨ it is dry
PA2: it is warm
PA3: ¬it is raining
PA4: ¬it is snowing
PA5: it is fine → it is a good day for a walk
PA6: [it is dry ∧ it is warm] → it is fine

This theory states: (PA1) that it is either raining, snowing, or dry, (PA2) that it is warm, (PA3) that it is not raining, (PA4) that it is not snowing, (PA5) that if it is fine then it is a good day for a walk and (PA6) that if it is dry and it is warm then it is fine. Notice that we have used strings such as 'it is warm' to stand for atomic formulas in this example.

Using the abbreviation definitions DF1, DF2 and DF3, the logical axiom schemas AS1, AS2 and AS3, the inference rules modus ponens and substitution and the proper axioms PA1 to PA6, we can now prove theorems in T. For example, to prove that the atomic proposition 'it is dry' is a logical consequence (i.e. a theorem) of T, we proceed as follows:

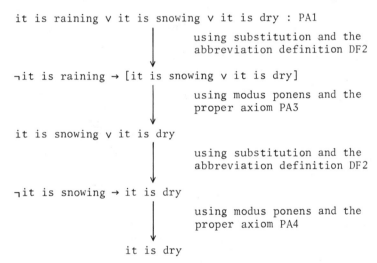

it is raining ∨ it is snowing ∨ it is dry : PA1

using substitution and the
abbreviation definition DF2

¬it is raining → [it is snowing ∨ it is dry]

using modus ponens and the
proper axiom PA3

it is snowing ∨ it is dry

using substitution and the
abbreviation definition DF2

¬it is snowing → it is dry

using modus ponens and the
proper axiom PA4

it is dry

Using a similar approach, it is also possible to prove that 'it is a good day for a walk' in the theory T above. Note that the above is an example of syntactic theorem-proving.

Another axiomatisation of classical propositional logic
Another complete axiom system for classical propositional logic is that defined by Hilbert and Ackerman (1928) which is based on ¬ and ∨ as primitive. This axiom system includes the abbreviations:

P → Q   for   ¬P ∨ Q
P ∧ Q   for   ¬[¬P ∨ ¬Q]
P ↔ Q   for   [P → Q] ∧ [Q → P]

and has the following set of logical axioms:

[P ∨ P] → P
      P → [P ∨ Q]
[P ∨ Q] → [Q ∨ P]
[P → Q] → [[R ∨ P] → [P ∨ Q]]

Hilbert and Ackermann's axiomatisation is less obscure than the one
defined by Lukasiewicz, but it is also less concise.

Equivalence rules
Various frequently used equivalence rules have been defined for classical propositional logic. These rules can be derived from the logical
axioms of any complete axiomatisation and therefore can be used in
proofs in any complete system. As example of such rules, consider the
following:

Idempotency   : P ∨ P ≡ P
                   P ∧ P ≡ P

Commutativity : P ∨ Q ≡ Q ∨ P
                   P ∧ Q ≡ Q ∧ P
                   P ↔ Q ≡ Q ↔ P

Associativity : [P ∨ Q] ∨ R ≡ P ∨ [Q ∨ R]
                   [P ∧ Q] ∧ R ≡ P ∧ [Q ∧ R]

Absorption   : P ∨ [P ∧ Q] ≡ P
                   P ∧ [P ∨ Q] ≡ P

Distributivity : P ∧ [Q ∨ R] ≡ [P ∧ Q] ∨ [P ∧ R]
                   P ∨ [Q ∧ R] ≡ [P ∨ Q] ∧ [P ∨ R]

Double negation : ¬¬P ≡ P

De Morgan   : ¬[P ∨ Q] ≡ ¬P ∧ ¬Q
                   ¬[P ∧ Q] ≡ ¬P ∨ ¬Q

Tautology   : P ∨ Q ≡ P if P is a tautology
                   P ∧ Q ≡ Q if P is a tautology

Unsatisfiability: P ∨ Q ≡ Q if P is unsatisfiable
                   P ∧ Q ≡ P if P is unsatisfiable

Conditional
elimination   : P → Q ≡ ¬P ∨ Q

Bi-conditional
elimination   : P ↔ Q ≡ [P → Q] ∧ [Q → P]

4.2.2 NATURAL DEDUCTION PROOF METHODS

So far, axiom systems for classical propositional logic have been described and we have shown how to construct purely syntactic proofs in
such systems. We now describe another method of purely syntactic
theorem-proving which is called 'natural deduction'.

The first systems of natural deduction were devised in 1934 independently by Gentzen and Kaskowski. Their investigations were motivated

by Lukasiewicz who noted that mathematicians, in practising their art, do not in general appeal to logical axioms but make use of sub-proofs involving to logical axioms but make use of sub-proofs involving 'suppositions', which are not theorems but are operating as temporary axioms assumed locally within the sub-proof.

All deduction systems can be thought of as containing a set of logical axioms and a set of inference rules. In natural deduction systems, the set of logical axioms is empty and the inference rules are divided into 'introduction' and 'exploitation' rules, as illustrated below. The idea of dividing rules in this way was developed by Fitch (1952) and independently by others who extended the methods devised by Gentzen.

Below is an example of a natural deduction system for classical propositional logic. The system contains the following rules:

Introduction rules

(a) from A and B infer A ∧ B
(b) from A infer A ∨ B
(c) from A infer B ∨ A
(d) from A ⊢ Ø infer ¬A
(e) from A ⊢ B infer A → B

Exploitation rules

(f) from A ∧ B infer A
(g) from A ∧ B infer B
(h) from A ∨ B, A ⊢ C, B ⊢ C infer C
(i) from A and ¬A infer Ø
(j) from ¬¬A infer A
(k) from A, A → B infer B

Ø stands for a logically false formula, (a) is called the ∧-introduction rule, and (b) the ∨-introduction rule, (f) the ∧-exploitation rule and so on. Rules (d) and (i) could both be replaced by the following rule without loss of power:

from A ⊢ B, ¬B infer ¬A

As example of a natural deduction proof, consider a theory which consists of the formal natural deduction system described above together with the following proper axiom:

PA: P ∨ [Q ∧ R]

Now suppose that we want to prove that the following formula is a theorem of this theory:

[P ∨ Q] ∧ [P ∨ R]

To construct the proof we might begin by 'supposing' P and then using appropriate rules to derive P ⊢ [P ∨ Q] ∧ [P ∨ R] as follows:

```
1.1   P                          supposition
1.2   P ∨ Q                      by ∨-introduction and 1.1
1.3   P ∨ R                      by ∨-introduction and 1.1
1.4   [P ∨ Q] ∧ [P ∨ R]         by ∧-introduction and 1.2 and 1.3

1.    P ⊢ [P ∨ Q] ∧ [P ∨ R]     from lines 1.1 to 1.4
```

We might then suppose Q ∧ R and use rules to derive
Q ∧ R ⊢ [P ∨ Q] ∧ [P ∨ R]:

```
2.1   Q ∧ R                      supposition
2.2   Q                          by ∧-exploitation and 2.1
2.3   P ∨ Q                      by ∨-introduction and 2.2
2.4   R                          by ∧-exploitation and 2.1
2.5   P ∨ R                      by ∨-introduction and 2.4
2.6   [P ∨ Q] ∧ [P ∨ R]         by ∧-introduction and 2.3 and 2.5

2.    Q ∧ R ⊢ [P ∨ Q] ∧ [P ∨ R] from 2.1 to 2.6
```

We could follow this by introducing the proper axiom PA:

```
3.    P ∨ [Q ∧ R]                given
```

We can now prove [P ∨ Q] ∧ [P ∨ R]:

```
[P ∨ Q] ∧ [P ∨ R]               from ∨-elimination (rule (h)) and
                                 1, 2 and 3 above.
```

It is clear from this example that natural deduction proofs rely in
large measure on the cleverness of the person constructing them.

Natural deduction proofs are so-called because the proofs parallel the
way in which humans construct them. In the example above, the proof
may be regarded as a tree (this is reflected in the numbering of the
proof steps):

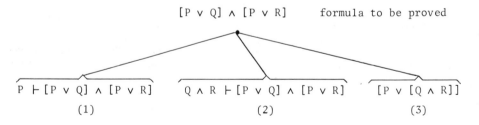

That is, to prove [P ∨ Q] ∧ [P ∨ R] from P ∨ [Q ∧ R] we first recognise
from the structure of P ∨ [Q ∧ R] that the ∨-elimination rule can be
used, and then go about constructing the sub-proofs of P ⊢ [P ∨ Q] ∧
[P ∨ R] and Q ∧ R ⊢ [P ∨ Q] ∧ [P ∨ R]. Each of these sub-proofs may
be regarded as a further branch on the tree.

Another feature of a natural deduction system is that it does not
require the proper axioms to be converted to some other form before the
proof can be performed (such transformation is required in some of the

proof techniques that we shall describe later). This means that the 'prover' can make use of the 'proof guidance information' which is embedded in the structure in which the proper axioms have been written down. For example, consider a theory which includes the following proper axioms, among others:

PA1: ¬P → [Q ∨ R ∨ S ∨ T]
PA2:   M → P

These could have been written as the equivalent formulas:

PA1': ¬[Q ∧ R ∧ S ∧ T] → P
PA2':   ¬P → ¬M

However, they were not written in this way, and it may be that in writing PA1 and PA2 the writer was indicating that in order to prove P one should first of all prove M. If the formulas are required to be converted to some standard equivalent form such as that shown below, the proof guidance information is lost.

P ∨ Q ∨ R ∨ S ∨ T
P ∨ ¬M

4.2.3 SEQUENT LOGIC/SEQUENT PROOFS

Sequent logic is a formulation of first order logic which was devised by Gentzen (1934) at the same time that he devised natural deduction. Sequent proofs involve inferring new sequents from proven sequents, where a 'sequent' is an expression of the form:

A1,...,Am → C1,...,Cn

where Ai (i ≤ m) are arbitrary formulas called 'antecedents' and Ci (i ≤ n) are arbitrary formulas called 'consequents' (or 'succedents').

Such a sequent may be interpreted as being equivalent to the following formula of classical logic:

A1 ∧ ,..., ∧ Am → C1 ∨ ,..., ∨ Cn

However, → is not exactly the same as →, nor is it the same as ⊢ , since it is also defined for cases in which m = 0 or n = 0. Tautologies are written as, for example, → P, ¬P and logically false formulas are written as, for example, P, ¬P →.

The inference rules of sequent propositional logic are divided into 'antecedent introduction rules', 'consequent introduction rules' and 'modification rules'. In the following, capital letters stand for sequences of formulas, e.g. T might represent A1,A2,...,Ak, and small letters stand for single formulas. In each case the sequent below the line is what can be inferred from the sequent(s) above the line.

Antecedent introduction rules

$$(A\rightarrow) \quad \frac{T \rightarrow U, a \qquad\qquad b, W \rightarrow X}{a \rightarrow b, T, W \rightarrow U, X}$$

(A∧) $\dfrac{a, \ T \ \rightarrow \ U}{a \ \wedge \ b, \ T \ \rightarrow \ U}$ $\dfrac{b, \ T \ \rightarrow \ U}{a \ \wedge \ b, \ T \ \rightarrow \ U}$

(A∨) $\dfrac{a, \ T \ \rightarrow \ U \qquad b, \ T \ \rightarrow \ U}{a \ \vee \ b, \ T \ \rightarrow \ U}$

(A¬) $\dfrac{T \ \rightarrow \ U, \ a}{\neg a, \ T \ \rightarrow \ U}$

The symbols in brackets on the left of each rule are shorthand for the name of the rule. For example (A→) may be read as 'the antecedent → introduction rule'. This particular rule indicates that the single sequent below the line can be inferred from the pair of sequents above the line. Notice that the notation used in the above examples differs from the language used in this section so far.

Consequent introduction rules

(C→) $\dfrac{a, \ T \ \rightarrow \ U, \ b}{T \ \rightarrow \ U, \ a \ \rightarrow \ b}$

(C∧) $\dfrac{T \ \rightarrow \ U, \ a \qquad T \ \rightarrow \ U, \ b}{T \ \rightarrow \ U, \ a \ \wedge \ b}$

(C∨) $\dfrac{T \ \rightarrow \ U, \ a}{T \ \rightarrow \ U, \ a \ \vee \ b}$ $\dfrac{T \ \rightarrow \ U, \ b}{T \ \rightarrow \ U, \ a \ \vee \ b}$

(C¬) $\dfrac{a, \ T \ \rightarrow \ U}{T \ \rightarrow \ U, \ \neg a}$

Modification rules

	In antecedent	In consequent
Thinning or weakening	$\dfrac{T \ \rightarrow \ U}{a, \ T \ \rightarrow \ U}$	$\dfrac{T \ \rightarrow \ U}{T \ \rightarrow \ U, \ a}$
Contraction	$\dfrac{a, \ a, \ T \ \rightarrow \ U}{a, \ T \ \rightarrow \ U}$	$\dfrac{T \ \rightarrow \ U, \ a, \ a}{T \ \rightarrow \ U, \ a}$
Interchange	$\dfrac{T, \ a, \ b, \ U \ \rightarrow \ W}{T, \ b, \ a, \ U \ \rightarrow \ W}$	$\dfrac{T \ \rightarrow \ U, \ a, \ b, \ W}{T \ \rightarrow \ U, \ b, \ a, \ W}$
Cut	$\dfrac{T \ \rightarrow \ U, \ a \qquad a, \ W \ \rightarrow \ X}{T, \ W \ \rightarrow \ U, \ X}$	

Sequent proofs are purely syntactic proofs. As example of a sequent proof, consider the following formula:

$$[a \rightarrow [b \rightarrow c]] \rightarrow [a \rightarrow c]$$

To show that this is a theorem of a theory with proper axiom a → b, we first of all create the formula:

$$[a \rightarrow b] \rightarrow [[a \rightarrow [b \rightarrow c]] \rightarrow [a \rightarrow c]]$$

and then show that this is a tautology. This is done by starting with two sequents b → b and c → c:

b → b c → c	

$$
\frac{
\frac{
\dfrac{b \to b \qquad c \to c}{a \to a \qquad b \to c, b \to c}
}{
a \to a \qquad b, a \to [b \to c], a \to c
}
}{
\begin{array}{c}
a, a \to [b \to c], a \to b \to c \\
a \to [b \to c], a \to b \to a \to c \\
a \to b \to [[a \to [b \to c]] \to [a \to c] \\
\to [a \to b] \to [[a \to [b \to c]] \to [a \to c]]
\end{array}
}
$$

by use of (A→) rule
by use of (A→) rule
by use of (A→) rule
by use of (C→) rule
by use of (C→) rule
by use of (C→) rule

This proof can be explained as follows: we start the proof with two sequents b → b and c → c, we then use the (A→) rule to infer b → c, b → c; we then introduce the sequent a → a and from this and the inferred sequent b → c, b → c we use the (A→) rule again to infer the sequent b, a → [b → c], a → c; once again, we introduce the sequent a → a, and so on.

The structural modification rule of interchange is used twice in this proof although this use is not stated explicitly.

In general, sequent proofs start with one or two instances of a logical axiom α → α and then use the inference rules in an attempt to derive the required formula.

Like natural deduction, sequent proofs rely heavily on the cleverness of the person constructing them.

Gentzen (1934) has shown that the cut rule described above is dispensable, i.e. that any proof involving it can be transformed to a proof in which the cut rule does not appear. This is the content of Gentzen's 'cut-elimination' or 'normal form' theorem. This theorem, together with Gentzen's notion of constructing a proof as a tree (as illustrated in natural deduction described earlier), influenced the development of very effective proof techniques called 'tableau' methods, which are described in sub-sections 4.2.5 and 4.2.6.

One final point regarding sequent logic should be mentioned: sequent logic was devised by Gentzen in order that he could use it as a tool to investigate properties of classical logics. As such, it may be described as a 'metatheoretical' logic.

4.2.4 TOP-DOWN PROOF METHODS

All of the syntactic proof methods described so far start with logical axioms, and/or proper axioms, and/or suppositions, and then apply inference rules in an attempt to derive the formula to be proven. Such methods are variously called 'deductive', 'bottom-up', 'forward-chaining' or 'data-driven' proof methods.

As mentioned earlier, proof methods of this kind rely to a large extent on the cleverness of the person constructing the proof. Any attempt to automate such proof techniques would either have to have such cleverness programmed in as heuristic rules (rules of thumb), or would have to use a 'blind' search strategy. A blind search would involve the system generating all the theorems it could, hoping that the required theorem would turn up. Neither of these two alternatives is satisfactory: in the first case, most of the heuristics which people apply when solving problems are not yet well defined, and those which have been well defined are generally only applicable in a particular domain (application area); in the second case even with relatively trivial theories the number of theorems which can be generated will be enormous, and in many cases will be infinite. In general, one would have to wait a very long time before the required theorem was generated (if it were generated at all), even using the fastest computers available.

As an alternative to bottom-up proof methods, people have developed methods variously called 'reductive', 'top-down', 'goal-driven' or 'backward-chaining' methods. In such methods, we begin with a formula which may or may not be provable and then apply rules to this formula, together with the proper axioms of the theory, to determine whether or not it is a theorem. Top-down methods are, in general, more mechanical than are bottom-up methods and as such are more amenable to automation. Top-down proof methods are described in the next few sub-sections.

4.2.5 TABLEAU PROOF METHODS

In sequent logic, we begin with one or two axioms of the form $\alpha \rightarrow \alpha$ and then by using rules develop longer and longer (in cut-free proofs) sequents until the required sequent is reached. Tableau proofs work in the opposite direction.

A tableau consists of two parallel columns each containing zero or more formulas. To construct a proof of a formula of the form $F1 \rightarrow F2$ we begin by writing F1 in the left column and F2 in the right column:

F1 | F2

We then proceed to decompose F1 and F2 using rules which are inverses of sequent logic rules. To illustrate this process, consider an example in which we want to prove that $R \rightarrow Q$ is a theorem of a theory with proper axiom $P \wedge Q$. In effect, we want to prove $[P \wedge Q] \rightarrow [R \rightarrow Q]$. We begin by constructing the tableau:

$P \wedge Q$ | $R \rightarrow Q$

Now, because the formula in the left-hand column is a conjunction, the sequent logic rule corresponding to it would be (A∧), i.e. the antecedent ∧-introduction rule. However, since we are working backwards we simply pull $P \wedge Q$ apart giving:

```
P ∧ Q | R → Q
   P  |
   Q  |
```

We now manipulate the right-hand side of the tableau using a rule corresponding to the 'consequent →introduction' rule of sequent logic. This rule tells us to put R on the left of the tableau and Q on the right, giving:

```
P ∧ Q | R → Q
   P  |
   Q  |
   R  | Q
```

Now, since Q occurs as a free-standing formula in both columns, we say that the tableau 'closes' and the proof is complete. Such closure corresponds to the beginning of a proof branch in sequent logic. Thus the tableau effectively tells us how we might construct a sequent proof:

Take all of the formulas for which there has been no rule application (i.e. P and R) and insert them into Q → Q by appropriate applications of the thinning rule by putting those on the left of the tableau into the antecedent and those in the right-hand column into the consequent:

$$\frac{Q \;\rightarrow\; Q}{P, \; Q, \; R \;\rightarrow\; Q}$$ by application of the sequent thinning rule

Now, in reverse order to the order used in constructing the tableau, we apply sequent rules corresponding to those rules used in constructing the tableau:

$$\frac{\dfrac{P, \; Q, \; R \;\rightarrow\; Q}{P, \; Q, \;\rightarrow\; R \rightarrow Q}}{P \wedge Q \;\rightarrow\; R \rightarrow Q}$$

(C→)

(A∧)

Finally, we can apply the (C→) rule to the last sequent giving:

$$\rightarrow\; P \wedge Q \rightarrow [R \rightarrow Q]$$

This illustrates the correspondence between the tableau and sequent proof methods.

The example above represents the simplest type of tableau proof. In general, tableau proofs can involve splitting the tableau into two tableaux and the subsequent splitting of these tableaux. For example, consider proof of the formula:

$$[[P \rightarrow Q] \rightarrow P] \rightarrow P$$

We begin by constructing the tableau:

tableau 1

[P → Q] → P | P

Because the formula in the left column is of the form F1 → F2, we split this column into two tableaux having a common upper part. F1 goes into the right column of one tableau and F2 goes into the left column of the other tableau. In our example this gives:

tableau 10			tableau 11	
[P → Q] → P	P		[P → Q] → P	P
	P → Q			P

Notice that both tableaux inherit formulas from their parent. As can be seen, tableau 11 is closed since P occurs in both columns. We proceed to manipulate the left tableau. Because it contains a formula of the form P → Q in the right column, we simply write P in the left column and Q in the right column of this tableau giving:

tableau 10

```
[P → Q] → P │ P
            │
            │ P → Q
          P │ Q
```

This tableau also closes because it contains P free standing in both columns. Since all split tableaux close, the proof is complete.

The binary numbering scheme (1,10 and 11) reflects the structure of the proof:

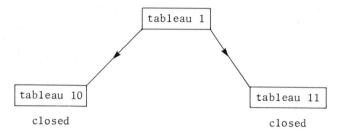

A more concise notation for tableau proofs is illustrated in the following which is equivalent to the proof above:

tableau 1

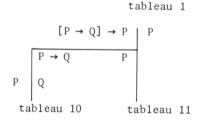

The contents above the horizontal line are inherited by both tableaux below the line.

The tableau construction rules are described more fully below. The symbols in brackets are an abbreviation for the name of the rule - for example, (L→) stands for 'left column → rule', and so on.

(R→):   When α → β occurs on the right, write α on the left and β on the right. This is the rule which was used at the beginning and end of the example proof above.

(L→):   When α → β occurs on the left, split the tableau writing α on the right of one of the new tableaux and β on the left of the other.

(RΛ): When α ∧ β occurs on the right, split the tableau writing α on the right of one of the new tableaux and β on the right of the other.

(LΛ): When α ∧ β occurs on the left, write both α and β on the left.

(Rν): When α ∨ β occurs on the right, write both α and β on the right.

(Lν): When α ∨ β occurs on the left, split that tableau and write α on the left of one of the new tableaux and β on the left of the other.

(R¬): When ¬α occurs on the right, write α on the left.

(L¬): When ¬α occurs on the left, write α on the right.

The following illustrates a tableau proof using the more precise notation given earlier. To prove that the formula:

$$[[P \wedge Q] \rightarrow [R \vee T]] \rightarrow [[\neg R \wedge \neg T] \rightarrow [\neg P \vee \neg Q]]$$

is valid, we begin by writing:

$$[P \wedge Q] \rightarrow [R \vee T] \mid [\neg R \wedge \neg T] \rightarrow [\neg P \vee \neg Q]$$

The proof proceeds as follows (the name of the rule being used is given on the right):

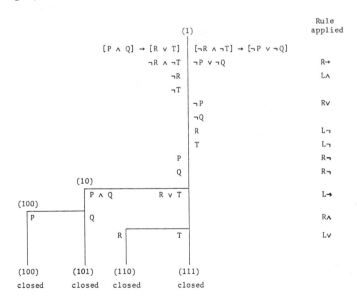

	Rule applied
	R→
	LΛ
	Rν
	L¬
	L¬
	R¬
	R¬
	L→
	RΛ
	Lν

The leftmost tableau (tableau 100) is closed since P occurs in the right column and in the left column (P in the left column is inherited

189

from the tableau above); similarly for all of the other tableaux. Consequently, the proof has succeeded.

The important property of tableau proofs is that they are mechanistic. They do not rely on the cleverness of the person constructing the proofs, only on his dexterity at manipulating symbols. As such, tableau proof methods are amenable to automation.

4.2.6 VALIDITY CHECKING BY SEARCHING FOR A COUNTEREXAMPLE USING SEMANTIC TABLEAUX

The idea behind this technique is to search for a 'counterexample' to the formula being tested. If all lines of search for a counterexample end in failure then the formula is valid.

Semantic justification

Assuming that $\top$ stands for true and $\bot$ for false, we know from the semantics of classical proposition logic that:

$$\alpha \rightarrow \beta = \bot \text{ iff } \alpha = \top \text{ and } \beta = \bot$$
$$\alpha \wedge \beta = \bot \text{ iff } \alpha = \bot \text{ or } \beta = \bot$$
$$\alpha \vee \beta = \bot \text{ iff } \alpha = \bot \text{ and } \beta = \bot$$
$$\neg\alpha = \bot \text{ iff } \alpha = \top$$

(etc.)

These definitions tell us how we can falsify a formula if it can be falsified. For example, given the formula:

$$F1 \rightarrow F2$$

the only way we can falsify this is by assigning $\top$ to F1 and $\bot$ to F2. If, however, in so doing we come up with a contradiction then the formula cannot be falsified and must therefore be valid.

Similar arguments can be applied to formulas containing the connectives $\vee$ and $\wedge$. For example, consider the following formula:

$$[P \wedge Q] \rightarrow [Q \vee R]$$

The only way that this formula can be falsified is by assigning $\top$ to $P \wedge Q$ and $\bot$ to $Q \vee R$. The only way in which $P \wedge Q$ can be true is if $P = \top$ and $Q = \top$. The only way in which $Q \vee R$ can be false is if $Q = \bot$ and $R = \bot$. Since Q is assigned both $\top$ and $\bot$ in this (the only) way in which the formula could be falsified, we can conclude that no falsifying truth assignment (counterexample) exists and therefore the formula $[P \wedge Q] \rightarrow [Q \vee R]$ is valid.

The examples given so far are all simple in that they involve 'non-branching' searches for falsifying truth assignments. Consider, now, the following formula:

$$[P \vee \neg P] \rightarrow P$$

In the first instance there is only one way to falsify this formula and that is to assign $\top$ to $P \vee \neg P$ and $\bot$ to P. However, there are now two ways in which P ∨ ¬P can be made true: either P can be assigned T or P can be assigned ⊥. In the first alternative we obtain a contradiction in our attempt to falsify [P ∨ ¬P] → P since we assign T to P on the left of → when we have previously assigned ⊥ to P on the right. However, no such contradiction occurs in the second alternative where ¬P is assigned T, and subsequently P is assigned ⊥. Therefore, we have identified a falsifying truth assignment (or counterexample), P = ⊥, which falsifies the formula [P ∨ ¬P] → P. As a consequence of this, we can conclude that the formula is not valid.

The method

There are various methods by which we can keep track of the truth assignments which we make when pursuing the alternative ways to falsify a formula. Use of tableaux happens to be one of the handier methods. The presence of a formula in the left column of a tableau signifies an assignment of T to that formula, and the presence of a formula in the right column signifies an assignment of ⊥. The splitting of a tableau into two tableaux occurs when there are two ways in which a sub-formula can obtain the required truth assignment.

Consider the formula [[Q ∨ ¬P] → P] → P. We begin our attempt to falsify this formula by writing it in the right-hand column of a tableau, thereby signifying an assignment of ⊥ to it:

$$| \quad [[Q \lor \neg P] \to P] \to P$$

The only way in which this formula can be falsified is if T is assigned to [Q ∨ ¬P] → P and ⊥ to P. We can indicate this truth assignment by writing [Q ∨ ¬P] → P in the left column and P in the right column of the tableau:

$$[Q \lor \neg P] \to P \quad \Big| \quad \begin{array}{l} [[Q \lor \neg P] \to P] \to P \\ P \end{array}$$

Now, there are two ways in which the sub-formula [Q ∨ ¬P] → P could be true. One way is if Q ∨ ¬P is false; the other way is if P is true. To signify these alternatives we split the tableau in a way similar to that in which we split tableaux in tableaux proofs:

$$
\begin{array}{c|c}
 & [[Q \lor \neg P] \to P] \to P \\
[Q \lor \neg P] \to P & P \\
\hline
\quad Q \lor \neg P \qquad\qquad P \\
\text{tableau 10} \qquad\quad \text{tableau 11}
\end{array}
$$

Note that tableau 11 closes since it has P in both columns (indicating a contradiction). Therefore this way of falsifying the original formula fails. We now turn our attention to tableau 10. The presence of Q ∨ ¬P in the right column of this tableau signifies an assignment of ⊥ to it. There is only one way in which this can occur: both Q and ¬P must be assigned ⊥. Therefore they are both written in the right column, giving:

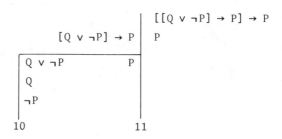

Now the only way in which ¬P can be assigned ⊥ is if P is assigned ⊤ giving the tableau:

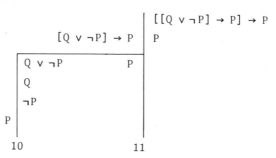

Tableau 10 has P in both columns and is therefore closed. Since we have exhausted all ways in which the formula [[Q ∨ ¬P] → P] → P might be falsified and have come up with a contradiction in each case, we can conclude that it must be valid.

The rules for constructing semantic tableaux when searching for a counterexample are equivalent to those for constructing tableau proofs as described in sub-section 4.2.5 so they will not be repeated here.

Determining the validity of formulas using semantic tableaux can be mechanised in a similar way to tableau proofs.

The importance of semantic tableaux will be apparent when modal logics are discussed in chapter 6. Many modal logic proof methods are based on the semantic tableau method.

A clear description of the use of tableaux in proofs and validity checking can be found in Zeman (1973).

4.2.7 UNIFORM PROOF AND VALIDITY CHECKING METHODS

All of the methods that we have described so far, both for constructing proofs and for determining validity, make use of more than one rule of inference. In addition, the formulas which they manipulate are irregular in that they do not conform to a simple standard format. For these reasons, such methods are called 'non-uniform' proof or validity checking methods.

This non-uniformity complicates the automation of the methods, as might be expected. However, such non-uniformity is not an essential feature

of proof and validity checking methods. Due to the interdefinability
of the logical connectives, it is possible to convert formulas to regular forms involving as few as two logical connectives and to reduce
the number of inference rules correspondingly. The proof method which
is described in the next sub-section does just this. All formulas are
converted to a particularly regular form called 'clausal form' involving disjunction, conjunction and negation of sub-formulas only. A
single inference rule, called the 'resolution' inference rule, is used
in proofs. As such, resolution is particularly amenable to automation.

However, it should be pointed out that conversion of formulas to a uniform format is not without disadvantage. Many researchers, particularly
in mathematical theorem-proving, believe that uniform proof methods are
unable to tackle difficult problems because in converting formulas to
uniform form we are throwing away proof guidance information which is
embedded in the original structure of the formulas. For this reason,
interest in uniform proof methods in certain applications such as mathematical theorem-proving is giving way to interest in methods based on
natural deduction. A very readable account of such methods can be
found in Bundy (1983).

In the present book, we are primarily concerned with uniform proof
methods since they are the ones most often used in knowledge base
systems. Resolution is used in many of the examples in subsequent
chapters since it is the most widely known uniform theorem-proving
method.

4.2.8 RESOLUTION

A uniform approach to theorem-proving and consistency checking in
propositional logic will now be described. The method, which is based
on principles developed by Robinson (1965), requires formulas to be
converted to a regular form called 'clausal form'. The methods described in this sub-section are particularly suitable for automation
owing to the simplicity of the single inference rule which is used.

Formulas can be converted to clausal form once they have been transformed to conjunctive normal form, as described next.

Conjunctive normal form
The equivalence rules described in sub-section 4.2.1, together with
the definitions for the logical connective abbreviations, can be used
to transform any formula of classical propositional logic into one of
either of two regular forms called 'conjunctive normal form' and 'disjunctive normal form'. A formula is in conjunctive normal form if it
is a conjunction of disjunctions of literals, where a literal is an
atomic formula (a simple proposition) or the negation of an atomic
formula. A formula is in disjunctive normal form if it is a disjunction of conjunctions of literals.

In this discussion we are interested in formulas which are in conjunctive normal form. As example, the conjunctive normal form of
¬[[P ∧ Q] ∨ R] is:

[¬P ∨ ¬Q] ∧ ¬R

The first conjunct is the disjunct ¬P ∨ ¬Q and the second conjunct is the 'disjunct' ¬R. We now describe, briefly, how formulas can be converted to conjunctive normal form:

Conversion of formulas to conjunctive normal form

(a) **→ elimination**
First, all implication signs must be eliminated. This is done by making the following conversion throughout the formula:

$$\neg P \lor Q \quad \text{for } P \to Q$$

(b) **Reducing the scope of ¬**
Now the scope of the negation signs is reduced so that each instance of ¬ applies to only one simple proposition. For example:

¬[P ∨ Q] becomes ¬P ∧ ¬Q } note that these are
¬[P ∧ Q] becomes ¬P ∨ ¬Q } de Morgan's rules
¬¬P becomes P

(c) **Application of a sub-set of the distributivity rules**
P ∨ [Q ∧ R] becomes [P ∨ Q] ∧ [P ∨ R]
[P ∧ Q] ∨ R becomes [P ∨ R] ∧ [Q ∨ R]

An example of conversion
As example of how the above method proceeds, consider the following formula:

[P → Q] → [¬R → [S ∧ T]]

The three implication signs are eliminated in three steps:

¬[P → Q] ∨ [¬R → [S ∧ T]]
¬[¬P ∨ Q] ∨ [¬R → [S ∧ T]]
¬[¬P ∨ Q] ∨ [¬¬R ∨ [S ∧ T]]

Now the scope of the negation sign is reduced in two steps:

[¬¬P ∧ ¬Q] ∨ [¬¬R ∨ [S ∧ T]]
[P ∧ ¬Q] ∨ [R ∨ [S ∧ T]]

Finally, we apply the distributivity rule four times (twice on last line):

[P ∧ ¬Q] ∨ [[R ∨ S] ∧ [R ∨ T]]
[P ∨ [[R ∨ S] ∧ [R ∨ T]]] ∧ [¬Q ∨ [[R ∨ S] ∧ [R ∨ T]]]
[P ∨ [R ∨ S]] ∧ [P ∨ [R ∨ T]] ∧ [¬Q ∨ [R ∨ S]] ∧ [¬Q ∨ [R ∨ T]]

In sub-section 4.2.11, a computer program written in Pascal which can be used to convert formulas of classical propositional logic to conjunctive normal form is outlined.

Clauses
Consider the following disjunction of literals:

¬P ∨ ¬Q

This formula is equivalent to the formula:

¬Q ∨ ¬P

That is, the order of the literals around the connective ∨ is irrelevant. Therefore, a disjunction of literals may be regarded as a set of literals - called a 'clause'. For example, the following clause is equivalent to the disjunction above:

{¬Q, ¬P}

This clause may be read as not Q *or* not P.

A clause which is empty is called the 'null clause' and is denoted by ⊠ .

A clause which contains at most one positive literal is called a 'Horn clause'. The following are examples of Horn clauses:

{P, ¬Q, ¬R}
{¬P, ¬Q, R}
{¬P, ¬Q, ¬R, ¬S}
{¬P, ¬Q, R, ¬S, ¬T}

Clause sets and clausal form
Now consider the following formula:

[¬Q ∨ ¬P] ∧ ¬R

This formula is equivalent to the formula:

¬R ∧ [¬Q ∨ ¬P]

That is, the order of the sub-formulas around the connective ∧ is irrelevant. Consequently, a formula in conjunctive normal form (as defined above) may be regarded as a set of clauses called a 'clause set'. For example, the formula above can be replaced by the following clause set:

{{¬Q, ¬P}, {¬R}}

Formulas in this form are said to be in 'clausal form'.

The empty clause set is denoted by φ. A clause set, all of whose members are Horn, is called a 'Horn clause set'. The above is an example of a Horn clause set.

Advantages of clausal form
Since any formula of propositional logic can be converted to conjunctive normal form, it can be converted to clausal form. The advantage of clausal form is its uniformity which makes it ideal for automatic processing. However, before describing how to reason about a formula or set of formulas in clausal form, we will outline the semantics of this form.

Semantics of formulas in clausal form

A truth assignment @ is appropriate to a clause set S if every atomic formula appearing in some clause in S is in the domain of @. @ satisfies a clause set iff it satisfies all of the clauses in the set. @ satisfies a clause iff it satisfies one of its members. For example, let S be the clause set:

$$\{\{P, Q\}, \{\neg R\}\}$$

If @ = {P := true, Q := false, R := false}, then @ satisfies S. We denote that @ satisfies S as follows:

$$@ \models S$$

Notice that:

(a) $@ \not\models \blacksquare$ for each @ (i.e. no assignment satisfies the null clause) because $\blacksquare$ has no members.

(b) $@ \models \varphi$ for each @ (i.e. all assignments satisfy the empty clause set) since @ satisfies each clause in φ of which there happen to be none.

(c) From (a) and (b) it follows that $@ \not\models \{\blacksquare\}$ for each @ (that is, no assignment satisfies the clause set containing the null clause).

A clause or clause set may be satisfiable, unsatisfiable or a tautology in the same way that a formula may be. For example, the empty clause set is a tautology but the null clause is unsatisfiable, as is any clause set containing the null clause.

The resolution inference rule

Consider the following pair of clauses:

C1:   {P, ¬Q}   meaning P or not Q
C2:   {Q, S}   meaning Q or S

Now consider the clause C3:   {P, S}. This clause is a logical consequence of C1 and C2 as can be demonstrated by the following truth table:

P	Q	S	C1: {P, ¬Q}	C2: {Q, S}	C3: {P, S}	
T	⊥	T	T	T	T	✓
T	⊥	⊥	T	⊥	T	
T	T	T	T	T	T	✓
T	T	⊥	T	T	T	✓
⊥	⊥	T	T	T	T	✓
⊥	⊥	⊥	T	⊥	⊥	
⊥	T	T	⊥	T	T	
⊥	T	⊥	⊥	T	⊥	

That is {P, S} is true in the four cases in which both {P, ¬Q} and {Q, S} are true.

Now suppose the formulas were not in clause form but were written out using the logical connective →. They would appear as follows:

    C1:   Q → P
    C2:   ¬S → Q
    C3:   ¬S → P

It is now clear that C3 follows from C1 and C2:

    from ¬S → Q and Q → P infer ¬S → P

Now we consider how to deduce C3 from C1 and C2 without having to resort to constructing truth tables or converting the clauses to some other form. The answer is quite straightforward. An inference rule which recognises the presence of the complementary literals ¬Q in C1 and Q in C2 is used. This rule, called the 'resolution inference rule' tells us that we can combine C1 and C2, by cancelling ¬Q in C1 with Q in C2, to form a new clause called the 'resolvent' of C1 and C2:

    C1: {P, ¬Q}
            {Q, S} : C2
       ↓
    C3: {P, S} the resolvent of C1 and C2.

We can generalise and specify the resolution inference rule more formally as follows:

    From a clause C1 containing some literal L and a clause C2 containing a literal ¬L we can infer the clause:

    C3 = {C1 - {L}} U {C2 - {¬L}}

For example:

C1	C2	C3: the resolvent of C1 and C2
{P, Q, R}	{S, T, ¬P}	{Q, R, S, T}
{P, Q}	{¬Q, S}	{P, S}
{T}	{¬T}	⊠
{P, Q, R, S}	{P, Q, ¬R, S}	{P, Q, S}

Thus, the 'resolvent' of two clauses is any clause obtained by striking out a complementary pair of literals, one from each clause, and merging the remaining literals into a single clause. Note that, as exemplified in line four of the table above, redundant literals must be removed from the resolvent.

The closure of a clause set under resolution
If S is a clause set then R is defined as follows, where i ⩾ 1:

    R0(S) = S
    R1(S) = S U all new resolvents of S
    R2(S) = R1(S) U all new resolvents of R1(S)
    Ri(S) = Ri-1(S) U all new resolvents of Ri-1(S)

R*S can now be defined, the closure of S under the operation of adding all resolvents of clauses to those already present, as follows:

$$R*(S) = U\ Rj(S)\ \text{where}\ j \geqslant 0\ \text{and}\ Rj(S) = Rj + 1(S)$$

For example, consider the following clause set:

$$S = \{\{P,\ Q\},\ \{\neg P,\ R\},\ \{\neg R,\ S\}\}$$

Applying the resolution rule gives us:

```
R0(S) = S
R1(S) = S U {{Q, R}, {¬P, S}}
R2(S) = R1(S) U {{Q, S}}
R3(S) = R2(S) U φ
R*(S) = {{P, Q}, {¬P, R}, {¬R, S}, {Q, R}, {¬P, S}, {Q, S}}
```

Notice that we did not have to consider R4(S) since the third resolution pass produced no new resolvents.

The resolution theorem

The resolution rule may be restated as follows:

If S is a clause set and D is a resolvent of two clauses in S, then S and S U{D} are equivalent.

The 'resolution theorem' which is based on the resolution rule states that a clause set S is unsatisfiable iff:

☒ ∈ R*(S)

That is, a clause set S is unsatisfiable iff the closure of S under resolution contains the null clause.

The 'if' part of this theorem is intuitively obvious since, by the resolution rule, S ≡ R0(S) ≡ R1(S) ≡ R2(S)...R*(S). The 'only if' part of the theorem is not so obvious. However, a clear exposition of this part of the theorem is given in Lewis and Papadimitriou (1981).

Consistency checking using resolution

Resolution can be used to determine the satisfiability or consistency of a formula or set of formulas as follows:

(a) Convert the formula(s) to conjunctive normal form.

(b) Form an equivalent clause set, call this set S.

(c) Form R1(S), R2(S) until Ri(S) = Ri-1(S) for some i.

(d) If ☒ ∈ Ri(S), then S is unsatisfiable (inconsistent); otherwise it is satisfiable (consistent).

Theorem-proving using resolution

Resolution may be used to see if a formula F is a theorem of some theory T. One method is to use a refutation procedure, as follows:

(a) Add ¬F to the logical and proper axioms of T.

198

(b)   Convert the formulas to conjunctive normal form.

(c)   Form an equivalent clause set, call this set S.

(d)   Form R1(S), R2(S) until Ri(S) = Ri-1(S) for some i.

(e)   If ⊠ ∈ Ri(S) then S is unsatisfiable, therefore F is a theorem; otherwise F is not a theorem.

Note that this is not an efficient method of using resolution. More efficient methods are described in sub-section 4.3.11.

4.2.9   NON-RESOLUTION UNIFORM THEOREM-PROVING METHODS

Various non-resolution uniform theorem-proving techniques have been developed. Some of these techniques are based on natural deduction and others are based on the idea of examining connections between the literals of the formulas of a theory.

Resolution-based methods are often criticised for being redundant and unnatural to follow and some of the non-resolution techniques may be regarded as serious competitors to the use of resolution for automated theorem-proving. Some of these techniques are described in sub-sections 4.4.8 and 4.4.9.

4.2.10   EXAMPLES OF THEOREM-PROVING IN PROPOSITIONAL LOGIC

As a reminder, three of the methods of theorem-proving which were described for propositional logic will now be illustrated. The first method is purely syntactic, the second is purely semantic, and the third is a refutation procedure using the resolution inference rule.

Consider a theory T which has as proper axioms:

    PA1:   P ∨ Q
    PA2:   P → ¬Q
    PA3:   ¬P

where, for example, P might stand for 'Pat is a man' and Q for 'Pat is a woman'.

The theorem which is to be proved is Q. That is, we are going to show that Q is a logical consequence of the theory T.

Syntactic method

(a)   Rewrite PA1 as PA1': ¬P → Q using conditional elimination and substitution rules.

(b)   Using modus ponens, Q can be inferred from PA3 and PA1'.

(c)   Therefore, Q is a theorem.

Semantic method

(a)   Construct the following truth table:

		PROPER AXIOMS			THEOREM
P	Q	P ∨ Q	P → ¬Q	¬P	Q
T	T	T	⊥	⊥	T
T	⊥	T	T	⊥	⊥
⊥	T	T	T	T	T ✓
⊥	⊥	⊥	T	T	⊥

(b)   Since Q is true in all cases in which all of the proper axioms of T are true, it can be concluded that Q is a theorem of T.

Using resolution

(a)   Add ¬Q to the proper axioms of T.   Convert the formulas to clausal form to obtain S:

S = {{P, Q}, {¬P,   ¬Q}, {¬P}, {¬Q}}

(b)   {P} is a resolvent of {P, Q} and {¬Q}.   Add this to S to obtain the clause set S':

S' = {{P, Q}, {¬P, ¬Q}, {¬P}, {¬Q}, {P}}

(c)   The resolvent of {¬P} and {P} is the null cause.   Add this to S' to obtain the clause set S".

(d)   S" contains the null clause, therefore it is unsatisfiable. Consequently S is unsatisfiable, therefore Q must be a theorem of T.

Using resolution might appear, in this example, to be a complicated method of proving an intuitively obvious theorem.   However, the important point is that it can be refined, automated and used for much more complicated proofs as will be seen in the following sections and in later chapters.

4.2.11   IMPLEMENTATION OF PROGRAMS FOR AUTOMATED REASONING IN PROPOSITIONAL LOGIC

In chapter 2, we described how to construct a parser which could be used to parse formulas of a propositional language called PROPLANG.

The grammar of PROPLANG is:

```
wff        ::=  exp;

exp        ::=  a
                [ exp list ]
                - exp

list       ::=  ∧ conjlist
                ∨ disjlist
                > exp

conjlist   ::=  exp conj

conj       ::=  ∧ conjlist
                ε
```

```
disjlist ::=  exp disj
disj     ::=  ∨ disjlist
              ε
```

where (a) 'a' stands for 'atomic formula' and (b) 'ε' means empty.

An example of a formula of PROPLANG is:

$$[[[(P) \wedge (Q)] \vee -[(S) \wedge (T)]] = > [(L) \wedge (M)]];$$

We now describe how to construct a program for converting formulas of PROPLANG to clausal form.

Conversion of formulas to clausal form
The method consists of three phases:

(a)   Convert the formula to a tree, e.g. the formula given above becomes the tree shown in fig. 4.1.

(b)   Process the tree so that the formula is in clausal form. This involves removal of → signs, etc., as discussed in 4.2.8.

(c)   Write the tree out as a set of clauses.

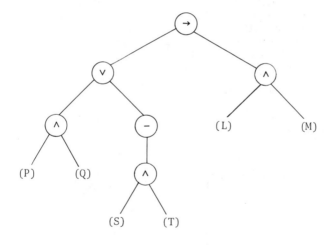

Figure 4.1   A tree representation of a formula

Phase 1: Constructing the tree
In chapter 3, section 3.4.14, we explained how actions can be placed in a grammar and corresponding procedure calls placed in a parser, so that a query expressed in a query language could be answered. We now explain how to place actions in the **grammar of** PROPLANG, and corresponding procedure calls in the PROPLANG parser, so that a tree can be built to represent a formula when that formula is parsed.

The method for constructing such trees makes use of a stack:

(a)   When an atomic formula is recognised in the exp procedure:

- create a new record with two fields
- put the character 'a' in the first field
- put the atomic formula in the second field
- put the record on to the stack

(b)   After a conj is recognised in the conjlist procedure:

- create a new record with three fields
- put the character '∧' in the first field
- pull a record from the stack and put a pointer to this record in the third field of the new record
- pull another record from the stack and put a pointer to this record in the second field of the new record
- put the new record on to the stack

(c)   After a disj is recognised in the disjlist procedure:

- as (b) but use 'v' instead of '∧'

(d)   After exp is recognised in the list procedure:

- as (b) but use '>' instead of '∧'

(e)   After -exp is recognised in the exp procedure:

- create a new record with two fields
- put the character '-' in the first field
- pull a record from the stack and put a pointer to this record in the second field of the new record
- put the new record on to the stack

Because (b), (c) and (d) are similar, a procedure called 'diadicop' which takes the character '∧', 'v' or '>' as parameter and performs the operations required can be used. The PROPLANG grammar with the embedded actions becomes:

```
wff       ::=  exp ;

exp       ::=  a <stackatf>
               [ exp list ]
               - exp <monadicop('-')>

list      ::=  ∧ conjlist
               v disjlist
               > exp <diadicop('>')>

conjlist  ::=  exp conj <diadicop('∧')>

conj      ::=  ∧ conjlist
               ε

disjlist  ::=  exp disj <diadicop('v')>

disj      ::=  v disjlist
               ε
```

For symmetry, a procedure called 'monadicop' has been used for dealing with the negation signs. Diadicop is short for 'diadic operation' and monadicop is short for 'monadic operation'. The procedure 'stackatf' creates a record for whatever atomic formula has just been read and stacks this record.

To illustrate how the tree would be constructed, consider the following formula:

[[(P) ∧ (Q)] → ¬R];

The parser would proceed as follows:

```
call wff
    call exp
        recognise [
        call exp
            recognise [
            call exp
                recognise a
                stackatf('P')
            call list
                recognise ∧
                call conjlist
                    call exp
                        recognise a
                        stackatf('Q')
                    call conj
                        recognise ε
                    diadicop('∧')
            recognise ]
        call list
            recognise >
            call exp
                recognise -
                call exp
                    recognise a
                    stackatf('R')
                monadicop('-')
            diadicop('>')
        recognise ]
    recognise ;
```

The operations on the stack which would be carried out during this parse are illustrated in fig. 4.2.

Phase 2: *Converting the tree to clausal form*

(a) *Removal of implication signs.* The tree is traversed recursively and implication signs are removed as follows:

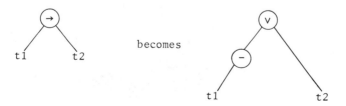

becomes

where t1 and t2 are sub-trees.

203

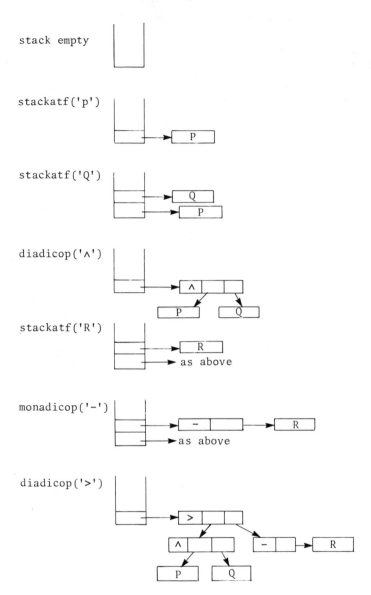

Figure 4.2   Stack operations during translation of a formula to tree form

(b)   *Reducing the scope of negation signs.*   The tree is traversed recursively and negation signs are pushed to the bottom of the tree using de Morgan's rules:

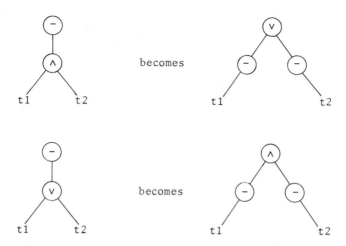

Whenever two negation signs are encountered, they cancel each other out:

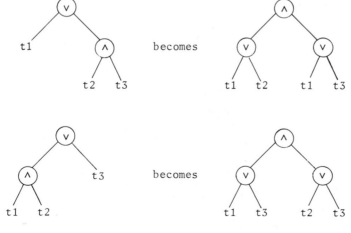

(c) *Converting to conjunctive normal form using distribution
rules.* The tree is traversed recursively in endorder order
such that no 'v' sign is above an 'ʌ' sign. The branches of
the tree (and of sub-trees) are processed before the root.
The transformations used are:

Whenever such a transformation is made, the two branches below the newly introduced '∧' sign must both be processed again recursively.

A Pascal program to convert formulas to clausal form
The program listed in the following pages reads formulas such as:

[(John walks) ∧ (Jill runs)] ∨ [(John runs) ∧ (Jill walks)]];

and converts them to clausal form:

{{ (John walks), (John runs)},
 { (John walks), (Jill walks)},
 { (Jill runs), (John runs)},
 { (Jill runs), (Jill walks)}}

When a formula is parsed, a tree is constructed to represent it. Pascal variant records are used for the tree nodes. After the tree has been constructed it is converted to conjunctive normal form using the procedures 'implication', 'negscope' and 'distribute' in that order. The procedure 'writetree' is then used to write out the clausal form of the formula.

```
program clause( input, output );
const
   stacksize = 40 ;
type
   treepoint = ^ treetype ;
   treetype = record
           case token : char of
              'a' : ( atf : packed array [1..20] of char );
              '-' : ( next : treepoint );
              '>', '^', 'v' : ( left, right : treepoint )
           end ;
var formula : array [1..80] of char ;
    charpos : integer ;
    k : char ;
    stack   : array[1..stacksize] of treepoint ;
    stacktop : integer ;
    p : treepoint ;
    atom  : packed array[1..20] of char ;
    j : integer ;
procedure readformula ;
var i : integer ;
begin
  for i := 1 to 80 do formula[i] := '';
  writeln( 'enter an formula' );
  i := 1 ;
  read ( formula[i] );
  while ( i < 79 ) and ( formula[i] < > ';' ) and not eoln
   do begin
        i := i + 1 ;
        read( formula[i] );
      end ;
  if formula[i] < > ';'
```

```
      then formula[i+1] := ',' ;
    readln ;
  end ;
function getok : char ;
  var i : integer ;
      c : char ;
      tok : char ;

  procedure error ;
     begin
       writeln ( 'lex error at pos', charpos ) ;
       tok := 'e'
     end ;
begin
  tok := '*' ;
   i := 1 ;
   atom :='          ' ;
   j := 1 ;
   while tok = '*'
     do begin
     charpos := charpos + 1 ;
     c := formula[charpos] ;
       case i of
         1 : begin
             if c = ' '
               then i := 1 ;
             if c in ['^', 'v', '-', ';', '[', ']']
               then tok := c ;
             if c = '='
               then i := 2 ;
             if c = '('
               then begin
                      atom[j] := '(' ;
                          j := j+1 ;
                          i := 3
                   end ;
            if not ( c in [' ', '^', 'v', '-', ';', '[', ']', '=', '('] )
               then error ;
             end ;
         2 : begin
             if c = ' '
               then i := 2 ;
             if c = '>'
               then tok := '>' ;
             if not ( c in [' ', '>'] )
               then error
             end ;

          3 : begin
             if c = ' '
               then i := 3 ;
             if c in ['a'..'z']
               then begin
                       i := 3 ;
                       atom[j] :=c ;
```

207

```
                     j := j+1 ;
                   end ;
             if c = ')'
                 then begin
                         atom[j] := ')' ;
                         tok := 'a'
                       end ;
             if not ( c in [' ', ')', 'a'..'z'] )
                     then error
                   end ;
         end ;
   end ;
  writeln( 'token is', tok ) ;
  getok := tok
end ;
procedure push( t : treepoint ) ;
 begin
   if stacktop < stacksize
          then begin
                  stack[stacktop] := t ;
                  stacktop := stacktop +1 ;
                end
          else begin
                  writeln( 'stack overflow' ) ;
                end
   end ;
procedure pull ( var t : treepoint ) ;
  begin
    if stacktop = 1
      then begin
           writeln( 'trying to pull from an empty stack' ) ;
           end
      else begin
             stacktop := stacktop-1 ;
             t := stack[stacktop] ;
           end
   end ;
procedure stackatf ;
   begin
     new( p ) ;
     p^ .token :='a' ;
     p^ .atf :=atom ;
     push( p )
   end ;
procedure diadicop( t :char ) ;

   begin
     new( p ) ;
     p^ .token :=t ;
     pull( p^ .right ) ;
     pull( p^ .left ) ;
     push( p )
   end ;
procedure monadicop( t :char ) ;
   begin
     new( p ) ;
```

```
      p^ .token :=t ;
      pull( p^ .next ) ;
      push( p )
    end ;
procedure parse ;
 var tok : char ;
 procedure wff ;      forward ;
 procedure exp ;      forward ;
 procedure list ;     forward ;
 procedure conjlist  ; forward ;
 procedure conj ;     forward ;
 procedure disjlist  ; forward ;
 procedure disj ;     forward ;

 procedure wff ;
  begin
     exp ;
     tok := getok ;
     if tok  < > ';'
        then writeln( ' ; expected' )
  end ;
 procedure exp ;
  begin
   if not( tok in ['a', '-', '[') )
     then writeln( 'a, -, or [ expected' )
     else case tok of
          'a' : begin
                  stackatf
                end ;
          '-' : begin
                  tok := getok ;
                  exp ;
                  monadicop( '-' )
                end ;
          '[' : begin
                  tok := getok ;
                  exp ;
                  tok := getok ;
                  list ;
                  tok := getok ;
                  if tok  < > ']'
                    then writeln( '] expected' )
               end
            end ;
    end ;
 procedure list ;
  begin
    if not ( tok in ['>', '^', 'v'] )
       then writeln ( ' >, ^, or v expected' )
       else case tok of
              '>' : begin
                     tok := getok ;
                     exp ;
                     diadicop( '>' )
                    end ;
```

```
        '^' : begin
                tok := getok ;
                conjlist
              end ;
         'v' : begin
                 tok := getok ;
                 disjlist
               end ;
       end ;
     end ;
procedure conjlist ;
  begin
    exp ;
    tok := getok ;
    conj ;
    diadicop( '^' )
  end ;
procedure conj ;
  begin
    if not ( tok in ['^', ']'] )
      then writeln( '^ or ] expected' )
      else case tok of
           '^' : begin
                    tok := getok ;
                    conjlist
                  end ;
            ']' : begin
                   charpos := charpos - 1
                  end
           end ;
    end ;
procedure disjlist ;
  begin
    exp ;
    tok := getok ;
    disj ;
    diadicop( 'v' )
  end ;
procedure disj ;
  begin
    if not ( tok in ['v', ']'] )
      then writeln( 'v or ] expected' )
      else case tok of
           'v' : begin
                   tok := getok ;
                   disjlist
                 end ;
            ']' : begin
                   charpos := charpos - 1
                  end
           end ;
    end ;
```

```
begin
  charpos := 0 ;
  stacktop := 1 ;
  tok := getok ;
  wff
end ;




  procedure implication( var p : treepoint ) ;
    var q, a : treepoint ;
    begin
      if not( p^ .token in ['>', 'v', '^', '-', 'a'] )
        then writeln( 'error in implication' )
        else case p^ .token of
              'a' : ;
              '-' : implication( p^ .next ) ;
          'v', '^' : begin
                      implication( p^ .left ) ;
                      implication( p^ .right )
                    end ;
              '>' : begin
                      new( q ) ;
                      q^ .token :='-' ;
                      q^ .next :=p^ .left ;
                      a :=p^ .right ;
                      p^ .token :='v' ;
                      p^ .left :=q ;
                      p^ .right :=a ;
                      implication( p )
                    end
            end
      end ;




  procedure negscope( var p :treepoint ) ;
    var
      a, b :treepoint ;
      op :char ;
    function opp( t :char ) :char ;
      begin
        if t='^' then opp :='v'
                else if t='v' then opp :='^'
                              else begin
                                    writeln( 'error in opp' )
                                  end
      end ;
```

```
begin
  if p < >nil
    then if not( p^ .token in['v', '^', '-', 'a'] )
        then writeln( 'error in negscope' )
        else case p^ .token of
                'a' : ;
            'v', '^' : begin
                        negscope( p^ .left ) ;
                        negscope( p^ .right )
                      end ;
                  '-' : case p^ .next^ .token of
                        'a' : ;
                        '-' : begin
                                p :=p^ .next^ .next ;
                                negscope( p )
                              end ;
                    'v', '^' : begin
                                op :=opp( p^ .next^ .token ) ;
                                new( a ) ;new( b ) ;
                                a^ .token :='-' ;
                                a^ .next :=p^ .next^ .left ;
                                b^ .token :='-' ;
                                b^ .next :=p^ .next^ .right ;
                                p^ .token :=op ;
                                p^ .left :=a ; p^ .right :=b ;
                                negscope( p )
                              end ;
                      end
        end
end ;


procedure distribute( p :treepoint ) ;
 var
   t1, t2 :treepoint ;
 begin
    if ( p^ .token in ['^', 'v'] )
      then begin
            distribute( p^ .left ) ;
            distribute( p^ .right )
          end ;
    case p^ .token of
    'a', '-', '^' : ;
        'v' : begin
                if p^ .right^ .token='^' then
                begin
                  new( t1 ) ;new( t2 ) ;
                  t1^ .token :='v' ;t2^ .token :='v' ;
                  t1^ .left :=p^ .left ;t1^ .right :=p^ .right^ .left ;
                  t2^ .left :=p^ .left ;t2^ .right :=p^ .right^ .right ;
                  p^ .token :='^' ;p^ .left :=t1 ;p^ .right :=t2 ;
                  distribute( p^ .left ) ;
                  distribute( p^ .right )
                end
```

```
              else if p^ .left^ .token='^ ' then
                begin
                  new( t1 ) ;new( t2 );

                  t1^ .token :='v' ;t2^ .token :='v' ;
                  t1^ .left :=p^ .left^ .left ;t1^ .right :=p^ .right ;
                  t2^ .left :=p^ .left^ .right ;t2^ .right :=p^ .right ;
                  p^ .token :='^ ' ;p^ .left :=t1 ;p^ .right :=t2 ;
                  distribute( p^ .left ) ;
                  distribute( p^ .right ) ;

                end ;
            end ;
    end
  end ;




procedure writetree( p :treepoint ) ;
  procedure writeout( p :treepoint ) ;
   begin
   case p^ .token of
     'a' : begin
             write( p^ .atf ) ;
           end ;
     '-' : begin
             write( '-' ) ;
             writeout( p^ .next )
           end ;
     'v' : begin
             writeout( p^ .left ) ;
             write( ',' ) ;
             writeout( p^ .right )
           end ;
     '^ ' : begin
             writeout( p^ .left ) ;
             writeln ;
             writeln( '..........' ) ;
             writeout( p^ .right )
           end ;
      '>' : begin
             writeout( p^ .left ) ;
             write( '>' ) ;
             writeout( p^ .right )
           end
     end
   end ;


begin
  writeln( 'clausal form' ) ;
  if p = nil
    then writeln( 'empty tree' )

      else writeout( p ) ;
    writeln
  end ;
```

```
procedure printformula ;
  var i : integer ;
  begin
    writeln( 'the formula you typed in is' ) ;
    for i := 1 to 80
      do write( formula[i] ) ;
    writeln
  end ;



begin
  writeln('THIS IS A PROPLANG CLAUSE FORM TRANSLATOR');
  writeln;writeln;
  writeln('enter formulas such as [(peter walks)=>(peter runs)];');
  writeln;writeln;



  repeat
    readformula ;
    printformula ;
    parse ;
    if p < > nil
      then begin
            implication( p ) ;
            negscope( p ) ;
            distribute( p ) ;
            writetree( p )
          end;
    writeln( 'type e to terminate,  any key to continue' ) ;
    readln( k ) ;
  until k = 'e'
end.
```

4.3 FIRST ORDER PREDICATE LOGIC

Relational structures

Propositional logic allows one to reason about propositions. However, there is no way to reason about the relationships which exist between individual 'entities' in some universe of discourse. Neither is there any way to express general assertions which apply to sets of similar cases. Consequently, logicians have developed more expressive logics called 'predicate logics'. Such logics can be used to describe and reason about parts of the universe viewed as 'relational structures', where a relational structure consists of a set of entities E, a set of relations defined on E and a set of functions defined on E. Entities in a sub-set of E are known as 'distinguished entities'.

A more formal definition of a relational structure is that it is a quadruple:

U = <E, N, R, H>

where:

(a) E is a set of entities {e1, e2, ...}, called the domain of U.

(b) N is a set of distinguished entities {n1, n2, ...} such that
     N is a sub-set of E.

(c) R is a set of relations {r1, r2, ...}, each of which is
     defined on E.

(d) H is a set of functions {h1, h2, ...}, each of which is
     defined on E.

The following is an example of a relational structure:

U1:-   E = the set of all entities which constitute the
               University of Glasgow
         N = {SUE, BOB, TWENTY, THIRTY, BILL, FORTY, FIFTY,
               SIXTY}
         R = {MARRIED, AGED}
         H = {DOUBLE}

where:

MARRIED   = {<SUE, BOB>, <BOB, SUE>}
AGED   = {<SUE, TWENTY>, <BOB, THIRTY>, <BILL, FORTY>}

DOUBLE   = | TWENTY → FORTY | i.e. DOUBLE(TWENTY) = FORTY
              | THIRTY → SIXTY | DOUBLE(THIRTY) = SIXTY

The relations and functions in a relational structure may be of various
arity (i.e. may have various numbers of arguments). For example MARRIED
has arity = 2, DOUBLE has arity = 1 and is called a one argument function. The structure U1 is illustrated diagrammatically in fig. 4.3.

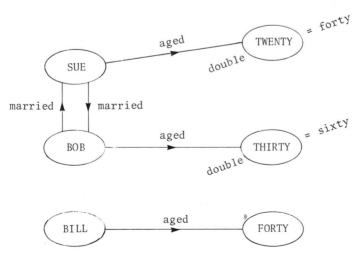

Figure 4.3 A graphical representation of a relational structure

In this chapter we restrict our attention to first order structures and logics. Higher-order structures and logics are described in chapter 6, section 6.10.

4.3.1 THE SYNTAX OF LANGUAGES OF FIRST ORDER PREDICATE LOGIC

The syntax of a formal language of first order predicate logic may be defined by a grammar whose terminal symbols include:

(a) A set of 'predicate symbols' P = {p1, p2, ...}

(b) A set of 'individual variables' Var = {v1, v2, ...}

(c) A set of 'individual constants' Cons = {c1, c2, ...}

(d) A set of 'function symbols' F = {f1, f2, ...}

(e) A set of 'logical connectives' which may include ∧, ∨, ¬, →, ↔, which stand for 'and', 'or', 'not', 'implies', and 'equivalent to', respectively.

(f) One or both of the 'quantifiers' ∀, ∃, which stand for 'for all' and 'there exists' respectively. ∀ is called the universal quantifier and ∃ is called the existential quantifier.

(g) Brackets.

The syntax of a first order predicate language is often defined using a sub-set of the logical connectives and only one of the quantifiers. The remaining connectives and quantifier are then defined as abbreviations. Whatever set is chosen, it should be complete in the sense that all other connectives and quantifiers may be defined in terms of the ones chosen. For example, if ∀ and ¬ are chosen, then ∃ may be defined as an abbreviation, as follows:

$$\exists x \ A \equiv \neg \forall x \ \neg A$$

where A is some formula and x is some variable. (This equivalence will become more meaningful when the following pages have been read.)

Similarly, → may be defined as:

$$A \rightarrow B \equiv \neg A \lor B$$

In the following, for simplicity, all connectives will be regarded as primitive.

The set of terms of a first order predicate language is defined as follows:

(a) All individual constants are terms.

(b) All individual variables are terms.

(c) If t1, ..., tn are terms, and f is an n-ary function symbol, then f(t1, ..., tn) is a term.

The set of atomic formulas of a first order predicate language is defined as follows:

If t1, ..., tn are terms, and p is an n-ary predicate symbol, then p(t1, ..., tn) is an atomic formula.

The set of well-formed formulas (wffs) of a first order predicate language is defined as follows:

(a)   If A is an atomic formula, then A is a wff.

(b)   If A and B are wffs, then so are:

> [A]
> ¬A
> A ∧ B
> A ∨ B
> A → B
> A ↔ B
> ∀v A   where v ∈ Var
> ∃v A   where v ∈ Var

(c)   The only wffs are those obtainable by finitely many applications of the above rules.

For ease of reading, the letters w, x, y, z will be used for individual variables, strings such as 'Sally' for individual constants, letters P, Q, R or strings such as 'has skill' for predicates, and the letters f, g, h or strings such as 'double' for function symbols. We shall also use the word 'formula' in place of 'wff' where the meaning is obvious.

As example of a language of first order predicate logic, consider the following informal definition of the syntax of a language which will be referred to as L1:

(a)   predicate symbols = {married, aged}, both of which are binary

(b)   variables   = {x, y, z}

(c)   constants   = {Sue, Bob, Bill, 20, 30, 40, 50, 60}

(d)   connectives   = {∧, ∨, ¬, →, ↔}

(e)   quantifiers   = {∀, ∃}

(f)   brackets   = {(,), [,]}

(g)   function symbols   = {double}

The set of terms of L1 is the set:

{Sue, Bob, Bill, 20, 30, 40, 50, 60, x, y, z, double(20), double(Sue), double(x), double(double(30)), etc.}

The atomic formulas and well-formed formulas of L1 are defined according to the rules given above. Examples of wffs of L1 are:

(a)   married(Sue, Bob)
      This atomic formula may be read as 'Sue is married to Bob'.

(b)   aged(Sue, 20)
      Read as 'Sue is aged twenty'.

(c)   aged(Bill, double(20))
      Read as 'Bill is aged double twenty'.

(d)   ¬married(Sue, Bill)
      Read as 'Sue is not married to Bill'.

(e)   ∀x∀y [married(x, y) → married(y, x)]
      Read as 'for all x and for all y, if x is married to y, then
      y is married to x'. This defines 'married' to be symmetric.

(f)   ∃x aged(x, 40)
      Read as 'there exists an x which is aged forty'.

(g)   aged(x, y)
      Read as 'x is aged y'.

The formulas (a) to (f) are called 'closed' formulas since they contain
no free variables (the variables, if any, are all bound by one or other
of the quantifiers ∀ and ∃). The formula (g) is an 'open formula'. If
A is a formula, then the scope of a quantifier occurrence, such as qx
in qx A, is A (where q = ∀ or ∃). An occurrence of a variable x in A is
'bound' iff it is immediately after a ∀ or ∃ sign, or if it is in the
scope of a quantifier occurrence. An occurrence of a variable which is
not bound is 'free'. Normal scope rules apply for binding variable
occurrences to quantifier occurrences. The 'matrix' of a formula is
the result of deleting all quantifier occurrences.

4.3.2 THE SEMANTICS OF A FIRST ORDER LANGUAGE

Interpretations

In order to express assertions about a first order relational structure
U we need to associate a first order language with it. To do this, we
need to define a language L such that we can assign each n-ary relation
in U to an n-ary predicate in L, each n-ary function in U to an n-ary
function symbol in L and each distinguished entity in U to a constant
in L. The function γ which defines these assignments is called an
'interpretation'.

It should be clear that we can associate the language L1 with the
structure U1 by defining an interpretation γ1 such that:

      γ1(Sue) = SUE
      γ1(Bob) = BOB
      γ1(married) = MARRIED
      γ1(20) = TWENTY   (etc.)

Valuations

A valuation or value assignment is a function which assigns entities
of a relational structure to variables of the associated language. For
example, consider the valuation α1 which is defined such that:

      α1(x) = BILL
      α1(y) = BOB
      α1(z) = TWENTY

Semantic values/denotations

The semantic value or denotation of an expression A with respect to a
structure U, an interpretation γ and a valuation α is denoted by:

⟦A⟧U,γ,α

or by the following, when the identity of the structure is obvious from the context:

⟦A⟧γ,α

For example, with respect to U1, γ1 and α1, we have:

(a)   ⟦Sue⟧γ1,α1 = SUE

(b)   ⟦x⟧γ1,α1 = BILL

(c)   ⟦double(20)⟧γ1,α1 = FORTY

Notice, in (c), that the denotation of a function expression is an entity in the associated structure. In general, the semantic value of a function expression f(t1, ..., tn), where t1, ..., tn are terms, is given by:

⟦f⟧γ,α(⟦t1⟧γ,α, ..., ⟦tn⟧γ,α)

That is, the semantic value of a function expression f(t1, ..., tn) is obtained by applying the function which is denoted by (i.e. is the semantic value of) f to the arguments which are denoted by t1 to tn.

Satisfaction of formulas
The satisfaction of a formula A of a language L by a structure U with respect to an interpretation γ and a valuation α, is denoted by:

U ⊨ A[γ,α]

and is defined as follows:

(a)   If p(t1, ..., tn) is an atomic formula of L then:

U ⊨ p(t1, ..., tn) iff <⟦t1⟧γ,α, ..., ⟦tn⟧γ,α> ∈ ⟦p⟧γ,α

i.e. U satisfies an atomic formula p(t1, ..., tn) with respect to an interpretation γ and a valuation α if and only if <e1, ..., en> ∈ r where r is the relation assigned to p by γ, and ei is the entity assigned to ti by γ or α (this may involve calculating the semantic value of terms if functions are involved).

(b)   If A and B are wffs of L, and v is a variable of L then:

(i)   U ⊨ [A][γ,α] iff U ⊨ A[γ,α], this takes care of square brackets

(ii)   U ⊨ ¬A[γ,α] iff it is not the case that U ⊨ A[γ,α]

(iii)   U ⊨ A ∧ B[γ,α] iff U ⊨ A[γ,α] and U ⊨ B[γ,α]

(iv)   U ⊨ A ∨ B[γ,α] iff U ⊨ A[γ,α] or U ⊨ B[γ,α]

(v)   U ⊨ A → B[γ,α] iff U ⊨ ¬A[γ,α] or U ⊨ B[γ,α]

(vi)   U ⊨ A ↔ B[γ,α] iff U ⊨ A → B[γ,α] and U ⊨ B → A[γ,α]

(vii) U ⊨ ∃v A[γ,α] iff there exists an entity e in U such
that U ⊨ A[γ,α'], where α' is identical to α except
that α'(v) = e whatever α(v) might be

(viii) U ⊨ ∀v A[γ,α] iff for all entities c in U, it is the
case that U ⊨ A[γ,α'] where α' is identical to α
except that α'(v) = e, whatever α(v) might be

For example, consider the language L1, the structure U1, the interpretation γ1 and the valuation α1 given above:

(a) U1 ⊨ married(Sue, Bob)[γ1,α1] since <SUE, BOB> ∈ MARRIED

(b) U1 ⊨ aged(Sue, 20)[γ1,α1] since <SUE, TWENTY> ∈ AGED

(c) U1 ⊨ aged(y, 30)[γ1,α1] since <BOB, THIRTY> ∈ AGED

(d) U1 ⊨ ∃x aged(x, 20)[γ1,α1] since <SUE, TWENTY> ∈ AGED that is,
we can define α' such that α'(x) = SUE

(e) U1 ⊨ ¬aged(Bob, 20)[γ1,α1] since it is not the case that
U1 ⊨ aged(Bob, 20)

(f) U1 ⊨ ∀x ¬aged(x, 60)[γ1,α1] since, for all entities e in U1,
U1 ⊨ ¬aged(x, 60)[γ1,α'] where α'(x) = e

To explain this last example, consider all entities e in U1. Since in
no case is <e, sixty> ∈ AGED, we can see that for no entity e can we
find a valuation α which assigns e to x such that U1 ⊨ aged(x, 60).

The satisfaction of a formula by a structure, with respect to an interpretation, does not depend on all the arguments of a valuation, but
only on those arguments which are free variables in that formula. Since
there are only a finite number of free variables in a given formula A,
the following notation may be used to denote satisfaction:

U ⊨ A[γ, e1, ..., en]

where e1, ..., en are the values of the valuation α on the free variables of A. For example, consider U1, γ1, and the formula 'married(x,
y)' of L1:

U1 ⊨ married(x, y)[γ1, SUE, BOB]

That is, 'married(x, y)' is satisfied in U1, with respect to the interpretation γ1, by any valuation α in which α(x) = SUE and α(y) = BOB.

Truth and models
If, for every possible valuation α, it is the case that U ⊨ A[γ,α], then
the formula A is said to be true in U with respect to γ. (In other
terminology, U is said to satisfy A with respect to γ.) This is denoted
by:

U ⊨ A[γ]

or by the following, if the interpretation is obvious from the context:

U ⊨ A

As example, consider U1, γ1 and L1 above:

    U1 $\models$ married(Sue, Bob)
    U1 $\models$ ∃x aged(x, 20)

The first example is obviously correct since there are no free variables in the formula, hence different valuations will have no effect. The second example is correct since in all valuations α there exists an entity SUE in U1 such that we can define a valuation α', where α'(x) = SUE, giving U1 $\models$ aged(x, 20)[γ1,α'].

If S is a set of formulas of a language L associated with a structure U, then U is a 'model' of the set S (denoted by U $\models$ S) iff for every formula A in S, U $\models$ A. Notice that we have assumed the existence of an appropriate interpretation γ in the above.

For example, consider the following set of formulas of L1:

    S1 = {married(Sue, Bob),
               ¬married(Sue, Bill),
               [aged(Sue, 20) ∧ aged(Bob, 30)],
               ∀x∀y[married(x, y) → married(y, x)],
               ∃x aged(20)   }

The structure U1 is a model of S1.

The above definition of truth may seem somewhat complex. However, such exact definition will be seen to be useful when we come to use logic to formalise various database notions such as 'integrity' which are often only described in vague terms.

Readers who are daunted by the definitions given above should not despair. They are difficult to everyone who is approaching logic for the first time. If you have difficulty in understanding them, ask someone to explain them to you. Familiarity with such concepts will help you understand many aspects of computer science normally regarded as being difficult. For example, the use of denotational semantics in the formal definition of programming languages (described in chapter 11) uses similar concepts and notation. Another example is the automatic translation of natural language using Montague's approach (described in chapter 6). This requires an understanding of the concepts described above.

Logical consequence (semantic consequence)
A formula F is a 'logical consequence' of a set of formulas S iff F is true in every model of S. This is denoted by:

    S $\models$ F

For example, 'married(Bob, Sue)' is a logical consequence of S1 above, i.e. S $\models$ married(Bob, Sue).

Note that the symbol $\models$ has now been used to denote two concepts. The intended use will always be obvious from the context.

Formal systems
A formal (or axiom) system consists of:

- a formal language
- a set of logical axioms
- a set of rules of inference

The logical axioms are formulas which are universally valid, e.g.:

$$A \wedge B \rightarrow A$$

The rules of inference allow new formulas to be generated from existing formulas as, for example, in this instance of the use of a rule called 'modus ponens':

From A and A → B, generate B.

The generated formula is said to be a 'theorem' of the formulas from which it was generated.

Axiomatisation of first order predicate logic
The following formal system is an axiomatisation of first order predicate logic:

(a) The language is a formal language as described earlier.

(b) The logical axioms are specified by the following axiom schemas:

$$A1 : \quad A \vee A \rightarrow A$$
$$A2 : \quad A \rightarrow A \vee B$$
$$A3 : \quad A \vee B \rightarrow B \vee A$$
$$A4 : \quad [A \rightarrow B] \rightarrow [[C \vee A] \rightarrow [C \vee B]]$$
$$A5 : \quad \forall v1 \ A(v1) \rightarrow A(v2)$$
$$A6 : \quad A(v1) \rightarrow \exists v2 \ A(v2)$$

Note that these are axiom schemas from which axioms can be generated by substitution of formulas for the 'formula variables' A and B. For example, substituting the formula P(x) for A, and the formula Q(x) for B in A3 gives the following logical axiom:

$$P(x) \vee Q(x) \rightarrow Q(x) \vee P(x)$$

In A5 and A6, the 'syntactic variables' v1 and v2 range over the 'individual variables' x,y,z, etc., of the language. In these two schemas, the presence of v1 or v2 after an A or B indicates that an allowed substitution is any formula of the language containing an 'individual variable'. For example, the formulas:

$$P(x), \ R(x,y), \ \neg Q(x), \ \forall x \ P(x), \ P(x) \rightarrow Q(x)$$

Hence, among the substitution instances of A5 are the axioms:

222

$\forall x\ P(x) \rightarrow P(y)$
$\forall x\ R(x,\ y) \rightarrow R(z,\ y)$
$\forall y\ R(x,\ y) \rightarrow R(x,\ z)$ (etc.)

Such substitution is subject to the restriction that no variable free in A before substitution becomes bound in A after the substitution.

(c)   The inference rules are the following, in which A and B are 'formula variables':

- modus ponens

  from A and A $\rightarrow$ B infer B

- replacement

from A $\rightarrow$ B	infer $\neg$A $\vee$ B
from $\neg$A $\vee$ B	infer A $\rightarrow$ B
from A $\wedge$ B	infer $\neg[\neg$A $\vee \neg$B$]$
from $\neg[\neg$A $\vee \neg$B$]$	infer A $\wedge$ B

- introducing the universal quantifier

  from B $\rightarrow$ A(v)   infer B $\rightarrow$ $\forall$v A(v)

  where A(v) stands for any formula in which a variable v occurs free, and B for any formula in which v does not occur free

- introducing the existential quantifier

  from A(v) $\rightarrow$ B   infer $\exists$v A(v) $\rightarrow$ B

  with the same proviso as above

This formal system will be referred to as FS1.

The theorems of predicate logic
The logical axiom schemas and inference rules of FS1 may be used to generate all of the theorems of first order predicate logic. Examples of some of these theorems are:

$\forall x\ P(x) \rightarrow \neg\exists x\ \neg P(x)$
$\forall x\ [Q(x) \vee \neg Q(x)]$
$\forall x\ [P(x) \wedge Q(x)] \rightarrow [\forall x\ P(x) \wedge \forall x\ Q(x)]$
$\forall x\ [\neg[P(x) \wedge Q(x)] \rightarrow [\neg P(x) \vee \neg Q(x)]]$

Because the language of predicate logic contains an infinite number of predicate symbols and variables, there are an infinite number of theorems.

For example, since 'person' is an allowed predicate symbol, the following is a theorem of predicate logic:

$\forall x\ person(x) \rightarrow \neg\exists x\ \neg person(x)$

Predicate logic can be axiomatised in various ways by choosing different logical axioms and inference rules. For the axiomatisation to be 'complete', all of the theorems of predicate logic must be derivable in it. FS1 is a complete axiomatisation of first order predicate logic.

Theories

A theory is a formal system plus a set of 'non-logical axioms' (sometimes called 'proper' axioms). The following is a theory in first order predicate logic, which will be referred to as T1:

> FS1
>
> +
>
> P1 : married(Sue, Bob) ⎞
> P2 : ¬married(Sue, Bill) ⎟
> P3 : [aged(Sue, 20) ∧ aged(Bob 30)] ⎬ S1 the set of
> P4 : ∀x∀y[married(x, y) → married(y, x)] ⎟ proper axioms
> P5 : ∃x aged(x, 40) ⎠

The theorems of this theory are all of those formulas which can be derived from the logical *and* proper axioms by use of the inference rules.

The existence of a derivation, or 'proof', of a formula F from a theory T consisting of a formal system FS and a set of proper axioms S, is denoted by:

> T ⊢ F
>
> or
>
> S ⊢ F
> FS

If the formal system is assumed to be known, then this can be abbreviated to:

> S ⊢ F

With respect to the theory T1 above, the following proofs exist, among others:

> S1 ⊢—— married(Bob, Sue)
> FS1
>
> S1 ⊢—— aged(Sue, 20)
> FS1

Consistency

A theory T is 'inconsistent' if for any formula F, F and ¬F are both theorems of T. That is, if the set of theorems of a theory contains a contradiction, then that theory is inconsistent. A theory which is not inconsistent, is 'consistent'.

Decidability

A formal system FS is 'decidable' if it is always possible to determine whether or not a theory T in FS is consistent or not. A formal system is 'semi-decidable' if it is always possible to determine inconsistency but only sometimes possible to determine consistency. Full predicate logic is semi-decidable. Function-free predicate logic is decidable. It is important to note that by 'function-free' we mean that no function symbols are allowed and, therefore, skolematisation of formulas (see later) must not result in skolem functions. We do not want to go into details here, and it is sufficient to state that no skolem functions will occur when skolematising, *provided that no existentially bound variable in an unskolematised formula is within the scope of a universal quantifier*. For example, the following formula would not be allowed:

$\forall x \exists y \, [\text{parent}(x) \rightarrow \text{child}(y)]$

This formula may be read as 'there exists a child for every parent'. However, the following would be allowed:

$\forall x \, \text{believes-in-god}(x) \rightarrow \exists y \, \text{god}(y)$

This may be read as 'if all things believe in god, then there exists a god'.

The relationship between formal systems and models
A formal system FS is sound iff:

$$S \vdash_{FS} F \text{ implies } S \vDash F$$

That is, a formal system FS is sound iff all theorems which can be proved from a set S of axioms in a theory in FS are also logical consequences of S.

A formal system FS is complete iff:

$$S \vDash F \text{ implies } S \vdash_{FS} F$$

That is, a formal system FS is complete iff for all formulas which are logical consequences of a set of axioms S there exists a proof from S in FS. The formal system FS1 described earlier is both sound and complete. Systems which include appropriate transformation rules together with the resolution inference rule are also sound and complete. (See later for a description of resolution in predicate logic.)

A theory in a sound and complete formal system is consistent iff it has a model (hence, this is another method of determining consistency which can be used in some cases). A consistent theory is said to 'admit' a set of one or more models. In effect, a consistent theory may be regarded as specifying a set of 'allowed' relational structures.

4.3.3 NATURAL DEDUCTION IN PREDICATE LOGIC
Some of the methods described in 4.2 for reasoning in propositional logic can be extended for use in predicate logic. Additional equivalence and inference rules are required, some of which are described below:

Equivalence rules (or quantifier replacement q.r. rules)

$$\forall x\ F \equiv \neg \exists x\ \neg F$$
$$\forall x\ \neg F \equiv \neg \exists x\ F$$
$$\neg \forall x\ F \equiv \exists x\ \neg F$$
$$\neg \forall x\ \neg F \equiv \exists x\ F$$
$$\left.\begin{array}{l} \forall x\ F \vee G \equiv \forall x[F \vee G] \\ \forall x\ F \wedge G \equiv \forall x[F \wedge G] \\ \exists x\ F \vee G \equiv \exists x[F \vee G] \\ \exists x\ F \wedge G \equiv \exists x[F \wedge G] \end{array}\right\} \text{ for closed formulas}$$
$$\forall x[F \wedge G] \equiv \forall x\ F \wedge \forall x\ G$$
$$\exists x[F \vee G] \equiv \exists x\ F \vee \exists x\ G$$

Inference rules

(a) Universal instantiation (u.i.):

   from $\forall x\ Fx$ infer Fa where a is any constant of the theory.

(b) Particular generalisation (p.g.):

   from Fa infer $\exists x\ Fx$

In this example Fa stands for any formula with a as a term. For example from the formula:

   person(John) $\wedge$ aged(John,24)

we can infer the following:

   $\exists x[person(x) \wedge aged(x, 24)]$

(c) Universal generalisation (u.g.):

   from Fa infer $\forall x\ Fx$

For this to be possible, a must not be the subject of a premise or an undischarged assumption. (See the example below for clarification.)

(d) Particular instantiation (p.i.):

   from $\exists x\ Fx$ infer H

See the example below for an illustratory explanation of this rule of inference.

All of the inference rules and equivalences of propositional logic also apply in predicate logic.

Example
The following is an example of a natural deduction proof in predicate logic. (Refer back to 4.2.2 if you have forgotten how to use the exploitation and introduction rules.)

1.	$\neg \exists x\ \neg[P(x) \wedge Q(x)]$	given
2.	$\forall x[S(x) \rightarrow T(x)]$	given
3.	$\neg \forall x\ \neg[S(x) \wedge L(x)]$	given
4.	$\exists x[S(x) \wedge L(x)]$	from 3 and q.r.
5.1	$S(a) \wedge L(a)$	supposition

5.2	S(a) → T(a)	from 2 and u.i.
5.3	S(a)	from 5.1 and ∧-exploitation
5.4	T(a)	from 5.2, 5.3, and modus ponens
5.5	∃x T(x)	from 5.4 and p.g.
6.	∃x T(x)	from 4, 5.1 to 5.5, and p.i.
7.	∀x[P(x) ∧ Q(x)]	from 1 and q.r.
8.	P(a) ∧ Q(a)	from 7 and u.i.
9.	P(a)	from 8 and ∧-exploitation
10.	∀x P(x)	from 9 and u.g.
11.	¬∃x ¬P(x)	from 10 and q.r.
12.	¬∃x ¬P(x) ∧ ∃x T(x)	from 11, 6 and ∧-introduction

For further information on reasoning in predicate logic using non-uniform techniques the reader is referred to Kozy (1974).

We now turn our attention to uniform proof procedures in predicate logic and begin by considering how to use equivalence rules, and other rules, to convert formulas to various simplified forms which can then be manipulated by uniform proof methods. The simplified forms which will be considered are called prenex form, functional form, skolem normal form, conjunctive normal form and clausal form.

4.3.4 PRENEX FORM
Let F and G be formulas. F and G are equivalent, F ↔ G, iff for every structure U and every function α appropriate to both, U ⊨ F[α] implies U ⊨ G[α], and U ⊨ G[α] implies U ⊨ F[α].

The following are examples of equivalences which hold for closed formulas:

$$
\begin{aligned}
\neg\forall x F &\equiv \exists x \neg F \\
\neg\exists x\ F &\equiv \forall x \neg F \\
\forall x\ F \lor G &\equiv \forall x[F \lor G] \\
\forall x\ F \land G &\equiv \forall x[F \land G] \\
\exists x\ F \lor G &\equiv \exists x[F \lor G] \\
\exists x\ F \land G &\equiv \exists x[F \land G] \\
\forall x[F \land G] &\equiv \forall x\ F \land \forall x\ G \\
\exists x[F \lor G] &\equiv \exists x\ F \lor \exists x\ G
\end{aligned}
$$

In addition all equivalences which hold in the propositional logic involving the logical connectives also hold in predicate logic.

If all the quantifiers of a formula are at the left end, that is F is of the form qv1, ..., qvn G where q = ∀ or ∃ and G has no quantifiers, then F is in 'prenex' form. Transforming a formula to prenex form involves:

(a) Rectifying the formula by renaming variables so that no variable has both free and bound occurrences, and so that there is at most one occurrence of a quantifier with any particular variable.

(b) Applying equivalences to pull the quantifiers to the left end.

For example, the prenex form of:

∃x[Q(x) ∧ [∀y P(x, y) ∨ ¬∀y Q(y)]] ∧ R(x)

is

∃z∀y∃w[[Q(z) ∧ [P(z, y) ∨ ¬Q(w)]] ∧ R(x)

4.3.5 FUNCTIONAL FORM AND SKOLEM NORMAL FORM

Any closed formula F may be transformed to a form called 'functional form' which is equivalent to F. This form is useful for reasons which will become apparent in later sub-sections. The transformation process involves:

(a)   Rectifying the formula, if it is not already rectified.

(b)   For each negative occurrence of a quantifier q, let x be the variable bound by that occurrence, let G be the scope of that occurrence, and let v1, ..., vn be in order the variables bound by those positive occurrences of quantifiers in whose scopes the sub-formula qxG occurs. Then choose a new n-place function sign f (called a 'skolem function') not used elsewhere in the formula, and replace the sub-formula qx G by H where H is identical to G except that x is replaced by f(v1, ..., vn). Where f is a nullary function it is called a 'skolem constant'.

Step (b) is repeated until no more negative occurrences of quantifiers remain.

Note that an occurrence of a universal quantifier is positive if it is in the scope of an even number of ¬ symbols; otherwise it is negative. The converse holds for existential quantifiers. For example, consider the formula:

∀x∃y hasfather(x, y) ∧ ∃x∀y ¬hasfather(y, x)

The following formula is the functional form of the above. Note that f is a skolem function and c is a skolem constant:

∀x∀z hasfather(x, f(x)) ∧ ¬hasfather(z, c)

This formula may be read as 'for all x and for all z, x has a father f(x), and there is someone, c, who is not the father of z'. That is, everyone has a dad but there exists someone who is no one's dad. An example of the use of functional form is given in sub-section 4.3.6.

The body of the functional form of a formula F is called the 'skolem normal form' of F. Bundy (1983, pages 214-216) describes a recursive procedure for transforming formulas to skolem normal form. Other procedures can be defined which involve converting F to prenex normal form first and then to skolem normal form.

Some examples are now given of formulas in standard and skolem normal form, together with an intuitive description of what they mean:

(a)   ∃x ¬secretary(x)
       read as 'there exists an x (i.e. an entity) which is not a

228

secretary'. The skolem normal form of this is:

¬secretary(c)

where c is a skolem constant. This can be read as 'c is not a secretary'.

(b) ∀x∃y[person(x) → hasfather(x, y)]
read as 'for all x, if x is a person then there exists an entity y such that x hasfather y'. The skolem normal form of this is:

person(x) → hasfather(x, dad(x))

which can be read as 'for all x, if x is a person then x has a father referred to as dad(x)'. In this example, 'dad' is a skolem function and 'dad(x)' identifies the entity which is the father of x.

(c) ∀x∃y[teacher(x) → [teaches(x, y) ∧ student(y)]]
which may be read as 'for all x, if x is a teacher then there exists an entity y such that x teaches y and y is a student'. The skolem normal form of this is:

teacher(x) → [teaches(x, pupilof(x))

∧ student(pupilof(x))]

Note that in these examples arbitrary but suitable names have been chosen for the skolem constants and functions.

All variables in the skolem normal form of a formula are implicitly universally quantified.

4.3.6 THE HERBRAND EXPANSION OF A CLOSED FORMULA
The 'Herbrand expansion' HE(F) of a closed formula F is a set of quantifier and variable-free formulas derived from F by the process described below.

(a) Transform F to skolem normal form.

(b) Obtain the 'Herbrand universe' HU(F) of F as follows:

(i) HU(F) includes all constant signs (skolem or not) which are present in the skolem normal form of F. If there are no constant signs then HU(F) includes a special constant 'h'.

(ii) If t1, ..., tn ∈ HU(F) and f is an n-place function sign (skolem or not) occurring in the skolem normal form of F, then f(t1, ..., tn) ∈ HU(F).

(c) The Herbrand expansion is obtained by consistently substituting terms from the Herbrand universe for variables in the skolem normal form of F in all possible ways.

It can be seen that the Herbrand universe of a formula F whose skolem normal form contains any non-nullary function signs (skolem or not) with any variable arguments, is infinite. If HU(F) is infinite, then HE(F) is infinite.

As example of an infinite Herbrand expansion, consider the following formula:

$$\forall x \exists y \text{ hasfather}(x, y) \land \exists x \forall y \neg \text{hasfather}(y, x)$$

which may be read as 'for all entities x in the universe of discourse there exists another entity y who is the father of x, and there exists in the universe of discourse an entity who is not the father of any entity'.

(a) Rectifying the formula gives:

$$\forall x \exists y \text{ hasfather}(x, y) \land \exists w \forall z \neg \text{hasfather}(z, w)$$

(b) The functional form is:

$$\forall x \forall z \text{ hasfather}(x, f(x)) \land \neg \text{hasfather}(z, c)$$

where f is a skolem function and c a skolem constant.

(c) The skolem normal form is:

$$\text{hasfather}(x, f(x)) \land \neg \text{hasfather}(z, c)$$

(d) The Herbrand universe is:

$$\{c, f(c), f(f(c)), f(f(f(c))), \ldots, \text{etc.}\}$$

(e) The Herbrand expansion is:

$$\{\text{hasfather}(c, f(c)) \land \neg \text{hasfather}(c, c),$$
$$\text{hasfather}(f(c), f(f(c))) \land \neg \text{hasfather}(c, c)$$
$$\text{hasfather}(c, f(c)) \land \neg \text{hasfather}(f(c), c)$$

(etc.)}

As example of a finite Herbrand expansion, consider the following closed formula which contains no function signs and no negative quantifiers (i.e. its skolem normal form contains only nullary function signs):

$$\forall x [\text{employed by}(x, \text{IBM}) \rightarrow \text{has tie colour}(x, \text{blue})]$$

(a) The skolem normal form is:

$$\text{employed by}(x, \text{IBM}) \rightarrow \text{has tie colour}(x, \text{blue})$$

(b) The Herbrand universe is:

$$\{\text{IBM}, \text{blue}\}$$

(c) The Herbrand expansion is:

$$\{\text{employed by}(\text{IBM}, \text{IBM}) \rightarrow \text{has tie colour}(\text{IBM}, \text{blue})$$
$$\text{employed by}(\text{blue}, \text{IBM}) \rightarrow \text{has tie colour}(\text{blue}, \text{blue})\}$$

4.3.7 CONSISTENCY OF CLOSED FORMULAS AND THE HERBRAND EXPANSION

There is no simple truth table method which can be used, in general, to determine the satisfiability of some formula F of predicate logic. One problem is that there are an infinite number of structures to be considered as interpretations of F. Another problem is that some structures have infinite domains and, even worse, some formulas have infinite satisfying interpretations but no finite satisfying interpretations. In fact, the problem of proving satisfiability is, in general, undecidable in predicate logic. However, it is possible in general to prove unsatisfiability and, in some cases, to prove satisfiability using standard methods. One of these methods involves the Herbrand expansion and is a consequence of Herbrand's theorem which states that 'a formula of predicate logic is satisfiable iff its Herbrand expansion is propositionally satisfiable'. (A proof of this theorem is given in Bridge (1977).) Two cases will be considered here.

To determine the consistency of a closed formula F whose Herbrand expansion is infinite

- (i) Let B = { }.

- (ii) Generate a larger sub-set B' of HE(F) such that B ⊆ B'.

- (iii) Test to see if B' is satisfiable by trying all permutations of truth assignments for the atomic formulas in B'.

- (iv) If B' is unsatisfiable then stop, since HE(F) must also be unsatisfiable (this is a consequence of the compactness theorem of propositional logic - see Bridge (1977)); otherwise let B = B' and go to (ii).

In this case, if F is unsatisfiable then we shall find some finite (although possibly very large) sub-set of HE(F) which is unsatisfiable. However, if F is satisfiable we shall go on for ever and never be able to prove satisfiability.

To determine the consistency of a closed formula F whose Herbrand expansion is finite

- (i) Generate the whole finite Herbrand expansion HE(F).

- (ii) Search for a satisfying truth assignment HE(F) by trying permutations of truth assignments for the atomic formulas in HE(F).

- (iii) If a satisfying truth assignment is found then F is satisfiable. If all permutations of truth assignments are tried and no satisfying truth assignment is found, then F is unsatisfiable.

In this case, satisfiability or unsatisfiability can be determined. As illustration, consider the following trivial example:

F = ∀x[employed by(x, IBM) → has tie colour(x, blue)]

The Herbrand expansion is:

HE(F) = {employed by (IBM, IBM) → has tie colour(IBM, blue),
          employed by(blue, IBM) → has tie colour(blue, blue)}

A satisfying truth assignment for this is:

```
{employed by(IBM, IBM) := false,
 employed by(blue, IBM) := false,
 has tie colour(IBM, blue) := false,
 has tie colour(blue, blue) := false}
```

Therefore, F is consistent.

In general, consistency checking and theorem-proving using the Herbrand expansion is not efficient enough to be of practical use. Other methods whose theoretical justifications derive from it and which use resolution are described in sub-sections 4.3.10 and 4.3.11. As introduction to these methods a brief description of conjunctive normal form, clausal form and resolution in predicate logic is given.

4.3.8 CONJUNCTIVE NORMAL FORM AND CLAUSAL FORM

A formula of predicate logic is in conjunctive normal form if it is a conjunction of disjunctions of 'literals', where a literal is an atomic formula or the negation of an atomic formula. For example, the following is in conjunctive normal form:

$$[\neg\text{secretary}(y) \vee \neg\text{lecturer}(y)] \wedge [\text{hasskill}(x, \text{typing}) \vee \neg\text{secretary}(x)]$$

All variables are implicitly universally quantified if the formula is closed.

Any formula of predicate logic can be transformed to an equivalent one in conjunctive normal form, as follows:

(a) Transform to skolem normal form.

(b) Remove → and ↔ using the equivalences:

$$A \rightarrow B \equiv B \vee \neg A$$
$$A \leftrightarrow B \equiv [B \vee \neg A] \wedge [A \vee \neg B]$$

(c) Transform to 'literal normal form' by moving ¬ signs down until they are directly next to atomic formulas, using the equivalences:

$$\neg[A \vee B] \equiv \neg A \wedge \neg B$$
$$\neg[A \wedge B] \equiv \neg A \vee \neg B$$
$$\neg\neg A \equiv A$$

(d) Transform to conjunctive normal form using the equivalences:

$$A \vee [B \wedge C] \equiv [A \vee B] \wedge [A \vee C]$$
$$[B \wedge C] \vee A \equiv [B \vee A] \wedge [C \vee A]$$

Clausal form

A 'clause' is a finite set of literals and a 'clause set' is a set of clauses. Any formula can be converted to clausal form by putting it in conjunctive normal form and then treating the disjunctions of literals as clauses. For example, the following is in clausal form:

```
{{¬secretary(y), ¬lecturer(y)},
 {hasskill(x, typing), ¬secretary(x)}}
```

The empty clause is denoted by ⊠ , and the empty clause set by φ.
Variable-free clauses are called 'ground clauses'. If C is a set of
clauses and D is some set of terms, then we write E(C,D) for the set
of all 'ground clause instances' of clauses in C which are obtained by
substituting variables in C by terms from D in all possible ways.

4.3.9 RESOLUTION IN PREDICATE LOGIC
Resolution can be used in predicate logic to generate new clauses
called 'resolvents' from sets of clauses. This use is similar to that
in propositional logic but involves a procedure called 'unification'
in which complementary literals in a pair of clauses are made identical,
apart from negation signs, by substitution of terms. Before any more
detailed description,use of the resolution inference rule can be illustrated by example:

$$\frac{C1 : \{employee(x), \neg manager(x)\}, C2 : \{manager(w), \neg senior\ manager(w)\}}{C3 : \{employee(x), \neg senior\ manager(x)\}}$$

In English, C1 states that if someone is a manager then he is an
employee, and C2 states that if someone is a senior manager then he is
a manager, and from these two formulas we can derive C3 using the
resolution rule. C3 states that if someone is a senior manager then he
is an employee.

Note that a clause {L1, ¬L2} is equivalent to the formula L2 → L1. The
English interpretation of the clauses which is given above regards the
clauses as being of the form L2 → L1 since this is a more natural way
of expressing this type of formula.

Note, also, that in this example the complementary literals which
cancel against each other are ¬manager(x) and manager(w). They are
made equal, apart from the negation sign, by the substitution [w/x].

The English interpretation has been described to show that the resolution inference rule is one that we use in everyday reasoning. The
notation:

$$\frac{C1, C2}{C3}$$

means C3 can be derived from C1 and C2. This is a convenient notation
which we shall use in a few more examples below.

$$\frac{\{hasskill(x, typing), \neg secretary(x)\}, \{secretary(Sally)\}}{\{hasskill(Sally, typing)\}}$$

This is an example showing the substitution of a variable by a constant.
In English, this states that 'if someone is a secretary then she has
skill typing', that 'Sally is a secretary' and that from these assertions we can infer that 'Sally has skill typing'.

$$\frac{\{>(x, y), \neg elephant(x), \neg rat(y)\}, \{elephant(w), \neg hastusk(w, y), \neg ivory(y)\}}{\{>(x, y), \neg rat(y), \neg hastusk(x, z), \neg ivory(z)\}}$$

This resolvent may not be the one you are expecting. However, it is correct, and its generation is explained as follows. The example illustrates that care must be taken when resolving two clauses with non-disjoint sets of variables. The coincidental presence of the variable y in both parent clauses should not be allowed to pollute the resolvent. That is, the following is not a correct resolvent:

$\{>(x, y), \neg rat(y), \neg hastusk(x, y), \neg ivory(y)\}$

Intuitively, we can see that this is an incorrect inference if we transform the parent clauses back to standard form giving:

F1 : $\forall x \forall y [[elephant(x) \land rat(y)] \rightarrow >(x, y)]$
F2 : $\forall w \forall y [[hastusk(w, y) \land ivory(y)] \rightarrow elephant(w)]$

We can now see that F3 but not F4 follows from F1 and F2:

F3 : $\forall x \forall y \forall z [[rat(y) \land hastusk(x, z) \land ivory(z)] \rightarrow >(x, y)]$
F4 : $\forall x \forall y [[rat(y) \land hastusk(x, y) \land ivory(y)] \rightarrow >(x,y)]$

In this example, the correct resolvent is obtained by making substitutions such that the resolving clauses have no variables in common. This process, called 'standardising apart' the variables in the two clauses, involves the consistent renaming of variables. In this example, the renaming, or substitution, used before resolution, was:

$\{elephant(w), \neg hastusk(w, y), \neg ivory(y)\}$
$\downarrow$ standardised to
$\{elephant(w), \neg hastusk(w, z), \neg ivory(z)\}$

The next example illustrates that more than one literal in a parent clause can be resolved away:

$$\frac{\{man(x), man(y), \neg inlovewith(x, y)\}, \{male(z), \neg man(z)\}}{\{male(z), \neg inlovewith(z, z)\}}$$

This is called 'full resolution', as opposed to binary resolution where only two literals, one from each parent, are involved.

Full resolution can be broken down into two phases: factoring and binary resolution. 'Factoring' involves one parent at a time and is concerned with merging unifiable literals in a single clause. For example:

$\{man(x), man(y), \neg inlovewith(x, y)\}$ factors to $\{man(x),$
$\neg inlovewith(x, x)\}$

The two-factored parent clauses may then be resolved using binary resolution.

Whichever method is used, it is necessary to find what is known as the 'most general unifier' of the literals being unified. (A unification algorithm is described shortly.)

To describe resolution and unification more fully, we introduce some terminology:

234

(a) A *substitution* is a finite set {v1/t1, ..., vn/tn} where every
     vi is a variable, and every ti is a term different from vi,
     and no two elements in the set have the same variable before
     the stroke symbol.   The following sets are examples of substi-
     tutions:

     {x/f(z), z/y}, {x/a, y/g(y), z/f(g(John))}

(b) Let θ = {v1/t1, ..., vn/tn} be a substitution and E be an
     expression.   Then Eθ is an expression obtained from E by re-
     placing, simultaneously, each occurrence of the variable vi
     ($1 \leqslant i \leqslant n$) in E by the term ti.   Eθ is called an *instance*
     of E.

(c) The *composition* of two substitutions, θ = {x1/t1, ..., xn/tn}
     and λ = {y1/u1, ..., ym/um}, is the substitution, denoted by
     θ ∘ λ, that is obtained from the intermediate set:

     {x1/t1λ, ..., xn/tnλ, y1/u1, ..., ym/um}

     by deleting any element xj/tjλ for which xj = tjλ, and any
     element yi/ui where yi is among {x1, x2, ..., xn}.   For
     example, suppose θ = {x/f(y), y/z} and λ = {x/John, y/Bill,
     z/y}.   Then the intermediate set is:

     {x/f(Bill), y/y, x/John, y/Bill, z/y}

     and the elements y/y, x/John, and y/Bill need to be deleted,
     according to the definition above.   This gives:

     θ ∘ λ = {x/f(Bill), z/y}

(d) A *disagreement pair* is a pair of non-identical terms which
     occupy the same position in the argument lists of two literals
     with the same predicate sign.

(e) A *non-redundant instance* of a clause C, denoted by Cγ, is any
     clause which is obtained from C by a substitution γ followed
     by the merging of identical literals in C.

(f) Two literals are a *complementary pair* if they have the same
     predicate sign and one is positive and the other negative,
     e.g. elephant(w) and ¬elephant(x).

(g) A *separating pair* of substitutions, γ, λ for two clauses C1
     and C2 are substitutions such that the instances C1γ and C2λ
     have no variable in common.

(h) A substitution γ is called a *unifier* for a set of expressions
     {E1, E2, ..., Ek} iff E1γ = E2γ = ... = Ekγ.   The set
     {E1, E2, ..., Ek} is said to be 'unifiable' iff there is a
     unifier for it.

(i) A unifier θ for a set of expressions {E1, E2, ..., Ek} is a
     most general unifier iff for each unifier γ for the set, there
     is a substitution λ such that γ = θ ∘ λ.

We can now describe a procedure for obtaining the resolvent of two clauses C1, C2 with respect to a complementary pair of literals $\langle L, \neg L\rangle$ where L $\in$ C1 and $\neg$L $\in$ C2:

(a)   Use the unification procedure described below to factor C1 w.r.t. L by unifying and merging L with all unifiable literals in C1.   Factor C2 w.r.t. $\neg$L in a similar way.   The factored clauses will be non-redundant instances which we shall denote by C1', C2'.   The unified literals will be L' and $\neg$L'.

(b)   Find a separating pair of substitutions γ, λ for C1' and C2'. This is necessary to overcome any problems which might arise from the coincidental presence of common variables in C1' and C2'.

(c)   Use the unification procedure to find the most general unifier θ, of L'γ and $\neg$L'λ. FAIL if no unifier exists (this means C1 and C2 cannot be resolved w.r.t. L and $\neg$L).

(d)   If a unifier exists then the resolvent of C1, and C2 w.r.t. L and $\neg$L is:

$$\{\{C1'\gamma - L'\gamma\} \cup \{C2'\lambda - \neg L'\lambda\}\}\theta$$

The following unification procedure is described using a mixture of English and Pascal.   This procedure may be used in factoring to find the most general unifier of a set of literals, or in binary resolution to find the most general unifier of two literals.   It is assumed that the literals to be unified have had their negation signs (if any) removed, and that in the case of binary resolution the literals have no variables in common, i.e. a separating pair of substitutions has already been applied if necessary.

```
procedure unify (C : a set of literals to be unified ; var S :
                                                  a substitution)

begin
    if there is only one literal in C or if the literals are identical
        then SUCCEED with S as the most general unifier
        else begin
                find the first disagreement pair <t1, t2> of any two
                                                  literals in C;
                if t1 is variable which does not occur in t2
                    then unify (C{t1/t2}, S U {t1/t2})

                    else if t2 is a variable which does not occur
                                                              in t1
                        then unify (C{t2/t1}, S U {t2/t1})
                        else FAIL, there is no unifier
             end
end
```

To use this procedure to unify a set of literals, SL, we would call unify (SL, { }).

The need for the 'occurs' tests in this procedure is clearly explained in Bundy (1983). As example of what is meant by 'occurs', consider the following: the variable x occurs in the term f(x) where f is a function sign.

A more formal description of resolution can be found in Chang and Lee (1973).

The unification algorithm - an example
Consider the following set of two literals:

W = {P(John, x, f(g(y))), P(z, f(z), f(u))}

(a)　We begin by calling unify(W, { }).

(b)　Since W contains more than one literal, we identify the first disagreement pair = <John, z>.

(c)　Since z is a variable which does not occur in John, we call

unify(W1, {z/John}), where W1 = W{z/John}
This evaluates to {P(John, x, f(g(y))), P(John, f(John),
f(u))}.

(d)　Since W1 contains more than one literal, we identify the first disagreement pair in W1 = <x, f(John)>.

(e)　Since x is a variable which does not occur in f(John), we call

unify(W2, {z/John, x/f(John)}), where W2 = W1{x/f(John)}
This evaluates to {P(John, f(John), f(g(y))), P(John,
f(John), f(u))}.

(f)　Since W2 contains more than one literal, we identify the first disagreement pair in W2 = <g(y), u>.

(g)　Since u is a variable which does not occur in g(y), we call

unify(W3, {z/John, x/f(John), u/g(y)}) where W3 =
W2{u/g(y)}
This evaluates to {P(John, f(John), f(g(y)))}.

Note: W3 contains only one literal, since after the substitution it contained two identical literals which were merged.

(h)　Since W3 contains only one literal, we terminate with success, and with the most general unifier = {z/John, x/f(John),
u/g(y)}.

Self-resolving clauses
A self-resolving clause is one that can resolve with itself. Note that this is different from factorisation. Note, also, that before a self-resolving clause may be resolved with itself, the two copies must have their variables standardised apart.

4.3.10 CONSISTENCY CHECKING USING RESOLUTION

The resolution theorem (see sub-section 4.2.2) also applies to predicate logic. Checking the consistency of a formula or a set of formulas, F, in this case can be carried out as follows:

(a) Transform F to a clause set S.

(b) Find new resolvents of pairs of clauses in S and add them to S.

(c) If ⊠ is ever generated as a resolvent, then stop: F is unsatisfiable.

(d) If no more resolvents can be generated from S, then stop: F must be satisfiable. Otherwise go back to (b).

Unsatisfiability can always be established in a finite amount of time if enough resources are available. Satisfiability can only be established if there are a finite number of resolvents of F.

4.3.11 THEOREM-PROVING IN PREDICATE LOGIC USING RESOLUTION

To prove, in some cases, that a formula F is or is not a theorem of some theory T, a refutation procedure similar to the one used in propositional logic can be used.

(a) Transform the logical and proper axioms of T to a clause set S.

(b) Transform ¬F to a clause set C.

(c) Let R = S ∪ C.

(d) Repeatedly form resolvents of R and add them to R. If ⊠ is ever generated then F is a theorem of T else if no more resolvents can be formed then F is not a theorem.

Note that for unrestricted predicate logic, in general, the problem of determining if a formula F is a theorem of a theory is semi-decidable. Consider the procedure above: if F is a theorem then it is theoretically possible to generate ⊠ in a finite amount of time given sufficient resources. On the other hand, if F is not a theorem then there are two possibilities: we run out of new resolvents, in which case we conclude that F is not a theorem; otherwise we go on generating new resolvents *ad infinitum*, in which case we cannot prove that F is or is not a theorem. Therefore, although the problem is semi-decidable in general, it is decidable in those cases where there are only a finite number of distinct resolvents.

As an example of this type of resolution theorem-proving, consider the following set S = {A1, A2} where:

A1 = ∀x (x. sameweightas. x)
or   {(x. sameweightas. x)} in clausal form

A2 = ∀x∀y∀z[(x. sameweightas. y) ∧ (z. sameweightas. y)] →
                                       (x. sameweightas. z)
or   {(x. sameweightas. z), ¬(x. sameweightas. y),
                     ¬(z. sameweightas. y)} in clausal form

We now illustrate how to prove that the formula F is a theorem of S, where:

F = ∀x∀y[(x. sameweightas. y) → (y. sameweightas. x)]

Negating F gives:

¬∀x∀y[(x. sameweightas. y) → (y. sameweightas. x)]

Replacing ∀v with ¬∃v¬ gives:

∃x∃y ¬[(x. sameweightas. y) → (y. sameweightas. x)]

(Note that ¬∀x∀y becomes ¬¬∃x¬∀y, which becomes ∃x¬¬∃y¬, which becomes ∃x∃y¬.)

Replacing existentially bound variables with skolem constants gives:

¬(c1. sameweightas. c2) → (c2. sameweightas. c1)   or
¬(c2. sameweightas. c1) ∨ ¬(c1. sameweightas. c2)   by definition
                                                   of →

Transforming to conjunctive normal form gives:

(c1. sameweightas. c2) ∧ ¬(c2. sameweightas. c1)

And finally converting to clausal form gives:

{{(c1. sameweightas. c2)}, {¬(c2. sameweightas. c1)}}

Let us call the two clauses in this clause set F1 and F2. All we have to do to prove that F is a theorem is generate the null clause by resolving F1 and/or F2 against the clausal form of A1 and A2:

$$\frac{F2,\ A2}{\{¬(c2.\ sameweightas.\ y),\ ¬(c1.\ sameweightas.\ y)\}}$$

$$\frac{\{¬(c2.\ sameweightas.\ y),\ ¬(c1.\ sameweightas.\ y)\},\ F1}{\{¬(c2.\ sameweightas.\ c2)\}}$$

$$\frac{\{¬(c2.\ sameweightas.\ c2)\},\ A1}{\boxtimes}$$

Notice that we have used infix notation in this example: the predicate is placed between its two arguments. In later chapters this notation will often be used for readability.

4.4 AUTOMATED THEOREM-PROVING IN FOPL

Various strategies have been developed to speed up theorem-proving in FOPL. Many are based on the procedure described in the last section but attempt to cut down on the amount of work that must be done. In particular, the 'bottom-up' method which has been described is not efficient for theorem-proving.

Some of the methods described in this section are 'top-down' methods which start with the theorem to be proved, negate it and try to find a contradiction to its negation. If a contradiction is found, then the proof is established. (Note that this is distinct from adding the negation to the set and repeatedly forming resolvents until the null clause is derived.)

239

4.4.1 LINEAR INPUT RESOLUTION

To prove F using this method we commence by resolving ¬F with one of the clauses in S to form a resolvent C. C is then resolved with a clause in S to form another resolvent, and so on. For example, suppose S = {A1, A2, A3, A4} where:

    A1 = {¬haswings(x), ¬layseggs(x), isbird(x)}
    A2 = {¬isbird(y), animal(y)}
    A3 = {layseggs(Sally)}
    A4 = {haswings(Sally)}

We now illustrate how linear input resolution would proceed for F = {animal(Sally)}:

$$\frac{\overset{\downarrow}{\{\neg animal(Sally)\}},\ A2}{\{\neg isbird(Sally)\}} \qquad\qquad \text{step 1}$$

$$\frac{\overset{\downarrow}{\{\neg isbird(Sally)\}},\ A1}{\{\neg haswings(Sally),\ \neg layseggs(Sally)\}} \qquad\qquad \text{step 2}$$

$$\frac{\{\neg haswings(Sally),\ \overset{\downarrow}{\neg layseggs(Sally)}\},\ A3}{\{\neg haswings(Sally)\}} \qquad \text{step 3}$$

$$\frac{\overset{\downarrow}{\{\neg haswings(Sally)\}},\ A4}{\boxtimes} \qquad\qquad \text{step 4}$$

The above proves that {animal(Sally)} is a theorem of S. The vertical arrows indicate which literal is unified in each resolution step. In linear input resolution any literal can be chosen for unification provided that the last produced resolvent is used as one parent and the other parent is taken from the clause set S (i.e. from an input clause rather than a derived clause).

Linear input resolution is only complete for Horn clauses.

4.4.2 LUSH RESOLUTION

LUSH stands for 'Linear resolution with Unrestricted Selection function for Horn clauses' (Hill, 1974). It is the same as linear input resolution except that at each resolution step the literal to be used as complement is selected from the last produced resolvent in a pre-defined order. Any order can be chosen, but once it has been chosen that order must be adhered to throughout the process. For example, suppose the order were 'use the leftmost literal which has a complement in the input clause set S'. The refutation search corresponding to the one above would proceed as follows:

    step 1 as above
    step 2 as above

$$\frac{\overset{\downarrow}{\{\neg haswings(Sally)},\ \neg layseggs(Sally)\},\ A4}{\{\neg layseggs(Sally)\}} \qquad \text{step 3'}$$

$\downarrow$
{¬layseggs(Sally)}, A3   step 4'
    ☒

LUSH resolution is only complete for Horn clauses.

4.4.3 SELECTED LITERAL (SL) RESOLUTION

SL resolution (Kowalski and Kuehner, 1971; Loveland, 1969; Reiter, 1971) is a refinement of resolution which is complete for non-Horn clauses. It is similar to LUSH resolution but differs in two respects: (i) the selected literal must be one of the most recently introduced literals and (ii) ancestor resolution is allowed. Ancestor resolution occurs when a clause resolves with one of its ancestors in the derivation which is not one of the original (input) set of clauses.

The following example of SL resolution is derived from one given in Kowalski (1975). Suppose that we have a theory which contains the following set of proper axioms in clausal form:

$\quad$ S = {{¬K, M}, {¬L, K}, {¬K, ¬L}, {¬M, L}}

To prove that the formula ¬[L ∨ K] is a theorem of S, using SL resolution, we proceed as follows:

(a) Negate the formula to be proved giving L ∨ K.

(b) Convert to clausal form giving {L, K}.

(c) Make this clause the top clause of an SL derivation:

$\quad\quad$ {L, K}

(d) Form resolvents and derive the null clause:

step 1	{L, K}, {¬K, M}	using 1st clause in S
	{L, M}	
step 2	{L, M}, {¬M, L}	using 4th clause in S
	{L}	
step 3	{L}, {¬L, K}	using 2nd clause in S
	{K}	
step 4	{K}, {¬K, ¬L}	using 3rd clause in S
	{¬L}	
step 5	{¬L}, {L}	using the ancestor clause
	☒	{L} which was derived in step 2

The above derivation is not the only SL derivation which is possible in this example. Other derivations may be obtained by choosing resolving clauses from S in a different order. The total set of such derivations is called the 'search space' and may be described using a tree structure as illustrated in fig. 4.4.

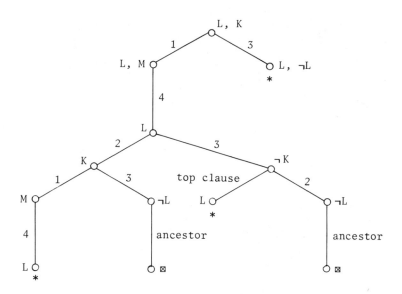

Figure 4.4 A search space for an SL derivation

This tree shows that there are two ways of deriving the null clause. The arc labels indicate which clause is used in the resolution. For example, at the top of the tree two resolutions are possible: one involves the first clause from the input set S (this gives rise to the left sub-tree) and the other involves the third clause from the input set S.

The asterisks in the tree indicate 'inadmissible' derivations, i.e. derivations which are pointless to pursue since, for example, the node marked with the asterisk is identical to one which has occurred higher up in the tree, or the node is a universally valid formula such as {L, ¬L}.

Deficiencies of SL-resolution

(a) The tree in fig. 4.4 illustrates one deficiency of SL resolution: contradictory unit clauses such as K and ¬K, which could result in an immediate derivation of the null clause, can appear on different branches of the search space and cannot therefore be taken advantage of unless the method is extended to include some book-keeping device which checks whenever a unit clause is generated to see if it contradicts some previously generated unit clause.

(b) Although SL resolution does not consider all of the n! ways in which a clause with n literals might be resolved away (as can happen in linear input resolution), other redundancies can occur in an SL search for the null clause. For example, consider the search space which would arise if we attempt to prove the formula ¬[R ∨ ¬M ∨ L] from a clause set which

242

includes the set S above. This search space is illustrated
in fig. 4.5.

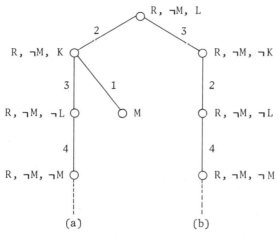

Figure 4.5 Duplication of work in an SL proof

Since R, ¬M, ¬L is derived on two branches, unless a book-
keeping device is used to recognise this, effort will be
duplicated if the branch labelled (a) does not result in the
null clause. That is, the system will search the branch (a)
and later search the branch (b) duplicating all derivations
from the node R, M, ¬L down.

4.4.4 SEARCH STRATEGIES

So far, two different methods for theorem-proving have been mentioned:
bottom-up and top-down. In the bottom-up method, we take the set of
clauses S of the theory and form resolvents of clauses in S, hoping
that the theorem F to be proved will be derived. Alternatively, we
add ¬F to S and repeatedly form resolvents, hoping to generate the
null clause. In this top-down method, we negate F and try to resolve
it away against S (i.e. we try to form the null clause by resolving ¬F
against S).

The bottom-up/top-down direction is not the only property by which
search strategies can be characterised. Consider the search space in
fig. 4.4. This search space illustrates that there are alternative
ways to prove that ¬[L ∨ K] is a theorem of S using the top-down
approach. We have two types of choice when searching for the null
clause: (i) we have the choice of which literal in {L, K} we want to
resolve away and (ii) we have a choice of which clause in S to resolve
with. The first type of choice is not really an alternative since all
literals in {L, K} must ultimately be resolved away and in SL resolution the choice is limited anyway. However, the second choice does
determine which of the alternative ways (if any) will be used to complete the proof.

Consider the tree in fig. 4.4. This tree illustrates that there are
two ways in which the null clause can be derived:

(a) Use clause 1 from S, then 4, then 2, then 3, and finally the ancestor clause {L}.

(b) Use clause 1 from S, then 4, then 3, then 2, and finally the ancestor clause {L}.

However, in many applications we will only be interested in identifying one of the ways in which the null clause can be derived. In such cases we will not want to search the whole tree, but only as much of it as is necessary to establish one proof.

Since trees can be traversed in various ways, this gives another property by which search strategies can be characterised. In particular, a tree may be traversed in a depth-first, breadth-first or heuristic manner, and each of these will now be considered in turn.

Depth-first traversal of a search tree

A depth-first search begins at the top of the tree and traverses the leftmost branch as far as it can until either (i) the null clause is derived, (ii) an inadmissible branch is detected (such as those marked by asterisks in fig. 4.4) or (iii) the branch cannot be extended any further since no more resolvents can be formed. The search then 'backs-up' to the last node visited and searches the unsearched space below that node using a depth-first method. Figure 4.6 illustrates the order in which nodes would be visited using a depth-first search.

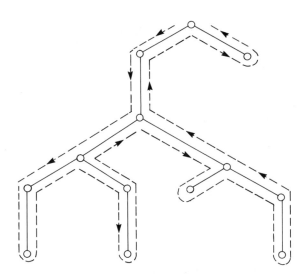

Figure 4.6 A depth-first search

Breadth-first traversal of a search tree

In a breadth-first search, all nodes at depth 1 are developed, and then all nodes at depth 2, and so on until all nodes have been examined This method is illustrated in fig. 4.7.

244

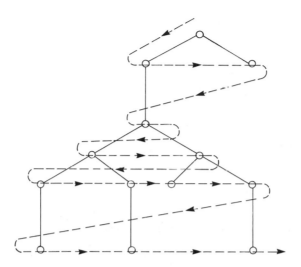

Figure 4.7 A breadth-first search

Heuristic search

Heuristic search is neither depth-first nor breadth-first but uses 'rules of thumb' to select the next node to be developed. An example of such a rule of thumb might be:

> 'Choose the node with the clause which has the least number of literals.'

This is called the 'unit preference strategy' since it choses clauses with a single literal if possible.

Depth-first search is the easiest to program since both the breadth-first and heuristic methods require an agenda to be maintained. An agenda contains a list of those nodes which are 'open' (i.e. waiting to be searched).

Depth-first, breadth-first and heuristic search strategies are described further in chapter 8 where similar methods are used in production rule based systems. Rather than expand upon these search strategies here, we refer the interested reader to chapter 8, section 8.3.

Simplification strategies

The direction of search is not the only factor which can affect the performance of a proof procedure. Sometimes a set of formulas can be 'simplified' by elimination of certain formulas or of certain literals in formulas. Such simplifications are permitted if the simplified set is equivalent to the original set.

There are various permitted simplification strategies:

    (a)   *Elimination of universally valid formulas*
           Universally valid formulas or clauses can be removed since an

unsatisfiable set of formulas containing universally valid
formulas remains unsatisfiable after these formulas are
removed.

(b) *Elimination by evaluatable predicates*
Sometimes it is possible to evaluate the truth value of a
formula or a sub-formula. For example, consider the following
formula:

$$P(x) \lor Q(y) \lor equal(4, 2)$$

Since equal(4, 2) can be evaluated to false, this formula can
be replaced by:

$$P(x) \lor Q(y)$$

(c) *Use of the purity principle*
With respect to resolution methods, the purity principle
(Robinson, 1965) states that a clause C may be deleted from
an unsatisfiable set of clauses S (without affecting the unsatisfiability of S) if it contains some literal L such that
no clause in S could resolve with C on L.

(d) *Elimination by subsumption*
A clause C1 'subsumes' a clause C2 if there exists a substitution θ such that C1 $\theta \subseteq$ C2. For example:

$$\{P(x)\}\text{subsumes}\{P(y) \lor Q(z)\}$$
$$\{P(x) \lor Q(a)\}\text{subsumes}\{P(f(a)) \lor Q(a) \lor R(y)\}$$

A clause in an unsatisfiable set of clauses S can be deleted
without affecting unsatisfiability if it is subsumed by
another clause in S.

Universally valid clauses may be deleted as they are produced,
but subsumed clauses should only be deleted after each 'level'
in the proof has been completed.

4.4.5 NON-CLAUSAL RESOLUTION
A criticism of clausal form is that it destroys useful information
which is implicit in the non-clausal structure of the formulas. Another
objection is that clausal form is difficult to read and is not human
oriented.

Various non-clausal theorem-provers have been developed; for example,
Storm (1974), Wilkins (1974), Bibel (1976), Nilsson (1977), Manna and
Waldinger (1980) and Murray (1982). The one described in this sub-
section is Murray's non-clausal resolution method which operates on
quantifier-free formulas and uses a single inference rule called 'non-
clausal resolution' (NC resolution).

Binary resolution may be regarded as replacing matched positive and
negative atoms by 'false' and 'true' and forming the disjunction of
the resultant clauses. The resolvent would then contain one or more
occurrences of the literals 'false' and 'true' which can be removed on

truth-functional grounds. In NC resolution, all occurrences of the resolved on atom are replaced by false/true in the formulas in which it occurs with positive/negative polarity. The resulting formulas are then disjoined and simplified by truth-functional reductions that eliminate embedded occurrences of true and false and optionally perform simplifications such as reducing P ∧ ¬P to false.

The notions of polarity, reduction and NC resolution will now be described in more detail.

Polarity
Let E, G and H be wffs, where H is a sub-formula of E:

(a) H is of positive polarity in E iff at least one occurrence of H is positive in E.

(b) H is negative in E iff at least one occurrence of H is negative in E.

(c) If ¬H is positive/negative in E then H is negative/positive in E and in E → G.

(d) If H is positive/negative in E then H is positive/negative in E ∨ G, E ∧ G and in G → E.

(e) If H occurs in E, then H is positive *and* negative in E ↔ G.

Reduction
Let > denote 'reduces to' and let ⊁ denote 'does not reduce to'. The following reduction rules can be used, there T stands for true and ⊥ for false:

(a) ¬T > ⊥ and ¬⊥ > T

(b) [T ∧ E] > E and [⊥ ∧ E] > ⊥

(c) [T ∨ E] > T and [⊥ ∨ E] > E

(d) [T → E] > E and [⊥ → E] > T

(e) [E → T] > T and [E → ⊥] > ¬E

(f) [T ↔ E] > E and [⊥ ↔ E] > ¬E

(g) If H occurs in E and H > G then E > E{H/G} where E{H/G} stands for the formula E in which occurrences of H are substituted by G.

(h) If E > G and G > H then E > H.

A wff is in 'reduced form' if no reduction rule can be applied to it.

NC resolution
Given that we have two formulas E and G, we can determine if they contain atomic formulas L1, ..., Ln such that these formulas can be unified by a most general unifying substitution θ such that L1θ = L2θ = , ..., Lnθ = L. If L is positive in E and negative in G, then we can generate the following NC resolvent of E and G:

Eθ{L/⊥} ∨ Gθ{L/T}

This resolvent can then be converted to reduced form using the reduction rules given above.

As an example, consider the following formulas:

E : P(x) ↔ R(Alan)
G : P(Bill) → [Q(Alan, Bill) ∨ ¬P(y)]

Now let L1 = P(x), L2 = P(Bill) and L3 = P(y). The most general unifying substitution for these atomic formulas is {x/Bill, y/Bill}. Therefore, L = P(Bill). L is positive and negative in E but is only negative in G. Therefore, we can generate the following NC resolvent:

[P(Bill) ↔ R(Alan){P(Bill)/⊥}]
        ∨ [P(Bill) → [Q(Alan, Bill) ∨ ¬P(Bill)]{P(Bill)/⊤}]

which reduces to:

¬R(Alan) ∨ Q(Alan, Bill)

Determining the unsatisfiability of a set of formulas
The method described by Murray is a non-clausal analogue to breadth-first binary resolution:

(a) Generate all NC resolvents of all pairs of formulas in S; if an unsatisfiable formula is generated then terminate with success.

(b) Add the generated NC resolvents to S and return to (a). If S is unsatisfiable, then an unsatisfiable formula (i.e. a contradiction) will ultimately be generated.

Theorem-proving
In order to prove that some formula F is a theorem of a set of formulas S, we can use the following procedures:

(a) Negate F and add the negation to S.

(b) Select a pair of formulas in S, and generate all of the NC resolvents of this pair of formulas. If an unsatisfiable formula is generated then terminate with success.

(c) Add the resolvents to S and return to (b).

This procedure is non-deterministic since it does not specify the order in which formulas should be selected at step (b). Various conflict resolution strategies can be used in this method. In order to avoid computing all NC resolvents of a set of clauses, Murray has shown that NC resolution can be restricted to operate only on atoms whose predicate symbol is the alphabetically earliest in the two formulas under consideration without loss of completeness. For example, consider the formulas:

E : A(x) ∨ ¬[P(John) → P(x)]
G : ¬A(y)

We could NC resolve E and G on A or we could NC resolve E with itself on P. The restriction above only allows the former, giving:

¬[P(John) → P(x)]

which may then be resolved with itself.

Resolving on sub-formulas
Moore has shown that NC resolution can be extended to resolve on non-atomic sub-formulas of pairs of formulas. For example, P ∨ Q and [P ∨ Q] → R can be resolved to obtain R. The advantage of this is that proofs are shorter and more readable.

Advantages of NC resolution

(a) The formulas need not be converted to clausal form.

(b) The method is not as redundant as clausal resolution.

Disadvantages of NC resolution
Use of NC resolution has the disadvantage that most operations are more complex than in clausal resolution. For example, in clausal resolution clauses can be represented as lists of literals and two lists can be concatenated to form a resolvent. This is not the case with NC resolution. In addition, in clausal resolution pointers can be used to share lists of literals between parents and resolvents as described by Boyer and Moore (1972). Such 'structure sharing' is more difficult in NC resolution. Also, a more complex definition of the purity principle must be used in NC resolution.

Stickel (1982) has listed several reasons why NC resolution on sub-formulas might not be a good idea. These reasons include the following:

(a) It might be difficult to recognise complementary sub-formulas. For example, P ∨ Q occurs positively in Q ∨ R ∨ P and in ¬P → Q.

(b) The effect of resolving on sub-formulas can be achieved by multiple resolution on atomic formulas. Resolution on both could lead to redundant derivations.

4.4.6 USE OF CONNECTION GRAPHS FOR THEOREM-PROVING
In sub-section 4.4.3, some of the deficiencies of SL resolution were mentioned. A further problem is the amount of effort which is required to identify potential resolvents. In the worst case it is necessary to search through the entire set of clauses in order to identify those clauses which resolve with a given literal.

To improve this situation, Kowalski and Kuehner (1971) used 'classification trees' to index clauses according to the literals with which they resolve. Figure 4.8 shows a simple classification tree which can be used to index the clauses shown at the top of the figure.

(1) {K(x), L(x)}
(2) {M(y), ¬K(f(y))}
(3) {¬M(Sue)}
(4) {¬M(u)}
(5) {¬L(f(Jim))}
(6) {¬L(Bill)}

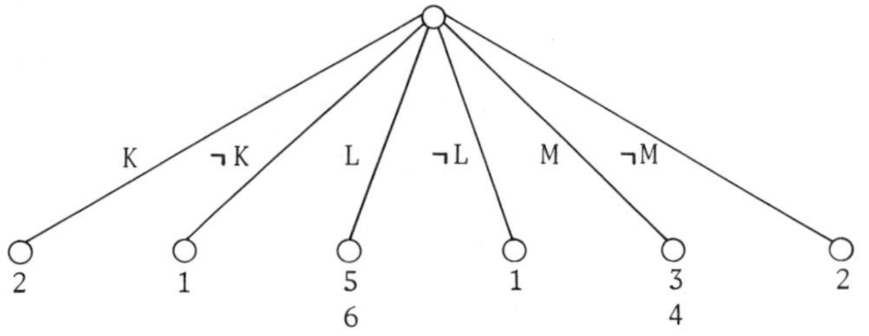

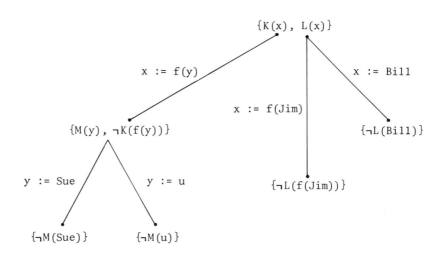

Figure 4.8 A simple classification tree

Connection graphs

Boyer and Moore (1972) suggested that matrices or graphs might provide
a useful alternative to classification trees. The idea is that every
literal occurrence in an input clause (i.e. every literal occurrence
in the original set of clauses S of a theory) should be related to a
node in a graph. Arcs are drawn between nodes if the literals are
potentially unifiable. Nodes corresponding to literals in the same
clause are grouped together in the graph. Each arc in the graph is
labelled with the most general unifying substitution of the two literals
which the arc connects. The resulting structure is called a 'connection
graph'. An example of a connection graph is given in fig. 4.9. This
graph relates the clauses given in fig. 4.8.

{K(x), L(x)}

x := f(y)   x := Bill

x := f(Jim)

{M(y), ¬K(f(y))}   {¬L(Bill)}

y := Sue   y := u   {¬L(f(Jim))}

{¬M(Sue)}   {¬M(u)}

Figure 4.9 A connection graph

A single resolvent is associated with each arc in a connection graph. This resolvent can be generated by resolving the two clauses C1 and C2 containing the literals E and ¬E which are at the ends of the arc. The new clause, if not empty, will contain literals L1, ..., Ln. A literal Li in this set can be connected to another node K in the graph if both of the following conditions are met:

(a) An arc must already exist connecting the 'parent' of Li to K. Note that the parent of Li will be some literal occurrence in one or other of the parent clauses C1 and C2.

(b) The substitution associated with the new arc between Li and K must be compatible with the substitution associated with the arc between E and ¬E.

Figure 4.10 illustrates the effect of adding the resolvent of the clauses {M(y), ¬K(f(y))} and {K(x), L(x)} to the graph shown in fig. 4.9. The dotted lines represent the new arcs.

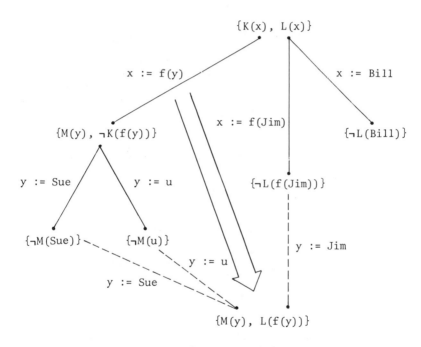

Figure 4.10   The effect of adding a resolvent to a connection graph

Determining unsatisfiability using a connection graph

A procedure for determining the unsatisfiability of a set of clauses S, which is based on the above method of generating resolvents, has been described by Kowalski (1975). An informal description of the method follows. This description is incomplete in that it does not take into account self-resolving clauses (i.e. clauses which resolve with a copy of themselves) and factoring operations. However, it should enable the reader to appreciate the philosophy behind the method.

The method consists of the following steps:

(a) Create a connection graph containing the clauses in S.

(b) Terminate with success if the graph contains the null clause.

(c) Select an arc A in the graph, generate the resolvent R associated with that arc and add R to the graph as described above.

(d) Modify the graph according to the following rules:

    (i) Delete the arc A.

    (ii) Delete any clause and all of its arcs if that clause contains a literal with no arc attached to it.

    (iii) Delete any clause and all of its arcs if it is a universally valid clause (i.e. if it contains two complementary literals).

(e) If there are no clauses left then terminate with failure else return to (b).

The deletion of arcs and nodes which can occur in step (d) is illustrated in fig. 4.11. This figure shows what happens when step (d) is applied to the graph in fig. 4.10. The deletions start with the arc A from which the resolvent was derived and 'fan out' from the nodes at the end of A.

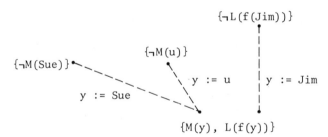

Figure 4.11 The effect of deleting arcs and clauses after a resolvent has been added to a graph

Step (d)(ii) follows from the purity principle (Robinson, 1965) which was described in sub-section 4.4.4.

Step (d)(iii) can be explained as follows. For a clause C to be universally valid it must contain some literal L and its negation ¬L. In order to resolve C away, both L and ¬L will need to be resolved away. Therefore, to resolve C away, S - C must contain both ¬L and L. Therefore, deleting C from S does not affect the unsatisfiability of S.

Theorem-proving using a connection graph
The following procedure can be used to determine if a formula F is a theorem of a theory T.

(a) Convert the proper axioms of T to a set of clauses S. Create a connection graph containing the clauses in S. Negate F, convert to clausal form and add it to the connection graph.

(b)
(c)
(d) } As above.
(e)

This procedure is non-deterministic in that it does not specify the order in which arcs should be selected in step (c). Various conflict resolution strategies can be used to decide which arc to select (note that the word 'resolution' is used with a different meaning here). For example, we might begin with an arc connected to a literal in the clause(s) corresponding to the negation of the theorem to be proved, and thereafter always select an arc connected to one of the most recently introduced literals. The resulting search will 'simulate' an SL resolution proof. In addition, we could use a heuristic which tells us to select an arc whose activation simplifies the graph to the greatest extent by reducing the total number of clauses, literal occurrences or arcs.

Unfortunately, there is not enough space in this book for a discussion of the various search strategies which can be used in connection graphs. The interested reader is referred to Kowalski (1975) for further information on this topic.

Advantages of the connection graph method

(a) The method solves the problem of identifying potential resolvents. Whenever a new clause is generated, it is immediately connected to other clauses with which it could be resolved. The new arcs are derived from the old arcs in the manner described above.

(b) 'Pre-processing' procedures, such as the ones making use of the purity principle and the deletion of universally valid clauses as described above, can be built into the method.

(c) It can be used to simulate other theorem proving methods by choice of conflict resolution strategy. Above, an example has been given of how the conflict resolution strategy can be chosen such that the method simulates an SL proof.

(d) If we want to prove another theorem of S then some of the work has already been done since we can use the connection graph containing the clauses in S which was created in step (a) of the previous proof (assuming that a copy of this graph were available).

4.4.7 NON-CLAUSAL CONNECTION GRAPH RESOLUTION THEOREM-PROVING

Stickel (1983) is developing a non-clausal connection graph theorem-prover. The use of NC resolution eliminates some of the redundancy and unreadability of clause-based systems. The use of a connection graph restricts the search space.

In this method, a connection graph is created in which arcs connect atoms which occur with positive polarity in one formula and negative polarity in the same or in another formula. NC resolution results in the creation of a new connection graph with the resolved on arc deleted and the NC resolvent added.

4.4.8 NON-RESOLUTION THEOREM-PROVING : NATURAL DEDUCTION
The uniform theorem-proving techniques, such as resolution, are not able to generate proofs for non-trivial theorems of mathematics. Such proofs require the use of sophisticated domain specific knowledge which cannot be accommodated by the uniform techniques. Consequently, people have developed automated theorem-provers which are based on 'natural deduction'. It is beyond the scope of this book to discuss these theorem-provers. The interested reader is referred to Bledsoe (1977) and Bundy (1983).

4.4.9 NON-RESOLUTION THEOREM-PROVING : MATRICES AND CONNECTIONS
Various theorem-proving methods have been developed which are based on the idea of examining 'connections' between the literals of formulas. These methods include Prawitz's matrix reduction method (Prawitz, 1976), Bibel's connection method (Bibel, 1976, 1982, 1983), and Andrews' matings method (Andrews, 1981).

To simplify the explanation of the method, we begin by describing how it can be used in propositional logic when the formulas have been transformed to clausal form. We then describe how the method can be extended for use in predicate logic, and conclude by showing how the method may be adopted for use with formulas that have not been transformed to clausal form.

Note that in Bibel's method formulas are converted to disjunctive normal form and then to negative clausal form. In order to keep the explanation as simple as possible we continue to use conjunctive normal form and clausal form. Interested readers should note this difference when referring to Bibel's papers.

The matrix connection method in propositional logic
Suppose that we have the following formulas:

F1 : $P \to Q$
F2 : P

To prove that Q is a theorem of these formulas, we proceed as follows:

(a) Convert F1 and F2 to a set of clauses S:

$\{\neg P, Q\}$
$\{P\}$

(b) Negate Q, convert to clausal form and add to S.

(c) Identify all of the 'paths' through S such that each path passes through exactly one literal in each clause. In this example there are only two such paths:

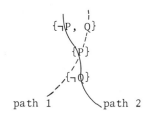

path 1   path 2

(d)   S is unsatisfiable iff each path through S contains at least
one complementary pair of literals. In our example, path 1
contains the complementary pair Q and ¬Q and path 2 contains
the complementary pair ¬P and P. Since these are the only
two paths through S, and since both of these paths contain a
complementary pair, S is unsatisfiable.

In the next example, consider the following formulas:

F1 : [¬P ∧ ¬Q] → R
F2 : ¬P → ¬Q
F3 : ¬P

To prove that R is a theorem of F1, F2 and F3, we proceed as follows:

(a)   Convert F1, F2 and F3 to a set of clauses S:

C1 : {P, Q, R}
C2 : {P, ¬Q}
C3 : {¬P}

(b)   Negate R, convert to clausal form and add to S.

(c)   Identify all of the paths through S. There are six paths:

path1 : P in C1, P in C2, ¬P in C3, ¬R
path2 : P in C1, ¬Q in C2, ¬P in C3, ¬R
path3 : Q in C1, P in C2, ¬P in C3, ¬R
path4 : Q in C1, ¬Q in C2, ¬P in C3, ¬R
path5 : R in C1, P in C2, ¬P in C2, ¬R
path6 : R in C1, ¬Q in C2, ¬P in C3, ¬R

(d)   Since each of these six paths contains a complementary pair,
S ∪ {¬R} is unsatisfiable. Therefore R is a theorem of S.

Why the method works
Each path through the clauses may be thought of as identifying a truth
assignment. For example, consider the following clauses:

{L1, L2, L3}
{L4, L5}
{L6}
{L7}

For this set to be satisfiable, one condition is that at least one
literal in each clause must be true. There are various ways in which

255

this condition may be met:

> 1st assignment :
> {L1 := true, L4 := true, L6 := true, L7 := true, all others false}
>
> 2nd assignment :
> {L1 := true, L5 := true, L6 := true, L7 := true, all others false}
>
> (etc.)

However, an assignment is not acceptable if it assigns a value of true and a value of false to the same atomic formula. For example, if L1 were equal to ¬L6, then the first assignment would not be acceptable.

It is not difficult to see the relationship between truth assignments and paths. If all paths through a set of clauses S contain a complementary pair of literals this means that there is no acceptable satisfying truth assignment for S. Therefore S is unsatisfiable.

Bibel refers to a complementary pair of literals in a path as a 'connection' and he calls a set of connections a 'spanning' for a set of clauses if each path in that set of clauses contains a connection.

An efficient algorithm for identifying a spanning set of connections
Not all literals in all paths need to be examined since a path PA, and all paths which contain PA as a sub-path, can be ignored as soon as a complementary pair is found in PA. For example, consider the following set of clauses:

> C1 : {P, ¬Q}
> C2 : {¬P, R}
> C3 : {¬R}
> C4 : {P, S}
> C5 : {Q}

We start by choosing any clause, say C1, and any literal in that clause, say P. All other literals in C1 are put on a stack. We then identify any clause which contains ¬P, say C2. Now all paths containing this connection need never be considered further. Therefore, we continue by selecting another literal from C2, say R, and stacking the rest of the literals in C2 (in this example, there are no more literals in C2). We now try to find a clause (not including C1, C2) which contains ¬R. This gives us C3. The connections that we have established so far are:

> C1 : {P, ¬Q}
> |
> C2 : {¬P, R}
>   /
> C3 : {¬R}
>
> C4 : {P, S}
>
> C5 : {Q}

Since there are no more literals in C3 we must 'back-up' by pulling an

entry off the stack which tells us that ¬Q in clause C1 is waiting to
be processed. We therefore look for a clause (not including C1) which
contains Q. C5 is such a clause. Since C5 does not contain any more
literals and since there are no more entries on the stack, we have
established that all paths through this set of clauses contain a complementary pair of literals. Note that clause C4 was not involved in
the process.

A more efficient algorithm based on this method can be found in Bibel
(1982). Current research is concerned with the analysis of various
algorithms for this method.

The connection method in predicate logic
The connection method in predicate logic involves the identification
of a spanning set of connections such that there is a substitution of
terms for variables which makes the connected literals complementary.
For example, consider the following formulas:

F1 : $\forall x\ P(x) \rightarrow Q(x)$
F2 : P(John)
F3 : Q(John)

To prove that F3 is a theorem of F1 and F2, we proceed as follows:

(a) Convert F1 and F2 to a set of clauses S:

$\{\neg P(x),\ Q(x)\}$
$\{P(John)\}$

(b) Negate F3, convert to clausal form and add to S:

$\{\neg P(x),\ Q(x)\}$
$\{P(John)\}$
$\{\neg Q(John)\}$

(c) Examine the two paths, ¬P(x), P(John), ¬Q(John) and Q(x),
P(John), ¬Q(John), to see if there is a substitution such
that there is a connection in both of these paths. The substitution {x/John} is such a substitution. Therefore the
proof is complete.

In general, in considering the nth path, the procedure must attempt to
find a substitution θn such that for two literals L1 and L2, $L1'\theta n$ =
$L2'\theta n$ where L = $L'\theta 1, \theta 2, \ldots, \theta n-1$. Whenever an acceptable substitution cannot be found, 'selective backtracking' must be used to consider
alternative substitutions in earlier paths.

There are two complications to the connection method, one concerning
skolematisation and the other the requirement to copy clauses.

Skolematisation
As in other proof methods, when a formula is converted to clausal form
it is sometimes necessary to introduce skolem constants. As example,
consider the following formula:

$\forall x \exists y [Q(x,\ x) \rightarrow Q(y,\ x)]$

To show that this is universally valid, we simply negate it, convert
it to clausal form and test the paths for a spanning set of connections.

$$\neg\forall x\exists y[Q(x, x) \to Q(y, x)]$$
$$\equiv \neg\neg\exists x\neg\exists y[Q(x, x) \to Q(y, x)]$$
$$\equiv \exists x\neg\neg\forall y \neg[Q(x, x) \to Q(y, x)]$$
$$\equiv \exists x\forall y \neg[\neg Q(x, x) \vee Q(y, x)]$$
$$\equiv \exists x\forall y[Q(x, x) \wedge \neg Q(y, x)]$$
$$\equiv \forall y[Q(sk, sk) \wedge \neg Q(y, sk)]$$
$$\equiv \{Q(sk, sk)\}, \{\neg Q(y, sk)\}$$

There is only one path and it contains a complementary pair. Therefore
the original formula is universally valid since its negation is unsatisfiable.

The need to copy clauses

Copies of clauses are sometimes required in order to complete a proof.
As example, consider the following formulas in which the function 'fac'
stands for factorial, 'tim' stands for times and 'plus' stands for plus,
i.e. fac(x) means factorial x, tim(x, y) means x times y, and plus(x, y)
means x plus y:

F1 : equals(fac(0), 1);
F2 : $\forall x\forall y[$equals(fac(x), y) $\to$
$\qquad\qquad\qquad$ equals(fac(plus(x, 1)), tim(y, plus(x, 1)))]
F3 : $\exists z$ equals(fac(2), z)

F1 states that the factorial 0 equals 1. F2 states that for all x and
for all y, if the factorial of x equals y, then the factorial of
(x+1)=y*(x+1). F3 states that there exists an entity which is equal to
the factorial of 2.

In order to prove that F3 is a theorem of F1 and F2, we proceed as
follows:

(a) Convert F1 and F2 to the set of clauses S:

$\qquad$ C1 : {equals(fac(0), 1)
$\qquad$ C2 : {$\neg$equals(fac(x), y), equals(fac(plus(x, 1)),
$\qquad\qquad\qquad\qquad\qquad\qquad$ tim(y, plus(x, 1)))}

(b) Negate F3, convert to clausal form and add to S:

$\qquad$ C3 : {$\neg$equals(fac(2), z)}

(c) There are two paths through this set of clauses; the first
contains the complementary literals equals(fac(0), 1) and
equals(fac(x), y) which can be unified with the substitution
{x/0, y/1}. However, given this substitution, there is no
compatible substitution which will make any pair of literals
complementary in the second path. Therefore, we need to make
copies of the self-resolving clause C2:

$\qquad$ C2' : {$\neg$equals(fac(x1), y1), equals(fac(plus(x1, 1)),
$\qquad\qquad\qquad\qquad\qquad\qquad$ tim(y1, plus(x1, 1)))}

258

C2" : {¬equals(fac(x2), y2), equals(fac(plus(x2, 1)),
                                   tim, (y2, plus(x2, 1))))}

There are now four paths in this set:

    P1 : C1, right C2', right C2", C3
    P2 : C1, right C2', left C2", C3
    P3 : C1, left C2', right C2", C3
    P4 : C1, left C2', left C2", C3

where 'left' and 'right' stand for 'left literal of' and
'right literal of' respectively. Each of these paths has a
connection:

Path	Complementary literals	Substitution
P1	C1, right C2'	{x1/0, y1/1}
P2	C1, right C2'	{x1/0, y1/1}
P3	left C2' and right C2"	{x2/plus(x1, 0), y2/tim(y1, plus(x2, 1))}
P4	left C2" and C3	{plus(x2, 1)/2, z/tim(y2, plus(x2, 1))}

These 'substitutions' are all compatible and the 'answer' to
z can be obtained if we compound them. Doing so gives a value
of 2 for z.

In general, several copies of a self-resolving clause might be required
to construct a proof.

*Using the connection method on formulas which have not been transformed
to clausal form*
The notion of a spanning set of connections can be redefined for arbitrary formulas (not just those in clausal form) by use of the equivalence
rules relating the logical connectives. This can give a slightly different method for constructing proofs. For example, consider the
following formulas:

    F1 : $\forall x \ [P(x) \rightarrow Q(x)]$
    F2 : P(John)
    F3 : Q(John)

To prove that F3 is a formula we simply look for a spanning set of connections in the formula:

    $[F1 \wedge F2] \rightarrow F3$

Using the redefined notion of paths and connections, we can obtain the
following proof:

$$[\forall x[P(x) \rightarrow Q(x)] \wedge P(John)] \rightarrow Q(John)$$

A complete description of the method can be found in Bibel (1982 and 1983) where several well substantiated claims are made regarding the superiority of the connection method over resolution and natural deduction based approaches. An efficient implementation of the connection method has been developed by Wallen (1984).

4.4.10 IMPLEMENTATION OF PROGRAMS FOR AUTOMATED REASONING IN FOPL

It should not be difficult to see how the programs given in sub-section 4.2.11, for propositional logic, might be extended for use with first order predicate logic:

(a) The parser would have to be modified to accommodate quantifiers, variables, constants and function symbols.

(b) The conversion of formulas to clausal form would have to include skolematisation, etc.

(c) Resolution would involve a unification procedure.

In order to simplify the implementation of such programs, it is useful, in the first instance, to restrict the logic such that:

(a) Only binary-relations are used.

(b) Function symbols are not allowed.

Systems which have been restricted in this way have been implemented by undergraduate students as part of their final year project work under the supervision of the author. As example, one such system allows the user to enter a set of assertions as formulas of restricted first order predicate logic. These assertions are then tested for consistency and, if consistent, the user may then enter formulas which are to be tested for theoremhood. In addition, the user can ask questions which are to be answered with respect to the set of assertions. The answers are provided by 'productive' theorem-proving (which is described in chapter 5). All formulas are converted to clausal form in this system and resolution is used for reasoning.

4.5 CONCLUDING COMMENTS

This chapter began with a general discussion of formal logic. Two logics, propositional logic and predicate logic, were then described in detail. This was followed by a discussion of automated theorem proving.

In this chapter, many different methods which can be used for theorem-proving have been introduced. Some readers may be a little perplexed by this, and may be wondering why we have described so many methods. The following summary may be helpful:

(a) 'Axiom systems' are often used to define logics, and to relate syntactic theorem-proving to semantic methods for determining logical consequences. We use an axiomatic approach to define various non-classical logics in chapter 6.

(b) It is often claimed that 'natural deduction' proof methods are the ones which most closely resemble the way in which people reason in everyday life. Those approaching logic for the first time often find natural deduction proofs the easiest to follow.

(c) 'Sequent' proof methods influenced the development of tableau methods. We included a brief description of sequent proofs to aid understanding of the tableau methods.

(d) The 'tableau' proof method was one of the first mechanistic methods to be developed. Tableau proofs do not depend on the cleverness of the person constructing them, only on his or her dexterity at manipulating symbols. As such, the tableau method is amenable to automation. However, it is little used in automated theorem-proving in classical logic since simpler methods (such as resolution) are available. The importance of the tableau proof method is that it has been extended for use in non-classical logics, particularly in modal logics which we describe in chapter 6. Although resolution based methods have been developed for modal logics in the last three or four years, they are very difficult to follow without an understanding of the tableau methods.

(e) 'Resolution' theorem-proving is perhaps the most commonly used method for performing deduction in knowledge base systems which are based on logic. It is particularly simple to implement due to the single inference rule which is used. Perhaps the most difficult part of a resolution based theorem-proving program is that part which converts formulas to clausal form.

(f) We have described several ways in which the efficiency of resolution theorem-proving can be improved. The various 'refinements' of the standard resolution method which we have discussed are:

> linear input resolution
> LUSH resolution
> selected literal resolution

We have also described how various 'search strategies' can be employed in resolution theorem-proving. We discuss search strategies in more detail in chapter 8 with respect to production rule based systems. Much of what we describe there is relevant to search strategies used in theorem-proving. The logic programming language PROLOG is based on a depth-first SL resolution theorem-prover and may be thought of as a type of production rule system.

(g) We have described various 'non-standard resolution' based theorem-proving methods:

> non-clausal resolution
> connection graph methods

We have included these methods since they go some way towards overcoming the inefficiency for which resolution is often criticised.

261

(h) We have briefly mentioned two non-resolution based automatic theorem-proving methods:

    natural deduction
    matrix connection method

Many researchers claim, with some justification, that clausal resolution is inherently inappropriate for complex theorem-proving as is required in, for example, mathematical theorem-proving. There is much support for the use of natural deduction based methods (which do not require conversion to clausal form) for complex problems. The matrix connection method, on the other hand, may be used with formulas in clausal form or with formulas in 'standard' form. When used with formulas in clausal form, this method is a serious rival to resolution since it is as simple to implement, and it has been claimed to be more efficient. When used with formulas in standard form, it is a serious rival to natural deduction based methods. At present, the matrix connection method is relatively little known. However, interest in this approach appears to be growing.

The method which we refer to most often in this book is the resolution theorem-proving method.

In the following chapter we show how some of the concepts which we have described here may be used to formalise various aspects of deductive and non-deductive database systems. In chapter 6 we describe various non-classical logics which have been developed to overcome some of the deficiencies of propositional and first order predicate logic.

5 Logic and Database Systems

5.1 INTRODUCTION

The objectives of this chapter

During the last fifteen years or so, there has been a great deal of
work carried out in relating database concepts to notions in formal
logic. Much of this work is based on one or other of two approaches:
in the first approach, the knowledge which constitutes a database and
its schema is viewed as defining a 'complete' relational structure
plus an associated formal theory; in the second approach, the knowledge
is regarded as defining a formal theory only. The first approach is
the one most often used in formalising aspects of conventional database
systems whereas the second is generally used in formalising aspects of
deductive database systems.

An excellent survey of work in this area is given in Gallaire, Minker
and Nicolas (1984). Unfortunately, the contents of their paper, and
much of the other literature on the subject, is inaccessible to many
people interested in databases since it requires an in-depth understanding of several relatively difficult subjects such as model theory,
proof theory, formal language theory, first order logic and non-monotonic logic. The objective of this chapter is to make this important
material more accessible by providing an introductory description of
how logic can be used to formalise various database concepts.

In addition, we introduce a new approach in which the knowledge in a
database system is viewed as defining an 'incomplete' relational structure plus a formal theory. We believe that this new approach may help
to resolve some of the problems which have been met when using the two
existing views to formalise concepts such as null values, indefinite
data, 'incompleteness' constraints and indefinite inference rules.

The three approaches discussed in this chapter are illustrated in fig.
5.1. To help the reader understand this figure, we introduce some
terminology:

> (a) Two structures are *isomorphic* if there is a 'one-to-one' cor-
> respondence between their 'parts'. That is, two relational
> structures A and B are isomorphic if there is a relation in
> A corresponding to each relation in B, and for each pair of

corresponding relations <RA, RB>, where RA is the relation in
A corresponding to the relation RB in B, RA and RB have the
same arity, the same number of tuples, and the tuples correspond, and so on. If two isomorphic structures were depicted
graphically, they would have the same shape but might differ
in the names of nodes and arcs.

(b)   A structure A is a *mathematical sub-structure* of a structure
      B if A is isomorphic to a 'sub-set' of the structure B.

These definitions are very informal. More precise definitions may be
found in Marciszewski (1981). The slice of reality which is of interest in each case is called the 'universe of discourse'.

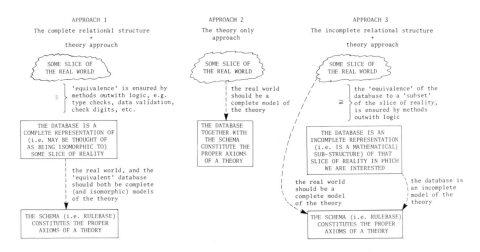

Figure 5.1   Three approaches to formalising database concepts

Advantages of using logic to formalise database concepts

Various advantages derive from using logic to formalise database concepts. In particular, since the semantics of logic are well-defined,
if a logical counterpart to a database concept can be found then the
semantics of that concept may also be well-defined. For example, in
the 'theory only' approach (the second approach mentioned above), the
maintenance of database integrity after an update may be regarded as
the well-defined problem of checking a theory for consistency. In
general, the advantage of formalising a database concept in this way
is twofold: firstly, the concept can often be better understood, and
secondly, in some cases, methods which have been developed in logic
can be used, or adapted for use, in the database context.

Deductive and non-deductive database systems

In the sections which follow we refer to 'deductive' and 'non-deductive'
database systems. In non-deductive systems, the only facts which can
be obtained from the database are those which are stored explicitly (or
which follow from certain assumptions described below). That is, new
facts cannot be deduced by the use of inference rules. Conventional
database systems are non-deductive, and the rules which constitute the

schemas in such systems all serve as integrity constraints which restrict the 'allowed' database states.

Deductive database systems also contain integrity constraints but, in addition, they contain inference rules which can be used to deduce new facts from those stored explicitly.

Database systems may also be categorised as 'definite' or 'indefinite'. The facts in a definite database system, whether stored explicitly or deduced, must all be definite. That is, facts such as the following are not allowed:

(Pat is a man) or (Pat is a woman)

Assumptions which are often made in database work
Three assumptions are often made when designing or using a database system:

(a) The 'domain closure assumption' which states that the universe of discourse contains only those individuals which are named. Different meanings are ascribed to the term 'named' in different situations. In some cases, the set of individuals includes only those whose names appear as values in the database, e.g. John, London, 21, etc. In other cases, the set of individuals includes only those whose names appear as values in the database and/or the database schema (i.e. in integrity constraints or inference rules). Often, the names are not all given explicitly but are specified by ranges, as for example in the integrity constraint 'ages must be in the range 0 to 120'.

(b) The 'unique name assumption' which states that all of the names which appear in the database or schema are unique identifiers of individuals.

(c) The 'closed world assumption' (CWA) which states that if an n-ary relationship is not known to hold between n individuals then that relationship is assumed not to hold. Different meanings are ascribed to the term 'known' in different situations. For example, if the database is non-deductive, then any relationship between individuals which is not represented explicitly is assumed not to hold. For example, if the relationship of marriage between John and Sue is not represented explicitly, then the CWA would imply that John and Sue are not married.

The appropriateness and formulation of these three assumptions depends on the application, on the type of database system and on the database designer's understanding of what the assumptions mean. The definitions given above are somewhat vague and the exact meaning of the assumptions, when so defined, is not clear. Such vagueness can lead to problems when interpreting answers to queries in database systems in which the assumptions are made. In what follows, we show how precise meanings can be ascribed to the assumptions when they are formalised according to the three approaches.

Restriction of the discussion to relational database systems
In the discussion, we refer mainly to relational database systems since
this is the area in which most of the work has been carried out. However, logic has been used to formalise concepts in other types of database system. In particular, Jacobs (1982) has developed a 'database
logic' which can be used in the context of hierarchical and network, as
well as relational, systems.

5.2   SOME RELEVANT NOTIONS FROM FORMAL LOGIC

The discussions in this chapter make use of the following notions from
first order predicate logic:

- relational structure
- formal first order predicate language
- interpretation
- valuation
- satisfaction
- truth and models
- logical consequence
- formal systems
- theories
- consistency
- decidability
- clausal form
- skolematisation
- resolution

(If you are not familiar with these notions, refer back to chapter 4.)

We now show how these notions from formal logic can be used to formalise various database concepts. The three approaches which will be
considered are illustrated in fig. 5.1.

5.3   THE THEORY AND COMPLETE RELATIONAL STRUCTURE APPROACH

The database
In this approach, the relations in a database D are regarded as being
'equivalent' to the relations in some slice of reality which is regarded as a complete relational structure W. If a tuple is not stored as
a member of a relation r in D, then it is assumed not to be a member of
the equivalent relation in W. (This is the closed world assumption.)

The domains of the database relations
The union of the domains of the relations in the database is regarded
as being 'equivalent' to the domain of the relational structure W, in
which all entities are assumed to be distinguished. Not all entities
need appear in tuples of the database. It is assumed that somewhere
there is an enumeration of them. Not all need be named explicitly;
some may be 'named' by specifying ranges, e.g. 0-120. The relations
and enumerated entities in the database are regarded as constituting
a 'complete' relational structure U. This structure, if correct, is
'equivalent' to the real world structure W. That is, a correct database and the slice of reality which it represents are regarded as being
'isomorphic' structures in this approach.

The database schema

The schema is regarded as comprising a set S of well-formed formulas of a language L which is the language of the relational structure U (i.e. there is a predicate symbol for each relation and a constant for each entity in U). Therefore U can be used to define a complete interpretation for S.

Schema analysis

If the language L is a language of predicate logic, then S may be regarded as the proper axioms of a theory T in predicate logic. T can be tested for consistency; for example, by use of resolution. If T is inconsistent, this means that it has no model. This is an indication that no database state (and therefore no state of the corresponding slice of reality) is compatible with the schema. The schema must therefore be in error and needs to be corrected.

5.3.1 INTEGRITY MAINTENANCE

In this approach, updating the database is regarded as creating a new relational structure U. Integrity checking is then equated with checking to make sure that U is a model of S, i.e. that all formulas in S evaluate to 'true' in the interpretation U. For example, consider the following schema rules:

$$S1 : \forall x[male(x) \rightarrow \neg female(x)]$$
$$S2 : \forall x \forall y[enrolledforclass(x, y) \rightarrow registeredstudent(x)]$$

For S1 to evaluate to true in U, it must be the case that:

$$U \models \forall x \, male(x) \rightarrow \neg female(x)[\alpha] \text{ for all valuations } \alpha$$

i.e. for all entities e_i in U, it must be the case that:

$$U \models male(x) \rightarrow \neg female(x)[e_i]$$

i.e. for all entities e_i in U, it must be the case that:

$$U \models \neg female(x)[e_i] \text{ or } U \models \neg male(x)[e_i]$$

i.e. for all entities e_i in U, it must be the case that:

$$\text{not} <e_i> \in \text{FEMALE or not} <e_i> \in \text{MALE}$$

In other words, for S1 to be satisfied, the unary relations 'FEMALE' and 'MALE' must be disjoint.

Using a similar line of argument, we can show that for S2 to be satisfied, all entities which appear in the first position in tuples of the relation ENROLLEDFORCLASS must also appear in a one-place tuple in the relation REGISTEREDSTUDENT.

In effect, S1 defines the constraint that 'no entity may be both male and female' and S2 defines the constraint that 'if an entity is to be enrolled for any class, that entity must be (known to be) a registered student'.

267

Consider, now, the following examples:

    S3 : ∀x[male(x) ∨ female(x)]
    S4 : ∀x∃y[parent(x) → child(y)]
    S5 : ∀x believes in god(x) → ∃y god(y)

    S3   means that all entities must be (known to be) male or female;
          hence, an 'empty' database does not satisfy this constraint.

    S4   means that for all entities ei in U, if ei is (known to be) a
          parent then there exists an entity which is (known to be) a
          child.

    S5   means that if all entities in U believe in god then there must
          be an entity which is (known to be) a god.

It is important to realise that in the theory and 'complete' interpretation approach, *all rules in the database schema are regarded as
integrity constraints.*

More efficient integrity checking

If we can assume that the database state before an update is a model
of the schema, then in order to check that the database state after the
update is also a model we need only examine those schema rules whose
evaluation might be affected. For example, if we were to insert JOHN
into the relation MALE, only S1 above is affected. If we were to
remove JEAN from the relation REGISTEREDSTUDENT, only S2 is affected.

Changing the domain by adding a new entity would violate rules such as
S3 unless other facts were also entered.

It is not difficult to see how algorithms might be constructed for (a)
detecting affected rules and (b) for determining if affected rules
evaluate to false. Such algorithms are described in Frost and Whittaker
(1983) and are outlined in chapter 3 sub-section 3.8.2.

5.3.2 QUERY EVALUATION

Closed queries

A closed query is a query whose answer is 'true' or 'false'. In the
theory and complete relational structure approach, queries are regarded
as formulas of the language of the relational structure U. Examples of
closed queries are:

    Q1 : parent(John)
    Q2 : [male(Pat) ∨ female(Pat)]
    Q3 : ∃x god(x)

Such queries can always be evaluated by reference to the relational
structure U. For example:

    Q1 is true if <JOHN> ∈ PARENT and false otherwise
    Q2 is true if <PAT> ∈ MALE or <PAT> ∈ FEMALE
    Q3 is true if there exists an entity e such that <e> ∈ GOD

Open queries

An open query is a query whose answer is a set of zero or more tuples.

For example, the answer to the open query (who are married?) might be {<Sue, Bob>, <Mary, John>}. Open queries may therefore be regarded as definitions of sets. For example, using standard set notation:

Q4 = {x | parent(x)}

The answer to this query is the set of constants corresponding to entities e for which:

U ⊨ parent(x)[c]   (refer to chapter 4 if the meaning of this equation is not understood)

That is, the answer to Q4 is the set of constants corresponding to entities which are assigned to x in valuations which satisfy the formula 'parent(x)'. For example, if <JOHN> ∈ PARENT is in U, then 'John' is in the set of answers if John corresponds to JOHN.

In general, an open query is of the form:

Q = {<v1, ..., vn> | F}

where v1, ..., vn are the free variables in the formula F.

The answer to an open query is the set of tuples of constants corresponding to tuples of entities which are assigned to the variables v1, ..., vn in valuations which satisfy the formula F. For example, consider the following open queries:

Q5 = {x, y | married(x, y) ∧ employee(x)}
Q6 = {x | ∀y likes(x, y)}

The answer to Q5 is the set of pairs of constants corresponding to pairs of entities ei, ej such that ei ∈ EMPLOYEE and <ei, ej> ∈ MARRIED.

The answer to Q6 is the set of constants corresponding to entities ei such that <ei, ej> ∈ LIKES for all ej ∈ E. In other words, all entities which like all other entities.

In the following, ‖Q‖ is used to denote the answer to a query Q.

Use of relational algebraic operations

It should not be difficult to see how relational algebraic operations can be used to evaluate queries in databases for which the theory and complete relational structure approach is appropriate. Consider the queries Q4, Q5 and Q6. The answers to these queries can be obtained as follows:

(a)   ‖Q4‖ = the relation PARENT.

(b)   ‖Q5‖ = join of MARRIED and EMPLOYEE on the first column of MARRIED.

(c)   ‖Q6‖ = (relational) division of LIKES on the second column with respect to E (i.e. with respect to the union of all of the domains of the database relations).

In optimising query evaluation we can make use of:

    (a) The equivalence rules in logic, e.g. $\neg[P(x) \wedge P(y)] \equiv \neg P(x) \vee \neg P(y)$.

    (b) Statistical information including size of relations, expected size of intersections, etc.

Note that relational algebraic operations are described in chapter 3.

Using the schema when evaluating queries

In some cases, the evaluation of queries can be made more efficient by reference to the schema. For example, suppose that we had the following schema rule:

    S6 : $\forall x \neg[p1(x) \wedge p2(x) \wedge p3(x) \wedge p4(x)]$

and that the following query is to be evaluated:

    Q7 = $\{x \mid p1(x) \wedge p2(x) \wedge p3(x) \wedge p4(x)\}$

If this query were evaluated without reference to the schema, then the evaluation would involve intersecting the four unary relations corresponding to p1, p2, p3 and p4. If the database were in a valid state, i.e. if it were a model of the schema, then the answer to Q7 would be the empty set. This answer could have been obtained immediately by reference to S6.

The schema can be used in various other ways to improve the efficiency of query evaluation.

5.3.3 DEFINED RELATIONS

As mentioned earlier, in this approach the schema rules are all regarded as integrity constraints. Since the relational structure is complete, the notion of inference does not arise. (Although we have shown how the schema might be used to improve the efficiency of query evaluation, when used in this way the schema is regarded as a kind of 'summary' of certain aspects of the relational structure.) However, this does not mean that the relations in the relational database have to be stored explicitly. The membership of database relations can be wholly or partly defined in terms of other relations. For example:

    D1 : PARENT = MOTHER U FATHER
    D2 : PARENT = the set of explicitly stored PARENT tuples U
                                                            MOTHER U FATHER

Although some of these definitions might be expressed in a language of logic, e.g. $\forall x[mother(x) \vee father(x)] \rightarrow parent(x)$, it is important to recognise that they are not proper axioms of a theory but are simply definitions of relation membership.

Compatibility of relation membership definitions

Since the relation membership definitions, as exemplified, can only be used to identify tuples which are members of relations (as opposed to identifying tuples which are not members), they can never be incompatible with each other (i.e. they can never lead to a contradiction). However, they could be incompatible with the database schema. If these definitions become too complex, then it would be better to regard the database as a deductive database and to formalise it according to one or other of the two approaches described in sections 5.4 and 5.5.

5.3.4 THE CLOSED WORLD, DOMAIN CLOSURE AND UNIQUE NAME ASSUMPTIONS

The 'closed world assumption' is implicit in the theory and complete relational structure approach. If a tuple t is not known to be a member of a relation r, then it is assumed not to be a member of r. The The notion of negative (false) facts is accommodated by the definition of satisfaction which states that U ⊨ ¬A iff it is not the case that U ⊨ A, where A is an atomic formula.

The 'domain closure assumption' is stated explicitly in this approach.

The 'unique name assumption' is implicit in this approach. The distinguished entities in a relational structure are distinct entities. Consequently, different values in the tuples of the database relations are regarded as representing distinct entities. Synonyms can be used. However, their transformation to a single identifier would be regarded as being outwith that part of the system which is being formalised.

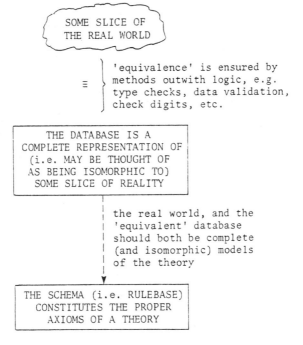

Figure 5.2 The complete relational structure and theory approach

5.3.5 THE APPLICABILITY OF THE THEORY AND COMPLETE RELATIONAL STRUCTURE APPROACH

Summary

In the theory and complete relational structure approach, the database relations together with the enumeration of their domains (and possibly

271

some relation membership definitions) are regarded as constituting a
complete relational structure U which, if correct, is isomorphic to the
real world structure which it represents. (See fig. 5.2.) The rules
in the database schema are regarded as the proper axioms of a theory T.
For the database to be in a valid state, U must be a model of T, i.e.
all of the rules in the schema must evaluate to true in the interpretation U. Closed queries are queries whose answers are true or false.
The answers to such queries are obtained by evaluating them in U. An
open query is regarded as an open formula. The answer to such a query
is the set of tuples of constants corresponding to tuples of entities
which are assigned to the free variables in valuations which satisfy
the formula.

Applications
The theory and complete relational structure view is appropriate when
the database is non-deductive and the closed world and domain closure
assumptions are appropriate. It is therefore appropriate in most conventional applications of databases.

5.4 THE THEORY ONLY APPROACH
In the theory only approach, the database together with the schema
rules are all regarded as proper axioms of a theory T. For example,
if there is a tuple <Pat, Jim> in a relation 'hasuncle', then this is
regarded as the 'ground atomic formula' 'hasuncle(Pat, Jim)'. A formula
is ground iff it is variable free. A schema rule which states that 'all
people have a dad' is regarded as the proper axiom:

$$\forall x \exists y [person(x) \rightarrow hasdad(x,y)]$$

In this approach, some part of the real world, called the 'universe of
discourse', is regarded as a complete relational structure which defines an interpretation of the theory T (see fig. 5.3).

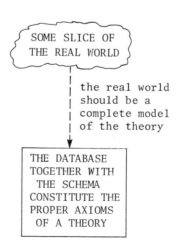

Figure 5.3 The theory only approach

T is in 'error' if either (a) it is inconsistent and therefore cannot have any satisfying interpretation (model) or (b) it is consistent but the universe of discourse is not a model of it. If the theory is decidable then we can detect errors of type (a). However, there is no method which is guaranteed to detect all errors of type (b) since we can never prove that the real world is a model of T. We can only check to see if the perceived world is a model. However, in practice we will not even want to do this since it would, in general, be too time-consuming to determine for all pairs of entities ei and ej, and all relations Rk, whether or not <ei, ej> ∈ Rk. Often, all that would be required is that the theory T be consistent and that it be an 'accurate' description of the universe of discourse. Such accuracy would have to be maintained by methods outwith the scope of logic; for example, by conventional error detection methods such as the use of parity bits, check sums, range checks, etc.

Since, in this approach, there is no distinction between the database and the schema, they will be referred to jointly as the 'knowledge base'.

In order to simplify the discussion, we restrict our examples to contain only binary predicates. This allows us to use the more readable 'infix' notation. For example, instead of 'hasuncle(Pat, Jim)', we write '(Pat.hasuncle.Jim)', and instead of 'person(David)', we write '(David. ∈ .people)' where ∈ stands for 'memberofset'.

We refer to the following example knowledge base in the next few sections:

```
KB1 = {A1 :  (Pat.hasuncle.Jim),
       A2 :  (Pat.hasdad.Bill),
       A3 :  ∀w[(w.brotherof.David) → (Pat.likes.w)],
       A4 :  (Jim.brotherof.David),
       A5 :  (Bob.brotherof.David),
       A6 :  (Bill.likes.Jim),
       A7 :  (Bill.likes.Bob),
       A8 :  ∀x∀y[(x.hasdad.y) → (y.haschild.x)],
       A9 :  ∀x∃y[(x.∈.people) → (x.hasdad.y)],
       A10: (David.∈.people),
       A11: ∀w (David.likes.w),
       A12: (Sue.likes.Pat),
       A13: (Sue.likes.Jim),
       A14: (Sue.likes.Bill),
       A15: (Sue.likes.David),
       A16: (Sue.likes.Bob),
       A17: (Sue.likes.people),
       A18: (Sue.likes.Sue)                         }
```

Notice that, although we have not used any function symbols, if A9 were converted to clausal form we would have to introduce a skolem function.

5.4.1 CONSISTENCY CHECKING
In the theory only approach, simple facts (i.e. tuples in database relations) and general rules (the schema) are treated in the same way with respect to consistency checking. They are all regarded as the proper

axioms of a theory T and, as mentioned earlier, T is in 'error' if either (a) it is inconsistent or (b) it is consistent but the universe of discourse is not a model of it. Since logic can only help us detect errors of type (a), we shall not consider errors of type (b) further in this section.

If a theory is 'decidable', then it is always possible to determine if it is consistent or not. Various methods, including methods based on resolution (as described earlier) can be used: When 'updating' a consistent theory T, by adding a proper axiom P, to obtain a theory T', we need only make certain that ¬P is not a theorem of T to ensure that T' is consistent. Deleting a proper axiom from a consistent theory always results in a consistent theory.

The notion of an 'integrity constraint' is not the same in the theory only approach as it was in the theory and complete relational structure approach. Consider a theory with the following proper axioms:

$$\forall x[(x.\in.\text{male}) \vee (x.\in.\text{female})]$$
$$\forall x \forall y[(x.\text{enrolledfor}.y) \rightarrow (x.\in.\text{registeredstudents})]$$

The first axiom does not mean that all entities must be known to be male or female. It states that all entities *are* either male or female (or both). In this respect it can be used for inference. When viewed as an 'integrity constraint' it states that no entity may be known to be both not male and not female.

The second axiom does not mean that for an entity to be enrolled it is necessary that the entity must be known to be a registered student. It states that if an entity is enrolled then that entity *is* a registered student. In this respect it can be used for inference. When viewed as an integrity constraint, it states that no entity may be known to be enrolled and known not to be a registered student.

It is important to note this distinction between the theory only and the theory and complete relational structure approaches. It derives from the fact that all proper axioms in a theory may be used for inference. When a proper axiom is regarded as an integrity constraint, this means that its negation cannot hold. For example:

Proper axiom	For inference	As an integrity constraint
the first one above	e.g. if an entity is known not to be male, then we can infer that it is female	$\exists x[\neg(x.\in.\text{male}) \wedge \neg(x.\in.\text{female})]$ may not be a theorem of T
the second one above	e.g. if an entity is known to be enrolled, then we can infer that it is a registered student	$\exists x \exists y[(x.\text{enrolledfor}.y) \wedge \neg(x.\in.\text{registeredstudents})]$ may not be a theorem of T

We see later that if the closed world assumption is implemented as a 'failure to prove' metarule then this view of proper axioms as inference rules and integrity constraints needs to be modified somewhat.

5.4.2 QUERY EVALUATION

Closed queries
In the theory only approach, a closed query is regarded as a closed formula F of the language of the theory T. The answer is 'yes' if F is a theorem of T, 'no' if ¬F is a theorem of T, and 'don't know' otherwise. As example, consider the knowledge base KB1 above and the question 'is it the case that David has a dad?' This closed query can be re-expressed as:

'is it the case that KB1 ⊢ ∃y (David.hasdad.y)?'

To answer this question, we can use a resolution based 'refutation' theorem-proving method. We begin by converting ∃y (David.hasdad.y) to the equivalent formula ¬∀y ¬(David.hasdad.y), negating this and converting to clausal form, giving:

{¬(David.hasdad.y)}

We now convert KB1 to clausal form and resolve {¬(David.hasdad.y)} away using A9 followed by A10 from KB1:

$$\frac{\{¬(David.hasdad.y)\}, \ \{(x.hasdad.f(x)), \ ¬(x.∈.people)\}A9}{\{¬(David.∈. \ people)\}}$$

$$\frac{\{¬(David.∈.people)\}, \ \{(David.∈.people)\}A10}{⊠}$$

The null clause, denoted by ⊠, is derived, therefore ∃y (David. hasdad.y) is a theorem of KB1 and the answer to the question is 'yes'. Notice that the clausal form of A9 contains a skolem function f.

Care must be taken to interpret answers to closed queries correctly:

- 'yes' means that the answer is definitely yes
- 'no' means that the answer is definitely no
- 'don't know' means that the answer could be yes or no but the problem of determining theoremhood is undecidable.

Open queries
Open queries may be expressed as follows:

{<v1, ..., vn> | F}KB

where (as before) v1, ..., vn are the free variables in the formula F. KB denotes the knowledge base concerned and may be omitted if it is obvious from the context.

Examples of open queries are:

Q1 : {x | ∃y (x.hasdad.y)}KB1
read as 'all entities which have a dad'

Q2 : {x | ∀y (x.likes.y)}KB1
read as 'all entities which like all other entities'

Q3 : {x, y | (x.likes.y)}KB1
read as 'all pairs of entities ei, ej where ei likes ej'

Q4 : {x | ∀y (y.brotherof.David) → (x.likes.y)}KB1
read as 'all entities which like all brothers of David'

In the theory only approach, the answer to an open query is the set of tuples of terms which, when substituted for the free variables in F, make the 'substitution instance' of F a theorem of KB. We use ‖Q‖ to denote the answer to a query Q.

For example, the answers to the queries above are:

‖Q1‖ = {Pat, David}
‖Q2‖ = {David}
‖Q3‖ = {<Pat, Jim>, <Pat, Bob>, <Bill, Jim>,
        <Bill, Bob>, <David, w>, <Sue, Pat>,
        <Sue, Jim>, <Sue, Bill>, <Sue, David>,
        <Sue, Bob>, <Sue, people>, <Sue, Sue>}
‖Q4‖ = {David, Pat}

The following points should be noted:

(a) 'Sue' is not in ‖Q2‖ as we might intuitively expect. We return to this point in the next sub-section.

(b) <David, w> ∈ ‖Q3‖ means that David likes all entities, i.e. a variable in an answer is regarded as being universally quantified.

(c) Neither 'Sue' nor 'Bill' are in ‖Q4‖ as we might intuitively expect. We return to this point in the next sub-section.

We now show how the answers above can be derived using a 'refutation' technique based on resolution. We begin with Q1. To see how this open query can be answered, consider the closed query:

'is it the case that KB1 ⊢ ∃x∃y (x.hasdad.y)?'

To answer this query positively (i.e. to obtain the answer 'yes'), we would attempt to refute the formula ¬∃x∃y (x.hasdad.y) by converting it to clausal form: {¬(x.hasdad.y)} and resolving this clause away. Any substitution for x which leads to the clause {¬(x.hasdad.y)} being resolved away against KB1, is a member of ‖Q1‖. The set of substitutions which represent all ways in which the clause can be resolved away is the complete answer to Q1.

As illustration:

$$\frac{\{¬(x.hasdad.y)\}, \ \{(Pat.hasdad.Bill)\}A2}{⊠}$$

Therefore, 'Pat' ∈ ‖Q1‖. Notice that the resolving axiom A2 has been annotated to help reference back to the knowledge base KB1. Another member of ‖Q1‖ is obtained as follows:

$$\frac{\{\neg(x.hasdad.y)\}, \ \{(z.hasdad.f(z)), \ \neg(z.\in.people)\}A9}{\{\neg(z. \in . people)\}}$$

with substitution $\{x/z, y/f(z)\}$, followed by:

$$\frac{\{\neg(z.\in.people)\}, \ \{(David.\in.people)\}A10}{\boxtimes}$$

with substitution $\{z/David\}$.

Notice that the variables in A9 have been standardised apart so that A9 has no variable in common with the clause with which it is resolved. Notice also that the partial answer 'David' is obtained by tracing back the substitutions from the null clause to x. Green (1968) has suggested a more efficient method which avoids such tracing. All we have to do is 'carry' the original (unnegated) clause throughout the process. It is tagged so as not to interfere with resolutions but its variables undergo (and thereby save) all substitutions which are made. For example, if the clause $\{(x.hasdad.y)\}$ were used in the example above, then it would eventually become $\{(David.hasdad.f(David)\}$, thereby providing the partial answer 'David'. In the following discussions such dummy clauses will be omitted for brevity. However, we shall assume that they are present and thereby provide us with the substitutions which give the answers required.

Problems occur with universally quantified variables
Problems occur with queries containing ∀. Consider, for example, Q2. To answer this query, we consider the corresponding closed query ∃x∀y (x.likes.y). Negating this gives ∀x∃y ¬(x.likes.y). Converting this to clausal form gives $\{\neg(x.likes.f(x))\}$ where f is a skolem function. The answer to Q2 consists of all substitutions for x such that this clause can be refuted in KB1.

The following shows how one such substitution may be identified:

$$\frac{\{\neg(x.likes.f(x))\}, \ \{(David.likes.w)\}A11}{\boxtimes}$$

That is, 'David' ∈ ‖Q2‖. However, by looking at KB1, we might also expect that 'Sue' ∈ ‖Q2‖, since she would appear to like all entities which are mentioned in KB1. In fact, as it stands, KB1 states that Sue likes all entities distinguished by constants in KB1. It does not state that Sue likes all entities since nowhere do we state that those entities distinguished by constants are the only entities in the domain of the relational structures which are models of KB1. One way to overcome this problem is to add what are called 'domain closure axioms' to the knowledge base. For example, the following could be added to KB1:

DC1 : ∀w[(Pat. = .w) ∨ (Jim. = .w) ∨ (Bill. = .w)...]
DC2 : ∀w∀y∀z[(y. = .z) ∧ (w.likes.y)] → (w.likes.z)
DC3 : ∀w∀y∀z[(y. = .z) ∧ (y.likes.w)] → (z.likes.w)
DC4 : ∀w∀y∀z[(y. = .z) ∧ (z.brotherof.w)] → (y.brotherof.w)
(etc.)

DC1 states that every entity in the domain is *equal* to Pat or Jim or

277

Bill ... . Note that this does not mean that Pat, Jim, Bill, etc. are the only entities. DC2, 3, 4, etc. state that two entities which are equal are indistinguishable as far as the relationships in which they are involved are concerned.

DC1 together with DC2, 3, 4, etc. effectively restrict the domain to Pat, Jim, Bill, etc., and may be regarded as implementing the domain closure assumption.

Assuming that the domain closure assumption is appropriate and that domain closure axioms have been added to KB1, we can obtain 'Sue' as a partial answer to Q2 as shown in equations (a) to (f) on the opposite page.

More complex queries
Consider the query Q4. The corresponding closed query is:

$$\exists x \forall y [\neg(y.brotherof.David) \lor (x.likes.y)]$$

The negation of this is to be refuted:

$$\forall x \exists y [(y.brotherof.David) \land \neg(x.likes.y)]$$

which in skolem form is:

$$(f(x).brotherof.David) \land \neg(x.likes.f(x))$$

which in clausal form is:

$$\{\{(f(w).brotherof.David)\}F1,$$ (Note that we have standardised
$$\{\neg(x.likes.f(x))\}F2 \qquad \}$$ the variables apart.)

This, the formula to be refuted, can be read as 'for all w there is someone f(w) who is the brother of David and for all x there is someone f(x) who is not liked by x'.

A partial answer to Q4 is any substitution for x which refutes either F1 or F2 or both. For example:

$$\underline{\{\neg(x.likes.f(x))\ F2,\quad (David.likes.w)\}A11}$$
$$\boxtimes$$

Therefore 'David' is a partial answer since David likes all entities. Another partial answer can be derived as follows:

$$\underline{\{(f(w).brotherof.David)\}F1,\ \{\neg(z.brotherof.David),\ (Pat.likes.z)\}A3}$$
$$\{(Pat.likes.f(w)\}$$

$$\underline{\{(Pat.likes.f(w))\},\ \{\neg(x.likes.f(x))\}F2}$$
$$\boxtimes$$

Therefore 'Pat' $\in$ $\|Q4\|$. Notice that we 'standardised apart' the variable in A3.

(a) $\{\neg(x.likes.f(x))\}, \{(w.likes.y), \neg(w.likes.y), \neg(y. = .z)\}DC2$

$\{\neg(x.likes.y), \neg(y. = .f(x))\}R1$

(b) $\{\neg(x.likes.y), \neg(y. = .f(x))\}R1, \{(Pat. = .w), (Jim. = .w), (Bill. = .w) \ldots\}DC1$

$\{\neg(x.likes.Pat), (Jim. = .f(x)), (Bill. = .f(x)) \ldots\}R2$

(c) $\{\neg(x.likes.Pat), (Jim. = .f(x)), (Bill. = .f(x)) \ldots\}R2, \{\neg(x.likes.y), \neg(y. = .f(w))\}R1$

$\{\neg(x.likes.Pat), \neg(x.likes.Jim), (Bill. = .f(x)) \ldots\}$

(d) Repeat until all literals with = are resolved away against R1.

(e) $\{\neg(x.likes.Pat), \neg(x.likes.Jim), \neg(x.likes.Bill), \ldots\}, \{(Sue.likes.Pat)\}A12$

$\{\neg(Sue.likes.Jim), \neg(Sue.likes.Bill)\} \ldots\}$

(f) Resolve literals away against A13 to A18 until the null clause is derived giving 'Sue' as an answer.

279

'Sue' can also be derived since F2 can be refuted using the domain
closure axioms. Intuitively, 'Sue' can be seen to be an answer since
Sue likes all entities whether or not they are brothers of David
(assuming that the domain closure axioms are present). Now, by looking
at KB1, we might also expect to be able to derive 'Bill' as an answer
since Bill likes Jim and Bob, and Jim and Bob appear to be the only
brothers of David. However, see what happens (assuming that the domain
closure axioms are present):

(a) F2 is expanded using DC1 and DC2 to give:

   {¬(x.likes.Jim), ¬(x.likes.Bob),
                         (Pat. = .f(x)), (Bill. = .f(x)) ...}

(b) This is resolved against A6 and A7 to give:

   {(Pat. = .f(Bill)), (Bill. = .f(Bill)) ...}

(c) This is resolved against DC4 to give:

   {(Pat.brotherof.w), ¬(f(Bill).brotherof.w),
                                  (Bill. = .f(Bill)) ...}

(d) This is resolved against F1 to give:

   {(Pat.brotherof. David), (Bill. = .f(Bill)) ...}

(e) Repeating the last two steps several times gives:

   {(Pat.brotherof.David), (Bill.brotherof.David), ...}

Now we are stuck. As KB1 stands, we cannot derive the null clause.
This is because Pat *could* be a brother of David, or Bill *could* be a
brother of David, or ... . There is nothing in KB1 to refute this.
What we need to do is to make the 'negative' facts (which we may have
assumed by default in our intuitive reasoning) explicit. That is, if
we add the following axioms to the knowledge base, then we can derive
the answer 'Bill' to the query Q4:

   ¬(Pat.brotherof.David)
   ¬(Bill.brotherof.David)
   ¬(David.brotherof.David)
   ¬(Sue.brotherof.David)
   ¬(people.brotherof.David)

Different approaches to dealing with negative facts are discussed in
sub-section 5.4.5.

5.4.3 REDUCTION OF ARBITRARY QUERIES TO COMPLETELY OPEN QUERIES

In many knowledge bases there will be a considerable number of constants. In such cases, the evaluation of queries containing universally quantified variables using domain closure and equality axioms as
described earlier will be very time-consuming. Referring back to the
example in 5.4.2, each constant in the domain closure axiom requires
three resolution steps for each answer. This problem can be alleviated
to some extent by reducing such queries to completely open queries,
answering these open queries using formal proof techniques and then
applying relational algebraic operators to these open query answers to

obtain the answers to the original query. The domain closure and equality axioms are not required at all in this approach.

In the following pages, the method is described informally using examples. A more rigorous description is given in Reiter (1978).

A simple query containing a universally quantified variable
We begin by considering a simple query containing a single universally quantified variable:

Q2 = {x | ∀y (x.likes.y)}KB1

which is read as 'retrieve all entities which are represented as liking all entities in the knowledge base KB1'. This query can be reduced to a completely open query:

Q2' = {x, y | (x.likes.y)}KB1

which may be read as 'retrieve all pairs <x, y> such that x is represented as liking y in the knowledge base KB1'. To answer this completely open query, we simply find all ways in which the clause ¬(x. likes. y) can be resolved away using axioms in KB1. The complete set of answers is:

‖Q2'‖	
x	y
Pat	Jim
Pat	Bob
Bill	Jim
Bill	Bob
David	w
Sue	Pat
Sue	Jim
Sue	Bill
Sue	David
Sue	Bob
Sue	people
Sue	Sue

The answer <David, w> means that David likes all entities, i.e.
<David, w> = {<David, Pat>, <David, Jim>, <David, Bill>, ... etc.}

If we now extract from ‖Q2'‖ only these values of x which are related to all values which y can stand for, then we have the answer to the original query. To be able to do this we need to enumerate the entities which y can stand for. In other words, a rule which is similar to the domain closure axiom given in 5.4.2 is needed.

As example, consider the following rule which states that the only entities which exist in the relational structure described by KB1 are those entities distinguished by the constants {Pat,Jim,Bill ... etc.}:

|entities in KB1| = {Pat, Jim, Bill, ...etc.}

281

Note that this rule is different from the domain closure axioms given earlier in that it is not part of the knowledge base nor is it part of the formal system. It is applied after the formal proof techniques have been used to obtain the answers to the completely open query. The rule simply lists those entities which exist in the universe of discourse. Using this rule we can see that the only values which y can assume are:

|values for y| = {Pat, Jim, Bill, ...etc.}

and, therefore, the only values of x which are related to all values of y are David and Sue. Therefore, the answer to Q2 is:

‖Q2‖ = those values of x in ‖Q2'‖ which are related to all
$$\text{values of } y$$
= {David, Sue}

Note that David is an answer since <David, w> is in ‖Q2'‖ and Sue is an answer since <Sue, Pat>, <Sue, Jim>, <Sue, Bill>, etc., are all in ‖Q2'‖.

The process of extracting from ‖Q2'‖ only those values of x which are related to all values which y can take is called 'division with respect to y'. Division is a relational algebraic operator as described in chapter 3. This division operator is denoted by δy which is defined as follows:

‖{x | ∀y F}‖ = δy‖{x, y | F}‖

A more complex query containing a universally quantified variable
We now present a slightly more complex example. Consider the query:

Q4 = {x | ∀y (y.brotherof.David) → (x.likes.y)}

which is read as 'retrieve all entities which like all brothers of David'. Reducing this to a completely open query in clausal form gives:

Q4' = {x, y | {(x.likes.y), ¬(y. brotherof.David)}}

which is read as 'retrieve all pairs of entities <x, y> such that either x likes y, or y is not a brother of David'. To answer this query, the clause {(x.likes.y), ¬(y.brotherof.David)} is negated to give the following clause set consisting of two clauses:

{{¬(x.likes.y)}C1, {(y.brotherof.David)}C2}

Notice that no skolem functions or constants need be introduced since Q4' contains no quantifiers.

To obtain the answers to Q4' we must add both of the clauses C1 and C2 to the axioms of KB1 and find all ways in which the null clause can be derived. This gives:

‖Q4'‖	
x	y
Pat	Jim
Pat	Bob
Bill	Jim
Bill	Bob
David	w
Sue	Pat
Sue	Jim
Sue	Bill
Sue	David
Sue	Bob
Sue	people
Sue	Sue
Pat	w

derived by resolving
axioms of KB1
against C1

The last tuple <Pat, w> is obtained as follows:

$$\frac{\{(y.brotherof.David)\}, \{\neg(w.brotherof.David), (Pat.likes.w)\}}{\{(Pat. likes. w)\}}$$

followed by:

$$\frac{\{(Pat.likes.w)\}, \{\neg(x.likes.y)\}}{⊠}$$

Applying the division operator δy to ‖Q4'‖ gives:

‖Q4‖
x
David
Sue
Pat

Notice, however, that <Bill> is not an answer to Q4.

Intuitively, we might expect <Bill> to be an answer since Bill likes Jim and Bill likes Bob, and Jim and Bob are the only brothers of David. The reason Bill has not been obtained as an answer is because, as it stands, KB1 is incomplete. Certain negative assertions are missing which are required if <Bill> is to be obtained as an answer. The missing assertions are:

¬(Pat.brotherof.David)
¬(Bill.brotherof.David)
¬(David.brotherof.David)
¬(Sue.brotherof.David)
¬(people.brotherof.David)

Note that we have already mentioned the need for such negative assertions in section 5.4.2.

Suppose, then, that these negative assertions are added to KB1. The answers to Q4' would now be:

‖Q4'‖	
x	y
Pat	Jim
Pat	Bob
Bill	Jim
David	w
Sue	Pat
Sue	Jim
Sue	Bill
Sue	David
Sue	Bob
Sue	people
Pat	w
-	Pat
-	Bill
-	David
-	Sue
-	people

The first group of rows is labelled "as before"; the second group of rows (with dashes in the x column) is "obtained by resolving C2 against the negative clauses".

The presence of a value in the y column with no corresponding value of x means that the value for y is an answer for all values of x. For example:

<-, Pat> = {<Pat, Pat>, <Jim, Pat>, (Bill, Pat>, ...etc.}

Applying the division operator to ‖Q4'‖ now gives:

‖Q4‖
x
David
Sue
Pat
Bill

which is the answer that we might intuitively expect.

Queries containing existentially quantified variables

The answers to queries containing existentially quantified variables can be obtained in a manner similar to that described above for universally quantified queries. The query is first reduced to a completely open query which is answered using formal proof techniques. This answer is then manipulated using a relational algebraic operator to obtain the answer to the original query. The difference is that the operator, used in this case, is the 'projection* operator'. For example, consider the query:

Q5 = {x | ∃y (x.likes.y)}

which may be read as 'retrieve all entities which are represented in
KB1 as liking some entity'. Reducing this to a completely open query
gives:

Q5' = {x, y | (x.likes.y)}

which is equivalent to Q2' described earlier. The answer to Q5' is
the same as the answer to Q2'. In order to obtain the answer to Q5,
we simply remove the y column from the answer ‖Q2'‖, (= ‖Q5'‖) and then
remove the redundant values of x, giving:

‖Q5‖
Pat
Bill
David
Sue

The projection* operator is denoted by π and is defined as follows:

‖{x | ∃y F}‖ = πy‖{x, y | F}‖

The projection* operator is derived from the relational algebraic projection operator as described in sub-section 3.4.7.

Arbitrary queries
The usefulness of the division and projection* operators should now be
apparent: we need only develop formal methods for the evaluation of
completely open queries. The answers to arbitrary queries, containing
universally and existentially quantified variables, can then be derived
by the appropriate application of δ and π to the answers obtained from
the corresponding open queries. For example, consider the query:

Q6 = {x | ∃y∀w∃z F}

which may read as 'retrieve all entities x for which there exists an
entity y such that for all entities w there exists an entity z which
makes the formula F true'. The answer to Q6 can be obtained by answering the completely open query:

Q6' = {x, y, w, z | F}

and then applying the operators πz, δw, πy, (in that order) to ‖Q6'‖.
That is:

‖{x | ∃y∀w∃z F}‖ = πyδwπz‖{x, y, w, z | F}‖

5.4.4 THE CLOSED WORLD ASSUMPTION/FAILURE TO PROVE AS NEGATION
Examples have been given of cases in which it is necessary to add negative assertions to a knowledge base in order that formal proof methods
will provide the answers which we would intuitively expect when queries
are evaluated. To illustrate this point further, we give another
example: suppose we want to find those entities which do not have Bill
as a dad:

Q8 = {x | ¬(x.hasdad.Bill)}KB1

With KB1 as it stands, we would obtain no answers to Q8 using the resolution proof method. Intuitively, we might expect the answer to be
{Jim, Bill, David, Bob, Sue, people}. The reason this answer is not
obtained is that the proof method treats the knowledge base literally.
The only things it knows are those things which are represented explicitly or can be derived from the knowledge base. Just because (Jim.
hasdad.Bill) is not in the knowledge base, there is no reason to assume
that ¬(Jim.hasdad.Bill) is true. As far as the logic is concerned, the
truth of (Jim.hasdad.Bill) is unknown. Therefore in order to obtain
the answer we might intuitively expect we could add the following assertions to KB1:

    ¬(Jim.hasdad.Bill)
    ¬(Bill.hasdad.Bill)
    ¬(David.hasdad.Bill)
    ¬(Sue.hasdad.Bill)
    ¬(people.hasdad.Bill)

Use of completion axioms and inequality axiom schemas
In many applications, it would be unreasonable to expect users to
explicitly express all negative assertions pertaining to some universe
of discourse. One solution to this probler is to add 'completion
axioms' and 'inequality axiom schemas' to the knowledge base. For
example, if we are certain that Pat is the only entity which has Bill
as father, then we could add the following completion axiom to KB1:

    ∀x (x.hasdad.Bill) → (x. = .Pat)

together with an inequality axiom schema for each literal on the right-
hand side of the completion axiom. In this example, there is only one
literal, and the inequality axiom schema is:

    ¬(c. = .Pat) for all constants c different from Pat

If KB1 also contained the formula (Gregory.hasdad.Bill), then the completion axiom would be:

    ∀x (x.hasdad.Bill) → (x. = .Pat) ∨ (x. = .Gregory)

and the inequality axiom schemas would be:

    ¬(c. = .Pat)
    ¬(c. = .Gregory)

Using first order proof techniques we can now prove, for example,
¬(Bill.hasdad. Bill) with respect to KB1. The proof of this formula
commences with resolving its negation against the completion axiom:

$$\frac{\{(Bill.hasdad.Bill)\}\{¬(x.hasdad.Bill), (x. = .Pat)\}}{\{(Bill. = .Pat)\}}$$

The inequality axiom schema is now used to generate the axiom
¬(Bill. = .Pat) which resolves against the resolvent above to give
the null clause.

This approach saves the user having to express all of the negative assertions explicitly. However, it is not a particularly good method for two reasons:

(a) The user still has to express what could be rather long completion axioms (though this could be partially automated).

(b) The proof might take a great deal of time since each literal on the right-hand side of the completion axiom will have to be resolved away against an appropriate inequality axiom.

The closed world assumption/'failure to prove as negation' metarule
Instead of using completion and inequality axioms, an alternative approach is to express all positive assertions and simply assume negative assertions by default. That is, if a formula F cannot be proved, then we assume ¬F. This assumption is equivalent to the 'closed world assumption' (CWA) and can be implemented using a failure as negation metarule:

if every possible proof of F fails, then infer ¬F

For example, consider the knowledge base KB1. Let us make the closed world assumption. We can now prove ¬(Bill.hasdad.Bill) as follows:

- Try to prove (Bill.hasdad.Bill).
- Because all proofs of (Bill.hasdad.Bill) fail, we can use the failure as negation rule to infer ¬(Bill.hasdad.Bill).

Notice that the CWA presumes total knowledge about the universe of discourse. In contrast, the 'open world assumption' (OWA) only assumes those assertions which can be proved (i.e. only those assertions which are explicitly present or which can be derived by inference rules other than the failure as negation rule). As such, the OWA permits gaps in our knowledge of the universe of discourse whereas the CWA does not.

Knowledge bases which are consistent with the CWA
Not every consistent knowledge base remains consistent under the CWA. For example, consider the following:

KB = {(x.∈.animals) ∨ (x.∈.minerals) ∨ (x.∈.vegetables)}

Since we cannot prove (John.∈.animals), nor can we prove (John.∈. minerals), nor can we prove (John.∈.vegetables) from KB, we can assume, under the CWA, that ¬(John.∈.animals), ¬(John.∈.minerals) and ¬(John.∈. vegetables) are all theorems of KB using the failure as negation metarule. But this now gives us a total set of formulas which is inconsistent:

{(x.∈.animals) ∨ (x.∈.minerals) ∨ (x.∈.vegetables),
¬(John.∈.animals),
¬(John.∈.minerals),
¬(John.∈.vegetables)}

This problem does not occur if the knowledge base is Horn; that is, if each clause in the clausal form of the knowledge base contains at most

one positive literal. This is an important restriction on the use of
the CWA.

Application of the CWA

We have indicated one restriction on the use of the CWA, i.e. it should
only be used when the knowledge base is Horn (if we require the knowledge base to remain consistent). However, this does not mean that it
is always appropriate to use the CWA when the knowledge base is Horn.
Use of the CWA depends on the application:

(a) If we have complete knowledge about the universe of discourse,
then it is appropriate to use the CWA. For example, consider
an airline booking system in which all flights and the cities
which they connect are explicitly represented. Failure to
find an entry connecting a particular flight to a particular
city permits one to conclude that no such connection exists.

(b) In some applications, it may only be appropriate to apply the
CWA to certain parts of the universe of discourse. For
example, the fact that we cannot prove, say, that (Jim.has
numberoflegs.2) would not generally permit us to conclude that
Jim has not got two legs. It would be quite wrong to apply
the CWA inappropriately since it could result in our inferring
facts as false which are really unknown.

The problem with the CWA and the failure as negation metarule is that
they apply to the whole knowledge base and not just to selected predicates. (Note, conversely, that completion and inequality axioms are
applied to particular predicates.) In section 5.5 an approach to
default negative assertions which overcomes this 'all or nothing' problem of the CWA is described. In effect, we apply the CWA to only those
parts of the knowledge base for which it is appropriate. Rules, called
'completion rules', are expressed which can be regarded as defining
sets of negative *or positive* formulas which can be assumed by default.
This is discussed in more detail in section 5.5.

Soundness of the failure as negation metarule

Suppose it is decided that for a particular knowledge base, the CWA is
appropriate. The question arises as to the soundness of the failure
as negation rule, i.e. is it correct to interpret a failure proof of
¬F as a valid first order inference that F is false? Clark (1978)
provides a validation of the failure as negation rule, which is constructive in the sense that it provides a method for evaluating CWA
queries. This method is similar to the approach used in the Prolog
logic programming language which is discussed in more detail later in
the book.

5.4.5 REDUCTION OF COMPLEX QUERIES TO SETS OF ATOMIC QUERIES

This section will show how, in certain constrained circumstances, the
evaluation of certain types of query can be reduced to the evaluation
of sets of very simple queries, called 'atomic queries', whose answers
are then manipulated using operations of division, projection, union,
intersection and difference, to obtain the answer to the original query.

An atomic query is of the form:

$\{\vec{x} \mid F\}$

where $\vec{x}$ stands for an n tuple $<x1, \ldots, xn>$ containing the free variables which occur in F, and F is an unquantified formula consisting of a single positive or negative predicate sign. The following is an example of an atomic query:

$\{x, y \mid (x.\text{likes}.y)\}$

In appropriate circumstances, as will be shown, we need only develop efficient methods for the evaluation of atomic queries and for the operations of division, projection, union, intersection and difference. Also, in certain circumstances, the OWA evaluation of atomic queries is equivalent to the CWA evaluation of atomic queries. This means that in these circumstances we need not use completeness axioms nor need we use the 'failure as negation' rule described in sub-section 5.4.4. It is, however, important to appreciate that the methods described in this sub-section only apply in the circumstances stated. A more general and formal treatment of these results is given in Reiter (1978).

We begin by showing how certain queries containing the logical connectives ∨ and ∧ can be reduced to sets of atomic queries whose answers are united and intersected to provide the answer to the original query.

Elimination of ∨ *and* ∧
The following identities hold for arbitrary knowledge bases under the CWA and for Horn knowledge bases under the OWA:

$$\|\{\vec{x} \mid \exists \vec{y} \ [F1 \lor F2]\}\| \ \equiv \ \|\{\vec{x} \mid \exists \vec{y} \ F1\}\| \ \cup \ \|\{\vec{x} \mid \exists \vec{y} \ F2\}\|$$
$$\|\{\vec{x} \mid F1 \land F2\}\| \ \equiv \ \|\{\vec{x} \mid F1\}\| \ \cap \ \|\{\vec{x} \mid F2\}\|$$

That is, ∨ and ∧ can be eliminated in favour of set union and set intersection. As example, consider the query:

$\{x \mid (x.\text{brotherof}.\text{David}) \lor (x.\text{brotherof}.\text{Sue})\}$

which may be read as 'retrieve all brothers of David or brothers of Sue'. The CWA answer to this query is equivalent to:

$\|\{x \mid (x.\text{brotherof}.\text{David})\}\|\text{CWA} \ \cup \ \|\{x \mid (x.\text{brotherof}.\text{Sue})\}\|\text{CWA}$

Notice that in the first identity the query must not contain universal quantifiers and in the second identity the query must be quantifier free. Notice also that although the identities hold for CWA evaluation of queries with respect to arbitrary knowledge bases, they fail under the OWA with respect to non-Horn knowledge bases. (As mentioned in 5.4.4, non-Horn knowledge bases may be inconsistent with the CWA; therefore, although the identities above hold for such knowledge bases, we will not use them in such circumstances.) Consequently, these identities are really only useful for Horn knowledge bases and, in this case, apply both to CWA and to OWA evaluation of queries.

As example of how the first identity above fails under OWA with respect to a non-Horn knowledge base, consider the following:

KB2 = {(Pat.∈.men) ∨ (Pat.∈.women)}
  Q = {x | (x.∈.men) ∨ (x.∈.women)}KB2

Hence ‖Q‖OWA = {Pat}
but ‖{x | (x.∈.men)}‖OWA ∪ ‖{x.∈.women)}‖OWA = { }

As example of how the second identity above fails under the OWA for
non-Horn knowledge bases, consider the following:

  KB3 = {(Alice.parentof.Bill) ∨ (Lucy.parentof.Bill),
         (Alice.∈.women),
         (Lucy.∈.women)}
  Q = {x | (x.parentof.Bill) ∧ (x.∈.women)}KB3

Hence, ‖Q‖OWA = {Alice or Lucy}
but ‖{x | (x.parentof.Bill)}‖OWA = {Alice or Lucy}
and ‖{x | (x.∈.women)}‖OWA = {Alice, Lucy}
and {Alice or Lucy} ∩ {Alice, Lucy} = { }

Notice that we have introduced indefinite answers such as {Alice or
Lucy} without really explaining how such answers would be obtained.
The interested reader is referred to Reiter (1978).

Elimination of occurrences of ¬ in queries
For CWA evaluation of quantifier-free queries with respect to Horn
knowledge bases, the following identities hold:

$$‖\{\vec{x} \mid ¬F\}‖CWA = |C|n - ‖\{\vec{x} \mid F\}‖CWA$$

$$‖\{\vec{x} \mid F1 ∧ ¬F2\}‖CWA = ‖\{\vec{x} \mid F1\}‖CWA - ‖\{\vec{x} \mid F2\}‖CWA$$

$\vec{x}$ stands for an n-tuple $\langle x1, \ldots, xn \rangle$ containing the free variables
which occur in the formula of the query, and $|C|n$ stands for the set
of n-tuples which can be obtained by selecting n constants, in all
possible ways, from the set C of constants which appear in the knowledge base. Notice that both of these equalities fail under the OWA.

As example of the use of the first identity, consider the knowledge
base KB1 which was introduced at the beginning of section 5.4. Suppose
we want to evaluate the query Q, below, under the CWA:

  Q = {x, y | ¬(x.likes.y)}KB1

This query may be read as 'retrieve all pairs of entities ⟨x, y⟩ such
that ¬(x.likes.y) is true in the knowledge base KB1'. Using the first
identity above gives:

‖Q‖CWA = |C|2 - ‖{x, y | (x.likes.y)}‖CWA
       = {⟨Pat, Pat⟩, ⟨Pat, Bill⟩, ⟨Pat, Tom⟩, ...etc.} -
                                        ‖{x, y | (x.likes.y)}‖
       = {⟨Pat, Pat⟩, ⟨Pat, Bill⟩, ⟨Pat, Tom⟩, ...etc.} -
                                 {⟨Pat, Jim⟩, ⟨Pat, Tom⟩,
                                  ⟨Bill, Tom⟩, ⟨Bill, Bob⟩,
                                       ⟨Sue, Pat⟩, ...}
       = {⟨Pat, Pat⟩, ⟨Pat, Bill⟩, ...etc.}

which is the answer that we would intuitively expect.

Notice that the evaluation of this query in this way does not require the use of completeness axioms nor the use of a 'failure as negation' metarule.

Reduction of arbitrary queries to atomic queries

So far it has been shown that, under appropriate circumstances, $\vee$, $\wedge$ and $\neg$ can be eliminated from certain types of query. These results are summarised in the following table:

Logical connective	Type of query	Assumption	Type of knowledge base
$\vee$	universal quantifier-free	CWA	arbitrary
$\vee$	universal quantifier-free	OWA	Horn
$\wedge$	quantifier-free	CWA	arbitrary
$\wedge$	quantifier-free	OWA	Horn
$\neg$	quantifier-free	CWA	Horn

The elimination of $\vee$, $\wedge$ and $\neg$, together with the methods described in sub-section 5.4.3, for the reduction of quantified queries to completely open queries, can be used to reduce arbitrarily quantified and complex queries to sets of atomic queries whose answers are then manipulated using the operations of division, projection, union, intersection and difference to obtain the answer to the original query. For example, suppose that we have a Horn knowledge base KB and a query Q:

$$Q = \{x \mid \exists y \ (x.P.y) \vee ((x.Q.y) \wedge \neg(x.R.y))\}KB$$

The OWA answer to this query can be obtained as follows:

$$\|Q\|OWA = \pi y (\|\{x, y \mid (x.P.y)\}\|OWA \cup (\|\{x, y \mid (x.Q.y)\}\|OWA \cap \|\{x, y \mid \neg(x.R.y)\}\|OWA))$$

and the CWA answer to this query can be obtained as follows:

$$\|Q\|CWA = \pi y (\|\{x, y \mid (x.P.y)\}\|CWA \cup (\|\{x, y \mid (x.Q.y)\}\|CWA \cap (|C|2 - \|\{x, y \mid (x.R.y)\}\|CWA)))$$

It should be pointed out that the unthinking reduction of quantified queries to open queries and then to atomic queries, as described above, may not always result in the most efficient method of query evaluation. For example, consider the following query which is to be evaluated under the CWA:

$$Q = \{x \mid \forall y \ \neg(x.likes.y)\}KB1$$

which is read as 'retrieve all entities which are represented in KB1 as not liking all entities'. Reducing Q to a completely open query gives:

$$\|Q\|CWA = \delta y \|\{x, y \mid \neg(x.likes.y)\}\|CWA$$

which may be reduced to an atomic query and application of the difference operator as follows:

$$\|Q\|CWA = \delta y (|C|2 - \|\{x, y \mid (x.likes.y)\}\|CWA)$$

where $|C|2 = \{<Pat, Pat>, <Pat, Jim> ... etc.\}$

Evaluation of $\|Q\|CWA$ in this way requires a fair amount of effort even for the very small knowledge base KB1. An alternative approach is to re-express the original query as:

$$Q = \{x \mid \neg\exists y \ (x.likes.y)\}$$

which may be read as 'retrieve all entities x for which there does not exist an entity y which x likes'.

Intuitively, we can see that under the CWA this query could be evaluated by retrieving the set of all entities which like anything and subtracting this set from the set of all entities:

$$\|Q\|CWA = C - \|\{x \mid \exists y \ (x.likes.y)\}\|CWA$$
$$= C - \pi y\|\{x, y \mid (x.likes.y)\}\|CWA$$

which should be easier to evaluate than the formulation above. This suggests that some strategy is required for the conversion of arbitrary queries to atomic queries such that optional evaluation procedures are found. Relatively little work has been done on developing such strategies and this may be regarded as an area for future research.

Reduction of CWA evaluation of arbitrary queries to OWA evaluation of positive atomic queries
If the knowledge base is consistent with the CWA (for example, if it is Horn) and Q is an atomic query, then:

$$\|Q\|CWA = \|Q\|OWA$$

This is one of the main results of Reiter's treatment of the closed world assumption. This result, together with those presented earlier, can be used to reduce CWA evaluation of arbitrary queries to OWA evaluation of atomic queries followed by the application of division, projection, union, intersection and difference operations. As illustration, a simple example derived from one given by Reiter (1978) is presented. Consider the Horn knowledge base KB4 defined as follows:

> KB4 : $\{\forall x \forall y \forall z \ (x.supplies.y) \wedge (z.subpart.y) \rightarrow (x.supplies.z),$
> $\forall x \ (x.\in.widget) \rightarrow (foobar.supplies.x),$
> $\forall x \forall y \forall z \ (z.subpart.y) \wedge (y.subpart.x) \rightarrow (z.subpart.x),$
> (Acme.supplies.p1),
> (AAA.supplies.w3),
> (AA.supplies.w4),
> (p2.subpart.p1),
> (p3.subpart.p2),
> (w1.subpart.p1),
> (w2.subpart.w1),
> (w1.∈.widget),
> (w2.∈.widget),
> (w3.∈.widget),
> (w4.∈.widget),}

Now suppose that we have the query Q:

$$Q = \{x \mid \exists y \ (x. \text{ supplies. } y) \land (y. \text{ subpart. } p1) \land \neg(x. \text{ supplies. } p3) \land (y. \in . \text{ widget})\}$$

which is read as 'retrieve all entities which supply a widget which is a subpart of p1, and which do not supply p3'.

The closed world answer to this can be obtained from OWA answers to atomic queries as follows:

$$\|Q\|CWA = \pi y(\|Q1\|OWA \cap \|Q2\|OWA \cap (|C| - \|Q3\|OWA) \cap \|Q4\|OWA)$$

where Q1 = {x, y | (x.supplies.y)}
      Q2 = {y | (y.subpart.p1)}
      Q3 = {x | (x.supplies.p3)}
      Q4 = {y | (y.∈.widgets)}

Open world assumption evaluation of these positive atomic queries gives:

||Q1||OWA		||Q2||OWA	||Q3||OWA	||Q4||OWA
x	y	y	x	y
Foobar	w1			
Foobar	w2	p2		w1
Foobar	w3	p3		w2
Foobar	w4		Acme	
AAA	w3	w1		w3
AAA	w4	w2		w4
Acme	w1			
Acme	w2			

Therefore:

$$|C| - \|Q3\|OWA = \{\text{Foobar, AAA, w1, w2, w3, w4, p1, p2, p3}\}$$

where |C| is the set of constants in KB4

and $\|Q1\|OWA \cap \|Q2\|OWA$ =

Foobar	w1
Foobar	w2
Acme	w1
Acme	w2

Hence:

$$\|Q\|CWA = \text{Foobar}$$

Notice that we have been somewhat liberal in the use of the terms

293

'union' and 'intersection'. From this example, it can be seen that we have defined ∩ and ∪ as follows:

$$\{<a,\ b>,\ <c,\ d>\} \cap \{<a,\ ->\} = \{<a,\ b>\}$$

and

$$\{<a,\ b>\} \cup \{<c,\ ->\} = \{<a,\ b>,\ <c,\ ->\}$$

where $<a,\ ->$ means that a is related to all other entities.

Removal of purely negative Horn clauses

Reiter (1978) also shows that for consistent Horn knowledge bases under the closed world assumption, purely negative clauses are irrelevant for deductive retrievel and function, instead, only as integrity constraints. In particular, Reiter shows that the evaluation of a query Q with respect to a consistent Horn knowledge base KB yields the same set of answers as when evaluated with respect to the knowledge base obtained by the removal of all clauses with no positive literal from KB. This result means that some clauses may be removed from the search space when evaluating a query, thereby reducing the effort required.

5.4.6 THE APPLICABILITY OF THE THEORY ONLY APPROACH

Summary
In the theory only approach, the database together with the schema are regarded as the proper axioms of a theory T. Integrity checking involves checking the consistency of the new theory T' after T has been updated. When viewed as integrity constraints, the schema rules specify that their negation cannot be a theorem of an updated theory. Data may always be deleted from the knowledge base without affecting consistency (see note on CWA below). The answer to a closed query is 'yes' if the formula is a theorem of the theory, 'no' if its negation is a theorem, and 'don't know' otherwise. A partial answer to an open query $Q = \{<v1,\ \dots,\ vn> \mid F\}$ is any substitution of constants for the free variables $v1,\ \dots,\ vn$ of F which make this substitution instance of F a theorem of T.

The domain closure assumption is not implicit in the evaluation of queries. If it is appropriate to make this assumption then it can be implemented by including domain closure axioms in the theory. Alternatively, a method which is more efficient, in some cases, is to convert the query to a completely open query, answer this query and then apply the projection and division operators (from relational algebra) as appropriate to obtain the answer to the original query.

The closed world assumption is also not implicit in this approach. Therefore, if an answer to a query relies on a 'negative' formula then this formula must be stated explicitly or must be a theorem of the theory. Hence, if the closed world assumption is not appropriate, then one must remember to write down all negative facts as proper axioms. For example, if Pat is not a brother of David, then ¬(Pat. brotherof. David) must be written as a proper axiom. If the closed world assumption *is* appropriate it can be implemented as the 'failure to prove as negation' metarule. However, this may only be done if the knowledge base is Horn since some consistent non-Horn knowledge bases can become inconsistent when this metarule is applied.

The evaluation of queries in a knowledge base which is consistent under the CWA metarule, when the domain closure and closed world assumptions are appropriate, can be reduced to the 'open world' evaluation of completely open atomic queries, followed by the application of relational algebraic operators to obtain the answers to the original query. This result can be used in query optimisation strategies.

Applicability

If the domain closure and closed world assumptions are not appropriate then the theory only approach may be used whereas the theory and complete relational structure approach may not.

If the domain closure and closed world assumptions are appropriate they can be implemented in various ways in the theory only view. If the knowledge base is Horn and the assumptions hold then efficient methods for answering queries can be developed.

The theory only view may be used to formalise deduction whereas the theory and complete relational structure view may not be so used.

If the domain closure and closed world assumptions are appropriate, the theory only view can handle null values. A 'null value' in conventional database work is a value which is known to exist but whose identity is not known. In the theory only approach, existentially quantified variables may be equated with null values. For example:

$$\exists x \ (x.\text{motherof}.\text{David})$$

This formula states that David has a mother, but we cannot identify her.

As mentioned earlier, the notion of an integrity constraint is different in the theory only and the theory and complete relational structure approaches. In particular, the theory only approach cannot accommodate integrity constraints such as 'before a student may be enrolled (for a class), he or she must be known to be a registered student.' Suppose that we try to express this rule as follows in some theory T:

$$R : \forall x \forall y[(x.\text{enrolledfor}.y) \rightarrow (x.\in.\text{registeredstudents})]$$

Whether or not the closed world assumption is in force, the only way we can contradict this 'rule' is by making the following formula a theorem of T:

$$\exists x \exists y[(x.\text{enrolledfor}.y) \land \neg(x.\in.\text{registeredstudents})]$$

For example, insertion of (John. enrolledfor. Maths123) and ¬(John. ∈ . registeredstudents) would contradict R. This is not really what was required. The problem is that in the theory only approach any formula of the form F1 → F2 can be used to infer F2 from F1. Hence it is not possible to use this formula to stand for the constraint that 'F1 is only allowed to be inserted into the knowledge base if F2 is present'. This shortcoming is one of the reasons for introducing the theory and incomplete relational structure approach.

5.5 THE THEORY AND INCOMPLETE RELATIONAL STRUCTURE APPROACH

We begin by listing some of the limitations of the two approaches that have been considered so far.

Limitations of the complete relational structure approach

- (a) The notion of an inference rule is not appropriate, hence this approach cannot be used to formalise deductive database systems.

- (b) The closed world assumption is implicit in this approach, hence it cannot be used to formalise systems in which the data in the database is incomplete.

Limitations of the theory only view

- (a) Integrity constraints such as 'before an entity may be enrolled for a class, it must be known to be a registered student', or 'everything must be known to be male or female', cannot be accommodated.

- (b) The closed world assumption can be implemented in two ways: (i) by use of completion axioms or (ii) by use of the 'failure to prove as negation' metarule. However, (i) is inefficient when queries involve universally quantified variables and (ii) can only be used with Horn databases if inconsistencies are to be avoided.

- (c) All of the proper axioms are used as inference rules *and* as integrity constraints. The notion of rules as inference rules *or* integrity constraints cannot be accommodated (this is related to (a)).

An alternative approach

In this alternative approach, which we call the 'theory and incomplete relational structure approach', the schema rules are regarded as proper axioms of a theory T which admits a set of models W = {W1, W2, ...}. Each of these models is an 'allowed' state of some slice of reality. The database relations are regarded as representing an incomplete relational structure IU which is a 'mathematical sub-structure' of one or more of the complete structures in W. For IU to be valid, it must be a sub-structure of at least one complete structure in W. For IU to be correct, it should be a sub-structure of the current state of the slice of reality which it is partially representing.

The theory and incomplete relational structure approach is depicted in fig. 5.4.

What do we mean by 'sub-structure'?

We are not using the word 'sub-structure' in the strict mathematical sense, although the meaning we ascribe to it is somewhat similar:

- (a) We assume that IU and all of the complete structures in W have the same domain E and the same relation names.

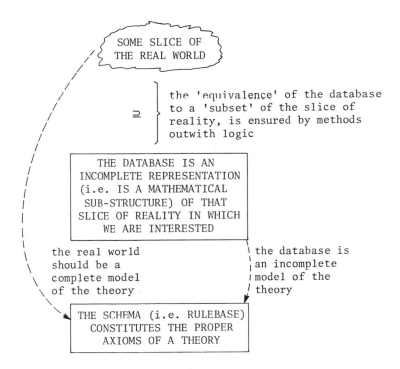

Figure 5.4 The incomplete relational structure and theory approach

(b)   Every structure Wi in W is complete in the sense that for
      every n-ary relation r in Wi and for every n-tuple t ∈ En, it
      is known whether or not t ∈ r, (note En is the set of all
      tuples which can be obtained by taking n entities from E in
      all possible ways).

(c)   IU is incomplete in the sense that for every n-ary relation r
      in IU and for every n-tuple t ∈ En, three cases can arise:

          (i)   it is known that t ∈ r

          (ii)   it is known that t is not a member of r (denoted
                 by t ∉ e)

          (iii) it is not known whether t is or is not a member of
                 r (denoted by the absence of t ∈ r and t ∉ r in IU)

(d)   IU is a mathematical sub-structure of a complete structure
      Wi ∈ U, iff for every n-ary relation r and for every n-tuple
      t ∈ En:

          (i)   if t ∈ r in IU then t ∈ r in Wi

          (ii)   if t ∉ r in IU then t ∉ r in Wi

That is, IU is a sub-structure of a complete structure Wi iff it is
isomorphic to Wi except for the unknown tuple/relation memberships.

Note that definition (d) is somewhat informal. A more precise definition of 'mathematical sub-structure' can be found in Marciszewski
(1981).

The 'relations' in IU are stored as in the following example:

∈	BOB	SUE
∉	ALAN	JANE

The notation t u r is used to signify that neither t ∈ r nor t ∉ r are
stored in IU. For example, <BOB, JANE> u MARRIED signifies that we do
not know whether Bob is married to Jane or not. Note that in conventional database systems, facts of the form t ∈ r are the only ones
allowed.

Evaluating atomic formulas in IU

Since IU is an incomplete structure, it is also an incomplete interpretation for the language L associated with the theory T. Hence it is not
always possible to determine the truth value of an atomic formula of L
by reference to IU. To accommodate this, we need to modify the notion
of satisfaction and truth with respect to an incomplete structure:

(a) An atomic formula pi(t1, t2, ..., tn) is *known to be satisfied*
by a valuation α, if <α(t1), α(t2), ..., α(tn)> ∈ ri. Where
α(t) is the entity in E which is assigned to the term t by the
valuation α, and ri is the relation in IU corresponding to the
predicate symbol pi.

(b) An atomic formula pi(t1, t2, ..., tn) is *known not to be satisfied* by a valuation α, if <α(t1) α(t2), ..., α(tn)> ∉ ri.

An atomic formula which is known to be satisfied in IU by all valuations, is *known to be true* and has the truth value T. An atomic
formula which is known not to be satisfied in IU by some valuation is
known to be false and has the truth value ⊥. An atomic formula which
is neither known to be true nor known to be false has an unknown truth
value. This is denoted by u.

For example, suppose IU contains the MARRIED relation above. The following 'truth values' would then follow:

```
married(Bob, Sue)   = T
married(Alan, Jane) = ⊥
married(Bob, Alan)  = u
married(Bob, Jane)  = u
married(Bob, Bob)   = u
```

Note that u does not mean that the truth value lies between true and
false; it simply means that the truth value is unknown.

Evaluating compound formulas

If a compound formula contains a sub-formula whose truth value is unknown, then it may not be possible to compute the truth value of that compound formula. In order to define exactly what to do in such cases, we extend the truth tables for the logical connectives as shown below:

A	B	A ∧ B	A ∨ B	¬A	A → B	uA
T	T	T	T	⊥	T	⊥
T	⊥	⊥	T	⊥	⊥	⊥
T	u	u	T	⊥	u	⊥
⊥	T	⊥	T	T	T	⊥
⊥	⊥	⊥	⊥	T	T	⊥
⊥	u	⊥	u	T	T	⊥
u	T	u	T	u	T	T
u	⊥	⊥	u	u	u	T
u	u	u	u	u	u	T

That is, if a formula A is known to be true and the truth value of B is unknown, then the truth value of [A ∧ B] is unknown, and so on.

The rightmost column states that the 'value' of the formula uA is true only in cases in which the truth value of A is unknown.

The definition of truth with respect to quantified formulas must also be modified so that:

(a) ∀x A is known to be true if for all entities ei in E, A{x/ei} is known to be true, where A{x/ei} is the formula A in which ei is substituted for x.

(b) ∀x A is known to be false, if for any entity e in E, A{x/e} is known to be false.

(c) ∀x A is unknown if for all entities ei in E, A{x/ei} is either known to be true or unknown (in at least one case).

(d) ∃x A is known to be true if for any entity e in E, A{x/e} is known to be true.

(e) ∃x A is known to be false if for all entities ei in E, A{x/ei} is known to be false.

(f) ∃x A is unknown if for all entities ei in E, A{x/ei} is either known to be false or unknown (in at least one case).

5.5.1 INTEGRITY CONSTRAINTS

In the complete relational structure approach, all schema rules are regarded as integrity constraints. Valid database states are defined as those representing structures in which all schema rules evaluate to true.

In the theory only approach, the database relations together with the schema rules are all regarded as proper axioms of a theory T. The role of a proper axiom R, as an integrity constraint, is restricted to pre-venting database updates which transform T to an inconsistent theory T'.

In the theory and incomplete structure approach, a schema rule R can be used for inference (described later) *and* for defining several integrity constraints. One of the uses of R for integrity checking is mandatory; the other uses are optional. For example, consider the rule R1 : ∀x male(x) v female(x). As in the complete structure approach, R1 must evaluate to true in all complete structures Wi ∈ W. However, with res-pect to the incomplete structure IU, R1 can be used to define several integrity constraints. For example:

(a) Since IU must be a sub-structure of at least one complete structure Wi ∈ W, it is mandatory that R1 does not evaluate to false in IU, i.e. ¬R1 must not evaluate to true.

(b) Various options are available which restrict the extent of incompleteness which is allowed in IU. For example, we might require that the formula ∃X[¬male(x) ∧ u female(x)] must not evaluate to true in IU. This would prevent us from entering PAT ∉ MALE into IU if PAT u FEMALE were the case.

In order to idenfity the mandatory and all of the optional integrity constraints which derive from an arbitrary rule R, we proceed as fol-lows:

(a) Convert R to clausal form.

(b) Construct a 'truth table' for R.

(c) The row in the truth table in which R evaluates to false is used to define a mandatory integrity constraint on IU, as shown in the example below.

(d) All rows in the truth table in which R evaluates to u can be used to define optional integrity constraints as shown below.

As example, consider the axiom R1. In clausal form, this axiom is {male(x), female(x)}. The 'truth table' which we construct is:

	male(x)	female(x)	{male(x), female(x)}
(a)	T	T	T
(b)	T	⊥	T
(c)	T	u	T
(d)	⊥	T	T
(e)	⊥	⊥	⊥
(f)	⊥	u	u
(g)	u	T	T
(h)	u	⊥	u
(i)	u	u	u

Row (e) is used to define the mandatory constraint:

'∃x[¬male(x) ∧ ¬female(x)] must not evaluate to true in IU'

The other rows can be used to define various optional constraints. For example, row (i) can be used to define the constraint:

'∃x[u male(x) ∧ u female(x)] must not evaluate to true in IU'

This constraint means that IU must never be in a state in which for any entity e it is not known whether e is or is not male or female.

The advantage of specifying constraints in the piecemeal way described above is that the database administrator has more flexibility than in either of the two approaches previously described. For example, suppose that we are wanting to maintain a database representing an organisation (a university) in which there is a prerequisite condition that for someone to enrol for any class, he or she must be known to be a registered student. In order to determine which integrity constraints to impose, we proceed as follows:

  (a) We begin by specifying the relevant schema rule as an axiom:

        R2 : ∀x∀y[enrolledforclass(x,y) → registeredstudent(x)]

        or

        R2 : ∀x∀y[¬enrolledforclass(x,y) ∨ registeredstudent(x)]

  (b) We note that in all valid states of the actual organisation, i.e. in all Wi ∈ W, R2 must evaluate to true.

  (c) We then convert R2 to clausal form and draw the 'truth table':

enrolledforclass(x, y)	registeredstudent(x)	{¬enrolledforclass(x, y), registeredstudent(x)}
(i)	T	T	T
(ii)	T	⊥	⊥
(iii)	T	u	u
(iv)	⊥	T	T
(v)	⊥	⊥	T
(vi)	⊥	u	T
(vii)	u	T	T
(viii)| u	⊥	u
(ix)	u	u	u

  (d) Row (ii) can be used to define the mandatory constraint:

        '∃x∃y[enrolledforclass(x,y) ∧ ¬registeredstudent(x)]
                           must not evaluate to true'

  (e) Row (iii) corresponds to the prerequisite condition, that we want to impose. We use this row to define the constraint:

        '∃x∃y[enrolledforclass(x,y) ∧ u registeredstudent(x)]
                           must not evaluate to true'

In general, if a truth table contains n rows which evaluate to u, then n optional integrity constraints may be defined. The process of defining integrity constraints is a little more complex when skolem constants or functions are present in the clausal form of the original schema rule. We do not go into details here.

The resulting set of constraints which is chosen for a given application is called a set of 'appropriate' constraints.

Minimal expanded sets of (appropriate) constraints
Consider the following set of schema rules:

        AS1 = {∀x[male(x) → [man(x) ∨ boy(x)]]
                 ∀x[female(x) → [woman(x) ∨ girl(x)]]
                 ∀x ¬[man(x) ∧ woman(x)]
                 ∀x ¬[man(x) ∧ girl(x)]
                 ∀x ¬[boy(x) ∧ woman(x)]
                 ∀x ¬[boy(x) ∧ girl(x)]
                 ∀x[king(x) → male(x)]   }

Suppose that the following set of appropriate constraints is chosen for some particular application:

        AIC1 =
        {∃x[male(x) ∧ ¬man(x) ∧ ¬boy(x)]   is not allowed ⎫
         ∃x[female(x) ∧ ¬woman(x) ∧ ¬girl(x)] is not allowed ⎪
         ∃x[man(x) ∧ woman(x)]   is not allowed ⎪
         ∃x[man(x) ∧ girl(x)]   is not allowed ⎬ mandatory
         ∃x[boy(x) ∧ woman(x)]   is not allowed ⎪
         ∃x[boy(x) ∧ girl(x)]   is not allowed ⎪
         ∃x[king(x) ∧ ¬male(x)]   is not allowed ⎭
         ∃x[king(x) ∧ u male(x)]   is not allowed } optional

The last constraint means that no one is allowed to be (known as) a king if it is unknown whether or not that person is male.

It should not be difficult to see that the constraints below 'follow' from the sets AIC1 and AS1:

        ∃x[male(x) ∧ female(x)]   is not allowed
        ∃x[man(x) ∧ female(x)]   is not allowed
        ∃x[male(x) ∧ ¬boy(x) ∧ woman(x)]   is not allowed
        ∃x[girl(x) ∧ male(x)]   is not allowed
        ∃x[woman(x) ∧ male(x)]   is not allowed
          .
          .
          .
        + several others

We call the union of AIC1 and all of the constraints which can be generated from AIC1 and AS1, a 'fully expanded' set of constraints. In general, a fully expanded set of constraints will contain some constraints which are subsumed by others. For example, consider the following pair of constraints:

        ∃x[male(x) ∧ ¬boy(x) ∧ woman(x)]   is not allowed
        ∃x[woman(x) ∧ male(x)]   is not allowed

302

The second constraint subsumes the first since, whenever the first is violated so is the second. If we remove all constraints which are subsumed by others from a fully expanded set of constraints, we are left with a set which we shall call a 'minimally expanded set of constraints'.

The following is the minimally expanded set of constraints which can be derived from AIC1 and AS1 above:

    MEIC1 = all constraints in AIC1

                        +

        $\exists x[male(x) \wedge female(x)]$ is not allowed
        $\exists x[man(x) \wedge female(x)]$ is not allowed
        $\exists x[boy(x) \wedge female(x)]$ is not allowed
        $\exists x[girl(x) \wedge male(x)]$ is not allowed
        $\exists x[woman(x) \wedge male(x)]$ is not allowed
        $\exists x[king(x) \wedge female(x)]$ is not allowed
        $\exists x[girl(x) \wedge king(x)]$ is not allowed
        $\exists x[woman(x) \wedge king(x)]$ is not allowed

Minimal expanded sets of constraints are used later, in sub-section 5.5.3.

5.5.2 AN ALTERNATIVE NOTION OF INFERENCE

In the theory only approach, 'inference' is related to the derivation of theorems of theories. In the theory and incomplete relational structure approach, a different view of inference is used: inference is regarded as the process of extending an incomplete relational structure so that it is less incomplete.

For example, consider the axiom $\forall x[king(x) \rightarrow male(x)]$ in AS1 above. This axiom can be used in three ways to extend an incomplete structure IU:

(a) If, for some entity e in E, e $\in$ KING is present in IU and e u MALE, then the axiom can be used to extend IU to IU' in which e $\in$ MALE is present.

(b) If, for some entity e in E, e $\notin$ MALE is present in IU and e u KING, then the axiom can be used to extend IU to IU' in which e $\notin$ KING is present.

(c) If, for some entity e in E, e u KING and e u MALE in IU, then the axiom R1 can be used to generate two incomplete structures IU' and IU'' from IU:

        IU' = IU U e $\notin$ KING
        IU'' = IU U e $\in$ MALE

One or other of IU' and IU'' is correct, but we do not know which.

In all cases, we do not have to explicitly store IU' (or IU''). We could store IU only. The presence of the axiom R1 in the schema implicitly represents the extension(s) which give IU' or (IU'').

A single axiom is therefore regarded as defining a set of 'structure extension rules'. Such rules are specified as follows:

(a) [∀x king(x) ∧ u male(x) →> male(x)]
(b) [∀x ¬male(x) ∧ u king(x) →> ¬king(x)]
(c) [∀x u king(x) ∧ u male(x) →> ¬king(x) ∨ male(x)]

Note that →> is not the same as logical implication. We call rules such as (a) and (b) 'definite' rules since they have a single literal on the right-hand side. Rules such as (c) are called 'indefinite' rules.

Now it may be apparent that the applicability of a structure extension rule can be restricted by the presence of certain integrity constraints. For example, if the following constraint were in force, then the extension rule (a) above would not be applicable:

'∃x[king(x) ∧ u male(x)] must not evaluate to true in IU'

In order to identify the set of applicable extension rules which derive from a set AS of schema rules and a set AIC of appropriate integrity constraints, we proceed as follows:

(a) Convert S to clausal form and identify the set ER of extension rules which can be derived from S.

(b) Remove all rules in ER whose left-hand side represents a state which is disallowed by any constraint in AIC.

Expanded sets of extension rules
Consider the following pair of rules:

∀x[male(x) ∧ ¬man(x) ∧ u boy(x) →> boy(x)]
∀x[boy(x) ∧ u woman(x) →> ¬woman(x)]

Another rule can be derived from these two:

∀x[male(x) ∧ ¬man(x) ∧ u woman(x) →> ¬woman(x)]

If all such derived rules are added to the set from which they were derived, we obtain an expanded set of extension rules.

Executing extension rules
We say that an extension rule is 'enabled' if an instance of its left-hand side evaluates to true in some structure. In addition, we say that a definite extension rule is 'executed' if the substitution instance of its right-hand side is made to evaluate to true by generating an appropriate definite fact. For example, ∀x[¬male(x) →> ¬king(x)] is a definite rule. This rule is enabled by the presence of the definite fact JAN ∉ MALE in a structure. Execution of the rule corresponding to the enabled instance would cause the definite fact JAN ∉ KING to be generated.

5.5.3 USING EXPANDED SETS OF INTEGRITY CONSTRAINTS AND STRUCTURE EXTENSION RULES

We now describe how integrity checking and deductive query evaluation might be carried out if expanded sets of constraints and extension rules are available. However, in many database applications it would be grossly inefficient to generate and use expanded sets in this way since such sets can be very large even for relatively simple schemas. The objective of this sub-section is to introduce a simple method which can be used as a basis from which more efficient methods may be developed.

Integrity checking on database initialisation

When a database is initialised, we begin by enumerating all entities in the domain E. Then some definite facts are added to IU. We must now make sure that no constraints are violated. In particular, we must check constraints which limit the extent to which IU is allowed to be incomplete. For example, if there is a constraint of the form:

'$\exists x[u\ p(x) \wedge u\ q(x)]$ is not allowed'

we must make sure that for every entity e, one or other of the following atomic formulas evaluates to true in IU:

$p(c)$, $\neg p(c)$, $q(c)$, $\neg q(c)$ where c is the constant corresponding to e

This does not mean that we have to enter one or other of the facts: $e \in P$, $e \notin P$, $e \in Q$, $e \notin Q$ into IU. What it means is that we have to enter sufficient facts into IU such that one or other of the atomic formulas evaluates to true in IU through the use of the extension rules. How extension rules can be used in the evaluation of formulas is shown later.

Integrity checking on database input

If an expanded set of constraints is available, integrity checking on database input is relatively straightforward. When a fact F such as PETER ∈ MALE is proposed for input, we proceed as follows:

(a)   Create a corresponding literal L, such as male(Peter).

(b)   Evaluate ¬L by reference to IU and the extension rules (as described later).

(c)   If ¬L evaluates to true, then F must be rejected; otherwise proceed as follows.

(d)   Identify all constraints which contain a literal which can be made equal to L through some substitution. For example in EIC1:

$\exists x[male\ (x) \wedge \neg man(x) \wedge \neg boy(x)]$	is not allowed
$\exists x[male(x) \wedge female(x)]$	is not allowed
$\exists x[girl(x) \wedge male(x)]$	is not allowed
$\exists x[woman(x) \wedge male(x)]$	is not allowed

(e)   For each identified constraint C: permeate the matching substitution throughout C, and evaluate all other substituted
literals in C with respect to IU and the extension rules (as
described later).

(f)   If in any identified constraint all other literals evaluate
to true, then F must be rejected; otherwise it may be accepted
for input.

Note that it is not necessary to generate and check all facts which can
be derived from F ∪ IU. This is because an expanded set of constraints
is being used.

Integrity checking on fact deletion
When a fact is deleted from IU we proceed as follows:

(a)   If the corresponding literal still evaluates to true in IU,
then do nothing (this will occur when the literal can be derived).

(b)   Otherwise:

(i)   Identify all constraints which have a matching
'unknown literal', e.g. if DAVID ∈ MALE is to be
deleted, the matching literal is 'u male(David)'.

(ii)   Make sure that the constraint is not violated (as
described above on database input).

(iii) Generate all facts which follow from the fact to
be deleted by use of extension rules. Apply steps
(a) and (b) to each of these facts.

If any constraint is violated then the deletion is not allowed. Otherwise the fact may be deleted.

Evaluating formulas
A literal L, such as male(John) or ¬king(John), may be evaluated as
follows:

(a)   If IU contains a fact corresponding to L, then L evaluates to
true; else if IU contains a fact corresponding to ¬L, then L
evaluates to false.

(b)   Otherwise, match L against the right-hand side of one of the
definite rules in the expanded set of extension rules. If the
substitution instance of the left-hand side evaluates to true
(which is determined by applying steps (a) and (b) recursively
to each literal) then L evaluates to true.

Answering atomic queries
Given a literal such as male(x), those entities e corresponding to constants c for which male(c) evaluates to true can be identified as
follows:

(a)   If for some entity e, e ∈ MALE is in IU, then e is a partial
      answer to the query {x | male(x)}.

(b)   Other partial answers can be obtained by making use of definite
      extension rules whose right-hand side = male(x). We identify
      all instantiations of these rules whose left-hand side evalu-
      ates to true, i.e. those instantiations in which all literals
      on the LHS evaluate to true. Such instantiations can be iden-
      tified by treating each literal on the left-hand side as an
      atomic query and combining the results of these queries using
      relational algebraic operations in a way similar to that des-
      cribed in the theory only approach.

Answering arbitrary queries
We begin by converting the formula of the query to conjunctive normal
form:

$$Q = \{<v1, v2, \ldots, vn> \mid \overline{qv} \; D1 \wedge D2 \wedge ,\ldots, \wedge Dm\}$$

where each Di is a disjunction of literals such as male(x) ∨ female(x).

The answer to Q is obtained by identifying the answers to each Di and
then manipulating these answers by use of relational algebraic operators as described in the theory only approach.

If a disjunction consists of a single literal, then it is treated as an
atomic query and answered as described above. If a disjunction D contains j literals (j ⩾ 2), then the answer to D is obtained as follows:

(a)   Answer each of the j literals and 'unite' these answers to
      obtain a partial answer to D.

(b)   If any sub-set of the j literals in d occurs on the right-hand
      side of an extension rule, then identify all instances of that
      rule whose left-hand side evaluates to true. Each such enab-
      ling substitution defines another partial answer to D.

5.5.4   ALTERNATIVES TO THE USE OF EXPANDED SETS OF RULES
The use of expanded sets is only feasible if the original schema is
relatively small and the rules have low interaction. If this is not
the case, then unexpanded sets of appropriate constraints and extension
rules must be used. Integrity checking and query evaluation is now
more complicated:

(a)   On database input, we have to generate all facts which follow
      from the one being proposed for input and check them for input
      as well.

(b)   When evaluating literals we have to make use of a different
      technique to the one described in 5.5.3. For example, suppose
      that we have the following set of applicable extension rules,
      where A, B, C and G stand for literals:

$\neg A \twoheadrightarrow B \lor G$

$\neg B \twoheadrightarrow A \lor G$

$\neg G \twoheadrightarrow A \lor B$

$\neg A \land \neg B \twoheadrightarrow G$ *

$\neg A \land \neg G \twoheadrightarrow B$

$\neg B \land \neg G \twoheadrightarrow A$

$A \twoheadrightarrow \neg C$ *

$\neg C \twoheadrightarrow B \lor G$

$\neg B \twoheadrightarrow C \lor G$

$\neg G \twoheadrightarrow G \lor B$

$\neg C \land \neg B \twoheadrightarrow G$ *

$\neg C \land \neg G \twoheadrightarrow B$

$\neg B \land \neg G \twoheadrightarrow C$

$\neg C \twoheadrightarrow A$

If we were to expand this set of rules, we would obtain the following rule, amongst others:

$\neg B \twoheadrightarrow G$

This is obtained from the rules above which are marked with an asterisk.

If $\neg B$ were true in IU, then G would only evaluate to true, using the method described in sub-section 5.5.3, if the expanded set (and hence $\neg B \twoheadrightarrow G$) were used.

It is beyond the scope of this discussion to describe how literals and compound formulas can be evaluated if expanded sets are not used. The method is somewhat similar to the use of resolution as described in section 5.4.

Deletion of data from a database causes problems both in the theory and in the theory and incomplete relational structure approaches (whether or not expanded sets are used). One 'solution' to this problem requires all 'potentially prerequisite' data to be made explicit whenever it can be inferred and for this data to be tagged with a counter indicating the number of ways in which it can be inferred from the other data in the database. By potentially prerequisite data we mean that data which may be 'required' to be present in IU before some other fact may be deleted. For example, if the following constraints apply:

$\exists x[u \ male(x) \land u \ female(x)]$ not allowed

$\exists x \exists y[enrolledforclass(x, y) \land u \ registered(x)]$ not allowed

then the potentially prerequisite data items are, for any entity e, e $\in$ MALE, e $\notin$ MALE, e $\in$ FEMALE, e $\notin$ FEMALE, e $\in$ REGISTERED, e $\notin$ REGISTERED.

Therefore, whenever a fact is entered all of the facts which can be derived from it must be generated. Any of these facts which are potentially prerequisite facts must either be made explicit and stored in IU and their counter set to 1, or else, if they are already in IU, their counter must be incremented by 1.

Now, whenever a fact is to be deleted all of the facts which derive from it are generated. The counter of each prerequisite fact so generated must be decremented by one. If a counter is reduced to 0 then the appropriate constraint(s) must be checked to make sure that none has been violated.

5.5.5 THE CLOSED WORLD AND DOMAIN CLOSURE ASSUMPTIONS

The domain closure assumption is implicit in this approach. We assume that, at all times, the domain E is finite and its members can be enumerated. If a new entity is added to IU we must make sure that we also enter sufficient facts so that constraints of the form:

$\exists x[u\ p1(x) \land u\ p2(x)...]$ is not allowed

are not violated.

The closed world assumption is not implicit in this approach. If we want to save the user the trouble of explicitly stating all negative facts, we can use rules called 'completion rules' which have the form:

$\forall x[u\ p(x) \twoheadrightarrow \neg p(x)]$

or

$\forall x[u\ p(x) \twoheadrightarrow p(x)]$

For example, we might have the following completion rules:

$\forall x[u\ brotherof(David, x) \twoheadrightarrow \neg brotherof(David, x)]$

and

$\forall x[u\ honest(x) \rightarrow honest(x)]$

That is, if we do not know whether someone is or is not a brother of David (respectively:honest), we shall assume that he is not a brother of David (respectively:that he is honest). Note that an advantage of this approach is that we can infer positive as well as negative facts by default.

The application of these rules has to be treated with care if related indefinite extension rules are present. Minker's notion of a generalised closed world assumption (Minker, 1982) has some relevance to this problem.

5.5.6 THE APPLICABILITY OF THE THEORY AND INCOMPLETE RELATIONAL STRUCTURE APPROACH

Summary
In this approach, the universe of discourse (i.e. the slice of reality which is being represented), is regarded as a complete structure Wi, which is one of a set W. The rules in the database schema are regarded as proper axioms of a theory T whose models comprise the set W. The database relations are regarded as constituting an incomplete structure IU which is 'valid' if it is a sub-structure of at least one structure in W and is absolutely correct (although incomplete) if it is a sub-structure of the real world structure which it represents. The domains of Wi and IU are regarded as being equivalent and are denoted by E. For

every n-ary relation r in the real world Wi and every n-tuple t ∈ En,
it is the case that t ∈ r or t ∉ r. However, in the incomplete structure IU, this is not the case: for some relations and tuples, neither
t ∈ r nor t ∉ r is denoted in IU. Hence it is not always possible to
determine the truth value of an atomic formula A by reference to IU. We
denote this by writing u A.

Since the truth value of a compound formula is dependent on its constituents, it is not always possible to determine the truth value of a
compound formula with respect to IU. We have shown how the definitions
of the logical connectives can be extended to accommodate this.

Schema rules can be used to derive various integrity constraints in
this approach. Some of these constraints are mandatory and their purpose is to ensure that IU is a sub-structure of at least one complete
structure which is a model of T. The other constraints are optional
and their use may be regarded as limiting the extent to which IU may be
incomplete. As such the use of these constraints is application dependent. The set of optional constraints which the database administrator
chooses to apply together with the mandatory constraints is called the
'set of appropriate constraints' (since they are appropriate for some
specific application). This set can be expanded so that all disallowed
states are explicitly specified.

Schema rules may also be used to derive various structure extension
rules. However, the application of some of these extension rules will
be prevented if certain integrity constraints are present. The set
which results from the elimination of inapplicable rules is called the
'set of applicable extension rules'. This set can also be expanded so
that all consequences of it are made explicit. For example, a conse-
quence of the two rules: $\forall x[p(x) \twoheadrightarrow q(x)]$ and $\forall x[q(x) \twoheadrightarrow l(x)]$,
is $\forall x[p(x) \twoheadrightarrow l(x)]$.

Methods which use expanded sets for integrity checking and deductive
retrieval have been described. However, it was noted that such use of
expanded sets is limited to systems which have relatively simple
schemas. Other methods which may be used as alternatives to the use
of expanded sets were mentioned briefly.

The development of efficient methods for integrity checking and deductive retrieval in the theory and incomplete relational structure
approach clearly requires further investigation. Related work is being
undertaken by Grant and Minker (1983), Minker and Perlis (1984), Reiter
(1984), and the author. Other work which is relevant includes Belnap's
work on four-valued logic (1977), Bossu and Siegel's work on non-monotonic reasoning and the closed world assumption (1985), Lipski's work on
incomplete databases (1981) and Levesque's work on the functionality of
knowledge bases which is specified in terms of what they are asked or
told about some universe of discourse (1984).

Applicability
The theory and incomplete relational structure approach can be used in
the following cases:

    (a)   When the closed world assumption is not appropriate for the whole database and where the 'truth values' of some facts are unknown.

(b)   Where the schema rules are not all Horn.

(c)   Where deductive retrieval is required.

(d)   Where more flexibility in specifying integrity constraints is required than is available in the theory only approach.

However, it would appear that it is less appropriate to use this approach to formalise database systems in which the schema rules are frequently changed than it would be to use the theory only approach. Hence it is not appropriate in applications where rules are being inserted and deleted as frequently as simple facts.

5.6   CONCLUDING COMMENTS

This discussion began with the revision of some relevant notions from formal logic. Then three approaches which use these notions to formalise various aspects of database systems were described.

The first of these approaches regards the schema as a theory and the database as a complete relational structure which, to be valid, must be a model of the theory and to be absolutely correct should be isomorphic with the real world structure which it represents. This approach can be used to formalise conventional non-deductive database systems.

The second approach regards the schema together with the database as comprising a theory and the real world as the structure. It is this approach which is adopted when the logic programming language PROLOG is used to implement a database system. This approach has the advantage of allowing the 'schema' as well as the 'database' to be easily updated. However, it does not allow us to formalise certain types of integrity constraints which are commonly required in database applications. In particular, PROLOG is restricted to Horn clauses and uses a 'failure to prove as negation' metarule to implement the closed world assumption. In addition, clauses which consist of negative literals only are regarded as 'goals' to be proved and not as assertions. This means that it is not possible to express negative facts as proper axioms in PROLOG. Consequently, it is not possible to construct an inconsistent theory in PROLOG, and therefore the notion of an integrity constraint is not supported at all in PROLOG.

In the third approach the schema is regarded as a theory and the database as an incomplete relational structure which is a sub-structure of the real world structure which it represents. This, in the author's opinion, is the most appropriate approach to use to formalise fifth generation database systems. This is particularly so if we regard fifth generation database systems as a special type of knowledge base system in which the general rules are relatively few and relatively static compared with the simple facts. In a typical database application, the schema rules represent an organisation's structure and policy, whereas the simple facts represent its current activity. It is generally the case that the activity of an organisation is 'governed' by its structure and policy. This being so, it would seem appropriate to regard the schema as a theory which effectively governs the way in which one relational structure (database state) may be transformed into another.

311

The first and second approaches have already been used extensively to aid the design of algorithms for integrity checking and query evaluation for certain types of database system. It is hoped that when the third approach has been developed further it will provide guidance for the design of algorithms for a wider class of database system.

However, it should be noted that the problem of formalising database integrity constraints and inference rules requires a good deal of further research. During March 1985, a number of people interested in this subject met for three days at a retreat called Ross Priory, which is owned by The University of Strathclyde. Participants included staff and research students from Strathclyde University, Glasgow University and Birkbeck College, London University, and representatives from the IBM Hursley Research Centre and Burroughs Machines Limited, Cumbernauld. During the course of this meeting an attempt was made to categorise various types of integrity constraint.

One difficulty encountered derives from the dichotomy which exists between 'static' constraints and 'dynamic' constraints. For example, consider the constraint that 'no student may be enrolled for any class unless that student is known to be registered'. This constraint may be regarded as a 'static' constraint which is applied to a database after update (see (a) below). Alternatively, it may be regarded as a 'dynamic' constraint which may be applied before update (see (b) below).

(a) When regarded as a static constraint, it may be specified as stating that the following formula must never evaluate to true:

$$\exists x \exists y [(x.\text{ enrolledforclass. } y) \wedge \neg(x. \in . \text{ registered})]$$

(b) When regarded as a dynamic (or transformation) constraint, it may be specified as follows:

'before (x. enrolledforclass. y) may be inserted, (x. $\in$. registered) must be known to be true'

At the Ross Priory meeting, one proposal which received some support was that all constraints should be regarded as static constraints, thereby allowing a uniform approach to be adopted. However, it was not clear what the repercussions of this approach would be.

Another difficulty which was identified concerned the insertion of constraints such as the one above into an existing database. In practice, there are various ways in which this constraint might subsequently be used:

(a) On input of data such as (John. enrolledforclass. Maths).

(b) 'Retrospectively' such that for all instances of enrolment which are in the database a check is made to determine registration.

(c) On deletion of data such as (John. $\in$. registered).

A further complication arises if the rule is only used as described in (a), but for reasons of saving storage space, as soon as data such as (John. enrolledforclass. Maths) gets over the 'hurdle' of requiring the presence of (John. ∈ . registered) this latter piece of data is deleted (since it can always be inferred from the presence of the former).

Before such problems can be resolved, it will be necessary to identify the various types (and uses) of integrity constraint which are required in real applications, and then to formalise these constraints according to one or other of the approaches described in this chapter. Preliminary work in this area is being undertaken by some of those present at the Ross Priory meeting, and also by Hugh Noble and Talib Abbod at Robert Gordon's Institute of Technology in Aberdeen. An alternative approach is being researched by Clifford and Warren, in which a logic called 'intensional logic' is used to formalise static and dynamic constraints. This approach is discussed in chapter 6, section 6.11.

6 The Use of Non-classical Logics in Automated Knowledge Processing

6.1 INTRODUCTION

The use of logic in automated knowledge processing has received much criticism, especially from many of the people who were working in artificial intelligence research in the early and mid seventies. Various criticisms have been raised, the most common being:

(a) That logic is not expressive enough, i.e. that there is too great a limit on what can be represented.

(b) That logic cannot handle incomplete, uncertain, imprecise, vague, and/or inconsistent knowledge.

(c) That the algorithms for manipulating knowledge, which derive from logic, are inefficient.

Such criticisms are largely due to a common misconception that 'logic' encompasses classical (first order propositional and predicate) logic only. This is not the case. There are many other logics, most of which were specifically designed to overcome certain deficiencies of classical logic (which, it could be argued, deserves some of the criticism which it has received).

It is important to understand that any system for manipulating knowledge may be regarded as a logic if it contains:

(a) A well-defined language for representing knowledge.

(b) A well-defined model-theory (or semantics) which is concerned with the meaning of statements expressed in the language.

(c) A proof theory which is concerned with the syntactic manipulation and derivation of statements from other statements.

In other words, a logic consists of a well-defined notation for the representation of knowledge, together with well-defined methods for interpreting and manipulating the knowledge which is represented. The important term is 'well-defined'. Therefore, it would appear that people who criticise logic are unwittingly condoning the use of ill-defined methods for knowledge processing.

In this chapter, the reader is introduced to several non-classical logics. The discussions of these logics are not intended to be comprehensive. The purpose of this chapter is to 'break the ice' covering what is often regarded by undergraduate students as an unfathomable subject area. The logics that we discuss are:

 many-sorted logic
 situational logic
 non-monotonic logic
 many-valued logic
 fuzzy logic
 modal logic
 temporal logic
 epistemic logic
 higher-order logic
 intensional logic

In each case, a brief description is given which, we hope, is sufficiently complete for the reader to acquire a feel for the capabilities of the logic described. Reference to more detailed accounts are included. These references were carefully chosen to be at a suitable level for readers who are unfamiliar with logic yet are wanting to continue their study of the non-classical logics mentioned in this chapter.

6.2 MANY-SORTED LOGICS

In classical first order predicate logic, a relational structure contains a single domain E of entities. Sub-sets of this domain are defined by use of 'unary' (one-place) predicates. In a many-sorted logic, the universe of discourse is regarded as comprising a relational structure in which the entities in the domain E are regarded as being of various sorts. The sorts are related to each other in various ways to form a 'sort structure'. There are different kinds of sort structure:

(a) Structures in which the sorts are all disjoint. For example, E might consist of entities of sorts: man, woman, bicycle, car.

(b) Structures in which the sorts are related in a 'sub-set' tree structure. For example:

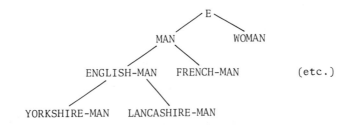

(c) Structures in which the sorts are related in a lattice. This is the most general sort structure. The following is an example of a lattice:

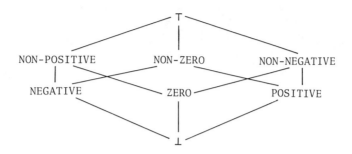

The advantage of dividing the entities in the domain of a relational structure into different sorts, is that it can help to improve the efficiency of mechanised reasoning by reducing the 'search space'.

For example, sorted logics prevent formulas from interacting as freely as they might in an unsorted logic. If the terms of two formulas have no sorts in common then they cannot interact directly with each other. In addition, meaningless assertions such as the 'ford is married to the mercedes' can be easily detected. It should be noted, however, that many-sorted logics are no more expressive than unsorted logics (Enderton, 1972).

In the following, two kinds of many-sorted logic are described and examples of how they can be used to improve the efficiency of automated reasoning are given. The first type to be considered is the simplest.

6.2.1 MANY-SORTED LOGICS WITH RESTRICTED QUANTIFICATION
We shall describe this kind of many-sorted logic with reference to disjoint sort structures, since it is for this kind of sort structure that the logic is most appropriate.

Restricted quantification
In classical first order predicate logic, universal quantification concerns *every* entity in the relational structure in question. That is, every entity is taken into account when determining the truth value of a universally quantified formula. For example, consider the following formula:

$\forall x[car(x) \rightarrow number\ of\ wheels(x, 4) \lor number\ of\ wheels(x, 3)]$

This formula, when written in clausal form is:

$\{\neg car(x), number\ of\ wheels(x, 4), number\ of\ wheels(x, 3)\}$

which means that for all entities in the domain, either e is not a car, or e has four or three wheels.

Instead of using universal quantification, an alternative method of representing the knowledge above is to use a formula containing a 'restricted quantifier':

$\forall x/car[number\ of\ wheels(x, 4) \lor number\ of\ wheels(x, 3)]$

The restricted quantifier, $\forall x/car$, ranges over a sub-set of the domain of the relational structure, i.e. over only those entities which are of sort car. The symbol which expresses the restriction on the quantifier (in this case 'car'), is called a 'sort symbol', and the sub-set of the domain which it denotes is called a 'sort'.

Using restricted quantification to improve the efficiency of answering queries

Suppose that we have the following 'sorted' knowledge base:

Disjoint sorts :   women = {Mary, Jane}
                   men = {Peter, Paul}

Proper axioms   {{(Mary. likes. Mary)} [note that these are
in clausal form: {(Mary. likes. Jane)} in infix notation]
                   {(Peter. likes. Mary)}
                   {(Jane. likes. Paul)}}

Consider the following query:

Q1 = {x | $\forall y/women$ (x. likes. y)}

which may be read as 'retrieve all entities which like all women'. The answer to this query, which is denoted by ‖Q1‖, may be obtained from the answer to the completely open query Q2 = {x, y | (x. likes. y)}, which is denoted by ‖Q2‖, as follows:

‖Q1‖ = $\delta y/women$‖Q2‖

where $\delta y/women$ is a sorted relational algebraic division operator. We obtain all tuples <x, y> for which (x. likes. y) is true, and then extract those values of x which are related to all values of y taken from the sort 'women'. That is:

‖Q2‖	
x	y
Mary	Mary
Mary	Jane
Peter	Mary
Jane	Paul

and

‖Q1‖ = $\delta y/women$
x
Mary

giving 'Mary' as answer.

317

Application of sorted division operators as described above is, in general, more efficient than application of unsorted division operators. In addition, certain 'negative' facts need not be stored (the assumption being that, if an entity is not represented as being of a particular sort, then it is assumed not to be of that sort). These two factors mean that certain types of query evaluation, and consistency checking, are more efficient in a sorted logic than in an unsorted logic.

6.2.2 MORE EXPRESSIVE MANY-SORTED LOGICS

We now describe a sorted logic in which the sortal behaviour of functions and predicates may be defined and in which restricted quantification is *not* used. This logic is described with respect to lattice sort structures, since it is for this kind of sort structure that the logic was developed. We begin by describing lattices in more detail.

Sort lattices

Consider the sort lattice given earlier. The symbol $\top$ at the top of the lattice is interpreted as the sort containing all entities in the domain of the relational structure. This sort is called 'top'. The symbol $\bot$ at the bottom of the lattice is interpreted as the empty sort. This sort is called 'bottom'.

The sorts immediately above bottom, e.g. {NEGATIVE, ZERO, POSITIVE} in our example lattice, are 'disjoint' sorts. Bottom is the most 'specific' sort. As one moves from bottom to top, the sort becomes more general, top being the most general. A sort which is higher in the lattice than another sort, and which is connected to that sort by downward traversal of arcs, is called a 'supersort' of the more specific sort. The more specific sort, in turn, is called a 'sub-sort' of the more general sort. The sub-sort/supersort relationship is denoted by:

$$S1 \subseteq S2$$

indicating that S1 is a sub-sort or is equal to S2. For example, POSITIVE $\subseteq$ NON-ZERO in the lattice above.

Sorts are related in other ways; for example, by the dyadic operators 'lub', 'glb' and 'comp':

(a) 'lub' (least upper bound): The sort S3 = S1 lub S2 is the most specific sort in the lattice which is the supersort of both S1 and S2. For example, in the lattice above, NON-POSITIVE = NEGATIVE lub ZERO. lub is related to the 'union' operator in set theory.

(b) 'glb' (greatest lower bound): The sort S3 = S1 glb S2 is the most general sort in the lattice which is a sub-sort of both S1 and S2. For example, in the lattice above, NEGATIVE = NON-POSITIVE glb NON-ZERO. glb is related to the 'intersection' operator in set theory.

(c) 'comp' (complement): The sort S3 = S1 comp S2 is the sort containing all entities in S1 minus those in S2. For example, in the lattice above, NEGATIVE = NON-POSITIVE comp ZERO.

lub, glb and comp may be used to define sorts without having to explicitly name them.

Sorting functions

Associated with every function symbol f in the language of the sorted logic is a 'sorting function' f̈, whose purpose is to define the sort of f's output given the sorts of f's inputs. For example, suppose that we have a function 'multiply' which takes two arguments, such that:

Sorts of arguments	Sort of result
ZERO, ZERO	ZERO
NON-POSITIVE, ZERO	ZERO
NEGATIVE, POSITIVE	NEGATIVE
(etc.)	

The sorting function multiply is then defined such that:

multïply(ZERO,ZERO) = ZERO
multïply(NON-POSITIVE, ZERO) = ZERO
multïply(NEGATIVE, POSITIVE) = NEGATIVE
(etc.)

That is, sorting functions map the set of sorts S to itself. Sorting functions are necessary to accommodate 'polymorphic' functions; that is, functions which can take arguments of different sorts (types). Sorting functions may also be used to define the sortal behaviour of predicate symbols. However, in this case the sorting functions map the set of sorts S into the 'boolean' set {EE, TT, FF, UU} where:

EE means that the atomic formula is ill-sorted; that is, the arguments of the predicate are of the wrong sort.

TT means that the atomic formula is well-sorted and is true.

FF means that the atomic formula is well-sorted and is false.

UU means that the atomic formula is well-sorted but that its truth value is not yet known.

These 'boolean' sorts also form a lattice:

Well-sortedness of functions, expressions, atomic formulas and arbitrary formulas

A function expression is well-sorted iff the sorts of its terms match the sorts required by their respective argument positions. In some of the many-sorted logics which have been defined, the sort S1 of a term only matches the sort S2 of an argument position if S1 ⊆ S2. However, a more expressive logic may be obtained if 'match' is defined such that a match fails only if S1 glb S2 = ⊥. For example, consider the function 'husbandof' and the following sort lattice:

```
              PERSON
             /      \
         MAN          WOMAN
             \      /
               ⊥
```

Suppose that the sorting function of 'husbandof' were defined such that:

    husbändof(MAN) = ⊥
    husbändof(WOMAN) = MAN

Suppose, further, that Pat is of sort PERSON but it is not known if Pat is a man or a woman. From the 'more expressive' definition of match, it follows that husbandof(Pat) is well-sorted even though if Pat is interpreted as a man then husbandof(Pat) fails to denote.

An atomic formula is well-sorted iff the sorts of its terms match the sorts required by their respective argument positions. For example, consider the predicate 'marriedto', the lattice above and the following sorting function for the predicate 'marriedto':

    marriedto(MAN, WOMAN) = UU
    marriedto(WOMAN, MAN) = UU
    marriedto(MAN, MAN)   = EE
    marriedto(WOMAN, WOMAN) = EE

If the more expressive definition of match is used then it follows that:

    marriedto(PERSON, PERSON) = UU

Note, however, that when the more expressive definition of 'match' is used, the most specific sort of an entity must be used when determining the well-sortedness of the expressions in which it occurs.

An arbitrary formula is well-sorted if there exists an assignment of sorts to its terms such that:

(a)   All sub-expressions are well-sorted.
(b)   The assignment is compatible with the pre-defined sorts of the constant symbols.

For example, suppose that John and Peter are of sort MAN, that Mary is of sort WOMAN and that the 'marriedto' predicate has the sortal behaviour as defined above. In this case, the following formulas are well-sorted:

    F1 :   married(John, Mary) ∧ ¬married(Peter, Mary)
    F2 :   ∀x∀y[married(x, y) → married(y, x)]

Note that in this approach restricted quantification is not used. This would reduce the value of allowing polymorphic functions since an instance of a variable would then have a unique sort associated with it. Instead of using restricted quantification, the sorts of variables are determined by the sorts of the argument positions in which they occur. When variables occur as arguments of a polymorphic function or predicate symbol, they may range over several sorts and the sort of the entire formula may then vary as a function of the sorts of such variables. For example, an instantiation of the second formula above is well sorted if the sort of x is MAN or PERSON and the sort of y is WOMAN or PERSON, or vice versa. In all other cases the formula is ill-sorted.

Using a more expressive many-sorted logic for integrity checking
Suppose that we are constructing a knowledge base using a language of a many-sorted logic as our representational formalism. We could proceed as follows:

(a) We begin by defining the sort lattice. This involves naming the sorts and indicating the relationships between them.

(b) We then define the sorts of the entities which are to be represented. Errors can be detected if an entity is specified as being of two disjoint sorts.

(c) We then define the sorting functions for the required functions and predicates. Errors may be detected if an inconsistent definition is given. For example, the following definition is incompatible with the lattice above:

        related(MAN, WOMAN) = UU
        related(WOMAN, MAN) = UU
        related(MAN, MAN)   = UU
        related(WOMAN, WOMAN) = UU
        related(PERSON, PERSON) = EE

(d) We then input assertions into the knowledge base. Errors may be detected if formulas are ill-sorted. For example, suppose that the 'marriedto' predicate has the sortal behaviour described earlier and that 'hasbrother' and 'hasbrother-in-law' are defined such that:

        hasbrother(MAN, WOMAN) = EE... (etc.)
        hasbrother-in-law(MAN, WOMAN) = EE... (etc.)

In this case, the following formula is ill-sorted:

$\forall x \forall y \forall z$[marriedto(x, y) $\land$ hasbrother(z, y)] $\rightarrow$
                                    hasbrother-in-law(z, x)

Using a more expressive many-sorted logic to improve the efficiency of automated reasoning
Efficiency can be improved if the deductive machinery is designed such that it does not attempt to perform inferences with ill-sorted formulas. For example, consider the formula F2 above. If we convert this formula to clausal form, we obtain:

321

{¬married(x, y), married(y, x)}

Suppose that Pat and Jan are both of sort MAN. The deductive machinery, if designed as suggested above, would never generate the following instantiation:

{¬married(Pat, Jan), married(Jan, Pat)}

6.2.3 CONCLUDING COMMENTS

Much of the material in section 6.2.2 was derived from Cohn (1983, 1984) who has developed algorithms which can be used to compute the sorts of formulas and terms. These algorithms can also be used to check the integrity of queries since a query whose sort is FF or EE may be rejected as unsatisfiable. An alternative method for checking queries in a sorted logic may be found in Reiter (1981).

Although it is well established that many-sorted logics can be used to improve the efficiency of automatic reasoning, there is some controversy as to whether this is the best way of achieving such improvement.

In the many-sorted approach, the knowledge which is represented by unary predicates in an unsorted logic is regarded as 'meta-knowledge' and held in a sort structure. An alternative approach would be to treat unary predicates (and formulas stating relationships between unary predicates) in a different way to other predicates in implementation rather than in principle. An advantage of the latter approach is that it does not result in the rather messy interface which exists, in many-sorted logics, between sort structures and formulas. For example, consider the following formula in an unsorted logic:

$$\forall x[\text{blood-temp}(x, \text{warm}) \wedge \text{number of legs}(x, 4) \wedge$$
$$\text{skin covering}(x, \text{fur}) \wedge \text{eats}(x, \text{eucalyptus leaves}) \wedge$$
$$\text{australian}(x)] \rightarrow \text{koala-bear}(x)$$

It is difficult to see how this might be expressed cleanly in any of the many-sorted logics which have been developed.

6.3 SITUATIONAL LOGIC

The logics described so far are primarily concerned with static relational structures. However, in many applications there is a need to store and manipulate knowledge which represents a changing universe of discourse. 'Situational logic' (McCarthy and Hayes, 1969) was developed for this type of application.

In situational logic, all predicates are given an extra argument which denotes the 'situation' in which the formula is true. For example, consider the following formula:

on(b1, b2, s1)

This formula states that b1 is on b2 in situation s1. Suppose that b1 and b2 are blocks. In a subsequent situation block b2 might have been moved elsewhere, resulting in the following formula:

¬on(b1, b2, s2)

The transformation of s1 to s2 was caused by an 'event': the event of moving b2 elsewhere.

Situations and events are related by a relation R, where R(e,s) denotes the situation which is obtained when event e occurs in situation s. For example, consider the following assertion concerning the movement of blocks:

$$\forall x[on(b1, b2, s) \land \neg on(x, b3, s) \rightarrow on(b1, b3, R(move(b2, b3), s))]$$

This states that if b1 is on b2, and no block is on b3, then the new situation denoted by R(move(b2, b3), s), which results from moving a block from b1's tower to b3's tower, will have b1 on b3.

The assertion above adequately describes the relative positions b1 and b3 in the new situation s' = R(move(b2, b3), s). However, one can infer nothing about the relative positions of all other blocks in s'. A solution to this problem is to write down assertions which state that a block stays where it is unless it is moved. In general, we need to write assertions of the form:

$$\varphi1[[s]] \land \alpha(e) \rightarrow \varphi2[[R(e, s)]]$$

where $\varphi[[s]]$ denotes a set of formulas, every situation in which is an occurrence of s. $\alpha(e)$ is a set of formulas which are affected by the event e. Hayes calls such assertions 'frame laws' and refers to the problem of determining adequate collections of such laws as 'the frame problem'. This problem will be referred to again in later sections.

Other problems arise as a consequence of a changing universe of discourse. Beliefs must change to accommodate a changing world. Consider the following example presented by Hayes (1981).

A robot concludes from a theory, which includes his beliefs as assertions, that he can drive to the airport. However, when he goes to the car he finds that it has a flat tyre. A human would simply add a new assertion, 'a tyre is flat', to his knowledge base and conclude that he cannot now drive to the airport. Adding the new belief renders an earlier conclusion false even though it was a valid conclusion from the earlier set of beliefs. If the robot is using a classical logic (see next section), then the only way in which he can make such an amendment to his beliefs is if his earlier conclusion were 'if the tyres are not flat, then I can drive to the airport'. However, there are a great number of potential mishaps which could prevent the robot from driving to the airport and it would be unreasonable to qualify the conclusion with all such possibilities.

Hayes calls this the 'qualification problem' and states that belief logics cannot be expected to obey the monotonicity property of classical logics. The 'monotonicity' property is defined in section 6.4.

In order to overcome the qualification problem associated with monotonic logics, Hayes introduced a new unary connective called 'proved' which means 'can be proved from the current set of beliefs'. Using this connective, it is possible to write assertions such as:

323

¬proved kaput(car, s) → at(robot, airport, R(drive(airport), s))

which means 'if it cannot be proved that the car is kaput in situation s, then the robot can drive to the airport giving situation R(drive (airport),s), and in this new situation the robot is at the airport'.

'Proved' could be defined as follows, where α and φ stand for arbitrary sets of formulas:

R1 : $\alpha \vdash$ proved α
R2 : $\varphi \vdash$ ¬proved α if $\varphi \not\vdash \alpha$

Unfortunately, R1 and R2 are inconsistent. Suppose that B $\not\vdash$ A but that A is consistent with B. By R2 we can conclude '¬proved A' from B. However, if we now add A to B (which we can do without obtaining an immediate inconsistency) then, by R1, we can conclude 'proved A'. A solution to this problem is to tag 'proved' with a belief state marker in a similar way to the way in which predicates are tagged with external situation markers. R1 and R2 become:

R1' : $\alpha \vdash$ proved(s) α(s)
R2' : $\varphi \vdash$ ¬proved(s)α(s), where $\varphi \not\vdash \alpha$(s), and every member of φ
has index s

Therefore, assertions of the form 'provedα' now have an extra index which identifies the 'state of belief' at the time the inference was made.

Use of the extended logic requires that:

(a) Whenever R2' is applied, φ contains all assertions with index s.

(b) Whenever an assertion is added, every belief index s is replaced by a new one s' except those on 'proved' assertions.

These notions led to the development of non-monotonic logics which are described in the next section.

6.4 NON-MONOTONIC LOGICS

6.4.1 WHAT IS MONOTONICITY?

In a 'monotonic' logic, if a proper axiom is added to a theory T to obtain a theory T', then all of the theorems of T are also theorems of T'. That is:

if T $\vdash$ P, and T $\subseteq$ T' then T' $\vdash$ P

In a 'non-monotonic' logic, the addition of an assertion to a theory may invalidate conclusions which could previously have been made.

There are three types of circumstance in which non-monotonic reasoning may be appropriate:

(a) When the knowledge is incomplete, default assumptions must be made which may be invalidated when more knowledge becomes available.

(b) When the universe of discourse is changing (as discussed in section 6.3).

(c) In problem solving where temporary assumptions are made.

These three circumstances are now discussed in more detail.

Incomplete knowledge/Default reasoning
Humans often use default reasoning when confronted with incomplete knowledge. For example, suppose that you are told that Ozzie is a pet bird. Subsequently you are told that someone has left the window open and Ozzie has escaped. You are likely to conclude that Ozzie flew away. However, if you are now told that Ozzie could not fly, because he had clipped wings, then you must revise your belief in how he escaped.

This example of default reasoning may be described as follows:

(a) Initially, you are not told that Ozzie cannot fly. Since you were told that he is a bird, you assumed by default that he could fly:

Ozzie is a bird ∧ not known Ozzie cannot fly $\rightarrow$
$$\text{(by default)}$$
$$\text{Ozzie can fly}$$

Hence, your belief set consists of:

Ozzie is a bird
∀x[x is a bird ∧ not known x cannot fly] → x can fly
Ozzie can fly

(b) Later, you are told that Ozzie cannot fly, hence you must retract your belief that he can fly. Your belief set is now:

Ozzie is a bird
∀x[x is a bird ∧ not known x cannot fly] → x can fly
Ozzie cannot fly

A changing world
Consider an example similar to the one above:

(a) Initially you are told that Ozzie is a bird and that he can fly.

(b) Subsequently you are told that someone left the window open and that Ozzie escaped.

(c) Finally you are told that Ozzie had his wings clipped after you were told (a) and before you were told (b).

This is similar to the example above, but differs slightly in that it is not concerned with default reasoning in the presence of incomplete knowledge but rather with reasoning with out-of-date knowledge.

The use of temporary assumptions in problem-solving
In many problem-solving tasks, humans make temporary assumptions which
allow them to pursue a 'possible' solution. Such assumptions may later
be validated or invalidated. For example, suppose that you want to
find a suitable time at which to arrange a meeting with colleagues. One
approach is to assume that the meeting can be held on a particular day,
say Monday, and then check all time slots on Monday to see if there is
one in which all colleagues are available. All consequences of the
meeting being on Monday will be temporarily assumed by colleagues when
they determine whether or not they will be available at a particular
time.

6.4.2 AN EXAMPLE OF A NON-MONOTONIC LOGIC

Extending a classical logic to a non-monotonic logic
McDermott and Doyle (1980) describe a non-monotonic logic which is
derived from a classical logic by adding a modal operator M standing
for 'consistent'. Informally, Mp means that p is consistent with
everything that is believed. (See section 6.7 for a discussion of
modal logic.)

For example, consider the following theory (in which infix notation is
used):

(a) $\forall x[(x. \in . \text{ birds}) \land M(x. \text{ hasability. flying}) \rightarrow$
$(x. \text{ hasability. flying})]$

(b) $(\text{Ozzie.} \in . \text{ birds})$

The first formula may be read as 'for all x, if x is a bird, and if (x
can fly) is consistent with everything that we believe, then we can
conclude that x can fly.'

From (a) and (b), we can deduce that Ozzie can fly.

However, if we were to add the belief that Ozzie cannot fly, then
(Ozzie can fly) is not consistent with our set of beliefs, and we must
retract our deduced belief that Ozzie can fly.

A proof procedure for non-monotonic logic
McDermott and Doyle have developed a proof procedure for non-monotonic
logic which is based on the tableau proof method of classical logic.
The proof method will not be described here since it is somewhat complex for an introductory discussion of this nature. However, we make
some comments which we hope will be useful to readers who are wanting
to follow up this discussion by referring to McDermott and Doyle's
work:

(a) The conventional tableau method is used to prove, for example,
T ⊢ p. However, if some tableau is constructed which has a
formula Mq in the right (false) column in an open branch, then
we must construct a tableau with goal T ⊢ ¬q if such a tableau
has not been constructed already.

(b) The resulting set of tableaux is called a 'tableau structure'.
When it has been built, it is checked for admissible labellings

(The admissibility test is described by McDermott and Doyle in their paper.)

(c)   If in all admissible labellings the initial tableau with goal T → p is labelled CLOSED, then p is a theorem of T; otherwise it is not.

(d)   The method is similar to the tableau proof method for the modal logic S5 described in section 6.7. One difference between the procedures is that the method for non-monotonic logic splits tableaux into branches before generating alternatives, while the S5 procedure splits the whole of alternatives into branches. (The reader will find these comments more meaningful after reading section 6.7.)

6.4.3 TMS - A TRUTH MAINTENANCE SYSTEM

Doyle (1982) has designed and implemented a system called TMS to support non-monotonic reasoning. TMS maintains consistency among a set of beliefs which are generated by the system it is supporting.

Statements of belief in TMS are called 'nodes'. A node is IN if it is believed to be true and OUT otherwise. Each node has a set of justifications linked to it, each of these justifications representing one way in which the node may be made true. An IN node has at least one justification that is currently valid. OUT nodes may have a set of justifications which show how that node may be made IN, but none of these justifications is itself currently justified. There are two kinds of justification in TMS: 'support list' justification, and 'conditional proof' justification. Only the former will be considered here.

Support list justification
In this case, the justification of a node N consists of a support list which identifies those nodes which are required to be IN, and those which are required to be OUT, for that particular justification of N to be valid. As example, consider the following set of TMS nodes and justifications:

		Status	Justification 1 IN	Justification 1 OUT	Justification 2 IN	Justification 2 OUT
1	Ozzie is a bird	IN				
2	Ozzie can fly	OUT	1	3		
3	Ozzie cannot fly	IN	4		5	
4	Ozzie has clipped wings	OUT				
5	Ozzie is a penguin	IN				

An empty justification list for a node which is IN means that the node is an assertion. An empty justification list for a node which is OUT means that that node was a previous assertion which has since been retracted.

The table above may be interpreted as follows:

1   'Ozzie is a bird' is an assertion.

2 'Ozzie can fly' is a belief which is not justified.

3 'Ozzie cannot fly' is a belief which is justified by justification 2, i.e. it is justified by node 5 being IN.

4 'Ozzie has clipped wings' is a previous assertion/belief which has been retracted.

5 'Ozzie is a penguin' is an assertion.

Now if assertion 5 were retracted then TMS would also retract belief 3; this in turn would cause belief 2 to become IN.

TMS does not create justifications. These are provided by the system which TMS supports. The role of TMS is to maintain a consistent set of beliefs.

The above description of TMS is very superficial. Many details have been omitted and some liberty has been taken in the example. The interested reader is referred to Doyle's paper for a more accurate and complete description.

6.5 MANY-VALUED LOGICS

The logics that we have described so far have all been two-valued, the two values being TRUE and FALSE. However, there is a large amount of literature concerned with logics which have more than two values. For example, Belnap (1977) has investigated a four-valued logic in which the four values are the four knowledge states that a knowledge base may be in with respect to a proposition P:

U = the knowledge base has not been told P and has not been told ¬P
T = the knowledge base has been told P
F = the knowledge base has been told ¬P
B = the knowledge base has been told P and has also been told ¬P

This system of four values is of relevance to the design of automatic question-answering systems, since a computerised knowledge base may be in any one of these four states with respect to a proposition P. (This was referred to in chapter 5.)

One of the best known many-valued logics is a three-valued logic proposed by Lukasiewicz. His justification for this logic was that assertions such as 'there will be a sea battle tomorrow' cannot really be assigned a value of true or false. Consequently, he introduced a third value I denoting an 'intermediate' truth value. McCawley (1981) shows how Lukasiewicz's three-valued logic may be modified such that I may be regarded as denoting the value 'sort of true'. A truth table corresponding to this interpretation is shown on the opposite page.

This interpretation of I as 'sort of true' may be generalised to accommodate degrees of truth. The systems which result from such generalisation are useful for dealing with 'vague' concepts such as 'fat'. (Fuzzy logic, discussed later, also attempts to accommodate vagueness.)

A survey of the literature on many-valued logic can be found in Rescher (1969).

A	B	A → B
T	T	T
T	I	I
T	F	F
T	T	T
I	I	T
I	F	F
F	T	T
F	I	T
F	F	T

6.6 FUZZY LOGIC

There is a great deal of 'commonsense' knowledge which cannot be accommodated by conventional logics. This is because commonsense knowledge typically contains a great deal of uncertainty. For example, consider the following piece of commonsense knowledge:

> 'If a car which is offered for sale is cheap and old, then it is probably not in good shape.'

There is much 'uncertainty' in this statement. Conventional logics do not admit gradations of truth and therefore cannot be used to represent and reason with statements of this kind.

Fuzzy logic (see, for example, Zadeh, 1983) can accommodate such uncertainty and does so by an approach to 'semantics' which is quite distinct from that used in conventional logic.

Test-score semantics

Test-score semantics is used to assign a meaning to a proposition in fuzzy logic. In test-score semantics, a proposition is regarded as a collection of 'elastic constraints'. For example, the proposition 'Mary is brunette' represents an elastic constraint on the colour of Mary's hair. And the proposition 'most fat men are not very agile' represents an elastic constraint on the number of fat men who are agile.

In test-score semantics, the meaning of a proposition is given by the procedure which is used to compute the test score of that proposition. In general, this procedure involves:

(a) Identifying the variables $x_1, \ldots, x_n$ whose values are constrained by the proposition. In the above, x_1 = colour of Mary's hair.

(b) Identifying the constraints $C_1, \ldots, C_m$ induced by the proposition (see below).

(c) Characterising each constraint C_i by describing a testing procedure (see below) that associates with C_i a test score t_1 representing the degree to which C_i is satisfied.

(d) Aggregating the partial test scores $t_1, \ldots, t_m$ into a smaller number of test scores $t_1, \ldots, t_k$ representing an overall vector test score t. In most cases, $k = 1$.

The testing procedure in (c) makes use of a collection of 'fuzzy' relations constituting an explanatory database (ED).

The meaning of the relations in ED is known to the person who is wanting to know the meaning of the proposition. Indirectly, the testing and aggregation procedures used in test-score semantics describe a process by which the meanings of propositions are composed from the meanings of the constituent relations in the explanatory database.

As example, suppose that we want to determine the meaning of the proposition:

usually snow is white

An appropriate explanatory database would include a relation WHITE and a relation USUALLY, such as:

WHITE

Snow sample	Degree to which the sample is white
S1	0.7
S2	0.8

USUALLY

Proportion	Degree to which the proportion represents 'usually'
0.1	0.0
0.2	0.0
0.3	0.0
0.6	0.1

Now, let S1, ..., Sm denote samples of snow and let ti $(1 \leqslant i \leqslant m)$ denote the degree to which the colour of Si is white. Thus ti is the test score for the constraint on the colour of Si induced by 'white'. Using this notation, the steps in the testing procedure are:

(a) Find the proportion of samples whose colour is white:

$$\alpha = \frac{t1 + \ldots + tm}{m}$$

(b) Compute the degree to which α satisfies the constraint induced by 'usually':

t = degree to which prop represents usually where prop = α

i.e. we simply use α to look up a value in the relation 'usually'.

The meaning of 'usually snow is white' is represented by the test procedure which is used to compute the value of t.

The example above was derived from Zadeh (1983) where another, more complex, example is given. We describe other aspects of fuzzy logic in chapters 7 and 8.

6.7 MODAL LOGICS

The logics which have been described so far are called 'truth-functional'
logics. When we determine consistency or prove theorems in theories of
such logics, we consider interpretations each of which assigns a value
of true or false to the atomic formulas of the theories concerned. This
is particularly obvious if truth tables are being used. For example,
consider the following pair of formulas:

    A → B
    B → C

which are read as 'A implies B' and 'B implies C'. From these two
formulas we can infer A → C by constructing the following truth table:

	A	B	C	A → B	B → C	A → C	
@1	T	T	T	T	T	T	✓
@2	T	T	⊥	T	⊥	⊥	
@3	T	⊥	T	⊥	T	T	
@4	T	⊥	⊥	⊥	T	⊥	
@5	⊥	T	T	T	T	T	✓
@6	⊥	T	⊥	T	⊥	T	
@7	⊥	⊥	T	T	T	T	✓
@8	⊥	⊥	⊥	T	T	T	✓

In effect, what we have done is to consider eight functions, @1 to @8,
each of which specifies a particular 'state of affairs' in which A, B
and C have various values of true or false. From the table, it can be
seen that A → C is true in all cases in which A → B and B → C are true.
Therefore, we can conclude that A → C is a logical consequence of A → B
and B → C.

The validity of this conclusion is intuitively obvious in the following,
where N is some number and:

    A stands for 'N is divisible by eight'
    B stands for 'N is divisible by four'
    C stands for 'N is divisible by two'

It is intuitively obvious that A → C is a logical consequence of A → B
and B → C, irrespective of what the number N actually is.

However, suppose that:

    A stands for 'Reagan was born in France'
    B stands for 'Reagan speaks French'
    C stands for 'Reagan speaks French in the White House'

In this case it is not intuitively obvious that A → C is a logical consequence of A → B and B → C. That is, given the two sentences S1 and
S2 below, it is not reasonable to infer the sentence S3:

    S1: 'Reagan was born in France implies that Reagan speaks French'

    S2: 'Reagan speaks French implies that Reagan speaks French in the
         White House'

S3:   'Reagan was born in France implies that Reagan speaks French
in the White House'

This inference is intuitively wrong because the sentences S1 and S2
relate to different states of affairs or 'possible worlds'. The first
sentence, S1, has to do with a state of affairs in which, other things
being as close as possible to the actual state of affairs, Reagan was
born in France rather than in the U.S. The second sentence, S2, has
to do with states of affairs in which, other things being as close as
possible to the actual state of affairs, Reagan was a French speaking
man living in the White House. But the 'other things' aren't the same
in the two cases, and as a result, the states of affairs that the first
sentence has to do with do not overlap with those that the second sentence has to do with: if Reagan had been born in France he wouldn't
have been President of the United States and thus presumably would not
be living in the White House. This example was derived from one given
by McCawley (1981) where other similar examples are discussed.

The logics considered so far cannot accommodate the distinction between
states of affairs, or possible worlds, such as those which occur in the
example above; neither can they accommodate states of affairs which
exist in people's beliefs, moral codes, etc. In order to deal with
such things, logicians have developed logics called 'modal logics'. It
is the objective of the next few sections to give a brief description
of modal logics and to discuss their use in knowledge base systems.

What is a modal logic?
Snyder (1971) has described a modal logic as a logic which allows us to
reason with statements which are in subjunctive moods rather than in
the indicative mood. Subjunctive statements assert what must be, ought
to be, might be, is believed to be, hoped to be, will be in the future,
and so on. Such statements are distinct from indicative statements
which simply assert what is. Classical truth-functional logics are
concerned with indicative statements. Modal statements can be detected
by the presence of modal operators. A formal feature of modal operators
is that they form statements whose truth values are not a function of
the truth values of the statement(s) being operated on. For example,
consider the following statements:

(a)   John has appendicitis.
(b)   It is the case that John has appendicitis.
(c)   It is possible that John has appendicitis.

Statements (a) and (b) are not modal. Statement (b) is true iff (a) is
true. Statement (c) is modal. It is true if (a) is true but may be
interpreted as true or false if (a) is false.

Early work on modal logic was primarily concerned with statements containing the operators 'it is possible that' and 'it is necessary that'
and their negations. Later, logicians considered statements containing
operators such as:

'it will always be the case that'
'it is obligatory that'
'it is permissible that'

'it is known that'
'it is believed that'

and so on. All of these qualify as modal under the description of
modality as given by Snyder. Modal logic, then, is concerned with
states of affairs or possible worlds in addition to the one that
exists.

Monadic and dyadic modal operators

Monadic modal operators range over single statements. All of the
examples above are monadic. Dyadic modal operators form new statements
from pairs of statements. Various attempts have been made to formalise
a dyadic modal 'if...then' operator. Two operators in particular have
been defined: 'strict implication' and 'entailment'. In classical
logic, the material implication formula P → Q is equivalent by definition to the negation of the conjunction P ∧ ¬Q. That is, P materially
implies Q iff it is not the case that P is true and Q is false. On the
other hand, the strict implication formula:

'P strictly implies Q'

is equivalent to the *impossibility* of the conjunction P ∧ ¬Q.

The distinction between material and strict implication is discussed
further in sub-section 6.7.3.

The following paragraphs describe, briefly, some types of modality.

Alethic modality

Modality which is concerned with necessity and possibility is called
'alethic' modality, from the Greek word for truth. In the same way
that our intuitions demand certain properties of the logical connectives of truth-functional logic, they also demand certain properties
of modal operators. For example, adequate systems of alethic modality
would be expected to have the following as theorems (tautologies):

    AS1 :   'if necessary P then possible P'
    AS2 :   'if necessary P then P'
    AS3 :   'if P then possible P'
    AS4 :   'if not possible P then not necessary P'
    AS5 :   'if not P then not necessary P'
    AS6 :   'if not possible P then not P'
    AS7 :   'possible not P iff not necessary P'
    AS8 :   'necessary not P iff not possible P'
    AS9 :   'either possible P or possible not P'
    AS10:   'not both necessary P and necessary not P'

There are various types of alethic modality depending on the interpretation of 'necessary' and 'possible'. For example, consider the following statements:

(a)   It is necessary that it will snow tomorrow or it will not snow
      tomorrow.

(b)   It is necessary that a bachelor be male.

(c) It is necessary that an action have an equal and opposite reaction.

The first is an example of logical necessity, the second of 'definitional' necessity and the third of physical necessity.

Temporal modality

The simplest temporal logics merely interpret the operators 'necessary' and 'possible' as 'always' and 'sometimes'. Formulas which are not in the scope of such operators are assumed to represent the present state of affairs. The logical axioms in such logics are the same as in alethic modality, as given above. More complex temporal logics include:

(a) Logics with tense operators such as 'it has been', 'it will be', 'it has always been' and 'it will always be'. Such logics have appropriate sets of logical axioms defined for them.

(b) Logics which include time variables as well as variables for entities.

Temporal logics are described in more detail in section 6.8.

Deontic modality

Deontic logics contain the modal operators 'it is obligatory' and 'it is permissible'. Deontic logics differ from alethic logics in that the ten logical axioms given above are not all appropriate. Whether or not something happens to be true has no bearing on whether it is obligatory or permissible from a moral or legal point of view. The axioms AS2, AS3, AS5 and AS6 have no counterparts in deontic logic. However, the following logical axioms should be theorems of any deontic logic:

    'if obligatory P then permissible P'
    'if not permissible P then not obligatory P'
    'permissible not P iff not obligatory P'
    'obligatory not P iff not permissible P'
    'either permissible P or permissible not P'
    'not both obligatory P and obligatory not P'

Epistemic modality

Epistemic logic is concerned with knowledge, belief and similar concepts. Simple epistemic logics involve modal operators 'it is known that' and 'it is believed that'. These two operators are not interdefinable as are the operators 'necessary' and 'possible'. Also our intuitions vary as to what we mean by 'known' and 'believed'. However, most simple epistemic logics contain the following logical axioms:

    'if known P then believed P'
    'if not believed P then not known P'
    'not both known P and known not P'

More complex epistemic logics include notions of agents or indexed modal operators which allow us to reason with statements such as 'John knows P.' Such logics are discussed in more detail in section 6.9.

334

A general comment
We could begin by describing each of these logics in more detail. However, this would involve a good deal of redundancy since they have much in common; for example, simple temporal logics have much in common with alethic logics. We have therefore decided to begin by discussing modal logics without much reference to application.

In the remainder of this section we discuss modal logics using the operators 'necessary' and 'possible' as example. A discussion of possible worlds (states of affairs) and the relationships between possible worlds is followed by a discussion of why some logical axioms are appropriate for some types of modal logic but not for others. Then some modal operators are defined more formally and a definition of a language for a modal propositional logic is given. This is followed by a description of various categories of modal logics which are related to different properties of the 'accessibility' relation between possible worlds. We then present a description of how to reason (prove theorems and check for consistency) in modal logic and conclude the section with a brief look at modal predicate logic.

This section is primarily concerned with the abstract properties of modality and modal logics. In subsequent sections (sections 6.8 and 6.9) two particular types of modal logic - temporal logic and epistemic logic - are described in more detail.

6.7.1 POSSIBLE WORLDS, ACCESSIBILITY RELATIONS AND THE NOTION OF NECESSITY

The world in which we live is the *actual* world. However, it is not the only world in which mankind is interested. Often, when engaged in discussions concerning politics, economics, science, morals and so forth, we introduce non-actual *possible* worlds with sentences like 'if such and such were the case then it would follow that...'. We go on to discuss these possible worlds in much the same way as we discuss the actual world.

Conjecture of possible worlds is useful in various circumstances for various reasons. For example, if politicians are considering a change in the voting system, then it is useful for them to consider the implications of such a change, i.e. the possible world which would arise if the new voting system were introduced.

Various types of possible world
The term 'possible world' can be used in various ways to distinguish 'possible' worlds from 'impossible' worlds. For example:

(a) A 'logically possible' world might be defined as a world which conforms to the rules of logic. A world in which London is *or* is not the capital of England is logically possible whereas a world in which London is *and* is not the capital of England is a logically impossible world.

(b) A 'physically possible' world might be defined as a world which has the same physical properties as the actual world. An example of a physically impossible world is one in which gravitational mass is distinct from inertial mass. Another example of a physically impossible world is a world in which particles (other than tachyons) can travel faster than the speed of light.

(c) A 'morally possible' world might be defined as one in which all laws of some particular moral code are obeyed.

(d) A 'conceivably possible' world might be defined as a world which can be conceived. We might conceive of a world in which there is no notion of colour.

(e) A 'temporally possible' world might be defined as a world which is at the same time or is in the future of the world under consideration. This definition captures, to some extent, the notion that we cannot go back in time.

The last two examples indicate the need for worlds to be defined as being possible with respect to other worlds rather than absolutely. For example:

(a) Given the above definition of 'temporally possible worlds', a world of 1988 is temporally possible with respect to a world of 1984 but not with respect to a world of 1994.

(b) A world w in which there is no notion of colour is conceivably possible with respect to the actual world. However, the actual world would not be conceivably possible with respect to w since the inhabitants of w have no notion of colour.

Accessibility relations
A concise way of describing relative possibilities between the worlds in some set of worlds W is to define a binary relation R, called an 'accessibility relation', over W, such that for any w_i, $w_j \in W$:

$\langle w_i, w_j \rangle \in R$ iff w_j is possible w.r.t. w_i

That is, a pair of worlds $\langle w_i, w_j \rangle$ is a member of the relation R if and only if w_j is possible with respect to w_i.

The terminology of relational theory can now be used to characterise R. For example:

(a) A relation R is 'reflexive' in the set W iff for all $w \in W$, $\langle w, w \rangle \in R$. That is, the accessibility relation is reflexive in a set of worlds W iff all worlds in W are possible with respect to themselves. In most of the examples above, the accessibility relation is reflexive. However, consider a set of worlds W, each member of which has a moral code. We might define R such that $\langle w_i, w_j \rangle \in R$ iff w_j obeys the moral code of w_i. It is most likely that $\langle w_i, w_i \rangle \notin R$ for some $w_i \in W$ (else why would it be necessary to create moral codes?). In this case R is not reflexive.

(b) A relation R is 'transitive' in the set W iff it satisfies the following condition for all w_i, w_j, $w_k \in W$:

if <wi, wj> ∈ R and <wj, wk> ∈ R then <wi, wk> ∈ R

The accessibility relation for temporal possibility (as defined above) is transitive.

(c)   A relation R is 'symmetric' in the set W iff it satisfies the following condition for all wi, wj ∈ W:

if <wi, wj> ∈ R then <wj, wi> ∈ R

The accessibility relation for physical possibility (as defined above) is symmetric, whereas the accessibility relation for temporal possibility is not symmetric.

(d)   A relation R is 'connected' in the set W iff it satisfies the following condition for all wi, wj ∈ W:

if wi ≠ wj then <wi, wj> ∈ R or <wj, wi> ∈ R

(e)   A relation R is an 'equivalence' relation in the set W iff it is reflexive, symmetric and transitive in W. For example, the accessibility relation for 'logical' possibility is an equivalence relation.

The notions of necessary and possible truth
The terms 'necessary' and 'possible' truth are defined more formally in sub-section 6.7.2, but for now the following informal descriptions will suffice:

(a)   A proposition P is necessarily true in a world w iff P is true in *all* worlds which are accessible from w. Necessary truth is denoted by □.

(b)   A proposition P is possibly true in a world w iff P is true in at least one world which is accessible from w. Possible truth is denoted by ◇.

Possible truth can be defined in terms of necessary truth:

DF1 : ◇P for ¬□¬P

i.e. a proposition is possibly true iff it is not necessary that it is not true.

As examples of the use of necessary and possible truth, consider the following propositions which we shall assume to be true in the current world. Possible worlds in this example are taken to be temporally possible worlds. In this case, the accessibility relation R is reflexive and transitive but not symmetric:

PA1 : JohnSmithisalive
read as 'John Smith is alive in the current world'.

PA2 : ◇John Smith is dead
read as 'in the current world or in some world in the future of the current world, John Smith is dead'.

337

PA3 :   □[John Smith is dead → □John Smith is dead]
         read as 'in the current world and in all worlds in the future
         of the current world, if John Smith is dead in that world,
         then he will be dead in all worlds in the future of that
         world' (i.e. once John Smith is dead, he will remain dead).

A more detailed discussion of possible worlds can be found in Bradley
and Swartz (1979).

6.7.2 SPECIAL INFERENCE RULES AND LOGICAL AXIOMS FOR PARTICULAR MODAL LOGICS

Alethic modal propositional logic includes (a) all of the machinery of
classical propositional logic extended to include the symbols ◇ and
□ , (b) the definition DF1 above and (c) some additional rules of inference and logical axioms. In this section, we describe one inference
rule and one logical axiom which are found in many basic modal systems.
Later, some additional logical axioms which may be added to the basic
systems of modal logic to produce extensions for particular applications are described.

The rule described is called 'Gödel's rule' or the rule of 'necessitation' (Gödel, 1933). This rule is appropriate for most modal systems
since it captures the notion that if something is logically true then
it is necessarily true. Since most modal systems deal only with possible worlds which are also logically possible, Gödel's rule is found
(or can be proved) in most modal systems. The rule may be defined as
follows:

        from ⊢ P infer □P

This rule means that if P is a theorem of the modal system being used
(that is, a logical axiom of the modal system), then □P is also a
theorem. Note that this does not mean that if P is a proper axiom of
some modal theory T, then □P is also a theorem of T.

In addition to the above rule of inference, many modal systems include
the following logical axiom:

        LAM :   □[P → Q] → [□P → □Q]

That is, if it is necessary that whenever P is true Q is also true, it
follows that if P is necessary then Q is necessary. The axiom, LAM,
follows from our intuitive understanding of the notion of necessity.

Additional logical axioms for particular modal systems
Basic modal systems can be extended by the addition of logical axioms.
Adding these axioms increases the number of valid formulas in such systems and therefore can increase the number of deductions which can be
made in their theories. The axioms described below are related to the
various properties of the accessibility relation. They can therefore
be added, as required, to a basic modal system to construct a system
which is more appropriate for a given application. For example, if the
application has a reflexive and transitive, but not symmetric, accessibility relation, then an appropriate modal system can be constructed
from a basic modal system plus axioms LA1 and LA2 below:

(a) If R is reflexive then the following axiom is appropriate:

   LA1 : $\Box P \to P$

That is, if $\Box P$ is true in some world w, then P is true in w since w is accessible from itself.

(b) If R is transitive then the following axiom is appropriate:

   LA2 : $\Box P \to \Box\,\Box P$

That is, if P is true in all worlds wj which are accessible from some world wi, then P is true in all worlds, wk, which are accessible from wj.

(c) If R is symmetric then the following axiom is appropriate:

   LA3 : $P \to \Box\Diamond P$

This means that if P is true in some world w, then $\Diamond P$ is true in all worlds that are accessible from w.

(d) If R is an equivalence relation then the following axioms are appropriate:

   LA1 : $\Box P \to P$
   LA4 : $\Diamond P \to \Box\,\Diamond P$

The following example concerns temporally accessible worlds. According to our earlier definition of temporal possibility, the accessibility relation R in this case is both reflexive and transitive. (We see later that this is not the only characterisation of R for temporal logic. However, for simplicity we shall assume that it is adequate for present purposes.)

Since R is reflexive and transitive, it is appropriate to use axioms LA1 and LA2 above. However, since R is not symmetric, nor is it an equivalence relation, it is not appropriate to use LA3 or LA4. As illustration, consider a modal theory T which contains the following proper axioms:

   PA1 :   John Smith is alive
   PA2 : $\Diamond$John Smith is dead
   PA3 : $\Box$[John Smith is dead $\to$ $\Box$John Smith is dead]
   PA4 : $\Box$[John Smith is alive $\to$ ¬John Smith is dead]

where PA4 might read as 'in all worlds which are accessible from the current world, if John Smith is alive then John Smith is not dead'.

As mentioned, since the accessibility relation that we are assuming is reflexive and transitive, the axioms LA1 and LA2 can be used, in addition to the machinery of propositional logic, when proving theorems in T. For example, to prove ¬(John Smith is dead), we proceed as follows:

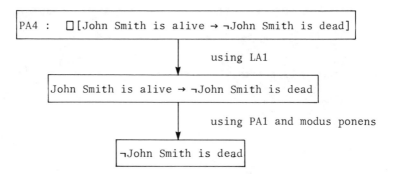

We now illustrate why it would be inappropriate to use LA4 in this example showing that (John Smith is dead) is also a theorem of T if LA4 is allowed as a logical axiom. Let Q stand for the proposition (John Smith is dead); the proof proceeds as follows:

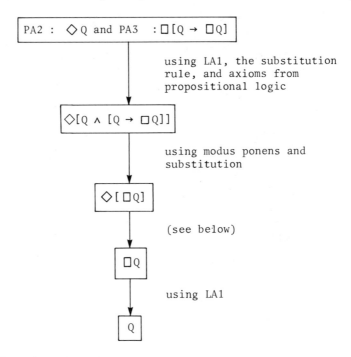

That is, if we include LA4 as a logical axiom, then we can prove (John Smith is dead) in T. This would make T inconsistent.

The penultimate step in the above proof is rather complex. The proof is outlined below, but we refer the interested reader to McCawley (1981) for a more detailed description. Our proof consists of showing that $\Diamond \Box P \to \Box P$ is a theorem of any modal system with LA4 as logical axiom:

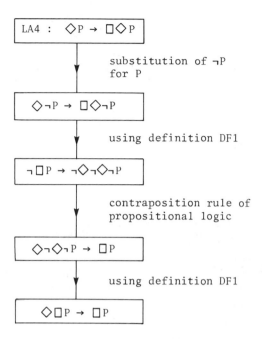

LA4 : $\Diamond P \rightarrow \Box \Diamond P$

↓ substitution of ¬P for P

$\Diamond \neg P \rightarrow \Box \Diamond \neg P$

↓ using definition DF1

$\neg \Box P \rightarrow \neg \Diamond \neg \Diamond \neg P$

↓ contraposition rule of propositional logic

$\Diamond \neg \Diamond \neg P \rightarrow \Box P$

↓ using definition DF1

$\Diamond \Box P \rightarrow \Box P$

This result can be used with the substitution inference rule to derive $\Diamond \Box Q \rightarrow \Box Q$.

In this example, we have illustrated how different modal logics can be constructed by the inclusion or exclusion of certain logical axioms. We have also indicated that these axioms relate to properties of the accessibility relation between worlds in some set of worlds. Therefore, we have shown that appropriate modal logics can be constructed for different applications in which different meanings are ascribed to the term 'possible world'. This feature has resulted in the construction of various types of modal logic such as temporal logic, epistemic logic and so on.

Before going on to discuss such logics in more detail, we present a more formal description of the notions introduced so far. This description includes axiomatisations for some of the better known modal systems, and a description of a proof technique which can be used with modal logics and which is intuitively easier than using logical axioms.

6.7.3 MODAL PROPERTIES OF PROPOSITIONS/FORMULAS
In each possible world, each atomic proposition has one or other of the values 'true' or 'false'. Consequent upon this, other properties of propositions, called modal properties, which determine the way in which the truth-values of propositions are distributed across the set of all possible worlds can be defined. For example:

(a) A proposition is *possibly true* iff it is true in at least one possible world. If this possible world is the actual world, then the proposition is *actually true*. For example, 'John

341

Smith lived for 108 years' is possibly true, and 'Reagan is the President of the United States' is actually true (at the time this book was written).

(b)   A proposition is *possibly false* iff it is false in at least one possible world.

(c)   A proposition is *contingent* iff it is true in at least one possible world and false in at least one possible world. For example, the proposition about Reagan above is contingent and happens to be true in the actual world.

(d)   A proposition is *necessarily true* if it is true in all possible worlds. The following is an example of a necessarily true proposition:

'John Smith lived 108 years or John Smith did not live 108 years.'

(e)   A proposition is *necessarily false* if it is false in all possible worlds. For example, 'John Smith lived 108 years and John Smith did not live 108 years' is a necessarily false proposition.

(f)   A proposition is *non-contingent* if it is necessarily true or necessarily false.

Notice that the discussion and examples above have been restricted to notions of 'logical possibility' and 'logical necessity'. As example of another type of necessity, consider the following proposition:

'If a good man knows that his neighbour is in difficulty, then he should help his neighbour.'

This proposition would be morally necessarily true in a moral modal logic based on the ten commandments.

Symbolisation
In this book the modal properties of propositions are symbolised as follows:

$\Diamond P$ means P is possibly true
$\Diamond \neg P$ means P is possibly false
∇P means P is contingent
$\Box P$ means P is necessarily true
$\Box \neg P$ means P is necessarily false
ΔP means P is non-contingent

Modal relationships between pairs of propositions
Propositions can be related to each other in various ways. In the following, some of the ways in which pairs of propositions can be related are described.

(a)   A proposition P1 is a *contradictory* of a proposition P2 if P1 is false in all possible worlds in which P2 is true and P1 is true in all possible worlds in which P2 is false. For example, the proposition 'John Smith lived 108 years' is a contradictory of the proposition 'John Smith did not live 108 years'.

(b) A proposition P1 is a *contrary* of a proposition P2 if although both may be false in some possible world, both may not be true in any possible world. For example, the propositions 'it is Wednesday' and 'it is Friday' are contrary propositions. Notice that a necessarily false proposition is a contrary of any and every other proposition including itself.

(c) Two propositions are *inconsistent* iff they are contradictory or contrary. A pair of propositions which includes a necessarily false proposition is always inconsistent.

(d) Two propositions are *consistent* iff they are not inconsistent.

(e) A proposition P strictly *implies* a proposition Q iff Q is true in all those possible worlds, if any, in which P is true. For example, the proposition 'John is married to Sue' strictly implies the proposition 'Sue is married to John'. Notice that false propositions may have implications according to this definition. The difference between the implications of a false proposition and the implication of a true proposition is that a false proposition has implications some of which may be false whereas a true proposition has implications all of which are true. Notice also that a necessarily false proposition implies any and every proposition and a necessarily true proposition is implied by any and every proposition. These consequences of the definition of implication given above may appear some what counterintuitive. However, arguments can be made for their acceptance; one such argument is given in Bradley and Swartz (1979).

(f) Two propositions are *equivalent* iff they imply one another, i.e. P is equivalent to Q iff P is true in all possible worlds in which Q is true and Q is true in all possible worlds in which P is true.

Symbolisation of relationships between pairs of propositions
In this book the relationships between pairs of propositions are symbolised as follows:

P o Q means P is consistent with Q
P φ Q means P is inconsistent with Q
P ⇒ Q means P strictly implies Q
P ↔ Q means P is equivalent to Q

Notice that modal implication denoted by ⇒ and modal equivalence denoted by ↔ are distinct from 'material implication' or 'conditionality', denoted by →, and 'material bi-conditionality', denoted by ↔, in truth-functional logic.

The modal connective ⇒ which is called 'strict implication' corresponds to ordinary language words such as 'if' and 'implies' better than the material implication → of truth-functional logic. A ⇒ B is equivalent to □[A → B] and therefore avoids some of the more bizarre theorems involving → (bizarre, that is, if → is identified with 'if'). For example, the following is a theorem of truth-functional propositional logic but not of S1, S2, S3, S4 or S5 (these are systems of modal logic which will be defined shortly):

   [A → B] v [B → A]

This is a theorem of truth-functional propositional logic even though A and B might be totally 'unrelated' propositions.

6.7.4 PROPERTIES OF, AND RELATIONS BETWEEN, PROPOSITION SETS
The following are definitions of some properties of sets of propositions in modal logic:

(a) A set of propositions is *true* iff every member of the set is true.

(b) A set of propositions is *possibly true* or *self-consistent* iff there exists a possible world in which every member of the set is true.

(c) A set of propositions is *possibly false* iff there exists a possible world in which at least one member of that set is false.

(d) A set of propositions is *necessarily true* iff every member of the set is necessarily true.

(e) A set of propositions is *necessarily false* or *self-inconsis-tent* iff in every possible world at least one proposition in the set is false.

(f) A set of propositions is *contingent* iff it is neither neces-sarily true nor necessarily false.

The following define relations between pairs of proposition sets:

(a) Two sets of propositions are *consistent* iff there exists some possible world in which all the propositions in both sets are true.

(b) Two sets of propositions are *inconsistent* iff they are not consistent.

(c) A set of propositions S1 *implies* a set of S2 iff all proposi-tions in S2 are true in all possible worlds in which all pro-positions in S1 are true.

(d) Two sets of propositions S1 and S2 are equivalent if S1 implies S2 *and* S2 implies S1.

6.7.5 THE SYNTAX OF A LANGUAGE OF MODAL PROPOSITIONAL LOGIC
The following context-free grammar defines the syntax of one example

344

of a language of modal propositional logic. We shall call this language L3:

$$\text{terminals} = \{p, q, r, s, \ldots, \wedge, \neg, [,], \square\}$$

```
          wff  ::= ¬ wff| wff ∧ wff|□ wff|atomic formula
atomic formula  ::= p | q | r | s, ...
```

The atomic formulas of L3 are denoted by the use of letters such as
p, q, r or by character strings. If P and Q are wffs, then the following abbreviations are also defined for L3:

```
P ∨ Q for ¬[¬P ∧ ¬Q]
P → Q for ¬P ∨ Q
P ↔ Q for [P → Q] ∧ [Q → P]
◇P    for ¬□¬P
P ⇒ Q for □[P → Q]
P ⇔ Q for □[P ↔ Q]
```

As example, consider the following wffs of L3 (in which strings are
used to denote atomic formulas):

(a) □[the moon is made of green cheese ∨ the moon is not made of
     green cheese]
     read as 'it is necessarily true that the moon is or is not
     made of green cheese'.

(b) □all triangles have three sides
     read as 'it is necessarily true that all triangles have three
     sides'.

(c) □[[John has a child ∧ John is male] → John is a father]
     read as 'it is necessarily true that if John has a child and
     John is male, then John is a father'. Notice that this
     formula may be re-written as:

     [John has a child ∧ John is male] ⇒ John is a father

(d) ◇[Reagan was born in France → Reagan speaks French]
     read as 'it is possible that if Reagan were born in France
     then Reagan would speak French'.

(e) ◇[Reagan speaks French → Reagan speaks French in the
     White House]
     read analogously to (d).

(f) □[N is divisible by 8 → N is divisible by 4]
     read as 'it is necessarily true (i.e. true in all possible
     worlds) that if N is divisible by 8 then N is divisible by 4'.

(g) □[N is divisible by 4 → N is divisible by 2]
     read as 'it is necessarily true that if N is divisible by 4
     then N is divisible by 2'.

The modal operators □, ◇ , ∇ and ∆, and the modal connectives o, φ, ⇒

and ↔ are not truth-functional as are the operators ¬, ∨, ∧, → and ↔. For example, given the truth value of P one cannot, in general, determine the truth value of □P. However, some truth values can be determined as illustrated in the following truth tables, in which I means 'indeterminate':

P	◇P	□P	∇P	ΔP
T	T	I	I	I
⊥	I	⊥	I	I

P	Q	P o Q	P φ Q	P ⇒ Q	P ↔ Q
T	T	T	⊥	I	I
T	⊥	I	I	⊥	⊥
⊥	T	I	I	I	⊥
⊥	⊥	I	I	I	I

These tables tell us, for example, that:

(a)   If P is true then ◇P is true, i.e. if P is true then P is true in some possible world.

(b)   If P is false then □P is false, i.e. if P is false then it cannot be necessarily true in all possible worlds.

These tables assume a reflexive accessibility relation.

Equivalence rules
For purposes of 'regularising' modal formulas for subsequent processing, the following equivalence rules can be used in addition to the abbreviation definitions given earlier:

$$P \text{ o } Q \leftrightarrow ◇[P ∧ Q]$$
$$P \text{ φ } Q \leftrightarrow ¬◇[P ∧ Q]$$
$$∇P \leftrightarrow ◇P ∧ ◇¬P$$
$$ΔP \leftrightarrow □P ∨ □¬P$$

For example:

P ⇒ P φ Q   may be replaced by   □[P → ¬[P ∧ Q]]

6.7.6   THE MODAL AXIOM SYSTEMS OF LEWIS
In this sub-section, five distinct systems of modal logic are described. These systems, called S1 to S5, were defined by Lewis (1918 and 1932). The system S5 dates back to Leibnitz but was named S5 by Lewis to indicate the position in the hierarchy of axiom systems defined by him. These systems all contain the same language and rules of inference but differ in their sets of logical axioms. The systems were defined independently of the notion of accessibility relations.

The language of S1 to S5
All five systems use the language L3 described above, or symbolic variants of this language.

Rules of inference

All five systems use the following rules of inference:

(a) Modus ponens for strict implication:
    given P and P ⇒ Q, infer Q.

(b) Uniform substitution:
    given P, infer Q where Q is the result of substituting some
    wff for a propositional variable uniformly throughout P.

(c) Conjunction:
    given P and Q, infer P ∧ Q.

(d) Replacement of equivalents:
    given P ⇔ Q and some propositional context ...P... involving
    P, infer ...Q... , where Q has replaced P in one or more of
    its occurrences in the initial context.

Logical axiom schemas for S1

AS1 : P ∧ Q ⇒ Q ∧ P
AS2 : P ∧ Q ⇒ P
AS3 : P ⇒ P ∧ P
AS4 : P ∧ [Q ∧ R] ⇒ Q ∧ [P ∧ R]
AS5 : [P ⇒ Q] ∧ [Q ⇒ R] ⇒ [P ⇒ R]
AS6 : P ⇒ ◇P

Logical axiom schemas for S2

Those for S1 plus AS7 : ◇[P ∧ Q] ⇒ ◇P.

Logical axiom schemas for S3

Those for S1 plus AS8 : [P ⇒ Q] ⇒ [◇P ⇒ ◇Q].

Logical axiom schemas for S4

Those for S1 plus AS9 : ◇◇P ⇒ ◇P.

Logical axiom schemas for S5

Those for S1 plus AS10 : ◇P ⇒ □◇P.

The modal logics S1 to S5 were defined and categorised before their
relationship to accessibility relations and possible worlds was fully
appreciated. To some extent, they were simply regarded as modal logics
in which different theorems could be proven. S5 is said to be 'stronger'
than S4 and S4 'stronger' than S3, etc. This is because all universally valid formulas of S4 can be derived in S5, and all universally
valid formulas of S3 can be derived in S4, and so on.

In 1963 Kripke provided a new understanding of modal logics which related them to properties of the accessibility relation (as discussed in
sub-section 6.7.1). He did this by defining various modal logics as
extensions to a basic modal logic which is variously called M, T, S2'
or the Feys/Van Wright system. This system, which we shall refer to as
M, was first axiomatised by Feys in 1937. M corresponds to an accessibility relation which is reflexive.

The following axiomatisation for M makes the relationship to a reflexive accessibility relation obvious.

An axiomatisation of M
M includes any complete axiomatisation for classical propositional
logic extended to include □, plus:

(a) The definitions:

DF1 : ◇P for ¬□¬P
DF2 : P ⇒ Q for ¬◇[P ∧ ¬Q]
DF3 : P ⇔ Q for [P ⇒ Q] ∧ [Q ⇒ P]

(b) The logical axioms:

AS1 : □P → P (this is the reflexiveness axiom)
AS2 : □[P → Q] → [□P → □Q]

(c) The inference rules:

R1 : modus ponens for →
R2 : uniform substitution
R3 : Gödel's rule : from ⊢ P infer ⊢ □P

Examples of theorems (universally valid formulas) of M

T1 : all tautologies of classical propositional logic
T2 : □P ⇒ P
T3 : P ⇒ ◇P
T4 : □P ⇒ ◇P
T5 : □[P ∧ Q] ⇔ [□P ∧ □Q]
T6 : ◇[P ∨ Q] ⇔ [◇P ∨ ◇Q]
T7 : [□P ∨ □Q] ⇒ □[P ∨ Q]
T8 : ◇[P ∧ Q] ⇒ [◇P ∧ ◇Q]
T9 : □P ⇔ □[¬P → P]
T10 : [[P ⇒ Q] ∧ P] ⇒ Q
T11 : [[P ⇒ Q] ∧ □P] ⇒ □Q
T12 : [[P ⇒ Q] ∧ ◇¬Q] ⇒ ◇¬P
T13 : [[P ⇒ Q] ∧ ¬Q] ⇒ ¬P
T14 : [[P ⇒ Q] ∧ [Q ⇒ R]] ⇒ [P ⇒ R]
T15 : [[P ∧ Q] ⇒ R] ⇒ [P ⇒ [Q → R]]
T16 : □Q ⇒ [P ⇒ Q]
T17 : □¬P ⇒ [P ⇒ Q]
T18 : □[P ⇒ P]
T19 : [P ∧ ¬P] ⇒ Q
T20 : Q ⇒ [P ∨ ¬P]
T21 : [P ⇒ Q] ⇒ [□P → □Q]

The addition of extra logical axioms to M results in various modal
logics. In particular, Kripke showed that S4, S5 and a logic called
the Brouwersche logic can be built from M as follows:

(a) S4 can be built from M by adding the axiom:

□P → □ □P   (this is the transitivity axiom)

(b) The Brouwersche logic can be built from M by adding the axiom:

  $P \rightarrow \Box\Diamond P$ (this is the symmetry axiom)

(c) S5 can be built from M by adding the axiom:

  $\Diamond P \rightarrow \Box\Diamond P$ (this is the equivalence axiom when used in conjunction with $\Box P \rightarrow P$)

It should be pointed out that M, S4, the Brouwersche logic, and S5 are not the only modal logics which can be so constructed. Other modal logics can be built which correspond to other types of accessibility relation. In fact, when we come to discuss temporal logic in more detail, in section 6.8, we find that a reflexive and transitive accessibility relation R is not the most appropriate type of relation for temporal necessity (as we have assumed it to be so far). A more appropriate accessibility relation and a correspondingly more appropriate logic for dealing with temporal expressions are identified in that section.

6.7.7 VALIDITY CHECKING AND THEOREM-PROVING USING SEMANTIC TABLEAUX
In order to determine the validity of modal propositional formulas, we can use a method which is an extension of the tableau method described in section 4.2.5 for propositional logic. However, before describing the method, it will be helpful to introduce the notion of 'world diagrams'.

World diagrams
We can represent individual worlds by rectangular boxes labelled with world identifiers. We can also depict the accessibility relation by drawing directed arcs between the boxes. For example, suppose that we have an accessibility relation which is not reflexive, not transitive, and not symmetric. This can be depicted as shown in fig. 6.1.

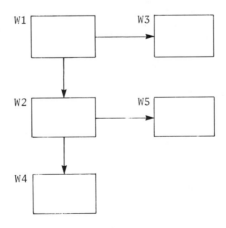

Figure 6.1

The diagram in fig. 6.1 can be interpreted as follows:

(a) W2 and W3 are accessible with respect to W1. Therefore any

349

formula which is necessarily true in W1 must be true in both W1 and W2, and any formula which is possibly true in W1 must be true in at least one of W2, W3 or some other world which is accessible to W1.

(b)   W4 is accessible to W2.

(c)   W5 is accessible to W2.

(d)   Because the accessibility relation is not reflexive, W1 is not accessible to itself.

(e)   Because the accessibility relation is not transitive, neither W4 nor W5 are accessible to W1.

(f)   Because the accessibility relation is not symmetric, W1 is not accessible to either W2 or W3.

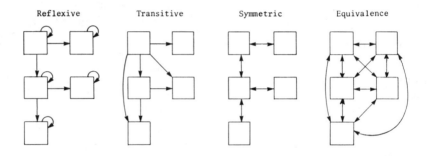

Figure 6.2 Different properties of the accessibility relation

Figure 6.2 shows similar diagrams for the cases in which the accessibility relation is:

(a)   Reflexive but not transitive or symmetric.
(b)   Transitive but not reflexive or symmetric.
(c)   Symmetric but not reflexive or transitive.
(d)   An equivalence relation.

We now show how such diagrams can be used to illustrate the effect of assigning a value of true to a modal formula in one of the worlds in a set of worlds.

Example 1
Suppose that we have an accessibility relation which is not reflexive, not transitive and not symmetric. Suppose, also, that we assign a value of true to the formula $\Box$P in world W1. Such an assignment requires that P be assigned a value of true in all worlds which are accessible to W1. This follows from the definition of $\Box$. (See fig. 6.3.)

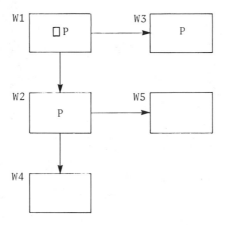

Figure 6.3

Example 2

Suppose that we have a similar accessibility relation, but assign the value true to the formula □ □P in W1. This means that □P must be true in all worlds accessible to W1, and that P must be true in all worlds accessible to these worlds. (See fig. 6.4.)

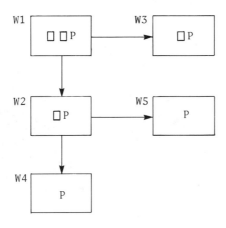

Figure 6.4

Example 3

Suppose that we have an accessibility relation which is both reflexive and transitive. Suppose also that we assign the value true to the formula □ □P in world W1. □P must be true in all worlds which are accessible to W1 (which includes itself) and P must be true in all worlds accessible to those worlds. (See fig. 6.5.)

Note that P in worlds W4 is a result of □P in W4, or □P in W1, or □P in W2. P in W2 is a result of □P in W1 or W2, etc.

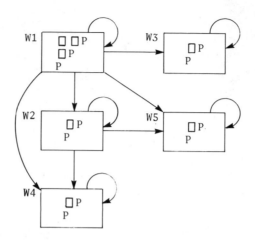

Figure 6.5

Example 4

Suppose that the accessibility relation is reflexive but not transitive and not symmetric. Suppose, also, that we assign the value true to the formula ◇P in W1. P must now be true in at least one of the worlds which are accessible to W1. (See fig. 6.6.)

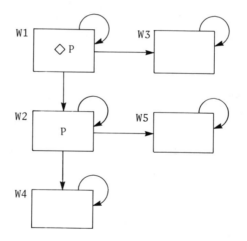

Figure 6.6

Alternatively, P could be true in W1 or W3, or in W1 and W2, or in W1 and W2 and W3, etc., in order that the assignment of ◇P in W1 be true.

Example 5

Suppose that we have an accessibility relation which is reflexive but not transitive and not symmetric. Suppose also that we assign a value of true to the formula ¬□P in world W1. For □P to be false in W1, ¬P must be true in some world which is accessible to W1. However, P could be true in some other world accessible to W1.   (See fig. 6.7.)

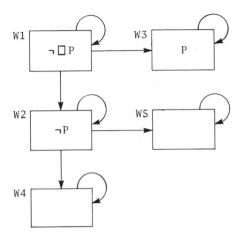

Figure 6.7

Example 6

Suppose that we have an accessibility relation which is not reflexive, not transitive, and not symmetric. Suppose also that we assign a value of true to the formula $\Box P \wedge \neg P$ in world W1. This means that P must be true in all worlds accessible to W1. This follows from the fact that if $\Box P \wedge \neg P$ is true in W1, both $\Box P$ and $\neg P$ must also be true. (See fig. 6.8.)

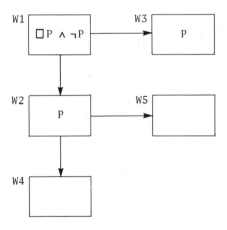

Figure 6.8

Example 7

Suppose now that we have the same situation as in example 6 but that the accessibility relation is reflexive. The situation becomes that illustrated in fig. 6.9. We can now see that we have a contradiction since $\neg P$ and P are both assigned a value of true in the same world.

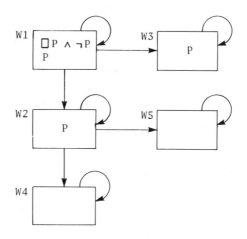

Figure 6.9

In this example, we have shown that if the accessibility relation is reflexive, □P ∧ ¬P cannot be assigned the value true (in any world) without resulting in a contradiction in that world. We can make the generality 'any world' since the world W1 was chosen arbitrarily.

Satisfiability checking
From the above, it can be seen that we have at our disposal a method for determining whether or not a simple modal formula can be satisfied with respect to a given type of accessibility relation. For example, □P ∧ ¬P is satisfiable if the accessibility relation is not reflexive, not transitive and not symmetric (example 6) but cannot be satisfied if the accessibility relation is reflexive (example 7).

Integrating world diagrams with semantic tableaux
Now the method that has been described so far is only applicable to 'simple' formulas - simple in the sense that they can only be satisfied in one way. In order to generalise the method we must integrate the use of world diagrams with the use of semantic tableaux. Referring back to section 4.2.5 (where semantic tableaux were used in classical propositional logic), we recall that semantic tableaux allow us to consider all of the various ways in which a formula might be assigned a value of true or false.

The following example illustrates the integration of the methods.

Example 8

Step 1: Suppose that we have an accessibility relation which is reflexive but not transitive and not symmetric. Suppose, also, that we assign a value of false to the following formula in world W1:

F1 : □[P → □[Q → R]] → ◇[Q → [□P → ◇R]]

We can depict this on a semantic tableau in W1 by putting the

354

formula in the right-hand column:

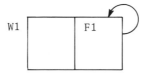

Step 2: Using the principles outlined for propositional logic in
section 4.2.5 we can now put □[P → □[Q → R]] in the left-hand
column and ◇[Q → [□P → ◇R]] in the right-hand column:

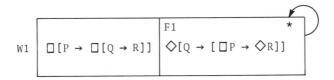

The asterisk indicates that formula F1 has been 'discharged'.
A formula is discharged when a tableau rule has been applied to it.

Step 3: We have now gone as far as classical tableau methods take us.
We now need to use the definitions of the modal operators □ and
◇ to obtain the world diagram in fig. 6.10.

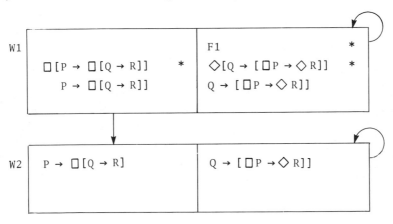

Figure 6.10

This is because if □α is true in W1 then α must be true in W1 and
in all worlds accessible to W1. Also, if ◇β is false in W1, then
β must be false in W1 and in all worlds accessible to W1.

Step 4: We can now apply the rules for →, giving the world diagram in
fig. 6.11.

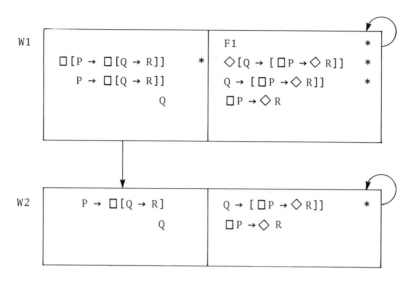

Figure 6.11

Step 5: Applying the rule for → again gives the world diagram in
fig. 6.12.

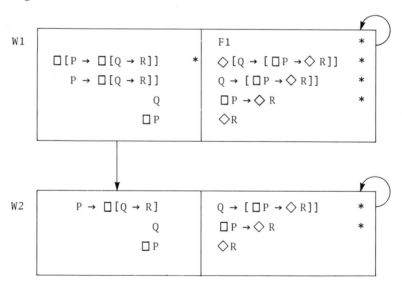

Figure 6.12

Step 6: Using the fact that $\Box P$ is true and $\Diamond R$ is false in W1 and
W2, we can write P true and R false in all worlds accessible to
W1 and W2. This is similar to step 3. The result is illustrated
in fig. 6.13.

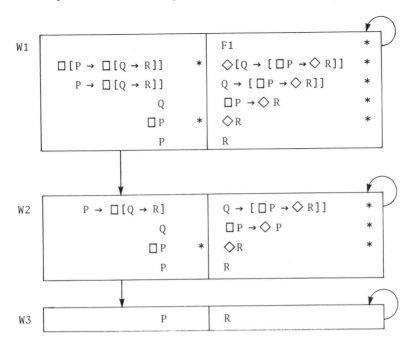

Figure 6.13

So far we have shown that if $\Box[P \to \Box[Q \to R]] \to \Diamond[Q \to [\Box P \to \Diamond R]]$ is to be false in W1, then (i) $\Box[P \to \Box[P \to R]]$ must be true and $\Diamond[Q \to [\Box P \to \Diamond R]]$ must be false in W1, (ii) $P \to \Box[Q \to R]]$ must be true, $Q \to [\Box P \to \Diamond R]]$ must be false, etc., in all worlds accessible to W1 (including itself since the accessibility relation is reflexive), and (iii) P must be true and R must be false in all worlds accessible to W1 and W2.

In fact, W2 contains those assignments which must hold in all worlds accessible to W1, and W3 contains those assignments which must hold in all worlds accessible to the set of worlds represented by W2.

Step 7: Now we can see that there is only one non-atomic formula to be discharged in world W1. This is the formula $P \to \Box[Q \to R]$ which is in the left column and has therefore been assigned a value of true. Now there are two ways in which this assignment can be discharged: either P is assigned false or $\Box[Q \to R]$ is assigned true. Therefore, we need to split the tableau in world W1 into two tableaux. We illustrate the split using the same notation as was used in section 4.2.5. The result is shown in fig. 6.14.

We can see that W1(1) contains an inconsistency since P is in both columns of the tableau. However, this only rules out one way in which the formula might be satisfied. We must look at W1(2) to test the other way.

357

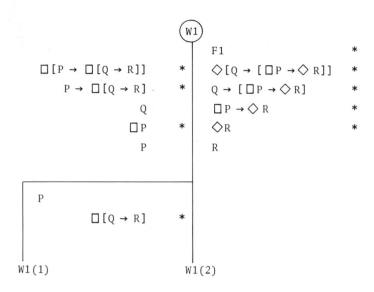

Figure 6.14

Step 8: Using the tableau rules for $\Box$ and $\rightarrow$ we obtain the situation shown in fig. 6.15.

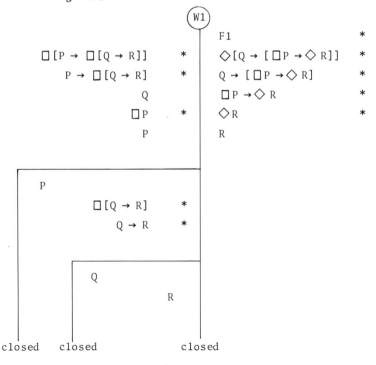

Figure 6.15

358

We see that W1(2) branches into two more tableaux each of which closes. Thus we can conclude that there is no truth assignment in world W1 that can assign a value of false to F1.

Notice that we need not consider the worlds W2 and W3 since no truth assignment can falsify F1 in W1.

Validity checking

The above procedure can be used for checking the validity of a formula. We simply put the formula in the false column of a tableau and test all possible ways in which this assignment can be satisfied. If all ways end in contradiction, then the original formula is valid. For example, the example above demonstrates the validity of the formula F1, since we explored all ways in which it might be assigned a value of false and found none.

Simplification if the accessibility relation is reflexive

Depending on the properties of the accessibility relation, the procedure above can be simplified. In particular, the generation of new worlds can be reduced. In fact, in the example above, because the relation is reflexive there was really no need to create any new worlds at all. This is explained in example 9 below.

To make the validity checks more concise, we introduce some additional notation. For example:

$$\begin{array}{c|ll} & 1: & A & :0* \\ 2: \quad B \qquad :1 & 3: & C & :1 \end{array}$$

This labels the 'assignment of false to the formula A' as 1, the 'assignment of true to the formula B' as 2, and the 'assignment of false to the formula C' as 3. The number to the right of a formula indicates the assignment above from which the given assignment was derived. The asterisk signifies that the assignment has been discharged.

Example 9

Suppose that the accessibility relation is reflexive but not transitive and not symmetric. Figure 6.16 illustrates the validity of the formula F1:

$$\Box[P \rightarrow \Box[Q \rightarrow R]] \rightarrow \Diamond[Q \rightarrow [\Box P \rightarrow \Diamond R]]$$

Note that in this example we do not need to create any new worlds since (i) the accessibility relation is reflexive and (ii) there are no cases of either ($\Diamond\alpha$ true and α false) or ($\Box\alpha$ false and α true) in W1. If either of these cases had occurred we would have had to create a new world (in the first case with α true and in the second case with α false).

We now give an example where a new world must be created. Note that when the new world is created we must put into it (i) α true for each $\Box\alpha$ true in W1 and (ii) α false for each $\Diamond\alpha$ false in W1.

Example 10

Suppose that we have an accessibility relation which is reflexive, but not transitive and not symmetric. Suppose also that we want to determine the validity of the formula:

F2 : $\Box[P \rightarrow \Box[Q \rightarrow R]] \rightarrow \Diamond[Q \rightarrow [\Box P \rightarrow \Diamond R]]$

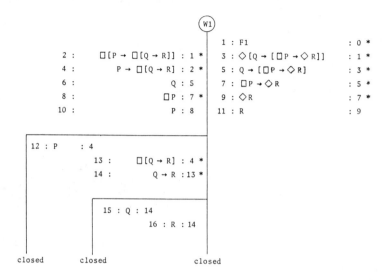

		1 : F1 : 0 *
2 :	$\Box[P \rightarrow \Box[Q \rightarrow R]]$: 1 *	3 : $\Diamond[Q \rightarrow [\Box P \rightarrow \Diamond R]]$: 1 *
4 :	$P \rightarrow \Box[Q \rightarrow R]$: 2 *	5 : $Q \rightarrow [\Box P \rightarrow \Diamond R]$: 3 *
6 :	Q : 5	7 : $\Box P \rightarrow \Diamond R$: 5 *
8 :	$\Box P$: 7 *	9 : $\Diamond R$: 7 *
10 :	P : 8	11 : R : 9

12 : P   : 4

   13 : $\Box[Q \rightarrow R]$: 4 *

   14 : $Q \rightarrow R$:13 *

   15 : Q : 14

      16 : R : 14

closed   closed   closed

Figure 6.16

Step 1:   Go as far as possible in world W1, as illustrated in fig. 6.17.

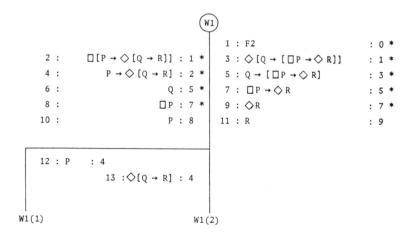

		1 : F2 : 0 *
2 :	$\Box[P \rightarrow \Diamond[Q \rightarrow R]]$: 1 *	3 : $\Diamond[Q \rightarrow [\Box P \rightarrow \Diamond R]]$: 1 *
4 :	$P \rightarrow \Diamond[Q \rightarrow R]$: 2 *	5 : $Q \rightarrow [\Box P \rightarrow \Diamond R]$: 3 *
6 :	Q : 5 *	7 : $\Box P \rightarrow \Diamond R$: 5 *
8 :	$\Box P$: 7 *	9 : $\Diamond R$: 7 *
10 :	P : 8	11 : R : 9

12 : P   : 4

   13 : $\Diamond[Q \rightarrow R]$: 4

W1(1)   W1(2)

Figure 6.17

Now we can see that the tableau labelled W1(1) is closed. W1(1) signifies that this is the first alternative in W1. We can now proceed in two ways:

360

(a) We could enter [Q → R] on the left of the tableau W1(2) since
     the assignment 13 tells us that Q → R must be true in some
     possible world. However, doing so would lead to an inconsis-
     tency in the same way as arose in example 9.

(b) Alternatively, since assignment 13 tells us that Q → R must
     be true in *some* possible world (not necessarily W1), we can
     explore this path by creating a new world W2:

W2
14: Q → R :13	

However, since this world is accessible from W1 we must assign
α true for all □α true in W1 and β false for all ◇β false in
W1:

W2
14: Q → R 13	16: Q → [□P → ◇R] :3
15: P → ◇[Q → R] : 2	
17: P : 8	18: R :9

We now develop the tableaux in W2 as illustrated in fig. 6.18.

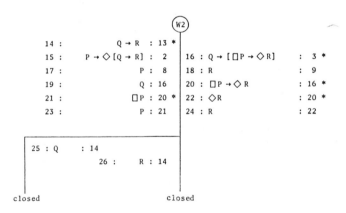

Figure 6.18

It can be seen that assignment 14 (i.e. Q → R true) cannot be discharged in W2 without producing a contradiction. Therefore no satisfying truth assignment can be found for W2, hence the original formula
must be valid. (Note that there is no need to discharge assignment 15.
Since 14 cannot be discharged it is irrelevant whether or not 15 can be
discharged.)

In this example there is really no need to consider the alternative of
assigning Q → R a value of true in W1. The reason for this is that if
a contraction were to occur in W2 it would always occur in W1 as well
(this is because the assignments in W2 will always be a subset of the
assignments in W1). Therefore we will not find a satisfying truth

assignment in W1 if one does not occur in W2. Consequently we can write down the following rules for dealing with assignment of true to ◇α and false to □α in any tableau in any world.

Rules for creating new worlds

(a) If in a world wi there occurs an assignment of true to a formula ◇α, then create a new world accessible to wi in which α is assigned true.

(b) If in a world wj there occurs an assignment of false to a formula □α, then create a new world accessible to wi in which α is assigned false.

(c) For every new world wj created, we must assign α true if □α is assigned true in any world wi from which wj is accessible

(d) For every new world wj created, we must assign α false if ◇α is assigned false in any world wi from which wj is accessible.

The following examples illustrate these rules.

Example 11

Suppose that we have an accessibility relation which is reflexive not transitive and not symmetric. Suppose also that we want to demonstrate the validity of the formula:

$$□[P \lor ◇Q] \rightarrow [□P \lor ◇Q]$$

We proceed by creating the tableau illustrated in fig. 6.19.

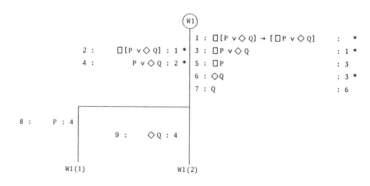

Figure 6.19

Now at this stage we must create two new worlds W2 and W3 (one for each tableau in W1), in which P is false (this results from assignment 5). In both of these worlds P ∨ ◇ Q must be true (due to assignment 2) and Q must be false (due to assignment 6), as illustrated in fig. 6.20.

World W2 is accessible from the first alternative in W1 (i.e. it relates to tableau W1(1)).

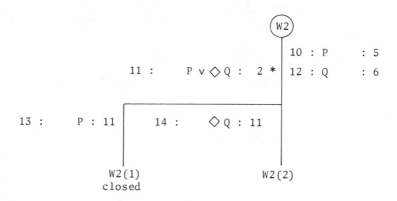

Figure 6.20

We can see that tableau W2(1) closes because of the occurrence of P in both columns. However, tableau W2(2) requires another world to be created (this follows from the presence of ◇Q in the left column). Let us call this world W4:

W4	15: Q :14	

The only requirement in W4 is that Q be true. Therefore, we have found a satisfying truth assignment which is illustrated in fig. 6.21.

	TRUE	FALSE
W1	□[P v ◇Q] P v ◇Q P	□[P v ◇Q] → [□P v ◇Q] □P v ◇Q □P ◇Q Q
W2	P v ◇Q ◇Q	P Q
W4	Q	

Figure 6.21

363

No contradictions occur and all sub-formulas are satisfied. Therefore the original formula is not valid (a satisfying truth assignment for its negation has been found).

If we had come up with a contradiction in this branch we would have had to develop world W3 corresponding to the tableau W1(2) in order to test all alternative ways in which the formula might be satisfied.

A *decision procedure for the system* M

In effect, the method described above is a procedure for checking the validity of formulas in system M since this system corresponds to an accessibility relation which is reflexive but not transitive and not symmetric.

A *decision procedure for the system* S4

System S4 corresponds to an accessibility relation which is reflexive and transitive but not symmetric. To accommodate the transitivity properly the method described above must be modified as follows:

> If an arrow is drawn from world wi to world wj, and an arrow is drawn from world wj to world wk, then we must draw an arrow from world wi to world wk, i.e. wk must be made accessible to wi.

The method is no different in any other respect. However, in S4-validity checks we can produce diagrams which have no counterpart in M-validity checks. For example, consider the formula:

$$\Box \Diamond P \rightarrow \Diamond \Box P$$

To test the S4-validity of this formula we proceed as illustrated in fig. 6.22. This diagram is not complete. For example, worlds W2 and W3 in the complete diagram would have two worlds accessible to them. However, the diagram illustrates a feature which can occur in S4 diagrams: worlds W2 and W6 are the same. Thus if allowed to do so the diagram would expand indefinitely. However, this situation can be easily overcome. We simply delete world W6 and run an arrow from world W4 to world W2. This then gives us a non-contradictory truth assignment

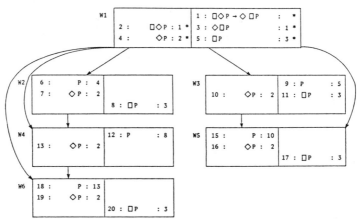

Figure 6.22

A decision procedure for S5
The method may also be used for checking for S5-validity. We simply
make the requirement that all worlds are connected to all other worlds
by arrows. This reflects the fact that S5 corresponds to an equivalence accessibility relation.

As example consider fig. 6.23 in which the S5-validity of the following
formula is demonstrated:

$$\Diamond\Diamond P \rightarrow \Box\Diamond P$$

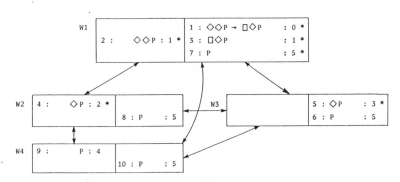

Figure 6.23

A more formal description of the use of semantic tableaux in decision
procedures for modal logic can be found in Hughes and Cresswell (1968).

6.7.8 A RESOLUTION-BASED METHOD FOR MODAL LOGIC
The resolution method for making deductions in classical propositional
logic has been extended for use in modal propositional logic by Farinas
del Cerro (1982). The method is rather complex and is not discussed
further in this book.

6.7.9 MODAL PREDICATE LOGIC

The Barcan axiom system
The Barcan axiom system for modal predicate logic (Barcan, 1946) contains S2, except for the axiom $P \Rightarrow \neg\neg P$, together with the following
axiom schemas:

    AS1 : ∀X[P → Q] ⇒ [∀XP ⇒ ∀XQ]
    AS2 : P ⇒ ∀XP, where X is not free in P
    AS3 : ◇∃X P ⇒ ∃X ◇P

The rules of inference are:

    R1: modus ponens for strict implication
    R2: conjunction
    R3: uniform substitution
    R4: generalisation:

        from PX infer ∀X PX, where X is free in P

365

The axiom AS3 above, which is known as the 'Barcan formula' has been much discussed in the literature because of certain counter-intuitive instances of it. The Barcan formula may be read as 'if it is possible that there exists an entity X such that P(X) is true, then this implies that there exists an entity for which P(X) is possibly true'.

The following counter-intuitive instance is given in Marciszcwski (1981). According to the Barcan formula, if it is possible that the first woman president of France will be a blonde, this implies that there exists someone who is possibly the first woman president of France. Such an existential conclusion is an undesirable result since we can easily per-ceive of a world in which the possible future woman president of France is not yet born. There is a way out of this problem:

(a) We accept that the Barcan formula is valid in modal systems in which all possible worlds have the same domain of entities.

(b) In modal systems where possible worlds have different domains of entities, we must use a modal predicate logic in which the Barcan formula cannot be derived (see below).

Prior's system
Prior's system for modal predicate logic (Prior, 1956) is a Gödel-type axiomatisation of S5 together with two rules for quantifiers taken from Lukasiewicz (1951). The complete system contains:

(a) Any complete axiomatisation of classical propositional logic.

(b) These additional axioms for modal concepts:

$$AS1 : \quad \Box[P \rightarrow Q] \rightarrow [\Box P \rightarrow \Box Q]$$
$$AS2 : \quad \Box P \rightarrow P$$
$$AS3 : \quad \neg\Box P \rightarrow \Box\neg\Box P$$

(c) Gödel's rule of inference:

$$R1 : \quad \text{from} \vdash P \text{ infer} \vdash \Box P$$

(d) Lukasiewicz's rules for quantification:

$$R2 : \quad \text{from} \vdash [P \rightarrow Q] \text{ infer} \vdash [\exists X[P \rightarrow Q]$$
$$\text{where X is not free in Q}$$
$$R3 : \quad \text{from} \vdash [P \rightarrow Q] \text{ infer} \vdash [P \rightarrow \exists X \, Q]$$

(e) The definition:

$$D1 : \quad \Diamond P \text{ for } \neg\Box\neg P$$

Thus Prior's system may be regarded as containing system M extended to S5 by the addition of the axiom $\neg\Box P \rightarrow \Box\neg\Box P$, together with the rules for quantification given above.

The Barcan formula is derivable in Prior's system, but is not derivable if the system is restricted in such a way that only closed formulas are allowed.

Kripke's semantic approach to modal predicate logic (Kripke, 1963)
In this approach, each possible world is an interpretation for a theory in the usual sense of the word 'interpretation'. However, there is a

constraint in that all possible worlds which are accessible from a particular world must contain the same set of entities and must agree in their assignments of entities to constants. This constraint means that possible worlds which are accessible from a particular world only differ in the relations in which entities take part.

The following section discusses temporal logics, and in sub-section 6.8.2 we consider a modal temporal logic. In section 6.9 a modal epistemic logic which can accommodate statements such as 'John knows P' is described.

6.8 TEMPORAL LOGIC
In the discussion so far, we have not really considered time-varying relational structures. Various approaches have been developed for dealing with time: some involve extensions to classical logics, others involve various types of modal logic, and one or two are based on intensional logic (which is discussed later in section 6.11). In this section, we describe some examples of the first two types. (How time is accommodated in intensional logic is shown in section 6.11.)

6.8.1 ACCOMMODATING TIME IN CLASSICAL FIRST ORDER PREDICATE LOGIC
Classical first order predicate logic may be used to reason about time, by regarding 'time points' as being like all other entities in the domain of a relational structure. Lundberg (1982) has described a logic based on this approach.

Time points are related to each other by predicates in the same way that other entities are related. For example, Lundberg defines two predicates 'et' and 'ss', such that et(t1,t2) signifies that the time point t1 is earlier than t2, and ss(t1,t2) signifies that t2 is the immediate successor of t1. The properties of the relations ET and SS, which are represented by the predicates et and ss, are expressed in an appropriately defined first order language as illustrated in the following examples:

(a) $\forall x \forall y [et(x, y) \rightarrow tpt(x) \wedge tpt(y)]$

where tpt(x) means that x is a time point.

(b) $\forall x \forall y [et(x, y) \vee (x = y) \vee et(y, x) \vee \neg tpt(x) \vee \neg tpt(y)]$

This may be read as 'for any two time points, either one is earlier than the other, or they are identical'.

(c) $\forall x \forall y [et(x, y) \wedge et(y, z)] \rightarrow et(x, z)$

This states that et is transitive.

(d) $\forall x \forall y [et(x, y) \rightarrow \neg et(y, x)]$

This states that if one time point is earlier than another, then the converse may not hold.

(etc.)

These examples are slightly modified versions of those given in Lundberg.

367

In order to describe aspects of time-varying relations, n-ary predicates are replaced by (n+1)ary predicates, where the (n+1)th argument
is a time point. For example, the assertion that 'an entity's age
never decreases' may be expressed as follows:

$$\forall v \forall w \forall x \forall y \forall z [age(x, y, z) \land age(x, w, v) \land et(z, v)] \rightarrow$$
$$\neg less\ than\ (w, y)$$

This approach is similar to the use of situation markers in situational
logic, as described earlier, and it also suffers from the frame problem
discussed in section 6.3.

6.8.2 TEMPORAL LOGICS BASED ON MODALITY

Many temporal logics have been developed which are based on notions
from modal logic. For example, in a relatively simple temporal logic,
'always' and 'sometimes' are defined analogously to 'necessary' and
'possible' in modal logic. The following formulas are generally included as theorems of such logics:

$$\begin{aligned}
always\ q & \rightarrow sometimes\ q \\
always\ q & \rightarrow q \\
q & \rightarrow sometimes\ q \\
sometimes\ q & \rightarrow \neg always\ \neg q
\end{aligned}$$

The modalities 'always' and 'sometimes' may be augmented with other
modalities such as P for past and F for future. The resulting logics
are often called 'tense' logics. Examples of formulas in such logics
are:

(it rains)	meaning	it is raining
P(it rains)	meaning	it rained
PP(it rains)	meaning	it had rained
F(it rains)	meaning	it will rain
FP(it rains)	meaning	it will have rained

Other modalities may be defined in terms of P and F. For example:

Hq $\equiv$ $\neg P \neg q$	meaning it has always been the case that q
Gq $\equiv$ $\neg F \neg q$	meaning it will always be the case that q

The relationship between H,G and 'always' may be expressed as follows:

$$always\ q \equiv Hq \land q \land Gq$$

KT: The minimal propositional tense logic
A minimal axiom system for a simple propositional tense logic has been
developed by Lemmon (1965). The logic is called KT. The language of
KT consists of the language of propositional logic, plus the modal
operators F,P,G and H with meanings as given above. The logical axioms
of KT include those of classical propositional logic, together with the
following:

$$\begin{aligned}
& G[q \rightarrow r] \rightarrow [Gq \rightarrow Gr] \\
& H[q \rightarrow r] \rightarrow [Hq \rightarrow Hr] \\
& \neg H \neg Gq \rightarrow q \\
& \neg G \neg Hq \rightarrow q
\end{aligned}$$

The inference rules are those of classical propositional logic plus:

> if q is a tautology infer Hq
> if q is a tautology infer Gq

The logic KT regards time as consisting of a linear sequence of states:

past   now   future

Hence, KT is called a 'linear temporal logic'.

An automated decision method (proof procedure) for linear temporal propositional logic has been developed by Cavali and Farinas del Cerro
(1984). Their method is based on an extension to the resolution method
as used in classical logic.

Branching temporal logics
Rather than regarding time as a linear sequence of states, an alternative approach is to treat the past as a linear sequence of states, up
to and including 'now', and to treat the future as a branching structure.

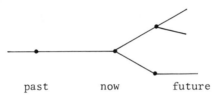

past   now   future

This approach accommodates the notion of several 'possible futures'.

Various branching temporal logics have been defined. One of the better
known is that developed by Ben-Ari, Manna, and Pneuli (1981). The one
described below was developed by Mays (1982) and incorporates much of
the logic developed by Ben-Ari et al. We begin by describing the language of the logic presented by Mays.

The syntax of the language
The terminals are:

    (a)   a set of atomic propositions {p,q,r, etc.}

    (b)   the boolean connectives ∨ and ¬ (→, ↔, ∧ are used as
                                          abbreviations)

    (c)   the temporal operators:

             AX - every next
             EX - some next
             AG - every always
             EG - some always
             AF - every eventually
             EF - some eventually

369

    L - immediately past
    P - sometime past
    H - always past

The meanings of some of these operators are given below. Well-formed formulas are constructed in the usual way.

The semantics of the language
In classical propositional logic, an interpretation consists of a single assignment of truth values to atomic propositions. In classical predicate logic, an interpretation consists of a single relational structure. In branching temporal propositional logic, an interpretation consists of a structure $u = \langle S, \pi, R \rangle$ such that:

(a)   S   is a set of states, i.e. points in the branching structure. For example, 'now' is the current state.

(b) π is a function mapping states to truth assignments. For example, suppose that there are two propositions p1 and p2, and three states: S1,S2 and S3, π might be defined such that:

$$\pi(S1) = \{p1 = \bot, p2 = \bot\}$$
$$\pi(S2) = \{p1 = \bot, p2 = \top\}$$
$$\pi(S3) = \{p1 = \top, p2 = \top\}$$

(c)   R   is an accessibility relation which relates states. Each state is required to have exactly one predecessor and at least one successor. For example:

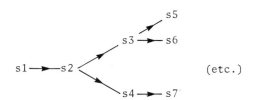

    (etc.)

s1 is the predecessor of s2; this is denoted by s1Rs2. s3 and s4 are the successors of s2; this is denoted by s2Rs3 and s2Rs4, etc.

(d)   branches, such as the branch s1, s2, s3 and s6 are called s-branches and are denoted by b.

The satisfaction of a formula p at a node s in a structure u, is denoted by $\langle u, s \rangle \models p$, and is defined as follows:

(a) $\langle u, s \rangle \models p$ iff $p = \top \in \pi(s)$

(b) $\langle u, s \rangle \models \neg p$ iff $p = \bot \in \pi(s)$

(c) $\langle u, s \rangle \models p \vee q$ iff $\langle u, s \rangle \models p$ OR $\langle u, s \rangle \models q$

(d) $\langle u, s \rangle \models AGp$ iff $\forall b \forall t [[t \in b \wedge t \geqslant s] \rightarrow \langle u, t \rangle \models p]$
     That is, p is true at every time of every future.

And so on. The complete set of definitions can be found in Mays (1983).

The logical axiom schemas
The logical axioms schemas of May's temporal logic are:

D1 : AFp ↔ ¬EG¬p
D2 : EFp ↔ ¬AG¬p
D3 : AXp ↔ ¬EX¬p
D4 : Pp ↔ ¬H¬p
D5 : Lp ↔ ¬L¬p
A1 : AG[p → q] → [EGp → EGq]

plus several others which are given in Mays.

Inference rules

R1 : if p is a tautology, then ⊢ p
R2 : if ⊢ p and ⊢ [p → q], then ⊢ q
R3 : if ⊢ p, then ⊢ AGp
R4 : if ⊢ p, then ⊢ Hp

Some example formulas
The following are examples of formulas of this logic and are derived from those given in Mays. We begin by letting:

q ≡ 'John has passed the maths course exam'
r ≡ 'John is registered for the maths course'

Consider the following:

(a) HAG[q → AXq]   (Note: HAG is explained below.)

This means that once John has passed the maths exam, it remains so.

(b) HAG[[¬q ∧ ¬r] → EXr]

This means that if John has not passed the maths exam and is not registered for the maths course, then it is next possible that John is registered for the maths course.

(c) HAG[r → EXq]

This means that if John is registered for the maths course, then it is next possible that he has passed the maths exam.

(d) HAG[[¬P[r ∧ L(Pr)] ∧ ¬Pq ∧ ¬r] → EXr

This means that it is next possible for John to register for the maths course if he has not registered for it twice before, and has not passed it, and is not currently registered for it.

Most non-logical axioms of a theory are taken to have held and to continue to hold forever, hence the operators HAG preceding each of the
above. Mays has developed a theorem-prover for the future fragment of
the logic above. The theorem-prover is based on the tableau method.
Mays' work is part of a project which is concerned with natural language database interactions.

A survey of temporal logics can be found in Rescher and Urquhart (1971).

Temporal logics also have uses in planning; for example, in planning the activities of a robot. One must model the effects of the robot's actions on the world to make sure that the plan is allowed and effective. They also have uses in program proving (see Ben-Ari et al, for example).

6.9 EPISTEMIC LOGIC
In the logics considered so far, we have only been concerned with a single reasoning agent. However, there are many applications in which an artificial reasoner would be required to cooperate with other reasoning agents.

In this section, a logic which can be used to reason about the knowledge possessed by several agents is described. As an example of how this logic can be used, we consider a puzzle which involves three agents who are initially given some common knowledge. By knowing the limit of the other agents' knowledge and reasoning ability, it is possible for an agent to infer new knowledge. Much of the discussion is derived from Konolige (1982).

We begin by describing Konolige's logic:

The logic
The logic which Konolige has defined is called KI4, and is based on a modal logic called K4 (Sato, 1976). K4 includes a set of indexed unary modal operators:

$$\{ \boxed{s} \mid s \in \text{a set of agents}\}$$

where the formula $\boxed{s}\alpha$ means that agent s knows α. The agent 0 is a fictitious agent called 'FOOL', whose knowledge is common knowledge.

The logical axiom schemas of K4
The logical axiom schemas of K4 are:

A1 : all propositional tautologies
A2 : $\boxed{s}\alpha \rightarrow \alpha$
A3 : $\boxed{s}\alpha \rightarrow \boxed{s}\,\boxed{s}\alpha$
A4 : $\boxed{s}[\alpha \rightarrow \beta] \rightarrow [\boxed{s}\alpha \rightarrow \boxed{s}\beta]$
A5 : $\boxed{0}[\alpha \rightarrow \boxed{0}\,\boxed{s}\alpha]$

where α and β denote arbitrary formulas, and s denotes an arbitrary agent.

A5 is the 'common knowledge axiom' = what any fool knows, any fool knows everyone knows.

Rules of inference of K4

(a) Modus ponens.
(b) If α is a tautology then infer $\boxed{s}\alpha$.

In this logic of knowledge, an agent's knowledge is represented as a theory called the 'agent's theory'.

Extending K4 to KI4

K4 is extended by the addition of 'circumscription modalities', which are written as $\langle\alpha\rangle$ where α is a formula of K4. $\langle\alpha\rangle$ stands for the α-theory of K4, hence $\langle\alpha\rangle\beta$ is true iff β is in the α-theory of K4. These modalities capture the notion of 'provability' when the following logical axioms are added:

A6 : $\langle\alpha\rangle\beta$ if $\alpha \vdash \beta$ in K4
A7 : $\neg\langle\alpha\rangle\beta$ if $\alpha \nvdash \beta$ in K4

Circumscription (McCarthy, 1980) is a form of default reasoning: the only propositions which are true are those which can be proved to be true. The circumscriptive nature of $\langle\alpha\rangle$ derives from the restriction of its meaning to the α theory in K4. If α is a knowledge operator, then $\langle\alpha\rangle$ may be translated as a circumscription of an agent's theory. For example,

(a) $\langle\boxed{s}q\rangle$ ≡ the theory of agent s for which q is the only proper axiom

(b) $\langle\boxed{s}q \vee \boxed{s}r\rangle\boxed{s}p$ ≡ the knowledge that s has about p is derived from the fact that he knows either q or r

An example of the use of KI4

Consider the following puzzle, which is called the 'wise men puzzle':

A king wants to know which is the wisest of his three wise men. He paints a single white dot on each of their foreheads, and tells them that their own dot could be black or white but that at least one dot is white. He then asks each man to determine the colour of his own dot. After a while, the wisest announces that his dot is white. How did he know?

The answer is that he reasoned as follows:

Suppose my dot were black, the second wisest would see a white dot and a black dot and would reason that if his dot were black, the least wise would see two black dots and would conclude that his dot is white on the basis of the king's assurance. Since he has not done this, the second wisest could conclude that his dot were white. But he did not do that, therefore my dot must be white.

Konolige simplifies the puzzle by having the king ask each wise man in turn what colour his dot is, starting with the least wise. He then formalises the solution as follows.

The agents are:
0	≡	fool
s1	≡	least wise man
s2	≡	next wise man
s3	≡	most wise man

The propositions are:
w1	≡	s1 has a white dot
w2	≡	s2 has a white dot
w3	≡	s3 has a white dot

An abbreviation used is:

$\{s\}p \equiv \boxed{s}p \lor \boxed{s}\neg p$ i.e. s knows whether or not p is true

The initial situation is defined as follows:

F1 :   w1 ∧ w2 ∧ w3
       in fact all three have white dots

F2 : $\boxed{0}$[w1 ∨ w2 ∨ w3]
       everyone knows at least one is white

F3 : $\boxed{0}$[{s1}w2 ∧ {s1}w3 ∧ {s2}w1 ∧ {s2}w3 ∧ {s3}w1 ∧ {s3}w2]
       every agent knows that each agent can see the other agents'
       dots

F4 : $\langle\alpha\rangle${s1}w1
       where α = F2 ∧ F3 ∧ $\boxed{s1}$w2 ∧ $\boxed{s1}$w3

F4 is a circumscription axiom: it states that if s1 knows that w1 holds,
this is solely on the basis of common knowledge (F2 and F3) and his own
observations.

Using F4, it is possible to prove that s1 does not know the colour of
his own dot in this initial situation. (See Konolige for an explanation of the proof.)

The next situation is similar, except that s2 has heard s1's reply to
the king that he does not know the colour of his dot. The axioms for
this situation are F1,F2,F3 together with:

F5 : $\boxed{s2}$¬{s1}w1
F6 : $\langle\alpha\rangle${s2}w2
       where α = F2 ∧ F3 ∧ F5 ∧ {s2}w1 ∧ $\boxed{s2}$w3

In this situation, it is possible to prove that s2 does not know the
colour of his dot.

Finally, s3 knows that s2 does not know the colour of his dot after
hearing s1's reply. The axioms for this situation are F1,F2,F3 together with:

F7 : $\boxed{s3}$ $\boxed{s2}$¬{s1}w1
F8 : $\boxed{s3}$¬{s2}w2
F9 : $\langle\alpha\rangle${s3}w3
       where α = F2 ∧ F3 ∧ F7 ∧ F8 ∧ $\boxed{s3}$w1 ∧ $\boxed{s3}$w2

It is possible, in this situation, to prove $\boxed{s3}$w3, i.e. to prove that
s3 knows that his spot is white.

Logics of knowledge may also be used in applications where the automatic reasoner has to co-operate with other agents; for example in
multi-agent planning. However, their use in such applications is still
at the research stage.

6.10 SOME MISCELLANEOUS TOPICS

In this section some miscellaneous topics which we refer to in later sections of this chapter, and in later chapters of the book, are introduced.

6.10.1 THE THEORY OF TYPES

The basic assumption underlying the theory of types is that there is a 'hierarchy' amongst the 'objects' to which the theory refers. Some of the objects are of primitive type, whereas others are constructed from objects of primitive type. In the simplest theory of types there is a primitive type called e which may be regarded as the type 'entity'. Other types are defined in terms of e, for example:

    (e)
    ((e))
    (e,e)

where objects of type (e) are classes (sets) of objects of type e, objects of type ((e)) are classes of classes of objects of type e, and objects of type (e, e) are two argument relations of objects of type e, and so on. For example, the class of symmetric relations between classes of individuals of type e, is of type (((e), (e))).

The functional theory of types

In the functional theory of types (Church, 1940), the universe is regarded as consisting of entities, truth values, and functions. There are two primitive types:

    e : the type 'entity'
    t : the type 'truth value'

Other types are constructed from e and t. For example:

(a) The type $<e, t>$ is the class of functions from entities to truth values.

(b) The type $<e, <e, t>>$ is the class of functions from entities to functions from entities to truth values.

An example of an object of type $<e, t>$ is the following function 'person':

Person		
Peter	→	T
Mary	→	T
Fido	→	⊥
John	→	T

where T = true, ⊥ = false. That is, person(Peter) = T, etc. An example of an object of type $<e, <e, t>>$ is the function 'married':

```
┌─────────────────────────────────────────┐
│                 Married                   │
│            ┌──────────────┐               │
│            │ Peter  →  T  │               │
│            │ Mary   →  T  │               │
│            │ John   →  T  │               │
│            └──────────────┘               │
│            ┌──────────────┐               │
│            │ Peter  →  T  │               │
│            │ Mary   →  T  │               │
│            │ John   →  ⊥  │               │
│            └──────────────┘               │
│            ┌──────────────┐               │
│            │ Peter  →  T  │               │
│            │ Mary   →  ⊥  │               │
│            │ John   →  T  │               │
│            └──────────────┘               │
│            ┌──────────────┐               │
│            │ Peter  →  T  │               │
│            │ Mary   →  ⊥  │               │
│            │ John   →  ⊥  │               │
│            └──────────────┘               │
│            ┌──────────────┐               │
│            │ Peter  →  ⊥  │               │
│            │ Mary   →  T  │               │
│            │ John   →  T  │               │
│            └──────────────┘               │
│            ┌──────────────┐               │
│  John  →   │ Peter  →  ⊥  │               │
│            │ Mary   →  T  │               │
│            │ John   →  ⊥  │               │
│            └──────────────┘               │
│            ┌──────────────┐               │
│  Mary  →   │ Peter  →  ⊥  │               │
│            │ Mary   →  ⊥  │               │
│            │ John   →  T  │               │
│            └──────────────┘               │
│            ┌──────────────┐               │
│  Peter →   │ Peter  →  ⊥  │               │
│            │ Mary   →  ⊥  │               │
│            │ John   →  ⊥  │               │
│            └──────────────┘               │
└─────────────────────────────────────────┘
```

which shows that Mary is married to John, and John is married to Mary.

Functions of type $\langle e, t \rangle$ correspond to entity sets. If E is a set of entities and A is a sub-set of E, we can define a 'characteristic function' fA on E such that:

$$fA(e) = \begin{array}{l} T \text{ if } e \in A \\ \bot \text{ if } e \notin A \end{array}$$

The characteristic function divides the set E into two parts, the sub-set mapped into T and the complementary sub-set which is mapped into ⊥.

The 'semantic' objects with which classical logic is concerned may be regarded as being of the types shown below:

Semantic object	Type
unary relation or entity set	⟨e, t⟩
two-place relation	⟨e, ⟨e, t⟩⟩
three-place relation	⟨e, ⟨e, ⟨e, t⟩⟩⟩
the notion of NOT	⟨t, t⟩
the notion of AND	⟨t, ⟨t, t⟩⟩
(etc.)	

That is, for example: NOT is a function which maps truth values into truth values; AND is a function which maps truth values into functions which map truth values into truth values. The function AND may be depicted as follows:

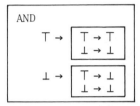

That is, the function AND, when applied to the argument ⊤, maps it into a function which maps ⊤ to ⊤ and ⊥ to ⊥. When applied to the argument ⊥, AND maps it into a function which maps ⊤ to ⊥ and ⊥ to ⊥.

In the functional theory of types, the universe is regarded as comprising an infinite set of types of object. This infinite set of types is defined recursively as follows:

- e is a type
- t is a type
- if a and b are types, then ⟨a, b⟩ is a type
- there are no other types

6.10.2 A TYPE THEORETIC LANGUAGE
The language LTYPE described below can be used to represent knowledge about objects of different types.

The syntax of LTYPE
Corresponding to each type of object in the universe of discourse, there is a 'syntactic category' in LTYPE. For example,

(a) For type e there is a syntactic category e.
(b) For type t there is a syntactic category t.
(c) For type ⟨e, t⟩ there is a syntactic category ⟨e, t⟩.

The same notation is used for 'labels' of types and syntactic categories. We assume that no confusion will arise as the meaning of a label such as ⟨e, t⟩ should always be obvious from the context.

The set of 'meaningful expressions' of a syntactic category a is denoted by MEa. The meaningful expressions of the categories of LTYPE are defined as follows:

(a) LTYPE contains constants and variables for each syntactic

377

category a. These are called 'basic expressions' and are members of MEa. Because there are variables of every type, LTYPE is a higher-order language. (In a first order language, variables may only range over entities; in a second order language, there are also variables which range over predicates, and so on.)

(b) If $X \in ME\langle a, b\rangle$ and $Y \in MEa$, then $X(Y) \in MEb$.

(c) If X and Y are members of MEt then so are:

$$[X]$$
$$\neg X$$
$$X \wedge Y$$
$$X \vee Y$$
$$X \rightarrow Y$$

(d) If $X \in MEt$, and v is a variable of any syntactic category, then $\forall v\ X \in MEt$ and $\exists v\ X \in MEt$.

The semantics of LTYPE

The 'denotation' or 'semantic value' of an expression X is the object which is assigned to X by some interpretation and/or valuation. The notation $[\![X]\!]\gamma,\alpha$ is used to stand for the denotation of X with respect to interpretation γ and valuation α. The notation DX is used to stand for the set of possible denotations of X.

We begin by specifying the possible denotations of expressions of various syntactic category:

(a) De = the set of entities.

(b) $Dt = \{\top, \bot\}$.

(c) For all syntactic categories a and b, $D\langle a, b\rangle$ = the set of all **functions** from Da to Db.

We now define the denotation of an expression X of LTYPE relative to an interpretation γ and a valuation α:

(a) If c is a non-logical constant (i.e. is not one of $\neg$, $\wedge$, $\vee$, $\rightarrow$, $\forall$, $\exists$), then $[\![c]\!]\gamma,\alpha$ = the object which is assigned to c by the interpretation γ.

(b) If v is a variable, then $[\![v]\!]\gamma,\alpha$ = the object which is assigned to v by the valuation α.

(c) If $X \in ME\langle a, b\rangle$ and $Y \in MEa$, then $[\![X(Y)]\!]\gamma,\alpha = [\![X]\!]\gamma,\alpha([\![Y]\!]\gamma,\alpha)$.

(d) If X and Y are in MEt, then:

$$[\![\neg X]\!]\gamma,\alpha = \bot \text{ iff } [\![X]\!]\gamma,\alpha = \top$$
$$[\![X \wedge Y]\!]\gamma,\alpha = \top \text{ iff } [\![X]\!]\gamma,\alpha = \top \text{ and } [\![Y]\!]\gamma,\alpha = \top$$
$$[\![X \vee Y]\!]\gamma,\alpha = \top \text{ iff } [\![X]\!]\gamma,\alpha = \top \text{ or } [\![Y]\!]\gamma,\alpha = \top$$
$$[\![X \rightarrow Y]\!]\gamma,\alpha = \top \text{ iff } [\![X]\!]\gamma,\alpha = \bot \text{ or } [\![Y]\!]\gamma,\alpha = \top$$

(e) If X ∈ MEt and v is a variable in syntactic category a, then
⟦∀vX⟧γ,α = T iff for all objects o in Da, ⟦X⟧γ,α = T, where
α(v) = o.

(f) If X ∈ MEt and u is a variable in syntactic category, a, then
⟦∃vX⟧γ,α = T iff for some object o in Da, ⟦X⟧γ,α = T, where
α(v) = o.

As in languages of classical predicate logic, the semantic value of an
expression in LTYPE does not depend on variables that are not free in
the expression. Hence, the denotation of a closed expression of LTYPE
relative to an interpretation γ, is defined as follows:

(a) For any expression X ∈ MEt, ⟦X⟧γ = T iff
⟦X⟧γ,α = T for every valuation α.

(b) For any expression X ∈ MEt, ⟦X⟧γ = ⊥ iff
⟦X⟧γ,α = ⊥ for any valuation α.

Examples of formulas of LTYPE
In order to indicate the syntactic category of a variable, the following notation is used:

vij ≡ the ith variable of category j

For example:

v1e = the first variable which ranges over the set of
entities.

v1⟨e, t⟩ = the first variable which ranges over the set of unary
predicates

We can now give some examples of formulas of LTYPE:

(a) ∀v1e[man(v1e) → male(v1e)]

This can be read as if it were a formula of a language of
first order predicate logic.

(b) ∀v1⟨e, t⟩[v1⟨e, t⟩(John) ↔ v1⟨e, t⟩(James)]

This says for all unary predicates if the predicate is true
of John, then the predicate is true of James and vice versa.
Effectively, this says that John and James are the same
individual. This is a second order formula.

(c) ∀v1⟨e, t⟩[NEM(v1⟨e, t⟩) → ∃v1e[v1⟨e, t⟩(v1e)]]

This says that all sets of entities in the set NEM, are non-
empty. NEM is a constant which, by the rules defining the
meaningful expressions of LTYPE, must denote a set of sets of
entities. Effectively, the formula states that NEM denotes
the set of non-empty sets of entities.

(d) ∀v1e∀v1⟨e, t⟩[non(v1⟨e, t⟩(v1e)) ↔ ¬v1⟨e, t⟩(v1e)]

This means that ⟦non⟧ is a function from D⟨e, t⟩ into D⟨e, t⟩

379

such that for any object P in D<e, t> and any entity X in De,
⟦non⟧(P(X)) = ⊤ iff P(X) = ⊥ else ⊤ otherwise. Non is called
a predicate modifier, since it 'takes in an entity set and
delivers the complement of that set'. For example, the following expression states that 'fido is not a person':

non(person(fido))

x,y,z are often used to denote variables of syntactic category e, and
P,Q,R to denote variables of syntactic category <e, t>.

In addition, we shall often use notation such as 'married(John,Sally)',
where we should really be writing 'married(John)(Sally)'.

6.10.3 THE LAMBDA OPERATOR

An operator is an expression which binds a variable. The quantifiers ∀
and ∃ are examples of operators. The 'lambda operator', which is also
known as the 'abstraction operator', is perhaps the most generally useful operator. It can be used for 'making' function symbols as described
below.

Consider the following lambda expression:

λx[...x...]

where ...x... denotes a formula which has x as a free variable. This
expression is the name of, or denotes, a function which when applied
to an argument makes of it that which is made with x according to the
formula '...x...'. For example:

(a) λx[x↑2] denotes the function 'the square of'.

(b) λx[loves(x,John)] denotes the (function of) the set of indi-
     viduals that love John.

(c) λP[P(John)] denotes the function 'a property of John'.

Note that, as illustrated in (c), the variable which is bound by λ need
not be an 'individual' variable (i.e. a variable which ranges over the
set of entities). The variable P in (c) is a predicate variable.

The lambda operator is useful since it allows us to create and name new
composite functions and thereby enables us to formally specify the properties of these new functions. For example, suppose that we have
defined the notion of 'increasing' as follows:

A function is increasing iff
$$\forall x \forall y[\text{lessthan}(x, y) \rightarrow \text{lessthan}(f(x), f(y))].$$

Now we can formally express the fact that an arbitrary function such as
2x↑3 + 5 is increasing as follows:

λx[2x↑3 + 5] is increasing

The linguistic operation of forming a function definition from an expression is called 'abstraction'.

380

The rule of lambda conversion
The use of the lambda operator is formally determined by the following rule:

$$\lambda x[...x...](a) = ...a...$$

which states that an expression of the form $\lambda x[...x...](a)$ may be replaced everywhere by the expression ...a... which results from ...x... when every occurrence of x in ...x... is replaced by a. For example:

$$\lambda x[loves(x, John)](Sally) = loves(Sally, John)$$

Application of the rule is restricted such that the argument a, whether it is a single term or a composite expression containing several terms, must not contain a free variable which becomes bound in the expression ...a... by an operator (lambda or other) which occurs in the expression ...x... .

We now describe a more complex example of lambda conversion. Consider the following expression:

(a) $\lambda P[P(John)](\lambda x[\exists y \; spouse(y, x) \wedge older(y, x)])$

This expression may be read as 'having a spouse who is older than oneself, is a property of John'. Since there are two instances of the lambda operator in (a), the lambda conversion rule must be applied twice:

(a)   becomes (a') $= \lambda x[\exists y \; spouse(y, x) \wedge older(y, x)](John)$

(a')   becomes (a'') $= \exists y \; spouse(y, John) \wedge older(y, John)$

Representing many-argument functions as functions of a smaller number of arguments

This can be done using lambda operators. For example, consider the following expression:

$$\lambda y[\lambda x loves(x, y)]$$

This expression denotes a one-argument function whose values are one-argument functions. For example, the expression $\lambda y[\lambda x loves(x, y)](John)$ becomes, by lambda conversion:

$$\lambda x[loves(x, John)]$$

6.10.4 A TYPE THEORETIC LANGUAGE WITH A LAMBDA OPERATOR
The language LTYPE, as described in section 6.10.2, may be extended to a language Lλ by the addition of the lambda operator. The syntactic and semantic definitions for LTYPE hold for Lλ, together with the additional definition:

> If X is an expression of syntactic category a and v is variable of syntactic category b, then $\lambda v[X]$ is an expression of syntactic category $<b, a>$.

For example:

λx[bald(x)] is of syntactic category <e, t>

That is, this expression is the name of a function which maps entities into {true, false}.

More complex expressions of Lλ

Consider the sentence 'every student walks'. The usual translation into predicate logic gives:

(a) ∀x student(x) → walks(x)

Now suppose that we let P be a predicate variable. The following lambda expression is equivalent to (a):

(b) λP[∀x student(x) → P(x)](walks)

Therefore, the denotation of (c): λP[∀x student(x) → P(x)] is 'every student'. Similarly:

(d) somestudent ≡ λP[∃x student(x) ∧ P(x)]

Now if we let Q be a predicate variable, the following lambda expression is equivalent to (c):

(e) λQ[λP[∀x Q(x) → P(x)]](student)

Similarly, the following is equivalent to (d):

(f) λQ[λP[∃x Q(x) ∧ P(x)]](student)

Hence, we may represent the notion of 'every' by the following expression:

(g) λQ[λP[∀x Q(x) → P(x)]]

and the notion of 'some' may be represented by:

(h) λQ[λP[∃x Q(x) ∧ P(x)]]

The advantage of incorporating the lambda operator into a type theoretic language is that it can be used to calculate the denotation or semantic value of a syntactic constituent of a larger expression whose semantic value is known. In addition, the semantic values of sentences which have a 'similar' structure in English can be represented by expressions with a similar structure in Lλ. For example, consider the following English sentences:

(a) Every student walks.
(b) John walks.

These have a similar 'noun phrase' + 'verb phrase' structure, but when translated into a language of classical predicate logic this similarity is obscured:

(a') ∀x student(x) → walks(x)
(b') walks(John)

However, when translated into Lλ, the similarity in structure is preserved:

(a") λQ[λP[∀x Q(x) → P(x)]](student)(walks)
(b") λP[P(John)](walks)

6.10.5 CO-ORDINATE SEMANTICS

It is possible to define a language that contains both temporal and other modal operators. For the interpretation of this language, a 'structure' is needed which includes a set of entities E, a set of worlds W *and* a set of times Tim. This structure may be thought of as having two 'dimensions'. A particular point in this structure which is called a 'state of affairs' can be thought of as being identified by a pair of co-ordinates <w, t> where w ∈ W and t ∈ Tim. w identifies the world, and t the point in time. Thus, the denotation of an expression is now given with respect to a structure (or universe of discourse) U, a valuation α, a world index and a time index. We can use the following notation to stand for the denotation of an expression X in structure U, in world w, at time t, under valuation α:

⟦X⟧U,w,t,α

There is an ordering, symbolised by OTim, on the set Tim. Therefore, a structure or universe of discourse, may be thought of as a quintuple:

U = <E, W, Tim, OTim>

For example, the following is such a structure:

U2 = <E = {e1, e2, e3},
        W = {w1, w2},
       Tim = {t1, t2, t3},
       OTim = {<t1, t2>, <t2, t3>, <t1, t3>}>

This can be depicted as follows:

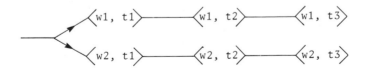

If, for example, <w1, t2> were 'actually now' then w1 is the world as it actually has been, is, and will be. The world w2 is as it might have been, might be, and would be, if things were different.

The semantics of modal operators may be defined, in co-ordinate semantics, as illustrated by the following example:

Suppose that we let ☐ stand for 'necessary everywhere and always'. We can define the semantics of ☐ as follows:

If X is a formula, then $[\![\Box X]\!] U,w,t,\alpha = \top$ iff $[\![X]\!] U,w',t',\alpha = \top$ for all $w' \in W$, and all $t' \in$ Tim. (Notice that this definition of $\Box$ is stronger than that given in our treatment of modal logic.)

Co-ordinate semantics has much in common with branching temporal logic which we described in section 6.8. We make further use of co-ordinate semantics in the following sub-sections.

6.10.6 INTENSIONS AND EXTENSIONS

The 'extension' of an expression is the semantic object which is assigned to it in a given world at a given point in time, i.e. the denotation in a given state of affairs. (Note: the notion of 'extension' has a longer history than suggested by this informal definition.) 'Intension' is a function which gives the extension of an expression in all possible states of affairs. For example, the extension of a formula is the truth value which is assigned to that formula in a given state of affairs. The intension of a formula is a function which assigns a truth value to that formula in all states of affairs.

As further example, the extension of a constant (of whatever type) is the object which is assigned to it in some given state of affairs, whereas the intension of a constant is a function which gives the objects which are assigned to it in all possible states of affairs.

We can make use of co-ordinate semantics to index the different states of affairs. For example, suppose that we have the structure U2 described in sub-section 6.10.5. Suppose also, that we define a type theoretic language LTYPE1 which contains the following:

(a)   Constants of syntactic category e = {Susan, Margaret, Mary, MissWorld}.

(b)   Constants of syntactic category $\langle e, t \rangle$ = {happy}.

We can use U2 as an interpretation of LTYPE1 by defining the function 'intension'. For example:

Values of 'intension'

Susan	t1	t2	t3	Margaret	t1	t2	t3	Mary	t1	t2	t3
w1	e1	e1	e1	w1	e2	e2	e2	w1	e3	e3	e3
w2	e1	e1	e1	w2	e2	e2	e2	w2	e3	e3	e3

MissWorld	t1	t2	t3	happy	t1	t2	t3
w1	e1	e2	e3	w1	{e1, e2}	{e1, e3}	{e2, e3}
w2	e3	e3	e2	w2	{e2, e3}	{e1}	{e1, e2, e3}

This intension tells us, for example, that:

(a)   In all worlds and at all times, the constant 'Susan' stands for the entity e1.

(b) In world w1 at time t1, the constant 'MissWorld' stands for the entity e1.

(c) In world w2 at time t2, e1 was the only entity who was 'happy'.

(d) If <w1, t2> were 'actually now', then we can see that, actually, e2 is MissWorld, e1 was MissWorld and e3 will be MissWorld. However, if things (not specified here) had been different then world w2 would have been, and e3 would now be MissWorld.

We can now evaluate formulas with respect to this intension. For example:

(a) 'happy(Susan)' is true in the actual world at the present time.

(b) 'happy(MissWorld)' is false in the actual world at the present time.

(c) 'F[happy(MissWorld)]' is true in the actual world at the present time where F is the temporal modal operator meaning 'in the future' (refer back to section 6.8).

As an alternative way of depicting an intension of an expression, we can use the notation illustrated in the following example:

$$
[\![\text{MissWorld}]\!]U2,\alpha \;=\; \begin{bmatrix} <\text{w1, t1}> \to \text{e1} \\ <\text{w1, t2}> \to \text{e3} \\ <\text{w1, t3}> \to \text{e2} \\ <\text{w2, t1}> \to \text{e3} \\ <\text{w2, t2}> \to \text{e3} \\ <\text{w2, t3}> \to \text{e2} \end{bmatrix}
$$

6.10.7 A TYPE THEORETIC LANGUAGE WHICH CAN ACCOMMODATE INTENSIONS AND EXTENSIONS

We now show how the language Lλ described in 6.10.4 may be extended to accommodate intensions and extensions:

(a) Intensional objects such as 'MissWorld' are denoted by constants such as:

   MissWorld'

(b) A notational device is used to make intension naming expressions out of extension naming expressions:

   If X is an expression, then ^X is an expression denoting the intension of X.

(c) A notational device to do the converse is also included:

   If X is an expression, then ˅X is an expression denoting the extension of X in some world, wi, and at some point in time, tj. wi and tj are determined by context (see below).

Examples of formulas in the extended language

(a) λP[λQ[∀x˅P(x) → ˅Q(x)]]

This stands for 'every'. Refer back to sub-section 6.10.4 to
compare this with the expression for 'every' in a non-coordi-
nate semantics where there is only one world and one time
point. The introduction of ˅ is necessary so that the expression above is applicable in particular states of affairs which
are determined by the context in which the expression occurs.

(b) man'

This stands for the object 'man' (which, we shall see, is of
type <e, t>) in some intensional structure.

(c) λP[λQ[∀x ˅P(x) → ˅Q(x)]](man')

This stands for every man. By lambda conversion we can transcribe (c) to:

(c') λQ[∀x ˅^man'(x) → ˅Q(x)

and by cancelling ˅ and ^, we obtain:

(c") λQ[∀x man'(x) → ˅Q(x)]

(d) talk'

This stands for the object 'talk' (which, we shall see, is of
type <e, t>) in some intensional structure.

(e) λQ[∀x man'(x) → ˅Q(x)](^talk')

This stands for 'every man talks'. By lambda conversion, we
obtain:

(e') ∀x man'(x) → ˅^talk'(x)

and by cancelling ˅ and ^, we obtain:

(e") ∀x man'(x) → talk'(x)

The difference between (e") and a similar-looking expression of a first
order predicate language is that (e") asserts that at a given index
(i.e. the one in which the expression is true) everything which has the
property of being a man also has the property of talking.

6.10.8 FURTHER READING
This section has briefly described some rather difficult notions:

- the theory of types
- a type-theoretic language
- the lambda operator
- co-ordinate semantics
- intensions and extensions

Due to constraints of space, the descriptions have been very cursory.

However, we feel that these notions are extremely important and that
it is useful to at least introduce readers to them. Interested readers
are referred to Dowty et al (1981) and McCawley (1981) for a more thorough discussion of the concepts.

6.11 INTENSIONAL LOGIC

6.11.1 MONTAGUE'S INTENSIONAL LOGIC

Many of the concepts described in this chapter have been used in a
logic, called 'intensional logic' (IL), which was developed by Montague
(see for example, Montague 1973 and 1974). IL employs a type hierarchy,
higher-order quantification (variables and quantifiers for each type),
lambda abstraction for all types, tenses, modal operators, syntactic
mechanisms for dealing with intensions and extensions, and has a model
theory which is based on co-ordinate semantics.

The view of the universe which underlies IL regards 'reality' as consisting of two truth values, a set of entities E, a set of possible
worlds W and a set of points in time T. A function space is constructed inductively from objects of these basic types. The set of types
(of objects and functions) is defined as follows:

(a) e is a type, which may be regarded as type 'entity'.

(b) t is a type, which may be regarded as type 'truth value'.

(c) If a and b are types, then $\langle a, b \rangle$ is a type. Objects of type
$\langle a, b \rangle$ are functions from objects of type a to those of type b.

(d) If a is a type, then $\langle s, a \rangle$ is a type. Objects of type $\langle s, a \rangle$
are functions from indices to objects of type a. Objects of
'type' s are called indices, and are pairs $\langle w, t \rangle$ where $w \in W$
and $t \in T$.

Objects of type $\langle s, a \rangle$ are 'special' functions which are related to intensions as we shall see later.

The syntax of the language of IL
Corresponding to each type in the universe of discourse, the language
of IL contains a syntactic category. The set of syntactic categories
is defined as follows:

(a) e is a syntactic category.

(b) t is a syntactic category.

(c) If a and b are syntactic categories, then $\langle a, b \rangle$ is a syntactic category.

(d) If a is a syntactic category, then $\langle s, a \rangle$ is a syntactic category.

The same notation is used to 'label' types of object in the universe
of discourse and syntactic categories in the language of IL. It is
assumed that no confusion will arise since the meaning of a label such
as $\langle e, t \rangle$ should be obvious from the context.

The syntactic components of the language of IL are as follows:

387

(a) For each syntactic category a, there is a set of non-logical constants Cona.

(b) For each syntactic category a, there is a set of variables, Vara.

The set of meaningful expression of a syntactic category a is denoted by MEa. The meaningful expressions of IL are defined as follows:

(a) All constants and variables of syntactic category a are in MEa.

(b) If $X \in$ MEa and u is a variable of syntactic category b, then $\lambda u\ X \in$ ME<a, b>.

(c) If $X \in$ ME<a, b> and $Y \in$ MEa, then $X(Y) \in$ MEb.

(d) If X and Y are both in MEa, then $X = Y \in$ MEt.

(e) If X and Y are in MEt, then so are the following:

$$X \wedge Y$$
$$X \vee Y$$
$$X \rightarrow Y$$
$$X \leftrightarrow Y$$

$\forall u\ X$ where u is a variable of any syntactic category
$\exists u\ X$ where u is a variable of any syntactic category
$\Box X$ where $\Box$ is the modal 'necessarily' operator
FX   where F is the 'future' tense operator
PX   where P is the 'past' tense operator

(f) If $X \in$ MEa, then $^\wedge X \in$ ME<s, a>. That is, $^\wedge$ is the 'intension forming' operator.

(g) If $X \in$ ME<s, a>, then $^\vee X \in$ MEa. That is, $^\vee$ is the 'extension forming' operator.

The rules (f) and (g) are explained below.

The semantics of the language of IL

Note: the word model is used below in a slightly different sense to the way in which it was used in first order predicate logic. A 'model' in modal logic and in IL is similar to a relational structure in predicate logic and is defined as below. The two uses of the word 'model' may be a little confusing. However, we have decided to use them as they are well established in the literature.

A model for the language of IL consists of:

- a set of entities, E
- a set of possible worlds, W
- a set of time-points, T
- a linear-ordering > on T (i.e. time is treated as in linear temporal logic)
- a function γ, which assigns an intension to each non-logical constant in IL

The function γ assigns to each constant of syntactic category a, a function mapping indices to objects of type a. In other words, γ gives the denotation of a constant in all possible worlds at all points of time.

For example, consider the following situation:

	t1 ———————→	t2 ———————→	t3
w1	the boss was e1	the boss was e1	the boss was e2
w2	the boss was e3	the boss was e3	the boss was e3

where w1 denotes what actually was the case, and w2 what might have been if ... This means that in the actual world the entity e1 was the boss at time points t1 and t2, but was then succeeded by e2 who became the boss at time t3. However, if things had been otherwise, (some particular conditions would be stated), then e3 would have been the boss at time points t1,t2 and t3.

The following is an 'intension' (i.e. a function from indices to objects) of type $\langle s, e \rangle$:

intension1

$\langle w1, t1 \rangle \rightarrow$ e1
$\langle w1, t2 \rangle \rightarrow$ e1
$\langle w1, t3 \rangle \rightarrow$ e2
$\langle w2, t1 \rangle \rightarrow$ e3
$\langle w2, t2 \rangle \rightarrow$ e3
$\langle w2, t2 \rangle \rightarrow$ e3

If IL contained the constant 'The Boss', then γ might be defined such that it assigns intension1 to this constant. That is:

γ(The Boss) = intension1

If we now apply the extension forming operator $\check{}$ to 'The Boss' in world w and time t, we obtain the extension (i.e. the denotation) of 'The Boss' in world w and time t. For example:

The Boss denotes e1 with respect to world w1 and time t1
The Boss denotes e3 with respect to world w2 and time t1 (etc.).

The set of possible denotations, Dx, of an expression of category x, of IL is given by the following:

(a) De = E, i.e. the set of possible denotations of expressions of syntactic category e are entities in the set E

(b) Dt = $\{\top, \perp\}$

(c) D$\langle a,b \rangle$ = the set of all functions from objects of type a to objects of type b

(d) D$\langle s,a \rangle$ = the set of all functions from indices to objects of type a.

We also introduce a function α (called a 'valuation' or an 'assignment of values to variables'), which assigns to each variable of syntactic category a, a member of Da.

The extension (or denotation) of an expression X, with respect to a model M, a world $w \in W$, a timepoint $t \in T$, and a valuation α, is denoted by $[\![X]\!]M,w,t,\alpha$. Such extensions are defined by the following rules:

(a) If c is a non-logical constant, then $[\![c]\!]M,w,t,\alpha = \gamma(c)(\langle w, t \rangle)$. That is, the extension of c in world w and at time t is obtained by applying the intension of c, which is supplied by $\gamma(c)$ to the argument $\langle w, t \rangle$.

(b) If v is a variable, then $[\![v]\!]M,w,t,\alpha = \alpha(v)$, i.e. the valuation determines the denotation of a variable irrespective of world and time.

(c) If $X \in ME_a$ and u is a variable of type b, then $[\![\lambda u[X]]\!]M,w,t,\alpha$ is that function h, with domain D_b such that for any object $o \in D_b$, $h(o) = [\![X]\!]M,w,t,\alpha'$ where α' is identical to α except that $\alpha'(u) = o$.

(d) If $X \in ME_{\langle a,b \rangle}$ and $Y \in ME_b$, then $[\![X(Y)]\!]M,w,t,\alpha$ is the result of applying the function $[\![X]\!]M,w,t,\alpha$ to the argument $[\![Y]\!]M,w,t,\alpha$.

(e) If X and Y are in ME_a, then $[\![X = Y]\!]M,w,t,\alpha = \top$ iff $[\![X]\!]M,w,t,\alpha$ is the same as $[\![Y]\!]M,w,t,\alpha$.

(f) If $X \in ME_t$, then $[\![\neg X]\!]M,w,t,\alpha = \top$ iff $[\![X]\!]M,w,t,\alpha = \bot$, and $\bot$ otherwise.

(g) If X and Y are in ME_t, then $[\![X \wedge Y]\!]M,w,t,\alpha = \top$ iff $[\![X]\!]M,w,t,\alpha = \top$ and $[\![Y]\!]M,w,t,\alpha = \top$.

(h) The rules for $[X \vee Y]$, $[X \rightarrow Y]$, $[X \leftrightarrow Y]$, $\forall u \ X$, and $\exists u \ X$ are as would be expected by reference to the rules for satisfaction of expressions in first order predicate logic (refer back to chapter 4).

(i) If $X \in ME_t$, then $[\![\Box X]\!]M,w,t,\alpha = \top$ iff $[\![X]\!]M,w',t',\alpha = \top$ for all $w' \in W$ and all $t' \in T$.

(j) If $X \in ME_t$, then $[\![FX]\!]M,w,t,\alpha = \top$ iff $[\![X]\!]M,w,t',\alpha = \top$ for some $t' \in T$ such that $t < t'$.

(k) The rule for PX is similar to j except that $t < t'$ is replaced by $t > t'$.

(l) If $X \in ME_a$, then $[\![^\wedge X]\!]M,w,t,\alpha$ is that function h with domain $W \times T$ (i.e. the Cartesian product of W and T) such that for all $\langle w', t' \rangle$ in $W \times T$, $h(\langle w',t' \rangle)$ is $[\![X]\!]M,w',t',\alpha$.

(m) If $X \in ME_{\langle s, a \rangle}$, then $[\![^\vee X]\!]M,w,t,\alpha$ is the result of applying the function $[\![X]\!]M,w,t,\alpha$ to the argument $\langle w, t \rangle$.

(n) If $X \in ME_t$, then X is true with respect to M and $\langle w, t \rangle$ (i.e. $[\![X]\!]M,w,t,\alpha = \top$ iff $[\![X]\!]M,w,t,\alpha = \top$ for all α).

(o) The intension of an expression Y with respect to M and α is denoted by $[\![Y]\!]M,\alpha$, and is that function h with domain W X T (where W X T is the Cartesian product of W and T) such that for all <w, t> in W X T, h(<w, t>) is $[\![Y]\!]M,w,t,\alpha$.

Note that the Cartesian product, W X T, of W and T is the set of all pairs <w, t> such that w ∈ W and t ∈ T.

6.11.2 MONTAGUE'S SYSTEM PTQ

The language of IL was used by Montague as an intermediate translation language in a system called PTQ (for Proper Treatment of Quantification in Ordinary English) which is used to derive a semantic (model-theoretic) interpretation of a fragment of the English language.

In PTQ, a sentence of English is first translated to an expression of IL according to a set of rules specified by Montague. The model-theoretic interpretation of the IL expression then serves, indirectly, as an interpretation of the English sentence. Translation of sentences of English to expressions of IL is a rigorously formalised procedure. Some of the features of this procedure are given below.

(a) Each 'basic' expression of English is translated into exactly one expression of IL. For example, 'every' translates into:

$$\lambda Q[\lambda P[\forall x \; Q(x) \rightarrow P(x)]]$$

(b) There is a strict correspondence between Montague's categories of English and the categories of IL. For example, all noun phrases in English are regarded as referring to sets of properties of entities. For example:

'every man' translates to $\lambda P[\forall x \; man'(x) \rightarrow P(x)]$
'John' translates to $\lambda P[P(John')]$

From this example, we can see that the proper name 'John' is taken to denote a set of properties of the entity John.

The correspondence between categories of English and categories of IL is illustrated by the following examples:

English category	Example
Noun phrase	John
intransitive verb	walk
sentence	John walks

IL category	Example
<<s, <e, t>>, t>	$\lambda P[P(John')]$
<<s, e>, t>	walk'
t	$\lambda P[P(John')](walk')$

(c) For each syntactic rule of English, there is a corresponding rule which specifies the translation of the output of an application of the syntactic rule in terms of the translations of the inputs to which the rule was applied. Therefore, the correspondence described in (b) above holds for derived as well as for basic expressions of English.

These requirements ensure that the translation of the whole English expression is determined by the translation of its parts and the syntactic rules used in forming it. Since the expressions of IL are themselves given a 'compositional' model-theoretic interpretation, it follows that the indirect model-theoretic interpretation of the English expression is compositional.

One of the advantages of Montague's approach is that it handles quantified noun phrases. For example, 'a woman' translates to the set of properties that are true of some woman:

$$\lambda P[\exists x\; woman'(x) \rightarrow P(x)]$$

Hence, the sentence 'a woman walks' translates to:

$$\lambda P[\exists x\; woman'(x) \rightarrow P(x)](walk')$$

which, by lambda conversion, becomes:

$$\exists x\; woman'(x) \wedge walk'(x)$$

Similarly, 'every woman talks' is:

$$\lambda P[\forall x\; woman'(x) \rightarrow talk'(x)]$$

which, by lambda conversion, becomes:

$$\forall x\; woman'(x) \rightarrow talks'(x)$$

Another advantage of Montague's approach is that it goes some way towards accommodating pronominalisation and co-reference. This is done by introducing syntactic variables as noun phrases, and then substituting a normal noun phrase and appropriate pronouns for subsequent occurrences of the same variable. For example, consider the sentence 'a man walks and he talks'. We begin by generating the sentence 'y walks and y talks'; then we substitute the noun phrase 'a man' to obtain 'a man walks and he talks':

$$\lambda P[\exists x\; man'(x) \wedge P(x)](\lambda y[walk'(y) \wedge talk'(y)])$$

which, by lambda conversion, becomes:

$$\exists x\; man'(x) \wedge \lambda y[walk'(y) \wedge talk'(y)](x)$$

which, by lambda conversion, becomes:

$$\exists x\; man'(x) \wedge walk'(x) \wedge talk'(x)$$

Other examples of translation from English to IL
We now give some more examples of translation from English to IL. However, in these examples, we do not give the translation rules used

(they may be found in Dowty et al, to which we refer at the end of this sub-section).

(a)   'John walks in a park', translates to:

    in' $(^\wedge\lambda Q[\exists x \; park'(x) \wedge \lor Q(x)])(^\wedge walk')(John')$

(b)   'John tries to walk', translates to:

    try'$(^\wedge walk')(John')$

(c)   'John walks slowly', translates to:

    slowly'$(^\wedge walk')(John')$

(d)   'John believes that Peter lies', translates to:

    $\lambda P[P(John')](^\wedge believe'(^\wedge lies'(Peter')))$

Montague rejected the commonly held belief that there exists an important theoretical difference between formal and natural languages. His contribution to natural language processing is that he built up a framework for the development of an explicit theory of semantics for natural language. Montague's work has attracted increasing attention in recent years among linguists, philosophers and a few people working in artificial intelligence (see below), since it offers the hope that semantics can be characterised with the same formal rigour that 'transformational' approaches (see Chomsky, 1965) have brought to the syntax of natural language.

Much of the discussion above was derived from a book by Dowty, Wall and Peters (1981). This book provides a clear and comprehensive guide to Montague semantics.

6.11.3 MONTAGUE'S METHODS USED IN ENGLISH/JAPANESE TRANSLATION

Montague's methods have been applied to the automatic translation of English into Japanese (Nishida and Doshita, 1983). Differences between English and Japanese occur at the conceptual level as well as at the syntactic level. Consequently, a large number of transformations at various levels are required in order to obtain high quality translation. The goal of Nishida and Doshita's work was to provide a framework for carrying out these transformations systematically. They began by identifying some basic requirements of an intermediate representation and decided to use an approach based on Montague's intensional logic.

Nishida and Doshita have implemented a prototype system and have shown that it is capable of translating real texts under plausible assumptions with some human assistance.

6.11.4 MONTAGUE'S METHODS USED IN A HISTORICAL DATABASE SYSTEM

In chapter 5, we showed how first order predicate logic could be used for formalising various aspects of relational database systems. Clifford and Warren (1983) have used intensional logic in an analogous way to formalise the temporal semantics of 'historical database systems', where a historical database contains knowledge representing some time-varying universe of discourse.

In Clifford and Warren's approach, all types in all relations are time-stamped. To accommodate this, they introduce a new attribute called STATE. In addition, since some entities do not 'exist' in all states, they introduce another attribute 'EXISTS?'. An example of a relation in a historical database is given in fig. 6.24.

STATE	EMP	EXISTS?	DEPT	SAL
S1	Jim	T	Software	13K
S1	Mary	T	Software	7K
S1	Edward	T	Sales	16K
S1	Larry	T	Hardware	20K
S1	Richard	T	Hardware	19K
S1	Paul	T	Hardware	19K
S1	Stephen	⊥	N/A	N/A
S1	Billy	⊥	N/A	N/A
S2	Jim	T	Software	15K
S2	Mary	T	Sales	10K
S2	Edward	T	Sales	17K
S2	Larry	⊥	N/A	N/A
S2	Richard	T	Hardware	18K
S2	Paul	⊥	N/A	N/A
S2	Stephen	T	Hardware	15K
S2	Billy	⊥	N/A	N/A
S3	Jim	⊥	N/A	N/A
S3	Mary	⊥	N/A	N/A
S3	Edward	T	Sales	17K
S3	Larry	⊥	N/A	N/A
S3	Richard	T	Hardware	18K
S3	Paul	T	Hardware	23K
S3	Stephen	T	Hardware	15K
S3	Billy	T	Software	13K

Figure 6.24 A relation in a historical database

The following are examples of queries which might be asked of such a database:

- Has Jim's salary risen?
- When was Paul re-hired?
- Did Richard work for the sales department last year?
- Has Jim ever earned the same salary as Paul?
- Will the average salary in the software department surpass $25,000 in the next five years?

Clifford and Warren introduce a logic called ILs which is a variation of Montague's intensional logic. One difference is that in ILs all indices have the same possible-world value (i.e. only the actual world is considered), and these indices are regarded as being of a basic type s as suggested in Gallin (1975). (Note that in Montague's formulation of intensional logic the set of indices, s, is not regarded as a type.)

To illustrate the use of ILs, Clifford and Warren set up a small language and a model for a language. This language and model are presented, with some alterations, below.

The language contains the following constants of the indicated semantic categories:

(a) Peter, Liz, Elsie, and THE Boss of category $\langle s, e \rangle$.
(b) 1977, 1978, 1979, 1980 and 1981 of category $\langle s \rangle$.
(c) EMP of category $\langle s, \langle e, t \rangle \rangle$.

The model M is a quadruple $\langle E, S, OS, \Upsilon \rangle$ where:

(a) $E = \{e1, e2, e3\}$
(b) $S = \{s1, s2, s3, s4, s5\}$
(c) OS is the linear ordering $\{\langle s1, s2 \rangle, \langle s2, s3 \rangle, \langle s3, s4 \rangle,$
$\quad\quad\quad\quad\quad\quad\quad\quad\quad\quad\quad\quad\quad\quad ...etc.\}$
(d) The 'interpretation' function Υ is defined such that:

$\Upsilon(\text{Peter}') =$
| s1 → e1 |
| s2 → e1 |
| s3 → e1 |
| s4 → e1 |
| s5 → e1 |

$\Upsilon(\text{Liz}') =$
| s1 → e2 |
| s2 → e2 |
| s3 → e2 |
| s4 → e2 |
| s5 → e2 |

$\Upsilon(\text{Elsie}') =$
| s1 → e3 |
| s2 → e3 |
| s3 → e3 |
| s4 → e3 |
| s5 → e3 |

$\Upsilon(\text{THEBoss}') =$
| s1 → e2 |
| s2 → e1 |
| s3 → c1 |
| s4 → e1 |
| s5 → e3 |

$\Upsilon(\text{EMP}') =$

S1 →
| e1 → ⊥ |
| e2 → ⊤ |
| e3 → ⊥ |

$\Upsilon(1982) = s1$

S2 →
| e1 → ⊤ |
| e2 → ⊤ |
| e3 → ⊥ |

$\Upsilon(1983) = s2$

S3 →
| e1 → ⊤ |
| e2 → ⊤ |
| e3 → ⊥ |

$\Upsilon(1984) = s3$

S4 →
| e1 → ⊤ |
| e2 → ⊥ |
| e3 → ⊥ |

$\Upsilon(1985) = s4$

S5 →
| e1 → ⊥ |
| e2 → ⊥ |
| e3 → ⊤ |

$\Upsilon(1986) = s5$

Note that since the constants Peter', Liz' and Elsie' each pick out the same individual at every index, they are called 'rigid designators'.

We can now consider the 'meaning' of expressions of the language with respect to this model:

(a) The expression EMP' (1983) is well-formed since EMP' is of category <s, <e, t>> and 1983 is of category s. The category of EMP' (1983) is therefore <e, t>. Its meaning (denotation) is obtained by applying the function which is denoted by EMP' (i.e. the intension of EMP) to the denotation of 1983, namely s2:

$$
\begin{array}{l}
s1 \rightarrow \{e2\} \\
s2 \rightarrow \{e1, e2\} \\
s3 \rightarrow \{e1, e2\} \\
s4 \rightarrow \{e1\} \\
s5 \rightarrow \{e3\}
\end{array}
\quad (s2) = \{e1, e2\}
$$

(b) Suppose that we want to form an expression whose meaning is a function from states to those individuals who were not THE Boss in those states. Such an expression will be of the same category as EMP', namely <s, <e, t>> and can be constructed from the constants given above using lambda abstraction. To do this, we need two variables t and v where t is a variable over states (i.e. of category s) and v is a variable over individuals (i.e. of category e). The expression that we want is:

$$\lambda t [\lambda v [\neg \text{THEBoss}(t)(v)]]$$

The denotation of this function is:

$$
\begin{array}{l}
s1 \rightarrow
\begin{array}{l}
e1 \rightarrow \top \\
e2 \rightarrow \bot \\
e3 \rightarrow \top
\end{array}
\\[1em]
s2 \rightarrow
\begin{array}{l}
e1 \rightarrow \bot \\
e2 \rightarrow \top \\
e3 \rightarrow \top
\end{array}
\\[1em]
s3 \rightarrow
\begin{array}{l}
e1 \rightarrow \bot \\
e2 \rightarrow \top \\
e3 \rightarrow \top
\end{array}
\\[1em]
s4 \rightarrow
\begin{array}{l}
e1 \rightarrow \bot \\
e2 \rightarrow \top \\
e3 \rightarrow \top
\end{array}
\\[1em]
s5 \rightarrow
\begin{array}{l}
e1 \rightarrow \top \\
e2 \rightarrow \top \\
e3 \rightarrow \bot
\end{array}
\end{array}
$$

(c) Consider the English sentence 'Peter was the boss'. This translates into:

$$\exists t [\text{OS}(t, \text{now}) \wedge \text{THEBoss}'(t)(\text{Peter}')]$$

If we assume that now is s4 then this expression is true. However, if we assume that now is s2, then the expression is false.

Clifford and Warren formalise various aspects of historical databases using ILs. One of the most interesting aspects of their approach is the formalisation of integrity constraints which are divided into two categories:

(a)   An 'extensional database constraint' is a constraint on individual states of the database. The violation (or non violation) of such constraints may be determined by reference to single states independently.

(b)   An 'intensional database constraint' is a constraint which defines valid progressions from one database state to another.

A more detailed account of intensional logic and historical databases is given in Clifford and Warren's paper. The work described there is part of their research into the larger domain of natural language database querying (NLQ). They hope to develop a framework for NLQ that is founded squarely on a fully formalised syntax and semantics.

Montague's work has been studied by various other researchers working in automated knowledge processing; for example Hobbs (1978), Friedman (1978) and Yonezaki (1980).

6.12   CONCLUDING COMMENTS

In this chapter, the reader has been introduced to several non-classical logics. The discussions have been somewhat brief and rather fragmented. However, they should facilitate the reading of the more comprehensive discussions which we have referred to in the text.

Interest in the use of logics, both classical and non-classical, to formalise aspects of database and knowledge base systems work has been growing over the last few years. In agreement with Clifford and Warren (1983) and Hayes (1981), we believe that this is a healthy trend and that the use of logic will facilitate the development and understanding of many ideas and techniques for advanced knowledge processing.

7 Theories for Dealing with Uncertainty

7.1 SOURCES OF UNCERTAINTY

Much of the knowledge which humans reason with is inexact or uncertain in some respect or other. This uncertainty is due to several factors:

(a) There are situations in which the universe of discourse is truly random. For example, the motion of gas molecules or the distribution of people's heights.

(b) There are situations in which the universe of discourse is not strictly random but for some reason there is insufficient data. For example, suppose that we want to represent the likelihood that a person has appendicitis. We could always operate to obtain a definite value. However, it may be inappropriate to do this and we must use probabilistic reasoning, based on the evidence which is readily available, to obtain a value.

(c) There are situations in which the knowledge available represents a 'gut feeling' (no relationship with the example in (b) is intended). Such judgemental knowledge can be useful when more sound knowledge is not available.

(d) There are situations in which the knowledge available is couched in terms which are themselves vague. For example, consider the word 'large' in 'a large animal collided with my car'.

(e) There are situations in which the source of knowledge is not totally reliable. For example, the source might be a perfectly honest but absent-minded professor.

Various theories have been developed to accommodate such uncertainty and in this discussion we provide a brief introduction to some of these theories. The subject of uncertainty is not trivial and we can do no more than scratch the surface in a discussion of this nature. The interested reader is advised to pursue the references given in the text.

7.2 PROBABILITY THEORY

The mathematical theory of probability provides a means of dealing with knowledge about truly random events. This theory includes the following law, among others:

L1: If the probability of A is pA and the probability of B is pB and A and B are independent events, then the probability of [A AND B] is pA * pB.

For example, suppose that we have a coin and an eight-sided die. Let A be the event of a head showing when the coin is tossed, and B be the event of a 7 being face up when the die is thrown. Now, if we simultaneously toss the coin and throw the die, then the probability of [A AND B] is:

$$p(A \text{ AND } B) = pA * pB$$
$$= 0.5 * 0.125$$
$$= 0.0625$$

That is, if we were to repeat this experiment 10,000 times we would expect to obtain roughly 625 instances of [head AND 7].

Another law of probability theory is:

L2: If the probability of A is pA then the probability of NOTA is 1.0 - pA.

A further law is:

L3: If the probability of A is pA, the probability of B is pB, and the probability of A AND B is p(A AND B), then the probability of A OR B is:

$$pA + pB - p(A \text{ AND } B)$$

If we ignore the condition in law L1 that A and B must be independent events then these three laws are contradictory, as can be illustrated by the following example.

Suppose that A is the probability of a coin landing face up. Suppose that B is the probability of the same coin landing face down. In this case pA = pB = 0.5. If we ignore the dependence of A and B, the laws above give:

(a) p(A AND B) = 0.5 * 0.5 = 0.25 by L1

(b) p(A OR B) = 0.5 + 0.5 - 0.25 = 0.75 by L3

However, the probability of a coin landing face up *and* down is obviously 0.0, contradicting (a), and the probability of a coin landing face up *or* face down is obviously 1.0, contradicting (b).

Baye's rule

Another component of probability theory is Baye's rule which provides a way of computing the probability of a hypothesis being true given some evidence related to that hypothesis. Before stating Baye's rule, we introduce some terminology:

(a) p(E/Hi)   is the probability that evidence E will be observed
given that hypothesis Hi is true. For example, E
might be a symptom and Hi a disease.

(b) p(Hi)   is the *a priori* probability that Hi is true. That
is, based on past experience, p(Hi) is simply the
probability that Hi is true irrespective of any
evidence for or against it in some particular case.
For example, if Hi were a disease then p(Hi) is the
probability of *any* person having that disease. The
a priori probability of a tossed coin landing face
up is 0.5.

(c) k   is the number of possible hypotheses which display
evidence E. For example, k might be the number of
diseases which display some symptom E.

Given these definitions, Baye's rule states that the probability that
hypothesis Hi is true given evidence E (which is denoted by p(Hi/E))
may be calculated as follows:

$$p(Hi/E) = \frac{p(E/Hi) * p(Hi)}{\sum_{n = 1 \text{ to } k} p(E/Hn) * p(Hn)}$$

That is, to obtain p(Hi/E) we calculate p(E/Hi) * p(Hi) and divide
this by the sum of the values of p(E/Hn) * p(Hn) for all possible
hypotheses.

An alternative expression of Baye's rule
Baye's rule may be expressed in a different form, as follows:

$$\emptyset(Hi/E) = LS * \emptyset(Hi)$$

where:

(a) $\emptyset$ stands for 'odds' and is related to probability as follows:

$$(i) \quad \emptyset(x) = \frac{p(x)}{1.0 - p(x)}$$

$$(ii) \quad p(x) = \frac{\emptyset(x)}{1.0 + \emptyset(x)}$$

(b) LS stands for 'likelihood ratio' and is calculated as follows:

$$LS = \frac{p(E/Hi)}{p(E/\neg Hi)}$$

where $p(E/\neg Hi)$ is the probability that E is displayed when
hypothesis Hi is false.

The LS value indicates the extent to which the presence of E supports the validity of the hypothesis Hi.

Complementary equations may also be written for the case in which E is absent (denoted by ¬E). The equations are:

$$\emptyset(Hi/\neg E) = LN * \emptyset(Hi)$$

where

$$LN = \frac{p(\neg E/Hi)}{p(\neg E/\neg Hi)}$$

The LN value indicates the extent to which the absence of the evidence E supports the non-validity of the hypothesis Hi.

An example of the use of Baye's rule
Suppose we are given a hypothesis X and values for $p(E/X)$, $p(E/\neg X)$, $p(\neg E/X)$, $p(\neg E/\neg X)$ for four pieces of evidence E = A,B,C,D. Suppose further that when we use these values, and the expressions above, to compute values for LS and LN for each piece of evidence, we obtain the following:

Evidence	Hypothesis	LS	LN
A	X	20.0	1.0
B	X	300.0	1.0
C	X	75.0	1.0
D	X	4.0	1.0

That is, the first row is calculated from $p(A/X)$, $p(A/\neg X)$, $p(\neg A/X)$ and $p(\neg A/\neg X)$, the second row from $p(B/X)$, etc., and so on. The values in the LS column show that the existence of evidence B is more suggestive of X than is the existence of A, C or D. The values in the LN column state that the absence of any one of A, B, C or D is unimportant to establishing X.

We now show how these values can be used to calculate the probability of X given that the *a priori* probability of X (i.e. $p(X)$) is 0.03 and that evidence A and B (but not C or D) have been observed:

(a) We begin by calculating the *a priori* odds of X:

$$\emptyset(X) = \frac{0.03}{1.0 - 0.03} = 0.030927$$

(b) Because the LS value for A is 20, we can compute the value of $\emptyset(X/A)$ as follows:

$$\emptyset(X/A) = 20 * \emptyset(X) = 0.61855$$

(c) From this we can calculate the new increased probability of X based on observing A:

$$p(X/A) = \frac{0.61855}{1.0 - 0.61855} = 0.382$$

401

That is, the effect of observing A is to increase the probability of X from 0.03 to 0.382.

(d) Now, because the LS value for B is 300, we can multiply the increased odds for X by 300, giving the new odds:

$$\emptyset(X/[A \text{ AND } B]) = \emptyset(X/A) * 300$$
$$= 0.61855 * 300$$
$$= 185.565$$

The value $\emptyset(X/[A \text{ AND } B])$ is the odds for X if A and B have been observed.

(e) Finally, we can compute the probability of X, given A and B, as follows:

$$p(X/[A \text{ AND } B]) = \frac{\emptyset(X/[A \text{ AND } B])}{1.0 + \emptyset(X/[A \text{ AND } B])}$$

$$= 0.99464$$

Such reasoning is only correct if A and B are independent. If they are not independent, then we should use values of p([A AND B]/X), p([A AND B]/¬X), p(¬[A AND B]/X) and p(¬[A AND B]/¬X) to compute values for LS and LN for [A AND B], and then use these in the calculations to compute p(X/[A AND B]), in place of LS and LN values for A and B.

Disadvantages of probability theory

There are several disadvantages of using probability theory to deal with uncertainty, some of which are mentioned below.

(a) It is often difficult to obtain exact values for *a priori* probabilities. In many domains, all that is available are subjective estimates.

(b) It is difficult to modify a Bayesian-based set of values because of the dependencies between them. For example, the probabilities of all possible hypotheses which display some evidence E must sum to 1.0. If we add a new hypothesis (e.g. if we identify a new disease with a symptom common to a set of existing diseases) we may have to re-compute many LS and LN values.

(c) When pieces of evidence are dependent, LS and LN values must be computed for the presence or absence of all combinations of these pieces of evidence. For example, if A, B and C are dependent, then LS and LN values would have to be computed for:

A
B
C
A AND B
A AND C
A AND B AND C
(etc.)

402

(d) The single probability value assigned to a hypothesis tells us nothing about its precision. To state that $p(X/A)$ is 0.5 might mean that $p(X/A)$ is 0.500 ± 0.001 or 0.5 ± 0.4.

(e) The single value combines evidence for and against a hypothesis without indicating how much there is of each.

More complete discussions of probability theory can be found in various books on statistics such as Fine (1973). Its use in the automated processing of uncertain knowledge in expert systems is described in chapter 8, sub-section 8.4.3.

7.3 CERTAINTY THEORY

Certainty theory (Shortliffe and Buchanan, 1975) is a theory developed for use in expert systems. It was developed in an attempt to overcome some of the problems associated with probability theory.

In certainty theory, a 'certainty measure' $C(S)$ is associated with every 'factual' statement S such that:

(a) $C(S) = 1.0$ if S is known to be true.
(b) $C(S) = -1.0$ if S is known to be false.
(c) $C(S) = 0.0$ if nothing is known about S.
(d) Intermediate values indicate a measure of certainty or uncertainty in S.

Knowledge which shows how factual statements are related is represented as a set of rules such as:

• if S1 then S2   with certainty factor 0.8
• if S2 and S3 then S4   with certainty factor 0.5

The 'certainty factors' associated with rules are measures of reliability of those rules. In general, rules are written with the following format:

if A then X   with certainty factor CF

where A is called the condition part and X the conclusion. If the condition part of a rule is true, i.e. if it has a certainty value of 1.0, then that rule can be used to compute a new certainty value for its conclusion as follows:

(a) If $C(X)$ and CF are both greater than 0.0 then the new certainty of X, denoted by $C(X/A)$, is computed according to the following equation:

$$C(X/A) = C(X) + [CF * [1.0 - C(X)]]$$

This equation can be explained as follows:

> If the certainty value $C(X)$ of a statement is positive, then the most that a rule with positive CF can increase the certainty of X is $1.0 - C(X)$. This amount is multiplied by CF and added to $C(X)$.

403

(b)   If C(X) and CF are both less than 0.0, then the new certainty of X is computed according to the following equation:

$$C(X/A) = C(X) + [CF * [1.0 + C(X)]]$$

(c)   If C(X) and CF are of opposite sign, then the new certainty of X is computed according to the following equation:

$$C(X/A) = \frac{C(X) + CF}{1.0 - \text{minimum of } \{|C(X)|, |CF|\}}$$

where $|\alpha|$ is equal to α if α is positive, and $-\alpha$ if α is negative.

Rules whose conditions have certainty values less than 1.0

In some cases the condition part of a rule R will be uncertain. That is, C(A) will be less than 1.0. Such cases can arise for two reasons:

(a)   A might be evidence which is empirically uncertain.
(b)   A might be a conclusion of another rule.

In either case, the certainty of the conclusion of R must be reduced accordingly.

One approach is to multiply the certainty factor of the rule by the certainty of the condition if this certainty is positive, and to ignore the rule if the certainty is negative. Another approach is to require that the certainty of the condition be above some threshold before the rule may be used.

Complex conditions

Rules may have complex conditions, as illustrated in the following examples:

    if [A AND B] then X with CF1
    if [A OR B] then Y with CF2
    if [A AND NOT B] then Z with CF3

In such cases, the certainty values of the complex conditions can be computed using results from the theory of fuzzy sets (Zadeh, 1965):

(a)   The certainty of [A AND B] = minimum of {C(A), C(B)}.
(b)   The certainty of [A OR B] = maximum of {C(A), C(B)}.
(c)   The certainty of (NOTA) = 1.0 - C(A).

An example

Suppose that we have the following rules:

    R1:   if A then X with certainty factor 0.8.
    R2:   if B then X with certainty factor 0.5.
    R3:   if [X AND E] then Y with certainty factor 0.8.

Suppose also that we have made observations such that C(A) = 1.0, C(B) = 1.0, and C(E) = 1.0, and that the initial certainty values of X and Y are both 0.0. We can calculate the revised certainties of X and Y as follows:

(a) Using R1:

$$C(X/A) = 0.0 + [0.8 * [1.0 - 0.0]]$$
$$= 0.8$$

Thus $C(X)$ is now 0.8.

(b) Using R2:

$$C(X/B) = 0.8 + [0.5 * [1.0 - 0.8]]$$
$$= 0.9$$

Thus $C(X)$ is now 0.9.

(c) The certainty of [X AND E] = minimum of $\{C(X), C(E)\}$
$$= 0.9$$

Hence the modified certainty factor for R3 is $0.8 * 0.9 = 0.72$.

(d) Using R3:

$$C(Y/[X \text{ AND } E]) = 0.0 + [0.72 * [1.0 - 0.0]]$$
$$= 0.72$$

Hence the revised certainty of Y is 0.72.

The rules of certainty theory described above are strictly only applicable if the pieces of evidence are statistically independent. When they are dependent, the rules must be carefully structured to minimise interactions.

Relationship of certainty theory to probability theory
The original definition of certainty factors (in certainty theory) related them to probability values:

(a) A positive certainty factor, CF, in a rule 'if A then X' is a *measure of belief* such that CF = 1.0 if $p(X) = 1.0$, and otherwise is calculated as follows:

$$CF = \frac{\text{maximum of } \{p(X/A), p(X)\} - p(X)}{1.0 - p(X)}$$

(b) A negative certainty factor, CF, in a rule 'if A then X' is a *measure of disbelief* such that CF = - 1.0 if $p(X) = 0.0$, and otherwise is calculated as follows:

$$CF = \frac{\text{minimum of } \{p(X/A), p(X)\} - p(X)}{p(X)}$$

However, in more recent developments of the theory, certainty factors have been used for quantifying subjective estimates which are not based on probabilities alone but include factors such as the importance of not missing the conclusion of the rule (see van Melle et al, 1981). For example, if the conclusion of a rule is the diagnosis of some high risk disease, then the certainty factor of this rule might be increased accordingly. Used in this way, certainty theory is a heuristic method based on pragmatic rather than theoretic grounds.

Advantages of certainty theory

Even if the exact values of probabilities cannot be obtained, certainty theory provides a means of manipulating subjective estimates of certainty such that the calculated certainty values are intuitively appealing:

(a) The resulting certainty values always lie between -1.0 and 1.0 and the meaning of the values -1.0, 0.0 and 1.0 are all well defined.

(b) If two contradictory rules are applied, such that the certainty of one is equal to the certainty of the other, then their effects cancel out.

The use of certainty theory in expert systems is discussed in chapter 8.

7.4 THE DEMPSTER/SCHAFER THEORY OF EVIDENCE

In this approach (see Schafer, 1976) a distinction is made between uncertainty and ignorance. Instead of probabilities, one specifies 'belief functions' by which one can put bounds on the assignment of probabilities to events instead of having to specify the probabilities exactly. The theory also provides methods for computing belief functions for combinations of evidence.

When the bounds determine the probabilities exactly, this theory reduces to probability theory.

Because the Dempster/Schafer theory includes probability theory as a special case, it inherits many of the problems associated with probability theory. It is also more complex and consequently less computationally efficient. However, it is important since it illustrates the effect of ignorance on reasoning with uncertain knowledge.

7.5 POSSIBILITY THEORY

Possibility theory (Zadeh, 1978) is a theory for dealing with vagueness as distinct from randomness and is based on Zadeh's earlier work on fuzzy sets (Zadeh, 1965).

The theory of 'fuzzy sets' provides a means for dealing with vagueness of terms such as 'large'. If S is a set and e is a member of S, then we can define a fuzzy subset F of S by introducing a membership function $@F$ such that $@F(e) = d$ where d is the degree to which e is a member of F. For example, if S is 'the set of all animals' and F is the 'set of large animals', then we can define $@F$ as follows:

```
@F (elephant)    = 1.0
@F (hippopotamus) = 1.0
@F (tiger)       = 0.8
@F (man)         = 0.6
@F (dog)         = 0.1
@F (mouse)       = 0.0001
(etc.)
```

A 'fuzzy' statement such as 'a large animal' is interpreted as having an imprecise denotation characterised by a fuzzy set.

A 'fuzzy variable' X is a variable which can take values in S as well as values 'assigned' to it by statements such as:

'X is an F'

If effect, the value of X is a possibility distribution such that the possibility that X = e is @F(e). For example, the statement:

'X is a large animal'

signifies that the possibility that 'X = elephant' is 1.0, the possibility that 'X = mouse' is 0.0001, and so on.

Possibility theory provides rules for computing the possibilities of expressions involving fuzzy variables. Such rules include:

(a) poss(X = a OR Y = b) = max{poss(X = a), poss(Y = b)}
(b) poss(X = a AND Y = b) = min{poss(X = a), poss(Y = b)}
(c) poss(X ≠ a) = 1 - poss(X = a)

Zadeh's fuzzy logic (which was described briefly in chapter 6) can help to detect redundancy in a set of fuzzy statements. For example, consider the following set of statements:

(a) People in the sixth form tend to run fast.

(b) Schoolchildren over 15 tend to run fast.

(c) A large number of runners were born in 1969.

(d) A child is much more likely to be in the sixth form if over the age of 16 than if under.

Given that Mary is at school, is 17, and was born in 1969, a naive reasoner might proceed as follows:

(e) From (b) above, conclude that Mary might run fast.

(f) From (d) and the given data conclude that Mary might well be in the sixth form.

(g) From (f), (a) and (e), conclude that Mary is likely to run fast.

(h) From the given data, and (c) together with (g), conclude that Mary must be a fast runner.

However, this conclusion is somewhat strong given the statements above. A discerning reasoner can see that it is too strong since he can detect the redundancy which is present. The problem a naive reasoner might have is due to the fact that the redundancy is implicit. The confusion arises because the statements above are expressed as equivalences or dispositions. That is the direction of causal implication has not been made clear. For example, it is not clear whether 17-year-olds run fast because they are in the sixth form or because they were born in 1969. Zadeh (1983) has described how fuzzy logic can be used to overcome such problems.

(The example above was derived from one given by Mamdani and Efstathion at Queen Mary College, London University.)

The use of possibility theory in expert systems is discussed in chapter 8.

7.6 INCIDENCE CALCULUS

'Incidence calculus' (Bundy, 1984) is a mechanism for reasoning with uncertainty which overcomes some of the problems associated with the methods described so far.

The methods described so far all involve the assignment of numerical values to assertions and rules, and the assignment of arithmetic functions to the connectives AND, OR and NOT. A problem with these methods is that the final value obtained for a goal assertion does not represent the probability of that assertion but rather is a measure whose exact meaning is ill-defined and which can, therefore, only be used to rank goal assertions in some order. As such, none of these methods can be correctly described as methods for probabilistic reasoning. Bundy (1984) argues that no method based purely on assigning numerical values can be so described. The following discussion derives from Bundy's work.

Limitations of a purely numerical mechanism
The laws of probability theory which were introduced in section 7.2 may be stated as:

    L1: p(A AND B) = p(A) * p(B)   if A and B are independent events
    L2: p(NOT A) = 1.0 - p(A)
    L3: p(A OR B) = pA + pB - p(A AND B)

As mentioned earlier, these laws are contradictory if we ignore the condition of independence of A and B in L1. In probability theory, a value 'corr(A,B)' called the correlation between two events is used to denote their degree of dependence. Correlation is defined such that:

    p(A AND B) = p(A) * p(B) + corr(A,B) * p(A) * p(NOTA) * p(B) *
                                                            p(NOTB)

This formula can be used in place of L1 when A and B are dependent. However, to use this formula in general requires us to provide values for the correlations of all combinations of the events involved. This would be reasonable if we had a calculus which allowed correlations of complex conjuncts to be calculated from values of their sub-formulas. For example, if we had rules which allowed us to calculate corr([A AND B],C) from p(A), p(B), p(C), corr(A,B), corr(A,C) and corr(B,C). Bundy (1984), however, has shown that it is not possible to provide such a calculus. Thus, the expert knowledge provider would have to provide correlations from all combinations of evidence and hypotheses. This is unfeasible in many applications.

Incidents
Incidence calculus is based on the set-theoretic roots of probability theory, in which the probability of a formula is based on a set of situations (interpretations, or possible worlds). Bundy calls such

situations 'incidents'. Suppose that we have an eight-sided die and a coin. There are sixteen possible incidents:

DIE	COIN
1	head
1	tail
2	head
2	tail

(etc.)

Let us use W to represent the set of all possible worlds or incidents in which the formulas of a theory are to be evaluated. In our example,

W = {<1,head>, <1,tail>, <2,head>, <2,tail>, etc...}

The incidence i(A) of a formula A with respect to W is the subset of W containing all those incidents in which A is true. In our example, if A represents 2 being face up on the die, then:

i(A) = {<2,head>, <2,tail>}

The dependence or independence of two formulas is the amount of intersection between their incidences. If two formulas are 'independent', then this intersection would be what would be expected from a random assignment of values to the elements of their incidences.

Incidence calculus
The following formulas constitute Bundy's incidence calculus:

(a) i(T) = W i.e. T (standing for true) is true in all incidents in W.

(b) i($\perp$) = { } i.e. false is true in no incidents.

(c) i(NOT A) = W - i(A).

(d) i(A AND B) = i(A) $\cap$ i(B), where $\cap$ stands for set intersection.

(e) i(A OR B) = i(A) $\cup$ i(B), where $\cup$ stands for set union.

To illustrate the use of these formulas, consider the example given above:

W = {<1,head>, <1,tail>, <2,head>, <2,tail>, etc...}
A = die with 2 face up
i(A) = {<2,head>, <2,tail> }
B = coin with head up
i(B) = {<1,head>, <2,head>, <3,head>, <4,head>, etc...}
i(A AND B) = {<2,head>}

Weighted probabilities
If w is an incident, let p(w) be the probability of w occurring. If W is a set of incidents, then the weighted probability of W, represented by p(W) is given by:

$$p(W) = \sum_{w \in W} p(w)$$

409

i.e. the weighted probability of W is the sum of the probabilities of the incidents in W.

In our example, since the incidents of W are disjoint, p(W) = 1.0 i.e.

p{<1,head> + p(<1,tail>) + p(<2,head>) etc...}

If A is a formula, then p(A) is the probability of A being true and:

p(A) = p(i(A))

For example, if A represents 'die with 2 face up' then

$$p(A) = \sum_{w \in i(A)} p(w) = p<2,head> + p<2,tail>$$

Representing incidents

Incidents may be represented by bit strings. For example, continuing with the eight-sided die and the coin, we can represent the sixteen disjoint incidents as follows:

w = 1 1 1 1 1 1 1 1 1 1 1 1 1 1 1 1

where the first 1 stands for <1,head>, the second for <2,head>, etc.

Now suppose that A stands for 'die with 2 face up', then i(A) may be represented as follows:

i(A) = 0 0 1 1 0 0 0 0 0 0 0 0 0 0 0 0

Similarly, i(NOTA), i(A AND NOTA) and i(A OR NOTA) can be represented as:

i(NOTA) = 1 1 0 0 1 1 1 1 1 1 1 1 1 1 1 1
i(A AND NOTA) = 0 0 0 0 0 0 0 0 0 0 0 0 0 0 0 0
i(A OR NOTA) = 1 1 1 1 1 1 1 1 1 1 1 1 1 1 1 1

Hence p(A AND NOTA) = 0
p(A OR NOTA) = 1

Thus, the method gives the required results for the two related events: 'die with 2 face up' and 'die not with 2 face up'.

Suppose now that B stands for 'coin with head up'. We can assign to B the following incidence:

B = 1 0 1 0 1 0 1 0 1 0 1 0 1 0 1 0

giving:

i(A AND B) = 0 0 1 0 0 0 0 0 0 0 0 0 0 0 0 0
i(A OR B) = 1 0 1 1 1 0 1 0 1 0 1 0 1 0 1 0

hence

$$p(A \text{ AND } B) = 1/16 \left.\right\}\quad \text{(assuming that each incident}$$
$$p(A \text{ OR } B) = 9/16 \left.\right\}\quad \text{is equally probable)}$$

In general, the user will not want to provide incidences but will prefer to give probabilities. For example, in the above, the user might prefer to state that the coin will be face up with probability 0.5, face down with probability 0.5, face up or face down with probability 1.0, face up and face down with probability 0.0, and that the die will be 1 face up with probability 0.125, 2 face up with probability 0.125, etc. The system must now generate incidences using some randomiser in conjunction with an algorithm which checks that all dependencies and independencies between events are respected.

Note that a simple mechanism which assigns, say, every other bit to an event with probability 0.5 will not in general work. Using such a simple approach we might obtain:

    i(coin with head up) = 1 0 1 0 1 0 1 0...
    i(coin with tail up) = 1 0 1 0 1 0 1 0...

This is obviously in error. For example, if we compute i(coin with head up AND coin with tail up) we obtain:

    1 0 1 0 1 0 1 0...

which is incorrect.

The assignment of incidences must take into account known probabilities of conjuncts and disjuncts such as p(coin with head up AND coin with tail up) = 0.0.

Bundy (1984) describes an incidence assignment algorithm which goes some way towards solving this problem.

Use of incidences
Given i(A) and a rule: 'if A then X', we need to be able to calculate i(X).

Unfortunately, there is a problem: from 'if A then X', all we can infer is that $i(A) \subseteq i(X)$ since X might also be true in incidents in which A is false. Thus, we can only calculate a lower bound on the incidence of X. However, if we have several rules each with the same consequent X, we can take the 'union' of the lower bounds as the lower bound for i(X).

For example, suppose that we have the rules:

    if A then X
    if B then X
    if C then X

We can then compute a lower bound for i(X) as follows:

    $(i(A) \cup i(B) \cup i(C)) \subseteq i(X)$

411

As example, continuing with our die/coin illustration, suppose that we have three rules:

    R1: if <3,tail> then <odd,tail>
    R2: if <5,tail> then <odd,tail>
    R3: if <7,tail> then <odd,tail>

A lower bound for an <odd,tail> event can be computed as follows:

    i(<3,tail>) U i(<5,tail>) U i(<7,tail>) =
                            0 0 0 0 0 1 0 0 0 1 0 0 0 1 0 0

giving a lower bound for p(<odd,tail>) of 3/16.

That is, if we knew nothing about a particular die/coin throw other than the facts (a) that each of the eight die faces were equally probable, (b) that each of the two coin faces were equally probable, (c) that (head AND tail) had probability 0.0 and (die 1 AND die 2) had probability 0.0, etc., (d) that the die and coin events were independent and (e) that the three rules R1, R2 and R3 above applied, then we would have a lower bound of: 3/16 for p(<odd,tail>). However, if we had another rule R4: if <1,tail> then <odd,tail>, then we could improve on this lower bound.

More information on incidence calculus can be found in Bundy (1984).

7.7 PLAUSIBILITY THEORY
Plausibility theory (Rescher, 1976) provides guidelines for reasoning with knowledge obtained from sources of less than total reliability. In particular, plausibility theory enables us to reason with inconsistent sets of knowledge obtained from imperfect sources. The following discussion of plausibility theory derives much from Rescher's book.

The inadequacy of probability theory
Probability theory is inadequate for dealing with knowledge from imperfect sources. As example, consider the following situation:

    S1 is a generally reliable but imperfect source.
    S1 asserts P.
    S2 is a generally reliable but imperfect source.
    S2 asserts ¬P.

What does probability theory allow us to infer from these statements? The answer is 'very little'. In fact, as far as probability theory is concerned, the assertion of P by a generally reliable but imperfect source tells us practically nothing about the probability of P. We can explain this as follows.

Suppose that the following inference rule R were valid:

    from

    $\left\{ \begin{array}{l} \text{S is a generally reliable but imperfect source} \\ \text{S asserts X} \end{array} \right\}$

    infer

        $pr(X) > 0.9$

412

According to this rule, the four statements above would be incompatible, since we can infer pr(P) > 0.9 and pr(¬P) > 0.9 using the rule R, and we can also infer pr(¬P) < 0.1 and pr(P) < 0.1 using probability theory which states that pr(¬X) = 1.0 - pr(X).

Consequently, rules such as R above are not compatible with classical probability theory.

The inadequacy of formal logic

Suppose that the following situation holds:

S1, S2, and S3 are generally reliable but imperfect sources.
S1 asserts ¬P.
S2 asserts ¬Q.
S3 asserts P v Q.

Formal logic would simply tell us that the set {¬P, ¬Q, P v Q} is inconsistent. It would not help us to identify assertions such as ¬P v ¬Q which may be regarded as being 'plausible' consequences of this inconsistent set.

The assertion ¬P v ¬Q may be regarded as being plausible since it follows from what remains when the set {¬P, ¬Q, P v Q} is made consistent in any one of the following minimally disruptive ways:

(a) Remove ¬P giving {¬Q, P v Q}.
(b) Remove ¬Q giving {¬P, P v Q}.
(c) Remove P v Q giving {¬P, ¬Q}.

Since ¬P v ¬Q follows from what is left in each case, this assertion may be regarded as being a plausible consequence of the inconsistent set.

P-sets and plausibility indexing

A p-set is a set of assertions which have been vouched for by sources of some degree of positive reliability.

Given the degrees of reliability of sources, the degrees of plausibility of assertions in some p-set, PS, can be determined according to the following principles:

(a) Every member of PS must be assigned a plausibility value, and the plausibility assigned to a member is determined by the standing of its most respectable source.

(b) Universally valid formulas must be given plausibility values of 1.0.

(c) All members of PS with a value of 1.0 must be logically consistent and materially compatible with each other.

(d) When a consistent sub-set, SPS, of PS implies some other member, Q, of PS, then the plausibility value of Q must not be less than the least plausible in SPS. That is, if
$p1,...,Pj \vdash Q$ and $P1,...,Pj,Q \subseteq PS$ and $P1,...,Pj$ are mutually

consistent, then the plausibility of Q must be equal or greater than the plausibility of the least plausible of P1,...,Pj.

(e) Any assertion P, and its negation ¬P, may both have relatively high plausibility values. There is nothing to prevent this happening. However both P and ¬P may not have plausibility values of 1.0, since this is not in keeping with principle (c).

(f) In a conflict, preference must be given to the assertion with the highest plausibility value.

A viable plausibility value assignment is one which is compatible with all of the above principles.

Some examples

(i) Suppose that the following knowledge has been obtained:

Source	Reliability	Assertion
S1	1.0	P → Q
S2	0.8	P, P ∨ R
S3	0.6	P, S ∨ ¬P

From the principle (a) above, we can assign the following viable plausibility values:

Thesis	Plausibility
P	0.8
P → Q	1.0
P ∨ R	0.8
S ∨ ¬P	0.6

That is, P has a plausibility value of 0.8 since S2 and S3 vouch for it, and S2 is the most respectable source with a reliability value of 0.8.

(ii) Suppose that the following knowledge has been obtained:

Source	Reliability	Assertion
S1	0.8	P
S2	0.6	P → Q
S3	0.4	R, Q
S4	0.2	Q, R → Q

From (a) and (d) above, we can assign the following viable plausibility values:

Thesis	Plausibility
P	0.8
P → Q	0.6
R	0.4
Q	0.6
R → Q	0.6

That is, Q has value 0.6 since it follows from P and [P → Q] (with plausibility values of 0.8 and 0.6 respectively). Also, [R → Q] has value 0.6 since it follows from Q with plausibility 0.6. That is, Q ⊢ [R → Q] and since Q has plausibility of 0.6, [R → Q] must have a plausibility of at least 0.6.

(iii) Suppose that the following knowledge has been obtained:

Source	Reliability	Assertion
S1	0.75	P v Q,
S2	0.5	¬Q, ¬P
S3	0.2	Q

From the principles above, we can assign the following viable plausibility values:

Thesis	Plausibility
P v Q	0.75
¬P	0.5
¬Q	0.5
Q	0.5

That is, Q has a plausibility value of 0.5 since it follows from [P v Q] and ¬P which have plausibility values 0.75 and 0.5 respectively. Hence Q must have a plausibility value of at least the smaller of these two.

Augmenting consistent p-sets

If a p-set is consistent, there is nothing to prevent our augmenting it with one or more of its logical consequences since these may be regarded as reasonable inferences. For instance, consider example 1 above. The augmented p-set would be:

Thesis	Plausibility
P	0.8
P → Q	1.0
P v R	0.8
S v ¬P	0.6
Q	0.8
S	0.6

That is, we can add Q to the p-set, since it can be inferred from P and [P → Q]. Also we can add S since S can be inferred from P and [S v ¬P].

Note that in some cases, such augmentation of a p-set may require plausibility values to be recalculated. For example, suppose that we begin with the following plausibility values:

Thesis	Plausibility
P	0.8
P → Q	0.4
¬P v R	0.6
R → Q	0.6

Since P, [P → Q] ⊢ Q and P, [¬P v R], [R → Q] ⊢ Q we can augment this set with the following:

    Q   0.6

The value of 0.6 is the minimum of the plausibilities of P, [¬P ∨ R] and [R → Q], and this minimum is greater than the minimum of P and [P → Q].

However, this augmentation now requires us to recompute the plausibility for [P → Q], since Q ⊢ [P → Q]. Therefore, the adjusted plausibilities are:

    P   0.8
    P → Q   0.6
    ¬P ∨ R   0.6
    R → Q   0.6
    Q   0.6

We could augment this set further by adding assertions such as [P ∧ Q] with plausibility 0.6. In fact, if a p-set is consistent we can add to it all of its logical consequences, should we so wish.

Augmenting inconsistent p-sets
Consider the following situation:

Source	Reliability	Assertion
S1	0.75	P, ¬P → R
S2	0.5	¬P, P → Q

Initially we have the following viable plausibility assignment, which is compatible with Rescher's principles(a) to (f) above:

    P   0.75
    ¬P → R   0.75
    ¬P   0.5
    P → Q   0.5

However, if we augment this set with the assertions which can be inferred from consistent sub-sets of it, we arrive at the set:

    P
    ¬P → R
    ¬P
    P → Q
    P ∧ ¬P
    Q
    R
    P ∨ Q
    ¬P ∨ R
    (etc.)

Now, we do not really want all of these additions since, for example, P ∧ ¬P is obviously false.

Consequently, we have to be careful when augmenting an inconsistent p-set. Rescher proposes that two principles can be used:

(a) Do not augment the p-set with assertions which are logically or materially untenable. This is called the 'exclusion principle'.

(b) If some extension P is known to be untenable, then add ¬P to the p-set with a high plausibility value. This is called the 'cancellation principle'.

For example, consider the following materially inconsistent set of assertions:

Source	Reliability	Assertion
S1	0.8	P: he drowned and his body was never found
S2	0.6	Q: he joined the foreign legion
S3	0.5	R: he was done in by his wife who buried him somewhere

It would be quite wrong to simply augment this set with P ∧ Q, Q ∧ R, P ∧ R, or P ∧ Q ∧ R since these are 'materially untenable'. Using Rescher's rules above, we have two choices:

(a) Exclude P ∧ Q, P ∧ R, Q ∧ R and P ∧ Q ∧ R from the augmented set on the grounds of material untenability,

(b) Augment the p-set with these inferences but also add ¬[P ∧ Q], ¬[P ∧ R], ¬[Q ∧ R] and ¬[P ∧ Q ∧ R] with appropriately high plausibility values.

Maximal consistent sub-sets
Given that we have an inconsistent p-set, we can restore consistency in various ways by removing one or more assertions from it. For example, consider the following inconsistent p-set:

PS = {P ∨ Q
$\quad$ P → R
$\quad$ Q → R
$\quad$ ¬R $\quad$ }

We can restore consistency in the following ways:

(a) Remove ¬R $\qquad\qquad\qquad\qquad$ from PS.
(b) Remove P → R $\qquad\qquad\qquad$ from PS.
(c) Remove Q → R $\qquad\qquad\qquad$ from PS.
(d) Remove P ∨ Q $\qquad\qquad\qquad$ from PS.
(e) Remove ¬R and P → R $\qquad$ from PS.
(f) Remove ¬R and Q → R $\qquad$ from PS.
(g) Remove ¬R and P ∨ Q $\qquad$ from PS.
(h) Remove P → R and P ∨ Q $\quad$ from PS.
(etc.)

The alternatives (a) to (d) are the least disruptive ways of restoring consistency to PS. The resulting p-sets in these cases are called 'maximal consistent sub-sets' (MCS) of PS. The following are the only MCSs of PS:

    MCS1 = PS - {¬R}
    MCS2 = PS - {Q → R}
    MCS3 = PS - {P → R}
    MCS4 = PS - {P ∨ Q}

A sub-set PSi of a p-set PS is a maximal consistent sub-set of PS if:

(a)   PSi is a non-empty sub-set of S.
(b)   PSi is logically consistent.
(c)   No member of PS can be added to PSi without generating an inconsistency.

According to this definition, the following is *not* an MCS of PS above:

    PS - {¬R, P → R}

This is not an MCS, since either one of ¬R or P → R can be added to it without generating an inconsistency.

The 'plausibilistically preferred' MCSs are MCS2 and MCS4 since MCS1 and MCS3 both reject PS elements of high plausibility.

    MCS2 = PS - {Q → R} = {P ∨ Q, P → R, ¬R}
    MCS4 = PS - {P ∨ Q} = {P → R, Q → R, ¬R}

Since P → R and ¬R are present in both of these preferred MCSs, we can regard these assertions as being plausibilistically acceptable.

In addition, we can regard all logical consequences of the set of plausibilistically acceptable assertions as also being acceptable. That is, ¬P, which follows from P → R and ¬R, is also a plausibilistically acceptable assertion.

Therefore, we have a method for identifying the plausibilistically acceptable assertions and logical consequences of an inconsistent set of assertions obtained from sources of less than total reliability:

(a)   Augment the set PS with its logical consequences, taking into account the exclusion and cancellation principles.

(b)   Construct a viable plausibility assignment.

(c)   Identify the MCSs of PS.

(d)   Reject those MCSs which eliminate assertions of high plausibility. The remaining MCSs are called 'preferred MCSs'.

(e)   Identify all assertions common to all preferred MCSs. These are the plausibilistically acceptable assertions.

(f)   Use standard logical deductive methods to identify all logical consequences of the set of plausibilistically acceptable assertions.

Rescher has called this method of plausibility screening a 'plausibility tropic' method, because it 'likes' (i.e. it prefers to keep) assertions of high plausibility.

The plausibility tropic method is not the only method that could have been employed in screening. An alternative, which Rescher calls an 'implausibility phobic' method, identifies preferable MCSs as those which do not contain assertions of low plausibility. Rescher provides a persuasive argument favouring the plausibility tropic approach.

An example of the use of plausibility theory
Rescher has shown how plausibility theory can be of use in data processing with inconsistent data, in understanding of counterfactuals and in explaining inductive inference. It is beyond the scope of this book to discuss all of these uses. Consequently, we have chosen to give a further example, which is relevant to applications involving knowledge bases.

Suppose that we have the following p-set, PS:

Source	Reliability	Assertions
S1	1.0	$R \rightarrow S$, $S \rightarrow \neg P$
S2	0.8	S
S3	0.7	$\neg S$, $Q \vee S$
S4	0.5	$P \wedge Q$, $\neg P$, $Q \wedge R$
S5	0.3	$\neg Q \wedge R$

What can be inferred from this p-set?

We begin by assigning initial plausibility values:

(a)	$R \rightarrow S$	1.0
(b)	$S \rightarrow \neg P$	1.0
(c)	S	0.8
(d)	$\neg S$	0.7
(e)	$Q \vee S$	0.7
(f)	$P \wedge Q$	0.5
(g)	$\neg P$	0.5
(h)	$Q \wedge R$	0.5
(i)	$\neg Q \wedge R$	0.3

Now, since $S \vdash Q \vee S$, we must increase the plausibility value of $Q \vee S$ to 0.8. Also, since S and $S \rightarrow \neg P \vdash \neg P$, we must increase the plausibility value of $\neg P$ to 0.8.

Next we identify the MCSs of this p-set:

$$MCS1 = PS - \{\neg P, \neg S, \neg Q \wedge R, S \rightarrow \neg P\}$$
$$MCS2 = PS - \{\neg S, P \wedge Q, \neg Q \wedge R\}$$
$$MCS3 = PS - \{\neg S, P \wedge Q, Q \wedge R\}$$
$$MCS4 = PS - \{\neg P, S, \neg Q \wedge R, R \rightarrow S\}$$
$$MCS5 = PS - \{\neg P, S, \neg Q \wedge R, Q \wedge R\}$$
$$MCS6 = PS - \{S, P \wedge Q, \neg Q \wedge R, R \rightarrow S\}$$
$$MCS7 = PS - \{S, P \wedge Q, \neg Q \wedge R, Q \wedge R\}$$
$$MCS8 = PS - \{S, P \wedge Q, Q \wedge R, Q \vee S, R \rightarrow S\}$$

Since MCS1, MCS4, MCS6 and MCS8 all reject assertions of plausibility value 1.0, these MCSs can be ruled out. Therefore, the preferable MCSs are: MCS2, MCS3, MCS5 and MCS7. These reject assertions with the following plausibility values:

```
MCS2 : 0.7, 0.5, 0.3
MCS3 : 0.7, 0.5, 0.5
MCS5 : 0.8, 0.8, 0.3, 0.5
MCS7 : 0.8, 0.5, 0.3, 0.5
```

Therefore MCS2 and MCS3 are the 'most preferred' MCSs:

$$MCS2 = \{R \rightarrow S, \ S \rightarrow \neg P, \ S, \ Q \vee S, \ \neg P, \ Q \wedge R\}$$

$$MCS3 = \{R \rightarrow S, \ S \rightarrow \neg P, \ S, \ Q \vee S, \ \neg P, \ \neg Q \wedge R\}$$

Now we can identify the following plausibilistically acceptable set of assertions:

$$\{S, \ \neg P, \ S \rightarrow \neg P, \ R \rightarrow S, \ R, \ Q \vee S\}$$

which can be expressed axiomatically (concisely) as follows:

$$\{S, \ \neg P, \ R\}$$

That is, if we were to be given the p-set above, we could use plausibility theory to identify its plausibilistically acceptable consequences which we could then axiomatise (reduce to the smallest sub-set from which the original set can be derived) and put into the knowledge base.

The use of plausibility theory in this way may be regarded as a pre-processing stage which inconsistent sets of knowledge must go through before formal deductive methods can be applied to them.

7.8 CONCLUDING COMMENTS

Several theories and calculi which were developed for dealing with uncertain knowledge have been briefly described. In chapter 8 we show how some of these approaches can be used in expert systems.

Also in chapter 8, we describe a relatively new calculus for dealing with uncertainty. The calculus is embedded in a system called INFERNO (Quinlan, 1983) which is a flexible and 'cautious' system for dealing with uncertainty. It is cautious since it does not depend on assumptions about joint probability distributions of events, and its conclusions about the probability bounds of statements are provably correct consequences of the given knowledge.

8 Production Rule Based Systems

8.1 INTRODUCTION

8.1 INTRODUCTION

8.1.1 WHAT IS A PRODUCTION SYSTEM?

A production system consists of:

- a database
- a rule base
- a rule application module (which is sometimes called a rule interpreter)

The 'database' is used to store data about the problem in hand. For example, it may contain data about a particular patient whose disease is to be diagnosed.

The 'rule base' contains rules, which are sometimes called 'production rules', which represent general knowledge about the problem domain. For example, the rule base might contain rules which are used in the diagnosis of infectious diseases. Each rule consists of a condition part C and an action part A, and is of the form:

> *if* C *then* A

As example, consider the following naive medical rule:

> *If* the patient has red spots *and* fever *and* is of school age *then* the patient has chicken-pox.

Whether or not the condition part of a rule is satisfied can be established by reference to the database and/or by questioning the user of the production system. The action part of a rule can denote different things. For example, it can denote a command to add something to the database about the problem in hand, to suggest undertaking a task to the user such as asking the patient a question, and so on.

The 'rule application module' selects and applies rules which may yield changes and/or additions to the database. In classical production systems the rule application module uses a data-driven approach whereby it cycles through the rules looking for one whose condition part is satisfied by the database. When it finds such a rule, it invokes the action

421

part. In many cases, the action results in changes to the database which enable other rules. The rule application module continues cycling until either (i) the problem is solved (the goal is achieved), or (ii) a state is reached where no more rules may be invoked.

An example production system

Consider a car fault diagnosis system which is implemented as a production system containing the following rules:

R1 : *if* the engine does not turn *and* the battery is not flat *then* ask the user to test the starter motor

R2 : *if* there is no spark *then* ask the user to check the points

R3 : *if* the engine turns *and* does not start *then* ask the user to check the spark

R4 : *if* the engine does not turn *then* ask the user to check the battery

R5 : *if* the battery is flat *then* ask the user to charge the battery *and* exit

.
.
.
.

Rn

Suppose that the rule application module cycles through the rules looking for one whose condition part is satisfied by the database. When it finds such a rule, it executes the action part. If the action part contains a statement of the form 'ask the user to check ....', then the rule application module causes an appropriate message to be displayed to the user requesting the check to be carried out and the results to be entered into the database.

As example of the use of the system, suppose that the database contains the following single statement relevant to a particular problem:

'the engine does not turn'

The rule application module cycles through the rules, recognises that the condition part of rule R4 is satisfied by the database and executes the action part of R4 by requesting the operator to check the battery. Suppose that the battery is not flat and a statement of this fact is entered into the database. The database will now contain the statements:

the engine does not turn
the battery is not flat

Suppose that the rule application module continues by looking at rules R5 to Rn and finds no rule whose condition part is satisfied by the database. It returns to R1 to begin a new cycle through the rules. R1 is satisfied; therefore the user is asked to test the starter motor and to enter the results of the test into the database. The process continues until either (i) a rule with an 'exit' is executed or (ii) the database remains unchanged throughout one complete cycle.

8.1.2 ORIGINS IN GENERAL PROBLEM-SOLVING SYSTEMS AND USE IN EXPERT SYSTEMS

The rule based methodology was originally proposed by Post (1943) and has since been used in various applications. A similar approach is used in the specification of grammars and the construction of parsers for programming languages (refer back to chapter 2 for an example of a grammar specified as a set of production rules).

In the late sixties and early seventies, the rule based approach was beginning to be used in the construction of expert systems such as DENDRAL (Buchanan et al, 1969) and MYCIN (Shortliffe, 1976), and in the HEARSAY speech recognition system (Lesser et al, 1975). Since then, the rule based approach has been used extensively in the construction of 'intelligent' systems.

In the following sections, the rule based approach is described in more detail and a brief description given of its use in expert systems.

8.2 APPROACHES TO PROBLEM-SOLVING

There are many ways in which rule application modules can select and apply rules. The simplest type act as follows:

(a) Evaluate the conditions in all rules with respect to the current database state, thereby identifying a set of applicable rules.

(b) If there are no applicable rules then terminate with failure, else arbitrarily choose one of the applicable rules and execute its action part.

(c) If the goal is achieved then terminate with success, else return to (a).

Such an approach is said to be 'non-deterministic' due to the arbitrary selection of an applicable rule in step (b). The approach is also said to be 'data-driven' since the database state is the sole identifier of applicable rules.

An alternative approach to problem-solving is one in which the system starts with the goal and works back through 'sub-goals' to show how the goal state follows from the original state. This approach, in which the system focuses its attention by only considering rules which are relevant to the problem in hand, is said to be 'goal-driven'.

In this section the data-driven and goal-driven approaches will be described in more detail. We also describe a mixed method which alternates between data-driven and goal-driven approaches until the goal is achieved or failure is identified.

8.2.1 THE DATA-DRIVEN APPROACH

The data-driven approach is also known as the 'bottom-up', 'forward-chaining' or 'antecedent reasoning' approach. (This approach was discussed with respect to theorem-proving in chapter 4, where it was referred to as the 'bottom-up' approach.)

In this method, rules are applicable only if their condition part is satisfied by the database. In using this method, one begins by entering data about the current problem into the database. The following recursive procedure written in pseudo-Pascal outlines the structure of a simple rule application module which is based on the data-driven approach:

```
procedure generate;
begin
   identify the set S of applicable rules;
   while S is non-empty
     do begin
        select a rule R from S;
        apply R;
        if the problem is solved by the application of R
          then indicate SUCCESS
          else call 'generate' recursively
        remove R from S and undo the effect of applying R
     end
end;
```

The procedure 'generate' generates new facts from the database by using the rules. These new facts are then added to the database.

We can illustrate how the procedure works with the following trivial example. Suppose that we have a production system which contains the following rules:

```
R1 : if X is divisible by 12 then X is divisible by  6
R2 : if X is divisible by 20 then X is divisible by 10
R3 : if X is divisible by  6 then X is divisible by  2
R4 : if X is divisible by 10 then X is divisible by  5
```

Suppose, also, that we know that some number N is divisible by 12 and by 20, and that the problem is to determine if N is divisible by 5. We begin by entering the following data into the database:

```
N is divisible by 12
N is divisible by 20
```

Execution of the procedure 'generate' above would begin by identifying the following set of applicable rules:

```
S = {R1, R2}
```

The condition parts of these rules are satisfied by the database if the substitution of N for X is made.

Suppose that the system now selects the first rule in S and applies it. This generates the new data that 'N is divisible by 6'. This is obtained by propagating the substitution 'N for X' throughout R1. This data is entered into the database giving the new state:

424

N is divisible by 12
N is divisible by 20
N is divisible by 6

The problem has not been solved by the application of R1; therefore the procedure 'generate' is called recursively. Execution of this recursive call commences by identifying the following set of applicable rules:

S' = {R2, R3}

R1 is not included in S' because its application would not change the current state of the database.

R2 would now be selected and applied giving the following database state:

N is divisible by 12
N is divisible by 20
N is divisible by 6
N is divisible by 10

The problem has still not been solved; therefore another recursive call of the procedure is made. This recursive call commences by identifying the following set of applicable rules:

S" = {R3, R4}

R1 and R2 are not in S" because they are not applicable. R3 is selected and applied giving the database state:

N is divisible by 12
N is divisible by 20
N is divisible by 6
N is divisible by 10
N is divisible by 2

The problem has still not been solved; therefore the procedure 'generate' is called recursively once again and commences by identifying the following set of applicable rules:

S''' = {R4}

R4 is the only applicable rule; therefore it is selected and applied, giving a solution to the problem. A trace of how this solution was achieved lists the order in which rules were used:

R1, R2, R3, R4

Note, however, that the process does not terminate here. The system finishes the last recursive call by undoing the effect of R4, i.e. it removes 'N is divisible by 5' from the database, and then returns to the previous call which continues as follows:

• R3 is removed from S"

- the effect of R3 is undone, i.e. 'N is divisible by 2' is removed from the database
- another pass through the while loop is embarked upon
- R4 is selected from S" and applied

Another solution is obtained. A trace of the rules used is:

    R1, R2, R4

The process has still not finished. The effect of R4 is undone, and since S" is empty the recursive call terminates. This brings us back to the call of the procedure in which S' = {R2, R3}. The effect of R2 is now undone, giving the database state:

    N is divisible by 12
    N is divisible by 20
    N is divisible by 6

R2 is removed from S' giving S' = {R3}. Another pass through the while loop is embarked upon: R3 is selected and applied giving the database state:

    N is divisible by 12
    N is divisible by 20
    N is divisible by 6
    N is divisible by 2

Application of R3 does not result in a solution; therefore the procedure is called recursively. This recursive call commences by identifying a set of applicable rules:

    S"" = {R2}

R2 is the only applicable rule; therefore it is selected and applied, giving a database state:

    N is divisible by 12
    N is divisible by 20
    N is divisible by 6
    N is divisible by 2
    N is divisible by 10

Application of R2 does not result in a solution; therefore the procedure is called again. This recursive call commences by identifying a set of applicable rules:

    S""" = {R4}

Selection and application of R4 results in a solution. A trace of rules used in this solution is:

    R1, R3, R2, R4

The process continues until all of the ways in which the solution can be achieved have been established.

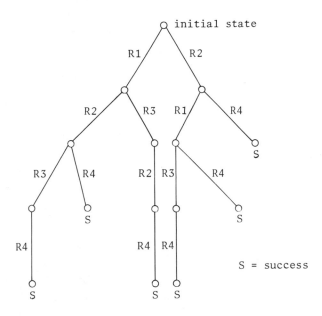

Figure 8.1

The whole 'search space' for the problem can be depicted by a tree
where each branch indicates an order in which applicable rules are
selected and applied (fig. 8.1). Essentially, this tree shows that:

(a)   In the initial state only rules R1 and R2 are applicable.

(b)   If R1 is the only rule that has been applied, then R2 and R3
      are the only rules which are applicable.

(c)   If R1, R2 and R3 have been applied, then R4 is the only
      applicable rule and its application gives a solution.

(etc.)

In this trivial example, there would appear to be little advantage in
identifying all ways in which a solution might be obtained. However,
in other applications the trace of rules might be used as a plan to
achieve a goal in an application area which is being modelled by the
production system. In such a case it might be useful to identify the
shortest path from initial state to goal. (Such an application might
be used in scheduling problems, for example.)

In other cases, there may be more than one goal, and it might then be
necessary to search the whole problem space.

Advantages of the data-driven approach include (i) its simplicity and
(ii) the fact that it can be used to provide all solutions to a given
problem.

A disadvantage of the data-driven approach is that the behaviour of the
system, in attempting to solve a problem, can be inefficient and can

427

also appear to be aimless since some of the rules which are executed could be unrelated to the problem in hand.

8.2.2 THE GOAL-DRIVEN APPROACH

The goal-driven approach is also known as the 'top-down', 'backward-chaining' or 'consequent reasoning' approach.

In the goal-driven approach, the system focuses its attention by only considering rules that are relevant to the problem in hand. In this approach, the user begins by specifying a goal by stating an expression E whose truth value is to be determined. For example, the expression might be 'N is divisible by 5'. The objective of the system would then be to establish the truth of this expression.

The following function, written in pseudo-Pascal, outlines the structure of a simple rule application module which uses the goal-driven approach:

```
function validate (X : expression) : boolean;
  var result : boolean;
  begin
    result : = false;
    scan the rule base to identify the set of applicable rules S
      which have X on the right-hand side;
    if S is empty
      then ask the user for some rules to add to S;
    while (result = false) and (S is non-empty)
      do begin
        select and remove a rule R from S;
        C : = the condition part of R;
        if C is true in the database
          then result : = true
          else if C is false in the database
            then do nothing
            else if validate (C) is true
              then result : = true
      end;
    validate : = result
  end;
```

In order to start the process off, the user asks for the truth value of 'validate (E)', where E is an expression such as 'N is divisible by 5'. The first thing that the system does is identify all of the rules which have E on the right-hand side assuming appropriate substitutions are made. These are rules which might be able to establish the truth of E and are the 'applicable' rules in this approach. If no such rules exist, the system asks the user to provide some. If there is more than one rule, the system selects one.

When a rule R is selected, its left-hand side (i.e. the condition part) C is checked against the database. If C is true in the database (with appropriate substitutions), then this establishes the truth of E and the process can terminate with success. If C is false in the database, then R cannot be used to establish the truth of E and another rule is selected from S. If C is unknown (i.e. it is neither true nor false

428

with respect to the database), then it is referred to as a 'sub-goal' and an attempt to establish its truth value is made by calling the function validate recursively with C as parameter. If validate (C) is true, then the rule R is applicable, the truth of E is established, and the process can terminate with success. If validate (C) is false, then another rule is selected from S. Thus, the process works back from the goal trying to attain sub-goals which can themselves establish the goal.

As example of the goal-driven approach, consider a production system with rules R1 to R4 as described in sub-section 8.2.1 together with a database containing the statements 'N is divisible by 12' and 'N is divisible by 20'.

Suppose that we want to determine if N is divisible by 5. We begin by calling validate (N is divisible by 5). Execution of the function call begins by scanning the rule base, giving:

S = {R4}

That is, R4 is the only rule with 'X is divisible by 5' on the right-hand side. (Note that the right-hand side of R4 can be made equivalent to the goal expression by the substitution of N for X.)

The process continues by selecting R4 and generating the sub-goal 'N is divisible by 10' by substituting N for X in the condition part of R4. Since 'N' is divisible by 20' is neither true nor false in the database, the function validate is called recursively with 'N is divisible by 10' as parameter. This recursive call begins by identifying the following set of rules:

S' = {R2}

R2 is included in this set since it has 'X is divisible by 10' on its right-hand side. The process continues by selecting R2 and generating the new sub-goal (N is divisible by 20). Since (N is divisible by 20) is true in the database, the recursive call terminates with validate (N is divisible by 10) = true. Thus, the initial call of validate can now terminate with value true.

Note that, in general, goal-driven systems query the user as well as the database when determining the truth of a sub-goal. Thus, the user need not enter all of the data at hand initially (as was the case in our example), but may wait until the system requests data. For example, in the above, instead of entering (N is divisible by 12) and (N is divisible by 20) into the database at the beginning, the user could wait until the system has (N is divisible by 12) or (N is divisible by 20) as a sub-goal. The goal-driven approach may also be depicted graphically as shown in the tree on page 430.

The function 'validate' which we have given as example terminates when a sub-goal is found to be true. However, if all of the ways in which E can be established are required, this can be achieved by changing the while loop control condition from ((result = false) and (S is non-empty)) to (S is non-empty).

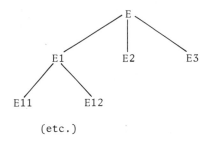

hypothesis to be validated

sub-goals each of which
can establish E

sub-sub-goals each of which
can establish a sub-goal

Note that the function 'validate' described above is simplistic in that
it assumes that the condition parts of rules consist of single statements such as 'X is divisible by 12'.   In many applications, the conditions will be compound expressions such as that in the following rule:

> *if* C1 *and* C2 *and* C3 *then* A

The function validate would have to be modified to accommodate this
kind of rule.   The changes required would be:

(a) Change   'if C is false in the database'
        to   'if (C1 is false) or (C2 is false) or (C3 is false)'.

(b) Change   'if validate (C) is true'
        to   'if (validate (C1) is true)
                               and (validate (C2) is true)
                               and (validate (C3) is true)'.

The main advantage of the goal-driven approach is that it does not seek
data and does not apply rules which are unrelated to the problem in
hand.

The goal-driven approach is the method of choice if a production system
is being used to check out a particular hypothesis (e.g. that N is divisible by 5).   However, it may also be used to check every possible
hypothesis, thereby providing all answers as can be done using a data-
driven approach.

8.2.3 MIXED METHODS
Data-driven and goal-driven approaches can be combined in various ways.
The following procedure outlines one such combination:

```
procedure mixed-method;
  begin
    repeat
      let user enter data into the database;
      call procedure 'generate' to generate new facts which are
          added to the database;
      call 'select-hypothesis' to select a goal statement E;
      call 'validate (E)';
    until the problem is solved
  end;
```

The function 'select-hypothesis' uses the facts which are generated by the preceding step to select a goal statement which the system then tries to validate.

8.3 SEARCH STRATEGIES USED IN PROBLEM-SOLVING

The data-driven and goal-driven approaches may both be regarded as attempts to find a path linking the initial problem state to the goal state. In the data-driven approach the system searches for a path by identifying sets of applicable rules whose condition parts are satisfied by the database, and selecting and applying rules from these sets. In the goal-driven approach the system searches for a path by identifying sets of applicable rules with some given right-hand side and selecting rules from these sets as sub-goals which it then attempts to establish.

In the data-driven approach the search moves from the initial problem state to the goal. In the goal-driven approach the search moves in the opposite direction. In both cases the system has to make decisions which have not yet been considered in any detail. For example, in both cases the system has to decide which rule to select from the set of applicable rules at each stage. This decision is determined by what is generally called a 'conflict resolution strategy', which is used by a scheduler. Other decisions involve considerations of how 'backtracking' should be employed, and the order in which the search space should be explored: 'depth-first', 'breadth-first' or in an order determined by some rules of thumb called 'heuristics'.

In this section, these characteristics of the search strategy will be discussed in more detail.

8.3.1 THE CONFLICT RESOLUTION STRATEGY

The way in which a rule is selected from a set of applicable rules is called the 'conflict resolution strategy'. Examples of such strategies include those based on one or more of the following principles:

(a) Select rules arbitrarily.
(b) Select a different rule in successive stages.
(c) Select the first applicable rule identified.
(d) Rules are given values which are used to determine which one to select.

8.3.2 BACKTRACKING

If a rule R is selected from a set S of applicable rules and is used (i.e. in the data-driven approach it is executed and in the goal-driven approach it is used as a sub-goal), then one of two situations might arise after one or more stages:

(a) The system reaches a dead end, i.e. it gets to a stage where no new applicable rules can be identified.

(b) A path is established linking the initial problem state to the goal.

If (a) occurs, then in many applications it would be useful to be able to 'backtrack' to the set S, possibly undoing the effects of selecting

R, and then to select another rule from S and use that rule in an attempt to identify a path.

If (b) occurs *and we are only interested in one solution*, then the process can terminate with success. However, if we are interested in more than one solution it would be useful to be able to backtrack in the manner described above.

Note that if the conflict resolution strategy works by selecting a single rule from a set of applicable rules and discards the rest, then no backtracking can take place. In this case, instead of acting to guide the search for a solution, the conflict resolution strategy determines the solution or non-solution of the problem.

8.3.3 DEPTH-FIRST / BREADTH-FIRST / HEURISTIC SEARCH

Depth-first search
The data-driven procedure 'generate' and the simplistic goal-driven function 'validate' which have been outlined may both be categorised as 'depth-first' search methods. They are so called because they traverse their respective problem-space trees in a depth-first manner. That is, they start at the root of the problem-space tree and work down the leftmost branch to the end-node (either success or failure) before they embark on any other branch. For example, given the problem-space tree in fig. 8.2, they would traverse the tree in the order indicated by the directed dotted line. In the case of the data-driven procedure 'generate', each branch of the tree depicts the application of a rule. In the goal-driven function 'validate', each branch represents a sub-goal. However, in both processes the search is depth-first.

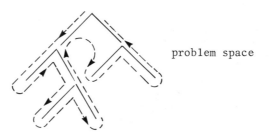

problem space

Figure 8.2 A depth-first search

There are two disadvantages of depth-first search:

(a)   In depth-first search we could pursue an infinite branch indefinitely and never backup to the rest of the tree. This would occur if the rule base inadvertently contained the following rule and we were using the function validate:

if N is divisible by 5 then N is divisible by 5

(b)   The depth-first search cannot guarantee to identify the shortest path to the solution before other longer paths have been followed. In depth-first search we may find a solution on one branch, but a shorter path to the solution may exist in part of the tree which has not yet been searched. This occurred in the example given to illustrate the use of the procedure generate: the first solution found had the following path of rule applications R1, R2, R3, R4. In fact, in our example, the shortest solution path R2, R4 would be the last path to be found.

An advantage of depth-first search is the simplicity with which it can be implemented. Another advantage is that it requires less memory than the alternative, breadth-first search.

Breadth-first search

In 'breadth-first' search, all of the nodes in the problem-space tree at depth 1 are developed first, then all of the nodes at depth 2 are developed and so on. For example, given the tree in fig. 8.3, the nodes would be developed in the order indicated by the node numbers.

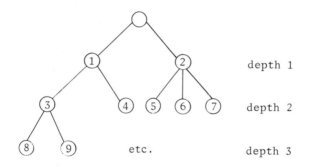

Figure 8.3 A breadth-first search

There are two characteristics of breadth-first search:

(a) All nodes will eventually be searched, given enough resources, even though one of the branches may be infinite.

(b) The first solution found will be the (or one of the) solution(s) with the shortest path.

Thus, breadth-first search overcomes the problems associated with depth-first search. However, the method can have huge overheads: at any stage, all nodes to the left *and* all nodes above the node being developed must be memorised. In our example illustrating the use of the generate procedure, we would have to store a database state and a list of applicable rules for each node that was developed if we were wanting to identify all ways in which the truth of (N is divisible by 5) could be established.

Heuristic search

Depth-first and breadth-first search both search the problem-space tree without regard to the particular problem being solved. Humans do not solve problems in this way. Generally, they use metarules to determine which node to develop next. As example, in a bottom-up search the rules might be given weightings indicating their proven usefulness for

433

past problems. A metarule might then be used which states that if a
choice exists, the rule with the highest score should be applied. The
resulting search will be neither depth-first nor breadth-first. Such
a search is called a 'heuristic' search.

For example, consider the example which was presented to illustrate the
use of the data-driven approach. Suppose the rules were given the following weightings:

    R1   7
    R2 10
    R3   5
    R4 20

A heuristic data-driven approach would develop the search tree in the
order indicated by the node numbers in the tree in fig. 8.4.

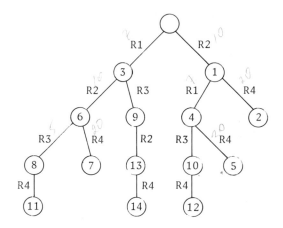

Figure 8.4   A heuristic search

That is, in the first step R1 and R2 would be the only applicable rules.
Since R2 has a higher weight than R1, it is applied first. At the next
step either **R1** or R4 can be applied. R1 is left over from the first
step and R4 was made applicable by application of rule R2. Since R4
has a higher weight than R1, it is applied. Since a solution was found,
R1 is the only rule which can now be applied, hence node numbers 3 and
4, and so on.

In order to keep track of nodes which are 'open', i.e. nodes which can
be developed, such nodes are generally kept on a list called an
'agenda'. The next node to be developed is always the one associated
with the highest weight.

Heuristic search and agendas can also be used with goal-driven methods.
In such cases the weight of a rule might be some value indicating the
expected cost or difficulty in achieving a sub-goal. The next node to
be developed is always the one with the lowest weight.

The conflict resolution strategy, backtracking strategy and order of search space development collectively determine the 'search strategy' employed to solve a problem. The search strategy controls the way in which the problem is solved.

8.3.4 THE EXPLICIT REPRESENTATION OF CONTROL KNOWLEDGE

In the examples which have been given, and in many of the systems based on production rules, the search strategy is coded as a procedure or function and the control knowledge is embedded in the code. There are two disadvantages of this approach:

(a) No particular mixture of data-driven, goal-driven, depth-first, breadth-first or heuristic search strategy is ideal for every problem. Different approaches are needed for different problems.

(b) Because the control knowledge is embedded in code, the system cannot explain its problem-solving strategy; neither can the user easily modify the strategy for a particular problem.

Consequently, there are good reasons for making control knowledge explicit. Over the last few years, various researchers have directed their attention to this problem; for example, Davis et al (1977) and Georgeff (1982).

Davis has represented certain types of heuristic search strategy knowledge as metarules. An example of such a metarule is:

if the infection is pelvic abscess
   and
   there are rule⌂ which mention enterobacteriacea in their premises
   and
   there are rules which mention gram-pos-rods in their premise
   then there is suggestive evidence (0.4) that the former rules
                                should be applied before the latter.

Such metarules, which are invoked as part of the conflict resolution strategy, can capture and implement strategic knowledge about a domain. However, as pointed out by Clancey (1983), metarules such as the one above have the disadvantage that they leave out the domain-dependent and domain-independent strategic principles that underly them. For example, the implicit strategic domain-dependent principle which underlies the rule above is that the most frequent causes of a disorder should be considered first. The implicit domain-independent principle which underlies the rule above is that the most 'useful' rule should be applied first. Clancey discusses ways in which domain-specific knowledge can be related to domain-independent strategies to produce more meaningful metarules.

Georgeff (1982) has proposed a general production system architecture that allows control knowledge to be directly represented using a control language. The architecture, which Georgeff calls a 'controlled production system', is based on the explicit specification of constraints on rule invocation. In Georgeff's scheme, control knowledge is represented by specifying a language whose set of wffs is the set of all allowable sequences of rules. Georgeff calls this language a 'control language'. A sequence of rule applications (i.e. a branch in the problem-space tree) is only allowed to be searched if the production rule sequence is a wff of the control language.

For example, consider a production system with rules R1 to R7. Suppose that the control language were defined by the following regular expression:

R1(R2R3R4)*R5R6R7

where the asterisk indicates repetition of the bracketed group. The only allowed rule sequences would be: R1, followed by the sequence R2R3R4 repeated an arbitrary number of times, followed by the sequence R5R6R7.

The restriction imposed by the control language can be invoked either when the set of applicable rules is being identified or as part of the conflict resolution strategy.

Ideally, search strategy control knowledge should be encoded explicitly at two levels:

    domain-independent metarules
    domain-specific metarules

Domain-independent metarules might include rules such as:

    if no domain-specific metarules exist and memory space is limited
       then
           use depth-first search.

CENTAUR (Aikins, 1980) is an example of a general purpose expert system in which control knowledge is represented explicitly.

8.4 RULE BASED EXPERT SYSTEMS

8.4.1 WHAT IS AN EXPERT SYSTEM?

An expert system is a system which is capable of carrying out a task generally regarded as being difficult and requiring some degree of human expertise.

Many of the expert systems which have been developed over the last fifteen years have been implemented as production rule based systems. One reason for this is that certain types of expert knowledge can be coded quite naturally as sets of rules.

We begin by classifying some of the better known expert systems. This may give the reader a feel for the range of problems which is being tackled by such systems.

Medical applications

MYCIN (Shortliffe, 1976) is a system which is capable of diagnosing infectious diseases and of selecting antibiotic therapy for bacteremia.

VM (Fagan et al, 1979) is a system which monitors a patient using a mechanical breathing device after surgery.

AI/COAG (Lindberg et al, 1981) is a system used for consultation about human hemostasis disorders.

CASNET (Weiss and Kulikowski, 1979) is a system used for medical decision making. It is based on production rules and semantic nets (see later).

INTERNIST (Pople, 1977) is a system used for medical consultation.

MDX (Chandrasekaran et al, 1979) is a system used for medical diagnosis. It is based on a hierarchy of experts (see later section on 'blackboard architectures').

KMS (Reggia et al, 1980) is an intelligent textbook of neurology.

PUFF (Kunz et al, 1978) is a system which interprets pulmonary function test results.

Mineral prospecting
PROSPECTOR (Hart et al, 1978 and Duda et al, 1979) is a system which provides advice on mineral exploration.

Mass spectroscopy
DENDRAL (Buchanan and Feigenbaum, 1978 and Buchanan et al, 1969).

Planning DNA experiments
MOLGEN (Martin et al, 1977) is a system used for planning experiments in molecular genetics.

Mathematical formula manipulation
MACSYMA (Moses, 1971) is a system used for the manipulation of mathematical formulas.

Speech recognition
HEARSAY-II (Erman et al, 1980) is a system which interprets spoken requests to a database.

Fault diagnosis
DART (Bennet and Hollander, 1981) is an expert system for computer fault diagnosis.

Legal consultancy
ELI (Leith, 1983) is a system which operates in the domain of legislation.

Computer configuration
R1 (McDermott, 1980) is a system which configures DEC VAX computer systems.

It is beyond the scope of this discussion to consider any of these systems in detail. However, work on such systems has identified several problems associated with the use of the rule based approach, and in some cases has provided partial solutions to these problems. In particular, (i) work on expert systems has identified some additional methods for dealing with large search spaces, (ii) the issue of representing and manipulating uncertainties was raised by Shortliffe while

437

working on the MYCIN system and (iii) the problem of providing users with explanations of how and why a system behaves in a particular way when solving a given problem has received a good deal of attention over the last few years by people working in the area. These and other issues are discussed in more detail in the following sub-sections.

8.4.2 TYPES OF TASK CARRIED OUT BY EXPERT SYSTEMS
Most expert tasks fall into one or other of the following categories:

Design   which involves the specification of a system or object such that the system or object satisfies some given set of requirements and can be built using some given set of resources.

Diagnosis   which involves fault-finding in a system given some set of symptoms.

Interpretation   which involves the analysis of data to determine its meaning.

Monitoring   which involves the continuous analysis of signals and the invocation of actions and/or alarms as appropriate.

Planning   which involves the creation of a plan of actions to achieve a given goal.

Nearly all expert tasks involve large search spaces, most involve reasoning with uncertain knowledge, and some involve reasoning with time-varying data. In the following three sub-sections, these problems are discussed in more detail and methods which have been developed to solve them are described.

8.4.3 ACCOMMODATING UNCERTAINTY
In many of the domains in which expert systems are applied, the knowledge available may be unreliable, incomplete, imprecise, vague and/or inconsistent. Various methodologies have been developed to reason with such knowledge. For example:

- probability theory
- certainty theory
- the Dempster-Schafer theory of evidence
- possibility theory/fuzzy logic
- incidence calculus
- plausibility theory

These methodologies were described in chapter 7. However, in chapter 7 we only gave a brief description of how the methodologies might be used to process uncertain knowledge. In this section, we extend that discussion and, in particular, consider how uncertain knowledge is accommodated in expert systems. Much of the following is derived from a paper by Quinlan (1983) in which a new approach (described later) is proposed. We begin by reviewing the various ways in which the uncertainty of a statement may be represented.

Representing uncertainty of statements

(a) Single value
The simplest method is to represent the uncertainty of a statement by a single value. In probability theory, this value stands for the probability of the statement being true. Initially, the value stands for the *a priori* probability. Subsequently, the value is updated, using Bayesian rules, in the light of evidence relevant to the statement. This is the method used in the PROSPECTOR expert system.

As mentioned in chapter 7, there are two shortcomings to this approach:

(i) The single value tells us nothing about its precision.

(ii) This single value combines evidence for and against a statement without indicating how much there is of each.

Furthermore, if the value is a true probability measure, three further problems arise:

(iii) It is not always possible to obtain accurate *a priori* probabilities.

(iv) Whenever a new hypothesis is added, many existing *a priori* probabilities are likely to require adjustment.

(v) Dependencies (correlations) between statements must be known.

(b) Two values: measure of belief and disbelief
An alternative approach is to maintain two separate values for each statement: $MB(X/A)$ is a probability-like measure of belief in X given A, and $MD(X/A)$ is a similar value for disbelief in X given A. These two values are combined into a single assessment of X given A, called the certainty measure $C(X/A)$. This is the approach underlying certainty theory which was developed for use in the MYCIN expert system.

This approach also has the shortcoming (i) above. However, (ii) is overcome since the existence of evidence for and against the statement is explicit.

(c) Use of sub-intervals
A third approach is to represent the probability of a statement by a sub-interval $[\ell(X), u(X)]$ of the interval $[0, 1]$. The sub-interval indicates that the probability of X lies between $\ell(X)$ and $u(X)$. The precision of the knowledge of the probability of X is explicit in this approach. This is the method used in the Dempster-Schafer theory of evidence.

Implication networks
An implication network is a directed graph in which nodes represent statements and arcs represent relationships between statements. An example of an implication network is given in fig. 8.5. Arcs between nodes are of two types: (i) those representing antecedent-consequent implications between statements, i.e. 'if-then' links, and (ii) those which are used to indicate that a statement is used as a component of a more complex statement. We shall call the former 'implication links' and the latter 'composition links'.

Implication networks can be used to indicate the relationships between evidence, production rules and hypotheses in an expert system. For example, the implication network in fig. 8.5 corresponds to the following set of production rules:

> *if* A AND B *then* X
> *if* X AND NOT C *then* Y
> *if* D *then* Y
> *if* Y AND E *then* Z

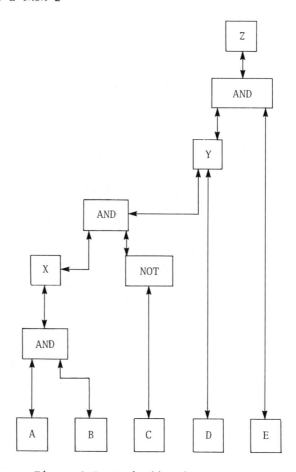

Figure 8.5 An implication network

Different values are associated with nodes and implication links depending on which theory (i.e. probability theory, certainty theory, etc.) is being used in the particular expert system in question. For example, if probability theory is being used, the values associated with nodes represent probabilities and the values associated with implication links represent LN and LS values (refer back to chapter 7). If certainty theory is being used, then two values are associated with each node, one representing measures of belief and the other of disbelief, and a single value is associated with an implication link representing a certainty factor (refer back to chapter 7).

Propagation of uncertainties in implication networks
The way in which uncertainty values are propagated through an implication network also depends on the theory which is being used:

(a) Probability theory
If the antecedent statement is definitely true, then the odds of the consequent are multiplied by the LS value of the link and the result is used to calculate the updated probability of the consequent. If the antecedent is definitely false, then the odds of the consequent are multiplied by the LN value of the link and the result is used to calculate the updated probability of the consequent (refer back to chapter 7 for a more detailed discussion). If the antecedent has some intermediate probability p, then the odds of the consequent are multiplied by some interpolated value determined by p together with the LS, LN values. Various interpolation schemes are discussed by Duda et al (1979).

A problem arises when a node is the consequent of more than one implication link; for example, node Y in fig. 8.5. In such cases, correlation factors may need to be used (as discussed in chapter 7).

(b) Certainty theory
As mentioned in chapter 7, certainty theory was developed for use in the MYCIN expert system. MYCIN was required to accommodate rules such as 'A suggests B' or 'C and D tend to rule out E'. Certainty factors are associated with MYCIN rules as, for example, in the following:

> *If* (i) the stain of the organism is gram-positive, and
> (ii) the morphology of the organism is coccus, and
> (iii) the growth conformation of the organism is clumps,
>
> *then* there is suggestive evidence (0.7) that the organism is
> staphylococcus.

The certainty value of 0.7 indicates that the evidence strongly suggests (0.7 out of 1.0) the conclusion, but not with certainty.

As mentioned earlier, evidence for a hypothesis is collected separately from that against it. The certainty of a hypothesis at any time (i.e. the certainty measure) is the algebraic sum of the measures of belief and disbelief in that hypothesis.

The calculation of certainty values of consequents of uncertain rules, when applied to uncertain antecedents, is carried out as described in chapter 7. In MYCIN, rules are only applied if the certainty value of the antecedent exceeds an empirical threshold of 0.2.

The certainty values of complex statements involving boolean operators is calculated as described below.

(c) Calculating the probability/certainty values of complex statements
Many expert systems, whether based on probability theory or certainty theory, use the following 'fuzzy' formulas for calculating values of combinations of statements:

```
cp(A OR B)  = max{cp(A), cp(B)}
cp(A AND B) = min{cp(A), cp(B)}
```

where cp stands for 'certainty or probability' depending on which
theory is being used.

Use of possibility theory/fuzzy logic

A difficulty associated with all of the methods described so far is
that they do not accommodate the notion of 'extent'. In chapter 7, we
gave an example to illustrate the difference between extent and certainty (as discussed so far): when asked the question 'how certain are
you that you suffer from stress?', many people would answer 'a little',
when they really mean that they are absolutely certain they suffer from
a little stress. Degree of belief in an assertion is being confused
with extent along a subjective scale. Possibility theory/fuzzy logic,
as described in chapters 6 and 7, accommodates the notion of extent
along scales, where the degree of extent is related to 'vagueness'.
Although this theory has not yet been used in many expert systems, the
distinction between uncertainty due to randomness and uncertainty due
to vagueness is now well accepted. It is likely that many of the
expert systems which will be built in the future will use some, if not
all, of the results of possibility theory/fuzzy logic.

Use of plausibility theory

Plausibility theory also has a role to play in expert systems due to
the fact that not all sources of knowledge are 100% reliable. One of
the methods described in chapter 7 allows plausible consequences to be
deduced from *inconsistent* sets of assertions which have been obtained
from sources of less than total reliability. Such techniques can be
used to pre-process knowledge before it is used by an expert system.

INFERNO

This sub-section concludes with a description of a relatively new calculus for dealing with uncertainty in expert systems. This calculus
is embedded in a system called INFERNO (Quinlan, 1983). The development
of INFERNO was motivated by several factors, including the following:

(a) Most of the methods for dealing with uncertainty in expert systems
are based on assumptions concerning the dependence/independence of the
probability distributions of statements (statements of evidence or
hypotheses). In many applications these assumptions are unjustified.
A better approach would be to allow users to state, for example, that
two statements are independent when such independence is known.

(b) In most systems the user is only allowed to enter probability
values or certainty measures for 'evidence' statements. The system
then calculates values for the 'conclusion' or 'hypothesis' statements.
A better approach would be to allow the user to enter values for any
statement (i.e. for any node in the implication network) and to observe
the consequences for the system as a whole. That is, it should be
possible to propagate uncertainties in all directions from a node, not
just towards a goal. For example, if values for A and B are known, the
system should be able to deduce a value for (A AND B). Also, if values
for (A OR B) and NOT A are known, the system should be able to deduce a
value for B.

(c) Most systems do not have a well-defined method for dealing with inconsistency. Ideally, systems should be able to detect inconsistency, signal to the user that an inconsistency has occurred and suggest ways in which consistency may be restored. Note that we have already described how plausibility theory might be used to achieve these aims. However, as yet no commercially available expert system makes use of plausibility theory in this way.

A more complete account of the deficiencies of many of the methods used for dealing with uncertainty in expert systems can be found in White (1984). We now describe how INFERNO deals with uncertainty:

INFERNO uses two values to represent the uncertainty of a statement. The two values are denoted by $t(x)$ and $f(x)$ where:

$$p(x) \geqslant t(x) \text{ and } p(NOT\ x) \geqslant f(x)$$

That is, $t(x)$ is a lower bound on $p(x)$ (i.e. on the probability of x), and $f(x)$ is a lower bound on the probability of NOT x. $t(x)$ is derived from statements in support of x and $f(x)$ is derived from statements against x.

A statement is regarded as supporting x if it enables the inference that $p(x) \geqslant R$, where R is some number in the range 0.0 to 1.0. A statement is against x if it enables the inference that $p(x) \leqslant R$. The knowledge concerning a statement x is regarded as being consistent if $t(x) + f(x) \leqslant 1.0$, in which case $t(x)$ is a lower bound on the value of $p(x)$ and $1.0 - f(x)$ is an upper bound on the value of $p(x)$.

The relations between statements in INFERNO are those named in the chart on page 444. The meaning of these relations is given in the right-hand column.

The relations 'inhibits', 'requires' and 'unless' can be defined in terms of 'enables' and 'negates'. Such definitions simplify the discussion of 'uncertainty propagation' which is discussed below.

Propagation of uncertainties in INFERNO
The certainty values of each statement A are initially set to 0.0, i.e. $t(A) = 0.0$ and $f(A) = 0.0$. As evidence is provided, the range within which the probability $p(A)$ of A is known to lie becomes smaller. Values for one or both of $t(A)$ and $f(A)$ become larger.

Certainties are propagated according to a set of 'propagation constraints', some of which are listed below. Each of these constraints may be read as:

If the previous value of the bound denoted by the left-hand side of the constraint is less than the value denoted by the right-hand side, *then* the bound on the left-hand side is increased to the value on the right-hand side.

Constraints are activated whenever the bound denoted by the right-hand side is changed.

RELATION NAME	MEANING
A enables X with strength S	$p(X/A) \geq S$
A inhibits X with strength S	$p(NOTX/A) \geq S$
X requires A with strength S	$p(NOTX/NOT\ A) \geq S$
X unless A with strength S	$p(X/NOT\ A) \geq S$
X negates Y	$X \equiv NOT\ Y$
X conjoins {A1, A2, ...}	$X \equiv A1\ AND\ A2\ AND\ ...$
X conjoins-independent {A1, A2, ...}	$X \equiv A1\ AND\ A2\ AND\ ...$ and for all $i \neq j$, $p(Ai\ AND\ Aj) = p(Ai) * p(Aj)$
X disjoins {A1, A2, ...}	$X \equiv A1\ OR\ A2\ OR\ ...$
X disjoins-independent {A1, A2, ...}	$X \equiv A1\ OR\ A2\ OR\ ...$ and for all $i \neq j$, $p(Ai\ AND\ Aj) = p(Ai) * p(Aj)$
X disjoins-exclusive {A1, A2, ...}	$X \equiv A1\ OR\ A2\ OR\ ...$ and for all $i \neq j$, $p(Ai\ and\ Aj) = 0.0$
{A1, A2, ...} mutually exclusive	for all $i \neq j$, $p(Ai\ AND\ Aj) = 0.0$

Examples of INFERNO propagation constraints
A enables X with strength S:

  (a) $t(X) \geqslant t(A) * S$

  (b) $f(A) \geqslant 1.0 - [1.0 - f(X)]/S$

X negates Y:

  (c) $t(X) = f(Y)$

  (d) $f(X) = t(Y)$

X conjoins {A1, A2, ... An}:

  (e) $t(X) \geqslant 1.0 - \sum_{1.0 \leqslant i \leqslant n} [1.0 - t(Ai)]$

  (f) $f(X) \geqslant f(Ai)$

  (g) $t(Ai) \geqslant t(X)$

  (h) $f(Ai) \geqslant f(X) - \sum_{j \neq 1} [1.0 - t(Aj)]$

X disjoins-independent {A1, A2, ..., An}:

  (i) $t(X) \geqslant 1.0 - \prod_{1.0 \leqslant i \leqslant n} [1.0 - t(Ai)]$

  (j) $f(X) \geqslant \prod_{1.0 \leqslant i \leqslant n} f(Ai)$

  (k) $t(Ai) \geqslant 1.0 - [1 - t(X)]/ \prod_{j \neq i} f(Aj)$

  (l) $f(Ai) \geqslant f(X)/ \prod_{j \neq i} 1.0 - t(Aj)$

  where $\sum_{1 \leqslant i \leqslant n} \alpha i$ is the sum of all αi for $1 \leqslant i \leqslant n$.

  and $\prod_{j \neq i} \alpha j$ is the average of all αj for $j \neq i$.

A complete list of INFERNO's propagation constraints can be found in Quinlan (1983).

Quinlan illustrates the propagation mechanism with the following example:

  Suppose that there are five statements A,B,C,D and E which are related as follows:

      C conjoins {A,B}
      E disjoins-independent {C,D}
      B enables E with strength 0.8

That is:

> C is the conjunction of A and B but nothing is known about the joint distribution of A and B

> E is the disjunction of C and D and these are known to be independent

> B directly suggests E with p(E/B) at least 0.8

These statements can be linked in an implication network (as shown in fig. 8.6).

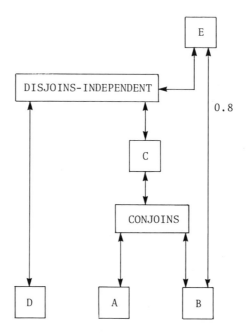

Figure 8.6   An example of an inferno implication network

Suppose that in a particular application, p(C) is found to lie in the interval [0.55, 0.65]. That is, t(C) = 0.55 and f(C) = 0.35. Using the relation 'C conjoins {A,B}', the constraint (g) above and the fact that t(C) = 0.55, we can update both t(A) and t(B) to 0.55. Assuming that t(D) and f(D) are initially zero, we can use the relation 'E disjoins-independent {C,D}', the constraint (i) above and the fact that t(C) = 0.55, to update t(E) to 0.55. Supposing that B is now found to have a probability of 0.9 (i.e. t(B) = 0.9 and f(B) = 0.1), the following inferences can be made:

    f(A) = 0.25 from constraint (h), f(C), and t(B)
    t(E) = 0.72 from constraint (a), and t(B)
    t(D) = 0.2 from constraint (k), t(E), and f(C)

INFERNO is also capable of identifying inconsistencies and of providing approximate, but nevertheless useful, suggestions for their remedy. We do not go into details here but refer the interested reader to Quinlan's paper.

In summary, INFERNO is a flexible and 'cautious' system for dealing with uncertain knowledge. It is cautious since it does not depend on assumptions about joint probability distributions of statements. Its conclusions about the probability bounds of statements are provably correct consequences of the given knowledge. The absence of assumptions would be expected to lead to weaker conclusions than would be obtained if the assumptions were made, but this is partially offset by enabling sets of statements which are mutually exclusive, or independent, to be identified by the user. This allows the probability bounds to be tightened in some cases. In addition, INFERNO does not distinguish between hypotheses and evidence and, therefore, can be used in data-driven or goal-driven searches.

8.4.4 ACCOMMODATING TIME-VARYING DATA

Many applications of expert systems involve situations which change with time. For example, in medical diagnosis, a patient's symptoms change with the progression of the disease and with the treatment given.

One of the earliest systems to deal with time-varying data was a robot planning system. The method used in this system was based on situational logic. (This logic was described in chapter 6.) The main idea is to tag all assertions with a situation identifier. A series of situations, S0, S1, S2, ..., is such that for any i > 0, Si temporally succeeds Si-1. The robot starts in situation S0 and performs a sequence of actions. After each action, the state of the robot's world is modelled by the next situation in the sequence.

VM is an example of an expert system which uses a variation of situational logic. This system monitors the post-surgical progress of patients whose breathing is assisted by a mechanical ventilator. VM's rule base consists of initialisation rules, status rules, transition rules and therapy rules. At regular intervals, VM receives an up-to-date set of instrument measurements against which it re-runs all of its rules. The transition rules are used to detect changes in a patient's state. When such a rule is satisfied, VM updates the situation to the one mentioned in that rule's conclusion. The initialisation rules are used to update the database so that it is compatible with the new situation.

The following is an example of a transition rule which is used in VM:

If (i) the patient transitioned from ASSIST to T-PIECE, or
    (ii) the patient transitioned from CMV to T-PIECE
then expect the following:

> A table containing acceptable ranges for pulse rates, etc.

Note: ASSIST, T-PIECE and CMV are patient states.

447

As mentioned in chapter 6, situational logic has several shortcomings, the most important of which are related to the 'frame problem' and to the fact that the logic can only accommodate a linear sequence of situations. In many expert tasks, especially those involving planning and/or prediction, it is necessary to deal with multiple possible futures. Modal logic, temporal logic and intensional logic, as used by Clifford and Warren (1983) in their work on historical databases, are relevant in such circumstances. (These logics were described in chapter 6.) However, the construction of expert systems which use such logics is still a research enterprise.

8.4.5 HANDLING LARGE SEARCH SPACES

Many expert tasks involve large search spaces. Some aspects of search strategy have already been described in sections 8.2 and 8.3. We now introduce some additional (and, in most cases, complementary) techniques which may be used in expert systems.

Reasoning by elimination

In many applications it is necessary to identify all of the solutions to a problem. For example, in medical diagnosis it is necessary to identify all diagnoses which are consistent with the symptoms presented by the patient. 'Reasoning by elimination' is an approach in which non-solutions (or solutions with low plausibility) are pruned from the search space as early as possible. To do this, the expert system must partition the search space in such a way that early pruning can be achieved. For example, symptoms can be used which partition the set of diagnoses cleanly (i.e. symptoms or lack of symptoms which rule out classes of disease).

DENDRAL and GA1 are examples of expert systems which use reasoning by elimination.

Use of abstraction

In some applications it is not possible to use reasoning by elimination. For example, in planning it is not really appropriate to consider dividing 'possible' plans into solutions and non-solutions. Most plans do not exist *a priori* and their creation as well as their evaluation is part of the expert system's task.

In certain types of planning problem, abstraction can be used. 'Abstraction' involves the identification of the important aspects of a problem and its subsequent partitioning into sub-problems.

R1 is an example of an expert system which is based on abstraction. In R1 the problem of configuring VAX computer systems is partitioned into five sub-problems:

(a) Checking the customer order for completeness and consistency.
(b) Configuring the CPU and CPU expansion boxes.
(c) Configuring the unibus expansion cabinet.
(d) Determining the layout of the system on the floor.
(e) Configuring the cabling.

Each of the sub-problems (b) to (e) is dependent on the solution to previous sub-problems.

Top-down refinement

In some applications of expert systems, the problem encountered cannot
be partitioned into a 'standard' set of sub-problems. However, the
principle of abstraction can still be used. The method of 'top-down
refinement' uses 'levels' of abstraction. Higher levels are more
abstract than lower levels. When the expert system has solved the
problem at one level it moves down to the next, more detailed, level.
The order and content of levels is pre-defined, whereas the order in
which sub-problems on a particular level are tackled is dependent on
the task in hand.

Programming is an example of a task in which top-down refinement is
used. At the top-level, data structures and algorithms are chosen; at
the next level, procedures and their relationships are specified; at
the next level the procedures are coded; and at the lowest level, the
code is compiled and tested.

An example of an expert system which uses top-down refinement is
ABSTRIPS, a robot planning program. Examples of high-level plans generated by ABSTRIPS are those concerned with the route which a robot
takes through rooms. Lower-level plans include details of how doors
are opened and closed, etc.

The least commitment principle

In top-down refinement it is assumed that, in a particular domain,
certain types of decision should *always* be made at a particular level
of abstraction. For example, in program design, decisions involving
specification of procedures should always be made at the second level
from the top, after all decisions in the top level have been made.
However, in some domains it is not always possible to make decisions
in the 'recommended' order, due to lack of data. In such cases, the
'least commitment principle' allows decision making to be co-ordinated
with the availability of data. The implementation of this principle
involves:

(a) Identifying points in time when there is enough data to make
a decision.

(b) Suspending activity on a sub-problem when the necessary data
is not available.

(c) Moving between sub-problems according to the availability of
data.

The least commitment principle ensures that decisions are not made
prematurely. MOLGEN is an example of an expert system which uses this
principle.

Guessing / use of heuristics

In some applications, circumstances can arise in which it is impossible
to determine the *best* decision to make at a given point in the problem-
solving activity. In such cases the expert system must make a 'guess'.
The rules which are used to guide guessing are called heuristics.

The problems associated with guessing include identifying wrong guesses and recovering from them. The use of heuristics and backtracking were mentioned in sub-section 8.3.3; the following comments are complementary to that discussion.

During the last few years, systems called 'belief-revision systems' have been built to support expert systems which use guessing (see, for example, Doyle, 1982). The responsibilities of a belief-revision system include storing, updating, analysing and accessing beliefs. Various approaches are used in such systems:

(a) Non-monotonic logic, as described in chapter 6, can be used to handle belief deletion as well as acquisition.

(b) Theories for dealing with uncertainty, as described in chapter 7, can be used to generate likely but uncertain beliefs from unreliable, incomplete, imprecise and/or inconsistent knowledge.

It is likely that future expert systems will contain belief-revision systems as components.

Multiple lines of reasoning

When humans tackle complex problems, they often use multiple lines of reasoning which may involve different representations (or views) of the problem in hand. The problem solver takes advantage of the particular strengths of the different approaches. The problem is solved by integrating various lines of argument such that weak points in one line are covered by strong points in other lines. An example of the use of this approach is given in section 8.4.6.

Multiple sources of knowledge (or expertise)

Certain types of problem are best solved by a number of experts, each of whom uses his own knowledge to tackle a particular aspect of the problem. In the following section, we describe an expert system architecture which is based on this notion.

8.4.6 BLACKBOARD ARCHITECTURES

We now describe the architecture of an expert system which uses multiple knowledge sources and mutliple lines of reasoning. The term 'knowledge source' is used here as it is the term which is used in the literature. A knowledge source is a set of rules used by an individual 'expert' to tackle a particular aspect of a problem.

The notion of multiple knowledge sources was first used in the HEARSAY-II system (Erman et al, 1980), which is a system capable of recognising spoken queries to a database system. The knowledge sources in HEARSAY-II include, amongst others, the following:

	SOURCE	FUNCTION
(a)	SEG	digitises the signal and produces labelled segmentations
(b)	POM	hypothesises the syllable class of a segment
(c)	MOW	hypothesises the word from the syllable classes
(d)	WORD-SEQ	hypothesises word sequences
(e)	PREDICT	predicts words that follow phrases
(etc.)		

450

The knowledge sources communicate via a shared data structure called a 'blackboard'. When a knowledge source is activated, it either creates a new hypothesis which it writes on to the blackboard or it modifies the certainty factor of an existing hypothesis. The hypotheses on the blackboard are arranged in two dimensions: level and time. The level dimension ranges from 'low-level' hypotheses concerning word segments to 'high-level' hypotheses concerning the meaning of the whole sentence. The time dimension ranges from when the utterance started to when it finished.

The application of knowledge sources is controlled by an 'opportunistic scheduler' which combines a least commitment strategy with strategies for managing limited computational resources. Different interpret-ations which occupy the 'same' location on the blackboard are called 'conflicting' hypotheses. For example, the blackboard might contain two word hypotheses for the same, or overlapping (in time), parts of the utterance. When conflicting hypotheses have the same certainty value, the scheduler has to decide which knowledge source to activate next. A discussion of scheduling in HEARSAY-II can be found in Hayes-Roth and Lesser (1977).

HEARSAY-II uses a mixture of data-driven and goal-driven search. For example, data-driven search is used in attempting to synthesise phrases from temporally adjacent word hypotheses, and goal-driven search is used to reduce hypothesised words into alternative sequences of phonemes.

8.4.7 EXPERT SYSTEM SHELLS

An 'expert system shell' is a system which can be used to build expert systems. Essentially it is an expert system with an empty rule base.

Ideally, in order to create an expert system, the user takes an expert system shell and simply adds the domain-dependent rules (i.e. the rules for the application in hand). Before discussing the extent to which this ideal has (or has not) been achieved, we describe an example of an expert system shell.

An example of an expert system shell
The techniques used in HEARSAY-II have since been developed and used in a domain-independent system called HEARSAY-III (Balzer et al, 1980). This system differs from HEARSAY-II in several respects:

(a) The time dimension has been removed from the blackboard since it is not appropriate to all domains.

(b) The blackboard in HEARSAY-III is based on a relational data-base system.

(c) A second blackboard and a set of knowledge sources is used for scheduling.

Scheduling was found to be such a complex task in HEARSAY-II that it was decided to regard it as an expert task. In HEARSAY-III, scheduling is handled by a separate blackboard which stores the dynamically crea-ted activation records of the knowledge sources. The knowledge sources in a HEARSAY-III implemented system include 'domain' knowledge sources and 'scheduling' sources. The scheduling sources consist of rules explicitly stating the control strategy which is to be used in problem-solving. (The advantage of explicitly represented control knowledge has already been discussed in section 8.3.4.)

HEARSAY-III has been used to implement various expert systems including (a) a system for building formal specifications of programs from informal specifications, (b) a system for producing natural language descriptions of expert system data structures and (c) a system which automatically transforms programs according to user requirements.

Other systems which may be categorised as expert system shells include:

(a) EMCYIN (van Melle, 1980) is a general purpose production system developed from the MYCIN system.

(b) PROLOG (Warren, 1977) is a logic programming language based on first order predicate logic. However, it may also be regarded as a general purpose production system.

(c) OPS4 (Forgy and McDermott, 1979) is a language for implementing production systems.

(d) EXPERT (Mizoguchi et al, 1979 and Weiss and Kulikowski, 1979) is a general purpose production system.

(e) CENTAUR (Aikins, 1980) is a general purpose expert system in which control knowledge is represented explicitly in slots of a frame-like data structure (see chapter 9 for a discussion of frame structures).

Criticism of expert system shells
The notion of a general purpose (domain-independent) expert system is regarded by some people as nonsense. Their criticisms often include statements such as:

(a) 'Some applications require data-driven search, others require goal-driven search, and in some cases a mixed-method is more appropriate.'

(b) 'Some applications, such as medical diagnosis, need to be able to handle uncertainty, whereas others, such as tax consultancy, do not have this requirement.'

(c) 'Some applications make use of very large collections of simple data and relatively few and static rules, whereas others need to handle large collections of time-varying rules.'

It is true that most of the shells currently available are better suited to certain applications than others. However, there is no reason why a shell could not be built which allows the user to choose among various combinations of search strategy, among various techniques for dealing with uncertainty, and among various data structures for storing simple facts and rules. The complexity of such a system is obviously going to be much greater than that of a domain-specific expert system. Nevertheless, such a system should not be regarded as being impossible to build.

8.4.8 HUMAN INTERFACE TO EXPERT SYSTEMS

Human interface to expert systems (and to knowledge base systems in general) is developing into a subject in its own right. Relevant ·techniques and notions from cognitive science, natural language understanding, knowledge engineering and database technology are being integrated and referred to collectively using terms such as 'man-machine interfacing'. In this discussion, we do no more than mention one or two of the important aspects of this subject.

The role of an expert system

It is important to differentiate between the various roles which an expert system can play:

(a) The expert system is regarded as 'slave' to the human user. In this case, the expert system carries out mundane tasks under the control of the user.

(b) The expert system is regarded as the 'controller' and the user as slave. For example, the user supplies results as requested by the system. The expert system makes the important decisions which are then put into practice by the user.

(c) The expert system is regarded as a 'colleague' of the user, for example as a fellow medical consultant, as a fellow lawyer. This role is by far the most difficult to achieve. The expert system must be capable of 'empathising' with the user, possibly by building some model of the user's knowledge, capabilities, etc.

Explanation

The credibility of an expert system is, to some extent, dependent on its ability to explain its reasoning. Explanation facilities can also be used for teaching purposes and for debugging the system. Originally, it was claimed that expert systems could be used by non-experts to help them tackle expert tasks. In practice, most expert systems which have been built are used by experts to help them in their work. This is partly due to the poor explanation facilities which are available in most expert systems.

A system, called BLAH, has been developed by Weiner (1980) in an attempt to overcome this problem. Weiner was particularly concerned with structuring explanations. A study of explanations used by humans (Weiner, 1979) was used as a basis for the design of BLAH.

The principles which Weiner identified as being important included the following:

(a) Explanations should be limited to what is not already known by the user.

(b) Details should not be given initially.

(c)   Details should be given in increments.

(d)   Explanations should be 'marked' in some way so that the
      underlying structure is more transparent.

More recently Coombs and Stell (1985) have been looking at ways in
which systems can construct models of the user's conception or misconception of the problem-solving strategy used in an expert task.   In
particular, they have developed a PROLOG program debugging aid, which
builds a PROLOG interpreter corresponding to the user's misconception
of how the PROLOG interpreter works. This incorrect interpreter is
then made explicit to the user, together with the correct interpreter,
and is used to help the user recognise his misconception. It is possible that modal logic (especially as used in epistemic logic as described in chapter 6) might be relevant to this type of explanation
facility.

Knowledge acquisition
There are three methods which are generally used for obtaining the
expert knowledge used in an expert system:

(a)   Transcription from text.
(b)   Elicitation from experts.
(c)   Induction from examples (see exercise in appendix 1).

(a) involves all of the problems associated with natural language
understanding.

(b) involves 'probing' rather than 'mining'. Difficulties have been
encountered when experts are regarded as containing chunks of knowledge
which can be 'mined' by asking them to write down the rules.

8.5 CONCLUDING COMMENTS
This discussion began with a description of the rule based approach to
problem-solving. We then described how the approach has been used in
expert systems and how such use has resulted in more sophisticated
search strategies and methods for dealing with uncertainty. We concluded our discussion with a very brief consideration of the human
interface to expert systems.

The fact that only a brief consideration was given to this last subject
should not be construed as an indication of the importance we attach to
it. Man-machine interface is, perhaps, one of the most important
aspects of expert systems. However, space limitations have prevented
us from giving a more detailed account.

Various advantages have been claimed for the production rule based
approach:

(a)   The modular stylised structure of production rules allows such
      rules to be easily coded and added to a production system.
      Where rules are independent, a new rule may be added to the
      knowledge base without change to other rules.

(b)   An expert system may be adapted for use in another problem
      domain by simply changing the set of production rules,

provided that the search strategy is appropriate for the new problem domain.

(c) Encoding knowledge as a set of production rules would appear to be a natural and appropriate method for many problem domains.

(d) Uncertain knowledge may be accommodated as described in sub-section 8.4.2.

(e) Explanation facilities may be added to production rule based systems as described in sub-section 8.4.8.

However, some of these claims (in particular (a), (b) and (e)) have since been refuted by many people working on expert systems. In particular, the following disadvantages have been found:

(a) Knowledge, when expressed as a set of production rules, is not always as easily understood as it would be if it were expressed in some other form. In part, this is due to the fact that all necessary contextual knowledge must be stated explicitly in the condition part of each rule.

(b) The choice of rules and search strategy, such that the system behaves in a comprehensive way, is not, in general, a trivial task.

(c) Most production rule based systems do not allow rules of the form:

for all X *if* condition(X) *then* A(X)

Most systems which do accommodate such rules accommodate them in an *ad hoc* way. (An exception to this is PROLOG, which is described later.)

(d) Most production rule based systems are not based on a well-defined semantics (PROLOG again being the exception). This results in unjustifiable, and in some cases unpredictable, behaviour.

(e) In most systems, the search strategy is embedded in the code. This limits the range of applications for which the expert system can be used. This problem can be alleviated by making the search strategy properties explicit and by giving the user a choice of such properties.

The advantages and disadvantages of the production rule based approach are discussed further in Davies et al (1977) and in Fox (1984).

In later chapters we show how the production rule based approach is related to other methods of knowledge processing.

455

9 Slot and Filler Knowledge Representations

9.1 INTRODUCTION

The languages of formal logic allow us to represent various aspects of the universe. However, they do not in general allow us to structure this knowledge to reflect the structure of that part of the universe which is being represented. For example, suppose we want to represent the facts that John is married to Sally, Bill is married to Jean, John is employed by IBM, Bill is employed by IBM, John has blue eyes and Bill has brown eyes. In a language of first order predicate logic, using infix notation, we can represent these facts as follows:

        F1:   (John.ismarriedto.Sally)
        F2:   (Bill.ismarriedto.Jean)
        F3:   (John.isemployedby.IBM)
        F4:   (Bill.isemployedby.IBM)
        F5:   (John.haseyecolour.blue)
        F6:   (Bill.haseyecolour.brown)

However, the order of these assertions is irrelevant and any other order would have been just as acceptable. The point is that in the languages of formal logic there is no facility for clustering formulas such as F1, F3 and F5 which are all related to a particular aspect of the universe (in this case, John).

The knowledge representations described in this chapter differ from formal logic in that they include facilities for representing the 'structure' of parts of the universe. The representations described include semantic nets, frames, conceptual dependency structures and scripts.

In 'frames', all assertions about a particular entity are held together. (For example, consider the instantiations of frames in fig. 9.4.)

In 'conceptual dependency structures', all assertions about a particular action or event are held together, and in 'scripts' all assertions about a particular sequence of events such as 'going to a restaurant' are held together.

The advantage of clustering assertions in this way is not simply an improvement in access to the knowledge although, from an implementation

point of view, it is often desirable to have related representations
stored in one place. A more important advantage is that 'stereotype'
structures can be represented. (For example, stereotype frames are
illustrated in fig. 9.3.) Such structures are called 'slot and filler'
structures since they contain slots such as the 'name slot', the
'parent of' slot, etc., which can be filled by values relating to a
particular entity.

Slot and filler structures facilitate pattern recognition, inference
of generic properties, handling of default values and the detection of
errors and omissions in bodies of knowledge. Each of these is described in detail in this chapter.

We begin with the least structured formalism, i.e. the semantic net,
which we shall show is closely related to first order logic. The
semantic net formalism is included in this chapter since it was the
precursor of the notions of frames, conceptual dependency structures
and scripts.

9.2 SEMANTIC NETS

9.2.1 WHAT IS A SEMANTIC NET?

A semantic net is a directed graph in which nodes represent entities
and arcs represent binary relationships between entities. Arcs are
labelled with the names of the relationship types, i.e. the binary
relation to which the relationship belongs. A single entity is represented by a single node. Semantic nets were first used by Quillian
(1968) and, independently, Raphael (1968). An example of part of a
semantic net is given in fig. 9.1.

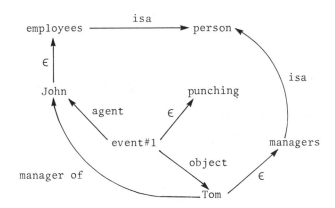

*Figure 9.1 A semantic net representing the situation in which
John punched his manager*

Semantic nets can be used to represent various types of knowledge.
For example:

(a) Set-membership relationships may be represented by ∈ arcs, e.g.

$$John \xrightarrow{\in} Employee$$

(b) Sub-set relationships may be represented by isa arcs, e.g.

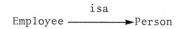

(c) n-ary relationships (with n>2) can be represented by 'creating' an entity to stand for the n-ary relationship. For example, the fact that machine#12 uses 20 instances of part#2 in its construction may be represented as follows:

(d) Events may be represented; for example:

which represents the event of John punching Tom.

(e) Statements such as 'Tom's height is 1.7 metres and is increasing' may be represented as follows:

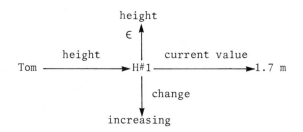

Note that the arcs are directed. If we want to represent facts in both directions we must do this explicitly. For example, to represent the facts that 'John is an employee' and that 'the set of employees includes John' we would have to use two arcs:

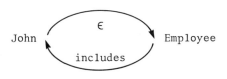

The basic notion of semantic nets has been adapted in various ways. For example, see Hendrix (1975), Fikes and Hendrix (1977), Schubert (1976), Shapiro (1971 and 1977), Simmons and Chester (1977) and Deliyanni and Kowalski (1979). Two of these adaptations are described below.

9.2.2 EXTENDED SEMANTIC NETS

Deliyanni and Kowalski (1979) have described an extended semantic net which can be interpreted as a variant syntax for the 'Kowalski clausal form' of first order predicate logic restricted to binary predicates:

Kowalski clausal form
A clause ¬C1 ∨ ,..., ∨ ¬Cm ∨ K1 ∨ ,..., ∨ Kn, where Ci and Ki are atomic formulas, is in Kowalski form if it is written as:

C1 ∧ ,..., ∧ Cm → K1 ∨ ,..., ∨ Kn

That is, all negated literals are collected in a conjunction called the 'condition' and all positive literals are collected in a disjunction called a 'conclusion'.

The meaning of → is extended to deal with the cases where either m or n is 0. When m is 0, we interpret the expression:

→ K1 ∨ , ..., ∨ Kn

as meaning:

K1 ∨ ,..., ∨ Kn

When n is 0, we interpret the expression:

C1 ∧ ,..., ∧ Cm →

as meaning:

¬[C1 ∧ ,..., ∧ Cm]

read as the denial of C1 ∧ ,..., ∧ Cm.

In the extended semantic net, terms are represented by nodes, and binary predicates by arc labels. Components of conclusions and conditions are represented by different types of arc. For example, consider the following:

(a) → ∈(John, human) ∧ married to(John, Sally), meaning John is a human and John is married to Sally, may be represented as:

$$\text{human} \xleftarrow{\quad \in \quad} \text{John} \xrightarrow{\quad \text{married to} \quad} \text{Sally}$$

$$\text{marriedto(John,Pat)} \longrightarrow$$

(b) marriedto(John,Pat) →, meaning John is not married to Pat, may be represented as:

$$\text{John} \xdashrightarrow{\quad \text{married to} \quad} \text{Pat}$$

459

(c) $\in(x, parent) \rightarrow \in(x, mother) \lor \in(x, father)$, meaning if some entity is a parent then that entity is a mother or a father, may be represented as:

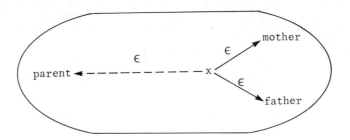

The enclosing line delimits the clause.

(d) $\in(x, y) \land isa(y, z) \rightarrow \in(x, z)$, meaning if x is a member of y and y isa z this implies that x is a member of z, may be represented as:

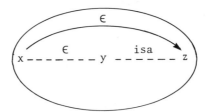

(e) Existentially quantified formulas may also be represented. Consider the following formula which is not in Kowalski form:

$$\forall x \exists y \ \in(x, parent) \rightarrow \in(y, offspring)$$

which states that for every parent there exists an offspring. This formula can be expressed in Kowalski form as follows:

$$\in(x, parent) \rightarrow \in(f(x), offspring)$$

which can be expressed in an extended semantic net as:

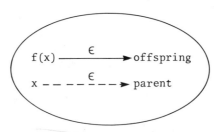

The correspondence between logic and extended semantic networks means that resolution can be used for inference. For example, consider the following semantic net:

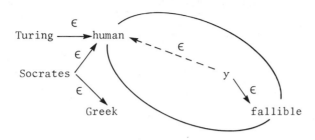

This corresponds to the following set of formulas:

$\in$(Turing, human)
$\in$(Socrates, human)
$\in$(Socrates, Greek)
$\in$(y, human) $\rightarrow$ $\in$(y, fallible)

In order to find a fallible Greek, we simply add the following denial to the net:

$\in$(x, fallible) $\wedge$ $\in$(x, Greek) $\rightarrow$

This gives:

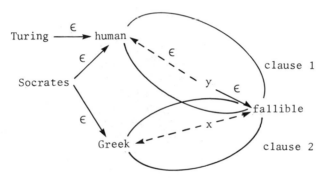

To obtain an answer, we now attempt to produce an explicit contradiction in the network. We use the following rules:

(a) Resolvents can be created by matching condition arcs with conclusion arcs in two clauses. For example, clause 1 and clause 2 match to form the clause:

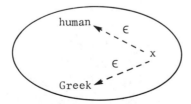

(b) Clauses can be deleted from the net if they contain an atom which matches no other atom in the net.

461

(c) Parents used in a resolution can be deleted if no other match exists for the atom being matched.

As example, consider the net above. To find a fallible Greek, we proceed as follows:

(a) Clause 1 matches clause 2 to form the resolvent clause 3. Clauses 1 and 2 are then deleted:

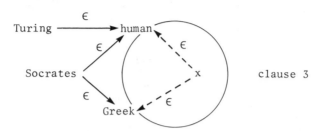

clause 3

(b) Clause 3 matches Turing---∈-->human to give:

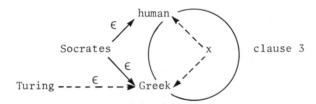

clause 3

(c) Since Turing---∈--->Greek has no match, it is deleted:

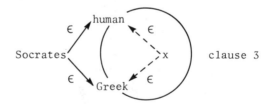

clause 3

(d) Clause 3 matches Socrates---∈-->human to form the resolvent Socrates----∈---->Greek. Both parents of this resolution can be deleted, giving:

(e) This is a contradiction. Hence the problem is solved.

Not only can the extended semantic net be regarded as a syntactic variant of the Kowalski form of logic, it may also be seen as an abstract data structure which can be used to guide proof procedures. This approach has been used in the development of the connection graph proof methods which we have already described in chapter 4, section 4.4.

9.2.3 PARTITIONED SEMANTIC NETS
We have demonstrated how semantic nets may be partitioned into spaces corresponding to clauses. An alternative approach to partitioning nets has been developed by Hendrix (1977).

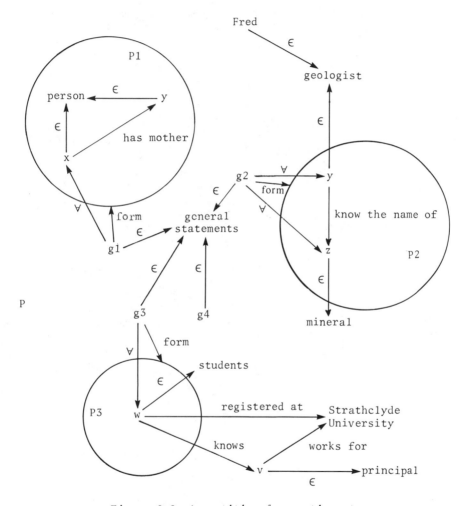

Figure 9.2 A partitioned semantic net

An example is given in fig. 9.2, which represents the following:

(a) Fred is a geologist.

(b) G1, G2 and G3 are all members of the set of general statements.

(c) G1 is the name of the statement in partition P1 which states

'for all x, if x is a person then there exists a person y who
is the mother of x'.

(d) G2 is the name of the statement in partition P2 which may be
read as 'all geologists know the names of all minerals'.

(e) G3 is the name of the statement in partition P3 which states
that 'all students of Strathclyde University know the principal of Strathclyde University'. The variable v is not in
the partition P3 since it is not an existentially quantified
variable but represents a single entity, as do all other nodes
in partition P.

The partitions of a partitioned semantic net are related in a hierarchy.
The hierarchy in fig. 9.2 may be depicted as follows:

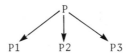

9.3 FRAME BASED SYSTEMS

Definition of a frame

A frame is a data structure which represents an entity type. A frame
consists of a collection of named 'slots' each of which can be 'filled'
by values or by pointers to other frames. Examples of frames are given
in fig. 9.3.

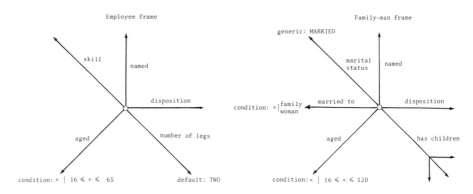

Figure 9.3 Examples of frames

Instantiation

When the slots of a frame are filled, the frame is said to be 'instantiated' and then represents a particular entity of the type represented
by the unfilled frame. Examples of instantiated frames are given in
fig. 9.4.

Representation of an entity from different points of view

Frames may be used to represent the same entity from different points
of view, as exemplified in fig. 9.4 in which the person called J SMITH
is viewed as an employee and as a family man.

464

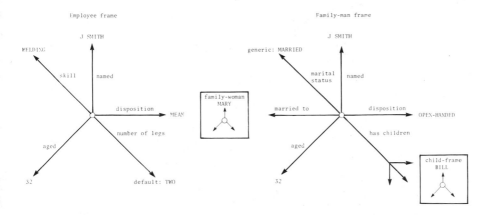

Figure 9.4   Examples of frame installations

Generic properties

Pre-set values in a frame, such as the value MARRIED in the 'marital status' slot in the family man frame in fig. 9.3, are called 'generic values' or 'generic properties'. They are values which occur in every instantiation of that frame. Thus, they correspond to properties which all entities of a particular entity type possess. For example, every family man has marital status MARRIED. (Note that the family man frame in fig. 9.3 represents one definition of 'family man' which may not accord with other, equally valid, definitions.)

Default values

Default values in a frame, such as the value TWO in the 'number of legs' slot in fig. 9.3, are values which can be assumed if no other value is known. For example, unless it is known otherwise one can assume that an employee has two legs.

Slot conditions

Conditions such as x|16 ≤ x ≤ 65 in the 'aged' slot in fig. 9.3 restrict the values with which a slot can be filled. Conditions may be more complex than this example and may refer to values in other slots. For example, the allowed age value of an employee may depend on whether the employee is male or female. This might be appropriate if there were different compulsory retirement ages for men and women.

Frame structures

Frames may be linked to other frames in various ways:

(a)   A slot in one frame might be filled by another frame (or by a pointer to another frame). For example, in fig. 9.3 the 'married to' slot in the family man frame can be filled by a family woman frame.

(b)   Frames may be linked in taxonomical structures as illustrated in fig. 9.5. The father/son links in such structures (depicted by continuous lines in the figure) represent sub-set relationships. For example, the entity set 'employee' is a sub-set of the entity set 'person'. Sibling links (represented by dotted lines in the figure) represent sub-sets which have the same father. Similarity links (represented by dashed lines in the figure) represent sub-sets which are similar in some specified sense of the word.

Such links between frames can be used to speed up matching and for the inference of generic properties (see below).

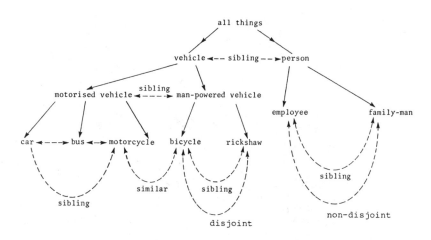

Figure 9.5 A frame structure

Matching

In many applications of frames, the type of an entity is not always known. For example, we might know the name, age and disposition of a person but we do not know if he/she is a family man, family woman, bachelor, spinster, etc. In such cases, it is not always a straight-forward matter of selecting a frame and then instantiating it to represent the entity concerned. We have to use the properties which are known to select a candidate frame. The system then tries to find values to fill the unfilled slots:

(i) If inappropriate values are found then another candidate frame must be selected. Identification of appropriate candidate frames can be facilitated by reference to the frame structures in some cases.

(ii) If no value is found then the system can proceed by assuming that the knowledge is simply missing.

In effect, the system tries to find a frame which best matches the known properties of an entity.

Inference

Three types of deductive inference can be made using frames:

(a) When a 'sufficient match' is made, the system can infer the existence of an entity of the entity type represented by the frame. For example, if a match is made between the values known for the properties of an entity and the values required to fill the slots of the 'family man frame', then the system can assume that a family man exists. (What is meant by 'sufficient match' is explained later.)

(b) When a sufficient match is made, we can infer that the entity represented by the instantiation has the generic values. For example, we can infer that a family man has marital status MARRIED. Generic properties of one entity type are passed down as generic properties of sub-sets of this type. (This is discussed in more detail later.)

(c) If the system has been told that 'the person Bill is like a bulldozer', it can use 'analogical' inference to deduce the values for various properties of Bill. For example, if both person and vehicle frames have slots for weight, and the bulldozer's instantiation of the vehicle frame has a relatively high value in this slot, then we can put a relatively high value in the weight slot of the person frame when we instantiate it to represent Bill.

Uses of frames

We have mentioned that frames can be used for inference. Another use is for checking a body of knowledge for inconsistencies and omissions. For example, if a person is said to be an employee but is known to have an age of 3, then this can be used to flag the possibility of an error.

Frame based systems were developed primarily as pattern recognition sub-systems of natural language understanding systems.

Procedural attachment/demons

Procedures called 'demons' may be attached to frames in various ways. For example, a procedure could be attached to the age slot in the employee frame such that if the condition is violated, i.e. the age is outside the range 16 to 65, then the procedure is invoked. The procedure might request the system user to explain the age range violation and may act according to the explanation given. This mixing of declarative and procedural knowledge is an important feature of frame based systems.

Each of these aspects of frames is now discussed in more detail.

9.3.1 FRAME INSTANTIATION AND THE REPRESENTATION OF AN ENTITY FROM DIFFERENT POINTS OF VIEW

Suppose that we know the values of several properties of some entity E. If these values are appropriate to fill all of the slots of some frame F, then we can use the instantiation of F to represent E. In effect, we have categorised E as being of the entity type represented by F.

Suppose that we learn more about E such that we can also fill the slots of another frame H. We can also use the instantiation of H to represent E. In effect, we have categorised E as being of the entity type represented by H.

There is no problem here. Entities may belong to more than one entity set; for example, a person might be an employee as well as a family man. The categorisation of an entity in this way may be regarded as seeing the entity from different points of view. We shall refer to frames which represent the same entity from different points of view as 'alternative view frames' with respect to each other. Of course, there are entity sets which are necessarily disjoint; for example, the sets: 'family man' and 'not family man'. The inclusion of an entity in both of these sets would signify an error. The extent to which sets are allowed to intersect must therefore be represented in the system in some form or other if such inconsistencies are to be detected.

Given that an entity is represented by two non-disjoint alternative view frames, inconsistencies can arise in other ways. For example, in fig. 9.4 we can see that the entity named J SMITH has apparently inconsistent values for the 'disposition' property when viewed as an employee and as a family man. There are three possible explanations for this:

(a) 'Disposition' at work and at home are really different concepts and should have distinct names.

(b) J SMITH may act differently at work and at home. There is no problem if we do not insist that an entity has the same value in identically named slots in alternative view frames. However, if this approach is adopted in all cases we would miss real inconsistencies such as a person having different values in the 'aged' slot in alternative view frames.

(c) The third explanation is that the alternative view frames do contradict each other and that there really is an error.

The use of frames for consistency checking is discussed in more detail in sub-section 9.3.7.

9.3.2 GENERIC PROPERTIES, DEFAULT VALUES AND SLOT CONDITIONS

Generic properties
We have used the term 'generic property' without defining exactly what is meant by this term. The dictionary defines the word 'generic' as 'pertaining to a genus' where a genus is equivalent to an entity set in the context of this discussion. However, in the literature on database and knowledge base systems, the term 'generic property' has a more specific meaning which may be expressed as follows:

A 'generic property' is a property associated with an entity set such that every member of that set displays that property.

For example, the entity set 'person' may have the following generic properties associated with it:

(a) Has blood temperature warm.
(b) Has some mother.
(c) Number of hearts is one.

Notice that the second property is somewhat different from the other two. Both (a) and (c) specify a type of property (has blood temperature, number of hearts) *and* a value for that property (warm and one, respectively), whereas (b) simply specifies a type of property. As such, (b) specifies the existence of a value for a named property without constraining what that value might be.

In sub-section 9.3.4, we discuss the use of generic properties in 'matching', i.e. in recognising that an entity is an instance of an entity set.

The use of entity sets and generic properties is very frequent in human discourse and reasoning. It can be found in the most mundane conversations. For example, suppose that you are asked the following question:

'Do you have a light?'

You would immediately start to use the concepts of the entity set and generic property. Depending on the circumstances you might attempt to match the word light with frames for 'torchlight' and 'cigarette lighter'. Supposing that 'cigarette lighter' were the best match (no pun intended), you might then use the generic property that 'all cigarette lighters can be used to light cigarettes' to re-express the question as follows:

'Have you anything that can be used to light a cigarette?'

You may then be able to deduce that the box of matches in your pocket might meet the requirements of what was asked for.

Default values
An example of a default value was given in fig. 9.3. A default value is one which is to be expected in the usual case. For example, most employed people have two legs, and unless we have contrary knowledge we can generally assume that this is the case. Such use of default knowledge is, in general, quite justified for the following reason: if there is contrary knowledge, and it is relevant, then we are likely to be given this knowledge. For example, if the number of legs which a person has is relevant to the application of the knowledge base then, in general, we would expect the knowledge base to contain knowledge of which people have only one or no legs. If no such knowledge is available for a particular person, then the default value of TWO is likely to be correct in most cases. If, however, the number of legs which a person has is irrelevant to the application of the knowledge base, then the knowledge base may not contain knowledge of which people have only one or no legs. The default value of TWO might then be incorrectly assumed in several cases. However, since for this application the number of legs is irrelevant, such incorrect default assumptions are unimportant.

Default values are frequently used in human reasoning and it is, therefore, most important that we can accommodate their use in knowledge base systems (this has already been discussed in the section on non-monotonic logic). However, we should also recognise that use of default values can be a hindrance to problem-solving in certain circumstances.

As example, consider the following party game. One person stands up and asks the others to act as detectives and solve a 'mystery problem'. The problem might be:

'John and Sally are lying dead in the middle of a living room surrounded by broken glass and water. The window is open. Who murdered them?'

The 'detectives' are allowed to ask questions to which the story teller may only answer 'yes' or 'no'. The following is an example of a dialogue which might follow:

Detective 1 : 'Were they stabbed to death?'
Storyteller : 'No'
Detective 2 : 'Were they poisoned?'
Storyteller : 'No'
Detective 3 : 'Did they have a fight?'
Storyteller : 'No'
Detective 4 : 'Did the murderer escape through the window?'
Storyteller : 'Yes'
Detective 2 : 'Did you say that they were surrounded by broken glass and water?'
Storyteller : 'Yes'
Detective 1 : 'Were they drowned?'
Storyteller : 'No'
Detective 3 : 'How old were John and Sally?'
Storyteller : 'You may only ask questions to which the answer is yes or no'
Detective 3 : 'Were John and Sally over 20 years old?'
Storyteller : 'No'
Detective 2 : 'Were John and Sally teenagers?'
Storyteller : 'No'
Detective 1 : 'Were John and Sally less than one year old?'
Storyteller : 'Yes'

Such dialogue could continue for some time until one of the detectives stops using the default assumption that John and Sally are human. The water and glass might then point to the 'fact' that John and Sally are goldfish and that the 'murderer' was a well-fed cat which came and left by the window.

When one has played such a game, other variations of it can be quickly solved. For example, there is the story about Bob who lives on the twelfth floor in a multi-storey block. Every morning he enters the lift on the twelfth floor and always gets out on the ground floor. Every evening he enters the lift on the ground floor but only gets out on the twelfth floor if there are other people in the lift. If he is by himself in the lift, he always gets out at the eighth floor and walks up four flights of stairs to the twelfth floor. If we do not make the default assumption that Bob is an adult then we might quickly determine that he is a very small child who is not tall enough to reach any button higher than that for the eighth floor.

It is thought by some (e.g. de Bono) that many difficult problems can only be solved if we deliberately prevent default values from blocking our thoughts. Brainstorming sessions in which people suggest most ludicrous solutions to problems, and lateral thinking in which the least likely paths are taken, are attempts to put this principle into practice.

There would seem to be some sense in the suggestion that very difficult problems that have been with us for a long time (e.g. the cause of cancer) will only be solved if people look at them from a new point of view, questioning all default assumptions that have been made by others who have attempted to solve them in the past.

Existing frame based systems do not accommodate such considerations of default reasoning but simply use default values when no contrary knowledge is available.

Slot conditions

Examples have been given, in fig. 9.3, of slots containing conditions restricting the values with which they are allowed to be filled. We have also mentioned the possibility of additional restrictions which take into account values to be found in identically named slots in alternative view frames.

More complex conditions can be expressed as formulas involving values in other slots both in the current frame and in other frames.

9.3.3 FRAME STRUCTURES

Frames may be related in various ways, as illustrated in fig. 9.5.

(a) Two frames F and G may be related by the 'sub-set' or 'isa' relationship, denoted by F isa G, if F represents an entity set which is a sub-set of the entity set represented by G. Note that this relationship is quite distinct from the set-membership relationship denoted by ∈. If F isa G then we say that F is a 'specialisation' of G.

(b) Two frames F and G may be related by the 'sibling' relationship if both F and G are related by the isa relationship to the same 'parent' frame. That is, F and G are siblings if, for some frame H, F isa H and G isa H.

(c) Two frames may be related by the 'disjoint' relationship if they represent disjoint entity sets. Two disjoint frames can never be instantiated to produce two alternative view frames w.r.t. each other.

(d) Two frames may be related by the non-disjoint relationship if they represent non-disjoint entity sets.

(e) Two frames may be related by the 'similar' relationship if they represent entity sets whose members have sufficient properties in common to be regarded as similar. The meaning of 'sufficient' is subjective and will depend on the use to which the frame system is put.

(f) Frames may be related by any relation at all. For example,

suppose that we have a frame F which represents an entity type
as seen from a particular angle. Suppose also that we have a
frame E which represents the same entity type as seen from a
different angle. Frames F and E may be related by a 'rotation'
relation.

(g) Frames can be related in more complex ways, as illustrated in
fig. 9.6.

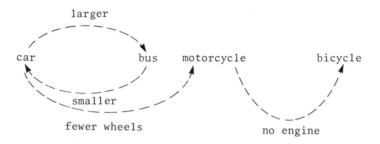

Figure 9.6 Relationships between entity sets

The 'isa' relation is very important in certain applications since it
defines a 'property inheritance' path. That is, if frame A isa B and
frame B isa C, then all of the generic properties associated with C
are also associated with B (and therefore inherited by the members of
B). Similarly, all of the generic properties of B, including those
inherited from C, are also associated with A. For example, if a maid
isa employee, and an employee isa person, and person has the associated
generic property 'has blood temperature WARM', then all instances of
the maid frame will inherit the property 'has blood temperature WARM'.

The 'isa' and 'similarity' relations are also important in matching and
pattern recognition, which are described in the next sub-section.

9.3.4 MATCHING AND PATTERN RECOGNITION

Frame systems are often used as components of pattern recognition systems, whether the patterns be visual patterns or abstract concepts.
For example, a frame system might consist of a set of frames, one for
each letter of the alphabet. The frame for the letter 'E' might contain slots and values such as 'number of straight lines=4', 'number of
corners=2' and 'number of curved lines=0', etc. Such a system might
then be used to recognise capital letters. In other applications, the
system could consist of frames for different types of people: male,
female, child, mother, father, etc. Such a system might be used to
'recognise' the existence of a particular type of person from textual
input.

In some applications, the problem to be solved is purely one of pattern
recognition. In other cases, when an entity has been recognised as
being of a particular entity type, all generic properties associated
with that type are inherited by that entity. The system is then acting
in a pattern recognition and inference mode. Inference is discussed in
more detail in the next sub-section. In this sub-section we are primarily concerned with pattern recognition.

In a frame system, pattern recognition involves 'matching' a set of values associated with an entity against the values required to fill the slots of a frame. If all of the slots of a frame, F can be filled with appropriate values relating to some entity E, then F can be instantiated to represent E and E can be categorised as being of type F.

However, F might represent a 'general' entity set such as 'person'. If we want to find a more specific match, we must look lower down the 'isa' hierarchy to see if a specialisation of F can be instantiated. For example, we might find that the values related to E are appropriate to fill the slots of a frame G representing 'computer scientist'. Matching E against G is more informative than matching E against F.

In some cases, we might not be able to find an exact match. Some slot values might not be known, others might be outside the allowed range. In such cases it will be necessary to find the best match. We now describe how this is carried out.

The process of matching
Suppose we know the values of various properties of an entity E. The system can use these properties to select a 'candidate frame'. This may be done in several ways:

(a) Start at the top of the isa hierarchy and select the frame with the best 'match value' (see below) at the first level.

(b) Index the frames by slot name. Select any frame which has a slot name which is the same as any of the property names for which there is a known value for E.

(c) Select a frame arbitrarily.

(d) Use other contextual information to select a frame. For example, if it is known that the entity E is a person then select a person frame.

When a candidate frame has been selected using one of the methods above, the system partially instantiates the frame by filling as many of its slots as possible. In some applications, the system may ask for additional knowledge in an attempt to fill more slots. A 'match value' is then computed which indicates the 'goodness' of the match. For example, if all slots are filled with appropriate values then the match value will be 1. If only half the slots are filled the match value might be 0.5. The method of computing the match value will differ from application to application. In some cases, the presence of an inappropriate slot value will set the match value to 0. For example, an entity with 'blood temperature COLD' would have a match value of 0 when matched against a person frame. In other cases, inappropriate slot values might not be so crucial and might simply reduce the match value.

Depending on the application, the match value will be regarded as signifying various degrees of success. If the match value is high enough, and the frame is specific enough for the application in hand, then the system will not look at other frames. However, if the match value is not high enough or the frame is not specific enough then the system will consider other frames. Rather than look at all other frames, the system can make use of the frame structure to identify relevant frames. It can do this in various ways:

(a) The system could move up the 'isa' hierarchy until it finds a perfect match. It could then search the 'isa' sub-tree below the perfectly matched frame in an attempt to find a more specific match. A depth-first, breadth-first or heuristic search could be used. For example, if we match an entity E with an ape frame and obtain a match value of 0.3, we could move up the 'isa' hierarchy and find a perfect match with (say) the mammal frame. We could then search the 'isa' sub-tree below the mammal frame in an attempt to match E with a more specific frame such as a dog frame.

(b) The system could look at frames related to the current one by the 'similar' or 'sibling' relation. For example, if an entity E matched the female human frame with a match value of 0.9 then the system could attempt to match E with frames such as male human in an attempt to find a better match.

(c) Complex relationships between frames as illustrated in fig. 9.6 can be used to identify candidates for matching. For example, if an entity matches the car frame except for its number of wheels which is TWO, then the relationship 'similar but fewer wheels' might be used to identify the motor cycle frame as a candidate frame.

9.3.5 INFERENCE

Frame systems use five types of inference: inferred existence, inferred generic properties, inferred default values, recognition of abnormal situations and inference by analogy. We have briefly described three of these already. In this sub-section, we describe all of them in a little more detail:

Inferred existence

When a match is made between an entity and a frame, the system is able to infer the existence of an entity of the entity type represented by that frame. The 'certainty' with which this inference can be made is related to the match value described earlier. It is not difficult to see how probability theory, certainty theory or possibility theory as used in production systems (see chapter 8) might be used in frame systems. There is nothing to prevent us representing a frame by a set of production rules. For example, a person frame could be represented by the following set of production rules:

    x is a person → x has blood temp WARM
    x is a person → x has number of hearts ONE
    x is a person → x has number of legs TWO with certainty 0.98

Inferred generic properties

When a match is made between an entity E and a frame F then the system can infer that E has all of the generic properties associated with F. The certainty of this inference depends on the match value between E and F and the certainty with which the generic properties are associated with F. The methods used in production systems for reasoning with uncertain knowledge could be adopted for use in frame systems.

Default properties

When a match is made between an entity E and a frame F, and the value for some slot S in F is not known for E, then if there is a default value for S the system can infer that E has this value for the property S. The certainty of such an inference depends on the match value and the certainty associated with the default value.

Recognition of abnormal situations

Since frames describe general or expected properties of the entities belonging to some entity set, the absence of a value for a slot (or the presence of an inappropriate value) may signify an unusual situation. For example, if an entity matches a car frame exactly except that it does not have brakes then this signifies an unusual situation: possibly the car is dangerous to drive and should be repaired.

9.3.6 INFERENCE BY ANALOGY

We have given an example of the use of analogy:

> *from* (Bill is like a bulldozer)
> *and* (a relatively high value in the weight slot of
>   the 'bulldozer instantiated' vehicle frame)
> *infer* (a relatively high value in the weight slot of the
>   'Bill instantiated' person frame)

In analogical reasoning, we use a statement such as 'X is like Y' to infer slot values for X given values for Y. The method involves selecting appropriate values from Y and using these values to select values appropriate for X. The following heuristics, derived from those presented in Rich (1983), could be used in this process.

To select values from Y

(a) Select values which are relatively high or relatively low compared with usual values for that slot.

(b) Select slots which are important in the sense that they contribute critically to match values.

(c) Select slots which no close relative of Y possesses. That is, select slots which do not occur in frames which are related to Y by the 'sibling' or 'similar' relation.

(d) Select values which no close relative of Y possesses. That is, relatives may have the same slot but the value of this slot, which Y has, is not to be found in any of Y's relatives.

(e) Use all of Y's values.

To filter the values

(a) Select slots that are not already filled in X.

(b) Select from those slots in (a) which are usually filled in X.

(c) Select all remaining slots from those selected in (a).

In our example of Bill being like a bulldozer, the use of heuristics was as follows:

(a) The bulldozer value for the weight slot is relatively high for the vehicle frame, therefore it is selected.

(b) Because no value for Bill's weight was known, a high value for the weight slot was selected to be analogous with the high value in the bulldozer weight slot.

Reasoning by analogy using a frame system is described in more detail in Winston (1980). Problem-solving by analogy is described in Carbonell (1982).

Analogy has also been used to couple the two distinct domains: a computer network and a graphics system (Stabile, 1982).

9.3.7 ERROR AND OMISSION DETECTION

The inference methods described in the previous sub-section may also be used to identify errors and omissions in a body of knowledge. For example, if a perfect match is made between an entity and a person frame except for a value of 22 in the 'number of legs' slot, the system might respond by asking the user to check that value.

More complex error detection may involve several slots. Engleman et al (1982) describe the form of a 'constraint' as:

name domain expr

where 'name' is used to identify a user-oriented description of the constraint, 'domain' is a list of slot names whose interrelationships are tested by the constraint and 'expr' is an expression which must be satisfied before the frame may be instantiated.

9.3.8 PROCEDURAL ATTACHMENT/DEMONS

We have mentioned that procedures may be attached to frame slots. Such procedures may be invoked when a slot is filled with a certain value. Such procedures are often called 'if-added demons'. For example, a person frame may have an if-added demon attached to the marital status slot. If the slot is filled with the value MARRIED in some instantiation then the demon is triggered. Its effect may be to instantiate another person frame to represent the wife/husband of the person represented by the first frame.

If-added demons can be used for error handling. For example, such demons might be triggered when slot values are out of range. The effect of the demon will depend on the application. It may involve asking the user to check a value to see if it is correct.

9.3.9 FRAME LANGUAGES AND EXAMPLES OF GENERAL PURPOSE FRAME BASED SYSTEMS

KRL

KRL (Bobrow and Winograd, 1977 and 1979) is a language which allows the user to build frame systems. In KRL frames are called 'units'. There are three types of unit:

(a) Basic units which represent disjoint entity sets, e.g. people, vehicles.

(b) Specialisation units which represent specialisations of other units, e.g. male person, unemployed person. These units are not necessarily disjoint.

(c) Abstract units which represent abstract entity types, e.g. travel.

Instantiations of frames which represent individual entities are also called units in KRL. Examples of KRL units are given in fig. 9.7.

```
[Person UNIT Basic
     <SELF>
     <Name (a String)>
     <Mother (a FemalePerson)>
     <Age (an Integer)>
     <Children's names (SetOf (a String))>]

[Employee UNIT Specialisation
     <SELF (a Person)>
     <Skills (SetOf (a String))>
     <Pays Tax {(OR Yes No) Yes; DEFAULT}>]

[Female Person UNIT Specialisation
     <SELF (a Person)>
     <Gender = Female>
     <Husband> = (a MalePerson)]

[Female Employee UNIT Specialisation
     <SELF {(a FemalePerson)(an Employee)}>]

[Person 1 UNIT individual
     <SELF {(a Person with
                 Name    = John
                 Mother  = FemalePerson20
                 Age     = 35
                 Children's Names = (Items Jack Sue Peter)}>]
```

Figure 9.7 Some KRL units

UNITS

The UNITS package (Smith and Friedland, 1980) is a frame system which was developed for application in molecular biology. Frames in UNIT represent 'disjoint' entity types.

In order to accommodate the potentially large number of frames, the UNITS package maintains a secondary store of frames on disk file. Frames are paged into mainstore on demand together with any 'ancestor' frames. The frame is timestamped whenever it is referenced. The garbage collector causes frames to be paged out when the mainstore becomes full. A first in first out/not used recently algorithm is used.

WHEEZE

WHEEZE (Smith and Clayton, 1980) is a system which performs medical pulmonary function diagnosis based on clinical test results. The system consists of a frame structured language to capture production rule knowledge together with an agenda based search control mechanism (see chapter 8) which allows considerable freedom in tailoring control.

The following is an example of a WHEEZE frame for obstructive airways disease (OAD).

> OAD with smoking
>
> | Manifestation | ((OAD-Present 10)(PatientHasSmoked 10) (PatientStillSmoking 10)) |
> |---|---|
> | SuggestiveOf | ((SmokingExacerbatedOAD 5)(SmokingInduced OAD 5)) |
> | ComplementaryTo | ((OADwithSmoking-None 5)) |
> | Certainty | 1000 |
> | Findings | discontinuation of smoking should help relieve the symptoms |
> | HowToDetermineBelief | function for computing minimum of the beliefs of the manifestations |

The numbers in the Manifestation, SuggestiveOf and ComplementaryTo slots are 'importance and suggestivity' weightings. The last slot indicates how the belief in the assertion is to be computed.

FRL

FRL (Roberts and Goldstein, 1977) was one of the first frame languages developed.

OWL

OWL (Szolovits et al, 1977) was another of the early frame languages to be developed.

AM

AM (Lenat, 1982) is a frame system designed to discover concepts in mathematics. In AM, each frame represents a concept such as INTEGER or PRIME NUMBER. One objective of AM is to create new concepts.

9.3.10 DESIRABLE PROPERTIES OF FRAME SYSTEMS

(a) The frame system should be able to efficiently identify the ancestors and progeny of any given frame. Inheritance of generic properties should be possible from several ancestors.

(b) The user should be able to easily enter a value for any slot in any frame at any time.

(c) The instantiation of one frame should be able to initiate the instantiation of other frames where appropriate. For example, the instantiation of a person frame with marital status slot value MARRIED should initiate the instantiation of a frame representing the spouse of that person.

(d) The system should respond as soon as an inconsistency arises.

(e) Analogical reasoning should be possible.

(f) The user should be able to specify how match values are to be computed.

(g) The user should be able to specify the extent to which a specialised match is required.

9.3.11 ADVANTAGES/DISADVANTAGES OF FRAME SYSTEMS

Advantages

(a) Frames are intuitively appealing. The clustering of properties relating to an entity or entity set is 'natural' in the sense that people are quite familiar with the approach and use it in everyday discourse.

(b) Frame structures accommodate a taxonomy of knowledge.

(c) Default values are accommodated.

(d) Generic properties are accommodated.

(e) Procedural as well as declarative knowledge can be represented.

(f) Frames facilitate analogical reasoning.

Disadvantages

(a) There is, as yet, no formal theory of frames. Consequently, the mechanisms for inference and consistency checking are not based on a well-defined semantics.

(b) The mechanism for reasoning with uncertain knowledge (i.e. by use of match values) is based on *ad hoc* expressions with no formal foundation.

9.3.12 THE RELATIONSHIP BETWEEN FRAME SYSTEMS AND LOGIC

There is much similarity between frames and logic as methods for representing and manipulating knowledge. For example:

(a) A frame with slot relationships Ri,...,Rn, representing an entity set E, can be described using a formula of predicate logic as:

$$\forall x \in (x, E) \rightarrow \exists y1,..., \exists yn (Ri (x, y1) \wedge ,..., \wedge Rn (x, yn))$$

(b) Generic properties in which values are specified may be represented as, for example:

$$\forall x \in (x, PERSON) \rightarrow numberofhearts (x, ONE)$$

(c) The isa relationship can be represented as, for example:

isa (Employee, Person)
isa (FemaleEmployee, Employee)

479

$$\forall x \forall y \forall z \ \in(x, y) \wedge isa(y, z) \rightarrow \in(x, z)$$

The last formula states that if an entity x is a member of a set y, and y is a sub-set of an entity set z, then x is a member of the set z. This enables an individual entity to inherit all generic properties of all of its ancestors.

(d) Slot constraints can be expressed as, for example:

$$\forall x \forall y \ aged(x, y) \wedge \in(x, EMPLOYEE) \rightarrow \geqslant(y, 16) \wedge \leqslant(y, 65)$$

(e) Matching can be represented as, for example:

$$\forall x \ numberofhearts(x, ONE) \wedge numberoflegs(x, TWO)$$
$$\wedge bloodtemp(x, WARM) \rightarrow \in(x, PERSON)$$

(f) Classical logic cannot accommodate default values, computation of match values, or analogical reasoning. However, some of the other logics, which we have described can be used. For example, using a non-monotonic logic:

$$\forall x \ \in(x, PERSON) \wedge Mnumberoflegs(x, TWO)$$
$$\rightarrow numberoflegs(x, TWO)$$

$$\forall x \forall y \forall z \ numberoflegs(x, y) \wedge numberoflegs(x, z)$$
$$\rightarrow ident(y, z)$$

The first formula states that if x is a person, and x having two legs is consistent with the knowledge base, then x has two legs. The second formula states that if x has y legs and x has z legs then y and z must be identical. Therefore, if a person P is known to have one leg then M numberoflegs(P,two) is false, then the default value may not be assumed. However, if the number of legs of P is not known, then M numberoflegs (P,two) is true and P can be assumed to have two legs.

Another difference is one which affects efficiency. In all theories of formal logic, the order of the formulas is irrelevant. Formulas relating to a particular entity set can be scattered throughout the theory. In a frame system, much of the knowledge relating to a particular entity set is located in one place. In certain applications this can be advantageous.

(g) Fuzzy logic can be used to accommodate inexact matching. (See chapter 6.)

The question, then, arises as to whether frames are simply a syntactic variant of formal logic. Anything that can be represented using frames can be represented in logic (if we include non-monotonic and fuzzy logic). However, there seems to be a difference of emphasis. Use of frames requires the user to view the universe of discourse as consisting of entity sets and entities. In formal logic, unary predicates are not given a distinguished position. The concept of an entity set is at the very heart of the notion of frames.

There is no reason why the formulas of a logical theory cannot be organised in such a way as to look like a frame system. For example, (a) all formulas which contain a particular unary predicate could be stored together, (b) all formulas involving the 'isa' predicate could be stored in one place and (c) all formulas relating to a particular entity could be stored in one place. Such a system would display many of the efficient implementation properties of a frame based system in addition to possessing a well-defined semantics which it would derive from formal logic.

Minsky (1975) was largely responsible for introducing the notion of frames. Frames are often used in text understanding systems.

9.4 CONCEPTUAL DEPENDENCY

9.4.1 THE BASIC IDEA

Most of the methods of knowledge representation that we have studied regard the universe as consisting of entities and relations. Some include notions of entity set, others of attribute, and a few of functions. The science which investigates the basic components of the universe is called 'metaphysics' or 'ontology'. We can therefore describe the methods of knowledge representation which we have studied so far as regarding the universe as consisting of various combinations of the ontological primitives: entity, relation, entity set, attribute and function.

Conceptual dependency (Schank, 1973, 1975 and 1977) differs in that it regards the universe as consisting of a larger set of ontological concepts. This set includes:

- various types of entity
- various types of action
- various conceptual cases
- various conceptual tenses
- various types of conceptual dependency

Schank claims that everything people talk or think about can be represented using his set of ontological concepts. In conceptual dependency theory the basic units of meaning are structured sub-sets of Schank's concepts and are called 'conceptualisations'. Conceptualisations can be linked to other conceptualisations to build infinitely complex structures. However, the basic building blocks are fixed and the way in which they may be interfaced is fixed by the rules of conceptual dependency theory.

We begin by describing the basic ontological building blocks of the theory.

Primitive entity types
There are four primitive entity types denoted as follows:

    PP - picture producers or actors (i.e. the causers of acts)
    PA - picture aiders
    ACT - actions
    AA - action aiders

Picture producers or actors are entities which perform acts. For example, if Bill jumped then Bill is a PP. Picture aiders are 'properties' of PPs. For example, if Bill is fat then 'fat' is a PA.

Types of ACT
Various types of primitive ACT have been defined by Schank. They comprise:

ATRANS - abstract transfer, e.g. of ownership or responsibility
ATTEND - focusing of a sense organ, e.g. to listen
CONC   - to think about
EXPEL - expulsion from the body of an animate entity, e.g. spit
GRASP - grasping of an entity, e.g. grip
INGEST - ingestion into the body of an animate entity, e.g. eat
MBUILD - to combine thoughts, e.g. decide
MOVE   - movement of part of a body by its owner
MTRANS - to bring into the conscious mind, e.g. remember
PROPEL - application of physical force, e.g. push
PTRANS - physical transfer of an entity from one location to
         another
SPEAK - production of sound

Schank claims that all verbs in everyday use can be analysed in terms of these twelve primitive actions. For example, he claims that all the various verbs of thought such as think, dream, remember, conclude, decide, realise, etc., can be constructed from CONC, MTRANS and MBUILD.

Note that Schank does not say that dreaming, for example, actually involves the primitive actions CONC, MTRANS or MBUILD, but simply that it can be *described* as comprising these primitive actions. That is, Schank is not putting forward a physiological theory about how one dreams, etc., but is simply providing a psychological theory which can be used to describe dreaming.

Acts are represented by double arrows linking actors to actions. For example:

Bill ↔ INGEST, meaning Bill ate or drank something

A single verb in English may translate into more than one ACT in conceptual dependency. For example, the fact that 'Jack pushed Jill down the hill' would be conceptualised as 'Jack PROPELled Jill *and* this caused Jill to be PTRANSed down the hill'.

Conceptual cases
Conceptual dependency theory includes four cases:

O - objective
D - directive
R - recipient
I - instrumental

These cases are crucial because every action involves one or more of them. For example, in English one may say that 'Bill drank' or 'Bill drank a cup of tea' but one can only conceive of Bill drinking some (perhaps unspecified) entity which is the object of the action.

As example of the use of a conceptual case, consider the following representation of the fact that Bill drank tea:

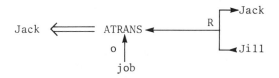

As another example, consider the situation in which 'Jack took the job from Jill', this is represented as follows:

```
                                        ┌──►Jack
                                      R │
   Jack ⇐══════ ATRANS ◄──────────────┤
              o ↑                       └──◄Jill
                │
              job
```

Conceptual tenses
The set of conceptual tenses used in conceptual dependency theory includes:

    c   - conditional
    delta - timeless
    f   - future
    k   - continuing
    p   - past
    nil   - present
    t   - transition
    tf   - finished transition
    ts   - start transition
    ?   - interrogative
    /   - negative

For example, 'Bill drank tea' can be represented as follows:

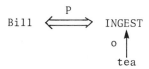

whereas 'Bill will drink tea' is represented as:

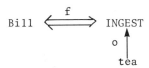

Tenses may be omitted where the tense is irrelevant.

Conceptual dependency structures

The basic building blocks described so far may be combined in various
ways according to the rules of conceptual dependency theory. The resulting structures are called 'conceptualisations'. Conceptualisations
can also be combined in various ways. The 'dependencies' between the
basic building blocks in a conceptualisation are represented diagrammatically by use of arrows. The direction of the arrow indicates the
direction of the dependency. The meaning of the word 'dependency' in
statements such as 'A depends on B' ranges from 'A is only meaningful
if B is present' to 'A is caused by B'.

The rules of conceptual dependency allow various types of dependency
structure. The following examples describe some of the allowed basic
structures:

(a) PP $\Longleftrightarrow$ ACT   e.g. Bill $\overset{p}{\Longleftrightarrow}$ MOVE

   Actors and acts which are mutually dependent may be related
   as illustrated.

(b) PP $\Longleftrightarrow$ PP   e.g. Bill $\Longleftrightarrow$ person

   Entities and the entity sets to which they belong may be related as shown. The entity is placed on the left of the arrow
   and the entity set to which it belongs is placed on the right.

(c)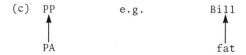

   A picture aider may be related to a picture producer as shown.
   The dependency is from PA to PP since, for example, the notion
   of 'fat' is meaningless without a PP.

(d)

   Two PP's can be related in various ways when one is a
   'property' of the other. The above depicts the conceptualisation 'the rabbit contained in the hutch'.

(e)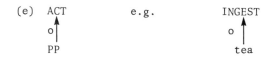

An ACT may be related to the PP which is the object of that ACT.

(f)

An ACT which involves movement can be related to a source and destination. The example depicts the conceptualisation 'something was physically transferred from room 1 to room 3'.

(g)

An ACT may be related to the source and recipient of the ACT.

(h)

$$\text{ACT} \xleftarrow{\quad I \quad} \text{ACT} \qquad \text{e.g.} \qquad \text{INGEST} \xleftarrow{\quad I \quad} \text{PTRANS}$$

An ACT may be related to an 'instrument' with which the ACT was carried out. The example represents the conceptualisation that something was INGESTed by the PTRANSing (physically movement) of something else.

(i)

A PP can be related to a state in which it started and finished. The example represents the conceptualisation that John went from being ill to being well, i.e. John got better.

(j)

Two ACTS may be related where one caused the other. The example represents the fact that 'John INGESTed because he PROPELled the weights'; that is, he got thirsty or hungry because he lifted, pushed or pressed (etc.) the weights.

(k)

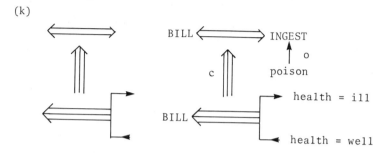

A state change may be related to an action which caused it, as illustrated. The example represents the conceptualisation that Bill 'changed' from being well to being ill because he INGESTed poison.

(l)

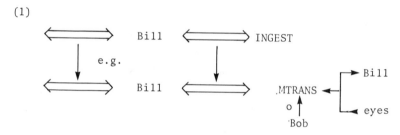

Two conceptualisations can be related if one occurred at the same time as the other. The example represents the situation which may be described in English as 'while Bill was INGESTing, he saw Bob'.

Various other basic dependency structures have been defined. However, we do not attempt to give a comprehensive set of allowed structures since conceptual dependency theory is in flux and the allowed structures vary from one description of it to another. The examples given should serve to illustrate the philosophy behind the theory.

9.4.2 EXAMPLES OF CONCEPTUAL DEPENDENCY REPRESENTATIONS
We now give examples of more complex situations.

Consider the situation in which Jill knocked Jack down the hill with a punch. This can be conceptualised as illustrated in fig. 9.8. The conceptualisation can be described as follows:

At some time in the past, Jill applied a force in the direction Jill to Jack, to the entity Jill's fist (POSS-BY stands for possessed-by). Jill did this by moving her fist in the direction from Jill to Jack. The effect of applying the force to her fist was to cause Jack to fall down the hill.

486

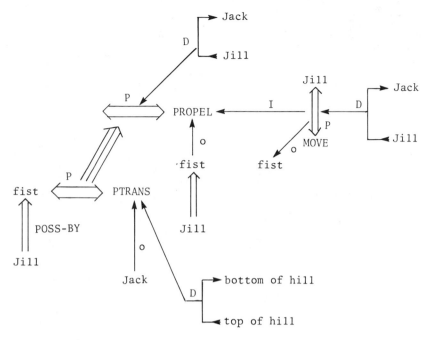

Figure 9.8 *Jill knocked Jack down the hill with a punch*

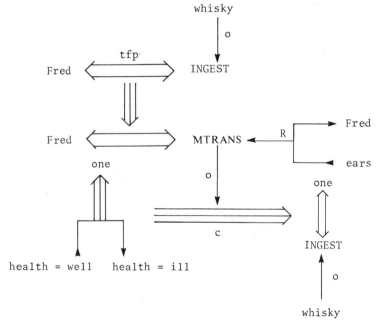

Figure 9.9 *Fred stopped drinking whisky because he heard that drinking whisky is bad for your health*

As another example, consider the situation in which Fred stopped drinking whisky because he heard that drinking whisky is bad for your health. This situation can be conceptualised as shown in fig. 9.9. The conceptual tense tfp indicates that drinking whisky happened in the past and has stopped.

Conceptual dependency structures are used in several text understanding systems.

9.5 SCRIPTS

9.5.1 WHAT IS A SCRIPT?

A script is a structure which represents a commonly occurring sequence of events such as 'going into a restaurant, and ordering, eating, and paying for a meal'. An example of a restaurant script is given in fig. 9.10. This script is a simplification of one given in Schank (1977).

Script name	:	restaurant
Roles	:	customer waiter cook owner
Entry condition	:	customer is hungry
Props	:	food table money
Scene 1	:	ENTER RESTAURANT customer PTRANs into restaurant customer MOVE customer to sit goto scene 2
Scene 2	:	ORDERING customer MTRANS signal to waiter waiter PTRANS waiter to customer customer MTRANS 'Bring me food' to waiter waiter PTRANS waiter to cook waiter MTRANS (ATRANS food) to cook cook DO (prepare food script) goto scene 3
Scene 3	:	EATING cook ATRANS food to waiter waiter ATRANS food to customer customer INGEST food *either* return to scene 2 to order more food *or* goto scene 4
Scene 4	:	customer ATRANS money to waiter customer PTRANS customer out of restaurant
Results	:	customer is not hungry customer has less money owner has more money restaurant has less food

Figure 9.10 A simple restaurant script

As illustrated in fig. 9.10, a script contains slots which can be filled by the entities that are involved in an instance of the sequence of events represented by the script. Typically, a script consists of:

(a) A set of *entry conditions* which must be satisfied before the script may be instantiated.

(b) A set of *roles* which are slots for people who would typically be involved in instances of the script.

(c) A set of *props* which are slots for objects which would typically be involved in instances of the script.

(d) A set of *scenes*, each of which represents one of the events making up the sequence of events represented by the script. A scene may be represented by a conceptual dependency graph as illustrated in figs 9.8 and 9.9.

(e) A set of *results* which will obtain after the sequence of events has been completed.

9.5.2 REASONING WITH SCRIPTS

A script may be activated by matching its name or its pre-conditions, roles, props, etc., or by matching some combination of these properties. Once a script has been activated it can be used to infer, through default reasoning, knowledge that has not been given explicitly. For example, if we know that Bill PTRANSed himself into a restaurant and that Bill ATRANSed money to a waiter, then we can infer that Bill was hungry, went into the restaurant, ordered and INGESTed some food, and left the restaurant with less money than he had when he went in.

9.5.3 EXAMPLES OF SCRIPT BASED SYSTEMS

(a) SAM (Cullingford, 1981) is a script based system which has been used to understand newspaper stories.

(b) IPP (Lebowitz, 1980) is a script based system which addresses the problems of integrating natural language parsing and memory updating. IPP was specifically designed to read and remember newspaper stories concerning international terrorism. IPP performs six tasks:

- it parses natural language into an internal representation
- it adds new stories to a long-term memory
- it recognises similarities with previous stories
- it notices interesting (unusual) aspects of stories
- it makes generalisations based on collections of similar stories
- it predicts likely future events based on the generalisations it has made

9.6 CONCLUDING COMMENTS

Various increasingly structured 'slot and filler' knowledge representations have been described: semantic nets, frames, conceptual dependency structures and scripts. We have shown that semantic nets may be regarded as syntactic variants for first order logic. We have also shown that the frame based approach has much in common with formal logic. However, when we considered the more structured slot and filler methods, the relationship to formal logic became more obscure.

Frame, conceptual dependency and script based methods are all founded very firmly on the 'entity, entity set, attribute and relation' view of the universe. This is what distinguishes these methods from formal logics, most of which are based on the 'entity, relation and function' view of the universe.

Slot and filler methods suffer from a lack of well-defined semantics. However, they can accommodate default reasoning, generic property inheritance, reasoning with uncertain knowledge and analogical reasoning.

Many people regard the slot and filler approaches as having the advantage of being more natural to use than formal logics. For example, the idea of constructing a set of stereotype frames and linking them together in an 'isa' hierarchy is easy to understand and novices can construct frame based systems in a very short time given a language such as KRL.

Although the more structured slot and filler approaches are quite distinct from formal logic and production rule based approaches, the reader should not regard them as being in competition with these other methods. There is no reason why systems should not be built which use concepts and techniques from formal logic, production rule based methods and the slot and filler approaches.

10 The Functional Approach to Knowledge Processing

10.1 INTRODUCTION

There is a growing interest in functional languages and the functional approach to knowledge processing. Many researchers believe that this approach offers an attractive alternative to the methods discussed so far in this book. It is attractive for a number of reasons, including the fact that it is based on relatively few semantic primitives and the fact that it accommodates higher-order relationships. Some aspects of the functional approach have been discussed in chapter 2, sub-section 2.2.7, and in chapter 6, sections 6.10 and 6.11. This approach is now described in more detail. We begin with a definition of the term 'function'.

10.1.1 WHAT IS A FUNCTION?

Before we can define precisely what a function is, we need to introduce the concepts of 'Cartesian product' and 'binary relation'.

Cartesian product

If A and B are sets then the set of ordered pairs {<a,b>, such that a ∈ A and b ∈ B} is called the 'Cartesian product' of A and B, and is denoted by:

A X B

Binary relations

A 'binary relation' r:A ↔ B from a set A to a set B is any set of ordered pairs which is a sub-set of A X B.

A binary relation has a 'domain' and a 'counter-domain'. The domain of a relation r is the set of objects x such that for some y, <x,y> ∈ r. The counter-domain of r is the set of all objects y such that for some x, <x,y> ∈ r.

Definition of a function

A 'function' f:A → B is a (one or many)-to-one binary relation. That is, a function is a set of ordered pairs <x,y> such that no two pairs have the same value for x and different values for y.

The domain of a function is often called its set of 'arguments', and

491

the counter-domain its 'range' or set of 'values'. A function is said to 'map' arguments to values.

The notation f(x) is used to denote the unique object y such that <x,y> ∈ f. As example of a function, consider the following:

<table>
<tr><td colspan="2">father</td><td></td><td colspan="2">father</td></tr>
<tr><td>Peter</td><td>Bill</td><td rowspan="4">often depicted as</td><td>Peter → Bill</td></tr>
<tr><td>Susan</td><td>Bill</td><td>Susan → Bill</td></tr>
<tr><td>John</td><td>David</td><td>John → David</td></tr>
<tr><td>Bill</td><td>Henry</td><td>Bill → Henry</td></tr>
</table>

(Note: the symbol → has a different meaning in this context to that in predicate logic.) In the above, the function 'father : PEOPLE → PEOPLE' is defined such that father(Peter) → Bill, father(Susan) → Bill, etc. The domain of father is the set of all people except two (since all people, except possibly ADAM and EVE, have had a father). The range of father is that sub-set of PEOPLE who are fathers.

Total functions, partial functions, onto functions, one-to-one functions and bijections

(a) A function f : A → B is a 'total' function if the domain of f = A.

(b) A function f : A → B is a 'partial' function if the domain of f ⊂ A.

(c) A function f : A → B is 'onto' if the range of f = B.

(d) A function f : A → B is 'one-to-one' if no two arguments in the domain of f are mapped to the same value.

(e) A function f is a 'bijection' if it is one-to-one and onto.

Multi-valued functions

A 'multi-valued function' is a function whose values are sets. For example, consider the following function:

<table>
<tr><td colspan="2">children</td></tr>
<tr><td>Bill</td><td>→ {Peter, Susan}</td></tr>
<tr><td>David</td><td>→ {John}</td></tr>
<tr><td>Sally</td><td>→ {Peter, Susan}</td></tr>
</table>

Multi-argument functions

In computer science, we often talk of functions having several arguments. More formally, such functions should be regarded as having a domain consisting of a set of tuples, i.e. a domain which is some appropriately defined Cartesian product. For example, consider the following function:

times

this is a function whose arguments are two-place tuples.

Multi-argument functions may be regarded as functions of one argument
As discussed in chapter 6, section 6.10, multi-argument functions may be regarded as functions of a smaller number of arguments. For example, the 'times' function above may be regarded as follows:

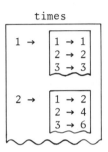

That is, 'times' may be regarded as a function which maps a single argument to a function which maps an argument to a value.

10.1.2 CHARACTERISTIC FUNCTIONS
The characteristic function f-r of an n-ary relation r is defined as follows:

$$f\text{-}r(x1,\ldots\ldots\ldots,xn) = \top \text{ if } \langle x1,\ldots\ldots\ldots,xn\rangle \in r$$
$$f\text{-}r(x1,\ldots\ldots\ldots,xn) = \bot \text{ if } \langle x1,\ldots\ldots\ldots,xn\rangle \notin r$$

For example, consider the relation 'loves' and its characteristic function 'f-loves':

loves

Bob	Sally
Paul	Jane
Bob	Paul

f-loves

$\langle$Bob, Sally$\rangle \rightarrow \top$
$\langle$Paul, Jane$\rangle \rightarrow \top$
$\langle$Bob, Jane$\rangle \rightarrow \bot$
$\langle$Paul, Sally$\rangle \rightarrow \bot$
$\langle$Paul, Paul$\rangle \rightarrow \bot$
$\langle$Bob, Paul$\rangle \rightarrow \top$
(etc.)

this assumes that the relation loves is defined on the set {Bob,Paul,Sally,Jane}

Sets may be regarded as unary relations and they also have characteristic functions. For example, consider the set 'male' and its characteristic function 'f-male':

493

```
        male                  f-male

   ┌──────────┐         ┌──────────────────┐
   │  Bob     │         │  Bob    → ⊤      │
   │  Paul    │         │  Paul   → ⊤      │
   └──────────┘         │  Sally  → ⊥      │
                        │  Jane   → ⊥      │
                        └──────────────────┘
```

This assumes that the unary relation 'male' is defined on the set {Bob, Paul, Sally, Jane}.

Notice that in first order predicate logic, a predicate symbol may be regarded as standing for the characteristic function of a relation. For example, consider the following wff of first order predicate logic:

married(John, Sally) ∧ ¬married(John, Jill)

If 'married' is regarded as standing for a characteristic function, then we could 'interpret' the above as meaning:

married(John, Sally) → ⊤ *and* married(John, Jill) → ⊥

10.2   DEFINING FUNCTIONS IN TERMS OF OTHER FUNCTIONS

Functions may be defined in terms of, or 'constructed' from, other functions. Various construction strategies may be used. These strategies include:

- composition
- generalised composition
- defining functions in terms of expressions
- defining functions by cases (conditional expressions)
- primitive recursion
- recursion
- inversion
- restriction

These strategies are each described below.

10.2.1   COMPOSITION

The 'composition' of two functions $f : A \to B$ and $g : B \to C$ is denoted by $f \circ g : A \to C$ and is defined as follows:

$$f \circ g = \{<a, c> \mid \exists b[<a, b> \in f \text{ and } <b, c> \in g]\}$$

As example of a function which is defined in this way, consider the function:

'maternal-grandfather' ≡ mother ∘ father

That is, if mother(a) → b and father(b) → c, then maternal-grandfather (a) → c.

Note that the 'relationship' between a and c may also be depicted, without introducing the maternal-grandfather function, by using 'nested' function calls:

> father(mother(a)) → c

10.2.2 GENERALISED COMPOSITION

'Generalised composition' is derived from the strategy of composition but is extended to allow functions to be defined in terms of functions which take a different number of arguments. It is defined as follows:

> if (a) h1,...,hn are functions each taking m arguments
> and (b) g is a function taking n arguments
> then (c) we can construct the following m-argument function by
> generalised composition:

> f(x1,...,xm) = g(h1(x1,...,xm),...,hn(x1,...,xm))

10.2.3. FUNCTIONS DEFINED IN TERMS OF EXPRESSIONS

Functions are often defined in terms of expressions. For example, f might be defined as that function which maps an argument y to the value which is obtained when the expression [2 * y * y + 5] is evaluated.

If operators such as * and + are regarded as functions, and constants such as 2 and 5 are regarded as constant functions, then this strategy may be regarded as equivalent to defining functions by composition (see later for a more complete explanation of this).

10.2.4 THE DEFINITION OF FUNCTIONS BY CASES/CONDITIONAL EXPRESSIONS

Definition of functions by cases
Functions may be defined by cases, as follows:

> f(x) → α   if c1(x)
>   → β   if c2(x)
>   → γ   if c3(x)
>   ⋮
>   ⋮
>   → ω   otherwise

where c1, c2, etc. are conditions which are applied to the arguments of f.

As example:

> (a) abs(x) → x   if x ⩾ 0
>   → -x   otherwise

i.e. abs maps positive numbers to themselves and negative numbers to their negation. For example, abs(3) → 3, abs(-5) → 5.

> (b) disjunction-of(x,y) → true   if x = true
>   → true   if y = true
>   → false   otherwise

Note that the logical connective 'v' in first order logic may be regarded as standing for the function 'disjunction-of'. Note also that the 'otherwise' case is optional and may be omitted provided that the other conditions cover all possible cases which it does not in examples (a) and (b).

Conditional expressions

McCarthy (1963) introduced an alternative notation for defining functions by cases. The resulting definitions are called 'conditional expressions' and have the general form:

$$f(x) = [c1(x) \rightarrow \alpha, c2(x) \rightarrow \beta, c3(x) \rightarrow \gamma, \ldots, true \rightarrow \omega]$$

For example, using this notation, 'abs' would be defined as:

$$abs(x) = [x \geq 0 \rightarrow x, true \rightarrow -x]$$

The 'condition' true in these conditional expressions corresponds to the 'otherwise' case above. It is also optional.

10.2.5 PRIMITIVE RECURSION

Hilbert (1925) defined a strategy for constructing 'numerical functions' (i.e. functions whose arguments and values are numbers) which is based on mathematical induction. The strategy is called 'primitive recursion'. Before describing this strategy, we give a brief description of mathematical induction.

Mathematical induction

Mathematical induction is a method for proving that a property holds for all but an initial segment of numbers. That is, we can use mathematical induction to prove that a property P holds for all $n \geq$ some number k. The proof consists of two steps:

(a) Prove that P(k) is true.
(b) Assuming that P(n) is true (where $n \geq k$), prove that P(n + 1) is true.

The first step is called the 'base step' and the second the 'inductive step'.

For example, to prove that 'for all $n \geq 0$, the sum (0 + 1 + ... + n) is equal to $\frac{1}{2} * n * (n + 1)$', we proceed as follows:

$$
\begin{aligned}
\text{base step:} \quad & \text{the sum } (0) = \tfrac{1}{2} * 0 * (0 + 1) \\
\text{inductive step:} \quad & \text{assume that sum } [0 + 1 + \ldots + n] = \tfrac{1}{2} * n * (n + 1) \\
& \text{then sum } (0 + 1 + \ldots + n + (n + 1)) \\
& \qquad = (\tfrac{1}{2} * n * (n + 1)) + (n + 1) \\
& \qquad = \tfrac{1}{2} * (n + 1) * ((n + 1) + 1)
\end{aligned}
$$

In this example, the base step is intuitively obvious and the inductive step simply involves the structural manipulation of an expression.

A procedure which is related to mathematical induction may be used to construct numerical functions. For example, consider the 'power' function, where power(x,y) is x raised to the power y. This function may be defined as follows:

```
power(x,y) → 1                 if y = 0
power(x,y) → x * power(x,y-1)   if y > 0
```

That is, 'power' may be defined in terms of the numbers 0 and 1 and the operator *. We show later that 0, 1 and * may be regarded as functions.

The strategy of primitive recursion

The strategy of primitive recursion is more general than that exemplified in the definition of 'power' above. The strategy is defined as follows.

If g and h are numerical functions with appropriate arguments, a numerical function f can be constructed from them, by primitive recursion:

$$f(x1,...,xn,y) \rightarrow g(x1,...,xn) \qquad\qquad \text{if } y = 0$$
$$f(x1,...,xn,y) \rightarrow h(x1,...,xn,y,f(x1,...,xn,y - 1)) \quad \text{if } y > 0$$

Applying this general strategy to the definition of the 'power' function, gives:

$$power(x,y) \rightarrow 1 \qquad\qquad\qquad\qquad\qquad\qquad \text{if } y = 0$$
$$power(x,y) \rightarrow \text{multiply-first-and-last-arguments-of}(x,y,power(x,y - 1))$$
$$\text{if } y > 0$$

In section 10.4 we show how functions such as 'multiply-first-and-last-arguments-of' can be regarded as 'basic' functions.

It should be recognised that 'primitive recursion' is quite distinct from 'recursion' as is generally understood in computer science, although the two concepts are related.

10.2.6 RECURSION

'Recursion', as is generally understood in computer science, is related to primitive recursion, but differs in two respects:

(a) It is not restricted to numerical functions (i.e. functions which map numbers to numbers).

(b) It is based on the more general notion that a function is recursive if its evaluation with one set of arguments ever requires the evaluation of a sub-expression involving an evaluation of itself with a different set of arguments.

McCarthy (1963) was one of the first to suggest that recursion should be incorporated into programming languages. In McCarthy's formalism, definitions of recursive functions involve conditional statements. For example, the 'power' function would be defined as follows:

$$power(x,y) = [y = 0 \rightarrow 1, true \rightarrow x * power(x,y - 1)]$$

In general, recursive functions are defined as follows:

$$f(x1,...,xn) = \text{some conditional expression involving}$$
$$x1,...,xn, \text{ and } f$$

Mutual recursion

A set of functions may be defined by mutual recursion. For example, two functions f and g may be defined by mutual recursion as follows:

$$f(x1,...,xn) = \text{some conditional expression involving}$$
$$x1,...,xn, \text{ and } g$$

g(y1,...,ym) = some conditional expression involving

y1,...,ym, and f

10.2.7 INVERSION AND RESTRICTION

Inversion
The 'inverse' of a one-to-one function f : A → B is the set of pairs
<b,a> such that <a,b> ∈ f.

Restriction
The 'restriction' of a function f : A → B to a set Q where Q ⊆ A, is
the function consisting of all pairs <a,b> such that a ∈ Q. The res-
triction of a function f to a set Q is denoted by f|Q.

Note that other notions of restriction have been defined. (We describe
one alternative in section 10.6.)

In later sections, we show how these various construction strategies
may be used in defining numerical functions and database queries.

10.3 THE LAMBDA CALCULUS
We have given some definitions of what a function is and how functions
may be constructed from other functions. We now describe a system in
which we can name and manipulate functions. The system is called the
'lambda calculus'.

The lambda calculus consists of a set of rules which can be used to
convert one lambda expression into another. The rules are concerned
with the renaming of bound variables, applying functions to arguments,
evaluation of expressions, and so on. The lambda calculus was devised
by Church (1941) who argued that this calculus embodied a precise definition of the notion of 'computability' (we return to this point
later).

Some aspects of the lambda calculus have been described in previous
chapters; for example, we have described lambda abstraction and lambda
conversion. We now give a more detailed account.

10.3.1 THE RULES OF LAMBDA CALCULUS

Lambda abstraction
The rule of lambda abstraction specifies how names can be constructed
for functions by use of an operator λ, called the 'lambda operator'.
For example, consider the function which maps an argument x to the
value which is obtained when the expression [2 * x + 5] is evaluated.
By lambda abstraction, we may name this function as λx[2 * x + 5].

The use of lambda names enables us to formally express properties of
defined functions. For example, we might express a property of the
function above as follows:

'λx[2 * x + 5] is increasing'

where the notion of increasing has been formally defined previously
(as in chapter 6, section 6.10). Lambda abstraction is useful when
we have an expression containing several free variables and we want

to consider it as a function of one variable. For example,
λx[x - y + 1] is increasing but λy[x - y + 1] is not.

Note that names of functions in the lambda calculus need not contain λ.
Names such as 'square', 'sum', etc. are also allowed. Note also that
a function name (as defined above) is a well-formed lambda expression.
If the name is of the form λ(x,y,...)[...x...y...], then λ(x,y...) is
called the 'bound variable part', and [...x...y...] is called the
'body' of the lambda expression.

Renaming of variables (α-conversion)
This rule states that a bound variable in a λ-expression may be consistently renamed, so long as no free occurrence of a variable, within the
body of the λ-expression, becomes bound. For example,

λx[x + y] may be renamed as λz[z + y] but may not be renamed as
$$λy[y + y]$$

(We have not described this rule explicitly in our previous discussions
of the λ-notation. However, we have made use of this rule implicitly
in our choice of examples, etc.)

Lambda conversion (β-conversion)
This rule determines how functions may be applied to arguments. We have
described one type of lambda expression (namely, function names); we
now describe another. Formulas such as λx[2 * x + 5](3) are also well-
formed lambda expressions and are called 'combinations'. The component
λx[2 * x + 5] is called the 'operator', and 3 the 'operand'.

The rule of lambda conversion tells us that a combination may be
reduced by substituting the operand for the bound variable in the body
of the operator provided that the argument contains no free occurrences
of variables which are bound in the body. For example:

λx[2 * x + 5](3) becomes [2 * 3 + 5] by lambda conversion
but λp[λx[p(x)]](x) is not allowed to become λx[x(x)]

The second expression may only be reduced if the bound variable is renamed:

λp[λx[p(x)]](x) is renamed to give λp[λy[p(y)]](x)
then λp[λy[p(y)]](x) becomes λy[x(y)] by lambda conversion

Lambda calculus also contains a rule called η-conversion.

10.3.2 THE CHURCH-ROSSER THEOREM
In all of the examples given of reduction of complex lambda expressions,
we have always applied the lambda conversion rule to the 'outermost'
lambda expression first. However, the 'evaluation sequence' need not
be restricted in this way. In general, lambda expressions may have
several evaluation sequences, some of which produce answers and some of
which do not. For example, consider the following lambda expression:

λx[5](λz[z(z)](λy[y(y)]))

If we apply lambda conversion such that (λz[z(z)](λy[y(y)])) is 'substituted' for the non-existent x in [5], we obtain the expression:

[5]

However, if we apply lambda conversion such that $\lambda y[y(y)]$ is substituted for z in z(z), we obtain:

$\lambda x[5](\lambda y[y(y)](\lambda y[(y)]))$

That is, we are back to where we started (apart from renaming of variables).

The question arises as to whether two different terminating sequences of reduction, applied to the same lambda expression, both of which result in irreducible expressions, produce the *same* irreducible expression. The answer is yes, according to the Church-Rosser theorem which states:

> If two different terminating evaluation sequences for a given lambda expression result in irreducible expressions, then the two irreducible expressions are equivalent up to the renaming of bound variables.

10.3.3 CURRIED FUNCTIONS

Functions with several arguments may be regarded as functions with a fewer number of arguments, as discussed earlier in this section. In the lambda calculus, this may be accommodated by a process called 'currying'. As example, consider a function which maps the argument tuple <x,y> to the value which is obtained when the expression [x * y] is evaluated. By lambda abstraction, this function may be named as:

$\lambda(x,y)[x * y]$

The curried version of this function is:

$\lambda x[\lambda y[x * y]]$

Combinations are constructed from curried functions by listing the operands in a sequence corresponding to the 'nesting' of the operators. For example:

$\lambda x[\lambda y[x * y]](3)(5)$

One application of the rule of lambda conversion gives:

$\lambda y[3 * y](5)$

A second application of the rule of lambda conversion gives:

$3 * 5$

We saw in chapter 6, section 6.11, how notions related to currying are used by Montague to determine the meaning of words such as 'every':

every $\equiv \lambda P[\lambda Q[\forall x P(x) \rightarrow Q(x)]]$

According to Montague, the translation of a sentence such as 'every man walks' to predicate logic may be carried out as follows:

(a) 'Every' is represented as the curried function given above.

(b) The sentence 'every man walks' becomes:

$\lambda P[\lambda Q[\forall x P(x) \rightarrow Q(x)]](man)(walks)$

(c) Application of the lambda conversion rule gives:

$\lambda Q[\forall x man(x) \rightarrow Q(x)](walks)$

(d) Further application of the lambda conversion rule gives:

$\forall x man(x) \rightarrow walks(x)$

Readers should refer back to chapter 6, sub-section 6.11, if necessary, for a more detailed description of Montague's approach to the semantics of natural language.

10.3.4 HIGHER-ORDER FUNCTIONS

Composition as a function
Earlier in this section, we explained how functions may be defined in terms of other functions. We mentioned 'composition' as one of the strategies for combining functions to form new functions. The composition strategy may itself be regarded as a function whose arguments are pairs of functions:

composition : the-set-of-pairs-of-functions →
the-set-of-composed-functions

For example:

composition(father, father) ≡ the-paternal-grandfather-function.

Composition may be regarded as a curried function, in which case:

composition(father)(father) ≡ the-paternal-grandfather-function.

Higher-order functions
A function which takes functions as arguments is called a 'higher-order function'. Composition is an example of a higher-order function. All of the other construction strategies may also be regarded as higher-order functions.

10.4 GENERAL RECURSIVE FUNCTIONS AND THE NOTION OF COMPUTABILITY

10.4.1 BASE FUNCTIONS AND CONSTRUCTED FUNCTIONS
Examples have been given of how functions may be defined or constructed from other functions. Obviously, some functions must be 'primitive' in the sense that they are not constructed from other functions. Such functions are called 'base functions'.

The methods which are used to construct non-base functions from other functions are called 'construction strategies'. We have mentioned several; for example, composition, generalised composition and primitive recursion. Suppose that we have a set F of base functions, and a set C of construction strategies; the total set of 'constructable' functions which can be derived is denoted by C(F).

For example, if F = {father, mother} and C = {composition}, then C(F) is:

{father ∘ father, father ∘ mother, mother ∘ father, mother ∘ mother,
father ∘ father ∘ father, etc.}

That is, C(F) includes all functions which can be constructed by the repeated application of the construction strategies to the base functions and to functions which have been constructed previously. That is, C(F) is the 'closure' of F under the operations in C.

10.4.2 COMPUTABLE FUNCTIONS

In an attempt to define the notion of 'computability', Hilbert (1925) defined a 'computable numerical function' as one that can be constructed from a particular set of base functions and construction strategies which were chosen by himself and Kleene. The base functions chosen were the following numerical functions:

(a) The constant 'zero function' : c0, which returns the value of zero irrespective of its argument.

$$c0(n) \rightarrow 0$$

(b) The 'successor function': succ, whose value is one greater than its argument.

$$succ(n) \rightarrow n+1$$

(c) The 'predecessor function': pred, whose value is one less than its argument:

$$pred(n) \rightarrow n - 1$$

(d) An infinite class of 'argument selector functions' each of which selects a particular argument from a list of arguments. For example, the selector function s25 selects the argument 2 from a list (tuple) of 5 arguments. For example:

$$s25(x1, x2, x3, x4, x5) \rightarrow x2$$

Note that s11 is the 'identity' function.

The construction strategies chosen by Hilbert and Kleene were generalised composition and primitive recursion, as defined in sub-section 10.1. We now give some examples of how other numerical functions may be constructed in Hilbert's system:

(a) The *constant function c1*, whose value is always 1, may be constructed as follows:

$$c1(n) \rightarrow succ(c0(n))$$
$$= succ(0)$$
$$= 1$$

(b) The *sum function* can be constructed, using primitive recursion, as follows:

$$sum(x,y) \rightarrow s11(x) \qquad \qquad \text{if } y = 0$$
$$sum(x,y) \rightarrow (composition(s33,succ))(x,y,sum(x,y - 1))$$
$$\text{if } y > 0$$

that is sum(x,y) → x if y = 0, otherwise sum(x,y) → the successor of the sum of x and y - 1.

10.4.3 THE GENERAL RECURSIVE FUNCTIONS

The numerical functions which can be constructed in Hilbert's system are 'computable' in the sense that an algorithm may be built such that the function can be implemented in terms of the base functions.

Hilbert conjectured that *all* of the computable numerical functions can be constructed using generalised composition and primitive recursion strategies extended to have higher-order functions as arguments. However, Ackerman identified an 'obviously' computable function that could not be so constructed. In order to overcome this problem, Kleene introduced an additional construction strategy called 'minimisation', which we now define:

If f is a function with n+1 arguments, and k is a number, we can construct a function g with n arguments, by minimisation, as follows:

g(x1,...,xn - 1) → the unique xn such that
      (a) f(x1,...,xn - 1,xn) → k
and (b) for all xn' < xn,   f(x1,...,xn - 1,xn') ≠ k

The set of numerical functions which can be constructed in Hilbert's system (extended to include the minimisation strategy) is called the set of 'general recursive functions'.

The relevance of the notions above to knowledge processing and knowledge base systems

Some readers may be wondering why the notions described in this sub-section have been introduced. The reason is that they are highly relevant to certain aspects of knowledge processing which we shall be describing in the remainder of this chapter and in chapter 11. In particular:

(a) McCarthy's pioneering work in the theory of computation (McCarthy, 1960 and 1963) included the development of a calculus of symbolic (non-numeric) expressions which was analogous to Hilbert's treatment of numerical functions. We describe McCarthy's calculus in the next sub-section and the programming language, LISP, which is based on the calculus, in chapter 11.

(b) The notion of computability is relevant to the discussion of programming languages as knowledge representation formalisms which is given in chapter 11.

(c) The discussion of Hilbert's approach to numerical functions demonstrates how the functional approach may be used to represent both simple and complex concepts in a systematic manner. It also demonstrates how a functional view of some slice of reality may be built using a very small set of semantic primitives, and how knowledge may be represented using a very small set of syntactic constructs.

10.5 McCARTHY'S APPROACH TO COMPUTATION

10.5.1 McCARTHY'S FORMALISM FOR THE THEORY OF COMPUTER SCIENCE

In the early days of computing, computers were primarily used to process numbers. McCarthy argued that numbers were inadequate to accommodate all of the knowledge processing that we might want to carry out on a computer. Consequently, he developed a formalism for the theory of computer science which included symbols as well as numbers. This formalism is similar to Hilbert's approach to numerical functions.

McCarthy proposed a set of construction strategies C which can be used to construct new functions from sets of base functions F which are chosen by users to be appropriate for the data structures they wish to use. The closure C(F), i.e. the set of all functions which can be so constructed, is regarded as comprising all of the computable functions relevant to the particular data structures concerned. For example, if the data structures are simply integer variables, then the set of base functions F might be chosen to be equivalent to those used by Hilbert. However, if the data structures are strings, then the set of base functions F might include LEN (giving the length of the string), APPEND (adding a single character to the end of a string) and so on. The closure C(F) would then comprise all of the computable functions on strings. (We show in the next sub-section, that LEN and APPEND are not the most appropriate primitives for symbolic processing.)

The construction strategies which McCarthy proposed were:

- generalised composition
- use of conditional expressions
- recursion

We shall refer to this set of strategies as CMc. All of these strategies have been described in section 10.2.

10.5.2 S-EXPRESSIONS AND THE BASE FUNCTIONS OF McCARTHY'S CALCULUS FOR SYMBOLIC PROCESSING

One of McCarthy's objectives was to develop a calculus for symbolic processing which was analogous to Hilbert's treatment of numbers. To this end, he developed a calculus which included CMc together with a set of base functions which operated on a particular type of symbolic expression called S-expressions.

S-expressions

S-expressions are data structures which are linearised representations of binary trees. Examples of S-expressions are:

```
S1 :    ((A . B) . (C . D))
S2 :    (A . (B . C))
S3 :    (A B C)
```

```
S4 :    A
S5 :    ((A . B) C D)
S6 :    NIL
S7 :    ( )
S8 :    ((A) (C D))
```

The binary trees corresponding to the first five of these S-expressions are:

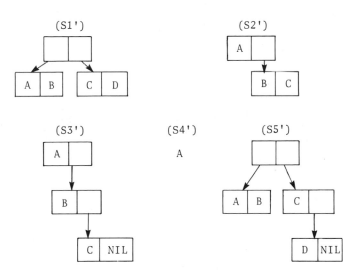

S-expressions are of different types:

    (a)   Atoms: expression S4 is an example of an atom.

    (b)   Dotted pairs: expressions S1 and S2 are examples of dotted pairs.

    (c)   Lists: expression S3 is an example of a list.

    (d)   List structures: expression S5 is an example of a list structure.

    (e)   NIL: a special atom which plays the role of list terminator.

    (f)   ( ): the empty list.

The list notation was introduced as a convenient shorthand for those S-expressions which 'represent' linear lists, where a linear list is of the following form (or of a form which we describe below):

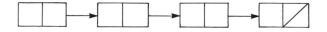

For example, the expression S3 above is shorthand for a dotted pair as shown below:

(A B C) is shorthand for (A . (B . (C . NIL))) where NIL is the empty list.

Notice that (A B C) is *not* shorthand for (A . (B . C)).

If the dotted pair and list notation are intermingled, then the result-ing S-expression is a list structure, as exemplified by S5 above. S5 is also shorthand for a dotted pair as shown below.

((A . B) C D) is shorthand for (A . B) . (C . (D . NIL)))

In McCarthy's calculus, an S-expression is of type 'list' if it rep-resents a binary tree in which every terminal right sub-tree is NIL. Consequently, the expression S8 is also of type list since it represents the following tree:

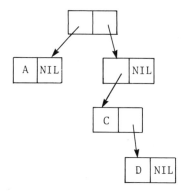

The base functions of S-expressions

McCarthy defined a set of base functions for S-expressions just as Hilbert defined a set of base functions for numbers. The base functions which McCarthy chose were 'atom', 'eq', 'car', cdr' and 'cons'.

(a)   'atom' is a function whose arguments are S-expressions and whose values are truth values. It is defined as follows:

$$\text{atom}(\alpha) \;\rightarrow\; \text{true if } \alpha \text{ is an atom}$$
$$\rightarrow\; \text{false otherwise}$$

(b)   'eq' is a function whose arguments are pairs of atoms and whose values are truth values. It is defined as follows:

$$\text{eq}(\alpha,\beta) \;\rightarrow\; \text{true if } \alpha \text{ and } \beta \text{ are equal}$$
$$\rightarrow\; \text{false otherwise}$$

eq is undefined if either of α or β are not atoms.

(c)   'car' is a function whose arguments are non-atomic S-expres-sions and whose values are S-expressions. It is defined as follows:

$$\text{car}((\alpha . \beta)) \;\rightarrow\; \alpha$$

In effect, car extracts the left sub-tree from an S-expression.

506

(d) 'cdr' is similar to car, but it extracts the right sub-tree, i.e.:

$$cdr((\alpha . \beta)) \rightarrow \beta$$

(e) 'cons' is a function whose argument is a pair of S-expressions whose value is a dotted pair formed from the two expressions:

$$cons(\alpha,\beta) \rightarrow (\alpha . \beta)$$

We shall refer to the five base functions given above as the set 'FS-exp'.

Examples of the application of the base functions FS-exp to S-expressions

(a) car((A . (B . C))) → A
(b) cdr((A . (B . C))) → (B . C)
(c) cons(A, (B . C)) → (A . (B . C))
(d) eq(A,A) → true
(e) eq(A, car(A . B)) → true
(f) atom(A) → true
(g) atom((A . B)) → false
(h) atom(cdr(cdr(A . (B . C))) → true
(i) car((A B C)) → A   (note that this is an atom)
(j) cdr((A B C)) → (B C)
(k) car(((A B) C)) → (A B)
(l) cdr(((A B) C)) → (C)   (note that this is a list)
(m) cdr((A)) → NIL

10.5.3 THE COMPUTABLE FUNCTIONS OF S-EXPRESSIONS AND THE PROGRAMMING LANGUAGE LISP

McCarthy claimed that the set of 'computable' functions of S-expressions are all those functions which can be constructed from FS-exp by application of the construction strategies CMc given in 10.5.1. That is:

The set of computable functions of S-expressions = all of those functions which may be constructed by the (possibly repeated) application of the strategies: generalised composition, conditional expressions, recursion, to the base functions atom, eq, car, cdr and cons.

This discussion concludes with some examples of constructed functions:

(a) The function 'null' takes an S-expression as argument and returns the value true if the expression is NIL. This function may be defined, using a conditional statement as follows:

$$null(\alpha) = [atom(\alpha) \rightarrow eq(\alpha,NIL), true \rightarrow false]$$

(b) The function 'append' takes a pair of lists as argument and joins the lists together. It is defined, using recursion and generalised composition:

$$append(\alpha,\beta) = [null(\alpha) \rightarrow \beta, true$$
$$\rightarrow cons(car(\alpha), append(cdr(\alpha),\beta))]$$

507

Append returns an error if either of the arguments
is atom.

(c)   The function 'equalatomiclists' takes a pair of lists of atoms
of equal length and returns the value true iff they are equal.
It is defined as follows:

$$\text{equalatomiclists}(\alpha,\beta) = [\text{null}(\alpha) \rightarrow \text{true}, \text{not eq}(\text{car}(\alpha),$$
$$\text{car}(\beta)) \rightarrow \text{false}, \text{true} \rightarrow \text{equalatomiclists}(\text{cdr}(\alpha),\text{cdr}(\beta))]$$

These examples are no more than basic string processing functions.
However, the set of functions which can be constructed from S-exp and
CMc includes much more powerful functions, as we shall see later.

McCarthy's calculus for S-expressions has been implemented in a programming language called LISP, in which all of the computable functions of
S-expressions can be expressed.   LISP is described in more detail in
chapter 11.

Some of the material in sub-sections 10.2 to 10.5 was derived from
Brady (1977).   Brady's book is a good introduction to the functional or
programming approach to the theory of computer science.

10.6   THE FUNCTIONAL VIEW OF THE UNIVERSE

Different types of functional view
Various views have been developed which may be categorised as 'functional' views.   For example, the view which underlies Montague's
approach to the semantics of natural language, which was discussed in
chapter 6, sub-sections 6.10 and 6.11, is a functional view in which
the universe is regarded as consisting of:

   • entities
   • truth values
   • functions
   • possible worlds
   • time points

In this approach, sets are conceptualised as characteristic functions,
logical connectives are regarded as functions and n-ary ($n \geqslant 2$) relations are conceptualised as functions which map single arguments into
n-1 argument functions.   For example:

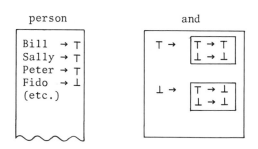

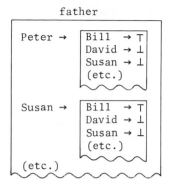

The advantage of this approach is its uniformity. This uniformity enables the definition of type-theoretic languages which have relatively simple syntax and semantics (an example of a type-theoretic language is described in chapter 6, section 6.10).

Other functional views have been developed. Some allow functions to have multiple arguments. For example:

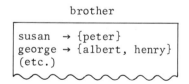

As such, these views conceptualise n-ary relations ($n \geqslant 2$) in a different way from the view used by Montague.

Some views allow functions to have sets as values (rather than viewing the world as consisting of characteristic functions of sets). For example:

brother

```
susan   → {peter}
george → {albert, henry}
(etc.)
```

What characterises a functional view?
The aspects of a view which characterise it as being a 'functional' view rather than a 'relational' view, or some other view, would appear to be (a) its regarding the universe as consisting of functions rather than arbitrary relations (remember that a function is a '(one or many)-to-one' binary relation) and (b) its allowing functions to be arguments or results of functions.

As such, the view on which first order predicate logic is based would not be regarded as a functional view since, although it does contain

509

the notion of a function, it also contains the notions of n-ary and
many-to-many relations, and it does not allow functions to be arguments
or results of functions.

According to the 'definition' above, functional views are 'higher-order'
views in that they allow us to conceptualise functions which have other
functions as arguments, or values, and therefore allow us to conceptualise functions as entities.

We now introduce two database languages which are based on a functional
approach to knowledge processing.

10.7 FQL: A DATABASE QUERY LANGUAGE

FQL is a database query language developed by Buneman and Frankel
(1979). FQL allows users to define functions in terms of the set of
base functions which are 'provided' by the database system they wish to
query. We begin by explaining what is meant by a 'base function' in
this context and then show how functions can be defined in terms of
base functions using FQL. Finally, we show how complex queries may be
expressed in FQL.

10.7.1 CHARACTERISING THE RETRIEVAL FACILITIES PROVIDED BY A DATABASE
SYSTEM AS A SET OF BASE FUNCTIONS

Access paths and retrieval facilities provided by a database system
Suppose that we have a database system which is characterised by the
database schema given in fig. 10.1. This schema is defined using a
notation which was introduced in chapter 3. (In that chapter, we defined a database schema as a schema depicting the data types and logical
access paths which are provided by a database system.)

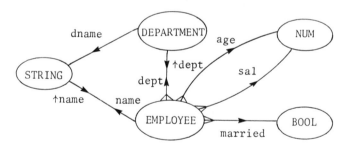

Figure 10.1 A database schema

Irrespective of how the database is stored, the database schema in fig.
10.1 tells us that:

(a) Five data types are supported: DEPARTMENT, EMPLOYEE, STRING,
     NUM and BOOL.

(b) Eight access paths are provided, each of which links objects
     of one type to objects of another type. For example, there
     is an access path from objects of type EMPLOYEE to objects of
     type STRING. This access path represents the NAME relation.

(c)   The AGE relation, for example, is many-to-one. That is, many employees may have the same age, but each employee may only have one age.

Access paths whose names begin with ↑ are 'inverses' of those paths whose names follow the up-arrow. For example, ↑NAME is the inverse of NAME.

In addition to the simple access paths mentioned above, the database system might provide some additional facilities for retrieving data. For example:

(a)   We may be able to retrieve a 'sequence' of all departments.

(b)   We may be able to retrieve the tuple, consisting of a name and salary, for a given employee.

(c)   We may be able to retrieve a hierarchically structured file (or record) containing the name for a given department together with the employees of that department.

In order to formalise the specification of the retrieval facilities provided by a database system, it is useful to introduce the notion of 'data types'.

Data types

We have already given examples of five simple data types: DEPARTMENT, EMPLOYEE, NUM, STRING and BOOL. More complex types may be defined in terms of these basic types. For example:

(a)   A sequence of departments is an instance of a constructed data type which we can denote by *DEPARTMENT.

(b)   A tuple, consisting of a name and a salary, is an instance of a constructed type which we can denote by [STRING, NUM].

(c)   A file such as that described in (c) above is an instance of a data type which we can denote by [STRING, *EMPLOYEE].

Given that data types can be constructed in this way, we can now define the facilities which are provided by the database system above.

Regarding the retrieval facilities provided by a database system as a set of base functions

The retrieval facilities provided by any database system, be it hier-archical, network, or relational, may be formally characterised by regarding them as functions which are provided by that database system. We shall call these functions 'base functions'. Continuing with the example, we could characterise the retrieval facilities provided by the database system above as the set of base functions on page 512. The types of these functions are defined in terms of the types of their arguments and values.

Functions whose names start with ! are called 'generating' functions since they require no argument and their values are sequences. As such they are 'constant' functions, although the sequence returned may change as the database is updated.

511

Function	Type	Meaning
NAME : EMPLOYEE → STRING		Given an employee, the database returns a string which is the name of that employee.
!DEPARTMENT : → *DEPARTMENT		The database provides a facility for retrieving a sequence of all departments.
MARRIED : EMPLOYEE → BOOL		Given an employee, the database returns a Boolean value indicating whether or not that employee is married.
EMPLOYEE-NAME-AND-SAL : EMPLOYEE → [STRING, NUM]		Given an employee, the database returns a tuple consisting of a string and number denoting the name and salary of that employee.
DEPT : DEPARTMENT → *EMPLOYEE		Given a department, the database returns a sequence of employees in that department.

```
!EMPLOYEE :                 → *EMPLOYEE ⎫
   DNAME  : DEPARTMENT → STRING          ⎪
    NAME  : EMPLOYEE   → STRING          ⎪
     SAL  : EMPLOYEE   → NUM             ⎬ Meanings as expected.
     AGE  : EMPLOYEE   → NUM             ⎪
    DEPT  : EMPLOYEE   → DEPARTMENT      ⎪
   ↑NAME  : STRING     → EMPLOYEE        ⎭
```

Characterising a database system by listing its base functions (as exemplified above) is a particularly powerful abstraction technique since (a) it can be used for any type of database system: hierarchical, network, relational or binary relational and (b) given the set of base functions which characterise a database system, the end-user need not concern himself with the type of DBMS used, nor with any aspect of the implemented storage structure (apart from efficiency considerations which are discussed later). As such, the end-user sees the database simply as a set of base functions, as illustrated in fig. 10.2.

Now, the user could use the base functions directly in queries; for example by calling them as follows:

!DEPARTMENT

where the result would be a sequence of departments.

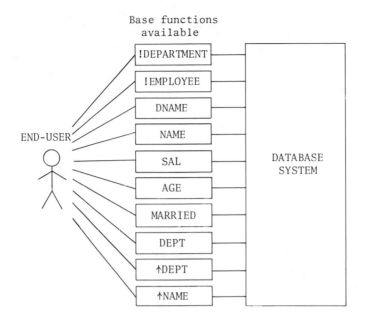

Base functions
available

Figure 10.2   The user's view of the database system as a set of base functions

The language FQL, which we describe in the remainder of this section, allows users to construct (a) new functions in terms of the base functions provided by the database in question, and (b) complex queries as expressions involving the base functions and/or the new functions. The facility to construct new functions allows users to adopt a 'modular programming' approach to query formulation.

We begin by describing the function construction strategies which are provided by FQL and then show how more complex functions may be defined in terms of base functions using the construction strategies. Our discussion of FQL concludes by showing how queries may be expressed in terms of base functions and defined functions.

Note that queries could be constructed from base functions alone, using the construction strategies available in FQL. However, the use of defined functions allows frequently used constructed functions to be defined, named and used as required. It also enables a 'modular' programming style, in which complex queries and functions may be defined in parts. As such, the use of defined functions in FQL is similar to the use of functions in conventional programming languages such as Pascal.

10.7.2   THE FUNCTION CONSTRUCTION STRATEGIES WHICH ARE AVAILABLE IN FQL
FQL provides various constructs (or higher-order functions) which allow new functions to be constructed from other functions. These higher-order functions implement construction strategies analogous to the construction strategies used in Hilbert's treatment of numbers and in

McCarthy's calculus for symbolic knowledge processing. (See sections 10.2, 10.3 and 10.4.) We describe FQL's construction strategies by giving some examples:

(a) *NAME denotes a function, constructed from the base function NAME, using the construction function *. The type of *NAME is *EMPLOYEE → *STRING. That is, the arguments of *NAME are sequences of employees and its values are sequences of strings denoting names of employees.

(b) DEPT ° DNAME denotes a function which maps objects of type EMPLOYEE to objects of type STRING. This function takes an employee as argument and returns the name of the department of that employee as value. The composition operator ° is similar to the one described in section 10.2.

(c) |MARRIED denotes a function which takes a sequence of employees and filters out those employees who are not married. That is, |MARRIED is of type *EMPLOYEE → *EMPLOYEE. In general, if f is a boolean-valued function, then |f restricts sequences according to whether f returns a value of true or false when applied to each element of the sequence.

(d) [NAME, SAL] denotes a function which maps employees into tuples consisting of a string (the name) and a number (the salary). That is, [NAME, SAL] is of type EMPLOYEE → [STRING, NUM]. Notice that square brackets have two meanings in FQL. When used for the definition of functions, their meaning is as given above. When used in the definition of types, they can be used to construct tuple types from other types as exemplified in sub-section 10.7.1.

(e) #1[NAME, SAL] denotes a function which is equivalent to NAME. The selector function #1 selects the first argument of the value returned by [NAME, SAL]. More useful examples involving selector functions are given later.

(f) &SUCC generates an infinite sequence which is obtained by applying 'successive powers' of SUCC to its argument. (This assumes that a function SUCC exists which maps numbers into their successors, i.e. it adds one to its argument as does Hilbert's base function SUCC.)

10.7.3 STANDARD FUNCTIONS WHICH ARE AVAILABLE IN FQL

In addition to the base functions which are provided by the database system in question, FQL provides a number of 'standard' functions. We list these functions, grouping them by type:

(a) Arithmetic functions: the following arithmetic functions are all of type [NUM, NUM] → NUM, and all have their 'expected' meanings:

   +

   -

```
×
/
MOD
```

The other arithmetic functions which are available are /+ and /× which perform 'addition' and 'times' on sequences of NUMs. That is, they are of type *NUM → NUM.

(b)   Relational and boolean functions: the following functions are available. All have their 'expected' meanings:

$$
\left.\begin{matrix} EQ \\ NE \\ GT \\ LT \\ GE \\ LE \end{matrix}\right\} \quad \begin{matrix} \text{all map [NUM,NUM]} \\ \text{or} \\ \text{[STRING,STRING]} \end{matrix} \left.\vphantom{\begin{matrix} a \\ b \\ c \end{matrix}}\right\} \quad \text{to BOOL}
$$

(c)   Constant functions: a numeric literal or a character string in quotes is regarded as a constant function whose value is the number or string denoted by the function name. For example, 1 is the constant function whose value is 1 and 'e2' is the function whose value is e2. Other constant functions are denoted by !<name> where name identifies a database type. !<name> denotes a generating function whose value is a sequence of objects of type <name>. The function NIL is a constant function whose value is the empty sequence of objects with type appropriate for the context in which NIL is used.

(d)   Basic sequence manipulating functions: the following basic sequence manipulating functions are available in FQL:

HD : *α → α   returns the first element of a
                        sequence

TL : *α → α   returns a sequence minus the
                        first element

CONS : [α, *α] → *α   takes an object and sequence and
                        appends them

(e)   Other sequence manipulating functions: the other sequence manipulating functions which are available in FQL are:

LEN : *α → NUM   computes the length of a
                        sequence

CONC : [*α, *α] → *α   concatenates two sequences

/CONC : **α → *α   forms a single sequence from
                        a sequence of sequences

DISTRIB : [*α, B] → *[α, B]   distributes the object B
                        over the objects in the
                        sequence *α

(f)   Other functions: the other functions provided by FQL are the 'construction' functions *, o, |, #1, #2, ..., ↑, ε and the

515

tuple forming function [ ], all of which have been described earlier. Another function which is available is ID : α → α, the identity function which maps an object to itself.

Note that since strings and numeric literals are regarded as constant functions in FQL, function calls are written as illustrated in the following example:

'E2' ° SAL

rather than the equivalent and more usual notation SAL(E2). The reason for treating strings and numeric literals as constant functions is that the 'order' of function composition corresponds to the 'navigation' of the access paths in the database. In the example above, we start with E2 and then follow the SAL path to the number denoting E2's salary.

10.7.4 DEFINING NEW FUNCTIONS IN FQL

New functions may be defined in FQL in terms of base functions, standard functions and previously defined functions by using the construction functions. For example:

(a) NAMEOFDEPTOFEMPLOYEE = DEPT ° DNAME ;

This function takes an employee as argument and returns the name of the department of that employee as value.

(b) !NAMESOFEMPLOYEES = !EMPLOYEE • *NAME ;

This function generates a sequence of the names of all employees.

(c) AVERAGE = [/+, LEN] ° / ;

This function takes a sequence of numbers as argument and returns a number, the average, as value.

(d) AVESAL = !EMPLOYEE ° *SAL ° AVERAGE ;

This function takes a department as argument and returns the average salary of employees in that department as value.

New functions may also be defined recursively in FQL. Details can be found in Buneman and Frankel (1979).

10.7.5 EXPRESSING QUERIES IN FQL

Queries in FQL are expressed as function calls. We give some examples: the first is a simple query involving a base function only, the next three are more complex queries involving base functions, standard functions and the construction functions, and the last is a 'structured' query which makes use of the defined functions given above.

(a) !DEPARTMENT ;

The answer to this query is a sequence of all departments.

(b) 'E2' ° AGE ;

The answer to this query is the age of employee E2.

(c) 'Smith' ∘ ↑NAME ∘ [AGE, SAL] ;

>   The answer to this query is a tuple consisting of the age
>   and salary of the employee named Smith.

(d) !DEPARTMENT ∘ |([DNAME, 'SALES'] ∘ EQ) ∘ *↑DEPT ∘ /CONC
     ∘ *[NAME, SAL]

>   The answer to this query is the names and salaries of all
>   employees in the sales departments.

(e) !EMPLOYEE ∘ |([[AGE, 30] ∘ LT, [SAL, AVESAL] ∘ GT] ∘ AND)
     ∘ *NAME ;

>   The answer to this query is a sequence of names of
>   employees whose age is less than 30 and whose salary is
>   greater than the average salary of employees.

Evaluating arithmetic expressions

FQL is more expressive than most database query languages since it
allows the user to evaluate arithmetic expressions without reference
to any database. For example, consider the following 'queries':

(a) [1, 2] ∘ + ;

>   The answer to this 'query' is 3.

(b) 0 ∘ &SUCC ;

>   This generates the sequence 0,1,2,... .

(c) [0,1] ∘ &[#2, +] ∘ *#1 ;

>   This generates the Fibonacci sequence of order 2.

Much of the material in this section was derived from a paper by
Buneman, Frankel and Nikhil (1982) in which an implementation technique
for database query languages is described using FQL as an example.

10.8 DAPLEX: A DATA DEFINITION AND MANIPULATION LANGUAGE

DAPLEX is a data definition and manipulation language which was developed by Shipman (1981). It has much in common with FQL and, in many
respects, DAPLEX is equivalent to FQL with a more user-friendly syntax.
However, it does have some additional facilities. For example, it
allows the user to declare sub-types, to assign values for variables,
to specify database updates and to specify constraints which are used
automatically.

Since the concepts which underly DAPLEX are similar to those underlying
FQL, we do not give a detailed description of DAPLEX. Instead, we present some examples of DAPLEX expressions in order to give the reader a
feel for the language. All of the examples below refer to the database
schema depicted in fig. 10.3.

Declaration of base functions

    DECLARE Student( ) ⇒⇒ ENTITY   Student is a generating function:
                                          it generates a sequence of
                                          students.

517

DECLARE Name(Student) ⇒ STRING   Name maps students to
                                          strings denoting their name.

DECLARE Department( ) ⇒⇒ ENTITY   Department generates a
                                          sequence of departments.

DECLARE Course(Student) ⇒⇒ Courses   Course maps students to
                                          sequences of courses.

DECLARE Dept(Student) ⇒ Department   Dept maps a student to his
                                          or her department.

DECLARE Course( ) ⇒⇒ ENTITY   Course generates a sequence
                                          of courses.

DECLARE Grade(Student, Course) ⇒ INTEGER   See note (c) below.

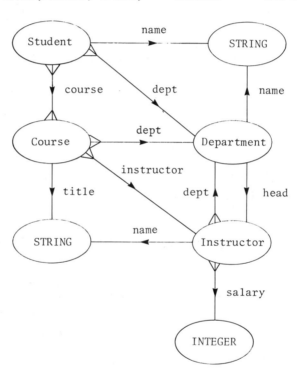

Figure 10.3 A database schema

Notes

(a) Name 'overloading' is possible in DAPLEX. That is, a name may
     be used to denote more than one thing. The correct denotation
     is determined by the context. For example, 'Course' can
     denote (i) a function mapping students to courses, (ii) an
     entity (or data) type or (iii) a generating function. Such
     name overloading is regarded by some as an advantage in that
     it is quite natural to use, while others regard it as a dis-
     advantage since it can be a source of confusion.

(b) The double-headed arrow signifies that the value returned by the function is a sequence.

(c) Multi-argument functions, such as 'Grade' above, may be declared. This function takes a tuple, consisting of a student and a course, as argument, and returns an integer, denoting the grade which the student obtained on that course, as value.

Sub-types and super-types

The functions declared above are defined over the 'base' types ENTITY, STRING and INTEGER. The generating functions may be thought of as declaring new types which are defined in terms of the base types.

In general, types may be declared and organised as a 'sort lattice' in DAPLEX. (We have already discussed sort lattices in chapter 6, section 6.2 with respect to sorted logics.) The following declarations show how a sort lattice may be constructed in DAPLEX:

```
DECLARE  Person( )      ⇒⇒  ENTITY
DECLARE  Student( )     ⇒⇒  Person
DECLARE  Employee( )    ⇒⇒  Person
DECLARE  Instructor( )  ⇒⇒  Employee
DECLARE  Department( )  ⇒⇒  ENTITY
DECLARE  Course( )      ⇒⇒  ENTITY
```

The lattice corresponding to these declarations is shown in fig. 10.4. This lattice is, in fact, a hierarchy. However, more general lattices may be constructed by use of the intersection and union operators which are available in DAPLEX.

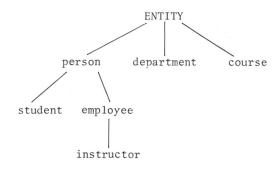

Figure 10.4 A lattice of entity types

Inheritance of functions

Suppose that, in addition to those above, we have the following declarations:

```
DECLARE Name(Person)     ⇒  STRING
DECLARE Dept(Student)    ⇒  Department
DECLARE Course(Student)  ⇒  Course
DECLARE Salary(Employee) ⇒  INTEGER
```

519

```
DECLARE  Manager(Employee)     ⇒  Employee
DECLARE  Rank(Instructor)      ⇒  STRING
DECLARE  Dept(Instructor)      ⇒  Department
DECLARE  Instructor(Course)    ⇒  Instructor
DECLARE  Title(Course)         ⇒  STRING
DECLARE  Name(Dept)            ⇒  STRING
```

Any function which is declared for an entity type is also declared for
its sub-types. Hence, for example, the 'Name' function is also declared
for Students, Employees, and Instructors, and the 'Salary' function is
also declared for Instructors.

Defined functions
New functions may be defined in terms of other functions in DAPLEX, as
illustrated in the following examples:

(a) DEFINE Instructor(Student) ⇒⇒ Instructor(Course(Student))

   This defines the instructors of a student to be the
   instructors of courses which the student takes.

(b) DEFINE Student(STRING) ⇒ INVERSE OF Name(Student)

(c) DEFINE Course(STRING) ⇒ INVERSE OF Title(Course)

   These two definitions introduce functions which are
   inverses of existing functions.

(d) DEFINE StudentTeacher( ) ⇒ INTERSECTION OF Student,
   Instructor

   This illustrates how new entity types may be defined in
   terms of others.

Queries in DAPLEX
Some examples of queries in DAPLEX follow. We do not give explanations
since the meaning in each case is self-evident.

(a) FOR EACH Student
   SUCH THAT FOR SOME Course(Student)
   Name(Dept(Course))   = "Computer Science"
   AND
   Rank(Instructor(Course))   = "Professor"
      PRINT Name(Student)

(b) FOR EACH Employee
   SUCH THAT Salary(Employee) > Salary(Manager(Employee))
      PRINT NAME(Employee)

(c) PRINT AVERAGE(Salary(Instructor)) OVER Instructor
   SUCH THAT Name(Dept(Instructor)) = "Computer Science")

Updating the database
The following DAPLEX statement causes 'Systems Analysis' to be dropped
from John's course, and 'Databases' to be added:

```
FOR THE Student SUCH THAT Name(Student)  =  "John"
     BEGIN
        EXCLUDE Course(Student)  =
           THE Course SUCH THAT Name(Course)  =  "Systems Analysis"
        INCLUDE Course(Student)  =
           THE Course SUCH THAT Name(Course)  =  "Databases"
```

Constraints

```
DEFINE CONSTRAINT Too many courses(Student)  ⇒
     COUNT(Course(Student)) > 6
```

This prevents the database from being updated in such a way that any student has more than six courses.

DAPLEX is a user-friendly data definition and manipulation language based on a functional view which regards the universe as consisting of entities and multi-valued functions. Although we have not described this facility, DAPLEX is also capable of accommodating multiple-user views which are implemented using defined functions. This facility allows DAPLEX to be used as an interface language in networks involving different types of database management system. However, in this respect it is not as powerful as FQL. This point is discussed further in section 10.9.

A version of DAPLEX, written in ADA and called ADAPLEX, has been implemented by CCA (1982).

10.9 CONCLUDING COMMENTS

This chapter began by defining what a function is, and went on to show how functions can be constructed from other functions. We then described lambda calculus, which is a calculus of functions, and followed this with an explanation of how Hilbert defined numbers in terms of a set of base functions and construction strategies. A description followed of McCarthy's calculus for symbolic expressions, which is analogous to Hilbert's treatment of numbers. McCarthy's calculus is embodied in the programming language LISP which is discussed further in the next chapter.

After discussing McCarthy's calculus, we attempted to characterise 'functional views' by identifying properties which distinguish functional views from other views.

In the last two sections, two 'database' languages which are based on functional views were described. In discussing the first of these, FQL, we introduced a powerful abstraction technique in which database systems of any type may be regarded as sets of base functions. New functions may then be defined in terms of the base functions using FQL's construction strategies, and queries can be expressed in terms of base functions and/or defined functions.

The second language which was discussed, DAPLEX, is similar to FQL in some respects, but it has a more user-friendly syntax and it provides facilities for constructing entity type (sort) lattices, for assigning values to variables, for specifying database updates and for specifying integrity constraints. However, DAPLEX is not as expressive as FQL in several other respects. In particular, in FQL, functions can return tuples as values. This would appear to simplify both the interfacing of FQL to database systems of various types and the construction of functions and queries whose values are something other than entities or sets of entities (e.g. hierarchically structured records).

At this point, the reader may be wondering how the functional approach relates to approaches based on predicate logic, and in particular how the use of defined functions relates to deduction. A discussion of this relationship is outside the scope of this book, and for now it will suffice to note the following points:

(a) Predicate symbols in languages of predicate logic may be regarded as standing for 'characteristic' functions. For example, consider the predicate 'married'. When this is 'applied' to a tuple such as <John, Mary> the value returned is true or false depending on whether <John, Mary> is in the relation MARRIED.

(b) The logical connectives ∧, ∨, ¬, →, etc. may be regarded as functions which map truth values to truth values as discussed earlier in this chapter.

(c) We have shown how the word 'every' may be regarded as a function. It is also possible to regard the quantifiers ∀ and ∃ as functions.

A comprehensive discussion of combinatory logic, the logic which is related to the functional view, can be found in Hindley, Lercher and Seldin (1972).

522

11 Programming Languages and Knowledge Processing

11.1 INTRODUCTION

In this chapter, we are concerned with the use of programming languages for (a) representing knowledge and (b) expressing commands to manipulate knowledge. This distinction is not fundamental since programs may themselves be regarded as constituting knowledge. However, it is useful to distinguish between writing declarative statements which 'tell a computer something' and writing imperative commands which 'tell a computer to do something'.

It is assumed that the reader is familiar with at least one high-level programming language and that he has some notion of how programming languages may be translated to executable code. However, as a refresher, we begin by giving some potted notes on grammars and translators and then show how the semantics of programming languages may be defined. This is followed by a discussion of various terms which are commonly used to describe programming languages, e.g. 'procedural', 'declarative', 'functional', 'database query', 'logic programming' and so on. Most of these terms are rather vaguely defined in the literature, yet they can serve to give the 'flavour' of a language. We conclude the chapter by discussing three languages which are particularly relevant to knowledge base systems work: LISP, Prolog and PS-algol.

The ability to design languages and to write translators is very useful for anyone wanting to embark on a career in knowledge base systems work. The notes which constitute this chapter are by no means comprehensive and should be regarded as an introduction to the topics with which they are concerned. References to suitable material for further reading are included.

We begin by discussing the syntax of programming languages.

11.2 SYNTAX

A language is defined by its 'syntax' and its 'semantics'. The syntax consists of rules for determining which sequences of symbols are 'well-formed' sentences of the language, and which are not. The semantics of a language comprises rules for ascribing meaning to well-formed sentences. For example, we might have a language L3 which is defined by the following syntax and semantics:

Syntax of L3

Well-formed sentences of L3 consist of an integer symbol, or
an integer symbol followed by '+' followed by an integer symbol. For example, the following are well-formed sentences of
L3:

3
3 + 2
17

Semantics of L3

(a) An integer symbol denotes an integer.
(b) A well-formed sentence of the form:

int.symbol-1 + int.symbol-2

denotes the integer which is the sum of the integers denoted
by:

int.symbol-1 and int.symbol-2.

A problem with such informal definitions of syntax and semantics is
that they are rather vague and hence may be misunderstood. In addition,
since the syntax rules are not specified in a standard format, it is
difficult to design general purpose processes by which syntax rules may
be transcribed to programs to automatically test a sentence to see if
it is well-formed.

In this section, some techniques for the formal specification of syntax
rules of a particular class of languages, called context-free languages,
are introduced. We also show how these formal specifications may be
used to manually recognise sentences which are well-formed. Later, we
show how the formal specifications of syntax rules may be transcribed
to programs which carry out the recognition task automatically.

We begin with some definitions.

11.2.1 CONTEXT-FREE GRAMMARS
A 'grammar' is a set of rules which determine which sequences of symbols are well-formed sentences of the language defined by the grammar.

A 'context-free grammar' (CFG) is a particular type of grammar. The
difference between a context-free and a context-sensitive grammar will
be discussed later.

A CFG consists of a finite set of 'terminal' symbols, a finite set of
'non-terminal' symbols, one of which is called the 'distinguished non-
terminal', and a finite set of 'production rules', each of which has a
single non-terminal on its left-hand side and a sequence of one or more
terminals or non-terminals on its right-hand side.

The terminal symbols are the symbols which are used when writing a sentence of the language defined by the grammar. They are atomic in the
sense that they are not composed of smaller symbols. Terminal symbols
may be composed of more than one character, for example ':='. However,
this symbol is considered to be atomic since it symbolises a single
concept (assignment in this case).

In chapter 2, sub-section 2.2.4, we described how to build a lexical
scanner. It is the job of the lexical scanner to recognise terminal
symbols in the source text. In the remainder of this chapter, we shall
assume that lexical scanners are available for the languages discussed.

Non-terminals represent classes of 'syntactic construct'. Examples of
non-terminals which are commonly used in the grammars of programming
languages are 'statement', 'while-loop', 'assignment', expression',
'operator', 'identifier', 'procedure' and so on.

Production rules, or 'productions', define how well-formed constructs
may be built. There may be any number of productions defining the same
non-terminal. Each of these productions defines an alternative way of
building the construct denoted by the non-terminal. (We shall use the
term 'production' from now on since the term 'production rule' was used
in a more general sense in the discussion of expert systems in chapter
8.)

There are various notations which may be used for defining CFGs, and
one is introduced in the following example:

Backus-Naur form (BNF)
The following context-free grammar G4, is specified using a variant of
BNF notation:

```
G4: terminals                      = {a, b, c, +, -, [, ]}
    non-terminals                  = {expression, primary, identifier}
    distinguished non-terminal     = expression

    productions:    expression ::= primary
                               | expression + primary
                               | expression - primary
                    primary    ::= identifier
                               | [ expression ]
                    identifier ::= a
                               | b
                               | c
```

The BNF notation may be explained as follows:

(a) n ::= α   means that the non-terminal n is composed of the
                sequence of terminals and non-terminals denoted
                by α.

(b) α β   denotes the sequence which consists of the sequence
                α followed by the sequence β.

(c) n ::= α⎫   means that n is composed of α or β. This is short-
         | β⎭   hand for the two rules 'n ::= α' and 'n ::= β'.

According to the grammar G4:

(a) a, b and c are identifiers in G4.

(b) a, [b] and [a+b] are examples of primaries in G4.

(c) a, [b], a - b and a + b - [c + d] are examples of expressions
     in G4.

To show that these are correct, we introduce the notion of a 'derivation'.

Derivations

In the following, the Greek letters α, β, γ and δ denote sequences of terminals and non-terminals.

We say that α 'directly derives' β in a grammar G, iff β can be obtained from α by replacing, in α, some non-terminal n by the right-hand side of some production in G whose left-hand side is n. We denote the fact that α directly derives β in a grammar G by:

$$\alpha \underset{G}{\Rightarrow} \beta \text{ or, if G is known, by } \alpha \Rightarrow \beta$$

For example, in the grammar G4 above:

    expression - primary = expression - identifier

If $\alpha \Rightarrow \gamma$ and $\gamma \Rightarrow \beta$, then we say that α 'derives' β. More generally, we can say that α derives β iff α directly derives β, or if α directly derives γ and γ derives β, i.e.:

$$\alpha \Rightarrow^+ \beta \text{ iff } \alpha \Rightarrow \beta \text{ or } [\alpha \Rightarrow \gamma \text{ and } \gamma \Rightarrow^+ \beta]$$

where $\alpha \Rightarrow^+ \beta$ denotes the fact that α derives β.

For example, in the grammar G4 above:

$$\text{expression} \Rightarrow^+ \text{expression - identifier}$$
$$\text{and expression} \Rightarrow^+ a - b + c$$

If we let E, P and I stand for expression, primary and identifier, respectively, then we can explain the last example above by listing the steps in the derivation together with the production used in each step:

Step	Production used
$E \Rightarrow E + P$	E ::= E + P
$\Rightarrow E + I$	P ::= I
$\Rightarrow E + c$	I ::= c
$\Rightarrow E - P + c$	E ::= E - P
$\Rightarrow E - I + c$	P ::= I
$\Rightarrow E - b + c$	I ::= b
$\Rightarrow P - b + c$	E ::= P
$\Rightarrow I - b + c$	P ::= I
$\Rightarrow a - b + c$	I ::= a
therefore $E \Rightarrow^+ a - b + c$	

Languages

A 'sentence' of a grammar G is a sequence of terminals α such that:

    the distinguished non-terminal $\Rightarrow^+ \alpha$

i.e. a sentence of a grammar G is any sequence of terminals that can
be derived in G from the distinguished non-terminal.

The 'language' of a grammar G is the set of all sentences of G. In
many cases, this set is infinite.

Syntax trees (derivation trees)
A 'syntax tree' can be used to illustrate how a sentence may be derived
in a grammar. A syntax tree is a tree such that:

   (a)   All leaf nodes are labelled with terminal symbols.
   (b)   All non-leaf nodes are labelled with non-terminals.
   (c)   The root node is labelled by the distinguished non-terminal.
   (d)   If a non-terminal node is labelled by n and its children are
         labelled by α, β, γ, etc., then 'n ::= α β γ ...' is a pro-
         duction in G.

As example, the syntax tree for a - b + c in G4 is given in fig. 11.1.

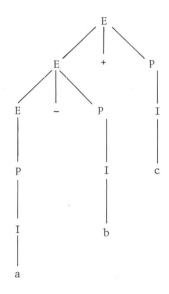

Figure 11.1 A syntax tree

A single syntax tree may correspond to more than one derivation. For
example, the tree in fig. 11.1 corresponds to the derivation given
above and also to the derivation shown on page 528.

Ambiguity
A sentence which has more than one syntax tree in a grammar is 'ambiguous' (note: this does not mean that sentences which have more than one
derivation are necessarily ambiguous).

A grammar which has one or more ambiguous sentences is itself ambiguous.
As example of an ambiguous grammar, consider the grammar G5.

Step

```
E ⇒ E + P          ⎤
  ⇒ E - P + P      ⎥
  ⇒ E - I + P      ⎥
  ⇒ E - b + P      ⎥
  ⇒ P - b + P      ⎬  an alternative derivation
  ⇒ P - b + I      ⎥  of a - b + c
  ⇒ I - b + I      ⎥
  ⇒ a - b + I      ⎥
  ⇒ a - b + c      ⎥
therefore E ⇒⁺ a - b + c ⎦
```

G5 is similar to G4 except that the productions are:

```
G5: E ::= P
      | E + E
      | E - E
    P ::= I
      | [E]
    I ::= a
      | b
      | c
```

We can demonstrate that G5 is ambiguous by constructing the two syntax trees shown in fig. 11.2 for the sentence 'a - b + c'.

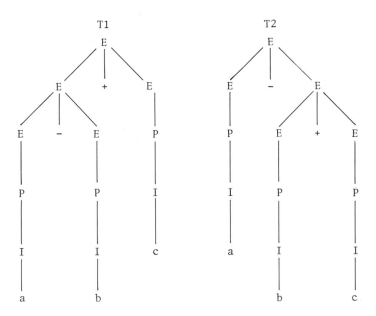

Figure 11.2 Demonstrating ambiguity

Syntax trees impose a syntactic structure on well-formed sentences which is, in some sense, related to the semantics of the language.

For example, T1 implies that a - b + c is equivalent to [a - b] + c, whereas T2 implies that a - b + c is equivalent to a - [b + c].

How to detect ambiguity

In general, it is not possible to determine whether or not a grammar is ambiguous; that is, the problem is undecidable. However, it is possible in some cases to determine whether a grammar is ambiguous. For example, a grammar is definitely ambiguous if:

(a) A production is both left- and right-recursive, e.g.:

> n ::= n α n   (see page 535 for a definition
> | γ   of recursive productions)

OR

(b) A non-terminal has both a left-recursive and a right-recursive production, e.g.:

> n ::= n α   (this is left-recursive)
> | β n (this is right-recursive)
> | γ

In general, it is desirable that grammars are not ambiguous. If a grammar is found to be ambiguous, it should be changed.

11.2.2 RECOGNITION AND PARSING

'Recognition' is the process of determining whether a given sequence of terminals is a sentence of a given grammar.

'Parsing' is recognition together with the implicit or explicit construction of the syntax tree.

There are various methods of parsing. We shall describe one method, called 'top-down parsing', with reference to an example. Consider the following grammar G6:

> G6:   terminals = {i, c, h, 1, ;}
>   non-terminals = {S, P}
>   distinguished non-terminal = S
>
>   productions
>   S ::= P ;
>   P ::= i
> | c P
> | h P 1 P

We now show how to parse the sequence 'chili;' in G6 using a top-down approach:

(a) Start by building a tree with the root labelled by the distinguished non-terminal S. Then attempt to 'reach down' to the sequence 'chili;' as shown in step 1 in fig. 11.3. That is, start by applying 'S ::= P ;',

(b) There are now three possibilities. That is, there are three productions that could be applied:

529

```
(i)   P ::= i
(ii)  P ::= c P
(iii) P ::= h P l P
```

The alternatives (i) and (iii) are no good since application
of (i) would lead to a tree corresponding to the sentence
'i;' and (iii) would lead to a set of trees corresponding to
sentences all of which start with 'h'. Therefore, (ii) is
the only choice. Application of (ii) is illustrated in step
2 in fig. 11.3.

(c)   Again, there are three possibilities since we could apply any
      one of the following:

```
(i)   P ::= i
(ii)  P ::= c P
(iii) P ::= h P l P
```

Alternative (iii) is the only 'valid' choice. This gives the
tree shown in step 3 in fig. 11.3.

(d)   Continuing in a similar fashion, we eventually obtain the
      final tree shown in fig. 11.3.

Notes

(i)   The 'parse' described above and illustrated in fig. 11.3 is
       top-down since we started with the distinguished non-terminal
       and worked down towards the sentence to be parsed.

(ii)   The parse was relatively easy since at each stage (other than
       in the first), although there was more than one production
       which could have been applied, only one of these productions
       was valid. That is, valid in the sense that its application
       was compatible with the sentence 'chili;'.

(iii) In the above example, and in all parses in G6, there is a
       simple method for determining which of the possible produc-
       tions should be applied: we look at the next terminal in the
       sequence to be parsed, which has not yet been linked into the
       syntax tree, and choose the production whose right-hand side
       starts with that terminal.

We can illustrate point (iii) by parsing 'chili;' again, emphasising
this method of determining which production to apply. The parse is
shown in fig. 11.4 on page 532.

Director sets
The grammar G6 is called a '1-lookahead' grammar. This is because we
need only look at the next unlinked terminal in the sentence being
parsed to determine which of the possible productions to apply.
1-lookahead grammars are useful since it is relatively easy to construct programs to automatically parse sentences of 1-lookahead
grammars. In non-1-lookahead grammars, if we were not able to determine which one from a set of possible productions to apply, we would

have to choose one arbitrarily and, if at some later stage we reached a 'dead end', would have to backtrack and choose another.

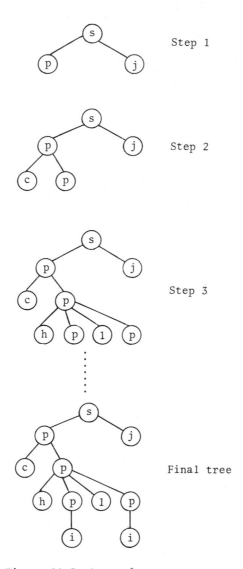

Step 1

Step 2

Step 3

Final tree

Figure 11.3 A top-down parse

The determination of which production to apply, when faced with a set of possible productions, in the grammar G6 is straightforward. We simply look at each of the possible productions and pick the one whose sequence on the right-hand side starts with the next unlinked terminal in the sentence being parsed. For example, consider the stages at which we had the following three possibilities:

```
apply P ::= i
apply P ::= c P
apply P ::= h P l P
```

In order to determine which one to apply, we simply looked at the next unlinked terminal, which was 'c' in the second step of our example, and matched this with the terminal starting the right-hand side 'c P'. This told us to apply the production 'P ::= c P'. This example is simple since in G6, whenever a choice is possible, the right-hand sides of the possible productions always start with a terminal. In general, this is not the case. Some right-hand sides might start with non-terminals.

(a) start with the distinguished non-terminal: Next terminal

(b) apply S ::= P; since only choice:

(c) apply P ::= c P since the next terminal is c

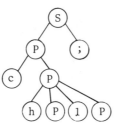

    c is linked in, so move to next terminal   c h i l i ;

(d) apply P ::= h P l P since the next terminal is h

    h is linked in so move to next terminal   c h i l i ;

(e) continue until all of the terminals have been
    linked into the tree

Figure 11.4 A top-down parse illustrating the use of director sets

However, there will always be other productions which can be used to
eventually derive one or more sequences which begin with terminals from
these non-terminals. Hence it is always possible to determine which
terminal or terminals will start the constructs denoted by the right-
hand side of any production in a grammar. This set of terminals is
called the 'director set' of that production.

We now give two examples of grammars and their director sets:

G6:   terminals = {i, c, h, l, ;}
       non-terminals = {S, P}
distinguished non-terminal = S

productions	director sets
S ::= P ;	{i, c, h} ← (this set is deter-
P ::= i	{i} mined by applying the
| c P	{c} productions for P)
| h P l P	{h}

G7:   terminals = {i, c, h, l, m, ;}
       non-terminals = {S, P}
distinguished non-terminal = S

productions	director sets
S ::= P ;	{i, c, h}
P ::= i	{i}
| c P	{c}
| h P l P	{h}
| h P m	{h}

Note two points with respect to these examples:

(a)   It is not always sufficient simply to look at the right-hand
      side of a production to determine the director set. If the
      right-hand side starts with a non-terminal, we need to follow
      through some derivations to determine the director set. More
      formally, if n is a non-terminal and α is a sequence of term-
      inals and non-terminals, then we can compute the director set
      DS of a production 'n ::= α' as follows:

              (i) If α starts with a terminal t, then DS = {t}
      else (ii) DS = {t| $\alpha \Rightarrow^+$ t β}

      where β is any sequence of terminals and non-terminals.

(b)   The grammar G7 is not 1-lookahead since the director sets for
      two of the productions for the non-terminal P are non-disjoint.
      That is, the productions 'P ::= h P l P' and 'P ::= h P m' do
      not have non-disjoint director sets, hence it is not possible
      to determine which one to apply by simply looking at the next
      unlinked terminal in the sentence being parsed.

Factorisation
Although the grammar G7 is not a 1-lookahead grammar, it is possible

to make it one by a process called 'factorisation'. This process simply involves the introduction of new non-terminals to stand for the common prefixes of troublesome productions.

For example, we can factorise G7 to obtain the following 1-lookahead grammar which is 'equivalent' to G7 in the sense that it defines the same language:

    G8:   terminals = {i, c, h, l, m, ;}
                     non-terminals = {S, P}
       distinguished non-terminal = S

productions	director sets	
S ::= P ;	{i, c, h}	
P ::= i	{i}	(note that Q is
| c P	{c}	the new non-
| h P Q	{h}	terminal introduced)
Q ::= l P	{l}	
| m	{m}	

The purpose of factorisation is to convert non-1-lookahead grammars to 1-lookahead grammars. Factorisation is useful since it is easier to construct automatic parsers for languages which are 1-lookahead than it is for those which are not.

Note: in general, factorisation is more complex than this. Two productions for the same non-terminal may have non-disjoint director sets yet may not have a common sequence at the beginning of their right-hand sides. For example, consider the following grammar G9:

    G9:   terminals = {a, b, c, d, e, f, ;}
                     non-terminals = {S, P, Q, R, T}
       distinguished non-terminal = S

productions	director sets	
S ::= P ;	{a, b, c}	
P ::= Q d	{a, b, c}	overlap
| R c	{a, b}	
Q ::= T	{a, b}	
| c	{c}	
R ::= a	{a}	
| b	{b}	
T ::= a f	{a}	
| b f	{b}	

Simple factorisation, as described above, will not help us convert this to a 1-lookahead grammar. However, a more complex rule can be used. We do not describe this rule here, but refer the reader to Waite and Goos (1984), Aho and Ullman (1979) or Backhouse (1979).

Left-recursion
Consider the following grammar:

G10:   terminals = {a, b, c, d, e, ;}
                           non-terminals = {S, P, Q}
           distinguished non-terminal = S

      productions   director sets
      S ::= P ;   {a, b, c}
      P ::= a   {a}
          | b P   {b}
          | c Q d   {c}
      Q ::= P   {a, b, c}⎫
          | Q e P   {a, b, c}⎬ non-disjoint

This grammar is called a 'left-recursive' grammar, due to the presence
of the production 'Q ::= Q e P'. As can be seen, this grammar is not
a 1-lookahead grammar. More importantly, it cannot be made into one
by factorisation. A left-recursive production, such as 'Q ::= Q e P',
can never have a director set which is disjoint from the director sets
of other productions with the same left-hand side, such as 'Q ::= P'.

One approach to this problem is to re-specify the grammar in such a way
that it does not contain a left-recursive production. The re-specified
grammar (if it is a 1-lookahead grammar) may then be transcribed to a
recogniser program as described later in this chapter.

However, removing left-recursion is not always a trivial task. Fortunately, there is a methodical approach to dealing with this problem.
This approach involves the use of another notation for specifying
grammars which is an extended form of the Backus-Naur notation.

Extended Backus-Naur form (EBNF)
EBNF is similar to BNF but includes some additional constructs:

   (a) $\langle\alpha\rangle$ means α occurs once or not at all.
   (b) $\{\alpha\}$ means α occurs zero or more times.
   (c) $(\alpha|\beta)$ means α or β occurs.

As example, consider the grammar G10 above specified in EBNF:

      S ::= P ;
      P ::= (a| b P| c Q d)
      Q ::= (P|Q e P)

Removal of left-recursion
The above does not really demonstrate the usefulness of EBNF since we
still have left-recursion. However, we can get rid of it now since:

      Q ::= (P|Q e P) may be re-written as Q ::= P{e P}

We can demonstrate that this is a valid conversion by building some
derivation trees (shown on page 536).

The general rule for the removal of left-recursion may be specified as
follows:

   Productions of the form 'N ::= $(\alpha|N\ \beta)$' may be re-written as
                                            'N ::= $\alpha\{\beta\}$'.

535

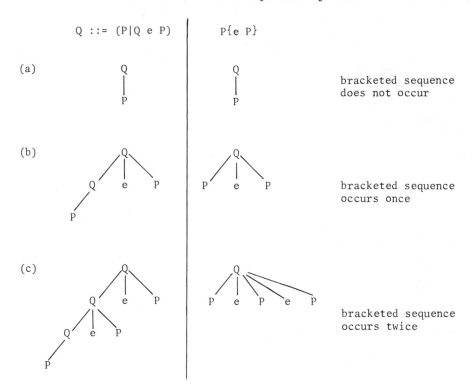

Q ::= (P|Q e P)   P{e P}

(a)

bracketed sequence
does not occur

(b)

bracketed sequence
occurs once

(c)

bracketed sequence
occurs twice

Removal of right-recursion

Right-recursion may also be removed by applying the following rule:

Productions of the form N ::= $(\alpha|\beta\ N)$ may be re-written as
$$N ::= \{\beta\}\alpha.$$

However, removal of right-recursion is not essential.

Factorisation in EBNF

Productions may also be factorised in EBNF. Two of the simpler factorisation rules are:

(a) Productions such as 'N ::= $(\alpha\ \beta\ \delta|\alpha\ \gamma\ \delta)$' may be factorised to 'N ::= $\alpha(\beta|\gamma)\delta$'.

(b) Productions such as 'N ::= $(\alpha\ \beta\ \delta|\alpha\ \delta)$' may be factorised to 'N ::= $\alpha <\beta> \delta$'.

Note that these simple factorisations are *not guaranteed* to produce 1-lookahead grammars. It is still necessary to determine the director sets for various cases when specifying a grammar in EBNF. For example:

(i) $(\alpha|\beta|...)$ Director sets of α, β, etc. must be disjoint.
(ii) $\{\alpha\}\beta$ Director sets of α and β must be disjoint.
(iii) $<\alpha>\beta$ Director sets of α and β must be disjoint.

If this is not the case then the grammar is not 1-lookahead, and the method for constructing recognisers given below will not work.

Note: these examples are not comprehensive. Suppose that we had two productions such that:

```
    n ::= mα
and m ::= γ{δ}
```

It is necessary that δ and α have disjoint director sets for the grammar to be 1-lookahead. For more details, we refer the reader to the references given earlier.

11.3 THE CONSTRUCTION OF RECOGNISER PROGRAMS

The advantage of using EBNF is that grammars which are specified in it, and which are 1-lookahead may be easily transcribed to recogniser programs. The transcription rules involved may be defined 'inductively' as follows, where the left-hand column gives an EBNF production schema and the right-hand column gives the corresponding piece of program:

Production schema	Program segment

(TR1) N ::= α	*procedure* Analyse-N;
	   begin
	      transcription of α
	   end;

(TR2) α β δ	transcription of α; transcription of β; transcription of δ;

(TR3) (β|γ|...)	*if* current-terminal is *in* the
	        director set of β
	  then transcription of β
	else if current-terminal is *in* the
	        director set of γ
	  then transcription of γ
	  (etc.)

(TR4) <β>	*if* current-terminal is *in* the
	        director set of β
	  then transcription of β
	  else do nothing;

(TR5) {β}	*while* current-terminal is in the
	        director set of β
	  do begin
	     transcription of β
	  end;

(TR6) α (where α is a single non-terminal)	Analyse-α;

(TR7) α (where α is a single terminal)	*if* current terminal = α
	  then fetch-next-terminal
	  else error;

Notes
The definition above is 'inductive' in the sense that the transcription
rules are applied repeatedly until all productions are transcribed to
program statements. All occurrences of 'transcription of ...' are reduced to program statements by repeated application of the transcription rules.

An example of constructing a recogniser for a grammar
Consider the following grammar G11 specified in BNF:

G11:   terminals = {a, b, c, d, +, -, *, [,]}
                            non-terminals = {E, T, P, I}
                distinguished non-terminal = E

        productions: E ::= T|E + T|E - T   (i)
                      T ::= P|T * P   (ii)
                      P ::= I|[E]   (iii)
                      I ::= a|b|c|d   (iv)

The following are examples of well-formed sentences of G11:

    a + b
    a + b - c
    a + b * c
    a + b * [c - d]

G11 is left-recursive and is not 1-lookahead. However, it may be converted to an equivalent grammar G11' in EBNF which is not left-recursive and is 1-lookahead:

    G11' similar to G11 except that the productions are:

            E ::= T{(+|-)T}   from (i) above   ⎫
            T ::= P{* P}   from (ii) above   ⎬ and the rules
            P ::= (I|[E])   from (iii) above ⎪ on page 535
            I ::= (a|b|c|d)   from (iv) above   ⎭

We can now create a recogniser program for this grammar.

If we apply the transcription rule (TR1) above to the first production,
we get:

    procedure Analyse-E;
        begin
                transcription of T{(+|-) T}
        end;

Applying the transcription rule (TR2) to this gives:

    procedure Analyse-E;
        begin
                transcription of T;
                transcription of {(+|-) T}
        end;

538

Applying rule (TR6) gives:

```
procedure Analyse-E;
    begin
            Analyse-T;
            transcription of {(+|-) T}
    end;
```

Applying rule (TR5) gives:

```
procedure Analyse-E;
    begin
            Analyse-T;
            while current-terminal in ['+', '-']
                do begin
                            transcription of (+|-) T
                    end
    end;
```

And so on.

Note: when the transcription rules are being applied it is often possible to simplify the code; for example, by removing redundant 'if-then-elses', and by using case statements, etc. If we do this with the example above, we will eventually obtain the following recogniser program for the grammar G11':

```
procedure    recogniser;
    var      current-terminal: token;
    procedure fetch-terminal;
                {fetches the next terminal from the input and
                assigns it to current-terminal - this may involve
                the use of a lexical scanner as discussed in
                chapter 2, sub-section 2.2.4 (called 'getok')}.

procedure error;
                {reports a syntax error}

procedure Analyse-E; forward;   ⎤
procedure Analyse-T; forward;   ⎥  accommodates any mutual recursion,
procedure Analyse-P; forward;   ⎬  and allows procedures to be
procedure Analyse-I; forward;   ⎦  written in natural order

procedure Analyse-E;
    begin
            Analyse-T;
                while current-terminal in ['+', '-']
                        do begin
                                fetch-terminal;
                                Analyse-T
                            end
    end;
```

```
procedure Analyse-T;
    begin
            Analyse-P;
            while current-terminal = '*'
                do begin
                            fetch-terminal;
                            Analyse-P
                    end;
    end;

procedure Analyse-P;
    begin
            if current-terminal = '['
                then begin
                            fetch-terminal;
                            Analyse-E;
                            if current-terminal = ']'
                                then fetch-terminal
                                else error
                    end
                else
                            Analyse-I
    end;

procedure Analyse-I;
    begin
            if current-terminal in ['a', 'b', 'c', 'd']
                then fetch-terminal
                else error
    end;

begin
        fetch-terminal; {i.e. first terminal on input}
        Analyse-E;
        if current-terminal not equal to some endmarker
            then error
end.
```

We have now described two methods for constructing recognisers for a certain class of context-free grammars known as LL1 grammars:

(a) In chapter 2, sub-section 2.2.4, we explained how a recogniser could be constructed from a BNF specification. However, this approach requires the grammar to be specified in BNF as a 1-lookahead, non-left-recursive grammar. This requires a certain amount of expertise from the person specifying the grammar.

(b) In the present section, we have explained a more 'mechanical' approach which requires the BNF specification to be converted to an EBNF specification which may then be transcribed to a recogniser procedure. This approach is not so dependent on the expertise of the person constructing the recogniser.

So far, we have only explained how to construct recognisers, i.e. programs which are able to identify well-formed sentences. Later, we shall

show how recognisers may be 'fleshed out' so that they do something
with the well-formed sentences which they recognise.

Note that the techniques which have been described only apply to LL1
grammars. Such grammars are only a sub-set of grammars and only define
a sub-set of languages. If the language for which you want to construct a translator cannot be defined by an LL1 grammar, then some
other parsing technique would have to be used. Again, we refer the
interested reader to the references given earlier.

11.4 CONTEXTUAL CONSTRAINTS

Context-free grammars are so called because the choice of production
from a set of possible productions at any point in any derivation is
independent of choices made earlier.

Consider the syntax tree in fig. 11.5 which corresponds to a block in
a Pascal program. This block is perfectly well-structured according
to the context-free grammar of Pascal. However, it is illegal with
respect to the contextual constraints of Pascal. In particular, it is
illegal with respect to the constraints (i) that an identifier may not
be declared twice in the same block and (ii) that the types of the
objects on the two sides of an assignment must be assignment compatible.

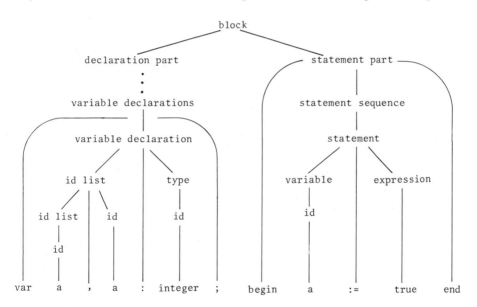

Figure 11.5 A syntax tree

The rules which define such constraints are called 'contextual
constraints'. Most programming languages are defined in terms of a
context-free grammar, which defines a set of sentences, together with
some contextual constraints which restrict the set to a set of legal
sentences of the language. Contextual constraints are typically defined in terms of 'scope rules' and 'mode rules'.

11.4.1 SCOPE RULES

The specification of scope rules involves:

(a) Designating certain constructs as *blocks*. For example, in Pascal there is only one type of block which is defined as consisting of a declaration part followed by a statement part.

(b) Defining the *scope* of identifiers in terms of that part of the enclosing block in which its declaration is effective. For example, in Pascal, the scope of an identifier extends from immediately after its declaration to the end of the immediately enclosing block, except for procedure and function declarations in which case the scope also includes the declaration itself.

(c) Defining the *visibility* of identifiers within their scope. For example, in Pascal, an identifier is visible throughout its scope, except for any enclosed block that contains another declaration of that identifier.

(d) Defining *restrictions* on declarations. For example, in Pascal, no identifier may be declared twice at the same level in a block.

Note that the examples above are not comprehensive with respect to Pascal which includes more complicated scope rules.

11.4.2 MODE RULES

The 'mode' of an identifier is the set of static properties bound to it by its declaration. Defining mode rules typically involves:

(a) Defining the mode bound to declared identifiers in different types of declaration. For example, in Pascal, a constant declaration of the form 'const c = some literal' defines c to be a constant of a type determined by the literal.

(b) Defining, for each operator, the mode of allowed operands and the mode of the result. For example, in Pascal, in an assignment of the form 'V := E', the modes of the operands must be 'assignment compatible'. And in expressions of the form 'E + E', the allowed combinations of operand modes are <integer, integer>, <integer, real>, <real, real>, etc. The mode of the result is, respectively, integer, real, real, etc. (Note the similarity of this to the use of sorting functions in many-sorted logics described in chapter 6, section 6.2.)

Contextual constraints are related to syntax and may be expressed formally by use of 'attribute grammars'. However, they are usually expressed in English as an annotation to a context-free grammar.

11.5 SEMANTICS

The semantics of a programming language tells us how to attach meanings to the well-formed constructs of that language. There are three commonly used methods for defining programming language semantics: 'denotational semantics', 'operational semantics' and 'axiomatic semantics'. Only the first of these will be considered in this discussion, and we will describe it primarily with respect to procedural, imperative languages such as Pascal.

11.5.1 DENOTATIONAL SEMANTICS

In 'denotational semantics', the meaning of a well-formed construct is defined in terms of the meanings of its constituents. The definitions are given as a set of 'semantic equations', one for each production in the grammar. For each production of the form N ::= α, there is a semantic equation of the form:

> meaning of a construct of type N = some formula expressed in terms of the meanings of the constituents of α

Different types of semantic equation are defined for different types of production. For example, a production whose left-hand side denotes a class of declarations has a different type of semantic equation from a production whose left-hand side denotes a class of statements.

In order to explain these differences, we introduce some terminology.

Expressible values

An 'expressible value' is a value which may be yielded by an expression. Examples of expressible values in Pascal are:

    integers
    reals
    characters
    enumerated values
    records
    arrays
    sets
    files
    pointers
    store addresses
    procedures
    functions

Stores

A 'store' is a set of 'locations' each of which may contain a 'storable value'. Examples of storable values in Pascal are:

    integers
    reals
    characters
    enumerated values
    records
    arrays
    sets
    files
    pointers

Denotable values

A 'denotable value' is a value to which an identifier is bound by a declaration. Examples of denotable values in Pascal are:

```
integers
reals
characters
strings
enumerated values
types
store locations
procedures
functions
```

For example, the constant declaration 'const pi = 3.142' binds the identifier 'pi' to the denotable value 3.142, and the variable declaration 'var x : integer' binds the variable x to a store location which can hold an integer.

Environments
An 'environment' of a construct is the set of all identifiers which are usable there, together with the denotable values to which they are bound. For example, consider the following:

```
program example (input, output) ;
const pi = 3.142 ;
var x : integer ;
begin
     read(x) ;← environment here is pi and its denotable value 3.142
     :          together with x and its denotable value which is
     :          some store location
end.
```

Semantic equations for expressions involving literals only
The meaning of an expression involving literals only is independent of both its environment and the store. Consequently, the meaning of such expressions may be defined by semantic equations of the form:

        value⟦expression⟧ = some well understood definition of an object
                                 such as an integer, real, etc.

For example, consider the following:

        value⟦3⟧ = the integer 3
        value⟦5 + 6⟧ = the integer which is the sum of the integers
                                 denoted by 5 and 6

Semantic equations for general expressions
In general, the meaning of an expression is dependent on both the environment and the store. Consequently, a more general semantic equation is used to define the meaning of expressions:

        eval⟦expression⟧(env, st) = some value defined in terms of the
                                 expression, environment and store.

For example:

        eval⟦a constant identifier⟧(env, st) = the value bound to the iden-
                                 tifier in the environment env.

544

eval⟦a variable identifier⟧ (env, st)   = the value stored in the location bound to the identifier in the environment env and store st.

eval⟦variableid. + variableid.⟧ (env, st) = the sum of the values stored in the locations bound to the identifiers in the environment env and store st.

Semantic equations for declarations

Declarations change the environment by creating new bindings of denotable values to identifiers. They also extend the store in the case of variable declarations since such declarations cause new locations to be added to the store.

The meaning of a variable declaration is defined by a semantic equation of the form:

    elab⟦declaration⟧ (env, st) = env', st'

where elab stands for elaboration, and env' and st' are the environment and store after the declaration has been elaborated. For example:

    elab⟦x : integer⟧ (env, st) = env', st'

where st' is st plus a new location L capable of storing a value of type integer, and env' is env plus the binding of x to L.

The semantic equations for constant declarations are similar except that the store is unaffected after the elaboration of a constant declaration.

Semantic equations for statements

Statements, when executed, may change the store but not the environment. However, their effect is dependent on both the environment and the store. Consequently, the semantic equations for statements are of the form:

    exec⟦statement⟧ (env, st) = st'

where st stands for the store before execution of the statement, and st' stands for the store after execution. For example:

    exec⟦x := 3⟧ (env, st) = st'

where st' is equal to st except that the location which is bound to x in the environment env now contains the value denoted by 3, i.e. the store location denoted by x contains val⟦3⟧ (val is short for value).

11.5.2 AN EXAMPLE OF THE SPECIFICATION OF THE SEMANTICS OF A SIMPLE LANGUAGE

As mentioned earlier, the semantics of a language may be specified by writing a semantic equation for each production in the grammar of that language. These equations are expressed in terms of semantic equations for declarations, expressions and statements. We illustrate this by giving an example of a language G12 which is a language with integer variables, declarations, blocks, assignment-statements, if-statements, and while-statements:

> terminals = {declare, begin, end, ;, integer, then, else, if,
> ::=, while, do, ⩾, 0, 1, ..., a,b,c, ...}
> non-terminals = {B, Q, S, E, P, DP, D, id, integerliteral}
> distinguished non-terminal = B

Notes

(a) B stands for block   Q stands for statement sequence
      S stands for statement   E stands for expression
      P stands for primary   DP stands for declaration part
      D stands for declaration   id stands for identifier

(b) Instead of writing, for example, 'Q ::= Q ; S' which tells us that a statement sequence consists of a statement sequence followed by ';' followed by a statement, we write 'Q0 ::= Q1 ; S'. This enables us to refer to the two statement sequences individually when expressing the semantic equations.

(c) The fact that this grammar is left-recursive is irrelevant as far as this discussion is concerned.

In order to illustrate how the equations on the following pages may be used to give meanings to sentences of the language G12, we can 'trace' the execution of a block written in G12, as illustrated in fig. 11.6.

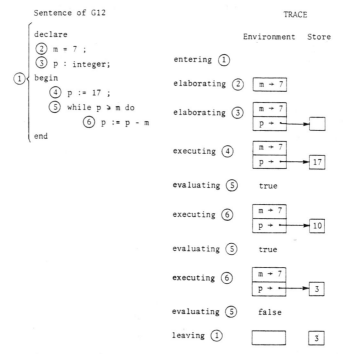

Figure 11.6   Tracing a program segment according to the semantic equations

546

Semantic equations

exec⟦B⟧(env, st) = exec⟦Q⟧(env', st')

where env', st' = elab⟦DP⟧(env, st)

exec⟦B⟧(env, st) = exec⟦Q⟧(env, st)

exec⟦Q⟧ = exec⟦S⟧

exec⟦Q0⟧(env, st) = exec⟦S⟧(env, st')
where st' = exec⟦Q1⟧(env, st)

exec⟦S⟧(env, st) = st'
where st' is equal to st except that the location, which is bound to id in environment env, now contains the value v,
where v = eval⟦E⟧(env, st)

exec⟦S⟧ = exec⟦B⟧

eval⟦E⟧(env, st) = eval⟦P⟧(env, st)

eval⟦E0⟧(env, st) = sum of eval⟦E1⟧(env, st) and eval⟦P⟧(env, st)

eval⟦P⟧(env, st) = value bound to id in env

eval⟦P⟧(env, st) = value contained at location L in st,
where L is bound to id in env

eval⟦P⟧(env, st) = val⟦integerliteral⟧

elab⟦DP⟧(env, st) = elab⟦D⟧(env, st)

Productions

B ::= declare DP;
       begin Q end

B ::= begin Q end

Q ::= S

Q0 ::= Q1 ; S

S ::= id := E

S ::= B

E ::= P

E0 ::= E1 + P

P ::= id   (if const.id)

P ::= id   (if variable.id)

P ::= integerliteral

DP ::= D

547

Productions

DP0 ::= DP1 ; D

D ::= id : integer

D ::= id = E

S0 ::= if C then S1 else S2

S0 ::= while C do S1

C ::= E1 $\geqslant$ E2

integerliteral ::= 0
integerliteral ::= 1
integerliteral ::= 2
(etc.)

id ::= a
id ::= b
id ::= c
(etc.)

Semantic equations

elab⟦DP0⟧(env, st) = elab⟦D⟧(env', st')
where env', st' = elab⟦DP1⟧(env, st)

elab⟦D⟧(env, st) = env', st'
where st' is st plus a new location L and env' is env plus the binding id to L

elab⟦D⟧(env, st) = env', st
where env' is env plus the binding id to eval⟦E⟧(env, st)

exec⟦S0⟧(env, st) = if eval⟦C⟧(env, st) is *true*
then exec⟦S1⟧(env, st)
else exec⟦S2⟧(env, st)

exec⟦S0⟧(env, st) = if eval⟦C⟧(env, st) is *false*
then st
else exec⟦S0⟧(env, st')
where st' = exec⟦S1⟧(env, st)

eval⟦C⟧(env, st) = if eval⟦E1⟧(env, st) $\geqslant$ eval⟦E2⟧(env, st)
then *true*
else *false*

val⟦integerliteral⟧ = val⟦0⟧
val⟦integerliteral⟧ = val⟦1⟧
val⟦integerliteral⟧ = val⟦2⟧
(etc.)

val⟦id⟧ = val⟦a⟧
val⟦id⟧ = val⟦b⟧
val⟦id⟧ = val⟦c⟧
(etc.)

548

11.5.3 THE DENOTABLE VALUES OF PROCEDURE AND FUNCTION IDENTIFIERS

We have seen that constant identifiers denote integers, reals, characters, etc. and that variable identifiers denote store locations. We now explain what procedure and function identifiers denote.

Procedure and function identifiers have different denotations in two different types of programming language. We will consider the most common type of language first.

Languages which have static procedure binding

In the following, 'procedure' stands for procedure or function. In most of the commonly used high-level languages, when a procedure is called its body is executed in the environment which existed at the time that the declaration of that procedure was elaborated. This is called 'static binding'. Therefore, to define the effect of a procedure call we must know both its body and the environment in which its declaration was elaborated. These are collectively known as the 'closure' of that procedure, and the procedure identifier denotes this closure. The closure of a procedure is all the data which is required to execute the procedure correctly.

We can illustrate the semantic equations pertaining to procedures by extending G12 to include three additional productions:

Production	Semantic equation
D ::= procedure id formalparameters ; body	elab⟦D⟧(env, st) = env', st where env' is env plus the binding id to the closure (body,env)
body ::= B (to simplify example)	see previous set of equations
S ::= call id actualparameters	exec⟦S⟧(env'', st) = exec⟦body⟧(env, st) where id is bound to the closure (body,env) with appropriate parameter substitution

As example of the use of these semantic equations, consider the trace in fig. 11.7 involving two procedures, both of which have empty parameter lists. (Note that more complex equations are required for recursion.)

Languages which have dynamic binding

In some languages, for example some dialects of LISP, the execution of a procedure call involves the execution of the related procedure body in the environment in which the procedure is called. This is referred to as 'dynamic binding'.

The semantic equations pertaining to procedures in languages with dynamic binding are illustrated by the examples shown on page 551.

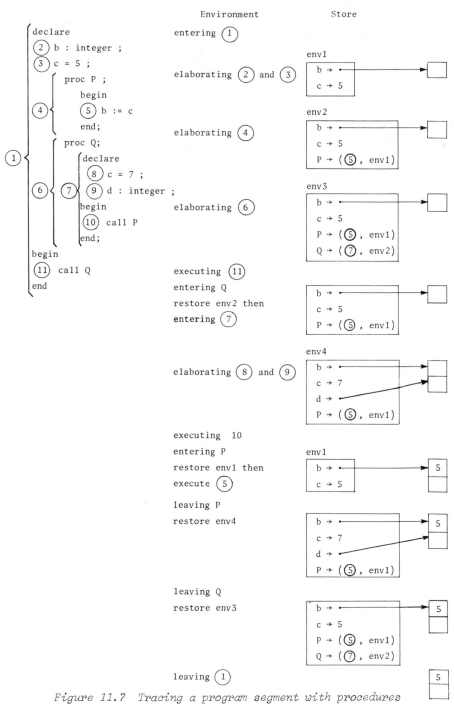

Figure 11.7 *Tracing a program segment with procedures*

Productions	Semantic equations
D ::= procedure id formalparameters ; body	elab⟦D⟧(env, st) = env', st where env' is env plus the binding id to (body)
body ::= B	see previous equations
S ::= call id actualparameters	exec⟦S⟧(env", st) = exec⟦body⟧(env", st) where id is bound to body with appropriate parameter substitution

If we were to outline a trace for the program given in fig. 11.7 in a dynamically bound language, execution of (5) would result in the following:

11.6 TRANSLATORS/COMPILERS/INTERPRETERS

11.6.1 DEFINITIONS

Translators
A 'translator' is a processor that accepts input in a source language and produces semantically equivalent output in a target language.

Compilers
A 'compiler' is a translator whose source language is a high-level programming language and whose output is some low-level language, such as machine code. A compiler typically consists of a lexical analyser which converts the source text to tokens, a parser which converts the sequence of tokens to a syntax tree, an attribute collector and distributor whose task is to make use of the contextual constraints of the source language, and a code generator and optimiser which transforms the syntax tree into the low-level code. These 'modules' typically interleave their operations. That is, the parser 'drives' the whole process requesting tokens from the lexical scanner as required. Often, the syntax tree is not explicitly built by the parser. More often, when a sufficient part of the tree becomes available it is used by the attribute collection and distribution modules to type check, and by the code generator to produce code.

It would not be appropriate to describe compiler construction in more detail here. We refer the interested reader to the literature referenced earlier.

Interpreters

An 'interpreter' is a processor that fetches and immediately executes
the instructions of a program one at a time.

Interpreters have the general structure:

```
begin
      initialise;
      repeat
            fetch the next instruction;
            analyse this instruction;
            case instruction type of
                  ......  ⎤
                  ......  ⎬ one case for each
                  ......  ⎦ type of instruction
            end
      until halted
end
```

Interpreters are useful when it is appropriate to have immediate response to instructions. Languages which are commonly interpreted
include command languages, query languages, and interactive programming
languages such as BASIC, APL and LISP.

The advantages of interpreted programming languages such as BASIC, APL
and LISP are twofold:

(a)   With simple languages such as BASIC, programming novices can
      quickly detect and correct errors in simple programs.

(b)   With languages such as LISP, experienced programmers can
      quickly detect and correct errors in complex programs.

The disadvantages of interpreted languages are twofold:

(a)   Type checking is limited.

(b)   Interpreted programs may be many times slower than compiled
      code since, for example, each instruction in a loop has to
      be analysed and translated each time it is executed.

Notice that this definition of an interpreter does not preclude machines from being regarded as interpreters. Machines, especially if they
are micro-coded, may be regarded as interpreters of the language defined by their instruction set.

Lexical scanners

The approach to constructing lexical scanners which was given in
chapter 2, sub-sections 2.2.3 and 2.2.4 is not the only approach. An
alternative method is to regard lexical analysis as a form of translation, i.e. translation from text to tokens. In this case, an appropriate grammar may be defined and the methods of translation described
in this chapter may be applied.

It is useful to consider lexical analysis separately from 'syntactic' analysis, for two reasons:

(a) It simplifies the translation from source to object text.

(b) The 'surface' syntax of a language may be easily changed to
     suit different users. For example, it may be appropriate to
     use the lexicon 'commence' instead of 'begin' in certain
     circumstances. Such modification involves the lexical scanner
     only.

11.6.2 MODIFYING RECOGNISERS TO OBTAIN TRANSLATORS

In this chapter we have shown how recognisers may be constructed.
However, we have not really described how recognisers may be extended
to translate the recognised text into some other form. In the case of
compilers, the whole of the input text would be converted to low-level
code which could later be executed. In the case of interpreters, the
output text is executed as it is produced. For example, with an interpreted database query language, the output text might consist of relatively high-level database commands, such as retrieve (...), intersect
(...), unite (...), etc.

In general, translators can produce various types of output. For
example:

       machine code
       database instructions
       text in some other language
       expressions in a particular form
       graphical output
       speech
       files in different format
       commands to control a robot
       (etc.)

Although we have not, in this chapter, described how recognisers may
be modified to produce output, we have given examples in previous
chapters of how this might be done. In chapter 3, sub-section 3.4.14
we explained how a recogniser for a database query language could be
'fleshed out' to produce database commands, and in chapter 4, sub-
section 4.2.11 we showed how a recogniser for PROPLANG, a language of
propositional logic, could be fleshed out to produce formulas in
clausal form from input in which formulas are expressed in standard
form. These two examples illustrate a technique which is of general
applicability: in order to convert a recogniser to a translator we
simply embed 'actions' in the recogniser at appropriate places. Whenever a parse 'traverses' an embedded action the translator acts
accordingly, for example, by issuing a database command. In order to
determine where to place the actions, it is common practice to extend
the BNF or EBNF notation to include statements, indicating where
actions should be placed in the recogniser procedures. For example,
consider the following simple grammar:

       G13:   terminals = {0,1,...,9,+,-,;}
                          non-terminals = {E,I,B}
              distinguished non-terminal = E

```
E ::= I B ;
B ::= + I| - I|ε        where ε stands for empty or nothing
I ::= 0|1|2|...|9
```

The following are sentences of the language defined by this grammar:

```
1 ;
8 ;
3 + 5 ;
2 - 6 ;
```

Suppose that we wanted to translate such expressions to the form:

```
one ;
eight ;
three plus five ;
two minus six ;
```

We could embed actions in the recogniser according to the following production rules, where angled brackets delimit actions:

```
E ::= I B ; <writeln ';'>
B ::= + <write'plus'> I| - <write 'minus'> I|ε
I ::= 0 <write'zero'> | 1 <write 'one'>| etc.
```

These rules tell us, for example, to flesh out the procedure Analyse-E, which recognises sentences of G13, to give:

```
procedure Translate-E;
    begin
           Translate-I;
           Translate-B;
           if current-terminal = ';'
               then writeln(';')        (this is an action)
               else error
    end;
```

The procedures for analysing B and I would be modified in a similar way.

Suppose, however, that instead of translating the expressions in this way we wanted to evaluate them. The productions could be written to include actions as follows:

```
E ::= <initialisestack> I B ; <writeouttopofstack>
B ::= + I <pull two from stack, add them and push result onto
                                                         stack>
    | - I <pull two from stack, subtract them and push result
                                                    onto stack>
    | ε
I ::= 0 <push 0 onto stack>| 1 <push 1 onto stack>| (etc.)
```

These productions tell us to modify the procedures Analyse-E, Analyse-B and Analyse-I to give:

```
procedure Translate-E;
  begin
    initialise stack;
    Translate-I;
    Translate-B;
    if current-terminal = ';'
      then writeln ('the answer is', topof-stack)
      else writeln ('error')
  end;

procedure Translate-B;
  begin
    if current-terminal = '+'
      then begin
             get-next-terminal;
             Translate-I;
             pull two from stack, add them, and push result
           end
      else if current-terminal = '-'
             then begin
                    get-next-terminal;
                    Translate-I;
                    pull two from stack, subtract them, and push
                  end                                      result
  end;

procedure Translate-I;
  begin
    if current-terminal is in ['0','1',...,'9']
      then begin
             push current-terminal;
             get-next-terminal
           end
      else error
  end;
```

Notes

The use of a stack is not really appropriate in this example. However, it illustrates a technique which is commonly used to evaluate expressions in more complex grammars.

Another point worth making is that the procedures could be simplified in various ways. For example, we could use a variable to store the operators + and -, and then we could amalgamate the stack manipulation code to give: 'pull-two from stack, if operator is + then add, else subtract, and then push the result'. This approach might be better specified using EBNF notation:

I ::= I [(+|-) <assign operator to variable> I <pull two, add or
                  subtract according to operator, and push>] ;

Here we are using square brackets to signify that the enclosed occurs one or zero times.

11.7 APPLICATION OF TECHNIQUES IN KNOWLEDGE BASE SYSTEMS WORK

An important point to note is that the techniques briefly described in this chapter have a wider application than just in the construction of compilers for programming languages. Much of the work of a knowledge base system is concerned with the translation of one representation of knowledge to some other representation, and with the interpretation of end-user instructions. For this reason, an understanding of grammars and translators is essential to anyone wanting to embark on a career in knowledge base systems work.

Much of knowledge processing may be regarded in many respects as the translation and interpretation of languages. All of the knowledge representation formalisms described in this book may be regarded as languages. Even the file and record formalism which is used in conventional database systems may be regarded as a language. For example, consider the following productions:

```
            file ::= record-sequence end-of-file-marker
 record-sequence ::= record | record-sequence record
          record ::= name-field age-field salary-field
      name-field ::= string
       age-field ::= 1|2|3|...|110
  (etc.)
```

11.8 CATEGORIES OF PROGRAMMING LANGUAGE

In this section, several terms which are often used to categorise programming languages are briefly discussed. This is in order to indicate the wide range of programming languages which are available for knowledge processing. The terms introduced are rather vaguely defined in the literature, and we do not attempt to give precise definitions here. The terms, when used to describe a language, should be regarded as giving no more than the 'flavour' of that language.

The reader will notice, when reading these notes, that most programming languages fall into several categories. For example, Pascal may be regarded as a high-level, procedural, imperative, statically bound language, which is functional to the extent that 'first order' functions may be defined and used in Pascal programs.

The set of terms considered below is by no means comprehensive. There are many books on programming languages and it would be worthwhile to supplement this discussion by reference to other material.

Low-level and high-level languages

Low-level languages include micro-code, machine code and assembler languages. The virtue of a low-level language is that a program written in it can be read and executed more or less directly by the computer. Programs can be tailored to the features of the machine and can, therefore, be designed to be very efficient. However, there are two major disadvantages: (a) low-level languages are usually so dependent on the structure of particular computers that programs written in them cannot be run on other computers, and (b) low-level code is difficult to understand and consequently programming in low-level languages is error prone.

High-level languages are languages whose constructs are abstracted away from the machine architecture. That is, programs can be written in a

high-level language without the programmer having to concern himself
with details of the machine on which the program is to run. High-level
languages have the following advantages:

(a) More difficult tasks can be programmed since the programmer
     does not have to worry about hardware details.

(b) The programs are generally easier to read and programming is
     consequently less error prone.

(c) Programs can often be run on other machines if suitable trans-
     lators are available.

The disadvantages of high-level languages are twofold: (a) high-level
programs need to be translated (compiled) into low-level code before
they can be executed, and (b) the compiled executable code is generally
less efficient than if the programs had been written in a low-level
language.

The distinction between low-level and high-level languages is, in some
ways, relative to the available hardware. Some languages previously
regarded as high-level may now be regarded as low-level because new
hardware has been developed which can execute instructions of that
language directly.

Procedural languages

This is, perhaps, one of the vaguest of the terms used to categorise
programming languages. Many people refer to 'procedural languages' as
those in which it is possible to explicitly express the sequence in
which statements are executed, i.e. those which contain for loops,
while loops, repeat-until loops, gotos, etc. and in which the order of
statements affects the order in which they are executed.

Others regard procedural languages as those in which imperative statements may be expressed, where an imperative statement may be thought
of as a statement which tells the computer to do something. For example,
in Pascal, the statement x := 3 is imperative since it tells the computer to put the value 3 into the store location denoted by x.

The term 'imperative language', which is discussed below, is perhaps a
better term to describe languages containing imperative statements and
the term 'procedural' is perhaps better reserved to describe those
languages in which the flow of control through the program statements
is expressed explicitly by the programmer. According to this definition, most low-level languages, and most conventional high-level
languages such as COBOL, FORTRAN, Algol, Pascal, C, Ada, etc. may be
regarded as being procedural. The database query languages based on
relational algebra would also be regarded as procedural.

Imperative languages

As mentioned above, the term 'imperative language' may be used to describe languages in which it is possible to express statements which
tell the computer to do something; for example, statements such as
'x := 3'; 'write ('hello')'; 'goto label'. However, some people would
argue that all programming languages are imperative in the sense that

they must all contain at least one imperative statement, otherwise the program would do nothing. Others maintain that languages exist in which every statement is simply a definition (or an assertion), and that the operating system command to 'run' the program is the only imperative statement used.

Non-procedural languages

'Non-procedural languages' are often defined as those languages in which the programmer specifies what is required rather than how it is to be obtained. For example, the following might be regarded as an example of a non-procedural statement:

solve the equation 'x = 5 * y + 3' for x and y

This notion of non-procedurality suggests that non-procedural languages are more high-level than procedural languages such as Pascal, FORTRAN, Algol, etc. However, it is not as straightforward as this. If a non-procedural program is regarded as a prescription for solving a problem which does not specify the details of how it is to be solved, then the distinction between 'procedural' and 'non-procedural' languages depends on the problem being solved. If a solution to a problem can be obtained by simply stating the problem in a language L, then L should be regarded as being non-procedural with respect to that problem. If, however, the details of the solution must be specified, then L should be regarded as being non-procedural with respect to that problem.

To avoid this confusion, it is perhaps better to use the term 'problem-oriented language' to describe languages in which problems, or requirements, rather than solutions may be stated. (We discuss this term later.) The term 'non-procedural' may be best reserved for languages in which the programmer does not have to express the flow of control through the program explicitly. The database query languages which are based on relational calculus may be regarded as non-procedural languages according to this definition.

Declarative languages

'Declarative languages' are languages which are not imperative languages. That is, there is no facility for the programmer to express statements which tell the computer to do something. All statements in a declarative language are either assertions or definitions. Note, however, that 'declarations' in languages such as Pascal are, in some sense, imperative statements since they tell the computer to change the environment.

As mentioned earlier, some people would argue that there is no such thing as a declarative (i.e. non-imperative) language since all programs require at least one imperative command to do anything. Others would argue that there are languages in which the only imperative command is the operating system command to 'run' the program.

Prolog is often described as a declarative language since most of the statements in a typical Prolog program are assertions. However, Prolog may also be described as 'procedural' since the order in which the assertions are written does affect the flow of control through the program (see later).

Problem-oriented languages

'Problem-oriented languages' are generally regarded as languages in which problems or requirements, rather than solutions, are specified. Such languages are always application dependent. For example, suppose that we have a problem-oriented language for controlling a robot builder. The following might be an example of a statement written in this language:

'a wall 2 metres long, 1 metre high'

The robot would then build such a wall without being told how to do it.

Logic-programming languages

The language Prolog, which is described in more detail later, is an example of a 'logic-programming language'. A Prolog program consists of a set of assertions which are regarded as constituting the proper axioms of a theory, together with a set of goal clauses which are regarded as theorems to be proved.

The only statements in a Prolog program which may be regarded as 'imperative' are those involving the input and output of data, and the goal clauses which may be regarded as instructions to the Prolog interpreter to apply a depth-first LUSH theorem-proving strategy. Consequently, Prolog may also be regarded as a declarative language to some extent.

Frame languages

'Frame languages' are special-purpose languages which can be used to define frames and frame structures and to perform operations such as matching on frames. Such languages can be used to implement frame based knowledge base systems. Examples of frame based languages were given in chapter 9.

Production rule languages

Such languages allow the implementation of production rule based systems. They have facilities for specifying production rules, for accessing databases and for initiating searches linking hypotheses to databases. Examples of such languages were given in chapter 8.

Functional or applicative languages

The terms 'functional language' and 'applicative language' have been used to describe languages such as LISP and DAPLEX, as well as languages such as SASL which do not support the notions of assignment or looping (iteration is achieved by use of recursion). A functional or applicative language may be thought of as a language in which:

(a) Functions are the 'main' objects.
(b) Most statements may be regarded as either function declarations, function definitions or function calls.

Database query languages

'Database query languages' are languages which can be used to express queries which are to be evaluated with respect to a database. We have described various types of query language in this book.

Data definition and database schema specification languages

A 'data definition' or 'schema specification' language is a language
which can be used to formally describe database schemas. Such languages are non-procedural, declarative languages. Several such languages have been mentioned in this book.

Database implementation languages

One or two languages are available which are specifically designed to
facilitate the implementation of database systems. One such language,
PS-algol, is described later in this chapter. A feature of PS-algol
is that it 'hides' the distinction between main store and backing
store. This frees the database system builder from having to worry
about backing store considerations.

11.9 LISP

In America, LISP is the most widely used language for writing 'AI'
programs. Several reasons have been put forward to explain this:

- (a) LISP supports dynamic data structures.

- (b) LISP is more flexible than most other high-level languages.
  For example, if a user does not like the syntax of LISP, he
  may change it to suit his requirements. Also, 'programs' may
  be treated like data.

- (c) LISP is oriented towards symbolic processing.

- (d) LISP, especially pure LISP, has a concise and precisely defined semantics.

It is not our intention in this section to describe LISP in detail.
There are many good texts on LISP (see the end of this sub-section).
The purpose of this section is twofold:

- (a) It is an introduction to LISP for readers who are not at all
  familiar with it.

- (b) It shows how McCarthy's calculus for symbolic processing has
  been embedded in LISP.

What type of language is LISP?

LISP is a high-level, functional, symbol processing language. There
are many 'dialects' of LISP. The early dialects, especially pure LISP,
did not have many procedural constructs, and functions had dynamic
binding. Later dialects have been extended to include a wide range of
procedural constructs, and most have static binding.

LISP is generally implemented as an interpreted interactive language,
i.e. LISP statements are typed at a terminal and are immediately translated and executed.

Calling functions in LISP

To call a function in LISP, enclose the name of the function and its
arguments inside round brackets. For example:

If you type (+ 3 5) the interpreter responds with 8.
If you type (* 4 6) the interpreter responds with 24.

Function calls may be embedded as, for example, in the following:

If you type (* (+ 2 3) 7) the interpreter responds with 35.

In the remainder of this discussion, the symbol '→' is used to stand for 'if you type' and '→→' to stand for 'the interpreter responds with'.

Defining functions in LISP

A 'program' in LISP is regarded as a function. This function may be defined in terms of other functions. Hence, the modular construction of programs involves the definition of functions. The following is an example showing how the function 'square' may be defined:

→ (defun square (num) (* num num))
→→ square

As can be seen, the definition of functions is regarded as a higher-order function call. The function being called is 'defun'. Its arguments are the name of the function being defined, its arguments and its body (which is specified as a function call). The value returned by 'defun' is the name of the function being defined. A 'side effect' of the function definition is that the interpreter memorises the definition so it can be used on subsequent occasions.

We show how more complex functions may be defined later.

Assignment

In most dialects of LISP, values may be assigned to variables by use of the function 'setq'. For example:

→ (setq z 10)
→→ 10

As indicated, the value returned by 'setq' is the value assigned to the variable z. The side effect of the function call is to change the store such that the variable z denotes a store location containing the number 10. Variables may be used as arguments to functions as, for example, in:

→ (square z)
→→ 100

Data types

Atoms, numbers, dotted pairs and lists are the basic data types in LISP.

Atoms

An 'atom' is an elementary data item. Syntactically, an atom is a string of letters and digits beginning with a letter. Within function definitions, atoms serve as identifiers of various kinds: function names, formal parameters, variables, statement labels and so on. In LISP data structures (which are described later), atoms serve as atomic data items.

When LISP is given a symbol (an atom) to evaluate, it assumes it to be a variable identifier and tries to find its value. For example, consider the following function call:

    (square z)

Here, z is treated as a variable identifier, its value of 10 is obtained and the result of the call is 100. However, there will be occasions when we might want 'z' to be considered literally. For example, suppose that we wanted to assign 'z' to the variable 'lastletter'. It would not be correct to write:

    (setq lastletter z)

since the interpreter would attempt to find the value of z, thinking it to be a variable, and would assign 10 to lastletter. This problem may be overcome by the use of a function called 'quote':

    (setq lastletter (quote z))

The value returned by the call (quote z) is the symbol 'z'.

Because quote is frequently used, there is an abbreviation which is illustrated by the following:

    (setq lastletter 'z)

Dotted pairs
'Dotted pairs' are data structures which contain a head and a tail, both of which may themselves be dotted pairs. In LISP, dotted pairs are represented as, for example:

    (a)   (a . b)
    (b)   (a . (b . (c . nil)))

Many LISP programmers claim that unrestricted use of dotted pairs is best avoided since they can be the source of program bugs which are difficult to locate. Hence they advocate the use of lists instead.

Lists
Dotted pairs such as (a . (b . (c . nil))) are 'lists', and may be represented graphically as follows:

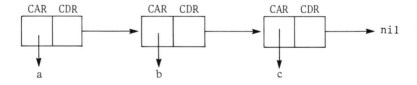

Each list element contains a pointer to a data item and a pointer to its successor. The successor of the last element is a special atom 'nil'. The pointer to the data is called CAR, and the pointer to the successor is called CDR.

An alternative notation is available, in all LISP dialects, for representing lists. Using this notation, the list above can be represented as follows:

    (a b c)

That is, a list is represented by writing its elements in sequence, separated by spaces, and enclosing the whole sequence in round brackets.

The data item pointed to by the CAR pointer of a list element may be an atom, a number, a dotted pair or another list. For example, the following are examples of lists in LISP:

    (one two three)
    (1 2 3 4)
    (1 (3 . a) 6)
    ((a b) c (d e f))

The last example is a list of three elements, the first and last of which are themselves lists.

Notice that ( ) and (( )) are distinct. The former represents an empty list, whereas the latter represents a list with a single element which is an empty list. ( ) is also represented by nil; nil is unique in that it is both an atom and a list.

Assignment of lists to variables
Suppose we wanted to assign the list (a b c) to the variable 'mylist'. It would not be correct to write:

    (setq mylist (a b c))

The reason this is not correct is that the interpreter would think (a b c) is a function call and would try to evaluate it. In order to prevent such evaluation, quote may be used as illustrated in the following, in which the abbreviated form of quote is used:

    (setq mylist '(a b c))

This tells the interpreter to treat (a b c) as a list rather than a function call.

The basic list processing functions available in LISP
We have mentioned car, cdr, cons, atom and equal in chapter 10. We now show how they are implemented and used in LISP by giving an example of a LISP interactive session:

    → (setq newlist '(a (b c) (d e)))
    ≫ (a (b c) (d e))
    → (car newlist)
    ≫ a
    →. (cdr newlist)
    ≫ ((b c) (d e))
    → (atom newlist)
    ≫ nil   (nil stands for false in many LISP dialects)

```
→   (cons 'x 'b)
⟫  (x . b)
→   (cons 'x newlist)
⟫  (x a (b c) (d e))
```

Other list processing functions available in LISP
Most dialects of LISP contain several other list processing functions.
These functions often include 'append' and 'list'. 'Append' strings
together the elements of all lists supplied as arguments, whereas
'list' makes a list out of its arguments. For example, in Franz LISP:

```
→   (append '(a b) '(c d))
⟫  (a b c d)
→   (list '(a b) '(c d))
⟫  ((a b) (c d))
```

Control structures in LISP
Many dialects of LISP contain various constructs for 'controlling the
flow' of execution of statements. We give some examples of the use of
such constructs:

Example 1

```
(defun abs (num)
    (cond ((< num 0) (* num -1)
                     (t num)))
```

This defines the function 'abs' which takes an argument num. If num
is less than 0, then the value returned by abs is num times minus 1;
otherwise the value returned is num. t stands for true and represents
the otherwise case. (Refer back to chapter 10 to see how this relates
to McCarthy's conditional expressions.)

The 'cond' function which takes a list of <condition,result> pairs is
available in most dialects of LISP.

Example 2

```
(1)   (defun power (x y)
(2)   (do ((result 1)
(3)   (exponent y))
(4)   ((zerop exponent) result)
(5)   (setq result (* x result))
(6)   (setq exponent (- exponent 1)))))
```

This defines the function 'power' which takes two parameters x and y
and returns the value x raised to the power y. Lines (2) and (3) bind
and assign parameters. Line (4) tests to see if the exponent is zero
and if so returns the value of result. Lines (5) and (6) are the
'body' of the do loop.

Note that this is how explicit iteration may be achieved in dialects
of LISP known as Franz LISP and COMMON LISP. Other dialects may have
different constructs for iteration.

Recursion

Some form of recursion is available in all dialects of LISP. The following is an example of the use of recursion in Franz LISP and COMMON LISP:

```
(defun power (x y)
    (cond ((zerop y) 1)
        (t (* x (power x (- y 1)))))))
```

This is an alternative way of defining the power function.

Lambda abstraction

Most dialects of LISP accommodate lambda abstraction, by which function descriptions can be used in places where ordinarily there would be a function name. Essentially, the lambda construct in LISP allows us to create and 'name' functions without having to introduce a new identifier. For example, consider the following:

```
(lambda (x y) (+ x y))
```

This 'names' a function which takes two arguments x and y and returns their sum.

The lambda construct has many uses, one of which is that it facilitates the treatment of functions as data. This topic is, however, beyond the scope of the present discussion.

Predicates

The functions 'atom' and 'equal' are predicates in that they test their arguments to see if they satisfy some condition. If not, the value nil is returned, indicating false. If the arguments do satisfy the condition, then something other than nil is returned. For example:

```
→  (equal '(a b) (cdr '(x a b))
≫ t
→  (atom '(a b))
≫ nil
```

Other predicates are also available. For example, the predicate 'member' is available in most modern dialects of LISP. This predicate takes two arguments x and y and tells us if x is a member of the list y. For example:

```
→  (member 'a '(x y z))
≫ nil
→  (member 'y '(x y z))
≫ (y z)
```

Notice that, in the second example, the value returned is not t standing for true but is the list starting with the element we are looking for. This signifies true *and* may be of use in further computation.

Properties

Many dialects of LISP contain functions which allow properties to be associated with symbols. In the dialect Franz LISP, the functions

'putprop' and 'get' allow properties to be associated and retrieved.
As illustration of their use, consider the following examples:

    → (putprop 'john 'spaghetti 'likes)
    ⟶ spaghetti
    → (putprop 'john 'sally 'marriedto)
    ⟶ sally
    → (get 'john 'likes)
    ⟶ 'spaghetti

The relationship of LISP to McCarthy's calculus for symbol processing
All dialects of LISP include the basic list processing functions car,
cdr, atom, equal and cons, and they provide constructs which allow new
functions to be defined using the strategies of composition, cases
(conditional expressions) and recursion. However, most dialects also
provide facilities for assignment and for explicitly controlling the
flow of execution (e.g. by use of do loops, etc.). In addition, most
dialects contain a set of pre-defined 'standard' functions such as
append, member, etc. as well as sophisticated library functions for
parsing, searching and so on.

The use of LISP in knowledge base systems work
It would appear that more AI programs have been written in LISP than
in any other language. This is most probably due to the flexibility
which it offers programmers, together with the many functions which
have been developed and are available.

As mentioned earlier, there are many books on LISP. Some of the more
recent ones are those by Charniak, Riesbeck, and McDermott (1980),
Winston and Horn (1981) and Wilensky (1984).

See section 11.12 for further comments on the use of LISP in knowledge
base systems work.

11.10 PROLOG
The Prolog programming language is quite different from the languages
which we have discussed in this chapter so far. A Prolog program consists of a set of assertions together with a set of goals. The assertions may be thought of as the proper axioms of a theory of a restricted
form of first order predicate logic and the goals as theorems to be
proved. Prolog is generally implemented as an interpreted language.
When the interpreter meets a goal, it uses a depth-first SL resolution
theorem-proving strategy in an attempt to prove that the goal is a
theorem of the assertions.

Assertions are not written using a conventional first order predicate
language, but in a form sometimes referred to as 'Kowalski clausal
form'. Examples of assertions written in this form are:

    (a) parent(john, susan).
    (b) parent(susan, peter).
    (c) grandparent(X, Z) :- parent(X, Y), parent(Y, Z).

Note: these examples are equivalent to the following formulas in first
order predicate logic:

```
parent(john, susan)
parent(susan, peter)
∀X∀Y∀Z[parent(X, Y) ∧ parent(Y, Z) → grandparent(X, Z)]
```

The first assertion (a) may be read as 'the parent of john is susan', the second (b) as 'the parent of susan is peter' and the third (c) may be read declaratively as 'if Y is the parent of X *and* Z is the parent of Y *then* Z is the grandparent of X'. The assertion (c) may also be read procedurally as 'in order to prove that Z is the grandparent of X, first of all prove that Y is the parent of X then prove that Z is the parent of Y'.

The following is an example of a Prolog goal:

(d) | ?- grandparent(john, X).

The symbols '| ?-' constitute the Prolog prompt when the system is in the 'enter goal' mode. This goal may be read as 'who is/are the grandparents of john?'.

If (a), (b) and (c) are entered as assertions, and then (d) is entered as a goal, the Prolog interpreter will initiate a depth-first SL resolution theorem-proving strategy and will respond by displaying:

X = peter

thereby indicating that peter is a grandparent of john.

We will now describe Prolog in a little more detail. The implementation we are using as example is cProlog which is available under the Unix operating system.

Our discussion is intended to serve as no more than a brief introduction to the language. For a more complete introduction, the reader is referred to Clocksin and Mellish (1981).

Initiating a Prolog session for learning purposes
Having logged on to Unix, type the word 'prolog'. The system will respond with:

cProlog version n   (where n is the version which is available)
| ?-

As such, the system is in the 'enter goal' mode. In order to insert assertions from the keyboard, type

| ?- [user].

Notice the full stop. This is the terminator which signals to Prolog to accept your input. The system now enters the 'accept assertions from the keyboard' mode, and responds with:

|
|

(Note that this mode should only be used for initial acquaintance with

Prolog. A better approach is to put assertions into a file which is then accessed by the Prolog interpreter. We explain how to do this later.)

Now enter assertions. After you have entered some assertions, you can return to the 'enter goal' mode by typing the end-of-file character which may be control-d or control-z depending on your system.

Before we describe what a Prolog assertion looks like, we will introduce some terminology.

Constants
A Prolog 'constant' may be an integer or an 'atom'. There are various types of atom:

		Example
(a)	character strings beginning with a lower case character	peter
(b)	a string of symbols	+-
(c)	character strings enclosed in quotes	'London'

Variables
A 'variable' is a character string beginning with a capital letter or an underline. For example:

    X
    Anyone
    _Y
    _

The single underline character is the 'anonymous variable' which can be used when a variable is required but its name is irrelevant.

Structures
A Prolog 'structure' consists of a functor followed by an opening round bracket followed by a set of components separated by commas, followed by a closing round bracket. Examples of structures are:

    parent(john, susan)
    grandparent(john, X)
    married(john, wifeof(john))
    owns(john, car(cavalier, blue))

Notice that the last two structures have structures as components. We see below that when structures appear as components of other structures they have different denotations to structures which are not components of other structures.

Prolog assertions - facts
A Prolog 'fact' is a structure in which the functor denotes a predicate. Examples of facts are:

    parent(susan, peter).
    parent(john, susan).

```
married(john, wifeof(john)).
owns(john, car(cavalier, blue)).
```

Notice that neither 'wifeof(john)' nor 'car(cavalier,blue)' are facts. When a structure appears inside another structure, it denotes an entity taking part in a relationship. For example, 'wifeof(john)' denotes the wife of john. The functor in this case represents a function.

Notice also, that Prolog 'facts' need not be variable free. For example, when the following is entered as an assertion, it is regarded as a fact stating that every entity knows john:

```
knows(X, john).
```

Prolog assertions - rules
A Prolog rule consists of a 'head', followed by the symbol ':-', followed by a 'body'. The head is a structure and the body is a set of structures separated by commas. For example:

```
grandparent(X, Z) :- parent(X, Y), parent(Y, Z).
male(X)           :- man(X).       (meaning if X is a man then X is
                                                                  male)
```

The body of a Prolog rule may be regarded as a conjunction of goals which must be satisfied, one after the other, for the head to be true.

Prolog goals
A Prolog 'goal' consists of a single structure or a set of structures separated by commas. For example:

```
?-married(john, sally).
?-grandparent(john, X).
?-grandparent(john, W), grandparent(henry, W).
```

These goals may be thought of as the questions:

```
is john married to sally?
who is/are the grandparents of john?
who is/are the grandparents of both john and henry?
```

A goal which consists of a set of structures separated by commas may be thought of as a 'complex' goal consisting of a set of sub-goals.

Prolog's method of answering questions/satisfying goals
When the Prolog interpreter recognises a goal clause, it attempts to 'answer it' by trying to satisfy its sub-goals from left to right. To do this, it starts with the leftmost sub-goal, makes this the current sub-goal and searches the 'knowledge base' of assertions from top to bottom, looking for facts or heads of rules which match this current sub-goal. If a match is found then Prolog instantiates the variables accordingly (see below). If the match is with a fact, Prolog attempts to satisfy the remaining sub-goals to the right of the current sub-goal in the original goal clause. If the match is with the head of a rule, sub-goals in the body of that rule are treated as additional sub-goals which need to be satisfied before the remaining sub-goals to the right

of the current sub-goal in the original goal clause are considered. Hence, Prolog commences by treating the leftmost goal in the body of the matching rule as the current sub-goal.

Whenever a sub-goal is satisfied, the Prolog interpreter marks the place in the knowledge base where that sub-goal was satisfied and proceeds with the next sub-goal, searching for a match by starting at the top of the knowledge base. If this sub-goal is satisfied, Prolog marks the place at which it was matched and continues with the next sub-goal. If all sub-goals are satisfied then Prolog has found a solution. If, however, a sub-goal cannot be satisfied (i.e. the whole knowledge base is scanned without finding a match) then Prolog backtracks to the previous sub-goal match (using the place marker), undoes the effect of this match and proceeds to search for another match by scanning the assertions below the place marker.

The matching algorithm which Prolog uses is similar to the unification algorithm described in chapter 4, sub-section 4.3.9. However, no occurs-test is carried out since this would slow down the execution of Prolog programs considerably. When a match is made, the substitutions which result are applied to all remaining sub-goals before an attempt to satisfy them is made.

Example
Suppose that we had entered the following set KB of assertions:

    A1: parent(henry, paul).
    A2: parent(john, susan).
    A3: parent(susan, peter).
    A4: parent(susan, jane).
    A5: grandparent(X, Z) :- parent(X, Y), parent(Y, Z).
    A6: parent(henry, susan).

Note: we use the assertion labels A1 to A6 below; they are not part of the Prolog program.

Suppose that we now enter the goal:

    ?-grandparent(john, W), grandparent(henry, W).

Prolog proceeds as follows:

(1)   Sub-goals are {grandparent(john, W), grandparent(henry, W)}.

(2)   Current sub-goal is grandparent(john, W).

(3)   Search KB starting with A1 to find a match with the current sub-goal.

(4)   The head of A5 matches, hence the substitutions are {john/X, W/Z}. A5 is place-marked.

(5)   The sub-goals in the body of A5 are added to the remaining sub-goals. Hence, the new set of sub-goals with substitutions is: {parent(john, Y), parent(Y, W), grandparent(henry, W)}.

(6)   The current sub-goal is parent(john, Y).

(7) Search KB starting with A1 to find a match.

(8) The fact A2 matches, hence the substitution is {susan/Y}. A2 is place-marked.

(9) The remaining sub-goals with substitutions are {parent(susan, W), grandparent(henry, W)}.

(10) The current sub-goal is parent(susan, W).

(11) Search KB starting with A1 to find a match.

(12) The fact A3 matches, hence the substitution is {peter/W}. A3 is place-marked.

(13) The remaining sub-goals with substitutions are {grandparent(henry, peter)}.

(14) The current sub-goal is grandparent(henry, peter).

(15) Search KB starting with A1 to find a match.

(16) The head of A5 matches, hence the substitutions are {henry/X, peter/Z}. A5 is place-marked.

(17) The new set of sub-goals with substitutions is {parent(henry, Y), parent(Y, peter)}.

(18) The current sub-goal is parent(henry, Y).

(19) Search KB starting with A1 to find a match.

(20) The fact A1 matches, hence the substitution is {paul/Y}. A1 is place-marked.

(21) The remaining sub-goals with substitutions are {parent(paul, peter)}.

(22) The current sub-goal is parent(paul, peter).

(23) Search KB starting with A1.

(24) No match is found, hence we need to backtrack. We undo the effect of the last match; this gives the remaining sub-goals {parent(henry, Y), parent(Y, peter)}. We now start the search for another match with the sub-goal parent(henry, Y) beginning at A2 (we know to start at A2 since the place marker which was set in (20) tells us where the last match of parent(henry, Y) was made).

(25) We continue to search from A2 and find that the fact A6 matches the current sub-goal. Hence the substitution is {susan/Y}. A6 is place-marked.

(26) The remaining sub-goals after substitution are {parent(susan, peter)}.

(27) The current sub-goal is parent(susan, peter).

(28) Search KB starting with A1.

(29) The fact A3 matches.

(30) There are no more sub-goals, hence the proof has succeeded. If we trace back through the substitutions, we find that W was instantiated to peter. Hence, Prolog displays the answer W = peter.

If we want more answers, we can type ';'. This tells Prolog to back-track and to search for another answer. If we do not want additional answers, we type '.'.

Tracing

To see Prolog's search strategy in action, enter the goal 'trace'. Prolog will then show every sub-goal which it generates during execution of the next subsequent goal entered. The trace can be turned off by entering the goal 'notrace'.

Operators

Functors may be declared as operators by use of a built-in predicate 'op'. For example, consider the functor '+'. This functor may be declared as an operator by entering the goal:

    op(31, yfx, +).

This causes + to be declared as an infix operator (i.e. yfx signifies that the operator denoted by f must appear between two arguments), and has a precedence of 31.

Arithmetic

In many implementations of Prolog, the standard arithmetic functors are pre-declared as operators. For example, consider the following goals:

    (a)   ?- 5 = 7.
    (b)   ?- 3 > 2.
    (c)   ?- 4 = (6/3).

The answer to (a) is no, to (b) is yes and to (c) is no. If the functors involved are not pre-declared as operators, one would have to write:

    (a)'   ? - =(5, 7).
    (b)'   ? - >(3, 2).
    (c)'   ? - =(4, /(6, 3)).

is

Prolog also provides a built-in predicate 'is' as an infix operator. 'is' takes a variable on the left and an arithmetic expression on the right, and causes the expression to be evaluated and the variable to be instantiated with the resulting value.

As example, consider the following rule:

    area(X, Y) :- len(X, L), wid(X, W), Y is L*W.

This rule may be read as:

    'The area of a surface X is Y if:
        the length of X is L, and
        the width of X is W, and
        Y is calculated by multiplying L by W.

The rule could be used in a Prolog program as follows:

```
len(mygarden, 20).
wid(mygarden, 30).
area(X, Y) :- len(X, L), wid(X, W), Y is L*W.
```

If we were to enter the goal 'area(mygarden, Ans).', the Prolog interpreter would respond with 'Ans = 600'.

Cut

Cut is a special mechanism which can be used in Prolog programs to prevent unnecessary or unwanted backtracking. To invoke this mechanism, a special predicate ! which takes no arguments is used. When this predicate is met as a goal, it is immediately satisfied and cannot be re-satisfied in the 'current problem'. It affects backtracking by signalling to the interpreter that if backtracking ever returns to this point then the parent goal should be failed immediately and no attempt to find another solution by re-matching previous sub-goals should be made. In other words, when a cut is encountered, the interpreter becomes committed to all choices made since the original goal was invoked. All other alternatives are discarded since all attempts to re-satisfy any goal between the parent goal and the cut will fail.

For example, suppose that we want to define a predicate 'sumcond' which takes a single argument N, which is an integer, and is true if the sum of the integers from N downto 1 is less than 12. We can define this predicate in two steps. Firstly, we define a 'sumto' predicate as follows, so that this recursively defined predicate allows us to compute the sum of integers from a number M downto 1:

```
sumto(1, 1) :- !.
sumto(M, Res) :- M1 is M-1, sumto(M1, Res1), Res is Res1+M.
```

If we now entered the goal 'sumto(4,X)', the Prolog interpreter would respond with 'X = 10'.

Using the predicate sumto, we can now define the predicate sumcond:

```
sumcond(N) :- sumto(N, Y), Y < 12.
```

If we now entered the goal 'sumcond(4)', the Prolog interpreter would respond with 'yes'. However, if we entered the goal 'sumcond(5)', the answer would be 'no'. That is, the sum of the integers from 4 downto 1 is less than 12, but the sum of those from 5 downto 1 is not less than 12. Suppose, however, that we had defined the predicate sumto as follows, omitting the cut:

```
sumto(1, 1).
sumto(M, Res) :- M1 is M-1, sumto(M1, Res1), Res is Res1+M.
```

If we entered the goal 'sumcond(5)', the interpreter would not answer with 'no' but would loop until the program ran out of resources. The reason is that when the sub-goal 'sumto(5,Y)' is met and satisfied, Y will have a value of 15, hence the subsequent sub-goal '15 < 12' will fail. Backtracking will be initiated in an attempt to find an alternative solution to 'sumto(5,Y)'.

If you trace through the whole process you will see that backtracking will take the process back to the point where the sub-goal 'sumto(1, Res1)' was matched with the fact 'sumto(1,1).'. The effect of this match is undone and the sub-goal 'sumto(1, Res1)' is now matched with 'sumto(M, Res)', i.e. with the head of the second rule defining sumto. The first sub-goal in the body of this rule is 'M1 is M-1', hence M1 is instantiated to 0. The second sub-goal is now 'sumto(0, Res1)'. This matches the head of the rule again and the process loops with M1 having values -1, -2, -3 ...

By using the initial definition of sumto, i.e. the definition in which the first rule is:

    sumto(1, 1) :- !

the problem of looping is avoided. When the sub-goal 'sumto(1,Res1)' is initially matched against the head of this rule, the cut prevents this match from ever being undone. Hence any attempt to backtrack past this point will fail.

The cut mechanism may also be used to improve efficiency of Prolog programs. However, its use can lead to programs which are more difficult to understand.

Lists in Prolog

Prolog has a special syntax for lists. They are written as a sequence of terms separated by commas and enclosed in square brackets. For example:

    [a,b,c,d]

The empty list, 'nil', is written as [ ], and a construct which is equivalent to the LISP 'cons(a,b)' can be written as:

    [a|b]

That is, a is the head and b the tail of the list [a|b].

As examples of list processing in Prolog, consider the following:

   (a) To append two lists:

        append([ ], L, L).
        append([Car,Cdr], L, [Car,Result]) :- append(Cdr, L,
                                                        Result).

       We have used the variable names 'Car' and 'Cdr' in this
       example to help comparison with LISP.

   (b) To see if a given object is a member of a list:

        member(X, [X|_]).
        member(X, [_|Y]) :- member(X, Y).

       If we entered the goal 'member(g,[a,d,g,x,y])', then Prolog
       would return the answer 'yes'.

574

Note that the order in which these assertions are written is important.

(c)   To delete an element from a list:

```
delete(X, [X|L], L) :- !.
delete(X, [Y|L], [Y|M]) :- delete(X, L, M).
```

Note that this deletes only the first occurrence of the element. For example, if we entered the goal delete (g, [a,b,g,h,g,k], Z), then Prolog would return the answer:

Z = [a,b,h,g,k].

fail
'fail' is a built-in predicate which is defined such that as a goal it always fails and initiates backtracking.

cut/fail combination
The combination of a cut followed by a fail is quite useful since it allows us to define 'selective' predicates. For example, suppose that we want to define a predicate 'suitablecoat' which takes one argument and evaluates to true if the argument denotes a coat suitable for purchase. The criteria for suitability are (a) under no circumstances may the coat be a fur coat and (b) the coat must be waterproof and cost less than £150. The predicate 'suitablecoat' can be defined as follows:

```
suitablecoat(X) :- furcoat(X), !, fail.
suitablecoat(X) :- waterproof(X), cost(X, Y), Y < 150.
```

Suppose that we also had the following facts

```
furcoat(coat_1).
waterproof(coat_1).
waterproof(coat_2).
cost(coat_1, 120).
cost(coat_2, 80).
```

If we now enter the goal 'suitablecoat(coat_1)', then Prolog would match this with suitablecoat(X) in the first rule. The current goal would now be furcoat(coat_1). This would match with the fact furcoat(coat_1) and would succeed. The current goal would now be ! which would succeed immediately. The next sub-goal would be fail which would fail immediately and would initiate backtracking. However, the cut would prevent backtracking past itself. Hence, the original goal 'suitablecoat(coat_1)' would fail.

not
not is a built-in predicate which is defined such that the goal 'not(G)' succeeds only if the goal 'G' fails. Hence, Prolog is based on the closed world assumption (as discussed in chapter 5) and uses a 'failure to prove as negation' metarule which is implemented through the built-in predicate 'not'.

As example, suppose that the Prolog knowledge base contains only the following facts:

```
flight(london, paris).
flight(london, milan).
```

If we enter the goal 'not(flight(london, paris))' then Prolog would
return the answer 'no'. However, if we enter the goal 'not(flight
(london, amsterdam))' then Prolog would answer 'yes' because it fails
to prove the goal 'flight(london, amsterdam)'.

Reading and writing

Prolog contains built-in predicates for reading and writing numbers
and characters from the keyboard and from files. As a simple example,
consider the following program:

```
compute :- read(X), Y is X*X, write(Y).
```

To use this program, you would begin by entering the goal 'compute'.
Prolog would then wait for you to enter a number. You would do this
as, for example:

    13.   (notice the full stop)

Prolog would return by writing 169 followed by 'yes'.

Reading assertions from files

Typing in clauses directly into Prolog is only recommended if the
clauses are not needed permanently and are few in number. Longer programs should be edited into a file and read into Prolog by giving the
following directive as a goal:

    ? |- [name].

where 'name' is the name of the (Unix) file containing the assertions.
If the file name contains any characters which are not allowed in
Prolog atoms then it must be enclosed in quotes, otherwise the name
only may be given. Any number of files may be accessed. For example:

    ? |- [myprogram, "people/greeks", sortroutine].

It is recommended that files be used when experimenting with the following example programs.

Some example Prolog programs

We conclude this very brief description of Prolog with some example
programs:

(a) Quicksort

```
        qsort([X|L], RO, R) :- partition(L, X, L1, L2),
                                        qsort(L2, RO, R1),
                                        qsort(L1, [X|R1], R).
        qsort([], R, R).
        partition([X|L], Y, [X|L1], L2) :- X =< Y, !,
                                        partition(L, Y, L1, L2).
        partition([X|L], Y, L1, [X|L2]) :- X, >, Y, !,
                                        partition(L, Y, L1, L2).
        partition([], _, [], []).
```

The goal qsort(L, RO, R) is true if the list R consists of
the members of list L sorted into order, followed by the members of list RO. To sort a list, enter a goal such as
'qsort([5,3,2,6],[ ],X)'. Prolog will respond with
X = [2,3,5,6].

(b) A simple parser
     The following program implements a parser for a grammar. The
     grammar defines a simple language which contains the follow-
     ing sentences, amongst others:

         the man likes the dog
         the man likes the girl
         the dog bites the man
         the dog bites the girl
         the man walks
         (etc.)

The grammar is:

         sentence(X, Y) :- noun-phrase(X, Z), verb-phrase(Z, Y).
         noun_phrase(X, Z) :- determiner(X, W), noun(W, Z).
         verb_phrase(Z, Y) :- verb(Z, Y).
         verb_phrase(Z, Y) :- verb(Z, P), noun-phrase(P, Y).
         determiner([the|X], X).
         noun([man|X], X).
         noun([dog|X], X).
         noun([girl|X], X).
         verb([likes|X], X).
         verb([bites|X], X).
         verb([walks|X], X).

If you were to enter the following goal:

         sentence([the,dog,bites,the,girl], []).

then the Prolog interpreter would answer 'yes', indicating
that the sentence 'the dog bites the girl' is a well-formed
sentence.

(c) A simple parser using Prolog's 'grammar rule' notation
     In many versions of Prolog there is a facility which enables
     you to enter grammar rules in a more readable form. These
     rules use a pre-defined infix operator -->. We demonstrate
     the use of this notation by giving a Prolog program which
     implements the same grammar as that given in (b) above:

         sentence --> nounphrase, verb_phrase.
         noun_phrase --> determiner, noun.
         verb_phrase --> verb.
         verb_phrase --> verb, noun_phrase.
         determiner --> [the].
         noun --> [man].
         noun --> [dog].
         noun --> [girl].

```
verb --> [likes].
verb --> [bites].
verb --> [walks].
```

(d) A translator from English to predicate logic formulas
     The translator described below was developed by Pereira and
     Warren at the University of Edinburgh. The operators ':',
     'and' and '⇒' are defined by entering the following goals
     before the grammar rules:

op(900, xfx, ⇒).	(Infix, neither left nor right associative)
op(800, xfy, and).	(Infix, right associative)
op(300, xfx, :).	(Infix, neither left nor right associative)

When these operators have been defined, the following assertions may be entered (preferably from a file).

```
sentence(P) --> noun_phrase(X,P1,P), verb_phrase(X,P1).

noun_phrase(X,P1,P) -->
 determiner(X,P2,P1,P), noun(X,P3), rel_clause(X,P3,P2).
noun_phrase(X,P,P) --> name(X).

verb_phrase(X,P) --> trans_verb(X,Y,P1), noun_phrase
                                               (Y,P1,P).
verb_phrase(X,P) --> intrans_verb(X,P).

rel_clause(X,P1,P1 and P2) --> [that], verb_phrase(X,P2).
rel_clause(_,P,P) --> [].

determiner(X,P1,P2, all(X):(P1 ⇒ P2) ) --> [every].
determiner(X,P1,P2, exists(X):(P1 and P2) ) --> [a].

noun(X, man(X) ) --> [man].
noun(X, woman(X) ) --> [woman].

name(john) --> [john].

trans_verb(X,Y, loves(X,Y) ) --> [loves].
intrans_verb(X, lives(X) ) --> [lives].
```

If we now enter the following goal:

```
sentence(P, [every,man,that,lives,loves,a,woman], []).
```

then the Prolog interpreter will respond with:

```
P = all(X) : (man(X) and lives(X) ⇒ exists(Y) :
                        (woman(Y) and loves(x, Y))).
```

A more complete introduction to Prolog can be found in
Clocksin and Mellish (1981).

Poplog
Poplog is a mixture of LISP, Prolog, and a language called Pop-II. The features of each of these languages are available for programmers to use, within a single program if required.

Poplog runs on Digital Equipment VAX machines under VMS or Unix, and is also available on a number of powerful micros such as the Bleasdale micro which has a 68000 processor.

11.11 PS-ALGOL

PS-algol (see, for example, Atkinson et al, 1984) is a language which has been designed and implemented as part of a project whose objective is to provide better programming techniques and environments for the construction of large dynamically evolving systems. In particular, one aim is to provide an environment in which the programmer never has to step outside the programming language for any computational activity. In order to achieve this aim, the traditional role of the programming language is being extended to provide facilities normally left to other modules such as the file system or linker.

PS-algol is a language which has been extended in this way. It is based on the notions of 'orthogonal persistence' and 'first-class procedures' which are discussed briefly below.

11.11.1 ORTHOGONAL PERSISTENCE

The 'persistence' of an object is the length of time that the object exists. In conventional programming languages, data does not exist longer than the activation of the program in which it was created unless some storage mechanism, such as a file system or database management package, is explicitly invoked. In persistent programming, data can outlive the program activation without the need to invoke such mechanisms. The method of accessing the data is uniform regardless of whether it is long or short term data. The term 'orthogonal persistence' means that all data objects, whatever their type, have the same rights to long and short term persistence. The persistence mechanisms of PS-algol include the operations 'open.database,' 's.enter,' 'commit' and 'abort', which may be illustrated by an example:

```
let db = open.database("library", "xyza", "write")
if db is error.record do write "database cannot be opened" ; abort
s.enter ("newdata", db, somerecord)
commit ( )
```

The open.database command opens the database "library" with "write" access rights by quoting the password "xyza". The s.enter command enters somerecord into an associative table (which was yielded by a successful open.database command). The identifier of somerecord is "newdata". The commit command causes the update to be committed. PS-algol includes other database operations including 's.lookup' which can be used to obtain entries from a table. For example:

```
let retrieved.data = s.lookup ("newdata", db)
```

11.11.2 PROCEDURES AS FIRST-CLASS OBJECTS

Procedures, in languages such as Algol 60 and Pascal, may only be

579

declared, passed as parameters, or executed. In this respect they do not have the same rights as data objects in the language. In order for them to become 'first-class' objects, they should have the same rights as any data object in the language. That is, they should be capable of being assigned, of being the result of expressions, of being elements of structures and arrays, etc.

LISP was the first language with first-class procedures. Since then, other languages have been developed with this feature. These languages include Pal, Gedankon, Clu, Sasl, ML and PS-algol.

11.11.3 PROCEDURAL ABSTRACTION
Most high-level languages allow statements to be grouped together into a procedure, function or sub-routine. The statements may then be referred to collectively by the procedure, function or sub-routine identifier. This mechanism is called 'procedural abstraction'.

There are three main advantages of procedural abstraction:

(a)   Large programs may be broken down into smaller, more manage-able parts.

(b)   Once a procedure has been coded, it can be used by a program-mer without that programmer having to know the internal code of the procedure (this is assuming that a correct specifica-tion of the function of the procedure is available).

(c)   Procedures may be tested separately. This facilitates more thorough testing than would be possible with a monolithic program.

11.11.4 ABSTRACT DATA TYPES
An abstract data type separates the implementation of a data object from its use. For example, the abstract data type 'integer-stack' defines an object 'integer-stack' as being something onto which integers may be pushed and from which integers may be pulled. The only way the integer-stack may be accessed and/or modified is through the procedures 'push' and 'pull'.

In a language such as Pascal, we can go some way towards implementing this abstract data type; for example, by writing statements such as:

```
type stackpointer = stackentry ;
     stackentry   = record
                           data : integer ;
                           next : stackpointer
                      end;
var stack : stackpointer ;
procedure push(x : integer) ;
    var p : stackpointer ;
    begin
        new(p) ;
        p↑.data := x ;
        p↑.next := stack ;
        stack := p
    end;
```

```
procedure pull (var x : integer) ;
    begin
        if stack = nil
            then writeln ('error stack underflow')
            else begin
                    x := stack↑.data ;
                    stack := stack↑.next
                end
    end;
```

It would still be possible to access the stack directly from within the program body without having to use push and pull. For example, we could write:

```
stack := nil ;
```

Hence, Pascal does not really support the notion of abstract data types. There are, however, languages which do support abstract data types, for example Simula, Clu, Algol 68R, Ada, PS-algol and several others.

The advantage of having abstract data types is twofold:

(a) It is a useful abstraction mechanism. For example, once the stack procedures push and pull have been implemented, the programmer can use the stack without having to think about how it has been implemented.

(b) The abstract data type mechanism also serves as a protection mechanism. In a language which supports abstract data types, not only would the programmer be freed from having to worry about how, for example, the stack was implemented, he would be unable to access the stack other than by use of the procedures push and pull.

11.11.5 FIRST-CLASS PROCEDURES AND ABSTRACT DATA TYPES

Relatively few languages support abstract data types *and* first-class procedures. Those languages which do include Clu, ML and PS-algol. Because procedures are first-class objects in PS-algol, data and procedural abstraction may both be obtained by the same mechanism which is closely related to the conventional mechanism for procedural abstraction. For example, consider the definition of an abstract object for a complex number given in fig. 11.8. This definition allows only the operations of addition, printing, and creation on the complex numbers.

One advantage of using a procedural mechanism for data abstraction is that it accommodates 'parametric' abstract types. That is, 'generic' types which can be used to create several instances which differ in some respect from each other according to parameters which are passed when the generic type is invoked. An example of a parametric data type is given in fig. 11.9. This is a generic type for 1-dimensional arrays which have different numbers of elements. The use of this abstract type is illustrated in fig. 11.10.

581

```
let add := proc( pntr a,b → pntr ) ; nullproc
let print := proc( pntr a ) ; nullproc
let complex := proc( real a,b → pntr ) ; nullproc

begin
    structure complex.number( real rpart,ipart )

    add := proc( pntr a,b → pntr )
            complex.number( a( rpart ) + b( rpart ),a( ipart ) +
                                                        b( ipart ) )

    print := proc( pntr a )
            write a( rpart ),
            if a( ipart ) < 0 then "-" else "+",
                                        rabs( a( ipart ) ), "i"

    complex := proc( real a,b → pntr)
            complex.number( a,b )
end

let a = complex( -1.0,-2.8 ) ; let b = complex( 2.3,3.2 )
print( add( a,b ) )
```

Figure 11.8   An abstract data type definition for complex numbers in PS-algol

```
structure vector.pack( proc( pntr,pntr → pntr )add ;
                        proc( pntr )print ;
                        proc( *real → pntr )create )

let make.vector.pack = proc( int n → pntr )
begin
    structure vec( *real rep )

    if n < 2 then { write "silly dimension" ; nil }
    else vector.pack(
        proc( pntr a,b → pntr ) !add
        begin
            let v = vector 1::n of 0.0
            for i = 1 to n do v( i ) := a( rep )( i ) +
                                                    b( rep )( i )
            vec(v)
        end,

        proc( pntr a ) !print
        begin
            write a( rep,1 )
            for i = 2 to n do write ", ",a( rep )( i )
        end,

        proc( *real r → pntr ) !create
        if upb( r ) = n and lwb( r ) = 1 then vec(r)
                                        else { write "wrong
                                                size" ; nil } )
end ! of make.vector.pack
```

Figure 11.9   A definition of a parameterised type in PS-algol

```
let Pack.2D = make.vector.pack( 2 )
let Pack.3D = make.vector.pack( 3 )

let add2 = Pack.2D( add ) ; let print2 = Pack.2D( print )
let mk2d = Pack.2D( create )
let add3 = Pack.3D( add ) ; let print3 = Pack.3D( print )
let mk3d = Pack.3D( create )

let v1 = mk2d( @1[ 1.1,2.2 ] )
let v2 = mk2d( @1[ 3.3,4.4 ] )
let v3 = add2( v1,v2 )

print2( v3 )

let w1 = mk3d( @1[ 1.1,2.2,3.3 ] ) ..........
```

Figure 11.10   An example of the use of a parameterised type

11.11.6   FIRST-CLASS PROCEDURES AND MODULES
A module is an object with the following properties:

(a)   It is a unit of program building which may be specified, com-
      piled, and tested separately, and later used in conjunction
      with other modules.

(b)   It may contain its own data which is bound to it for its
      lifetime.

(c)   It serves as an abstraction mechanism; for example, for
      implementing abstract data types.

Languages which support modules include Algol 68R, Clu, Ada, ML,
Modula-2, and PS-algol.

In PS-algol, first-class procedures, in conjunction with orthogonal
persistence, provide all the facilities of modules. In addition, the
normal parametric mechanisms of procedures mean that PS-algol supports
parameterised modules.

11.11.7   USING PS-ALGOL TO IMPLEMENT KNOWLEDGE BASE SYSTEMS
We have mentioned one or two of the features of PS-algol. These and
other features of the language facilitate the construction of complex
dynamically evolving systems.

Hence, PS-algol is an appropriate language for building knowledge base
systems.

Further information on PS-algol can be found in Atkinson et al (1984).

11.12   THE ROLE OF PROGRAMMING LANGUAGES IN KNOWLEDGE BASE SYSTEMS
WORK
It is important to recognise that programming languages may be used in
two quite distinct ways in knowledge base systems work:

(a)   They can be used *as* knowledge base systems.
(b)   They can be used *to write programs to implement* knowledge
      base systems.

For example, the logic-programming language Prolog may be used as a knowledge base system capable of storing assertions which are proper axioms of a theory of first order predicate logic (which is restricted to Horn clauses, in which there is no negation and in which the closed world assumption is made).

The Prolog interpreter is based on a depth-first SL theorem-prover, and a 'failure-to-prove as negation' metarule is implemented through a predicate 'not'. When used in this way, Prolog may be regarded as a knowledge base system with fairly severe limitations:

(a) It may only be used for applications in which it is correct to make the closed world assumption.

(b) It may only be used for applications in which Horn clauses are adequate.

(c) It is an example of the 'theory only' approach to knowledge base systems (see chapter 5), and consequently inherits all of the limitations of that approach.

(d) The combination of the theory only approach, the inability of users to enter negative assertions and the 'failure-to-prove as negation' metarule means that a Prolog program can never be inconsistent. Hence, the notions of integrity and integrity maintenance are completely missing when Prolog is used as a knowledge base system.

(e) There is, as yet, no implementation of Prolog which can efficiently handle very large collections of assertions, although some systems have been extended to handle reasonably large 'databases'.

These comments should not be read as a criticism of Prolog. They are intended to indicate some of the limitations of using Prolog *as* a knowledge base system. More importantly, these restrictions do not mean that Prolog cannot be used *to write programs to implement* other types of knowledge base system. For example, it is possible to write programs in Prolog which translate formulas of unrestricted predicate logic which are expressed in standard form to formulas expressed in clausal form. It is also possible to write programs which can test such formulas for inconsistency using any one of the methods described in chapter 4.

Similarly, LISP may be used as a knowledge base system or for writing programs to implement a knowledge base system. When used as a knowledge base system, the built-in functions for manipulating property lists can be used for storing and retrieving data and the facilities for function definition and function calling can be used for 'inference'.

Alternatively, LISP may be used to write programs to implement knowledge base systems. For example, LISP programs which perform depth-first and breadth-first searches may be found in McDermott and Charniak (1984).

11.13 CONCLUDING COMMENTS

We began this chapter by discussing the syntax and semantics of programming languages. We included some introductory notes on how to
construct translators for those languages which can be defined by a
class of context-free grammars called LL1 grammars. The notes given
are by no means comprehensive, but are sufficient for students to
construct simple translators. We have given references to additional
literature which readers are strongly encouraged to pursue. The description of translators was followed with a brief discussion of several
terms which are frequently used to categorise languages. We did this
to illustrate the variety of programming languages available for knowledge processing. We then went on to describe three languages which
are particularly relevant to knowledge base systems work: LISP, Prolog
and PS-algol.

We have mentioned that an ability to construct translators is extremely
useful to anyone wanting to embark on a career in knowledge base systems work. This is because many of the tasks which a knowledge base
system carries out involve the translation of one knowledge representation to another. For example:

(a) The input to a knowledge base can take many forms. It may
     consist of files of records or of natural language text, for
     example. Whatever the form of the input, it is likely that
     it will need to be translated to some 'canonical' form in
     order that it may be stored and retrieved efficiently.

(b) There is no single canonical form which is ideally suited to
     all of the 'reasoning' processes which have been developed for
     knowledge base systems. For example, those knowledge repres-
     entation formalisms which are well suited for efficient
     theorem-proving (as used in deductive question answering or
     consistency checking) are not well suited for theorem-provers
     which are required to explain their behaviour to end-users.
     In such cases, the stored knowledge, which may be in some
     canonical form, will have to be translated to a form suitable
     for the particular reasoning process in question.

(c) Output from a knowledge base system is likely to be required
     in various forms: as text, as tables, graphically, etc. A
     translator will have to be built for each of the output form-
     alisms required.

12 Special-purpose Hardware for Knowledge Processing

It would be both inappropriate and impractical to discuss hardware in detail in an introductory book of this nature. It would be inappropriate because the hardware which is being developed for knowledge base systems can only be appreciated if one has a relatively advanced understanding of conventional computer architecture. It would be impractical because there are many developments taking place and the subject really deserves a book on its own. Hence, we have decided to give some very brief notes under miscellaneous headings together with some references to further reading.

12.1 LIMITATIONS OF CONVENTIONAL VON NEUMANN ARCHITECTURES

There are several limitations to conventional computer architectures:

- (a) It is based on serial processing.
- (b) The instructions and data are rigidly separated.
- (c) It is primarily designed for efficient numeric processing only.

In order to overcome these limitations, various developments have taken place.

12.2 DATAFLOW ARCHITECTURES

Dataflow architectures provide high-speed computing by exploiting software parallelism in parallel processing hardware. Dataflow architectures have an advantage over other approaches to high performance computing in that the scheduling and synchronisation of concurrent processes is handled at the hardware level. However, in order to take advantage of the concurrency, a new approach to programming is required. Functional (applicative) languages may provide a solution. The basic idea in a dataflow machine is that the initial task is broken down into sub-tasks each of which is executed as soon as the data it requires becomes available.

Initially, the primary goal of the dataflow architecture was to reduce the execution time of large numerical computations. However, more recent developments have shifted the emphasis to symbolic processing. For example:

- (a) Dataflow techniques have been applied to database machines. An example of this is 'Direct', a multiprocessor, multiple

instruction stream, multiple data stream (MIMD), relational
database machine. In this system, groups of processors can,
for example, work on different instructions from the same
query. The strategy for processor allocation is based on a
variation of dataflow techniques. See Boral and Dewitt (1982)
for an introductory discussion.

(b) Alice (for applicative language idealised computing engine) is
a desk-top computer capable of running 'parallel' programs in
languages such as LISP and Prolog up to two orders of magnitude
faster than conventional hardware of the same complexity.
Alice, which is being developed in Britain at Imperial College,
London, was one of the first systems to use the Inmos 'trans-
puter' chip which is regarded by many as a useful fifth generation building block because of its efficiency at handling
large dataflows. See Smith (1983) for a dated but simple
introduction to Alice.

12.3 MACHINE ARCHITECTURES FOR PRODUCTION RULE BASED SYSTEMS

DADO (Stolfo and Shaw, 1982) is a parallel tree structured machine designed to improve the performance of large production rule based systems.
DADO comprises many thousands of processing elements, each containing
its own processor, a few K bytes of RAM and a specialised I/O switch.
The processing elements are interconnected to form a binary tree. Each
processing element (PE) is capable of executing in two distinct modes:
(a) the single instruction, multiple data stream (SIMD) mode, in which
the PE executes instructions which are broadcast by some ancestor PE
within the tree, and (b) the multiple instruction, multiple data stream
(MIMD) mode, in which the PE executes instructions stored in its own
local RAM independently of other PEs.

12.4 PARALLEL COMPUTATION - THEORETICAL CONSIDERATIONS

Future computer systems will need to use parallism much more than they
do at present. This brings challenges to computer designers and programmers. In addition to the engineering problems, there are various
theoretical issues which need to be resolved. A review of work relating to these issues can be found in Valiant (1983).

12.5 AI WORKSTATIONS

There are now available a large number of workstations which have been
specifically developed to run LISP-like languages. For example:

(a) *Explorer* is a symbolic processing system developed by Texas
Instruments. It contains 16K of 56-bit word writable control
store, microprogrammed for LISP processing. It has 128M bytes
of virtual address space and is centred around two high-speed
32-bit buses. It has a detached mass storage sub-system with
112M bytes of disk capacity, four of which can be daisychained
together. Explorer also supports Prolog.

(b) *Advent AI Workstation* from Advent Data Systems is an implementation of Common LISP on a Perq workstation.

(c) *KPS 10* from Racal Norsk is a LISP processor, based on the
Norsk Data 570 Series 32-bit supermini, which can also be used

to run the commercial application programs that have been developed for Norsk Data's existing commercial computers. Up to 168M bytes of physical memory can be accommodated, sixteen 500M byte disk drives, and additional processors can be added to expand capacity or support special functions.

(d)   *Symbolics 3600* from Symbolics is a descendent of the LM-2 which was a repackaged version of the 'LISP machine', the first hardware system specifically designed for LISP. The 3600 series has a 36-bit architecture which can support up to one G byte of demand paged virtual memory and it is claimed that most simple LISP instructions can be executed in one machine cycle. The system also supports Prolog as well as several conventional languages.

(e)   *Xerox 1108* is a single user workstation which runs Interlisp-D and the Loops knowledge engineering software. The system includes a 16-bit, bit-sliced processor, 1.5 to 3.5M bytes of main memory, and 10 to 315M byte disk store. This system is at the lower end of the price range for AI workstations.

(f)   The *Lambda* range from LISP Machine Incorporated are LISP machines which have a 32-bit processor designed around a high-speed multiprocessor bus, with 169 to 474M byte disks. The systems run Zetalisp-Plus which contains 10,000 pre-compiled LISP functions. Prolog is also supported.

12.6   THE CONNECTION MACHINE

The connection machine is a parallel processing computer with 65,000 separate processors. It was designed by Minsky at MIT and developed by the company Thinking Machines. The connection machine was originally designed to speed up the searching of semantic nets. (The MIT solution was to provide a processor for every node and every link in the network.) However, the connection machine is now finding use in other applications such as design rule checking, circuit simulation, and 3-D modelling.

12.7   TEXT RETRIEVAL MACHINES

These machines store and retrieve data which is archival in nature and whose usage is not generally known in advance. Search typically involves the pattern matching of stored text against words, combinations of words or phrases input by the end-user. Machine architectures for text retrieval are required to have very large on-line store and to support very fast pattern matching.

A discussion of machine architectures for text retrieval may be found in chapter 9 of Hsiao (1983).

12.8   MACHINES WHICH SUPPORT ASSOCIATIVE RETRIEVAL

When retrieving a record or tuple in a conventional system using direct access, the record or tuple key is transformed (by use of hashing or indexes, for example) to the physical address of the record or tuple. Such direct access is typically faster than searching for the record using a sequential technique in which records or tuples are brought into memory in some sequential order and tested to see if they are the one searched for. In both cases, some form of software is responsible for finding the required record. However, there are storage systems, called 'associative stores' in which the location of a record or tuple with a given key is carried out in hardware. Examples of such systems are:

(a) CASSM, content addressable segment memory (Su and Lipovski, 1975).
(b) RAPS (Ozkarahan et al, 1975).
(c) STARAN (Batcher, 1977).
(d) CAFS (ICL, 1977).
(e) DBC (Banerjee et al, 1979).

These and other systems are described in Bray and Freeman (1979). More recent developments are discussed in Hsiao (1983).

12.9 TRIPLE STORES
Throughout this book we have used examples based on the binary relational approach to knowledge processing. Two hardware systems have been developed explicitly to support this approach. One is called IFS (Lavington et al, 1984) and the other is called the FACT machine (McGregor and Malone, 1984).

12.10 PSM - THE PERSISTENT STORE MACHINE
PSM is a persistent store machine being developed at the University of Glasgow. The machine is designed to be suitable for the execution of a variety of high level languages, in particular block-structured languages, languages which treat procedures and functions as first-class objects, and database languages which require efficient indexing facilities. The PSM project is related to the project which is developing the language PS-algol described in chapter 11.

Details of PSM can be found in Cockshott (1985).

12.11 SUM - THE SYRACUSE UNIFICATION MACHINE
SUM is a coprocessor which carries out unification. The unification algorithm has a number of uses: in resolution in logic programming and in theorem-proving, and in functional programming. The SUM interface is tailored to the LISP Machine Incorporated Lambda range but could easily be adapted for other machines. When a Lambda machine, which is executing a LISP program, comes up to the point where it needs to do a unification, that task is handed over to the SUM machine which can execute it more efficiently.

An introductory description of SUM is given in Robinson (1985).

12.12 CONCLUDING COMMENTS
In this short chapter we have given a rather cursory description of some of the special-purpose hardware which is available to support knowledge base systems. The notes given are by no means comprehensive; they do, however, provide an introduction to the references which have been included.

One of the problems which hardware designers are currently facing is in identifying the type of processing which is required in knowledge base systems. During the last few months, the author of this book has been involved in discussions with hardware designers representing several major computer manufacturers. In many of these discussions, the author has been asked if he can define the processing requirements of knowledge base systems. The answer has been negative. Of course, there are requirements to support languages such as LISP, Prolog and PS-algol. However, these are likely to be short-term requirements.

At present, there is no consensus as to what knowledge processing techniques are fundamental and, in the author's opinion, it would be inappropriate to expend too much effort in hardware design for those languages and techniques which are currently in vogue. The computer industry would, in fact, appear to have adopted this view. For example, many of the AI workstations currently available are simply based on conventional systems which have been microprogrammed to support some particular language or approach to knowledge processing.

This view does not mean that it is inappropriate to experiment with new designs for hardware. The connection machine is an example of innovative hardware which has 'found' more applications than that for which it was originally designed. The development of new computer architectures should be encouraged, provided that such work is regarded as exploring other avenues to the identification of useful knowledge processing techniques.

If one accepts this approach, it appears strange that computer architectures based on the physiology of the human brain are typically regarded as being the product of crackpots. Many research programs in AI still regard any attempt to emulate the physiology of the brain as being outside the domain of 'realistic' research. This seems somewhat incongruous when one considers the aims of AI work.

The brain, which consists of several hundred thousand neurons, may be regarded as a set of interconnected analog computers. Each neuron is an analog to digital converter. The dendrites of a neuron collect signals, through their synaptic connections to other neurons, which are 'weighted' and summated in the body of the neuron. If the sum of these weighted signals exceeds some threshold, then the neuron responds by 'firing', i.e. sending an output signal down its axon, a channel connecting it to the dendrites of other neurons. The conductivity of synaptic connections may be affected by the activity of 'inhibitory' and 'excitatory' neural circuits located nearby. This structure would appear to account for much of the pattern matching ability of the human brain. However, computer architectures which are based on this structure have received very little support during the fifteen to twenty years since it was first put forward by neurophysiologists.

In chapter 9, we described Schank's approach to natural language processing. This approach involved the use of scripts built from semantic primitives such as INGEST, MOVE, etc. Schank explicitly disclaimed any attempt to model the physiology involved in human understanding. Perhaps, in the next few years, we shall see models of human cognitive abilities which are based on primitives closely related to the physiology of our own 'central processors'.

13 A List of Knowledge Base Systems and Related Products

When the notion of this book was first conceived some two years ago, the intention was to include a survey of knowledge base systems at this point. However, since that time we have decided that this would be impractical. Due to the increased activity in this area, there are many more systems available than there were two years ago. Consequently, we have decided to include:

(a) A list of systems mentioned in previous chapters together with references to the sections in which they appear.

(b) A short list of systems which have been released in the last few months.

(c) Some references to literature in which up-to-date descriptions of new products can be found.

13.1 SYSTEMS WHICH HAVE BEEN MENTIONED IN THE BOOK

The numbers indicate sections or sub-sections in which the systems were mentioned.

Database management systems

IMS	3.5.1
IDMS	3.5.2
TOTAL	3.5.3
ADABAS	3.5.4
dBASE II	3.5.5
INGRES	3.5.6
DB2	3.5.7
NDB	3.5.8

Database query languages and deductive facilities

McAIMS	3.4.11
IS/1	3.4.11
LINUS	3.4.11
ASTRID	3.4.11
Alpha	3.4.11

Frame based systems and languages

KRL	9.3.9
UNIT	9.3.9
WHEEZE	9.3.9
FRL	9.3.9
OWL	9.3.9
AM	9.3.9

Script based systems

SAM	9.5.3
IPP	9.5.3

Languages for implementing knowledge base systems

Prolog	11.10
LISP	10.5.2, 11.9
PS-algol	11.11
Abset	Appendix I, exercises for chapter 11

Special hardware for database and knowledge base systems

CASSM	3.8.5
RAPS	3.8.5
STARAN	3.8.5
CAFS	3.8.5
DBC	3.8.5
FACT	3.8.5
IFS	3.8.5
ALICE	12.2
DADO	12.3
Explorer	12.5
Advent AI workstation	12.5
KPS 10	12.5
Symbolics 3600	12.5
Xerox 1108	12.5
Lambda	12.5
Connection Machine	12.5
FACT	12.9
IFS	12.9
PSM	12.10
SUM	12.11

13.2 SOME RECENTLY RELEASED SYSTEMS

For each of these systems, we give a very brief description, a list
of the machines on which it runs, and the name and address of the
vendor.

EXSYS

- A goal-driven production rule based system.
- IBM PC and Apple Macintosh.
- EXSYS, P.O. Box 75158, Contract
  Station 14, Albequerque, NM 87194, USA.

LOOPS

- A LISP object oriented programming system.
- Runs under Interlisp-D on the Xerox 1108.
- Artificial Intelligence, 58 Merton Road, Watford,
  WD1 7BY, UK.

M.1

- A software tool for rapidly prototyping knowledge base systems
  to tackle 'structured selection' type problems such as diagnosing
  illness. Data-driven search is used and certainty factors are
  accommodated.
- IBM PC.
- Teknowledge, Palo Alto, CA 94301-1982, USA.

S.1

- A sophisticated knowledge engineering tool used for 'structured
  selection' type problems.
- Xerox 1108, Symbolics 3600 and DEC VAX.
- Teknowledge (see above).

Knowledge Craft

- A frame based expert system shell.
- Symbolics 3600, Texas Instruments Explorer and DEC VAX.
- Carnegie Group Inc., Commerce Court, Station Square,
  Pittsburgh, PA 15219, USA.

MP-LRO

- An object oriented language dealing with hierarchies of entity
  sets and inheritance of properties.
- Any machine with a Le-Lisp environment, such as VAX, Sun and
  Apollo.
- CRIL, 12 bis rue Jean Jaure, 92807 Puteaux, France.

EXPER OPS5

- An expert system shell which includes a data-driven inference
  engine and graphics facilities.
- Apple Macintosh 512K plus add-on hard or floppy disk.
- Expertelligence, 559 San Ysidro Road, Santa Barbara,
  CA 93018, USA.

ADVISOR

- An expert system shell for developing small production rule
  based systems. Data and goal-driven search strategies are
  available.
- Commodore 64, Apple II, and Atari 800.
- Ultimate Media Inc., 275 Magnolia Avenue, Larkspur,
  CA 94939, USA.

INSIGHT 2

- A Pascal programming environment, a dBase II compatible database
  editor, and a Wordstar-lookalike word processor. Knowledge bases

594

may be set up using standard word processing packages or text editors, and data can be taken from dBase II files. Data and goal-driven search strategies and probabilistic reasoning are provided.
- IBM PC and DEC Rainbow with hard disk.
- Level 5 Research Inc., 4980 South, Melbourne Beach, Fla. 32951, USA.

KEE

- An expert system shell with hybrid knowledge representation facilities integrating frames, production rules and object oriented programs. Data and goal-driven search strategies are provided.
- All LISP machines.
- Intellicorp, Knowledge Systems Division, 707 Laurel Street, Menlo Park, CA 94025-3445, USA.

HULK2

- A system which helps users create rule bases from dBASE II databases. Bayesian methods are used to calculate whether or not the rules are 'good' at prediction.
- Runs under CP/M80, CP/M86, PC/DOS, MS/DOS and UNIX.
- Brainstorm Computer Solutions, 103a Seven Sisters Road, London, N7 7QN, UK.

KES

- An expert system shell with hybrid knowledge representation facilities integrating frame and production rules. Statistical reasoning is accommodated.
- A range of machines including mainframes and the IBM PC.
- Software A and E, 1500 Wilson Boulevard, Suite 800, Arlington, Va 22209, USA.

ESP-ADVISOR

- An expert system shell written in Prolog.
- Data General's THE ONE, ACT Apricot, IBM PC, Sirius, DEC Rainbow, Logica VTS, TI Professional, Torch Graduate, HP 150 and Grid Portable.
- Expert Systems International, 9 West Way, Oxford, OX2 0JB, UK.

TESS

- An expert system shell using Bayesian inference.
- IBM PC and compatibles.
- Helix Expert Systems, 11 Ludgate Circus, London, EC4, UK.

SAVOIR

- An expert system shell.
- IBM PC under MS/DOS and VAX under VMS.
- ISI Ltd., 11 Oakdene Road, Redhill, Surrey, RH1 6BT, UK.

Xi

- An expert system shell written in Prolog.
- IBM PC
- Expertech, 172 Bath Road, Slough, SL1 3XE, UK.

13.3 SOURCES OF DATA ON NEW PRODUCTS

There are numerous sources of data on new products. It would be inappropriate to attempt to give a comprehensive list here since new
sources are continually coming onto the market. However, it may be of
interest to list the sources which the author has used in the writing
of this book.

(a) *Directory of Software* This directory is published in the UK
by Computing Publications Ltd., Evelyn House, 62 Oxford
Street, London, W1A 2HE. It is also available in the US from
Computing Publications Inc., 101 College Road East, Princeton
Forrestal Centre, Princeton, NJ 08540.

(b) *Expert Systems User* Subscription to this magazine may be
obtained from Expert Systems User, Cromwell House, 20 Bride
Lane, London, EC4 B4AH, UK.

(c) A catalogue of expert system shells, knowledge engineering
tools and artificial intelligence companies in the US and
Europe is published by Research Data Publications, 58 White-
ford Road, Plymouth, PL3 5LY, UK.

14 Summary

14.1 SYNOPSIS OF CONCEPTS AND TECHNIQUES DESCRIBED IN THE BOOK
We began, in chapter 1, by defining what we meant by a knowledge base
system. We followed this by describing how the development of knowledge base systems is benefiting from an integration of concepts and
techniques from database technology, formal logic, artificial intelligence work and linguistics. We also introduced the notion of a 'view
of the universe' which we have used (mostly implicitly) throughout the
book to define the systems of semantic concepts (or ontologies) which
underly the various techniques described.

In chapter 2, we gave an overview of the various knowledge representation formalisms which were to be discussed in detail in subsequent
chapters. We also included a brief description of how to construct a
parser program for a simple language of propositional logic. Our
reason for introducing parser construction so early in the text was
that languages were to figure in nearly every one of the following
chapters. We felt that an early introduction to parser construction,
followed in later chapters by descriptions of how parsers could be converted to query languages and formula translators, would emphasise the
relevance of chapter 11 (in which parser construction was described in
greater detail).

In chapter 3, we included a comprehensive discussion of conventional
database techniques followed by a brief description of one or two of
the better known commercially available database management systems.
The final sections in chapter 3 were concerned with what we called
fifth generation database systems. We stated that such systems should
be capable of providing, amongst other things, automatic maintenance
of semantic integrity, inference capabilities, and more user-friendly
interfaces. We then described an *ad hoc* approach to the automatic
maintenance of a limited type of semantic integrity. This description
served two purposes: (a) it provided an introduction to the notion of
semantic integrity and (b) it demonstrated the need for a more formal
(well-defined) approach such as that provided by formal logic.

Chapter 4 introduced the reader to classical logic. We began with a
general discussion, followed this with a description of propositional
logic and first order predicate logic, and concluded with a description

of various automatic theorem-proving techniques. We introduced a large number of theorem-proving techniques in our discussion. The reason for this was twofold: (a) an understanding of some of these techniques would be useful when the more complicated techniques used in non-classical logics were discussed later in the book and (b) at present there is no consensus as to which theorem-proving techniques are most appropriate for particular types of knowledge processing.

Chapter 5 explained how first order predicate logic could be used to formalise various aspects of database systems. We introduced three approaches: (a) the theory and complete relational structure approach, which may be used to formalise aspects of conventional non-deductive database systems, (b) the theory only approach (this is the approach used in Prolog) which may be used to formalise certain types of deductive database system and (c) the theory and incomplete relational structure approach which may be used to formalise a more general class of database system. We indicated, in the latter part of chapter 5, that there are certain aspects of database systems which are not yet fully understood and for which efficient techniques have not yet been developed. An example is the maintenance of semantic integrity when data is deleted from a deductive database system.

The use of first order predicate logic as the basis for knowledge base systems work is limited in several respects. In chapter 6, we introduced some of the non-classical logics which have been developed, and briefly described how they may be used to overcome these limitations.

One property of knowledge which we had virtually ignored in the first six chapters is the uncertainty which is associated with it. In chapter 7, we described some of the calculi which have been developed for dealing with uncertainty.

In chapter 8, we introduced the reader to an approach to knowledge processing which is not based on logic. This is the production rule based approach. Many instances of a particular type of knowledge base system, called expert systems, are implemented as production rule based systems. We discussed various aspects of expert systems in the latter half of chapter 8.

In chapters 9 and 10, we described two other approaches to knowledge processing: the frame based approach and the functional approach. Both of these approaches are regarded by many as important developments in knowledge base systems work.

Chapter 11 discussed the use of programming languages in knowledge processing. We began by giving some potted notes on grammars and on translator construction. These topics were included since much of the processing which is carried out by a knowledge base system involves the translation of one knowledge representation to some other representation. We believe that an ability to design languages and to construct translator programs is essential to anyone wanting to embark on a career in knowledge base systems work. We concluded chapter 11 by giving brief descriptions of three languages: LISP, Prolog and PS-algol, which typify three classes of programming language particularly relevant to knowledge base systems work.

Chapter 12 described some of the special-purpose hardware which has been developed for knowledge base systems. This discussion was kept very brief for two reasons: (a) there have been many developments which would require a separate book to describe adequately and (b) there is, as yet, no consensus as to what knowledge processing techniques should be supported in hardware. In the author's opinion, it would be inappropriate to spend a great deal of effort developing hardware to support those techniques and languages which are currently in vogue. A better approach is to regard innovative hardware development as empirical research providing another avenue to the identification of useful knowledge processing techniques.

In chapter 13, we listed some of the knowledge base systems which were available when the book was written. The author did not spend a great deal of time in compiling this list since it is likely to be out of date very quickly. References were given to sources which maintain up-to-date lists of commercially available systems.

Due to the nature of this book, and the broad subject area, it has not been possible to give anything other than introductory descriptions of the topics covered. In particular, we have not attempted to analyse the techniques and systems which we have described. Consequently, on completing this book, the reader should not regard him/herself as having acquired an expertise in the subject of knowledge base systems work. The experts are few and far between. Typically, they have a deep understanding of the strengths and limitations of one particular approach to knowledge base systems work which they have gained through years of involvement in the development or use of that approach.

There are many aspects of knowledge processing which deserve more research and we list some of these in appendix 2. Hopefully, this book will encourage some students to embark on such research and to establish themselves as experts in, as yet, uncharted aspects of knowledge base systems work.

14.2 PUTTING THE CONCEPTS AND TECHNIQUES IN PERSPECTIVE

Currently, there is much controversy as to which approaches to knowledge processing are 'better' than others. Disputes include:

- n-ary relational data models versus binary-relational data models
- classical logic based approaches versus non-classical logic based approaches
- logic based approaches versus other approaches
- production rules versus frames
- Bayesian probability theory versus certainty theory
- classical logic based approaches versus the functional approach
- Prolog versus LISP

In the author's opinion, such argument contributes little to the development of the subject. All of the methods described in this book have their limitations, some more than others. However, all have advantages over other techniques with respect to particular applications.

When taken together, the techniques described constitute a powerful arsenal with which to attack knowledge processing problems. For example:

(a)   Database techniques can be used to manage large collections
      of data which are used by more than one person or for more
      than one purpose.

(b)   Formal logic, with its well-defined semantics, provides us
      with the means to formalise various aspects of the knowledge
      base systems which we build. This, together with the notions
      of soundness, completeness and decidability, enables us to
      clearly understand the capabilities of our products. Formal
      logics, classical and non-classical, also provide us with vari-
      ous consistency checking and theorem-proving techniques which
      we can adapt for integrity maintenance and deductive retrieval.

(c)   If the knowledge that we are dealing with is uncertain in some
      respect or other, then we have various calculi for dealing
      with this. Bayesian probability theory is useful when accu-
      rate *a priori* probabilities and correlation coefficients are
      available. Certainty theory can be used in systems where such
      values are not available and the certainty measures which are
      available represent subjective estimates. Possibility theory
      and fuzzy logic may be used when we need to distinguish between
      extent and probability. Plausibility theory is useful for pre-
      processing inconsistent sets of assertions in order to derive
      plausible consequences which can subsequently be manipulated
      by other means. Incidence calculus is useful when more infor-
      mation about events is required than can be supplied by simple
      numerical probabilities.

(d)   Many of the search strategies which have been developed for
      production rule based systems are similar to strategies which
      have been developed for automated theorem-proving in formal
      logic. Many production rule based systems are also capable of
      'propagating' certainty values and of explaining their behav-
      iour to end-users.

(e)   The slot and filler approaches, such as those based on frames
      or scripts, are particularly useful for knowledge acquisition
      (e.g. from natural language text), and for making use of gen-
      eric and default values in question answering.

(f)   Finally, the functional approach can be used to characterise
      database systems (in terms of the retrieval functions they
      provide) and to facilitate their interface to other database
      systems and end-users. The functional approach also provides
      us with a framework for higher-order knowledge processing in
      which, for example, we can reason about properties of sets of
      relations, and so on. Various higher-order logics have been
      developed which are closely related to the functional approach.

14.3   THE NEED FOR A SEMANTIC FRAMEWORK WITH WHICH TO CATEGORISE DIFFERENT TECHNIQUES AND SYSTEMS

A large number of techniques have developed and are being developed for
knowledge processing. Integration of these techniques and systems is
problematical for a number of reasons, not least of which is the different terminologies and knowledge representation formalisms they use. The

compatibility or incompatibility of the techniques and systems is obscured by the different terminologies and knowledge representation formalisms.

A possible solution to this problem is to identify a commonly used set of semantic concepts which can subsequently be employed to characterise the various techniques and systems available. This should help us to determine the type of knowledge which can be represented and processed by the techniques and systems being considered. Note that we are not suggesting that we should try to identify a universally acceptable set of semantic primitives. We are saying that we should try to identify a commonly used set of semantic concepts.

By 'semantic concept' we mean an abstract notion which can be represented in various ways using syntactically different notations. An example of a semantic concept is 'logical negation', which may be represented in various ways, including the following:

(a) 'not'
(b) ¬
(c) 'it is false that'
(d) by omission (this involves the closed world assumption as discussed in chapter 5)

Other semantic concepts which might be of relevance are:

- proposition (a semantically indivisible statement which is true or false)
- truth
- falsehood
- unknown truth value
- uncertainty value
- entity
- entity set
- attribute
- attribute set
- relation (different types: 1 to 1, 1 to many, etc.)
- binary relation
- the set membership relation
- the sub-set relation
- relationship
- function
- name
- variable
- logical conjunction
- logical disjunction
- material implication
- equality
- possible world
- possible truth
- necessary truth
- strict implication
- agent (the knower or believer in belief logic)
- proof
- entity set membership rule
- relation cardinality rule (i.e. 1 to 1, 1 to many, etc.)

601

In order to avoid confusion, it would be useful to name and define semantic concepts using some well-established terminology such as that found in Marciszewski's *Dictionary of Logic* (1981).

The concepts listed above were chosen intuitively. It is recognised that they require a good deal of re-working before a really useful set can be identified. It is suggested that the list should be refined and extended by using the set on some typical techniques and systems. We feel that this pragmatic approach is likely to be more rewarding than lengthy philosophical discourse on what does or does not constitute a useful semantic concept.

As example of the use of semantic concepts, we give two examples of systems which are described in terms of them.

The hierarchical approach to database systems work

In the hierarchical approach, knowledge is represented by the use of files, records and fields which are related in tree structures. We have given examples of the hierarchical approach in chapter 3. Using the semantic concepts listed above, we can characterise the hierarchical approach as follows:

Semantic concept	Corresponding hierarchical terminology/concept
entity	record instance
attribute	field value
entity set	record type
attribute set	field type
one-to-many relation between entity sets	record links between father and son records in files
many-to-many relation from entity set to attribute set	record-field links
negation	(by omission)
entity set membership rules	record type structure
attribute set membership rules	field format
relation domain and counter-domain rules	field specification, record specification

The representation of rules in the hierarchical approach is embedded in the structure of the files, records and fields:

(a) Entity set membership rules are implicitly defined by restricting records to have a particular structure.

(b) Attribute set membership rules are implicity defined by restricting fields to have a fixed format.

(c) Relation domain and counter-domain rules are implicitly defined by restricting the type of records allowed in files and by restricting the types of field allowed in records.

Negation may only be represented by omission if it is appropriate to make the closed-word assumption. From this example, we can see that

our list of concepts should include specific types of rule in addition
to the relation domain and counter-domain rules.

Prolog
Using some of the concepts listed above, Prolog may be characterised
as follows:

Semantic concepts underlying Prolog

- entities
- unrestricted n-ary relations ($n \geqslant 1$)
- functions
- variables
- conjunction
- disjunction
- material implication
- any rule which can be expressed as a Horn clause with at least
  one positive literal
- negation by omission (failure to prove)

Note that no distinction is made between entities and attributes. There
is no notion of an entity set in 'standard' Prolog. Any rule which can
be expressed as a Horn clause with at least one positive literal can be
represented in Prolog. The 'not' operator in Prolog really means fail
to prove. There is no way of expressing, for example, the fact that
'John is not married to Sally' other than by omission of the fact that
John is married to Sally, or by introducing a predicate 'notmarriedto'.

This example also demonstrates the need for our list of concepts to
include more specific types of rule.

14.4 SOME PERSONAL OPINIONS
We have covered a large number of concepts and techniques in this book.
In describing these concepts and techniques, we have attempted to be as
objective as possible. In this section, some personal opinions which
the author holds are presented.

(a) Logic should form the basis of all knowledge base systems work.
    The syntax and semantics of any knowledge representation which
    is used should be defined using the techniques which have been
    developed for defining logics.

(b) The theory and incomplete relational structure approach (see
    chapter 5) is the most appropriate approach for formalising
    first order knowledge base systems.

(c) The binary relational view of the universe (see chapter 3) is
    the most promising of the many views that have been developed.
    The database should consist of a set of binary relationships
    such as:

fact id.	universe id.	time	sign	entity	relation id.	entity	source	certainty value

(d)   There should be more than one type of inference engine. A
      suitable set of inference engines might include one based on
      sorted predicate logic (see chapter 6), one based on sorted
      non-monotonic logic, one based on production rules using
      INFERNO's calculus for handling uncertainty (see chapter 8)
      and one based on the functional approach (see chapter 10) used
      in conjunction with a sort lattice. (We have not described
      this combination in the book. However, it is not difficult
      to see how the use of sort lattices, as used in sorted logic,
      could be adapted for use with a functional language such as
      LISP.)

(e)   Various interfaces to the knowledge base system should be pro-
      vided. A suitable set of interfaces might include one based
      on relational calculus (see chapter 3), one based on FQL (see
      chapter 10) and a natural language interface based on
      Montague's work (see chapter 6).

(f)   Many of the concepts which have been developed for expert sys-
      tems could be used in the design of the inference engines. In
      particular, the results of work on explanations and on know-
      ledge acquisition could be so used.

(g)   The frame based approach may be regarded as a sorted non-mono-
      tonic logic. Some of the techniques which have been developed
      for frame based systems could be used in the design of the
      inference engines. In particular, the pattern matching and
      'reasoning by analogy' capabilities of frame based systems
      could be so used.

(h)   Ideally, a single inference engine would be capable of effic-
      iently accommodating time, modality, uncertainty, default pro-
      perties, generic properties, higher-order properties, actions
      and so on. However, the construction of such an inference
      engine is currently not possible. Before such an inference
      engine could be built, a sorted, non-monotonic, modal, situa-
      tional, higher-order action logic would have to be developed.
      The work of Montague (see chapter 6), Martin-Löf (1982) and
      Goguen and Meseguer (1985) may be regarded as providing a
      basis for the development of such a logic.

(i)   The knowledge base system should include an automatic semantic
      integrity checking module. At present, there are very few
      well-defined approaches to dealing with semantic integrity.
      The approach which was described in chapter 5 could form the
      basis of a simplistic integrity checker for first order know-
      ledge bases. There is a need for much more research in this
      area.

14.5 SUGGESTIONS FOR FURTHER READING

We conclude the main text of this book by referring to a number of publications which we regard as being particularly useful:

      Alvey (March, 1984)
      Alvey (May, 1984)
      Alvey (Sept., 1984)

* Bundy (1983)
  Bibel (1983)
  Buneman and Frankel (1979)
  Clifford and Warren (1983)
* Clocksin and Mellish (1981)
  Cohn (1984)
* Dowty et al (1981)
  Gaillaire and Minker (1978)
  Gaillaire, Minker and Nicolas (1984)
  Goguen and Meseguer (1985)
* Hayes-Roth, Waterman, and Lenat (1983)
* Kowalski (1979)
  Li (1984)
  McCawley (1981)
* Marciszewski (1981)
  Nilsson (1971)
* Sell (1985)
  Turner (1984)
* Winston and Horn (1981)

Those marked with an asterisk are books which are worth purchasing if you are wanting to continue your study of knowledge base systems work.

Appendix 1
Exercises

1.1 At the beginning of chapter 1, we mentioned that the development
of mathematical notations and systems, formal logics, libraries,
filing systems, database management systems, expert systems and
natural language understanding systems have all contributed to an
increase in mankind's ability to store and process knowledge. What
other developments may also have played a part in this increase?

1.2 We have defined a knowledge base as 'a collection of simple facts
and general rules representing some universe of discourse'. Would
it have been better to use the term 'complex facts' in place of
'general rules' in this definition? Explain your answer.

1.3 Write a first order predicate logic expression corresponding to
the sentence:

   'There exists a man who loves all women.'

The following sentence may be interpreted in two ways:

   'Every man loves some woman.'

What are these two interpretations? Write first order predicate
logic expressions corresponding to these two interpretations.

1.4 Is the following sentence true?:

   'A database is necessarily a knowledge base but a knowledge
   base is not necessarily a database.'

Explain your answer.

1.5 In what way is the study of 'views of the universe' related to
ontology or metaphysics?

1.6 The term 'knowledge base system' has been deliberately used in
this book instead of the term 'knowledge based system'. What is

the difference between a knowledge base system as described in chapter 1 and a knowledge based system? (You will need to refer to other literature to determine the usual meaning of the latter term.)

EXERCISES FOR CHAPTER 2

2.1 We have defined the word 'knowledge' as 'the symbolic representation of aspects of some named universe of discourse'. Why is it important to include the adjective 'named' in this definition?

2.2 Peter and Paul both have a great deal of knowledge, but Henry is not so knowledgeable. However, Peter prefers to hear what Henry has to say rather than listen to Paul. Give a possible explanation which exemplifies the distinction between knowledge and information.

2.3 Consider the sentence:

'If Robert is over 65 years old, then he is eligible for a state pension.'

How might this sentence convey information to someone who does not know if Robert is eligible for a pension? Consider the sentence:

'If Robert could travel faster than the speed of light, then he could go back in time.'

Could this sentence convey information to anyone?

2.4 What is the difference between a knowledge representation and a knowledge representation formalism?

2.5 What are the meanings of the terms 'syntax' and 'semantics'?

2.6 Give BNF rules defining the syntax for the structure of books such as this one. The first rule may look something like:

book ::= front-cover body back-cover

2.7 Construct a state diagram for a lexical scanner for a language PROPLANG' which is equivalent to PROPLANG except that '¬', '⇒', '∧' and '∨' are replaced by 'not', 'implies', 'and' and 'or' respectively.

2.8 Insert comments at appropriate places in the PROPLANG parser program to show that you understand how it works.

2.9 Trace the execution of the PROPLANG parser for the following input:

[[(john is hungry) ∧ (john has money)] ⇒ (john buys food)];

Use the same notation for the trace as that used in the example trace in sub-section 2.2.4.

2.10 Write down a set of production rules for 'noughts and crosses' ('tic-tac-toe') which a complete beginner could use to play the game.

2.11 Consider the following body of knowledge:

'All people have two parents. John's parents are Betty and Bill. Betty is younger than Bill. John is 25 years old.'

Construct representations of this knowledge using the following formalisms:

- file/record
- n-ary relations
- binary relations
- first order predicate logic
- frames
- Pascal

2.12 Why would it be useful to identify a set of semantic concepts which are commonly used in knowledge base systems work?

EXERCISES FOR CHAPTER 3

3.1 In what respects could the ancient library at Alexandria be regarded as a database system? How might the notion of 'data independence' have been useful in the design and operation of this library?

3.2 What are the differences between a conceptual schema and a data dictionary? Who uses them and for what purpose?

3.3 Suppose that you are responsible for designing a database system. Would it be better to create the conceptual schema before the data dictionary or vice versa? Explain your answer.

3.4 It is generally good practice to construct the conceptual and database schemas using the unconstrained network view or binary relational view, in the first instance, and then to transcribe the database schema to one based on the particular view underlying the DBMS being used. For example, if the IDMS database management system were being used, it would be good practice to construct the conceptual and database schemas using the unconstrained network or binary relational view and then to transcribe the database schema to one based on the DBTG network view. Why do you think it is good practice, in general, to proceed in this way? Would this be an appropriate approach if a relational database management system were being used? Explain your answer.

3.5 Give examples of circumstances in which it would be more appropriate to use dynamic hash tables than B-trees, and vice versa. Explain your choices.

3.6 Discuss the relative merits of multi-lists, inverted lists, inverted files, bit lists and transposed files. Which do you think would be the easiest and the hardest to implement in Pascal (assuming that routines for accessing direct access backing store files are available)? Explain your answer.

3.7 The logical-to-physical mapping module is generally one of the most difficult parts to construct in a fully data-independent database system, and whenever the data storage structure is changed this module will need to be modified. Explain how the construction and modification of the logical-to-physical mapping module may be facilitated if it is regarded as a language translator (see chapter 11 if you are not familiar with translator construction).

3.8 What is the difference between syntactic and semantic integrity in the context of a database system?

3.9 Suppose that you are in charge of a filing cabinet containing 100 extremely important records. Several people require access to these records in order to read or update them. How could you use the notions of 'locking', 'transaction', 'back-up files', 'roll-back' and 'roll-forward' to ensure that you could recover from various 'accidents' which might otherwise corrupt this manual database which is in your charge?

3.10 Draw a diagram of an ideal DBMS showing the interactions between the parts.

3.11 The early database views, i.e. the hierarchical and DBTG network views, are closely related to the notions of files and records. The newer views, i.e. the entity relationship attribute, relational and binary relational views, are not so closely related to these notions. Why do you think that this is the case?

3.12 Until recently, the recommended approach to the design of a relational database system involved (a) identifying relations corresponding to the input/output requirements of users, and then (b) normalising these relations in order to obtain a relational model in 'third normal form' which could be used as a basis for the design of the required database system. However, this approach is now being questioned and an alternative approach has been put forward. The new approach proceeds as follows: (a) construct an entity relationship attribute model or a binary relational model of the application area (note that this provides a model which is already in fourth or fifth normal form) and then (b) take into account the access requirements in order to 'de-normalise' this model to obtain a more efficient one in third normal form. Both approaches should result in the same model. What are the relative advantages of the two approaches? (See Date (1981), for example, for a definition of first, second, third, fourth and fifth normal forms.)

3.13 In sub-section 3.4.9, we defined the relational algebraic operations of projection, selection, join, and division. We did not mention the relational algebraic operations of intersection and union. Write down what you think would be adequate definitions for these two operations. Give some examples of their use. Refer to other literature to see if your definitions are correct.

3.14 In sub-section 3.4.9, we gave nine examples of relational algebraic commands and queries. What are the equivalent relational calculus commands and queries?

3.15 In sub-section 3.4.10, we gave six examples of relational calculus queries. What are the equivalent relational algebraic queries?

3.16 What are the advantages and disadvantages of the binary relational view compared with the relational view?

3.17 What are the advantages and disadvantages of the hierarchical view compared with the relational view?

3.18 How could the query language described in sub-section 3.4.14 be modified to handle queries such as:

[not(x . works for . IBM) ∧ not(x . aged . 24)];

What additional data would have to be made available to the query processor?

3.19 How could dBASE II, as described in sub-section 3.5.5, be improved?

3.20 What would be involved in converting a set of relations to a set of hierarchical files of records?

3.21 Why is the DBMS architecture outlined in fig. 3.48 likely to result in database systems which are more data independent than those resulting from the use of the architecture outlined in fig. 3.1?

3.22 In sub-section 3.8.2 we described a simple method for automatically maintaining the semantic integrity of databases. What are the limitations of this method?

3.23 Can the method described in 3.8.2 be used to automatically enforce constraints such as:

'Before someone may be employed by MI5, he must definitely be known not to be a member of the Communist Party.'

3.24 What do we mean when we say that SCHEMAL is based on a sub-set of a language of first order predicate logic?

3.25 What would be the practical advantages of having a deductive retrieval facility in a database system?

EXERCISES FOR CHAPTER 4

4.1 State which of the following are universally valid (i.e. tautolo-
     gies), which are satisfiable and which are unsatisfiable:

        (a) P ∧ ¬P
        (b) P ∨ ¬P
        (c) P
        (d) P ∧ [[Q ∧ ¬P] ∨ [¬Q ∧ P]] ∧ Q
        (e) [P ∧ Q ∧ R] → [P ∨ Q ∨ R]
        (f) [P ∧ S] ∨ [Q ∧ ¬S]

4.2 Why is it important that a deduction system be both sound and
     complete?

4.3 Suppose that H is a theory consisting of a sound and complete
     axiomatisation of propositional logic, such as that given in sub-
     section 4.1.5, together with the following proper axioms:

        P1: if polly went up then polly must come down
        P2: polly went up

Construct syntactic proofs showing that the following are theorems
of H:

        F1: polly must come down
        F2: either polly did not go up or she must come down

(Hint: begin by translating the expressions above into formulas,
e.g. with, say, P standing for 'polly went up' and Q for 'polly
must come down'.)

4.4 Use a purely semantic method to show that F1 and F2 above are
     logical consequences of P1 and P2 above.

4.5 Use resolution to show that the following set of assertions is
     inconsistent:

        {P → Q ∨ S;
         T → P;
         Q → S;
         T → ¬S;
         T ;   }

4.6 Consider the theory T in sub-section 4.2.1. Outline a syntactic
     proof showing that the proposition 'it is a good day for a walk'
     is a theorem of T.

4.7 Using natural deduction and the introduction and exploitation
     rules given in sub-section 4.2.2, prove that the formula [C ∨ A]
     is a theorem of a theory of propositional logic which has the
     proper axiom:

        [A → C] ∧ [B → C] ∧ [A ∨ B]

4.8   Re-write the sequent proof given in sub-section 4.2.3 so that the use of the structural modification rule of interchange is made explicit.

4.9   Use the tableau-proving method as described in sub-section 4.2.5 to prove that the formula [C ∨ A] is a theorem of the formula [A → C] ∧ [B → C] ∧ [A ∨ B].

4.10 What is the difference between a tableau proof and a semantic tableau proof?

4.11 Convert the following formulas to clausal form:

      (a) ¬P → ¬Q
      (b) P ∧ Q → S
      (c) P ∨ Q → S ∧ T
      (d) ¬[¬P ∧ ¬R] → [S ∨ ¬T]

4.12 Use the resolution theorem-proving method to show that the formula [C ∨ A] is a theorem of the formula [A → C] ∧ [B → C] ∧ [A ∨ B].

4.13 Use resolution to prove that the set of assertions given in exercise 4.5 is inconsistent.

4.14 Insert comments at appropriate places in the program 'clause' given in sub-section 4.2.11 to show that you understand how it works.

4.15 Trace the execution of the 'clause' program given in sub-section 4.2.11 for the following input:

      [[(johnwalks) ∧ (jillruns)] ∨ [(johnruns) ∧ (jillwalks)]];

      For your trace use the same notation that was used in the example trace in sub-section 4.2.11.

4.16 Describe an electric kettle as a relational structure. The kettle must consist of a spout, a body, an element, a handle, four feet and so on. These parts are either metal or plastic. Some parts are attached to other parts. Some parts are inside other parts.

      (Hint: the set E will be defined such that E = {spout, body, element, handle, foot#1, foot#2, ...}. The relations will include metal = {body, spout, ...}, plastic = {handle, foot#1, foot#2, ...}, attached = {<handle, body>, <spout, body>, <foot#1, body>, ...}).

4.17 Define a first order predicate language which can be used to state assertions about the electric kettle described in exercise 4.16. Write some assertions in your language. Include the assertion: 'all feet are plastic and are attached to the body.'

4.18 Determine whether or not the assertion 'all feet are plastic and are attached to the body', which is written in the language you defined in exercise 4.17, is true with respect to the kettle you described as a relational structure in exercise 4.16. Show the steps carried out and state the interpretation assumed.

4.19 What is the difference between an interpretation and a model?

4.20 Convert the following formula to clausal form showing the steps involved in the process:

$$\forall x[[man(x) \wedge lives(x)] \rightarrow \exists y[woman(y) \wedge loves(x, y)]]$$

4.21 Can the methods described in sub-sections 4.3.6 and 4.3.7, which are based on Herbrand's theorem, be used to demonstrate that the formula given in exercise 4.20 is satisfiable?

4.22 Why is the 'occurs' test needed in the unification procedure?

4.23 Give an example of a self-resolving clause.

4.24 Use the resolution theorem-proving method to prove that the formula likes(peter, paul) is a theorem of the following assertions:

$$\forall x \forall y[brother\ of(x, y) \rightarrow relativeof(x, y)]$$
$$\forall x[relative\ of(john, x) \rightarrow likes(peter, x)]$$
brother of(john, paul).

4.25 What is the difference between linear input resolution and selected literal resolution? Illustrate your answer with an example which is different from the example given in sub-sections 4.4.1 and 4.4.2.

4.26 Use the matrix connection method to demonstrate that the set of assertions given in exercise 4.5 is inconsistent.

4.27 At present, resolution based methods are the most commonly used methods in automatic theorem-proving systems. However, there is a growing interest in the use of the matrix connection method. What are the relative advantages and disadvantages of the two approaches?

EXERCISES FOR CHAPTER 5

5.1 In section 5.1, when discussing the theory and complete relational structure approach, we used the term 'isomorphic' to describe the relationship between the database and that slice of reality which it represents. We gave an informal definition of the term 'isomorphic'. Refer to the literature to obtain a better definition and determine whether or not it would be correct to say that a caricature of a person is isomorphic with a photograph of the same person in the same pose.

5.2 What are the advantages of using logic to formalise database concepts?

5.3 Give examples of how the domain closure, unique name, and closed world assumptions might be made in the design of an airline booking system. (For example, the closed world assumption will be made with respect to data concerning cities which are connected by flights: if there is no data indicating that there is a flight from London to Hull, then it will be assumed that no such flight exists.)

5.4 In sub-section 5.3.1 we stated that adding a new entity to the domain E of a relational structure would violate schema rules such as $\forall x[male(x) \lor female(x)]$ unless appropriate facts were also added. Describe, in English, an algorithm that could be used to identify those schema rules which might be violated in this way.

5.5 In sub-section 5.3.2 we gave examples of how relational algebraic operations can be used to evaluate queries when a database is formalised according to the theory and complete relational structure approach. Using the same techniques, show how relational algebraic operations can be used to evaluate the following queries:

$$Q1 = \{x \,|\, male(x) \land employee(x)\}$$
$$Q2 = \{x \,|\, \exists y\; likes(x,\, y)\}$$
$$Q3 = \{x,\, y \,|\, \exists y[likes(x,\, y) \land employee(y)]\}$$

5.6 Give two examples of applications in which it would be appropriate to use the theory and complete relational structure approach to the formalisation of database concepts and two examples of applications in which it would not be appropriate to use this approach. Explain the reasoning behind your choices.

5.7 In the theory only approach, 'facts' such as 'hasuncle(Pat, Jim)' and 'rules' such as '$\forall x \exists y[person(x) \rightarrow hasdad(x,\, y)]$' are all regarded as proper axioms of a theory T. They have the same status in this approach and are manipulated in the same way during query evaluation and integrity checking. However, in practice it may be appropriate to store 'facts' and 'rules' separately. Why might this be the case?

5.8 Convert the knowledge base KB1, which is given at the beginning of section 5.4, to clausal form.

5.9 Explain why deleting a proper axiom from a consistent first order predicate logic theory always results in a consistent theory.

5.10 State, in English, what the following proper axiom means when viewed as an integrity constraint in the theory only approach:

$$\forall x[[man(x) \land lives(x)] \rightarrow \exists y\; woman(y) \land loves(x,\, y)]]$$

(Hint: refer to sub-section 5.4.1.)

5.11 Using the theory only approach, determine the answer to the
      following closed query with respect to the knowledge base KB1
      given at the beginning of section 5.4:

    ∃x[(pat . likes . y) ∧ (pat . hasuncle . y)]

5.12 Using the theory only approach, derive the answer to the follow-
      ing open query with respect to the knowledge base KB1. Use the
      resolution based refutation technique described in sub-section
      5.4.2.

    {x|∃y[(x . hasdad . y) ∧ (x . likes . pat)]}

    i.e. all x such that x has a dad and x likes Pat.

5.13 Using the theory only approach, derive three answers to the
      following open query with respect to the knowledge base KB1.
      Use the resolution based refutation technique described in sub-
      section 5.4.2:

    {x|∀y[[(y . brotherof . david) → (x . likes . y)]
                                    ∧ (sue . likes . x)]}

    i.e. all x such that x likes all brothers of David and Sue likes
    x. (Hint: to obtain three answers, you will have to add domain
    closure and completion axioms to KB1.)

5.14 Using the theory only approach, derive the answer to the follow-
      ing open query with respect to the knowledge base KB1. Use the
      technique described in sub-section 5.4.3 in which (a) the query
      is first reduced to a completely open query, (b) the completely
      open query is answered using a resolution based method and (c)
      the answer to the original query is obtained by the appropriate
      application of the relational division and projection* operations.

    {x|∀y[[(y . brotherof . david) → (x . likes . y)]
                                    ∧ ∃z (z . likes . x)]}

    i.e. all x such that x likes all brothers of David and there is
    some entity which likes x.

5.15 Add a completion axiom and an inequality axiom schema to the
      knowledge base KB1 to represent the knowledge that David has no
      more brothers than those stated explicitly in KB1. That is, Jim
      and Bob are the only brothers of David. (Hint: an example of
      the use of completion axioms is given in sub-section 5.4.4.)

5.16 What are the advantages and disadvantages of using a 'failure to
      prove as negation' metarule compared with the use of completion
      and inequality axioms?

5.17 Determine the CWA answer to the following query with respect to
      KB1 by reducing the evaluation to the OWA evaluation of atomic
      queries followed by the application of relational algebraic
      operations as discussed in sub-section 5.4.6:

$$\{x | \forall y [[(y \, . \, brotherof \, . \, david) \rightarrow (x \, . \, likes \, . \, Y)] \\ \land \exists z \, (z \, . \, likes \, . \, x)]\}$$

5.18 Give two examples of applications in which it would be appropriate to use the theory only approach and two examples of applications in which it would be inappropriate to use this approach. Explain the reasoning behind your choices.

5.19 Describe, in your own words, the difference between the theory and complete relational structure approach and the theory and incomplete relational structure approach.

5.20 Derive a minimally expanded set of integrity constraints, expressed as formulas, which correspond to the following constraints expressed in English:

  (a) An entity may not be a full-time and a part-time student.

  (b) An entity may only set an exam if he is known to be a lecturer.

  (c) An entity may only be eligible to sit an exam if he is known to be a full-time student, a part-time student or a lecturer.

  (d) No entity is eligible to sit an exam which he has set.

  (e) If an entity is eligible to sit an exam, this implies that either he is not a lecturer or he did not set that exam.

5.21 What is the set of structure extension rules corresponding to the following axiom:

$$\forall x [[hungry(x) \land hasmoney(x)] \rightarrow buysfood(x)]$$

5.22 In sub-section 5.5.3 we described a method for evaluating formulas such as male(John) by reference (first of all) to the 'facts' in the incomplete structure IU and then (if the facts do not provide an answer) by reference to the definite rules in the expanded set of extension rules. Why is it that only the definite rules in the expanded set are used in this process?

5.23 Describe in English an algorithm which can be used to evaluate formulas when only an unexpanded set of extension rules is available. (See sub-section 5.5.4.)

5.24 What is the difference between 'completion rules' in the theory and incomplete relational structure approach and 'completion axioms' in the theory only approach?

5.25 Give two examples of applications in which it would be appropriate to use the theory and incomplete relational structure approach and two applications in which it would be inappropriate to use this approach. Explain the reasoning behind your choices.

EXERCISES FOR CHAPTER 6

6.1 Give examples illustrating limitations on what can be expressed in first order predicate logic.

6.2 Give reasons why theorem-proving in first order predicate logic might use up a great deal of computing resources even for relatively simple proofs.

6.3 Explain why theorem-proving in a many-sorted logic can be more efficient than in an expressively equivalent one-sorted logic.

6.4 What are the advantages of many-sorted logics which use sort lattices and sorting functions compared with many-sorted logics which are based on restricted quantification?

6.5 Explain, in your own words, the 'frame problem' of situational logic.

6.6 Explain, in your own words, the 'qualification problem' of situational logic.

6.7 Give three examples of the non-monotonic reasoning which humans employ in day-to-day living. The first example should be related to incomplete knowledge, the second to a changing world and the third to the use of temporary assumptions in problem solving. Give examples which are different from those given in sub-section 6.4.1.

6.8 Read Belnap's paper on a four-valued logic. Write notes (about 500 words) discussing the relationship of Belnap's approach to the 'theory and incomplete relational structure approach' described in chapter 5.

6.9 Refer to the literature and write short notes (about 500 words) describing applications of many-valued logics.

6.10 Read Zadeh's paper (referenced in section 6.6) and explain in your own words the meaning which is conveyed by the sentence 'usually snow is white', given the explanatory database presented in Zadeh's paper.

6.11 At the beginning of section 6.7 we gave an example of a 'situation' in which the proposition $A \rightarrow C$ may *not* be an intuitive consequence of the propositions $A \rightarrow B$ and $B \rightarrow C$. Explain why the problem illustrated by this example derives from inappropriately equating $A \rightarrow B$ with the usual meaning of the sentence 'if A then B'.

6.12 Give an example of modal statements involving the operators $\wedge$, $\vee$, $\rightarrow$ and $\neg$.

6.13 Give examples of statements illustrating the following types of modality:

- alethic modality
- temporal modality

- deontic modality
- epistemic modality

6.14 Explain Gödel's rule of necessitation in your own words.

6.15 Describe, in your own words, Kripke's contribution to the under-standing of modal logics.

6.16 For each of the following types of modal logic, give an example of an application in which its use would be appropriate:

- M
- S4
- Brouwersche logic
- S5

Explain your choice of examples.

6.17 Use the proof method described in sub-section 6.7.7 to prove that the formula '(John Smith is dead)' is a theorem of the following proper axioms in a modal logic in which the accessibility rela-tion is reflexive, transitive and symmetrical:

(John Smith is alive)
$\Diamond$(John Smith is dead)
$\Box$[(John Smith is dead) $\rightarrow$ (John Smith is dead)]
$\Box$[(John Smith is alive) $\rightarrow$ ¬(John Smith is dead)]

6.18 Use the techniques described in sub-section 6.7.7 to determine whether or not the following formula is valid:

$$\Diamond[P \rightarrow \Box[Q \rightarrow R]] \rightarrow \Box[Q \rightarrow [\Diamond P \rightarrow \Box R]]$$

6.19 Explain, in your own words, why the material presented in section 6.7 is important in the context of knowledge base systems work.

6.20 What advantages do temporal logics which are based on modal logic have compared with temporal logics such as Lundberg's which we briefly described in sub-section 6.8.1?

6.21 Search the literature to identify examples of applications of temporal logic.

6.22 Give two examples of applications in which it might be appro-priate to use an epistemic logic such as that described in section 6.9.

6.23 Give an example of a function of type $\langle e, \langle e, \langle e, t \rangle\rangle\rangle$.

6.24 Why is the language LTYPE, which we described in sub-section 6.10.2, more expressively powerful than languages of first order predicate logic?

6.25 Explain, in your own words, the advantages which the language Lλ, described in sub-section 6.10.4 has compared with the language LTYPE described in sub-section 6.10.2.

6.26 Translate the following sentences into formulas of Montague's intensional logic:

- Every man that lives loves a woman.
- John is interested in all relations which are symmetric.
- All future kings of England will know the names of all the previous kings of England.

6.27 Refer to the literature and write notes (about 500 words) on the use of intensional logic in natural language translation.

6.28 Explain, in your own words, the difference between extensional database constraints and intensional database constraints as discussed in sub-section 6.11.4. Give examples of each type of constraint.

6.29 Write short notes (about 500 words) discussing the relationship between the approach to integrity constraints adopted by Clifford and Warren in their paper on historical databases and the approach adopted in the theory and incomplete relational structure approach described in chapter 5.

EXERCISES FOR CHAPTER 7

7.1 In section 7.1 we mentioned five types of sources of uncertainty. Give an example of each type. (Use examples which are different from those given in the text.)

7.2 Suppose that we have a coin and two six-sided dice. What is the probability of the coin landing head up and one of the dice landing 5 up with the other not landing 3 up?

7.3 Suppose that we are given a hypothesis X and the following values for $p(E/X)$, $p(E/\neg X)$, $p(\neg E/X)$, $p(\neg E/\neg X)$ for four pieces of evidence $E = A, B, C, D$:

	$p(E/X)$	$p(E/\neg X)$	$p(\neg E/X)$	$p(\neg E/\neg X)$
E = A	1.0	0.0	0.0	1.0
E = B	1.0	0.5	0.0	0.5
E = C	0.5	0.2	0.5	0.8
E = D	0.3	1.0	0.7	0.0

Calculate the LS and LN values for X and each of A, B, C and D.

7.4 Using the values calculated in exercise 7.3, calculate the probability of X given that:

- The *a priori* probability of X = 0.2.
- Evidence A or B has been observed with certainty.
- ¬C is known with certainty.
- Nothing is known about D.

619

7.5 In the last part of section 7.2, we mentioned several disadvantages of probability theory. What are its advantages? Give an example of an application in which it would be more appropriate to use probability theory than any of the other calculi mentioned in chapter 7.

7.6 Use certainty theory to calculate the new certainty of X given that the initial certainty of X is 0.4, that the initial value of Y is 0.2, that A has been observed with certainty 1.0, that B has been observed with certainty 0.5, that D has been observed with certainty 0.3 and that the following rules are available:

    R1: if A then Y with certainty factor 0.7
    R2: if B then Y with certainty factor 0.8
    R3: if (D or Y) then X with certainty factor 0.6

7.7 Write short notes (about 500 words) explaining the relationship of possibility theory to fuzzy logic. (Note: we described fuzzy logic very briefly in chapter 6, but you should also refer to other literature.)

7.8 What are the advantages and disadvantages of incidence calculus compared with probability theory?

7.9 Use plausibility theory to obtain the plausible consequences of the following set of assertions:

P ∨ Q	0.75
¬Q	0.5
¬P	0.5
Q	0.2
S	0.8
¬S → R	0.8
¬S	0.4
S → P	0.4

7.10 For each calculus, other than probability theory, which is described in chapter 7 give an example of an application in which it would be more appropriate to use that calculus than any of the other calculi.

EXERCISES FOR CHAPTER 8

8.1 Trace the execution of the data-driven procedure 'generate' when trying to determine if N is divisible by 2, given the rules R1 to R4 in sub-section 8.2.1 and a database containing the facts 'N is divisible by 10' and 'N is divisible by 12'.

8.2 Trace the execution of the goal-driven procedure 'validate' when trying to determine if 'N is divisible by 2', given the rules R1 to R4 in sub-section 8.2.2 and a database containing the facts 'N is divisible by 10' and 'N is divisible by 12'.

8.3   Describe a procedure in pseudo-English which implements a data-driven breadth-first search strategy. (Hint: modify the procedure 'generate' given in sub-section 8.2.1.)

8.4   Describe a procedure in pseudo-English which implements a goal-driven breadth-first search strategy. (Hint: modify the procedure 'validate' given in sub-section 8.2.2.)

8.5   Explain, in your own words, the difference between 'domain-independent metarules' and 'domain-specific metarules' with reference to production rule based systems.

8.6   What is the difference between a production rule based system and an expert system?

8.7   Find out more about the MYCIN and PROSPECTOR expert systems. What are the differences between these two systems?

8.8   How does possibility theory differ from each of the following in the way it handles uncertainty:

- probability theory
- certainty theory
- the Dempster-Schafer theory of evidence

8.9   How does Quinlan's method differ from each of the following in the way it handles uncertainty:

- probability theory
- certainty theory
- the Dempster-Schafer theory of evidence
- possibility theory

8.10 The INFERNO relations 'inhibits', 'requires', and 'unless' can be defined in terms of the relations 'enables' and 'negates'. What are these definitions?

8.11 Derive INFERNO propagation constraints for the relations 'conjoins-independent' and 'disjoins'. Look up Quinlan's paper to see if your constraints are correct.

8.12 In sub-section 8.4.4 we gave a very brief description of how the expert system VM handles time-varying data. Search the literature and write notes describing the various ways in which other expert systems deal with time-varying data.

8.13 In sections 8.2 and 8.3 and sub-section 8.4.5 we described various techniques which can be used in expert systems as part of the problem-solving search strategy; for example, the data-driven technique, the top-down technique, use of abstraction, multiple lines of reasoning, etc. Some of these techniques can be used in conjunction with other techniques (e.g. goal-driven and depth-first may be used together), some are alternatives to other techniques (e.g. depth-first and breadth-first) and some are refinements of other techniques (e.g. use of abstraction is a refinement of the goal-driven approach). Categorise the various techniques which we have discussed, showing which can be used together, which are alternatives and which are refinements of other techniques.

8.14　Find out what the term 'ladder of abstraction' means and discuss how this concept can be used to advantage in expert systems work.

8.15　Refer to the relevant literature and describe the design of the opportunistic schedulars which are used in HEARSAY II and HEARSAY III.

8.16　How does an expert system shell differ from a deductive database management system?

8.17　In sub-section 8.4.8 we described three roles which an expert system can play with respect to the user. Explain how epistemic logic, as discussed in chapter 6, could be used in the design of expert systems which play the role of colleague to the user.

8.18　In sub-section 8.4.8 we mentioned three methods by which expert knowledge may be acquired by an expert system. The last of these, 'induction', is used in an expert system shell called EXPERTEASE, developed by Donald Michie at The University of Edinburgh, Scotland. EXPERTEASE applications have been very successful in the U.S. Find out what you can about EXPERTEASE and write notes describing it.

8.19　Write an essay discussing the relationship between problem-solving in expert systems and theorem-proving in formal logic.

EXERCISES FOR CHAPTER 9

9.1　Why is the term 'slot and filler structure' an appropriate generic name for semantic nets, frames, conceptual dependency structures and scripts?

9.2　Write an essay discussing the relationship between semantic nets and the binary relational approach to database management described in chapter 3.

9.3　Draw an extended semantic net corresponding to the following formulas:

> parent(phillip, susan)
> parent(henry, sally)
> parent(peter, sally)
> parent(sally, george)
> $\forall x \forall y \forall z [[parent(x, y) \land parent(y, z)] \rightarrow grandparent(x, z)]$

Using the proof technique exemplified in sub-section 9.2.2, show that the following is a theorem of these formulas:

> $\exists x \; grandparent(x, george)$

That is, prove that George is a grandparent.

9.4 Construct a frame which would be appropriate for storing data about students in a student record system. Try to incorporate examples of generic slots, default slots and conditional slots.

9.5 Frame based systems were primarily developed for use in pattern recognition modules of natural language understanding systems. What type of frames and frame structures might be used in such systems?

9.6 At the beginning of section 9.3 we described the use of procedural attachment in frame based systems. Procedural attachment has other uses in computing: give some examples.

9.7 Make up a mystery problem, such as the murder mystery given in sub-section 9.3.2, in which default reasoning hinders the solution to the problem.

9.8 What is the relationship between a frame structure and a sort lattice as described in chapter 6?

9.9 The knowledge which is stored in a set of frames and in a frame system could be represented as a set of production rules. Give an example of this. What are the disadvantages of using production rules?

9.10 Refer to the literature concerning reasoning by analogy and write notes on this topic.

9.11 What type of knowledge can be handled by frame systems but not by formal logic?

9.12 Show how fuzzy logic can be used to accommodate the inexact matching which is possible in a frame system.

9.13 Use conceptual dependency theory to depict the situation in which Richard thought of eating his dinner while he was making up exercises in the pub.

9.14 Construct a script for the sequence of events involved in registering for and graduating from a degree in computing science. Do not include a great deal of detail. Use pointers to associated scripts.

9.15 Search the literature to identify work that has been done on providing formal semantics for the various slot and filler approaches.

EXERCISES FOR CHAPTER 10

10.1 In a university, the function which maps students to student numbers is a one-to-one, total, single-valued function since every student has exactly one unique student number. Give examples of the following types of function which may be found in a university organisation:

- A total multi-valued function.
- A partial function.
- A multi-argument function.
- A bijection.

10.2 Consider the tuple <machine#1, part#6, 4> which represents the fact that 4 of part#6 are used in the construction of machine#1. This is an example of a tuple which is a member of a 3-ary (tertiary) relation. Describe the characteristic function corresponding to this relation using the example tuple above and others as illustration.

10.3 Give examples of functions which are constructed using the following strategies:

- composition
- generalised composition
- definition by expression
- definition by cases
- primitive recursion
- recursion
- inversion
- restriction

Your examples should be different from those presented in the text.

10.4 (a) Use lambda abstraction to express the fact that the 'married' relation is symmetric.

(b) When might it be necessary to re-name variables in a lambda expression?

(c) Describe the Church-Rosser theorem in your own words. (Refer to other literature to obtain a more precise definition than that given in the text.)

10.5 What are the advantages of using curried functions instead of multi-argument functions?

10.6 Show how the 'multiplication' function may be constructed in Hilbert's system.

10.7 What was the 'obviously computable' function which Ackerman identified and which required Kleene to introduce an additional construction strategy to Hilbert's system? (You will need to refer to other literature.)

10.8 The function 'reverse' takes a list and returns a copy of the list with the elements in reverse order. Show how the function 'reverse' may be constructed in McCarthy's calculus for S-expressions (that is, from the set of functions FS-exp using the construction strategies CMc).

10.9 Write notes comparing the functional view of the universe with the binary relational view described in chapter 3.

10.10 In FQL, constants are treated as constant functions and sequences (sets) are treated as constant generating functions. What are the advantages of this approach?

10.11 Consider a student database consisting of a student file and a class file. The records in these files have the following formats:

Student file records:
- student name
- student number
- department name
- a repeating group of <class attended, mark obtained> pairs
- a boolean 'flag' indicating whether the student is an honours student or not

Class file records:
- class name
- lecturer name
- a repeating group of <student name, mark obtained> pairs

The retrieval facilities provided by the database system allow student records to be retrieved by student name and by department name. The class records may be retrieved by class name and by lecturer name. Describe the database system as a set of base functions in the language FQL. State clearly any assumptions which you make.

10.12 Using the base functions which you defined in exercise 10.11 and the construction strategies which are available in FQL, define the following functions:

(a) A function which returns the average mark for a given student.

(b) A function which returns a list of the classes taught by a given lecturer.

(c) A function which returns the average mark for all students taught by a given lecturer.

(d) A function which returns a list of honours students taught by a given lecturer.

Hint: you should define some intermediate functions, such as 'average', which may be used in your definitions of the functions above.

10.13 Write notes discussing how relational algebraic operators such as selection, projection, join, etc. might be defined as FQL functions.

10.14 Write notes discussing the advantages and disadvantages of FQL compared with relational calculus query languages such as QUEL or SEQUEL.

10.15 Name overloading is possible in DAPLEX. Discuss the advantages and disadvantages of this facility, giving examples to illustrate your answer.

10.16 Refer to the literature and explain why DAPLEX is not a strictly functional language.

10.17 In 1978 a paper was published describing a functional language called FP. This paper was written by Backus. Use the citation index in your library to identify this paper, and obtain a copy.

10.18 Write introductory notes (about 500 words) describing the language FP.

10.19 Write a short essay (about 500 words) discussing the notion of inference in a knowledge base system based on the functional view.

10.20 Write a short essay (about 500 words) discussing the notion of semantic integrity constraints in a knowledge base system based on the functional view.

EXERCISES FOR CHAPTER 11

11.1 Explain, in your own words, the relationship between the syntax and the semantics of a programming language.

11.2 What is the difference between a context-free grammar and a context-sensitive grammar?

11.3 Construct a derivation tree showing that the string 'a + b - [c + d]' is a well-formed sentence of the grammar G4 given in sub-section 11.2.1.

11.4 Show that the following grammar is ambiguous by identifying a sentence of it which has two syntax trees:

```
E   ::=   P + E
    |     P - E
    |     I

P   ::=   E
    |     [E]
    |     I

I   ::=   a
    |     b
    |     c
```

11.5 Why is it necessary, in general, to remove ambiguity from a grammar?

11.6   Use a top-down approach to construct the parse tree for the sentence 'hhilili;' in the grammar G6 given in sub-section 11.2.2.

11.7   Determine the director sets of the non-terminals of the grammar G11 given in section 11.3. Show that G11 is not 1-lookahead.

11.8   Refer to the literature to identify a more powerful factorisation rule than that given in sub-section 11.2.2. Use the more powerful rule to convert the grammar G9 given in sub-section 11.2.2 to a 1-lookahead grammar.

11.9   Use the method described in sub-section 11.2.2 to remove the left recursion from the grammar G12 given in sub-section 11.5.2. (Note: ignore the semantic equations for the purpose of this exercise.)

11.10   Convert the grammar G10 to an equivalent EBNF grammar, then transcribe the EBNF productions to a recogniser program using the transcription rules given in section 11.3. You may assume the existence of a 'fetch-terminal' procedure.

11.11   Use the methods described in chapter 11 to construct a recogniser for the PROPLANG grammar given in chapter 2.

11.12   What are the advantages and disadvantages of the method for constructing recognisers which is given in chapter 11 compared with the method given in chapter 2?

11.13   Define the following terms in your own words:

   • contextual constraints
   • scope rules
   • mode rules

   Explain what a 'closure' is and describe the difference between static and dynamic binding with respect to procedures.

11.14   Refer to the literature and write short notes (about 500 words) on operational and axiomatic semantics.

11.15   Write suitable semantic equations for the following productions:

   (a) declarations ::= singledeclaration
                        | declarations ";" singledeclaration

   (b) block ::= "declare" declarations "begin" statements
                                                         "end"

   The strings enclosed in quotes are terminals. You should assume that the terms 'block', 'declarations', 'statement', etc. have their usual meaning.

11.16   Use the semantic equations given in sub-sections 11.5.2 and 11.5.3 to trace the following program segment which is a well-formed sentence of the grammar G12:

```
declare
     a : integer;
     b : integer;
     c = 2;
     d = 3;
     proc P;
          begin
               declare
                    c = 5;
                    proc Q:
                         declare
                              d = 4;
                              begin
                                   a := d
                              end;
                    begin
                         call Q;
                         b := a + c
                    end
     end
end
```

11.17 In sub-section 11.6.2 we showed how to design a program to evaluate well-formed sentences of the grammar G13. At the end of that sub-section we gave an indication of how this program could be simplified by using a variable to store the operator and by amalgamating the stack manipulation code. Use this approach to design a new and simpler program to evaluate expressions of the grammar G13.

11.18 Write short notes (about 500 words) on the application of parsing and translation techniques in knowledge base systems work.

11.19 In section 11.8 we introduced various terms which are often used to categorise programming languages. Use these terms to describe your favourite programming language and the language you least like.

11.20 Define a LISP function which takes two integers as arguments and returns the highest common factor of these two arguments.

11.21 Define a LISP function which takes a list of numbers and returns the list sorted into ascending order.

11.22 LISP may be used as a knowledge base system rather than as a language for implementing knowledge base systems: the functions 'putprop' and 'get' may be used to store and retrieve simple facts and function definitions may be regarded as more complex rules. Which of the three approaches given in chapter 5 would be the most appropriate for formalising the use of LISP as a knowledge base system in this way? Explain your answer.

11.23 Write Prolog statements corresponding as closely as possible to the knowledge base KB1 given at the beginning of section 5.4 in chapter 5. Enter the statements and run Prolog to determine which of the queries Q1 to Q4, given in sub-section 5.4.2, may be expressed as goals in Prolog and which may not.

11.24 Write a parser, in Prolog, for a variant of the PROPLANG language given in chapter 2. For simplicity, you may assume that
atomic propositions are represented by the letters P, Q, R, S
and T, that all expressions which are typed in are 'space-free'
and that round brackets are used instead of square brackets.
The following is an example of a well-formed formula in this
language:

$$((P \lor Q) \Rightarrow -(S \lor T)):$$

(You may use > instead of $\Rightarrow$.)

11.25 Prolog may be used as a knowledge base system rather than as a
language for implementing knowledge base systems. Its use in
this way may be formalised using the 'theory only approach'
described in chapter 5. Using the terminology of such a formalisation, explain why Prolog when used in this way cannot accommodate the notions of semantic integrity or semantic integrity
constraint.

11.26 Prolog uses a depth-first SL resolution theorem-proving technique. This is not a complete proof procedure for full first
order predicate logic but is a sufficient method for proving
goals in Prolog. Why is this?

11.27 There is a language called ABSET which was developed by Ted
Elcock when he was at The University of Aberdeen. ABSET has
much in common with Prolog but was developed many years earlier.
Search the literature to find out as much as you can about
ABSET and write notes (about 500 words) comparing ABSET with
Prolog.

11.28 What advantages derive from treating procedures as first-class
objects in a programming language?

11.29 Write notes (about 500 words) explaining how the features of
PS-algol facilitate the construction of complex dynamically
evolving systems and hence facilitate the construction of
sophisticated knowledge base systems.

11.30 List those tasks in a sophisticated knowledge base system that
may be regarded as language translation tasks.

EXERCISES FOR CHAPTER 12

12.1 In section 12.1 we mentioned three limitations of conventional
computer architecture. Explain these limitations in your own
words using examples to illustrate your answer.

12.2 Refer to relevant literature and write short notes (about 500
words) on the relationship between functional languages and
dataflow machines.

12.3   In section 12.3 we mentioned a machine called DADO which was specifically designed to improve the performance of large production rule based systems. Read Stolfo and Shaw's paper describing DADO and explain, in your own words, how the machine works.

12.4   In section 12.5 we described several LISP workstations. Search the literature to see if any Prolog workstations have been developed.

12.5   What is the difference between a text retrieval machine and an associative store machine?

12.6   Read the literature and compare the connection machine with the FACT machine.

12.7   Write short notes (about 500 words) listing the advantages and disadvantages of attempting to develop computers whose design is based on the physiology of the human brain.

EXERCISES FOR CHAPTER 13

13.1   Search the literature and make a list of knowledge base systems which are available but which are not referred to in chapter 13.

13.2   Determine whether or not your own library subscribes to any sources of data on new knowledge base systems products such as those mentioned in section 13.3.

EXERCISES FOR CHAPTER 14

14.1   In section 14.2 we voiced the opinion that argument over which approaches to knowledge processing are 'better than others' contributes little to the development of the subject. However, we did not say that it contributes nothing. Write short notes (about 200 words) discussing how controversy over approaches to knowledge processing might improve our understanding of the subject.

14.2   Suggest some additions to the list of useful semantic concepts given in section 14.3. Give reasons for your suggestions.

14.3   Read Goguen and Meseguer's paper which is referenced in section 14.5. Write short notes (about 500 words) which would serve as an introduction to this paper.

14.4   Explain why research such as that described in Goguen and Meseguer's paper is important to the development of knowledge base systems technology.

Appendix 2
Research Topics

This appendix lists several research topics each of which could be used as the basis for work leading to a Master's degree or for the first year of a Ph.D. programme.

The list is not meant to be comprehensive. It reflects the author's interests and his opinions on which topics are important.

- Identify the various classes of integrity constraint which are required in different types of database application.

- Investigate the use of the language FQL as a means of converting databases structured according to one view of the universe to databases based on other views.

- Investigate the use of non-clausal resolution in deductive database systems.

- Investigate the use of non-resolution based theorem-proving methods in deductive database systems.

- Formalise the meanings of the domain closure, closed world and unique name assumptions as used in knowledge base systems work.

- Investigate the relationship between inference rules and semantic integrity constraints in knowledge base systems.

- Survey the use of non-classical logics in knowledge base systems work.

- Investigate the use of Cohn's many-sorted logic in knowledge base systems work.

- Survey algorithms for the manipulation of inference rules expressed as formulas of sorted logic.

- Investigate methods for theorem-proving in non-monotonic logic.

- Investigate the use of Belnap's four-valued logic in knowledge base systems work.

- Survey the use of fuzzy logic in knowledge base systems work.

- Investigate the use of modal logic in the maintenance of semantic integrity of knowledge bases.

- Analyse methods of automated theorem-proving in modal logic.

- Investigate the application of Manna's temporal logic to knowledge base systems.

- Survey the use of epistemic logics in knowledge base systems work.

- Analyse the relative merits of using a type-theoretic language as a basis for knowledge base systems work compared with a first order predicate language.

- Investigate methods of semantic integrity maintenance which are based on Montague's intensional logic.

- Survey methods for resolving inconsistencies in knowledge bases which include certainty values.

- Analyse the calculus for reasoning with uncertainty which was developed by Quinlan for use in the INFERNO system.

- Survey different approaches to providing explanation facilities in expert systems.

- Investigate the use of graphics in explanation facilities for expert systems.

- Use formal logic to formalise the notions which underly frame-based systems.

- Investigate the use of combinatory logic in knowledge base systems work.

- Investigate the relationship between Prolog-like languages and functional languages. Goguen's work on EQLOG is an example of such synthesis.

- Determine the need for persistent data structures in large-scale knowledge base systems.

- Identify a commonly used set of semantic concepts which can be used to compare and contrast different knowledge representation formalisms.

References

Abrial, J. R. (1974) 'Data semantics'. In Klimbie, J. W. K. and Koffeman, K. L. *Data Management Systems*. Amsterdam : North Holland.

Addis, T. R.(1982)'A relation based language interpreter for CAFS'. *ACM TODS* **7** (2), 125-163.

Aho, A. V. and Ullman, J. D. (1979) *Principles of Compiler Design*. Reading, Massachusetts : Addison-Wesley.

Aikins, J. (1980) 'Representation of control knowledge in expert systems'. *Proceedings of the First AAAI Conference*, Stanford University, California.

Alvey (March 1984) *Expert Systems Workshop Report*. London : Queen Mary College, London University.

Alvey (early May 1984) *IKBS Special Interest Group : Reasoning under Uncertainty, Workshop Report*. London : Queen Mary College.

Alvey (late May 1984) *Proceedings of the Workshop on Architectures for Large Knowledge Bases*. Manchester : Department of Computer Science, Manchester University.

Alvey (September 1984) *Inference Workshop Report*. London : Imperial College.

Andrews, P. B. (1981) 'Theorem proving via general matings'. *JACM* **28** (2), 193 - 214.

ANSI/X3/SPARC (1977) 'Study group final report'. *Bulletin of the ACM SIGMOD* **7** (2).

Aqvist, L. (1974) 'A new approach to the logical theory of actions and causality'. In Stenlund, S. *Logical Theory and Semantic Analysis*. Holland : D. Reidel Publishing Co.

Ash, W. L. and Sibley, E. H. (1968) 'TRAMP : an interpretive associative processor with deductive capabilities'. *Proceedings of the ACM 23rd National Conference*. Princeton, New Jersey : Brandon/Systems Press.

Asher, J. (1982) *The Design and Implementation of a Conceptual Schema Definition Language : Final Year Project Report*. Glasgow : Department of Computer Science, Strathclyde University.

Astrahan, M. M. and Chamberlin, D. D. (1975) 'Implementation of a structured English query language'. *CACM* **18 (10)**, 580 - 588.

Atkinson, M. P. , Bailey, P. J. , Chisholm, K. J. , Cockshott, W. P. and Morrison, R. (1984) *Procedures as Persistent Data Objects : Computing Science Report CSC/84/R3.* Glasgow : Department of Computing Science, Glasgow University.

Azmoodeh, M. (1984) 'Automatic maintenance of integrity rules in a binary relational database'. In Alvey *Proceedings of the Workshop on Architectures for Large Knowledge Bases.* Manchester : Department of Computer Science, Manchester University.

Babb, E. (1983) 'The logic language PROLOG-M in database technology and intelligent knowledge based systems'. *ICL Technical Journal* **3 (4)**, 373 - 392.

Backhouse, R. C. (1979) *Syntax of Programming Languages, Theory and Practice.* London : Prentice-Hall.

Balzer, R. , Erman, L. , London, P. and Williams, C. (1980) 'Hearsay - III : a domain independent framework for expert systems'. *Proceedings of the First AAAI.* Stanford University, California.

Banerjee, J. , Hsiao, D. K. and Kannan, K. (1979) 'DBC : a database computer for very large databases'. *IEEE Transactions on Computers C-28* **6**, 414 - 429.

Barcan, R. C. (1946) 'A functional calculus of first order logic based on strict implication'. *Journal of Symbolic Logic* **11**, 1 - 16.

Batcher, K. E. (1977) 'STARAN Series E'. *Proceedings of the 1977 International Conference on Parallel Processing.*

Batory, D. S. (1979) 'On searching transposed files'. *ACM TODS* **4 (4)**, 531 - 544.

Bayer, R. and McCreight, E. (1972) 'Organisation and maintenance of large ordered indexes'. *Acta Informatica* **1 (3)**, 173 - 189.

Bays, C. (1973) 'Reallocation of hash coded tables'. *CACM* **16 (1)**.

BCS (1976) *Interim Report of the Data Dictionary Systems Working Party.* London : British Computer Society.

BCS (1978) *Proceedings of the BCS Conference on Data Analysis for Information Systems Design.* London : British Computer Society.

Belnap, N. D. (1977) 'A useful four-valued logic'. In Dunn, J. M. and Epstein, G. *Modern Uses of Multiple Valued Logic.* Holland : D. Reidel Publishing Co.

Ben-Ari, Manna, Z. and Pneuli, A. (1981) 'The temporal logic of branching time'. *The Eighth Annual ACM Symposium on Principles of Programming Languages.* Williamsburg, Vancouver.

Bennet, J. S. and Hollander, C. R. (1981) 'DART : an expert system for computer fault diagnosis'. *Proceedings of the the Seventh IJCA.* Vancouver, Canada.

Beth, E. W. (1955) 'Semantic entailment and formal derivability'. Reprinted in Hintikka, J. (1969) *Philosophy of Mathematics.* Oxford : Oxford University Press.

Bibel, W. (1976) 'A syntactic connection between proof procedures and refutation procedures'. *Second Conference on Automated Deduction*. Oberwolfach, West Germany.

Bibel, W. (1982) 'A comparative study of several proof procedures'. *Artificial Intelligence* **18**, 269 - 293.

Bibel, W. (1983) 'Matings in matrices'. *CACM* **26 (11)**, 844 - 852.

Biller, H. and Neuhold, E. J. (1978) 'Semantics of data bases : the semantics of data models'. *Information Systems* **3 (1)**, 11 - 30.

Bledsoe, W. W. (1971) 'Splitting and reduction heuristics in automatic theorem proving'. *Artificial Intelligence* **2,** 55 - 77.

Bledsoe, W. W. (1977) 'Non-resolution theorem proving'. *Artificial Intelligence* **9 (1)**, 1 - 35.

Bobrow, D. G. and Winograd, T. (1977) 'An overview of KRL, a knowledge representation language'. *Cognitive Science* **1 (1)**, 3 - 46.

Bobrow, D. G. and Winograd, T. (1979) 'KRL : another perspective'. *Cognitive Science* **3 (1)**.

Boral, H. and Dewitt, D. J. (1982) 'Applying dataflow techniques to data base machines'. *Computer* **15 (8)**, 57 - 63.

Borgida, A. and Wong, H. K. T. (1981) 'Data models and data manipulation languages : complementary semantics and proof theory'. In *Proceedings of the Seventh International Conference on Very Large Data Bases*. Cannes, France. New York : IEEE.

Bossu, G. and Siegel, P. (1985) 'Saturation, non-monotonic reasoning and the closed world assumption'. *Artificial Intelligence* **(25)**, 13 - 63.

Boyce, R. F. , Chamberlin, D. D. , King, W. F. , and Hammer, M. M. (1975) 'Specifying queries as relational expressions : the SQUARE data sublanguage'. *CACM* **18 (11)**, 621 - 628.

Boyer, R. S. and Moore, J. S. (1972) 'The sharing of structure in theorem proving programs.' In Melzer, B. and Michie, D. *Machine Intelligence 7*. New York : Edinburgh University Press.

Boyer, R. S. and Moore, J. S. (1979) *A Computational Logic*. New York : Academic Press.

Bracchi, G. , Paolini, P. and Pelagatti, E. (1976) 'Binary logical associations in data modelling'. In Nijssen, G. M. *Modelling in Data Base Management Systems*. Amsterdam : North Holland.

Bradley, R. and Swartz, N. (1979) *Possible Worlds : An Introduction to Logic and its Philosophy*. Oxford : Basil Blackwell.

Brady, J. M. (1977) *The Theory of Computer Science : A Programming Approach*. London : Chapman and Hall.

Bray, O. H. and Freeman, H. A. (1979) *Data Base Computers*. Toronto : Lexington Books.

Bridge, J. (1977) *Beginning Model Theory*. Oxford : Clarendon Press.

Brodie, M. L. (1980) 'The application of data types to database semantic integrity'. *Information Systems* **5**, 287 - 296.

Buchanan, B. G. , Sutherland, G. and Geirgenbaum, E. (1969) 'Heuristic DENDRAL : a program for generating explanatory hypotheses in organic chemistry'. In Meltzer, B. and Michie, D. *Machine Intelligence 5*. New York : Elsevier.

Buchanan, B. G. and Feigenbaum, E. A. (1978) 'DENDRAL and META-DENDRAL'. *Artificial Intelligence* 11 (1), 5 - 24.

Bundy, A. (1983) *The Computer Modelling of Mathematical Reasoning*. London : Academic Press.

Bundy, A. (1984) 'Incidence calculus : a mechanism for probabilistic reasoning'. *Research Paper No. 216*. Edinburgh : Department of Artificial Intelligence, Edinburgh University.

Buneman, O. P. , and Frankel, R. E. (1979) 'FQL : a functional query language'. In *Proceedings of the ACM SIGMOD International Conference on the Management of Data*. Boston, Massachusetts. New York : ACM.

Buneman, O. P. , Frankel, R. E. and Nikhil, R. (1982) 'An implementation technique for database query languages'. *ACM TODS* 7 (2), 164 - 186.

Byres, R. A. (1984) *dBASE II For the First Time User*. Rockville, Maryland : Computer Science Press.

Canning, R. G. (1981) 'A computational model of analogical problem solving'. In *Proceedings of the Seventh IJCA*. Vancouver, Canada.

Carbonell, J. G. (1982) 'Experimental learning in analogical problem solving'. In *Proceedings of the AAAI 82*. University of Pittsburgh, Pennsylvania.

Cardenas, A. F. (1979) *Data Base Management Systems*. London : Allyn and Bacon.

Carnap, R. (1946) 'Modalities and quantification'. *Journal of Symbolic Logic* 11, 33 - 64.

Cavali, A. R. and Farinas del Cerro, L. (1984) 'A decision method for linear temporal logic'. In *Lecture Notes in Computer Science 170*, 113 - 127.

CCA (1982) *ADAPLEX Reference Manual*. CCA, 575 Technology Square, Cambridge, Massachusetts 02139, USA.

Chamberlin, D. D. (1976) 'Relational data base management : a survey'. *Computing Surveys* 8 (1).

Chamberlin,D.D. , Astrahan, M. M. , Eswaran, K. P. , Griffiths, P. P. , Lorie,R. A. , Mehl, J. W. , Reisner, P. and Wade, B. W. (1976) 'SEQUEL 2 : a unified approach to data definition, manipulation and control'. *IBM Journal of Research and Development* 20, 560 - 575.

Chamberlin,D.D. , Astrahan, M. M. , Blasgen, M. W. , Gray, J. N. , King,W. F. , Lindsay, B. G. , Lorie, R. , Mehl, J. W. , Price, T. G. , Putzolu, F. , Selinger, P. G. , Schkolnick, M. , Slutz, D. R. , Traiger, I. L. , Wade, B. W. and Yost, R. A. (1981) 'A history and evaluation of System R'. *CACM* 24 (10), 632 - 646.

Chandrasekaran, B. et al (1979) 'An approach to medical diagnosis based on conceptual structures'. In *Proceedings of the Sixth IJCA*. Tokyo.

Chang, C. and Lee, R. C.(1973) *Symbolic Logic and Mechanical Theorem Proving*. New York : Academic Press.

Chang, C. L. (1976) 'DEDUCE : a deductive query language for relational data bases'. In Chen, C. H. *Pattern Recognition and Artificial Intelligence*. New York : Academic Press.

Chang, C. L. (1978) 'DEDUCE II - further investigations of deduction in relational data bases. *IBM Research Report RJ2147*. San Jose, California.

Charniak, E. , Riesbeck, C. K. and McDermott, D. V. (1980) *Artificial Intelligence Programming*. Hillsdale, New York : Laurance Erlbaum Associates.

Charniak, E. and McDermott, D. V. (1985) *Introduction to Artificial Intelligence*. Reading, Massachusetts : Addison-Wesley.

Chellas, B. F. (1980) *Modal Logic : An Introduction*. Cambridge : Cambridge University Press.

Chen, P. P. (1976) 'The entity-relationship model : towards a unified view of data'. *ACM TODS* **1**, 9 - 36

Chomsky, N. (1965) *Aspects of the Theory of Syntax*. Cambridge, Massachusetts : Massachusetts Institute of Technology Press.

Church, A. L.(1940)'A formulation of the simple theory of types'. *Symbolic Logic* **5** (1), 56-68.

Church, A. L. (1941) *The Calculi of Lambda-Conversion*. Princeton, New Jersey : Princeton University Press.

Clancey, W. J. (1983) 'The epistomology of a rule-based expert system : a framework for explanation'. *Artificial Intelligence* **20** (3), 215 - 252.

Clark, K. L. (1978) 'Negation as failure'. In Gallaire, H. and Minker, J. *Logic and Databases*.

Claybrook, B. G. and Yang, C. S. (1978) 'Efficient algorithms for answering queries using unsorted multilists'. *Information Systems* **3**, 93 - 97.

Clifford, J. and Warren, D. S. (1983) 'Formal semantics for time in databases'. *ACM TODS* **8** (2), 214 - 254.

Clocksin, W. F. and Mellish, C. S. (1981) *Programming in Prolog*. Berlin and New York : Springer Verlag.

Cockshott, W. P. (1985) 'The persistent store machine'. *Persistent Programming Research Project Report 18*. Glasgow : Department of Computing Science, The University of Glasgow.

Codd, E. F. (1970) 'A relational model of data for large shared data banks'. *CACM* **13** (6), 377-387.

Codd, E. F. (1971) 'A data base sublanguage founded on the relational calculus'. In Codd, E. F. and Dean *Proceedings of the ACM SIGFIDET Workshop on Data Description, Access and Control*. San Diego : ACM.

Codd, E. F. (1972) 'Further normalisation of the data base relational model'. In Rustin, R. *Courant Computer Science Symposia 6 : Data Base Systems*. Englewood Cliffs, New Jersey : Prentice-Hall.

Codd, E. F. (1974) 'Seven steps to RENDEZVOUS with the casual user'. In Nijssen, G. M. *Proceedings of the IFIP TC-2 Working Conference on Data Base Management Systems.* Amsterdam : North Holland.

Cohn, A. G. (1983) 'Mechanising a particularly expressive many sorted logic. (Ph.D. Thesis). Colchester : Essex University.

Cohn, A. G. (1984) 'A note concerning the axiomatisation of Schubert's steamroller in many sorted logic'. In Alvey *Inference Workshop Report.* London : Imperial College.

Conway, R. W. , Maxwell, W. L. and Morgan, H. L. (1972) 'On the implementation of security measures in information systems'. *CACM* 15 (4).

Coombs, M. J. and Stell, J. (1985) *Personal Communication.* Glasgow : Department of Computer Science, University of Strathclyde.

Cougar, J.D., Colter, M.A. and Knapp, R.W.(1982) *Advanced System Development/Feasibility Techniques.* New York : John Wiley and Sons.

Cowie, J. (1983) 'Building databases from NL input'. In *Proceedings of the Conference on Applied Natural Language Analysis.* Santa Monica, California.

Crick, M. F. and Symonds (1970) 'A software associative memory for complex data structures'. *IBM Technical Report G320-2060.*

Cullinane Corporation (1980) *IQS Summary Description.*

Cullingford, R. (1981) 'SAM'. In Schank, R. C. and Riesbeck, C. K. *Inside Computer Understanding.* Hillsdale, New Jersey : Erlbaum.

Date, C. J. (1977) *An Introduction to Database Systems.* 2nd. edn. Reading, Massachusetts : Addison-Wesley.

Date, C. J. (1981) *An Introduction to Database Systems.* 3rd. edn. Reading, Massachusetts : Addison-Wesley.

Davis, R. (1976) 'Applications of meta-level knowledge to the construction, maintenance, and use of large knowledge bases'. *AIM - 283.* Stanford University AI Laboratory, California.

Davis, R. , Buchanan, B. G. and Shortliffe, E. H. (1977) 'Production rules as a representation of a knowledge base consultation program'. *Artificial Intelligence* 8, 15 - 45.

Davis, R. and King, J. (1977) 'An overview of production systems'. In Elcock, E. W. and Michie, D. *Machine Intelligence 8.* New York : Wiley and Sons.

DBTG (1971) *The Data Base Task Group of the CODASYL Programming Language Committee Report.* Available from the ACM, BCS and IAG.

Dowty, D. R. , Wall, R. E. and Peters, S. (1981) *Introduction to Montague Semantics.* Dordrecht, Holland : D. Reidel Publishing Co.

Doyle, J. (1982) 'A truth maintenance system'. *Artificial Intelligence* 12, 231 - 272.

Deen, S. M. (1977) *Fundamentals of Data Base Systems.* London : Macmillan.

Deliyanni, A. and Kowalski, R. A. (1979) 'Logic and semantic networks'. *CACM* 22 (3), 184 - 192.

Denning, D. E. and Denning, P. J. (1979) 'Data security'. *ACM Computing Surveys* **11** (3), 227 - 249.

Duda, R. , Gashnig, J. and Hart, P. (1979) 'Model design in the Prospector consultant system for mineral exploration'. In Michie, D. *Expert Systems in the Micro-Electronic Age.* New York : Edinburgh University Press.

Duda, R. O. , Hart, P. E. , Konolige, K. and Reboh, R. (1979) 'A computer based consultant for mineral exploration'. *Technical Report.* SRI International.

EDP (1982) 'Query systems for end users'. *EDP Analyser* **20** (9).

Elcock, E. W. , Foster, J. M. , Gray, P. M. D. , McGregor, J. J. and Murray, A. M. (1971) 'ABSET, a programming language based on sets : motivation and examples'. In Melzer, B. and Michie, D. *Machine Intelligence 6.* New York : Edinburgh University Press.

Enderton, H. B. (1972) *A Mathematical Introduction to Logic.* New York : Academic Press.

Engleman, C. Scarl, E. A. and Berg, C. H. (1982) 'Interactive frame instantiation'. *AAAI 82 Conference.* University of Pittsburgh, Pennsylvania.

Erman, L. D. , Hayes-Roth, F. , Lesser, V. R. and Reddy, P. R. (1980) 'The HEARSAY-II speech understanding system : integrating knowledge to resolve uncertainty'. *ACM Computing Surveys* **12** (2), 213 - 253.

Eswaran, K. P. and Chamberlin, D. D. (1975) 'Functional specification of a subsystem for data base integrity'. In *Proceedings of the International Conference on Very Large Data Bases.* Framington, Massachusetts.

Fagan, L. M. , Kunz, J. C. , Feigenbaum, E. A. and Osborn, J. J. (1979) 'Representation of dynamic clinical knowledge : measurement interpretation in the intensive care unit'. In *Proceedings of the Sixth IJCA.* Tokyo.

Farinas del Cerro (1982) 'A simple deduction method for modal logic'. *Information Processing Letters* **14** (2), 49 - 51.

Feldman, J. A. (1965) 'Aspects of associative processing'. *Technical note 1965 - 13.* Massachusetts Institute of Technology, Lincoln Laboratory, Lexington, Massachusetts.

Feldman, J. A. and Rovner, P. D. (1969) 'An Algol based associative language'. *CACM* **12** (8), 439 - 449.

Fernandez, E. B. , Summers, R. C. and Coleman, C. D. (1974) 'An authorization model for shared data bases'. *Proceedings of the 1975 ACM SIGMOD International Conference on the Management of Data.*

Feys, R. (1937) 'Les logiques nouvelles de modalites'. *Revue Neoscolastique de Philosophie* **40**, 517 - 533 and 214 - 252.

Fikes, R. E. and Hendrix, G. G. (1977) 'A network based knowledge representation and its natural deduction system'. *Proceedings of the Fifth IJCA.* Massachusetts Institute of Technology, Cambridge, Massachusetts.

Fine, T. (1973) *Theories of Probability.* New York : Academic Press.

Fitch, F. B. (1952) *Symbolic Logic : An Introduction.* New York : Ronald.

Florentin, J. J. (1974) 'Consistency auditing of databases'. *The Computer Journal* **17**, 52 - 58.

Forgy, C. and McDermott, J. (1979) 'OPS, a domain independent production system language'. *Proceedings of the Sixth IJCA.* Tokyo.

Fox, J. (1984) 'Formal and knowledge-based methods in decision technology'. In Alvey *Expert Systems Workshop Report.*

Friedman, J. (1978) 'Evaluating English sentences in a logical model'. *Abstract 16, COLING.*

Frost, R. A. (1982) 'Binary relational storage structures'. *The Computer Journal* **25** (3), 358 - 367.

Frost, R. A. (1983) 'SCHEMAL : yet another conceptual schema definition language'. *The Computer Journal* **26** (3), 228 -234.

Frost, R. A. (1985) 'Using semantic concepts to characterise various knowledge representation formalisms. A method of facilitating the interface of knowledge base system components'. *The Computer Journal* **28** (1), 112 -116.

Frost, R. A. and Whittaker, S. A. (1983) 'A step towards the automatic maintenance of the semantic integrity of databases'. *The Computer Journal* **26** (2), 124 - 133.

Futo, I. , Daruas, F. and Szeredi, P. (1977) 'Application of Prolog to development of QA and DBM systems'. In Gallaire, H. and Minker, J. *Logic and Data Bases.* New York : Plenum Press.

Gallaire, H. and Minker, J. (1978) *Logic and Data Bases.* New York : Plenum Press.

Gallaire, H. , Minker, J. and Nicolas, J. (1984) 'Logic and databases : a deductive approach'. *ACM Computing Surveys* **16** (2), 153 - 185.

Gallin, D. (1975) *Intensional and Higher Order Modal Logic.* Amsterdam : North Holland.

Gane, C. and Sarson, T. (1977) *Structured Systems Analysis.* New York : 1st. Data Books.

Gentzen, G. (1934) 'Untersuchungen uber das logische Schliessen'. *Mathematische Zeitschrift* **39**, 176 - 210 and 405 - 431.

Georgeff, M. P. (1982) 'Procedural control in production systems'. *Artificial Intelligence* **18**, 175 - 201.

Ghosh, S. P. and Lum, V. Y. (1973) 'An analysis of collisions when hashing by division'. *Technical Report RJ-1218.* IBM.

Godel, K. (1933) 'Eine Interpretation des intuitionistischen Aussagenkalkuls'. *Ergebnisse eines Mathematischen Kolloquiums* **4**, 34 - 50 (translated in Hintikka 1969).

Goguen, J. A. and Meseguer, J. (1985) 'EQLOG : equality, types and generic modules for logic programming'. In *Working Material for International Summer School in Advanced Programming Technologies.* Faculty of Informatics, University of San Sebastian, Spain.

Gradwell, J. L. (1975) 'Why data dictionaries?'. *Database* **6** (2), 15 - 18.

Grant, J. and Minker, J. (1983) 'Answering queries in indefinite databases and the null value problem'. *Technical Report 1374.* Computer Science Department, University of Maryland.

References

Gray, P. M. D. (1984) *Logic, Algebra, and Databases*. Chichester : Ellis Horwood.

Gray, P. M. D. and Bell, R. (1978) 'An introduction to relational algebra'. *Research Report AUCS/78003*. Aberdeen : Department of Computing Science, Aberdeen University.

Green, C. C. (1969) 'Theorem proving by resolution as a basis for question answering systems'. In Melzer, B. and Michie, D. *Machine Intelligence 4*. New York : Edinburgh University Press.

Hall, P. , Owlett, J. and Todd, S. (1976) 'Relations and Entities'. *Proceedings of the IFIP TC-2 Working Conference on Modelling in Database Management Systems*. Amsterdam : North Holland.

Hammer, M. M. and McLeod, D. J. (1978) 'The semantic data model : a modelling mechanism for database applications'. *ACM SIGMOD*, 26 - 35.

Harman, P. and King, D. (1985) *Expert Systems : Artificial Intelligence in Business*. New York : John Wiley and Sons.

Harris, L. R. (1977) 'User oriented data base query with the ROBOT natural language query system'. *Proceedings of the Third International Conference on Very Large Data Bases*. Tokyo.

Harrison, C. (1969) 'Kripke's semantics for modal logic'. In Davis, J. W. , Hockney, D. J. and Wilson, W. K. *Philosophical Logic*. Holland : D. Reidel Publishing Co.

Hart, P. E. , Duda, R. O. and Einaudi, M. T. (1978) 'PROSPECTOR : a computer based consultation system for mineral exploration'. *Math Geology* 10 (5), 589 - 610.

Hayes, P. J. (1981) 'The frame problem and related problems in artificial intelligence'. In Webber, B. L. and Nilsson, N. J. *Readings in Artificial Intelligence*. Palo Alto, California : Tioga Publishing.

Hayes, P. J. (1981) 'The logic of frames'. In Webber, B. L. and Nilsson, N. J. *Readings in Artificial Intelligence*. Palo Alto, California : Tioga Publishing.

Hayes-Roth, F. and Lesser, V. R. (1977) 'Focus of attention in the HEARSAY III system'. In *Proceedings of the Fifth IJCA*. Massachusetts Institute of Technology, Cambridge, Massachusetts.

Hayes-Roth, F. , Waterman, D. A. and Lenat, D. B. (1983) *Building Expert Systems*. Reading, Massachusetts : Addison-Wesley.

Hendrix, G. G. (1975) 'Expanding the utility of semantic networks through partitioning'. In *Proceedings of the Fourth IJCA*. Tiblis.

Hendrix, G. G. (1977) 'Human engineering for applied natural language processing'. In *Proceedings of the Fifth IJCA*. Massachusetts Institute of Technology, Cambridge, Massachusetts.

Hilbert, D. (1925) 'On the infinite'. In van Heijenoot (1967).

Hilbert and Ackerman (1928) In Rescher (1969), 333.

Hill, R. (1974) 'LUSH resolution and its completeness'. *DCS Memo No. 78*. School of Artificial Intelligence, Edinburgh University.

Hindley, J. R. , Lercher, B. and Seldin, P. (1972) *Introduction to Combinatory Logic.* London : Cambridge University Press.

Hintikka, J. (1969) *The Philosophy of Mathematics.* Oxford : Oxford University Press.

Hobbs, J. R. and Rosenchein, S. J. (1987) 'Making computational sense of Montague's intensional logic'. *Artificial Intelligence* **9**, 287 - 306.

Honeywell (1976) 'WWMCCS : worldwide data management system user's guide'. *DB97 Review 3.* Honeywell Information Systems.

Honeywell (1978) 'Logical inquiry and update system (LINUS)'. *Reference Manual.* Honeywell Information Systems.

Hsiao, D. K. (1983) *Advanced Database Machine Architecture.* Englewood Cliffs, New Jersey : Prentice-Hall.

Hughes, G. E. and Cresswell, M. J. (1968) *Introduction to Modal Logic.* London : Methuen .

ICL (1977) 'ICL first with DB processor'. *Computer Weekly* **573**, 1.

Jacobs, B. E. (1982) 'On database logic'. *JACM* **29 (2)**, 310 - 332.

Johnson, C. I. (1968) 'Interactive graphics in data processing : principles of interactive systems'. *IBM Systems Journal* **3 (4)**, 147 - 173.

Johnson, L. and Keravnou, E. T. (1985) *Expert Systems Technology : A Guide.* Abacus Press.

Johnson, R. G. and Martin, N. J. (1984) 'Triples as a substructure for more intelligent databases'. In Alvey *Proceedings of the Workshop on Architectures for Large Knowledge Bases.* Manchester : Department of Computer Science, Manchester University.

Jaskowski, S. (1934) 'On the rules of supposition in formal logic'. *Studia Logica* **1**.

Kellogg, C. H. , Burger, J. F. , Diller, T. and Fogt, K. (1971) 'The CONVERSE natural language data management system : current status and plans'. *Proceedings of the ACM Symposium on Information Storage and Retrieval.* University of Maryland.

Kent, W. (1983) 'A simple guide to five normal forms in relational database theory'. *CACM* **26 (2)**, 120 - 125.

King, P. J. H. (1977) 'Information systems analysis for database design'. *Online Database Conference.* Pinner, Middlesex : Online Publications.

King, P. J. H. (1984) *Databases - A Technical Comparison : Pergamon State of the Art Report.* London : Pergamon Press.

Klopprogge, M. P. (1981) 'Term : an approach to include the time dimension in the entity-relationship model'. In Chen, P. P. *Entity-Relationship Approach to Information Modelling and Analysis.* California : ER Institute.

Konolige, K. (1982) 'Circumscription ignorance'. *Proceedings of the AAAI 82.* University of Pittsburgh, Pennsylvania.

Kowalski, R. A. (1975) 'A proof procedure using connection graphs'. *JACM* **22 (4)**, 572 - 595.

Kowalski, R. A. (1979) *Logic for Problem Solving*. New York : Elsevier, North Holland.

Kowalski, R. A. (1984) 'Logic databases'. In Alvey *Proceedings of the Workshop on Architectures for Large Knowledge Bases*. Department of Computer Science, University of Manchester.

Kowalski, R. A. and Kuehner, D. (1971) 'Linear resolution with selection function'. *Artificial Intelligence* **2**, 227 260.

Kozy, J. (1974) *Understanding Natural Deduction*. Encino, California : Dickenson Publishing Co. Inc.

Kripke, S. (1963) 'Semantic analysis of modal logic I : normal modal propositional calculi'. *Math. Log. Grundl. Math.* **9**, 67 - 96.

Kroenke, D. (1977) *Database Processing*. Palo Alto, California : Science Research Associates.

Kunz, J. C. , Fallet, R. J. , et al (1978) 'A physiological rule based system for interpreting pulmonary function test results'. *HPP-78-19 Working Paper*. California : Heuristic Programming Project, Department of Computer Science, Stanford University.

Lacroix, M. and Pirotte, A. (1974) 'ILL : An English structured query language for relational data bases'. In Nijssen, G. M. *Proceedings of the IFIP TC-2 Working Conference on Modelling in Data Base Management Systems*. Amsterdam : North Holland.

Lacroix, M. and Pirotte, A. (1976) 'Example queries in relational languages'. *MBLE Technical Note N107*.

Larson, P. (1978) 'Dynamic Hashing'. *BIT* **18**, 184 - 201.

Lavington, S. H. , Standring, M. and Rubner, G. B. (1984) 'A 4 Mbyte associative predicate store'. In Alvey *Proceedings of the Workshop on Architectures for Large Knowledge Bases*.

Lebowitz, M. (1980) 'Languages and memory : generalization as a part of understanding'. *Proceedings of AAAI 80*. Stanford University, California.

Leith,P.(1983)'Hierarchically structured production rules'. *The Computer Journal* **26** (1), 1-5.

Lemmon, E. (1965) *See* Rescher and Urquhart (1971).

Lenat, D. B. (1977) 'Automated theory formation in mathematics'. *Proceedings of the Fifth IJCA*. Massachusetts Institute of Technology, Cambridge, Massachusetts.

Lenat, D. B. (1982) 'AM : an artificial intelligence approach to discovery in mathematics as heuristic search '. In Davis, R. and Lenat, D. B. *Knowledge Based Systems in Artificial Intelligence*. New York : McGraw-Hill.

Lesser, V. R. , Fennell, R. D. , Erman, L. D. and Reddy, D. R. (1975) ' Organisation of the HEARSAY II speech understanding system'. *IEEE Transactions on Acoustic Speech Signal Processing* **23**, 11 - 24.

Levesque, H. J. (1984) 'Foundations of a functional approach to knowledge representation'. *Artificial Intelligence* **23** (2), 155 - 212.

Levien, R. E. and Maron, M. E. (1967) 'A computer system for inference execution and data retrieval '. *CACM* **10** (11), 715 - 721.

Lewis, C. I. (1918) *A Survey of Symbolic Logic.* Berkeley : University of California Press.

Lewis, C. I. (1932) 'Alternative systems of logic'. *The Monist* **42,** 481 - 507.

Lewis, H. R. and Papadimitriou, C. H. (1981) *Elements of the Theory of Computation.* Englewood Cliffs, New Jersey : Prentice-Hall.

Li, D. (1984) *A Prolog Database System.* Letchworth, UK : Research Studies Press Ltd (and John Wiley and Sons).

Lindberg, D. A. B. , Gaston, L. W. , Kingsland, L. C. and Vanker, A. D. (1981) 'A knowledge based system for consultation about human hemostasis disorders : progress report'. *Proceedings of the Fifth Annual Symposium on Computer Applications in Medical Care.*

Lipski, W. (1981) 'On databases with incomplete information'. *JACM* **28 (1),** 41 - 70.

Lloyd, J. W. (1984) *Foundations of Logic Programming.* Berlin and New York : Springer-Verlag.

Lomax, J. D. (1978) *Data Dictionary Systems.* London : NCC Publications.

Lorie, R. A. (1974) 'XRM : an extended (n-ary) relational memory'. *Report No. G320-2096.* Cambridge, Massachusetts : IBM Cambridge Scientific Centre.

Lorie, R. A. and Symonds, A. J. (1971) 'A relational access method for interactive applications'. In *Database Systems, Courant Computer Science Symposia* **6.** Englewood Cliffs, New Jersey : Prentice-Hall.

Loveland, D. (1969) 'Theorem provers combining model elimination and resolution'. In Meltzer, B. and Michie, D. *Machine Intelligence 4.* New York : Elsevier North Holland.

Lukasiewicz, J. (1929) *Elementy Logiki Matematycznej.* Warsaw : Panstowowe Wydawnictwo Nawkowe.

Lukasiewicz, J.(1951)'Aristotle's *Syllogistics from the Standpoint of Modern Formal Logic.* Oxford : Clarendon Press.

Lum, V. Y. (1971) 'General performance analysis of key-to-address transformation methods using an abstract file concept'. *CACM* **16 (10).**

Lundberg, B. (1981) 'On consistency of information models'. *BIT* **21,** 37 - 45.

Lundberg, B. (1982) 'An axiomatization of events'. *BIT* **22,** 291 - 299.

McArthur, R. P. (1976) *Tense Logic.* Holland : D. Reidel Publishing Co.

McCarthy, J. (1960) 'Recursive functions of symbolic expressions and their computation by machine : Part 1'. *CACM* **3,** 184 - 195.

McCarthy, J. (1963) 'A basis for a mathematical theory of computation'. In Bradford, P. and Hirschberg, D. *Computer Programming and Formal Systems.* Amsterdam : North Holland.

McCarthy, J. (1978) 'On the model theory of knowledge'. *Memo AIM 312.* Stanford University, California.

McCarthy, J. (1980) 'Circumscription - a form of non-monotonic reasoning'. *Artificial Intelligence* **13 (1)**, 27 - 40.

McCarthy, J. and Hayes, P. J. (1969) 'Some philosophical problems from the standpoint of artificial intelligence'. In Meltzer, B. and Michie, D. *Machine Intelligence 4.* New York : Edinburgh University Press.

McCawley, J. D. (1981) *Everything That Linguists Have Always Wanted to Know About Logic.* Oxford : Basil Blackwell.

McDermott, D. V. and Doyle, J. (1980) 'Non-monotonic logic I'. *Artificial Intelligence* **13 (12)**, 41 - 72.

McDermott, J. (1980) 'R1 : a rule based configurer of computer systems'. *Report CMU-CS-80-119.* Department of Computer Science, Carnegie-Mellon University, Pittsburgh, Pennsylvania.

McGettrick, A. D. (1980) *The Definition of Programming Languages : Cambridge Computer Science Texts - 11.* Cambridge : Cambridge University Press.

McGregor, D. R. and Malone, J. R. (1984) 'An integrated high performance, hardware assisted, intelligent database system for large scale knowledge bases'. In Alvey *Proceedings of the Workshop on Architectures for Large Knowledge Bases.* Department of Computer Science, Manchester University.

McSkimmin, J. R. and Minker, J. (1979) 'The use of a semantic network in a deductive question answering system'. In *Proceedings of the Sixth IJCA.* Tokyo.

Mamdani, E. H. and Gaines, B. (1981) *Fuzzy Reasoning and its Applications.* London : Academic Press.

Manna, Z. and Waldinger, R. (1980) 'A deductive approach to program synthesis'. *ACM Transactions on Programming Languages and Systems* **2 (1)**, 90 - 121.

Marciszewski, W. (1981) *Dictionary of Logic.* The Hague : Martins Nijhoft.

Martin, J. (1975) *Computer Database Organisation.* Englewood Cliffs, New Jersey : Prentice-Hall.

Martin N. et al (1977) 'Knowledge base management for experiment planning in molecular genetics'. *Proceedings of the Fifth IJCA.* Massachusetts Institute of Technology, Cambridge, Massachusetts.

Martin, N. J. (1984) 'The construction of interfaces to triple based databases'. In Hammersley, P. M. *Proceedings of the British National Conference on Databases.* Cambridge : Cambridge University Press.

Martin-Lof, P. (1982) 'Constructive mathematics and computer programming'. In *Logic, Methodology and Philosophy of Science VI : Proceedings of the Sixth International Conference in Hanover.* Amsterdam : North Holland.

Massey, G. J. (1970) *Understanding Symbolic Logic.* New York : Harper and Row.

Mays, E. (1982) 'Monitors as responses to questions : determining competence'. In *Proceedings of the National Conference on Artificial Intelligence.* University of Pittsburgh, Pennsylvania.

Minker, J. (1978a) 'Search strategy and selection function for an inferential relational system'. *ACM TODS* **3 (1)**, 1 - 31.

Minker, J. (1978b) 'An experimental relational database system based on logic'. In Gallaire, H. and Minker, J. *Logic and Data Bases*. New York : Plenum.

Minker, J. (1982) 'On indefinite databases and the closed world assumption'. In *Proceedings of the Sixth Conference on Automated Deduction : Lecture Notes in Computer Science No. 138*. Berlin and New York : Springer Verlag.

Minker, J. and Perlis, D. (1984) 'Application of protected circumscription'. In *Proceedings of the Seventh Conference on Automated Deduction*. Napa, California. Berlin and New York : Springer-Verlag.

Minsky, M. (1975) 'A framework for representing knowledge'. In Winston, P. H. *The Psychology of Computer Vision*. New York : McGraw-Hill.

Mizoguchi, F. , Maruyama, K. , Yamada, T. , Kitazawa, K. , Saito, M. and Kulikowski, C. A. (1979) 'A case study of EXPERT formalism : an approach to a design of a medical consultation system through EXPERT formalism'. In *Proceedings of the Sixth IJCA*. Tokyo.

Montague, R. (1973) 'The proper treatment of quantification in ordinary English'. In Hintikka, K. J. J. *Approaches to Natural Languages*. Germany : Dordrecht.

Montague, R. (1974) *Formal Philosophy : Selected Papers of Richard Montague*. New Haven : Yale University Press.

Moses (1971) 'Symbolic integration : the stormy decade'. *CACM* **14 (8)**, 548 - 560.

Moulin, P. , Randon, J. , Teboul, M. , Savoysky, S. , Spaccapietra, S. and Tardieu, H. (1976) 'Conceptual model as a database design tool'. In Nijssen, G. M. *Modelling in Data Base Management Systems*. Amsterdam : North Holland.

Munz, R. (1978) 'The WELL system : a multi-user database system based on binary-relations and graph matching'. *Information Systems* **3 (2)**, 99 - 115.

Murray, N. V. (1982) 'Completely non-clausal theorem proving'. *Artificial Intelligence* **18 (1)**, 67 - 85.

Mylopoulos, J. (1980) 'An overview of knowledge representation'. *ACM SIGMOD Rec.* **11 (2)**, 5 - 12.

Mylopoulos, J. , Borgida, A. , Cohen, P. , Roussopoulos, N. , Tsotsos, J. and Wong, H. K. T. (1976) 'TORUS : a step towards bridging the gap between data bases and the casual user'. *Information Systems* **2**, 71 - 77.

Mylopoulos, J. , Bernstein, P. A. and Wong, H. K. T. (1980) 'A language facility for designing interactive database intensive applications'. *ACM TODS* **5 (2)**, 185 - 207.

Nakamura, T. and Mizoguchi, T. (1978) 'An analysis of storage utilization factors in block split data structuring scheme'. In *Proceedings of the Fourth International Conference on Very Large Data Bases*. New York : IEEE.

Nijssen, G. M. (1984) 'From databases towards knowledge bases : a technical comparison'. In King, P. J. H. *Databases : State of the Art Report*. London : Pergamon Press.

Nilsson, N. J. (1971) *Problem Solving Methods in Artificial Intelligence.* New York : McGraw-Hill.

Nilsson, N. J. (1977) 'A production system for automated deduction'. *Technical Note 148.* SRI International, Menlo Park, California.

Nishida, T. and Doshita, S. (1983) 'An application of Montague grammar to English-Japanese machine translation'. In *Proceedings of the Conference on Applied Natural Language Analysis.* Santa Monica, California.

Online (1983) *Database Techniques : Software Selection and Systems Development.* Pinner, Middlesex : Online Publications.

Ozkarahan, E. A. , Schuster, S. A. and Smith, K. C. (1975) 'RAP : an associative processor for data base management'. In *AFIPS Conference Proceedings 44.*

Pelagatti, E. , Paolini, P. and Bracchi, G. (1978) 'Mapping external views to a common data model'. *Information Systems 3,* 141 - 151.

Perkinson, R. C.(1984) *Data Analysis : The Key to Data Base Design.* Wellesley, Massachusetts : QED Information Sciences, Inc.

Petofi, J. (1978) *Logic and the Formal Theory of Natural Language.* Hamburg : Buske.

Pirotte, A. (1978) 'High level database query languages'. In Gallaire, H. and Minker, J. *Logic and Data Bases.* New York : Plenum Press.

Pirotte, A. and Wodon, P. (1974) 'A comprehensive formal query language for a relational data base : FQL. *RAIRO. Informatique / Computer Science II,* 165 - 183.

Pople, H. E. (1977) 'The formation of composite hypotheses in diagnostic problem solving : an exercise in synthetic reasoning'. In *Proceedings of the Fifth IJCA.* Massachusetts Institute of Technology, Cambridge, Massachusetts.

Post (1943) 'Formal reductions of the general combinatorial decision problem'. *American Journal of Mathematics 65,* 197 - 215.

Prawitz, D. (1976) 'A proof procedure with matrix reduction'. In *Lecture Notes in Mathematics 125.* Berlin and New York : Springer-Verlag.

Prior, A. N. (1956) 'Modality and quantification in S5'. *Journal of Symbolic Logic 21,* 60 - 62.

Quillian, R. (1968) 'Semantic memory'. In Minsky, M. *Semantic Information Processing.* Cambridge, Massachusetts : Massachusetts Institute of Technology Press.

Quinlan, J. R. (1983) 'Inferno : a cautious approach to uncertain inference'. *The Computer Journal 26* (3), 255 - 268.

Raphael, B. (1968) 'A computer program for semantic information retrieval'. In Minsky, M. *Semantic Information Processing.* Cambridge, Massachusetts : Massachusetts Institute of Technology Press.

Ravin, J. and Schatzoff, M. (1973) 'An interactive graphics system for analysis of business decisions'. *IBM Systems Journal 12* (3), 238 - 256.

Rayward-Smith, V. J. (1983) *A First Course in Formal Language Theory.* Oxford : Blackwell Scientific Publications.

Reggia, J. et al (1980) 'Towards an intelligent textbook of neurology'. In *Proceedings of the Fourth Annual Symposium on Computer Applications in Medical Care.* Washington, District of Colombia.

Reiter, R. (1971) 'Two results on ordering for resolution with merging and linear format'. *JACM* **18,** 630 -646.

Reiter, R. (1978) 'On closed world databases'. In Gallaire, H. and Minker, J. *Logic and Databases.* New York : Plenum Press.

Reiter, R. (1978) 'Deductive question-answering in relational databases'. In Gallaire, H. and Minker, J. *Logic and Databases.* New York : Plenum Press.

Reiter, R. (1981) 'On the integrity of typed first order data bases'. In Gallaire, H. , Minker, J. and Nicolas, J. M. *Advances in Data Base Theory : Volume I.* New York : Plenum Press.

Reiter, R.(1984)'Towards a logical reconstruction of relational database theory'. In Brodie,M. , Mylopoulos, J. and Schmidt, J. W. *On Conceptual Modelling.* Berlin and New York : Springer - Verlag.

Rescher, N. (1969) *Many Valued Logic.* New York : McGraw-Hill.

Rescher, N. (1976) *Plausible Reasoning.* Amsterdam : Van Gorcum.

Rescher, N. and Urquhart, A. (1971) *Temporal Logic.* Berlin and New York : Springer-Verlag.

Rich, E. (1983) *Artificial Intelligence.* New York : McGraw-Hill.

Roberts, R. B. and Goldstein, I. P. (1977) 'The FRL manual'. *Technical Report.* Massachusetts Institute of Technology Artificial Intelligence Laboratory, Cambridge, Massachusetts.

Robinson, H. M. (1981) *Database Analysis and Design.* Bromley, UK : Chartwell-Bratt.

Robinson, J. A. (1965) 'A machine oriented logic based on the resolution principle'. *JACM* **12,** 25 - 41.

Robinson, J. A. (1967) 'A review of automatic theorem proving'. In *Proceedings of the Symposia in Applied Mathematics 19.* Providence, Rhode Island : American Mathematical Society.

Robinson, P. (1985) 'The SUM : an AI coprocessor'. *BYTE* **10 (6),** 169 - 184.

Roussopoulos, N. (1979) 'A conceptual schema definition language for the design of data base applications'. *IEEE Transactions on Software Engineering* **SE-5,** 481 - 496.

Russell, B. and Whitehead, A. N. (1925) *Principia Mathematica.* Cambridge : Cambridge University Press.

Sato, M. (1976) *A Study of Kripke-type Models for Some Modal Logics by Gentzen's Sequential Method.* Kyoto, Japan : Research Institute for Mathematical Sciences, Kyoto University.

Scha, R. J. H. (1977) 'Phillips question-answering system PHLIQA I'. *SIGART Newsletter* **61.**

Schafer, G. (1976) *A Mathematical Theory of Evidence.* Princeton, New Jersey : Princeton University Press.

Schank, R. C. (1973) 'Identification of conceptualizations underlying natural language'. In Schank, R. C. and Colby, K. *Computer Models of Thought and Language.* San Francisco : W. H. Freeman and Sons.

Schank, R. C. (1975) *Conceptual Information Processing.* New York : Elsevier, North Holland.

Schank, R. C. and Abelson, R. P. (1977) *Scripts, Plans, Goals and Understanding.* Hillsdale, New York : Erlbaum.

Schubert, L. K. (1976) 'Extending the expressive power of semantic networks'. *Artificial Intelligence* 7, 89 - 124.

Sell, P. S. (1985) *Expert Systems : A Practical Introduction.* London and New York : MacMillan.

Severance, D. G. and Duhne, R. (1976) 'A practioner's guide to addressing algorithms'. *CACM* 19 (6), 314 - 326.

Shannon, C. E. (1948) 'A mathematical theory of communication'. In Slepian, D. *Key Papers in the Development of Information Theory.* New York : IEEE 1974.

Shapiro, S. C. (1971) 'The mind system : a data structure for semantic information processing'. *Report R-837-PR USAF Project Rand.* Santa Monica, California : Rand Corporation.

Shapiro, S. C. (1977) 'Representing and locating deduction rules in a semantic network'. In *Proceedings of the Workshop on Pattern-Directed Inference Systems. ACM/SIGART Newsletter* 63, 14 - 18.

Sharman, G. O. and Winterbottom, N. (1979) 'NDB : Non-Programmer Database Facility'. *IBM Technical Report TR 12.179.* Winchester : IBM UK Laboratories Ltd.

Shave, M. J. R. (1981) 'Entities, functions and binary relations : steps to a conceptual schema'. *The Computer Journal* 24 (1), 42 - 46.

Shipman, D. W. (1981) 'Functional data model and DAPLEX'. *ACM TODS* 6 (1), 140 - 174.

Shneiderman, B. and Goodman, V. (1976) 'Batched searching of sequential and tree structured files.' *ACM TODS* 1, 268 - 275.

Shortliffe, E. H. (1976) *MYCIN : Computer Based Medical Consultation.* New York : American Elsevier.

Shortliffe, E. H. and Buchanan, B. G. (1975) 'A model of inexact reasoning in medicine'. *Mathematical Biosciences* 23, 351 - 379.

Simmons, R. F. and Chester, D. (1977) 'Inferences in quantified semantic networks'. In *Proceedings of the Fifth IJCA.* Massachusetts Institute of Technology, Cambridge, Massachusetts.

Smith, D. E. and Clayton, J. E. (1980) 'A frame based production system architecture'. In *Proceedings of the AAAI 80.* Stanford University, California.

Smith, K. (1983) 'A new computer breed uses transputers for parallel processing'. *Electronics* 56 (4), 67 - 68.

Smith, R. G. and Friedland, P. (1980) 'A user guide to the UNITS system'. *Technical Report.* Heuristic Programming Project, Stanford University, California.

Snyder, D. P. (1971) *Modal Logic and its Applications.* New York : Van Nostrand.

Sowa, J. F. (1984) *Conceptual Structures : Information Processing in Mind and Machine.* Reading, Massachusetts : Addison-Wesley.

Sparck-Jones, K. and Boguraev, B. K. (1983) 'How to drive a database front end using general semantic information'. In *Proceedings of the Conference on Applied Natural Language Analysis.* Santa Monica, California.

Stabile, L. A. (1982) 'Frame based computer network monitoring'. In *Proceedings of the AAAI 82.* University of Pittsburgh, Pennsylvania.

Stefik, M. , Aikins, J. , Balzer, R. , Benoit, J. , Birnbaum, L. , Hayes-Roth, F. and Sacerdoti, E. (1982) 'The organisation of expert systems : a tutorial'. *Artificial Intelligence* 18, 135 - 173.

Stickel, M. E. (1982) 'A non-clausal connection-graph resolution theorem proving program'. In *Proceedings of the AAAI 82.* University of Pittsburg, Pennsylvania.

Stickel, M. E. (1983) 'Theory-resolution : building-in non-equational theories'. In *Proceedings of the AAAI 83.* Washington, District of Colombia.

Stolfo, S. J. and Shaw, D. E. (1982) 'DADO : a tree-structured machine architecture for production systems'. In *Proceedings of the AAAI 82.* University of Pittsburg, Pennsylvania.

Stonebraker, M. R. (1975) 'Implementation of integrity constraints and views by query modification'. In *Proceedings of the ACM SIGMOD Conference.* San Jose, California.

Stonebraker, M. R. , Held, G. D. and Wong, E. (1975) 'INGRES : a relational data base system'. *Proceedings of the NCC 44.*

Storm, E. F. (1974) 'Evaluation procedures for resolution without normal forms'. *Systems and Information Science Report.* Syracuse University, Syracuse, New York.

Strnad, A. J. (1971) 'The relational approach to the management of data bases'. In *Proceedings of the IFIP Conference.*

Su, S. Y. W. and Lipovski, G. J. (1975) 'CASSM : a cellular system for very large data bases'. in *Proceedings of the International Conference on Very Large Data Bases.* Framington, Massachusetts. New York : ACM.

Symonds, A. J. (1968) 'Auxiliary storage associative data structure for PL/I'. *IBM Systems Journal* 7 (3/4), 229 - 245.

Szolovits, P. , Hawkinson, L. R. and Martin, W. A. (1977) 'An overview of OWL : a language for knowledge representation'. *Report Massachusetts Institute of Technology/LCS/TM-86.* Massachusetts Institute of Technology, Cambridge, Massachusetts.

Taylor, R. J. B. (1984) 'Relational memory'. In Alvey *Proceedings of the Workshop on Architectures for Large Knowledge Bases.* Department of Computer Science, Manchester University.

Templeton, M. and Burger, J. (1983) 'Problems in natural language interface to DBMS with examples from EUFID'. In *Proceedings of the Conference on Applied Natural Language Analysis.* Santa Monica, California.

Thompson, F. B. and Thompson, B. H. (1975) 'Practical natural language processing : the REL system as prototype'. In Rubinoff, M. and Yovits, M. C. *Advances in Computers* **13**. New York : Academic Press.

Titman, P. (1974) 'An experimental database system using binary relations'. In Klimbie and Koffeman *Data Base Management : Proceedings of the IFIP TC-2 Working Conference.* Cargesa, Corsica. Amsterdam : North-Holland.

Todd, S. (1976) 'The Peterlee relational test vehicle : a system overview'. *IBM Systems Journal* **15 (4)**, 285 - 307.

Tremblay, J. and Sorenson, P. G. (1985) *An Introduction to Data Structures with Applications.* New York : McGraw-Hill.

Tsichritzis, D. S. and Lochovsky, F. H. (1977) *Data Base Management Systems.* New York : Academic Press.

Tsichritzis, D. S. and Lochovsky, F. H. (1982) *Data Models.* Englewood Cliffs, New Jersey : Prentice-Hall.

Tyson, M. (1982) 'Proof methods in an agenda based natural deduction theorem prover'. *Proceedings of the AAAI 82.* University of Pittsburgh, Pennsylvania.

Valiant, L. G. (1983) 'Parallel computation'. In Bakker, J. W. and van Leeuwen, J. *Foundations of Computer Science IV : Distributed Systems ; Part I : Algorithms and Complexity.* Amsterdam : Mathematisch Centrum.

Vandijke, E. (1977) 'Towards a more familiar relational retrieval language'. *Information Systems* **2**, 159 - 169.

van Duyn, J. V. (1982) *Developing a Data Dictionary System.* Englewood Cliffs, New Jersey : Prentice-Hall.

van Griethuysen, J. J. (1982) 'Concepts and terminology for the conceptual schema and the information base'. *Preliminary Report ISO TC 97/SC5/WG5.*

van Heijenoot, J. (1967) *From Frege to Godel : A Source Book on Mathematical Logic 1879 - 1931.* Cambridge, Massachusetts.

van Melle, W. (1980) 'A domain independent system that aids in constructing knowledge based consultation programs' (Ph.D. Dissertation). Department of Computer Science, Stanford University, California.

van Melle, W. , Scott, A. C. , Bennett, J. S. and Peairs, M. A. (1981) 'The EMYCIN Manual'. *Technical Report.* Heuristic Programming Project, Stanford University, California.

Waite, W. M. and Goos, G. (1984) *Compiler Construction.* Berlin and New York : Springer-Verlag.

Wallen, L. (1984) *Personal Communication.* Edinburgh University, Edinburgh.

Walsh, M. E. (1979) *Information Management System / Virtual Storage.* Reston, Virginia : Reston Publishing Co.

Walther, C. (1985) 'A mechanical solution of Schubert's steamroller by many-sorted resolution'. *Artificial Intelligence* **26 (2)**, 217 - 224.

Waltz, D. C. (1978) 'An English language question answering system for a large relational database'. *CACM* **21 (7)**, 526 - 539.

Warnier, J. D. (1974) *Logical Construction of Programs.* Leiden, Netherlands : H. E. Stenfert Kroese BV.

Warren, D. H. D. (1977) 'Implementing Prolog : compiling predicate logic programs'. *AI Report.* Edinburgh University, Edinburgh.

Warren, D. H. D. (1981) 'Efficient processing of interactive relational database queries expressed in logic'. In *Proceedings of the Seventh Conference on Very Large Data Bases.* Cannes, France. New York : IEEE.

Weiner, J. L. (1979) 'The structure of natural explanations : theory and application'. *Report SP - 4025.* System Development Corporation.

Weiner, J. L. (1980) 'BLAH : a system which explains its reasoning'. *Artificial Intelligence* **15,** 19 - 48.

Weiss, S. and Kulikowski, C. (1979) 'EXPERT : a system for developing consultation models'. *Proceedings of the Sixth IJCA.* Tokyo.

White, A. P. (1984) 'Inference deficiencies in rule based expert systems'. In Bramer, M. A. *Research and Development in Expert Systems.* Cambridge : Cambridge University Press.

Wiederhold, G. (1977) *Database Design.* New York : McGraw-Hill.

Wiederhold, G. (1983) *Database Design.* 2nd. edn. New York : McGraw-Hill.

Wilensky, R. (1984) *LISPcraft.* New York : Norton.

Wilkins, D. (1974) 'A non-clausal theorem proving system'. *Proceedings of the AISB Summer Conference.* Brighton, UK.

Winston, P. H. (1980) 'Learning and reasoning by analogy'. *CACM* **23 (12),** 689 - 703.

Winston, P. H. and Horn, B. K. P. (1981) *LISP.* Reading, Massachusetts : Addison-Wesley.

Wirth, N. (1976) *Algorithms + Data Structures = Programs.* Englewood Cliffs, New Jersey : Prentice-Hall.

Woods, W. A. (1975) 'What's in a link'. In Bobrow, D. and Collins, A. *Representation and Understanding.* New York : Academic Press.

Woods, W. A. , Kaplan, R. M. and Nash-Webber, B. (1972) 'The lunar sciences natural language information system'. *Final Report No. 2378.* Cambridge, Massachusetts : Bolt, Beranek and Newman Inc.

Yonezaki, H. and Enomoto, H. (1980) 'A database system based on intensional logic'. In *Proceedings of COLING 80.*

Yuen, P. S. T. , Lum, V. Y. and Dodd, M. (1971) 'Key to address transform techniques : a fundamental performance study on large existing files'. *CACM* **14 (4).**

Zadeh, L. A. (1965) 'Fuzzy sets'. *Information and Control* **8,** 338 - 353.

References

Zadeh, L. A. (1978) 'Fuzzy sets as a basis for a theory of possibility'. *Fuzzy Sets and Systems.* Amsterdam : North Holland.

Zadeh, L. A. (1983) 'Commonsense knowledge representation based on fuzzy logic'. *Computer* **16** (10), 61 - 65.

Zeman, J. J. (1973) *Modal Logic : The Lewis Modal Systems.* Oxford : Oxford University Press.

Zloof, M. M. (1977) 'Query-by-example : a database language'. *IBM Systems Journal,* 324 - 343.

Index